PRAISE FOR
THE SEVEN MILITARY CLASSICS OF ANCIENT CHINA

"Ralph Sawyer's excellent work fills a serious gap for anyone interested in the history of ancient warfare. There are many sources in translation for ancient Greek and Roman war. Now scholars and others will be able to consult this fascinating and significant book for comparable material on ancient China."

—Arther Ferrill, author of *The Origins of War*

"Ralph Sawyer's translation of the *Seven Military Classics,* combined with his groundbreaking study of warfare in ancient China, is a tour de force of scholarship and a significant contribution to the historical literature."

—Robert L. O'Connell, author of *Of Arms and Men: A History of War, Weapons, and Aggression*

Also by Ralph D. Sawyer

The Tao of Deception

The Essential Art of War

Ling Ch'i Ching

The Essence of War

The Tao of Spycraft

The Art of War

The Tao of War

One Hundred Unorthodox Strategies (Paperback)

The Complete Art of War

Sun Pin

Sun Tzu

HISTORY AND WARFARE
Arther Ferrill, *Series Editor*

The SEVEN MILITARY CLASSICS of Ancient China
Ralph D. Sawyer, *translator*

FEEDING MARS: Logistics in Western Warfare from the
Middle Ages to the Present   John Lynn, *editor*

ON WATERLOO
The Campaign of 1815 in France by Carl von Clausewitz
Memorandum on the Battle of Waterloo by the Duke of Wellington
Christopher Bassford, *translator*

THE CHIWAYA WAR: Malawians in World War One
Melvin Page

THE ANATOMY OF A LITTLE WAR: A Diplomatic and
Military History of the Gundovald Affair, 567–585
Bernard S. Bachrach

THE HALT IN THE MUD: French Strategic Planning
from Waterloo to the Franco-Prussian War
Gary P. Cox

THE HUNDRED YEARS WAR FOR MOROCCO:
Gunpowder and the Military Revolution in the
Early Modern Muslim World   Weston F. Cook, Jr.

THE CAVALRY OF ANCIENT GREECE
Leslie J. Worley

ORDERING SOCIETY: A World History of
Military Institutions   Barton C. Hacker

WARFARE AND CIVILIZATION IN THE
MEDIEVAL ISLAMIC WORLD   William J. Hamblin

The SEVEN MILITARY CLASSICS of ANCIENT CHINA

translation and commentary by
RALPH D. SAWYER

with Mei-chün Sawyer

BASIC BOOKS
A Member of the Perseus Books Group
New York

To our parents

Copyright © 1993 by Ralph D. Sawyer

Published in 1993 in the United States by Westview Press, Inc.,
Boulder, Colorado
Published in 2007 in the United States by Basic Books,
A Member of the Perseus Books Group,
387 Park Avenue South, New York, NY 10016-8810

Books published by Basic Books are available at special discounts
for bulk purchases in the United States by corporations, institutions,
and other organizations. For more information, please contact
the Special Markets Department at the Perseus Books Group,
2300 Chestnut Street, Philadelphia, PA, or call (800) 255-1514,
or e-mail special.markets@perseusbooks.com.

Library of Congress Cataloguing-in-Publication Data
Wu ching ch'i shu. English.
    The Seven military classics of ancient China = [Wu ching ch'i shu]
/ translation and commentary by Ralph D. Sawyer, with Mei-chün Sawyer.
        p. cm. — (History and warfare)
    Includes bibliographical references and index.
    ISBN: 0-8133-1228-0
    1. Military art and science—China—Early work to 1800.
I. Sawyer, Ralph. II. Sawyer, Mei-chün. III. Title. IV. Title: Wu
ching ch'i shu. V. Series.
U101.W8413 1993
355.02—dc20   92-39146
                                                           CIP

Paperback: ISBN-13: 978-0-465-00304-4; ISBN-10: 0-465-00304-4

10 9 8 7 6 5 4

Contents

Preface to the Paperback Edition

CHINA HAS BEEN markedly transformed over the fifteen years since the original preface to *Seven Military Classics* was written. The economy has expanded at an unprecedented rate, unrelenting modernization affects virtually every dimension of life, and the physical and intellectual horrors of the Cultural Revolution have become fading, albeit still painful, memories. Achievement of superpower status seems assured, but whether the PRC's ascension will foster worldwide prosperity or entail pervasive destruction remains uncertain.

Paradoxically, even as modern cities proliferate and the latest technologies are adapted, many aspects of its long-forgotten, vociferously deprecated traditional culture have not only reappeared but also been deliberately revitalized, in a desperate attempt to suppress escalating social unrest and retard a zealous plunge into corruption and hedonism. Even Confucianism, long viewed as a feudal anathema, is being brandished as a reformist tool by draconian authorities in the vacuum created by Marxism's demise.

Amid this turbulent milieu, China's classic military writings have soared in popularity and become virtually ubiquitous. Works such as the *Art of War* and *Six Secret Teachings* now appear in many guises, ranging from heavily annotated scholarly editions through cheap vernacular paperbacks. Comic book and lavishly illustrated editions of immense fame and popularity abound, and versions purporting to apply their contents to every conceivable realm proliferate. Numerous military terms have entered the language while the concepts and principles ground strategic thinking and continue to affect the mindset, shaping and delimiting the very categories of thought and response. The contents also provide essential materials for lengthy martial arts dramas, crucial themes for movies, and vital content for other mass media presentations.

More significantly, the classic military writings are playing an important role as the PRC consciously reformulates its martial doctrine to create "contemporary military science with unique Chinese characteristics." As discussed in our *Tao of Deception*, PRC think tanks such as the Academy of Military Science are examining every passage for concepts and tactical principles that can be adopted to the contemporary battlefield so as to ensure that China's comparatively deficient armed forces will, through unexpected and unorthodox measures, be able to wrest a localized advantage and prevail. In conjunction with paradigm battles abstracted from its three-thousand-year military history, the seven books that are contained in the *Seven Military Classics*, previously confined to the martial realm, thus enjoy unprecedented readership and vibrancy.

Ralph D. Sawyer
2007

Preface

RECENT DECADES have witnessed explosive growth in American and European interest in the Far East. Books and articles about China have enjoyed popularity since the 1970s; those on Japan, especially on Japanese management practices, have proliferated since the early 1980s; and those focusing on business in terms of "corporate warfare" and theories of strategy, including Asian practices and their underlying philosophies, retain currency. The writings of Musashi, the famous Japanese swordsman, and Sun-tzu, the ancient Chinese military theorist, have been repeatedly translated, investigated, and discussed. However, as interesting as they and a few books from the martial arts have proven to be, the vast Chinese military corpus—despite its historical importance and contemporary significance—remains unknown in the West.

Chinese military thought probably originated with neolithic village conflicts four or five thousand years ago, perhaps even as mythologized in the clash of legendary cultural heroes and Sage Emperors. Subsequently, because men were compelled to direct their ingenuity toward combat, weapons were developed, tactics evolved, and power structures arose. Eventually, dominant figures—perhaps clan or lineage chiefs commanding more-warlike peoples—imposed their wills over other groups and widening domains and some groups became significant political powers. At the dawn of the historical age, as preserved in early written materials and revealed by artifacts, frequent, intense clashes were already occurring between these contending forces as they evolved into states and as powerful individuals sought to establish sole rule over the realm and to found dynastic houses. Thereafter the scope of battle expanded; the strength and effectiveness of weapons increased; and military organization, tactics, and technology all developed. Eventually, battlefield lessons and command experience became the focus of conscious study; efforts were made to preserve the insights and avoid the errors of the past; and the science of military tactics and strategy was born.

By the second century B.C. China had already passed through a thousand years of almost unremitting conflict and had been brutally unified into a vast, powerful, imperially directed entity. Along the way, skilled commanders appeared, and major battles were fought. Campaigns became interminable, and the scale of destruction was immense, consuming both men and the thoughts they had committed to writing. However, among the small number of military writings that survived until unification, there were six major ones, including Sun-tzu's famous *Art of War.* They continued to be studied and transmitted down through the centuries until the remnants were collected and edited in the Sung dynasty around twelve hundred years later. Combined with a T'ang dynasty work, they compose the *Seven Military Classics,* a compilation that comprised the orthodox foundations for military thought and the basis for the imperial examinations required for martial appointment.

In the early 1970s, archaeologists excavating the Han dynasty tomb of a high-ranking official discovered a large number of immensely valuable texts written on remarkably well preserved bamboo slips. The military works among them include major portions of several of the *Seven Military Classics* and extensive fragments of Sun Pin's *Military Methods.* Although this book—by Sun-tzu's descendant—appeared in the bibliographic listings compiled in the Han dynasty, it had apparently vanished in the Han and been lost for over two thousand years. This important find thus increased the total extant military materials from the ancient period to eight classic works in all, supplemented by a few hundred other writings of various, but definitely later, dates.

Although tactical studies continued to be written throughout Chinese history, much of the vast military corpus has undoubtedly been lost over the centuries through carelessness, natural disasters, deliberate destruction, and warfare. However, ancient epigraphic materials and such early historical records as the *Tso chuan* and *Shih chi* also chronicle the exploits of generals and kings; the *Twenty-five Histories* preserves extensive information about men and actions; and Warring States philosophical works contain discussions of military issues. Thus resources abound, but only a part of the historical writings, including the complete *Tso chuan,* and essentially two of the *Seven Military Classics* (Sun-tzu's *Art of War*—three major versions, several minor ones—and the *Wu-tzu*—which appears as an appendix to Griffith's translation) have been translated and published.

Far from having vanished and being forgotten, these ancient Chinese military works have extensively influenced twentieth-century thought and are experiencing a new vitality in Asia. Not only in the military realm—throughout the century they have been thoroughly studied in Japan and China—do they continue to be discussed, but also in the business and personal spheres their resurgence is particularly evident. In the 1980s a management book that revived Sun-tzu's thought and employed the revitalized figures of several ancient martial heroes to instruct companies in the basics of business and marketing became a bestseller in the draconian Communist environment of the People's Republic of China and eventually in capitalist Hong Kong as well. Japanese companies have regularly held study groups to seek insights that may be implemented as corporate strategy. Koreans, enduring intense international pressure to revalue their currency, open their markets, and submit to trade limitations just when prosperity is attainable, are discovering strategies for international business warfare in these books.

In Taiwan, where companies confront a situation similar to Korea's, books applying the thoughts of the ancient strategists to life, business, sports, and the stock market have suddenly surged in popularity, even though modernists have ignored and scorned them for decades. Perhaps more astounding is the penchant of Japanese writers to apply principles and tactics from the *Seven Military Classics* to all the complexities of modern society; they use such tactics, for example, for successful human relations, romantic liaisons, and company infighting. In addition to at least one scholarly translation, several new paperbacks offering simplified renditions and popularized expansions of selected teachings are published annually in Japan. The ubiquitous *salaryman* may be seen reading them while commuting to work, and there are even comic-book editions to satisfy those so inclined. Naturally, tactics from the classics also frequently appear in novels, movies, and on television, and their words are quoted in contemporary media throughout Asia.

There is a great temptation, given the extensive materials rapidly becoming available from diverse sources, to undertake a truly comprehensive introduction to the entire military enterprise in Ancient China. Many topics critical to understanding strategy, tactics, and the evolution of military thought merit exploration and analysis. However, we have consciously focused upon depicting the historical context and reviewing the essential material aspects, such as armor and weapons, rather than ineffectually sketching comprehensive intellectual issues. Although we have not totally neglected the latter, exploring topics such as the relationships of Taoism and military thought in at least cursory fashion in the introductions and the extensive notes, these areas must largely be consigned to another work and to expert monographs. Similarly, although we have outlined the essentials of various concepts, such as unorthodox/orthodox, we have not analyzed them in depth, nor have we discussed the details of technology; concrete tactics of deployment; or the overall implementation of strategy beyond the discussions found in the *Seven Military Classics.* Furthermore, except in an occasional note, we have not explored the relationship of these texts to the *Kuan-tzu,* the *Book of Lord Shang,* or other Warring States philosophical writings that prominently espouse military policies, administrative measures, and strategic concepts. These and many other topics, including the systematic analysis and integration of ideas and methods in each of the classics, require extensive studies in themselves. Because their inclusion would be premature and would also make an already massive book more unwieldy, we will focus upon them in a future work integrating the interactive development of military technology and tactical thought.

Because this book is intended for the general reader, a rubric we assume encompasses everyone except those few specialists in ancient Chinese studies with expertise in the previously neglected military writings, we have provided somewhat fuller notes on many general aspects than might otherwise be necessary. Overall the notes have been designed for several different audiences; although much of the translation cries out for detailed annotation, in order to minimize the number of notes, we have refrained from exploring deeply every thought, concept, and strategy. Many of the notes simply provide contextual information or identify figures and terms for the convenience of readers unfamiliar with Chinese history and writings. Others are intended for those students of Asia—professional or not—who might benefit from further historical, technical, or military information or from the citation of certain seminal articles. Many notes comment upon the intricacies of translation matters: They provide alternative readings; note emendations we have accepted and commentaries followed; and sometimes indicate where we have relied upon our own judgment contrary to traditional readings. Finally, some amplify those portions of the introductory material where we sought to avoid dogmatic assertions about the numerous issues, such as textual authenticity, that have only tentatively been resolved or remain the subject of scholarly controversy. Every reader is encouraged to peruse them all, at least briefly, focusing upon those of greatest relevance in the quest to understand these texts.

Full bibliographic information is provided for each work at its first appearance in each chapter, with abbreviated titles thereafter. Consequently, for the bibliography we have departed from the usual format and instead provided a selected listing by subject for those who might wish to investigate the literature on a single topic. Numerous books with only tangential connections with the *Seven Military Classics* and solely of interest to specialists have been excluded. For matters of general knowledge that have not been annotated, the reader should consult the Western-language works listed in the bibliography for further reading.

A work of this scope, in our case undertaken enthusiastically without fully realizing the many thorny issues it would entail, is necessarily the product of years of reading, study, pondering, sifting, and effort. We have benefited vastly from the commentaries and essays of a hundred generations of Chinese scholars and from the growth of detailed knowledge deriving from the work of Western and Asian scholars in the present century. However, having left the academic community two decades ago, we have enjoyed a rather different, vibrant perspective on these ideas and philosophies—the result of twenty-five years of technical and business consulting at all levels in Japan, China, Taiwan, Korea, Hong Kong, Singapore, and Southeast Asia. For a startling number of our Asian associates, the various military classics remain compendiums of effective tactics and strategies, providing approaches and measures that can be profitably adopted in life and employed in business practices. Their discussions and understanding of many of the concrete lessons, although not necessarily orthodox or classically based, stimulated our own enlightenment on many issues. In particular, conversations over the decades in Asia with Guy Baer, Cleon Brewer, Ma Shang-jen, Kong Jung-yul, Professor W. K. Seong, Professor Ts'ai Mao-t'ang, and especially C. S. Shim have been both stimulating and illuminating.

Certain early teachers had a lasting influence on my approach to Chinese intellectual history. In particular, as a graduate student at Harvard in the turbulent 1960s I was greatly influenced by Professors Yang Lien-sheng, Yü Ying-shih, Benjamin Schwartz, and especially Dr. Achilles Fang, under whom I was privileged to be thrust into the true study of classical Chinese. Thereafter I was fortunate to read intermittently for more than a decade with Professor Chin Chia-hsi, a *Chuang-tzu* specialist and university professor of Chinese at National Taiwan University. However, my greatest intellectual debt is to Professor Nathan Sivin, initially a Sage at M.I.T.; a friend for more than twenty-five years; and ultimately responsible for both illuminating the Way and making the path accessible. However, these are all general intellectual obligations, not specific, for these scholars have not seen any portion of this work, and the survivors from Harvard would perhaps be astonished to learn that I have been carrying on the Chinese tradition of private scholarship over these many years.

Whereas I am responsible for the translations, introductions, and notes, Mei-chün Lee (Sawyer) has not only been an active participant in our discussions and studies over the years but also undertook numerous burdens associated with the detailed research of such historical issues as the evolution of weapons. She also contributed immeasurably through her insightful readings of the translations and the tedious investigation and comparison of various modern commentaries. Her collaborative efforts greatly aided my understanding of many issues and improved the overall work significantly, all while she continued to fulfill her responsibilities in our consulting operations.

Finally we would like to thank Westview Press, in particular, Peter Kracht, senior editor, for his efforts on this project. We have benefited greatly from Westview's editorial support and from the intensive, detailed reading of the translation provided through their auspices by Professor Robin D.S. Yates. Many of his numerous emendations and general suggestions substantially improved the work, and all his criticisms stimulated a careful reexamination of the texts and many additional materials; nevertheless, final responsibility for their evaluation and integration, where accepted, remains with the translators.

Others who assisted, especially in locating articles and textual materials in the United States and Asia, include Miao Yong-i, Marta Hanson, Yuriko Baer, Anton Stetzko, and Zhao Yong; Lorrie Stetzko provided expertise on horses and the intricacies of riding; and Bob Matheney and Max Gartenberg essentially made the project possible. We express our deep appreciation to all these people and to Lee T'ing-jung, who has honored the work with his calligraphy.

Ralph D. Sawyer

A Note on the Translation
and Pronunciation

The translation is based upon and rigorously follows the so-called Ming edition of the (Sung dynasty) *Seven Military Classics*, which contains and benefits from Liu Yin's consistent commentary—the *chih-chieh*, or "direct explanations"—throughout all seven books. However, although many of his comments are illuminating and even critical to understanding the actual text, scholarship continued to advance, and over the centuries, a few valuable commentaries and several variant editions that have furthered the process of understanding—particularly of the *Art of War*—have come out. Where the Ming text appears obviously defective, recourse for emendation is made first to the Sung edition and then to other variants. Full information on the individual variants employed is given in the introduction and the notes for each book, and the basic editions are listed in the bibliography.

We have sought to employ judiciously contemporary scholarship irrespective of its political perspective and to integrate insights provided by archaeological discoveries. The discovery of early versions, although dramatic and invaluable, precipitates the problem about which text to translate: the "original" versions, which entail numerous problems of their own, or the Sung *Seven Military Classics* edition, which has been historically available and influential for nine centuries. Because most of the *Seven Military Classics* have not previously been translated, we have chosen to make the traditional edition available first. Accordingly, we have used the newly recovered textual materials to make emendations only where they resolve highly problematic or completely incomprehensible passages, always annotating appropriately. Although we have refrained from indiscriminately revising the traditional text, significant differences between the newly recovered fragments and the historically transmitted edition are generally recorded in the notes.

In providing a translation for a general readership, rather than a somewhat more literal (and some would claim precise) version for sinologists, we hope to emulate the vibrant translations of Professor Burton Watson and thereby make these amazing texts accessible to the widest possible audience. We have thus avoided military jargon because, apart from the thorny question about each term's appropriateness, such terms would render the translation less comprehensible to anyone lacking military experience or unacquainted with military history.

Unfortunately, neither of the two commonly employed orthographies makes the pronunciation of romanized Chinese characters easy. Each system has its stumbling blocks and we remain unconvinced that the Pinyin *qi* is inherently more comprehensible than the Wade-Giles *ch'i,* although it is certainly no less comprehensible than *j* for *r* in Wade-Giles. However, as many of the important terms may already be familiar to Western readers and previous translations have employed Wade-Giles, we have opted to use that system throughout our work. Well-known cities, names, and books—such as Peking—are retained in their common form, and books and articles published with romanized names and titles also appear in their original form.

As a guide to pronunciation, we offer the following notes on the significant exceptions to normally expected sounds:

t, as in *Tao:* without apostrophe, pronounced like *d*
p, as in *ping:* without apostrophe, pronounced like *b*
ch, as in *chuang:* without apostrophe, pronounced like *j*
hs, as in *hsi:* pronounced *sh*
j, as in *jen:* pronounced like *r*

Thus, the name of the famous Chou dynasty is pronounced as if written "jou" and sounds just like the English name "Joe."

Chronology of Approximate Dynastic Periods

Dynastic Period	Years
LEGENDARY SAGE EMPERORS	2852–2255 B.C.
HSIA	2205–1766
SHANG	1766–1045
CHOU	1045–256
Western Chou	1045–770
Eastern Chou	770–256
Spring and Autumn	722–481
Warring States	403–221
CH'IN	221–207
FORMER HAN	206 B.C.–8 A.D.
LATER HAN	23–220
SIX DYNASTIES	222–589
SUI	589–618
T'ANG	618–907
FIVE DYNASTIES	907–959
SUNG	960–1126
SOUTHERN SUNG	1127–1279
YÜAN (*Mongol*)	1279–1368
MING	1368–1644
CH'ING (*Manchu*)	1644–1911

General Introduction and
Historical Background of the Classics

Military thought, the complex product of both violent war and intellectual analysis, suffered from disparagement and disrepute during almost all the past two millennia in Imperial China. Ignoring the original teachings of Confucius, self-styled Confucians eschewed—whether sincerely or hypocritically—the profession of arms and all aspects of military involvement from the Han dynasty on, growing more vociferous in their condemnation with the passing of centuries.[1] However, regardless of these people's civilized and cultured self-perception, the nation could not be without armies or generals, particularly in the face of constant "barbarian" threats and ongoing conflicts with volatile nomadic peoples. Accordingly, a number of early military treatises continued to be valued and studied and thereby managed to survive, while the turmoil of frequent crises inevitably fostered generations of professional military figures and additional strategic studies. Yet compared to the Confucian classics and various other orthodox writings, the military corpus remained minuscule, numbering at most a few hundred works.

Individual chapters of several writings by influential philosophers of the Warring States period (403–221 B.C.),[2] such as Lord Shang, also focused upon military matters, often with radical impact.[3] Many famous thinkers, including Hsün-tzu and Han Fei-tzu,[4] pondered the major questions of government administration and military organization; motivation and training; the nature of courage; and the establishment of policies to stimulate the state's material prosperity. The *Tso chuan* and other historical writings similarly record the thoughts of many key administrators and preserve the outlines of famous strategies, although their presentation of battlefield tactics is minimal.

A number of the ancient strategic monographs became relatively famous, and scholars in the Sung period (circa A.D. 1078) collected, edited, and assembled the six important survivors, augmenting them with a T'ang dynasty book; the final product was the *Seven Military Classics*. Thus codified, the seven works thereafter furnished the official textual foundation for government examinations in military affairs and concurrently provided a common ground for tactical and strategic conceptualization.

Despite incessant barbarian incursions and major military threats throughout its history, Imperial China was little inclined to pursue military solutions to aggression—except during the ill-fated expansionistic policies of the Former Han dynasty, or under dynamic young rulers, such as T'ang T'ai-tsung, during the founding years of a dynasty. Rulers and ministers preferred to believe in the myth of cultural attraction whereby their vastly superior Chinese civilization, founded upon Virtue[5] and reinforced by opulent material achievements, would simply overwhelm the hostile tendencies of the uncultured. Frequent gifts of the embellishments of civilized life, coupled with music and women, it was felt, would distract and enervate even the most warlike peoples. If they could not be either overawed into submission or bribed into compliance, other mounted nomadic tribes could be employed against the troublemakers, following the time-honored tradition of "using barbarian against barbarian."[6]

According to Confucian thought, which became the orthodox philosophy and prescribed state view in the Former Han, the ruler need only cultivate his Virtue, accord with the seasons, and implement benevolent policies in order to be successful in attracting universal support and fostering stability. Naturally, there were dissenting views, and even Mencius (371–289 B.C.), the second great Confucian, advocated punitive military expeditions to chastise evil rulers and relieve the people's suffering. However, except under rulers such as Sui Yang-ti (reigned A.D. 605–617), who sought to impose Chinese suzerainty on external regions—and thereby impoverished the nation—military affairs were pressed unwillingly; most of the bureaucracy tended to disdain anything associated with the military and the profession of arms.

Evolution of Conflict and Weapons in China

The Shang

Over the centuries Chinese military thought mirrored the evolution in weapons, economic conditions, and political power while creating the framework for strategic conceptualization and stimulating the development of battlefield methods. Tactics appropriate to the dawn of the historical Shang period changed in response to increased manpower, greater speed and mobility, and the invention of more-powerful shock and missile weapons. However, a critical kernel of thought that focused on basic questions, including organization, discipline, evaluation, objectives, and fundamental principles, retained its validity and continued to be applied until the Ch'in eventually conquered and unified the empire, thereby signifying the end of the Warring States period.

The Shang dynasty was a theocratic state whose power arose initially from, and continued to depend upon, the military skills of the nobility, in conjunction with its religious beliefs and institutions.[7] The populace was effectively divided into four classes: ruling families; royal clan members, many of whom were enfeoffed or served as officials, and other members of the nobility; common people, who were essentially serfs; and slaves.[8] The king exercised great power over a central area and enjoyed the allegiance of various lords in the peripheral territory. The nobility, which was educated and cultured, lived in well-organized cities marked by massive complex buildings, such as palaces and temples.[9] The common people, who dwelled in semi-earthen huts, farmed or practiced various specialized crafts during most of the year, although they were also required to provide conscript labor and even to mobilize to assist military campaigns.

Bronze technology advanced rapidly from the official inception of the Shang (traditionally dated as 1766 B.C., when T'ang I mounted his victorious campaign over the Hsia) until its collapse at the hands of the Chou, about 1045 B.C.[10] Intricately detailed ritual vessels, essential to the ancestor worship that underlay the king's power, provide dramatic evidence of the technological achievements and the government's effective management and monopoly of productive resources.[11] Although the weapons for the nobility were fashioned primarily from bronze, the raw materials for agricultural implements and the arms carried by the commoners were largely confined to stone, wood, and animal bones.[12] Millet and, later, wheat, were the staple crops, and they were stored in centralized granaries after harvesting. Rice was known, but it remained an expensive luxury even for the ruler because it was cultivated mainly in the south.[13] The level of material culture had progressed sufficiently to sustain cities with large populations based upon organized farming and systematic exploitation of the hunt. Some animals—such as sheep, oxen, pigs, and dogs—had been domesticated,[14] and both silk and hemp were produced. Vessels for ordinary use were made of pottery, which was marked by intricate designs.

Prior to the Shang dynasty, armed conflict essentially consisted of raids by and engagements between neolithic villages, although certain clan chiefs apparently developed local power bases and some regional strongmen emerged, such as those who founded the Hsia dynasty. However, with the rise of the Shang and the imposition of significant central authority (although not administration), a royal standing army of about a thousand was maintained. The number could be expanded as needed: The subservient lineage chiefs and state rulers would be ordered to furnish supporting armies. Although the king normally commanded in person, a rudimentary military bureaucracy with specialized officials already existed.[15] A royal campaign against border enemies might require three to five thousand men, and a campaign directed toward an insolent state as many as thirteen thousand.[16] Military actions required from a few days to perhaps three months; the actual battles generally were settled in a single confrontation, although engagements lasting several days have also been recorded.[17] The army was divided into three sections—left, right, and middle[18]—formed from two types of units: loosely organized infantry, conscripted from the privileged populace,[19] which acted in a supporting role; and chariots, manned by the nobles fulfilling their martial responsibilities as warriors and sustainers of the state.

Shang warfare objectives included the imposition or reinforcement of royal suzerainty, the mass capture of prisoners, and the seizure of riches.[20] Control over areas outside the central core continued to be imposed through a vassal-like network, rather than through integration under a centrally administered bureaucracy. Plunder increased the wealth of the royal house and also furnished the means to reward loyal service. Some prisoners were enslaved and forced to work in either agricultural or domestic tasks, but large numbers were sacrificed as part of Shang religious ceremonies.[21]

During the several hundred years of Shang rule, bronze weapons formed an integral part of every Shang warrior's arsenal.[22] The preferred weapon was the *ko* (halberd, or dagger-ax),[23] supplemented by spears[24] and the compound bow.[25] Bronze-tipped arrows, propelled by reflex bows whose pull may have reached 160 pounds, provided effective action at a distance. Daggers and hatchets were available for close fighting; leather armor and large shields—the latter used in coordinated fighting tactics—offered considerable protection against shock weapons and projectiles.[26] Bronze helmets were fabricated to deflect missiles and glancing blows, and thin bronze plates were affixed as outer protection on both armor and shields. According to Warring States theory, weapons were usually of mixed type, providing the means for both aggressive and defensive action at close and long ranges. However, the sword evolved slowly, apparently from daggers or perhaps the dagger-ax, and true swords did not become common until the middle of the Warring States period.[27]

The chariot functioned as the basic fighting unit during the late Shang, Western Chou, and Spring and Autumn (722–481 B.C.) periods; it remained important until well into the Warring States (403–221), when it was gradually supplanted by large infantry masses and eventually, during the third century B.C., began to be supplemented by the cavalry. Chinese tradition portrays the Shang as having employed seventy chariots during the campaign of rectification to oust the evil Hsia dynasty.[28] However, twentieth-century archaeological discoveries, supplemented by textual research, indicate that the chariot, rather than being an indigenous development, did not reach China from Central Asia until the middle of the Shang dynasty—approximately 1300 to 1200 B.C.[29] Initially, the use of chariot was probably confined to ceremonies and transportation and only gradually was expanded to the hunt and eventually to warfare. Epigraphic materials provide evidence that the Shang relied upon infantry units of nobility to confront their enemies even after the integration of the chariot into their military organization. In fact, throughout the Shang, the chariot may have remained a prestige symbol; its function during military engagements was restricted to providing transport mobility and serving as a command platform rather than constituting a significant military weapon.

The chariots of the late Shang and subsequent Chou periods normally carried three men: the driver in the center, the archer on the left, and a warrior with a dagger-ax on the right. Five chariots constituted a squad, the basic functional unit, and five squads composed a brigade. Each chariot had a complement of 10 to 25 close-supporting infantry, with an additional vanguard of perhaps 125 men in later times.[30] A Shang team consisted of two horses, and the rectangular chariot rode on two sturdy, multispoked wheels. Training for warfare included large-scale royal hunts that utilized chariots, although given the difficulty of developing driving skills and the fighting expertise appropriate to a racing chariot, far more practice must have been necessary.[31] It was an expensive weapon that required craftsmen to build and maintain; thus its use was confined to the nobility, minimally supported by conscripted commoners. Battles accordingly resolved into a number of individual clashes, with personal combat supposedly governed by appropriate ceremonial constraints (probably a later romanticization). A few scholars have seen references to hunting on horseback in certain sentences, but these claims are generally discounted: The horse was employed only in conjunction with the chariot. However, lacking stirrups and a saddle and hampered by his long robes, the mounted rider could not become an effective military element until the third century B.C.

The Chou

The Chou came to power by overthrowing the Shang in a decisive battle at Mu-yeh after many years of stealthy preparation and the gradual expansion of their power base through carefully wrought alliances, the submission of some smaller states, and the subjugation of other clans and peoples. Possibly descendants of the Hsia,[32] the Chou originally dwelled to the north but had been forced south into the Wei River valley by more-aggressive peoples.[33] As the Chou were situated on the periphery of Shang culture, they were able to assimilate many of the material and cultural achievements of Shang civilization in relative freedom while successfully developing a strong agricultural base, indigenous technology, and their own cultural identity. External barbarian pressures stimulated their military skills, organizational abilities, and tactical thought simultaneously, and the Shang even entrusted them with the task of subjugating rebellious peoples in the west, which allowed the Chou to increase their military prowess.[34] When they mounted their final campaign against the debauched, enervated Shang, the Chou's weapons and implements were similar to the Shang's. Perhaps the only Chou innovation was the extensive employment of chariots, facilitating more-rapid movement and the conveying of greater quantities of weapons and supplies.[35] The Chou's victory probably stemmed in large part not only from the Shang's disorganization but also from the exhaustion suffered by the Shang in fighting off hostile nomadic peoples to the north and east and from their large-scale commitment to a southern military expedition at the moment of attack.[36] The Chou's overall campaign and tactics (particularly if the *Book of Documents* and the *Six Secret Teachings* preserve any reliable material) approached the conflict from a new perspective—abandoning ritualistic, formal combat for effective revolutionary activity.[37]

The Chou kings were confronted with the immediate problem of ruling an empire of disparate peoples and far-flung territories with only a small Chou population. Although the Chou had apparently enjoyed the allegiance of roughly eight hundred states in the final campaign against the Shang, many had also opposed them. These enemy peoples, the tens of thousands of Shang nobility, and even the populace of their own allies all had to be effectively controlled, and smoldering rebellions quenched. Immediately after the famous battle at Mu-yeh, King Wu had the T'ai Kung secure the Chou hold over the surrounding area. Next, when returning to the capital, the Chou vanquished a number of recalcitrant states lying along the corridor of their march.[38] Finally, the Western Chou consolidated their rule through several political and military measures, the most important of which was the enfeoffment of powerful clan members among both allied and dissident states. Each person so enfeoffed would establish a collateral family line and would emigrate with his family members, retainers, and military forces. They would constitute a Chou enclave among the local people and would immediately construct a walled town, which would function as the Chou military, political, economic, administrative, and cultural center.[39]

The Chou also forced thousands of Shang noble families to emigrate to the eastern capital region, where they could be adequately supervised and controlled, although they were allowed to retain most of their own officials, customs, and laws.[40] Thereafter, the early Chou kings imposed their rule and consolidated their power through close connections with all the vassals thus established. The obedience of these feudal lords was ensured by their participation in clan activities and power, was reinforced by their military and political inferiority, and was emphasized by their relative isolation—all of which necessitated mutual cooperation under the king's directives. The Shang's theocratic character was displaced by a more worldly approach, although the Chou king preserved and emphasized his right to sacrifice to the ancestors, whose intimate involvement in state affairs remained necessary, and to Heaven, which had sanctified Chou's revolutionary activity.

In addition to maintaining six royal armies[41] and posting garrison units throughout the realm, the Chou also incorporated eight armies from the vanquished Shang and could summon the forces of their own vassals as necessary. These units were still composed essentially of nobility, although they were assisted by commoners, personal retainers, and servants in a secondary role. No doubt the *shih*—minor descendants of the ruling house, younger sons of earls and dukes, and other members of the lesser nobility—also furnished many of the combatants and foot support. Throughout the Western Chou period, the actual fighting was conducted by men of rank and was marked increasingly by mutual deference and respect, with the chariot dominating as the focus of power and mobility.

The Western Chou

Following the final conquest of the peripheral areas and their integration under central authority through the imposition of a feudal system, the first few hundred years of the Western Chou period witnessed no dramatic changes in military technology or strategy. Armor more suited to the increasingly active role played by infantrymen appeared and evolved, thanks to improvements in tanning and leather-working capabilities. Coincident with the consistent advances in metallurgical skills, the shape of weapons continued to evolve slowly, becoming longer, stronger, and more complex, eventually resulting in the development of the true sword, which appeared in limited quantities by the end of the Western Chou in 771 B.C. However, long weapons persisted—for fighting either from chariots or dismounted—with the halberd (dagger-ax) predominating.

After only four generations, the central power of the Western Chou began to erode, dissipated partly by fatal expansionist campaigns into the south. Early on, the Western Chou became preoccupied with barbarian threats from the north and west, and they were impoverished as the kings continued to grant fiefs and rewards to the loyal vassals who sustained the government. Consequently, the feudal lords gradually rose in power, and although still reluctantly obedient to the king's demands, they became increasingly self-conscious about their regional identities, particularly as they interacted with local peoples and cultures. The ruling house was also plagued by weak and incompetent rulers, some of whom had obviously forgotten that King Chou's debauchery was among the justifications cited when King Wu presumptuously claimed the sanction of the Mandate of Heaven. Eventually, in 771 B.C., a Chou king, restored to the throne through the efforts of vassal states, was compelled to move the capital ignominiously to the east to avoid barbarian pressures and prolong the myth of dynasty. Ironically, one of his defensive actions was to enfeoff the ancestors of the state of Ch'in as a reward for their horsebreeding efforts, in the expectation that they (who were semibarbarians themselves) would form a bulwark against the nomadic tide.

The Spring and Autumn

The Spring and Autumn period (722–481 B.C.), named after the famous Confucian classic chronicling the era, witnessed the rise of state power, development of internecine strife, and destruction of numerous political entities. At its inception, descendants of the various Chou feudal lords still ruled in most states, generally in conjunction with other members of their immediate families and the local nobility. Although they appeared to exercise supreme power, their positions depended largely upon the kinship system and the state as extensions of the greater clan. With the Chou's continued decline, the states were effectively freed of their subservient status and therefore were able to exercise increasing independence in their activities. Their new assertiveness reflected not only the shift in the balance of power from a central authority to peripheral actors but also the distinct weakening of the original ties of kinship upon which enfeoffment had been based. The passing of generations, combined with the inherent difficulties of traveling to the capital to participate actively in the Chou court, had contributed to this estrangement. Although the feudal lords continued to seek Chou sanctification and strongmen later appeared to wield power as hegemons in the dynasty's name, their acquiescence in major political and military affairs had to be sought—rather than being mandated—by the king. Freed of old constraints, the feudal lords focused on internal strife and interstate conflict instead of devoting themselves to performing the duties of vassals.

The locus of state power also tended to shift from the enfeoffed ruling house to the contending parties. From the beginning to the middle of the era, the ministerial families—mostly collateral descendants of the first feudal lord—grew more powerful. In many states they even wrested control of the government from the legitimate line, only to exterminate each other in the next century. By the end of the period the surviving states all had effective despots—either members of the founding family who had managed to reseize power or survivors from one of the great families that had usurped the throne. Because more than a hundred states were annexed or extinguished during the Spring and Autumn period—with their ruling clans and great families reduced to commoners, enslaved, or killed—much of the original feudal nobility ceased to exist.[42]

As a result of the predatory campaigns of the stronger states, the scope of warfare in the Spring and Autumn period increased dramatically. It necessarily involved greater numbers of peasants as integral elements because it could not depend solely upon the nobility. Sustained combat, at least on open terrain, apparently remained centered on the chariot supported by infantry forces, which grew more and more numerous. Concepts of chivalry initially prevailed, and the ethics of battle dictated adherence to the *li* (forms of propriety), although conscripted infantry were little bound by them. Within a century, however, only the foolish and soon-to-be-defeated were burdened by the old code of ethics, and the ancient style of individual combat—despite personal challenges still offered to instigate battles—was outmoded.[43]

Early in the period, campaign armies consisted of roughly several hundred to a thousand chariots, accompanied by perhaps ten thousand men. However, by the end of the Spring and Autumn period in 481 B.C., the strong states of Ch'in and Ch'i fielded approximately four thousand chariots each, supported by forty thousand infantrymen. Cavalry remained unknown, and in 541 B.C. the Chin commander even compelled his reluctant chariot forces to dismount and—as infantrymen—engage barbarian foot soldiers.[44]

Combat weapons throughout the period were similar to those of the Western Chou, with the infantrymen depending more upon spears and short swords than the dagger-ax (halberd), which was the weapon par excellence of charioteers.[45] Metalworking skills continued to advance, resulting in stronger, sharper, larger, and more-deadly combat tools. Yet bronze technology remained the norm, with the newly discovered processes of iron and steel technology (in the late Spring and Autumn period) confined largely to the production of agricultural implements.[46]

Wars occurred frequently, and even the most powerful state, should it fail to prepare its defenses and train its soldiers, could be vanquished. Consequently, the recognition and retention of individuals proficient in the military arts became essential, and rewards—including position, honors, and rank—for valor, strength, and military achievements were initiated. Basic physical qualifications for members of the standing army and for those selected to more elite units were maintained.[47]

As talent grew in importance, resulting in social mobility, bureaucracies staffed by capable individuals began to expand, supplementing and then displacing government by members of the ruler's clan and the entrenched nobility. More-direct forms of administration, through the establishment of districts rather than through enfeoffment, apparently emerged, permitting the central government to wield greater power over the entire state. Peasants slowly began to gain land tenancy instead of being serfs; they prospered economically as property gradually became a transferable commodity rather than the sole possession of the king.

The Warring States Period

At the beginning of the Warring States period in 403 B.C., the pace of events accelerated. The conflicts of the Spring and Autumn period had segmented China into seven powerful survivor-states,[48] each contending for control of the realm, and fifteen weaker states for them to prey upon. The feudal lords had by then evolved into despotic monarchs who were compelled to nurture the development of extensive economic and political bureaucracies just to survive. In order to suppress external threats effectively, virtually every ruler had to expand his state's agricultural base. The immigration of disaffected people from other states was encouraged by policies providing them with land, and tenancy and landownership continued their swift development. After 500 B.C. iron implements came into general use, and drainage and irrigation projects vastly increased the food reserves—and therefore strength—of some areas. Trade and commerce flourished, and as a result, a class of influential merchants arose, although they continued to be officially despised.

During the Warring States period, the scale of conflict surged phenomenally, sustained by the increasing agricultural productivity and expanding material prosperity. In the Shang a few thousand men once had constituted an army, whereas now the weaker states easily fielded 100,000 and the strongest, in the third century B.C., reportedly maintaining a standing army of nearly a million, is said to have even mobilized 600,000 for a single campaign. In the battle between Ch'in and Ch'u the total number of combatants apparently exceeded a million, an astounding figure even after discounting for inaccuracy and exaggeration. Numerical strength had become critical, for in the previous campaign Ch'in, with 200,000 soldiers, had suffered a severe defeat. Naturally, casualties also escalated rapidly, with 100,000 from Wei dying at the battle of Ma-ling in 341 B.C.; 240,000 in the combined forces of Wei and Han perishing at I-ch'üeh in 295 B.C.; and 450,000 men of Ch'u being slaughtered at Ch'ang-p'ing in 260 B.C. Campaigns of such magnitude required lengthy periods for logistical preparation, mobilization, and engagement. Instead of a few days or weeks on the march, with perhaps a couple of days in battle, as in the Shang, months and even years were necessary, with the battles raging for tens of days, or stalemates persisting for a year or more.

Managing the employment of such vast resources and manpower demanded great expertise, and the profession of arms quickly developed. Whereas the newly free masses were generally registered and subjected to military training on a seasonal basis and were conscripted for combat when needed, the army's core had to be composed of practiced, disciplined officers and soldiers. Drill manuals and deployment methods, as well as the tactics they would be designed to execute, suddenly became indispensable. An extensive body of military theory appeared, stimulated not only by battlefield and training requirements but also by new political theories and individual philosophies. Numerous military books—remnants of which survive—were no doubt composed during the early part of the Warring States, and their theories found rigorous employment thereafter.

The commander's qualifications and responsibilities also changed during the period, with strategy becoming so complex that the replacement of a general could, and frequently did, result in an army's defeat and the endangerment of an entire nation. Although rulers continued to meddle in army matters—with catastrophic results—often at the instigation of jealous ministers or corrupt officials acting on behalf of foreign powers, in general, professional officers who specialized solely in military affairs appeared. Early in the Warring States period the ideal commander was normally an effective, even exemplary, civilian administrator, such as Wu Ch'i, but toward the end, the civilian realm became increasingly estranged from the realities of warfare.[49]

During the Shang and early Chou periods, battles were fought on agricultural and otherwise open, undefended terrain, with mobilized armies encountering only scattered cities during their advances. Some fortifications seem to have always existed—such as the famous thick neolithic and Shang dynasty stamped-earth walls that are still being discovered—but forces could essentially roam through the countryside unhampered until encountering them. In the Warring States period the feudal lords undertook the expanded defense of borders, constructing "great walls," ramparts, forts, and guard towers throughout the countryside to defend the entire territory against incursion.[50] States protected their land more than their people, and the objective of warfare changed as each state sought not to capture prisoners and plunder for riches but to vanquish its enemies by seizing their lands, exterminating their armies, gaining political control of their populace, and administratively annexing their territory.

Fortified cities, previously military and administrative centers, grew enormously in significance as industry, trade, and population all flourished, and they became focal points in the road network. Accordingly, whereas in the Western Chou and Spring and Autumn periods it was advisable to circumvent these isolated cities rather than to waste men and resources besieging and assaulting them, their capture or destruction now assumed critical importance. Techniques for assault and defense advanced simultaneously, with siege engines, mobile shields, battering rams, catapults, mobile towers, and similar mobile devices appearing in substantial numbers. Specialists in the technologies of assault and defense were needed: The Mohists, who created and mastered defensive techniques and measures, became famous for their dedication to assisting the targets of aggression. Therefore, Sun-tzu's condemnation of besieging and assaulting cities had become outdated by the time of Sun Pin's analysis of vulnerable and impregnable targets in his *Military Methods*.[51]

The growth of mass infantry armies was also accompanied by the perfection and widespread use of the crossbow during the fourth century B.C.;[52] by further developments in articulation, deployment, and maneuvering capabilities; and by the reluctant adoption of barbarian practices to create the cavalry.[53] Under constant pressure from mounted steppe horsemen, various perceptive commanders and rulers realized the need to develop their own cavalry. Although the history of the horse in China is still emerging, it appears that in 307 B.C. King Wu-ling of North Chao, over vehement objections, deliberately—to facilitate adoption of the cavalry—forced on his troops the "barbarian style of dress" (short jacket and trousers) instead of the indigenous and much-revered long coat of the Chinese. Since the fifth century mounted horsemen had apparently been challenging the Chinese states. The skill of riding probably evolved from Iran and the steppe region, and foreign horses had long been famous in China for their speed and endurance. Wu-ling created the first known cavalry, immediately providing the state with a vastly increased offensive potential.

The saddle, when there was one, was extremely primitive—only a rolled blanket, and stirrups did not appear until the end of the Han. Consequently, the rider was burdened with the task of simultaneously controlling his horse and either shooting his bow or striking with his shock weapon. The effectiveness of the horsemen, acting from such an unstable platform, was inevitably limited and stemmed more from their great speed and mobility than inherent fighting power. However, the development of the cavalry—mentioned only briefly in the military books prior to T'ang T'ai-tsung—freed armies from being confined to open, chariot-accessible terrain and allowed their diffuse deployment in ravines, valleys, forests, hilly fields, and mountains, fully exploiting the terrain.[54] Supported by vast hordes of armored infantrymen wielding spears, crossbows, and swords (possibly of iron),[55] warfare on an unprecedented scale suddenly became both possible and inevitable. In the final century of conflict, the third century B.C., which witnessed the growth and decisive triumph of Ch'in, massive campaigns requiring hundreds of thousands of men executing both "explosive" and "persisting" strategies decimated the populace and the countryside. In those days the strategies and methods of the famous tacticians were repeatedly tested and applied and were proven to have a timeless validity.

The State of Wei

The history of Wei, an important participant in the politics of the era, reflects the evolution of military affairs during the Warring States period. Wu Ch'i[56] became a famous general and military administrator in Wei, whereas both Mencius, the early Confucian standard-bearer, and Wei Liao-tzu, reputed progenitor of the military classic bearing his name, squandered their persuasive skills on King Hui. One of the seven powers in the Warring States period, Wei had become an independent political entity in 434 B.C. when three powerful families carved the large, formerly mighty state of Chin into Wei, Chao, and Han. In 403 B.C. the Chou king recognized the de facto rulers as feudal lords, and in 376 B.C. they completely exterminated the remnants of the Chin ruling house. Situated in the central part of China between the contending powers of Ch'in to the west and Ch'i to the east, Wei was the strongest of the so-called three Chin. Initially, the capital was at An-i, but the fertile plains area in which it was located lacked such natural defenses as mountains and ravines, and the government suffered from constant pressure from hostile neighbors in all directions. When the government was strong and prosperous, it could retain control over the West Ho region and thus fend off any threat from the belligerent Ch'in; when weak—through the ruler's ineptitude or some disaster—it suffered repeated defeats in the incessant warfare. Furthermore, whereas Ch'in had been successfully stymied by the strength of the great Chin, once the latter was segmented, the successor states—indifferent to mutual cooperation—lacked the power necessary for independent survival.

King Wen, who reigned from the inception of Wei until 387 B.C., realized the need for talented advisers and welcomed worthy men irrespective of their regional origin. Li K'o, one of the outsiders who responded to this policy, was appointed to high office and had great impact. He rewrote the laws, promulgated measures to increase agricultural production, established private property, and fostered a stable commodity-price policy. Hsi-men Pao focused his efforts upon irrigation, thereby greatly increasing the nation's wealth. Wu Ch'i, appointed commanding general, conducted numerous successful campaigns against the Ch'in and secured the defense of the West Ho region. King Wen's son King Wu continued Wu Ch'i's basic policy, thereby compelling the other Chin states of Han and Chao to respect Wei's might and prosperity, although Wu Ch'i was ignominiously forced by court intrigues to flee for his life.

Unfortunately, King Hui—who assumed power in 370 B.C.—was more successful in antagonizing people than in employing them, and he forfeited the services of many talented individuals, such as Lord Shang (who subsequently was instrumental in strengthening Ch'in). Instead of nurturing harmonious relations with his neighbors, he appears to have constantly annoyed them, greatly exacerbating the pressures and conflicts on all sides. Furthermore, he eventually lost the West Ho region, thereby opening the state to incursions by Ch'in, and was forced to move the capital to Ta-liang, thereafter calling the state Liang.

Two famous battles illustrate the nature of warfare in this period. The first, at Kui-ling, stemmed from King Hui's desire to recoup losses suffered at the hands of Ch'in in the west. Wei's army, under the command of P'ang Chüan, attacked Chao in the north. Finding itself hard-pressed, Chao requested aid from Ch'i, in the east, on the premise that as Chao presented a natural barrier and defense against Wei, it would be strategically advantageous for Ch'i to support Chao's efforts. Although the Ch'i ruler assented, Sun Pin—the famous strategist whose book has recently been rediscovered—advised waiting for the two antagonists to exhaust themselves, thereby ensuring maximum gain with minimum risk and effort. In 352 B.C., under the command of T'ien Chi, Ch'i mobilized an army to effect an indirect strike at the Wei homeland, the critical city of Ta-liang, in accord with the principles of "first seize what they love," "attack vacuity," and "strike where undefended." P'ang Chüan, flushed with his victories in Chao, reacted as predicted, racing back to mount a counterattack. Ch'i then feigned concern and withdrew to its chosen battlefield to await the Wei army, thereby following a number of basic tactical principles from Sun-tzu and Sun Pin, such as "with ease await the tired." From its fortified positions and high terrain Ch'i was able to quickly defeat the exhausted Wei army, inflicting severe casualties at minimal cost.

Some years later, Wei found itself being increasingly squeezed by a newly vigorous Han, to the south, Ch'in, to the west, Ch'i, to the east, and Chao, to the north. King Hui embarked on a campaign against Han, which had become formidable through the administrative efforts of the famous theorist Shen Pu-hai and by forming an alliance with and returning to Chao the cities previously lost. P'ang Chüan, again entrusted with command, struck directly at the Han capital. Han, as Chao had before, sought aid from Ch'i, citing the benefits of mutual defense. Again Sun Pin advised waiting for the forces to decimate each other, further weakening Wei. Han mounted a total defensive effort but lost five major battles in succession and was forced to submit to Ch'in in a desperate effort to survive. Ch'i then sallied forth, following the previous strategy, with Sun Pin as strategist and T'ien Chi in command. P'ang Chüan immediately abandoned his campaign in Han, turning back toward his home state. Meanwhile, King Hui mobilized all his resources, placing his son in command of the home-defense troops, with the sole aim of seeking a decisive confrontation with Ch'i.

Under Sun Pin's direction the Ch'i armies, which were advancing into Wei, followed the dictum "be deceptive." P'ang Chüan arrogantly believed the men of Ch'i to be cowards who would flee rather than engage mighty Wei in battle. Therefore, Sun Pin daily reduced the number of cooking fires in the encampment to create a facade of ever-increasing desertion. He also effected a tactical withdrawal to further entice P'ang Chüan into the favorable terrain at Ma-ling where the Ch'i commander concealed ten thousand crossbowmen among the hills. P'ang Chüan, apparently afraid that he would miss an opportunity to inflict a severe blow on the retreating Ch'i army, abandoned his heavy forces and supply train and rushed forth with only light units. Arriving at night, the combined Wei forces were ambushed as soon as they penetrated the killing zone. In addition to being decisively defeated by Ch'i's withering crossbow fire, 100,000 Wei soldiers needlessly perished because of their commander's character flaws and hasty judgment.[57]

Thereafter, Wei not only never regained its former power but also suffered numerous incursions by the now-unchecked mighty Ch'in, which would eventually subjugate all China. In 340 B.C. Wei was forced to cede 700 *li* to Ch'in after sustained defeats, and felt compelled to move its capital to Ta-li-ang to avoid the incessant danger. Although a strong figure occasionally emerged to effect a temporary resurgence in Wei's strength, its territory continued to shrink until the state, together with the royal house, was finally extinguished in 225 B.C.

The Military Writings

In order to appreciate the great value and inherent importance of the Chinese military classics, one should note several brief historical and political points. First, military works were not normally permitted in private hands, and their possession could be construed as evidence of a conspiracy. (Possession of the T'ai Kung's *Six Secret Teachings*—a book advocating and instructing revolution—would be particularly fatal.) Second, almost all these teachings were at first transmitted down through the generations, often orally and always secretly. Eventually they were recorded—committed to written form on bamboo slips—and sometimes became public knowledge. Government scribes and designated officials gathered the slips for state use, depositing them in imperial libraries, where they were so highly valued that they were exempted from the infamous book burnings of the Ch'in dynasty. Once stored away, they were accessible to a few professors of the classics, a restricted number of high officials, and the emperor himself. Even these privileged individuals might still be denied access to the critical writings, especially if they were related to the imperial family.

Even after the teachings were recorded in manuscript form on bamboo, silk, or eventually paper (after the Han dynasty), patriots sometimes felt compelled to remove them from public domain. General Chang Liang, who played a fundamental role in the overthrow of the tyrannical Ch'in dynasty and in the establishment of the Han, for example, supposedly had the sole copy of the *Three Strategies of Huang Shih-kung,* from which he had personally profited, buried with him in his casket. According to one tradition, however, the text resurfaced when his tomb was vandalized in the fourth century A.D. Another example is the well-known (although perhaps apocryphal) refusal of Li Wei-kung, a famous strategist and effective general, to provide the T'ang emperor with more than defensive knowledge and tactics. In the view of Li Wei-kung, strategies for aggressive action should not be disseminated because, with the empire already at peace, they could only aid and interest those who wanted to precipitate war and incite revolution.

The seven military books, as they have been traditionally arranged in the *Seven Military Classics* since the Sung dynasty, are

> *Sun-tzu's Art of War*
> *Wu-tzu*
> *The Methods of the Ssu-ma (Ssu-ma Fa)*
> *Questions and Replies Between T'ang T'ai-tsung and Li Wei-kung*
> *Wei Liao-tzu*
> *Three Strategies of Huang Shih-kung*
> *T'ai Kung's Six Secret Teachings*

Although uncertainly abounds regarding the authorship and dates of several of the classics, as well as to what extent they are composite books drawing upon common ground and lost writings, the traditional order unquestionably is not chronological. Sun-tzu's *Art of War* has generally been considered the oldest and greatest extant Chinese military work, even though the purported author of the *Six Secret Teachings*—the T'ai Kung—was active hundreds of years earlier than the (possibly) historical Sun-tzu. Materials preserved in the *Ssu-ma Fa* reputedly extend back into the early Chou; the *Wu-tzu* may have been recorded by Wu Ch'i's disciples, although suffering from later accretions; and the *Three Strategies* probably follows the *Wei Liao-tzu*, yet traditionalists still associate it with the T'ai Kung. Accordingly, one possible order (with many caveats and unstated qualifications) might well be

INITIAL PERIOD	*Ssu-ma Fa*
	Art of War
SECOND PERIOD	*Wu-tzu*
THIRD PERIOD	*Wei Liao-tzu*
	Six Secret Teachings
	Three Strategies
T'ANG–SUNG	*Questions and Replies*

Biographies of the purported authors, along with summary discussions of the evidence for ascribing dates of composition to particular periods, are found in the introductions to the individual translations. Much of the evidence is tenuous and often circular, and the systematic study of the evolution of strategic thought and military concepts remains to be undertaken. However, the preceding sequence—although possibly infuriating Sun-tzu advocates—seems sustainable in the light of both traditional textual scholarship and recent tomb discoveries. The relative order of books in the third period (which probably coincides with the latter half of the third century B.C.) remains to be defined.[58] Although we recognize these chronological issues, for purposes of continuity in introducing essential historical material and developments, our order of presentation places the *Six Secret Teachings* first, discussing the T'ai Kung as an active participant in the great Chou drama that would affect and color Chinese history for three millennia. The *Ssu-ma Fa,* which makes frequent references to Chou practices, follows, and then the *Art of War.* The *Wu-tzu,* which might have been composed close to the time of the *Art of War,* completes the early Warring States works. Thereafter, the sequence continues in likely chronological order, with the *Wei Liao-tzu,* the *Three Strategies,* and finally the medieval *Questions and Replies.*

1

T'ai Kung's Six Secret Teachings

太公六韜

IV   Tiger Secret Teaching   76

V   Leopard Secret Teaching   89

VI   Canine Secret Teaching   96

Translator's Introduction

*T*HE *Six Secret Teachings* purportedly records the T'ai Kung's political advice and tactical instructions to Kings Wen and Wu of the Chou dynasty in the eleventh century B.C. Although the present book evidently dates from the Warring States period (as is discussed at the end of this introduction), some scholars believe it reflects the tradition of Ch'i military studies[1] and therefore preserves at least vestiges of the oldest strata of Chinese military thought. The historic T'ai Kung, to whom the *Six Secret Teachings* is nominally attributed, has been honored throughout Chinese history to be the first famous general and the progenitor of strategic studies. In the T'ang dynasty he was even accorded his own state temple as the martial patron and thereby attained officially sanctioned status approaching that of Confucius, the revered civil patron.[2]

A complete work that not only discusses strategy and tactics but also proposes the government measures necessary for forging effective state control and attaining national prosperity, the *Six Secret Teachings* is grounded on—or perhaps projected back into—monumental historical events. The Chou kings presumably implemented many of these policies, thereby enabling them to develop their agricultural and population bases, gradually expand their small border domain, and secure the allegiance of the populace until they could launch the decisive military campaign that defeated the powerful Shang dynasty and overturned its six-hundred-year rule.

The *Six Secret Teachings* is the only military classic written from the perspective of revolutionary activity because the goal of the Chou was nothing less than a dynastic revolution. Attaining this objective required perfecting themselves in the measures and technologies of the time and systematically developing policies, strategies, and even battlefield tactics not previously witnessed in Chinese history. The Chou kings were compelled to ponder employing limited resources and restricted forces to attack a vastly superior, well-entrenched foe whose campaign armies alone probably outnumbered the entire Chou population. In contrast, many of the other strategic writings focus on managing military confrontations between states of comparable strength, with both sides starting from relatively similar military and government infrastructures. Furthermore, although nearly all the military texts adhere to the basic concept of "enriching the state (through agriculture) and strengthening the army," many tend to emphasize strategic analysis and battlefield tactics rather than the fundamental measures necessary to create even the possibility of confrontation.[3]

The epoch-making clash between the Chou and Shang dynasties, as envisioned by the Chou and idealistically portrayed in later historical writings, set the moral tone and established the parameters for the dynastic cycle concept. The archetypal battle of virtue and evil—the benevolent and righteous acting on behalf of all the people against a tyrant and his coterie of parasitic supporters—had its origin with this conflict. The Shang's earlier conquest of the Hsia, although portrayed as having been similarly conceived, occurred before the advent of written language and was only a legend even in antiquity. However, the Chou's determined effort to free the realm from the yoke of suffering and establish a rule of Virtue and benevolence became the inspirational essence of China's moral self-perception. As dynasties decayed and rulers became morally corrupt and increasingly ineffectual, new champions of righteousness appeared who confronted the oppressive forces of government, rescued the people from imminent doom, and returned the state to benevolent policies. Moreover, in the view of some historians, the Shang-Chou conflict marked the last battle between different peoples because starting with the Chou dynasty, military engagements within China were essentially internal political clashes.[4] However, confrontations between inhabitants of the agrarian central states and the nomadic steppe peoples continued throughout Chinese history, reflecting in part the self-conscious identity emphasized by the people of the central states in contrast with their "barbarian" neighbors.

As portrayed in such historical writings as the *Shih chi*,[5] and in accord with good moral tradition and the plight of the people, the Shang had ascended to power by overthrowing the last evil ruler of the previous dynasty—the Hsia.[6] After generations of rule, the Shang emperors—due perhaps to their splendid isolation and constant indulgence in myriad pleasures—are believed to have become less virtuous and less capable.[7] Their moral decline continued inexorably until the final ruler, who history has depicted as evil incarnate. The many perversities attributed to him included imposing heavy taxes; forcing the people to perform onerous labor services, mainly to provide him with lavish palaces and pleasure centers; interfering with agricultural practices, thereby causing widespread hunger and deprivation; indulging in debauchery, including drunkenness, orgies, and violence; brutally murdering innumerable people, especially famous men of virtue and loyal court officials; and developing and inflicting inhuman punishments. However, as the following brief excerpt from the Shang Annals in the *Shih chi* records, the king was also talented, powerful, and fearsome:

> In natural ability and discrimination Emperor Chou was acute and quick; his hearing and sight were extremely sensitive; and his physical skills and strength surpassed other men. His hands could slay a fierce animal; his knowledge was sufficient to ward off criticism; and his verbal skills [were] sufficient to adorn his errors. He boasted to his ministers about his own ability; he was haughty to all the realm with his reputation; and [he] believed that all were below him. He loved wine, debauched himself in music, and was enamored of his consorts. He loved Ta Chi, and followed her words.[8] Thus he had Shih Chüan create new licentious sounds, the Pei-li dance [of licentious women], and the [lewd] music of "fluttering down." He made the taxes heavier in order to fill the Deer Tower with coins, and stuffed the Chü-ch'iao storehouses with grain. He increased his collections of dogs, horses, and unusual objects, overflowing the palace buildings. He expanded the Sha-ch'iu garden tower, and had a multitude of wild animals and flying birds brought there. He was disrespectful to ghosts and spirits. He assembled numerous musicians and actors at the Sha-ch'iu garden; [he] made a lake of wine and a forest of hanging meat, and had naked men and women pursue each other in them, conducting a drinking feast throughout the night. The hundred surnames looked toward him with hatred, and some of the feudal lords revolted.[9]

According to traditional sources, the Chou state was dramatically established when Tan Fu, the Chou leader, emigrated over the mountains south into the Wei River valley to avoid endangering his people and subsequently abandoned so-called barbarian customs to embrace the agricultural destiny of his ancestors. These actions immediately characterized him as a paragon of Virtue and endowed the Chou—and subsequently China—with a sedentary, agrarian character. The *Shi chi* records it as follows:

> The Ancient Duke, Tan Fu, again cultivated the [agricultural] occupation of Hou Chi[10] and Duke Liu, accumulated his Virtue and practiced righteousness, and the people of the state all supported him. The Hsün-yü of the Jung and Ti [barbarians] attacked them, wanting to get their wealth and things, so he gave them to them. After that they again attacked, wanting to take the land and people. The people were all angry and wanted to fight. The Ancient Duke said, "When people establish a ruler, it should be to their advantage. Now the barbarians are attacking and waging war because they want my land and people. What difference is there if the people are with them, or with me? The people want to fight because of me, but to slay people's fathers and sons in order to rule them, I

cannot bear to do it." Then, with his relatives, he went to Pin, forded the Ch'i
River, the Chü River, crossed over Mt. Liang, and stopped below Mt. Ch'i. The
people of Pin, supporting their aged and carrying their weak, again all flocked
to the Ancient Duke below Mt. Ch'i. When the nearby states heard of the Ancient Duke's benevolence, many also gave their allegiance. Thereupon the Ancient Duke discarded their barbarian customs, constructed walls and buildings,
and established cities to have them dwell separately. He set up officials for the
five offices. The people all sang songs and took pleasure in it, praising his Virtue.[11]

General Hsü Pei-ken, a twentieth-century Chinese military historian, believes the Chou easily managed to develop alliances with various peoples—
including disenchanted Hsia groups conquered by the Shang—because of
their agricultural heritage and specialization. In perpetuating the Hsia's agricultural offices, for many years the Chou had dispatched advisers to instruct
other peoples and states in farming practices and seasonal activities. This not
only garnered them respect and goodwill but also gave them an opportunity
to gain a thorough knowledge of the inhabitants, customs, and terrain outside the Wei River valley.[12]

However, Chi Li—Tan Fu's third son and heir through the virtuous deference of his two elder brothers—aggressively waged successful campaigns
against neighboring peoples and rapidly expanded the Chou's power base.
At first the Shang recognized his achievements and sanctioned his actions,
granting him the title of earl, but he was eventually imprisoned and died at
Shang hands despite having married into their royal house. Although the history of Shang-Chou relations remains somewhat unclear, awaiting further
archaeological discoveries, several other members of the Chou royal
house—including King Wen—seem to have married Shang princesses. Generations before the Chou had migrated into the Wei River valley, commencing with King Wu Ting, the Shang had conducted several military expeditions to subjugate the Chou. Shang kings had also frequently hunted in the
Chou domain but apparently grew apprehensive and abandoned this practice as Chou's might increased.[13]

In his old age, King Wen was also imprisoned by the tyrannical Shang
ruler for his loyal remonstrance, but he gained his freedom through lavish
bribes gathered by his family and other virtuous men.[14] The gifts presented
were so generous and impressive that King Wen, who continued to profess
his submission and fealty to the Shang, was even designated the Western
Duke, or Lord of the West. When the title was conferred, he was presented
with a bow, arrows, and axes—symbols of the attendant military responsibilities that ironically required that he actively protect the empire from exter-

nal challenges. He immediately returned to his small state on the western fringe of the Shang empire where the remoteness of the Wei River valley proved immensely advantageous. Dwelling in essentially barbarian territory, the people enjoyed the stimulus of vigorous military activity,[15] the harvests of a fertile area, and the secrecy relative isolation allowed. Because King Wen could implement effective policies to foster the state's material and social strength without attracting undue attention, Chou had the luxury of seventeen years to prepare for the ultimate confrontation.[16]

The T'ai Kung

Into this state of Chou—insignificant when compared with the strength and expanse of the mighty Shang, which continued to assert at least nominal control over roughly three thousand small states and fiefs—came the eccentric T'ai Kung, whose personal name was Chiang Shang. An elderly, somewhat mysterious figure whose early life was shrouded in secrecy, he had perhaps found the Shang ruler insufferable and feigned madness to escape court life and the ruler's power. He disappeared, only to resurface in the Chou countryside at the apocryphal age of seventy-two and become instrumental in Chou affairs. After faithfully serving the Chou court for approximately twenty years subsequent to his first encounter with King Wen, the T'ai Kung was enfeoffed as king of Ch'i following the great conquest—as much to stabilize the eastern area (and perhaps remove him as a military threat) as to reward him for his efforts.

Apart from the T'ai Kung's storied longevity, the initial interview between him and King Wen is also marked by the mythic aura that frequently characterizes predestined meetings between great historical figures. As recorded in the *Six Secret Teachings,* the Grand Historian had noted signs portending the appearance of a great Worthy and accordingly informed King Wen. The king therefore observed a vegetarian fast for three days to morally prepare for the meeting and to attain the proper spiritual state of mind. When he finally encountered him, the T'ai Kung quickly broached the ultimate subject of revolution—of overthrowing the Shang—by responding to the king's inquiry about fishing in allegorical terms. He then abandoned metaphors to openly advise the king that the realm—indeed, the entire world—could be taken with the proper humanitarian measures and an effective government. Surprised by his directness, although probably assuming it was the working of Heaven, the king immediately acknowledged the T'ai Kung as the true Sage who was critical to realizing Chou dreams and resolved to overthrow the Shang dynasty. Thereafter, the T'ai Kung served as adviser, teacher, confidant, Sage, military strategist, and possibly commander-in-chief of the armed forces to kings Wen and Wu over the many years necessary before final victory could be realized.

The *Shih chi* chapter on the state of Ch'i contains a biography of its founder, the T'ai Kung, that provides additional information and records the developments that led to the famous interview (which purportedly is preserved in Chapter One of the *Six Secret Teachings*).

T'ai Kung Wang, Lü Shang, was a native of the Eastern Sea area.[17] His ancestor once served as a labor director, and in assisting Yü in pacifying the waters, had merit. In the interval between Emperor Shun and the Hsia dynasty he was enfeoffed at Lü, or perhaps at Shen, and surnamed Chiang. During the Hsia and Shang dynasties some of the sons and grandsons of the collateral lines were enfeoffed at Lü and Shen, some were commoners, and Shang was their descendant. His original surname was Chiang, but he was [subsequently] surnamed from his fief, so was called Lü Shang.

Lü Shang, impoverished and in straits, was already old when, through fishing, he sought out the Lord of the West [King Wen].[18] The Lord of the West was about to go hunting, and divined about [the prospects]. What [the diviner] said was: "What you will obtain will be neither dragon nor serpent, neither tiger nor bear. What you will obtain is an assistant for a hegemon[19] or king." Thereupon the Lord of the West went hunting, and indeed met the T'ai Kung on the sunny side of the Wei River. After speaking with him he was greatly pleased and said, "My former lord, the T'ai Kung, said 'There should be a Sage who will come to Chou, and Chou will thereby flourish.' Are you truly this [one] or not? My T'ai Kung looked out [*wang*] for you for a long time." Thus he called him T'ai Kung Wang,[20] and returned together with him in the carriage, establishing him as strategist.[21]

Someone said, "The T'ai Kung has extensive learning, and once served King Chou [of the Shang]. King Chou lacked the Way [Tao], so he left him. He traveled about exercising his persuasion on the various feudal lords,[22] but didn't encounter anyone [suitable], and in the end returned west with the Lord of the West."

Someone else said, "Lü Shang was a retired scholar who had hidden himself on the seacoast.[23] When the Lord of the West was confined at Yu-li, San-i Sheng and Hung Yao, having long known him, summoned Lü Shang. Lü Shang also said, 'I have heard that the Lord of the West is a Worthy, and moreover excels at nurturing the old, so I guess I'll go there.' The three men sought out beautiful women and unusual objects on behalf of the Lord of the West, and presented them to King Chou in order to ransom the Lord of the West. The Lord of the West was thereby able to go out and return to his state."

Although the ways they say Lü Shang came to serve the Lord of the West differ, still the essential point is that he became strategist to Kings Wen and Wu.

After the Lord of the West was extricated from Yu-li and returned [to Chou], he secretly planned with Lü Shang and cultivated his Virtue in order to overturn Shang's government. The T'ai Kung's affairs were mostly concerned with military authority and unorthodox stratagems,[24] so when later generations speak about armies and the Chou's secret balance of power [ch'üan,][25] they all honor the T'ai Kung for making the fundamental plans.

The Lord of the West's government was equitable, [even] extending to settling the conflict between the Yü and Jui. The poet [in the *Book of Odes*] refers to the Lord of the West as King Wen after he received the Mandate [of Heaven]. He attacked Ch'ung, Mi-hsü, and Chüan-i,[26] and constructed a great city at Feng. If All under Heaven were divided into thirds, two-thirds had [already] given their allegiance to the Chou.[27] The T'ai Kung's plans and schemes occupied the major part.

When King Wen died, King Wu ascended the throne. In the ninth year, wanting to continue King Wen's task, he mounted an attack in the east to observe whether the feudal lords would assemble or not. When the army set out, the T'ai Kung wielded the yellow battle ax in his left hand, and grasped the white pennon in his right, in order to swear the oath.

Ts'ang-ssu! Ts'ang-ssu![28]
Unite your masses of common people
with your boats and oars.
Those who arrive after will be beheaded.

Thereafter he went to Meng-chin. The number of feudal lords who assembled of their own accord was eight hundred. The feudal lords all said, "King Chou can be attacked." King Wu said, "They cannot yet." He returned the army and made the Great Oath with the T'ai Kung.[29]

After they had remained in Chou for two years, King Chou killed prince Pi-kan and imprisoned Chi-tzu. King Wu, wanting to attack King Chou, performed divination with the tortoise shell to observe the signs. They were not auspicious, and violent wind and rain arose. The assembled Dukes were all afraid, but the T'ai Kung stiffened them to support King Wu.[30] King Wu then went forth.

In the eleventh year, the first month, on the day *chia-tzu* he swore the oath at Mu-yeh and attacked King Chou of the Shang. King Chou's army was completely defeated. King Chou turned and ran off, mounting the Deer Tower. They then pursued and beheaded King Chou.[31] On the morrow King Wu was established at the altars: The Dukes presented clear water; K'ang Shu-feng of Wei spread out a variegated mat; the Shih Shang-fu [the T'ai Kung] led the sacrificial animals; and the Scribe I chanted the prayers, in order to announce to the spirits the punishment of King Chou's offenses. They distributed the money from the Deer Tower, and gave out grain from the Chü-ch'iao granary, in order to relieve the impoverished people. They enfeoffed Pi-kan's grave, and released Chi-tzu from imprisonment. They moved the nine cauldrons,[32] rectified the government of Chou, and began anew with All under Heaven. The Shih Shang-fu's [T'ai Kung's] plans occupied the major part.[33]

Thereupon King Wu, having already pacified the Shang and become King of All under Heaven, enfeoffed the T'ai Kung at Ying-ch'iu in Ch'i. The T'ai Kung went east to go to his state, staying overnight on the road and traveling slowly. The innkeeper said, "I have heard it said that time is hard to get but easy to lose. Our guest sleeps extremely peacefully. Probably he isn't going to return to his state." The T'ai Kung, overhearing it, got dressed that night and set out, reaching his state just before first light. The Marquis of Lai came out to attack, and fought with him for Ying-ch'iu. Ying-ch'iu bordered Lai. The people of Lai were Yi people who, taking advantage of the chaos under King Chou and the new settlement of the Chou dynasty, assumed Chou would not be able to assemble the distant quarters. For this reason they battled with the T'ai Kung for his state.

When the T'ai Kung reached his state he rectified the government in accord with their customs[34]; simplified the Chou's forms of propriety [li]; opened up the occupations of the merchants and artisans; and facilitated the realization of profits from fishing and salt. In large numbers the people turned their allegiance to Ch'i, and Ch'i became a great state.[35]

Then when King Ch'eng of the Chou was young,[36] Kuan Shu and Ts'ai Shu revolted, and the Yi people of the Hua River valley turned against the Chou. So [King Ch'eng] had Duke Chao K'ang issue a mandate to the T'ai Kung: "To the east as far as the sea, the west to the Yellow River, south to Mu-ling, and north to Wu-ti, completely rectify and put in order the five marquis and nine earls."[37] From this Ch'i was able to conduct a campaign of rectification and attack [the rebellious], and became a great state. Its capital was Ying-ch'iu.

When the T'ai Kung died he was probably more than a hundred years old. ...

r   r   r

The Grand Historian says: "I went to Ch'i—from Lang-yeh which belongs to Mt. T'ai, north to where it fronts the sea, two thousand li of fertile land. Its people are expansive,[38] and many conceal their knowledge. It's their Heaven-given nature. Taking the T'ai Kung's Sageness in establishing his state, isn't it appropriate that Duke Huan flourished and cultivated good government, and was thereby able to assemble the feudal lords in a covenant. Vast, vast, truly the style of a great state!"[39]

Despite this detailed biography of the T'ai Kung in Ssu-ma Ch'ien's generally reliable *Shih chi,* over the millennia Confucian skeptics even denied his very existence. Others, perturbed by the confusing traditions regarding his origin, consigned him to a minor role. Both groups justified their views by citing the absence of references to the T'ai Kung in the traditionally accepted archaic texts that supposedly provide an authentic record of these epoch-making events—the *Shang shu*[40] and *Ch'un ch'iu* [*Spring and Autumn Annals*.] Thus, skeptics generally appear to follow the thinking of the second great Confucian, the pedantic Mencius, in refusing to accept the brutal nature of military campaigns and the inevitable bloodshed.[41] King Wu's herculean efforts over the many years prior to the conquest, and his achievements in imposing rudimentary Chou control over the vast Shang domain also tend to be slighted. Consequently, the two figures historically associated with sagacity, virtue, and the civil—King Wen and the Duke of Chou—are revered while the strategist and final commander, the representatives of the martial, are ignored and dismissed. However, after examining numerous stories and references in disparate texts and winnowing away the legendary and mythic material, other scholars and historians have concluded that the T'ai Kung not only existed but also played a prominent role in Chou history—much as described in the *Shih chi* biography.[42] Although the details of his initial encounter with King Wen seem likely to remain unknown, the T'ai Kung was probably a representative of the Chiang clan with whom the Chou were militarily allied and had intermarried for generations.[43] No doubt, as with the Hsia dynasty, whose formerly mythic existence assumes concrete dimensions with the ongoing discovery of ancient artifacts, the T'ai Kung will eventually be vindicated by historical evidence.[44]

Policies and Strategies of the T'ai Kung

In order to realize their objectives of surviving and then conquering, the Chou needed a grand strategy to develop a substantial material base, undermine the enemy's strength, and create an administrative organization that could be imposed effectively in both peace and war. Accordingly, in the *Six Secret Teachings* the T'ai Kung is a strong proponent of the doctrine of the benevolent ruler, with its consequent administrative emphasis on the people's welfare. He advocates this fundamental policy because he believes a well-ordered, prosperous, satisfied people will both physically and emotionally support their government. Only a society with sufficient material resources is able to train and instruct its people,[45] to generate the spirit and provide the supplies essential to military campaigns, and to establish the environment necessary to furnish truly motivated soldiers. Moreover, a benevolent government immediately becomes an attractive beacon to the oppressed and dispirited, to refugees, and to other states that are under the yoke of despotic powers. It creates the confidence that if a new regime is established, its rulers will not duplicate the errors of recently deposed evil monarchs.

The T'ai Kung's basic principles, general policies, and strategic concepts as expressed in the *Six Secret Teachings* are briefly summarized as follows.[46]

Civil Affairs

Profit the People   The T'ai Kung strongly advocates policies similar to Mencius's historically significant emphasis on the welfare and condition of the people. Stimulating agriculture must be primary and should encompass positive measures to increase productivity as well as conscious efforts to avoid interfering with the agricultural seasons, thus minimizing the negative impact of government actions. Virtues can only be inculcated in and demands successfully imposed on the populace if an adequate material base exists. A prosperous, well-governed state inhabited by a contented people will inevitably be respected by other powers.[47]

Institute a Strong Bureaucracy and Impose Controls   Although government must be founded on moral standards and should assiduously practice virtue, it can only govern effectively by creating and systematically imposing a system of rewards and punishments. These policies must invariably be implemented by a strong bureaucracy composed of talented men selected carefully after insightful evaluation. Values inimical to the state, such as private standards of courage, should be discouraged. However, tolerance must be extended to allies and efforts made to avoid violating their local customs.

Rewards and punishments must be clear, immediate, and universal so they will become part of the national consciousness. Although laws and punishments should be restrained and never multiplied, those necessary to the state's survival should be rigorously enforced. Punishments should extend to the very highest ranks and rewards to the lowest.[48] Only then will they prove effective and will people be motivated to observe them regardless of their positions and of whether their potential transgressions might be detectable.

Personal Example and Sympathy of the Ruler   The ruler, and by implication all the members of government, should intensively cultivate the universally acknowledged virtues: benevolence, righteousness, loyalty, credibility, sincerity, courage, and wisdom. Because all men love profits, pleasure, and virtue and detest death, suffering, and evil, the ruler should develop and foster these in common with the people. Ideally, he must perceive their needs and desires and avail himself of every possible source of information to understand their condition. Personal emotions should never be allowed to interfere with the impartial administration of government, nor should the ruler's pleasures or those of the bureaucracy become excessive, thereby impoverishing the people and depriving them of their livelihood. The ruler should strive to eliminate every vestige of evil in order to forge a persona that contrasts dramatically with an enemy's perversity, vividly presenting the people diametrically opposed alternatives. Righteousness must always dominate personal emotions and desires, and the ruler should actively share both hardship and pleasure with his people and also project an image of doing so. This will bind the people to him and guarantee their allegiance to the state.

Total Warfare   One reason the *Six Secret Teachings* was excoriated over the centuries is because the T'ai Kung insisted on utilizing every available method to achieve victory, as did the historical figure—as conventionally portrayed—in the Chou effort to conquer the Shang. Important measures include always anticipating the possibility of hostilities by consciously planning to employ the normal means of production for warfare[49]; feigning and dissembling to deceive the enemy and allay suspicions; using bribes, gifts, and other methods to induce disloyalty among enemy officials and to cause chaos and consternation in their ranks; and further increasing the enemy's profligacy and debilitation by furnishing the tools for self-destruction—such as music, wine, women, and fascinating rarities (jade carvings and the like). Complete secrecy is mandated, and when the battle is joined, constraints should not be imposed.[50]

Military Affairs

Much of the book is devoted to detailed tactics for particular situations. However, the T'ai Kung also gave advice on many topics, including campaign strategy, the selection of generals and officers, training, preparation and types of weapons, creation of new weapons, communications, battle tactics, and organization. Many of his observations and strategies are obsolete, but others have enduring value. Articulation, segmentation and control, independent action, and specialized weapons systems and their forces are discussed extensively. The following particularly merit summary introduction.

The General   The general must be carefully selected and should be properly invested in his role as commander-in-chief with a formal ceremony at the state altars, after which he is entrusted with absolute authority over all military matters. Once he has assumed command, the ruler cannot interfere with the general's actions or decisions, primarily because valuable opportunities might be lost or actions forced that endanger the army, but also to prevent any officers from questioning the general's authority by presuming on their familiarity with the king.[51]

Generals and commanders should embody critical characteristics in balanced combinations to qualify them for leadership and be free of traits that might either lead to judgmental errors or be exploitable and thereby doom their forces. Several chapters enumerate these essential aspects of character and their correlated flaws and suggest psychological techniques for evaluating and selecting military leaders.[52]

Organization and Unity Both the military and civilian spheres must be marked by unity and thorough integration if they are to be effective. Individual sections must be assigned single tasks, and an integrated system of reporting and responsibility should be implemented. A command hierarchy must be created and imposed, with a full staff of general officers and technical and administrative specialists.[53]

Battle Tactics The T'ai Kung analyzes numerous battle situations and formulates some general principles to guide the commander's actions and his efforts to determine appropriate tactics based on objective classifications of terrain, aspects of the enemy, and relative strength of the confrontational forces.[54] There are two basic categories: one in which the army is about to engage an enemy, and one in which it suddenly finds itself at a disadvantage in a forced encounter. The topics covered include selection of advantageous terrain, assault methods against fortifications,[55] night attacks, counterattacks, escape from entrapment, forest warfare, water conflict, mountain fighting, valley defense, survival under fire attack, situations and topography to avoid, techniques for psychological warfare, probing and manipulating the enemy, ways to induce fear, and methods for deception.

Despite the passage of millennia, certain prominent principles, strategies, and tactics from the *Six Secret Teachings* retain validity and continue to be employed in both the military and business spheres. Clearly, the most important of these are deception and surprise.[56] To maximize an attack's effectiveness, unorthodox measures should be implemented to manipulate the enemy psychologically and physically. Several techniques are possible, but among the most effective are false attacks, feints, and limited encounters designed to constantly harry deployed forces. Following these the main attack can be launched, taking advantage of the enemy's surprise and its expectation that the attack is merely another ruse.

Additional tactics include inciting confusion in the enemy's ranks, through such tactics as disinformation, then taking advantage of the ensuing chaos; overawing the enemy through massive displays of force; being aggressive and never yielding the initiative; stressing speed and swiftness; availing oneself of climatic and terrain conditions that trouble and annoy the enemy, such as rain and wind; attacking from out of the sun or at sunset; and mounting intensive efforts to gather intelligence. The enemy must be evaluated and judgments properly rendered before a decision to attack or defend can be made. Weaknesses in the opposing general should be fully exploited, and assaults should be directed toward the enemy's undefended positions. Traps and ambushes need to be avoided but should always be deployed when in difficulty. Forces should normally be consolidated for effective concentration of power rather than dispersed and weakened. Those who surrender should be spared to encourage the enemy to abandon its resistance. The troops should be mobile, and their specializations should be fully utilized. No general should ever suffer a defeat from lack of training or preparation.

Date and Authorship of the Text

The historic T'ai Kung's relationship to the *Six Secret Teachings* remains somewhat controversial and is marked by widely differing opinions. The present Chinese title, *T'ai Kung Liu-t'ao,* first appeared in the "Treatise on Literature" incorporated into the *Sui shu*—the history of the short-lived Sui dynasty written in the T'ang era. Prior to this, both Liu Pei and the great general Chu-ko Liang are noted by a *San-kuo chih* commentator as having high regard for a book entitled *Liu-t'ao.*[57] Yen Shih-ku, the famous exegete (perhaps erroneously) identified this work with another, similarly titled book extant in the Han dynasty that was thought to be a Chou dynasty historical work.[58]

The meaning of the title is not completely clear; however, the first character, *liu,* incontrovertibly means "six." The second character, *t'ao,* has the primary meaning of a "wrap," or "cover"; within a military context it meant the cloth wrapped around a bow or perhaps a bowcase used to carry it.[59] By extension it means "to conceal" or "to secret," and by implication it probably came to refer to the skills involved in using a bow in warfare and thus in military arts in general.[60] Thus, the *Liu-t'ao* should be understood as a book containing six categorical discussions about the skills and tactics of warfare. The title has occasionally been translated as the *Six Cases.* However, we have opted to emphasize the aspect of wrapping things and thereby keeping them secret together with the putative author's role in teaching and advising and have chosen the title *Secret Teachings.*

Members of the Confucian school, including a number of prominent Sung dynasty scholars, disparaged the *Six Secret Teachings* as a forgery of the Warring States period, during which the other military writings were developed.[61] Thereafter, other pedants attributed it to the T'ang dynasty, vociferously denying it any claim to antiquity. Their main criticism focused on the realistic nature of the work and the "despicable policies" the T'ai Kung clearly advocates. As mentioned in the preceding discussion of the T'ai Kung's historicity, they dogmatically insisted that true Sages, such as the founders of the Chou dynasty and the T'ai Kung, would not debase themselves or be compelled to use artifice, deception, sex, and bribes to achieve their ends. Therefore, from their narrow perspective, the conquest of the Shang can only be understood as the victory of culture and Virtue over barbarism and perversity.[62] Unfortunately, these pedants have systematically ignored the ancient emphasis on both the civil and the martial and thereby overlooked the decisive nature of the final battle and the conditions preceding it wherein after an extensive forced march, the vastly outnumbered Chou army decimated the Shang forces. (A few professional soldiers have contradicted the pedants, emphasizing that the realistic character of the Chou's military activities and their total commitment to employing every means possible to vanquish the evil and preserve the populace should be construed as a clear and certain attestation to the validity of the text.)

Some traditionalists, especially historians with career military service backgrounds, are apparently anxious to uphold the authenticity of the work and still claim that it dates from the founding of the Chou dynasty.[63] Others with more moderate viewpoints believe the core teachings could have been preserved in terse form on bamboo and been transmitted orally by the T'ai Kung's descendants in the state of Ch'i, becoming the foundation for Ch'i military studies. They acknowledge that over the centuries the original discussions probably suffered numerous accretions and losses, as is the case with *Chuang-tzu* and *Han Fei-tzu,* which were finally compiled and revised late in the Warring States period.[64]

The confident assertions that the entire work is a T'ang forgery were dramatically destroyed with the discovery of a virtually identical, although only partial, bamboo slip edition in a Han dynasty tomb in the early 1970s.[65] Combined with other Han historical references, this finding proves that portions of the text assumed their present form by at least the early Han era and has been cited by proponents of the T'ai Kung's essential connection with the book as evidence for their position. However, even those advocates who staunchly believe a prototype text underlies the current *Six Secret Teachings* are compelled to acknowledge several historical anachronisms. The language and style of writing indicate extensive revisions, and the final commitment to written form could not have occurred before perhaps the fourth century B.C.[66] The frequent mention of advanced weapons, such as the crossbow and sword,[67] and entire chapters devoted to cavalry tactics prove that the penultimate author lived seven to eight hundred years later than the T'ai Kung. For example, Chapter 55, "Equivalent Forces," discusses the relative effectiveness of chariots, cavalrymen, and infantrymen even though the infantry did not become significant for centuries and the cavalry only emerged in the third century B.C.

Several scholars have asserted that the *Six Secret Teachings* extensively quotes passages and borrows concepts from the other military classics, such as Sun-tzu's *Art of War*.[68] However, questions of priority must always be considered subjects for debate. The *Art of War* may in fact be terse and abstract because Sun-tzu benefited from this tradition of military thought and, as with the authors of such other works as the *Wei Liao-tzu*, availed himself of concepts from the embryonic text of the *Six Secret Teachings* and assiduously assimilated common sayings.[69] In the Warring States period, thorough familiarity with all extant military thought would have been essential if states and commanders were to survive. Therefore, the absence of both conceptual and textual borrowing would probably be more remarkable than the presence thereof because it would indicate highly segmented and strictly preserved schools of tactics and secret strategy.

One final viewpoint regarding the text's transmission holds that the famous military writing given to Chang Liang in the turbulent years preceding the Han dynasty's founding was the *Six Secret Teachings* rather than the *Three Strategies of Huang Shih-kung*.[70] This book would be particularly appropriate because of its historical echoes: Its readers were committed to the populist overthrow of another brutal, oppressive ruling house—the Ch'in. Accordingly, it has been suggested that the book was actually composed by a military expert in the third century B.C. when the Ch'in were relentlessly destroying their enemies and consolidating their power.[71] This would explain the mature development of concepts and strategies, the extensive knowledge of weapons and defensive equipment, the emphasis on benevolent government, and the efforts to preserve the book's secrecy.

The Six T'ao

Most commentators characterize the first two Secret Teachings as focusing on grand strategy and planning for war and the last four as falling within the category of tactical studies.[72] However, because either the original authors of the *Six Secret Teachings* failed to provide any explanations for their apparently thematic groupings or such prefatory material has been lost, it is difficult to perceive any intrinsic connection between titles such as "dragon" and the contents of the section. Only the first two Secret Teachings, the Civil and the Martial, which focus on the two foundations for conducting warfare—an economically sound, well-administered state with a motivated populace, and a strong army—have contents that justify their titles. Although a few attempts have been made to discern thematic issues underlying the six individual classifications, such distinctions often appear inadequate to support assigning a particular chapter to one Teaching or another without knowledge of the extant work.

Although the Table of Contents for this section provides a general indication of each Teaching's topics and the translator's introduction surveys the main subjects in some detail, a brief characterization of the individual Teachings may still be useful.

Civil T'ao

Moral, effective government is the basis for survival and the foundation for warfare. The state must thrive economically while limiting expenditures, foster appropriate values and behavior among the populace, implement rewards and punishments, employ the worthy, and refrain from disturbing or harming the people.[73]

Martial T'ao

The Martial Secret Teaching continues the Civil T'ao's discussion of political, rather than military, measures. It begins with the T'ai Kung's analysis of the contemporary political world and his assessment of the Chou's prospects for successfully revolting against the Shang if their avowed objective is to save the world from tyranny and suffering. Attracting the disaffected weakens the enemy and strengthens the state; employing subterfuge and psychological techniques allows manipulation of the enemy and hastens its demise. The ruler must visibly cultivate his Virtue and embrace government policies that will allow the state to compete for the minds and hearts of the people; the state will thus gain victory without engaging in battle.[74]

Dragon T'ao

The Dragon Secret Teaching focuses primarily on military organization, including the specialized responsibilities of the command staff, the characteristics and qualifications of generals and methods for their evaluation and selection, the ceremony appropriate for commissioning a commanding general to ensure that his independence and awesomeness are established, the importance of rewards and punishments in creating and maintaining the general's awesomeness and authority, and essential behavior if the general is to truly command in person and foster allegiance and unity in his troops. Secondary issues concern military communications and the paramount need for secrecy; evaluation of the situation and how to act decisively when the moment arrives; an understanding of basic tactical principles, including flexibility and the unorthodox, and avoiding the common errors of command; various cues for fathoming the enemy's situation; and the everyday basis for military skills and equipment.

Tiger T'ao

The Tiger Secret Teaching opens with a discussion of the important categories of military equipment and weapons, then continues with widely ranging expositions on tactical principles and essential issues of command. Although types of deployment are considered briefly, and the necessary preparation of amphibious equipment is addressed, most of the chapters provide tactics for extricating oneself from adverse battlefield situations. The solutions generally emphasize speed, maneuverability, unified action, decisive commitment, the employment of misdirection, the establishment of ambushes, and the appropriate use of different types of forces.

Leopard T'ao

The Leopard Secret Teaching emphasizes tactical solutions for particularly difficult types of terrain, such as forests, mountains, ravines and defiles, lakes and rivers, deep valleys, and other constricted locations. It also contains discussions of methods to contain rampaging invaders, confront superior forces, deploy effectively, and act explosively.

Canine T'ao

The most important chapters in the Canine Secret Teaching expound on detailed principles for appropriately employing the three component forces—chariots, infantry, and cavalry—in a wide variety of concrete tactical situations and discuss their comparative battlefield effectiveness. Another section describes deficiencies and weaknesses in the enemy that can and should be exploited immediately with a determined attack. Finally, several chapters address general issues that seem more appropriate to the Dragon Secret Teaching: the identification and selection of highly motivated, physically talented individuals for elite infantry units and for the cavalry and chariots; and methods for training the soldiers.

I

CIVIL SECRET TEACHING

1. King Wen's Teacher

King Wen intended to go hunting, so Pien, the Scribe, performed divination to inquire about his prospects. The Scribe reported: "While hunting on the north bank of the Wei river you will get a great catch. It will not be any form of dragon, nor a tiger or great bear. According to the signs, you will find a duke or marquis there whom Heaven has sent to be your teacher. If employed as your assistant, you will flourish and the benefits will extend to three generations of Chou kings."

King Wen asked: "Do the signs truly signify this?"

The Scribe Pien replied: "My Supreme Ancestor, the Scribe Ch'ou, when performing divination for the Sage Emperor Shun,[1] obtained comparable indications. Emperor Shun then found Kao-yao to assist him."

King Wen then observed a vegetarian regime for three days to purify himself, then mounted his hunting chariot. Driving his hunting horses, he went out to hunt on the northern bank of the Wei river. Finally he saw the T'ai Kung sitting on a grass mat fishing. King Wen greeted him courteously and then asked: "Do you take pleasure in fishing?"

The T'ai Kung replied: "The True Man of Worth[2] takes pleasure in attaining his ambitions; the common man takes pleasure in succeeding in his [ordinary] affairs. Now my fishing is very much like this."

"What do you mean it is like it?" inquired the king.

The T'ai Kung responded: "In fishing there are three forms of authority:[3] the ranks of salary, death, and offices. Fishing is the means to obtain what you seek. Its nature is deep, and from it much greater principles can be discerned."

King Wen said: "I would like to hear about its nature."

The T'ai Kung elaborated: "When the source is deep, the water flows actively. When the water flows actively, fish spawn there. This is nature. When the roots are deep, the tree is tall. When the tree is tall, fruit is produced. This is nature. When True Men of Worth have sympathies and views in common, they will be drawn together. When they are drawn together affairs arise.[4] This is nature.

"Speech and response are the adornment of inner emotions. Speaking about true nature is the pinnacle of affairs. Now if I speak about true nature, without avoiding any topic, will you find it abhorrent?"

King Wen replied: "Only a man of true humanity[5] can accept corrections and remonstrance. I have no abhorrence of true nature, so what is your meaning?"

The T'ai Kung said: "When the line is thin and the bait glittering, only small fish will eat it. When the line is heavier and the bait fragrant, medium-sized fish will eat it. But when the line is heavy and the bait generous, large fish will eat it. When the fish take the bait, they will be caught on the line. When men take their salary, they will submit to the ruler. When you catch fish with bait, the fish can be killed. When you catch men with remuneration, they can be made to exhaust their abilities for you. If you use your family to gain the state, the state can be plucked. If you use your state, the world can be completely acquired.

"Alas, flourishing and florid, although they assemble together they will be scattered! Silent and still, the Sage Ruler's glory will inevitably extend far! Subtle and mysterious, the Virtue of the Sage Ruler as it attracts the people! He alone sees it. Wondrous and joyful, the plans of the Sage Ruler through which everyone seeks and returns to their appropriate places, while he establishes the measures that will gather in their hearts."

King Wen inquired: "How shall we proceed to establish measures so that All under Heaven will give their allegiance?"

The T'ai Kung said: "All under Heaven is not one man's domain. All under Heaven means just that, *all* under Heaven. Anyone who shares profit with all the people under Heaven will gain the world. Anyone who monopolizes its profits will lose the world. Heaven has its seasons, Earth its resources. Being capable of sharing these in common with the people is true humanity. Wherever there is true humanity, All under Heaven will give their allegiance.

"Sparing the people from death, eliminating the hardships of the people, relieving the misfortunes of the people, and sustaining the people in their extremities is Virtue. Wherever there is Virtue, All under Heaven will give their allegiance.

"Sharing worries, pleasures, likes, and dislikes with the people constitutes righteousness. Where there is righteousness the people will go.

"In general, people hate death and take pleasure in life. They love Virtue and incline to profit. The ability to produce profit accords with the Tao. Where the Tao resides, All under Heaven will give their allegiance."

King Wen bowed twice and said: "True wisdom! Do I dare not accept Heaven's edict and mandate?"

He had the T'ai Kung ride in the chariot and returned with him, establishing him as his teacher.

2. Fullness and Emptiness[6]

King Wen inquired of the T'ai Kung: "The world is replete with a dazzling array of states—some full, others empty, some well ordered, others in chaos. How does it come to be thus? Is it that the moral qualities of these rulers are not the same? Or that the changes and transformations of the seasons of Heaven naturally cause it to be thus?"

The T'ai Kung said: "If the ruler lacks moral worth, then the state will be in danger and the people in turbulence. If the ruler is a Worthy or a Sage, then the state will be at peace and the people well ordered. Fortune and misfortune lie with the ruler, not with the seasons of Heaven."

King Wen: "May I hear about the Sages of antiquity?"

T'ai Kung: "Former generations referred to Emperor Yao, in his kingship over the realm in antiquity, as a Worthy ruler."

King Wen: "What was his administration like?"

T'ai Kung: "When Yao was king of the world he did not adorn himself with gold, silver, pearls, and jade.[7] He did not wear brocaded, embroidered, or elegantly decorated clothes. He did not look at strange, odd, rare, or unusual things. He did not treasure items of amusement nor listen to licentious music. He did not whitewash the walls around the palace or the buildings nor decoratively carve the beams, square and round rafters, and pillars. He did not even trim the reeds that grew all about his courtyards. He used a deerskin robe to ward off the cold, while simple clothes covered his body. He ate coarse millet and unpolished grains and thick soups from rough vegetables. He did not, through the [untimely imposition of] labor service, injure the people's seasons for agriculture and sericulture. He reduced his desires and constrained his will, managing affairs by nonaction.

"He honored the positions of the officials who were loyal, upright, and upheld the laws, and made generous the salaries of those who were pure and scrupulous and loved people. He loved and respected those among the people who were filial and compassionate, and he comforted and encouraged those who exhausted their strength in agriculture and sericulture. Pennants distinguished the virtuous from the evil, being displayed at the gates of the village lanes. He tranquilized his heart and rectified the constraints [of social forms].[8] With laws and measures he prohibited evil and artifice.

"Among those he hated, if anyone had merit he would invariably reward him. Among those he loved, if anyone were guilty of an offense he would certainly punish him. He preserved and nurtured the widows, widowers, orphans, and solitary elderly and gave aid to the families who had suffered misfortune and loss.

"What he allotted to himself was extremely meager, the taxes and services he required of the people extremely few. Thus the myriad peoples were prosperous and happy and did not have the appearance of suffering from hunger and cold. The hundred surnames revered their ruler as if he were the sun and moon and gave their emotional allegiance as if he were their father and mother."

King Wen: "Great is the Worthy and Virtuous ruler!"

3. Affairs of State

King Wen said to the T'ai Kung: "I would like to learn about the affair of administering the state. If I want to have the ruler honored and the people settled, how should I proceed?"

T'ai Kung: "Just love the people."

King Wen: "How does one love the people?"

T'ai Kung: "Profit them, do not harm them. Help them to succeed, do not defeat them. Give them life, do not slay them. Grant, do not take away. Give them pleasure, do not cause them to suffer. Make them happy, do not cause them to be angry."

King Wen: "May I dare ask you to explain the reasons for these?"

T'ai Kung: "When the people do not lose their fundamental occupations, you have profited them. When the farmers do not lose the agricultural seasons, you have completed them. [When you reduce punishments and fines, you give them life.[9]] When you impose light taxes, you give to them. When you keep your palaces, mansions, terraces, and pavilions few, you give them pleasure. When the officials are pure and neither irritating nor troublesome, you make them happy.

"But when the people lose their fundamental occupations, you harm them. When the farmers lose the agricultural seasons, you defeat them. When they are innocent but you punish them, you kill them. When you impose heavy taxes, you take from them. When you construct numerous palaces, mansions, terraces, and pavilions, thereby wearing out the people's strength, you make it bitter for them. When the officials are corrupt, irritating, and troublesome, you anger them.

"Thus one who excels at administering a state governs the people as parents govern their beloved children or as an older brother acts toward his beloved younger brother. When they see their hunger and cold, they are troubled for them. When they see their labors and suffering, they grieve for them.

"Rewards and punishments should be implemented as if being imposed upon yourself. Taxes should be imposed as if taking from yourself. This is the Way to love the people."

4. The Great Forms of Etiquette

King Wen asked T'ai Kung: "What is the proper form of etiquette (*li*)[10] between ruler and minister?"

The T'ai Kung said: "The ruler only needs to draw near to the people; subordinates only need to be submissive. He must approach them, not being distant from any. They must be submissive without hiding anything. The ruler wants only to be all-encompassing; subordinates want only to be settled [in their positions]. If he is all-encompassing he will be like Heaven. If they are settled, they will be like Earth. One Heaven, one Earth—the Great Li is then complete."

King Wen: "How should the ruler act in his position?"

T'ai Kung: "He should be composed, dignified, and quiet. His softness and self-constraint should be established first. He should excel at giving and not be contentious. He should empty his mind and tranquilize his intentions, awaiting events with uprightness."

King Wen inquired: "How should the ruler listen to affairs?"

The T'ai Kung replied: "He should not carelessly allow them nor go against opinion and oppose them. If he allows them in this fashion, he will lose his central control; if he opposes them in this way, he will close off his access.

"He should be like the height of a mountain which—when looked up to—cannot be perceived, or the depths of a great abyss which—when measured—cannot be fathomed. Such spiritual and enlightened Virtue is the pinnacle of uprightness and tranquility."

King Wen inquired: "What should the ruler's wisdom be like?"

The T'ai Kung: "The eye values clarity, the ear values sharpness, the mind values wisdom. If you look with the eyes of All under Heaven, there is nothing you will not see. If you listen with the ears of All under Heaven, there is nothing you will not hear. If you think with the minds of All under Heaven, there is nothing you will not know. When [you receive information from all directions], just like the spokes converging on the hub of a wheel, your clarity will not be obfuscated."

5. Clear Instructions

King Wen, lying in bed seriously ill, summoned T'ai Kung Wang and Imperial Prince Fa [King Wu] to his side. "Alas, Heaven is about to abandon me. Chou's state altars will soon be entrusted to you. Today I want you, my teacher, to discuss the great principles of the Tao in order to clearly transmit them to my son and grandsons."

T'ai Kung said: "My king, what do you want to ask about?"

King Wen: "May I hear about the Tao of the former Sages—where it stops, where it begins?"

T'ai Kung: "If one sees good but is dilatory [in doing it], if the time for action arrives and one is doubtful, if you know something is wrong but you sanction it—it is in these three that the Tao stops. If one is soft and quiet, dignified and respectful, strong yet genial, tolerant yet hard—it is in these four that the Tao begins. Accordingly, when righteousness overcomes desire one will flourish; when desire overcomes righteousness one will perish. When respect overcomes dilatoriness it is auspicious; when dilatoriness overcomes respect one is destroyed."

6. Six Preservations

King Wen asked the T'ai Kung: "How does the ruler of the state and leader of the people come to lose his position?"

The T'ai Kung said: "He is not cautious about whom he has as associates. The ruler has 'six preservations' and 'three treasures.'"

King Wen asked: "What are the six preservations?"

The T'ai Kung: "The first is called benevolence, the second righteousness, the third loyalty, the fourth trust [good faith], the fifth courage, and the sixth planning. These are referred to as the 'six preservations.'"

King Wen asked: "How does one go about carefully selecting men using the six preservations?"

T'ai Kung: "Make them rich and observe whether they do not commit offenses. Give them rank and observe whether they do not become arrogant. Entrust them with responsibility and see whether they will not change. Employ them and see whether they will not conceal anything. Endanger them and see whether they are not afraid. Give them the management of affairs and see whether they are not perplexed.

"If you make them rich but they do not commit offenses, they are benevolent. If you give them rank and they do not grow arrogant, they are righteous. If you entrust them with office and they do not change, they are loyal. If you employ them and they do not conceal anything, they are trustworthy. If you put them in danger and they are not afraid, they are courageous. If you give them the management of affairs and they are not perplexed, they are capable of making plans.

"The ruler must not loan the 'three treasures' to other men. If he loans them to other men the ruler will lose his awesomeness."

King Wen: "May I ask about the three treasures?"

T'ai Kung: "Great agriculture, great industry, and great commerce are referred to as the 'three treasures.' If you have the farmers dwell solely in districts of farmers, then the five grains will be sufficient. If you have the artisans dwell solely in districts of artisans, then the implements will be adequate. If you have the merchants dwell solely in districts of merchants, then the material goods will be sufficient.[11]

"If the three treasures are each settled in their places, then the people will not scheme. Do not allow confusion among their districts, do not allow confusion among their clans. Ministers should not be more wealthy than the ruler. No other cities should be larger than the ruler's state capital. When the six preservations are fully implemented, the ruler will flourish. When the three treasures are complete, the state will be secure."

7. Preserving the State's Territory

King Wen asked the T'ai Kung: "How does one preserve the state's territory?"

T'ai Kung: "Do not estrange your relatives. Do not neglect the masses. Be conciliatory and solicitous toward nearby states and control the four quarters.

"Do not loan the handles of state to other men.[12] If you loan the handles of state to other men, then you will lose your authority [ch'üan]. Do not dig valleys deeper to increase hills. Do not abandon the foundation to govern the branches. When the sun is at midday you should dry things. If you grasp a knife you must cut. If you hold an ax you must attack.

"If, at the height of the day, you do not dry things in the sun, this is termed losing the time. If you grasp a knife but do not cut anything, you will lose the moment for profits. If you hold an ax but do not attack, then bandits will come.

"If trickling streams are not blocked, they will become great rivers. If you do not extinguish the smallest flames, what will you do about a great conflagration? If you do not eliminate the two-leaf sapling, how will you use your ax [when the tree has grown]?

"For this reason the ruler must focus on developing wealth within his state. Without material wealth he has nothing with which to be benevolent. If he does not bespread beneficence he will have nothing with which to bring his relatives together.[13] If he estranges his relatives it will be harmful. If he loses the common people he will be defeated.

"Do not loan sharp weapons to other men.[14] If you loan sharp weapons to other men, you will be hurt by them and will not live out your allotted span of years."

King Wen said: "What do you mean by benevolence and righteousness?"

The T'ai Kung: "Respect the common people, unite your relatives. If you respect the common people they will be at peace. And if you unite your relatives they will be happy. This is the way to implement the essential cords of benevolence and righteousness.

"Do not allow other men to snatch away your awesomeness. Rely on your wisdom, follow the constant. Those that submit and accord with you, treat generously with Virtue. Those that oppose you, break with force. If you respect the people and are decisive, then All under Heaven will be peaceful and submissive."

8. Preserving the State

King Wen asked the T'ai Kung: "How does one preserve the state?"

T'ai Kung: "You should observe a vegetarian fast, for I am about to speak to you about the essential principles of Heaven and Earth, what the four seasons produce, the Tao of true humanity and sagacity, and the nature of the people's impulses."

The King observed a vegetarian regime for seven days, then, facing north, bowed twice and requested instruction.

The T'ai Kung said: "Heaven gives birth to the four seasons, Earth produces the myriad things. Under Heaven there are the people, and the Sage acts as their shepherd.

"Thus the Tao of spring is birth and the myriad things begin to flourish. The Tao of summer is growth; the myriad things mature. The Tao of autumn is gathering; the myriad things are full. The Tao of winter is storing away;

the myriad things are still. When they are full they are stored away; after they are stored away they again revive. No one knows where it ends, no one knows where it begins. The Sage accords with it and models himself on Heaven and Earth. Thus when the realm is well ordered, his benevolence and sagacity are hidden. When All under Heaven are in turbulence, his benevolence and sagacity flourish. This is the true Tao.

"In his position between Heaven and Earth, what the Sage treasures is substantial and vast. Relying on the constant to view it, the people are at peace. But when the people are agitated it creates impulses. When impulses stir, conflict over gain and loss arises. Thus it is initiated in yin, but coalesces in yang. If someone ventures to be the first leader, All under Heaven will unite with him.[15] At the extreme, when things return to normal, do not continue to advance and contend, do not withdraw and yield. If you can preserve the state in this fashion, you will share the splendor of Heaven and Earth."

9. Honoring the Worthy

King Wen asked the T'ai Kung: "Among those I rule,[16] who should be elevated, who should be placed in inferior positions? Who should be selected for employment, who cast aside? How should they be restricted, how stopped?"

The T'ai Kung said: "Elevate the Worthy, and place the unworthy in inferior positions. Choose the sincere and trustworthy, eliminate the deceptive and artful. Prohibit violence and turbulence, stop extravagance and ease. Accordingly, one who exercises kingship over the people recognizes 'six thieves' and 'seven harms.'"

King Wen said: "I would like to know about its Tao."

T'ai Kung: "As for the 'six thieves':

"First, if your subordinates build large palaces and mansions, pools and terraces, and amble about enjoying the pleasures of scenery and female musicians, it will injure the king's Virtue.

"Second, when the people are not engaged in agriculture and sericulture but instead give rein to their tempers and travel about as bravados, disdaining and transgressing the laws and prohibitions, not following the instructions of the officials, it harms the king's transforming influence.[17]

"Third, when officials form cliques and parties—obfuscating the worthy and wise, obstructing the ruler's clarity—it injures the king's authority [ch'üan].

"Fourth, when the knights are contrary-minded and conspicuously display 'high moral standards'—taking such behavior to be powerful expression of their *ch'i*[18]—and have private relationships with other feudal lords—slighting their own ruler—it injures the king's awesomeness.

"Fifth, when subordinates disdain titles and positions, are contemptuous of the administrators, and are ashamed to face hardship for their ruler, it injures the efforts of the meritorious subordinates.

"Sixth, when the strong clans encroach on others—seizing what they want, insulting and ridiculing the poor and weak—it injures the work of the common people.

"The 'seven harms':

"First, men without knowledge or strategic planning ability are generously rewarded and honored with rank. Therefore, the strong and courageous who regard war lightly take their chances in the field. The king must be careful not to employ them as generals.

"Second, they have reputation but lack substance. What they say is constantly shifting. They conceal the good and point out deficiencies. They view advancement and dismissal as a question of skill. The king should be careful not to make plans with them.

"Third, they make their appearance simple, wear ugly clothes, speak about actionless action in order to seek fame, and talk about non-desire in order to gain profit. They are artificial men, and the king should be careful not to bring them near.

"Fourth, they wear strange caps and belts, and their clothes are overflowing. They listen widely to the disputations of others and speak speciously about unrealistic ideas, displaying them as a sort of personal adornment. They dwell in poverty and live in tranquility, deprecating the customs of the world. They are cunning people, and the king should be careful not to favor them.

"Fifth, with slander, obsequiousness, and pandering, they seek office and rank. They are courageous and daring, treating death lightly, out of their greed for salary and position. They are not concerned with major affairs but move solely out of avarice. With lofty talk and specious discussions, they please the ruler. The king should be careful not to employ them.

"Sixth, they have buildings elaborately carved and inlaid. They promote artifice and flowery adornment to the injury of agriculture. You must prohibit them.

"Seventh, they create magical formulas and weird techniques, practice sorcery and witchcraft, advance unorthodox ways, and circulate inauspicious sayings, confusing and befuddling the good people. The king must stop them.

"Now when the people do not exhaust their strength, they are not our people. If the officers are not sincere and trustworthy, they are not our officers. If the ministers do not offer loyal remonstrance, they are not our ministers. If the officials are not evenhanded, pure, nor love the people, they are not our officials. If the chancellor cannot enrich the state and strengthen the army, harmonize yin and yang, and ensure security for the ruler of a state of ten thousand chariots—and moreover properly control the ministers, set names and realities, make clear rewards and punishments, and give pleasure to the people—he is not our chancellor.

"Now the Tao of the king is like that of a dragon's head. He dwells in the heights and looks out far. He sees deeply and listens carefully. He displays his form but conceals his nature. He is like the heights of Heaven, which cannot be perceived. He is like the depths of an abyss, which cannot be fathomed. Thus if he should get angry but does not, evil subordinates will arise. If he should execute but does not, great thieves will appear. If strategic military power is not exercised, enemy states will grow strong."

King Wen said: "Excellent!"

10. Advancing the Worthy

King Wen asked the T'ai Kung: "How does it happen that a ruler may exert himself to advance the Worthy but is unable to obtain any results from such efforts, and in fact the world grows increasingly turbulent, even to the point that he is endangered or perishes?"

T'ai Kung: "If one advances the Worthy but doesn't employ them, this is attaining the name of 'advancing the Worthy' but lacking the substance of 'using the Worthy.'"

King Wen asked: "Whence comes the error?"

T'ai Kung: "The error lies in wanting to employ men who are popularly praised rather than obtaining true Worthies."

King Wen: "How is that?"

The T'ai Kung said: "If the ruler takes those that the world commonly praises as being Worthies and those that they condemn as being worthless, then the larger cliques will advance and the smaller ones will retreat. In this situation groups of evil individuals will associate together to obscure the Worthy. Loyal subordinates will die even though innocent. And perverse subordinates will obtain rank and position through empty fame. In this way, as turbulence continues to grow in the world, the state cannot avoid danger and destruction."

King Wen asked: "How does one advance the Worthy?"

T'ai Kung replied: "Your general and chancellor should divide the responsibility, each of them selecting men based on the names of the positions. In accord with the name of the position, they will assess the substance required. In selecting men, they will evaluate their abilities, making the reality of their talents match the name of the position. When the name matches the reality, you will have realized the Tao for advancing the Worthy."[19]

11. Rewards and Punishments

King Wen asked the T'ai Kung: "Rewards are the means to preserve the encouragement [of the good], punishments the means to display the rectification of evil. By rewarding one man I want to stimulate a hundred, by punishing one man rectify the multitude. How can I do it?"

The T'ai Kung said: "In general, in employing rewards one values credibility; in employing punishments one values certainty. When rewards are trusted and punishments inevitable wherever the eye sees and the ear hears, then even where they do not see or hear there is no one who will not be transformed in their secrecy. Since the ruler's sincerity extends to Heaven and Earth and penetrates to the spirits, how much the more so to men?"

12. The Tao of the Military

King Wu asked the T'ai Kung: "What is the Tao of the military?"[20]

The T'ai Kung said: "In general, as for the Tao of the military, nothing surpasses unity. The unified can come alone, can depart alone. The Yellow Emperor said: 'Unification approaches the Tao and touches on the spiritual.' Its employment lies in the subtle;[21] its conspicuous manifestation lies in the strategic configuration of power; its completion lies with the ruler. Thus the Sage Kings termed weapons evil implements, but when they had no alternative, they employed them.

"Today the Shang king knows about existence, but not about perishing. He knows pleasure, but not disaster. Now existence does not lie in existence, but in thinking about perishing. Pleasure does not lie in pleasure, but in contemplating disaster. Now that you have already pondered the source of such changes, why do you trouble yourself about the future flow of events?"

King Wu said: "Suppose two armies encounter each other. The enemy cannot come forward, and we cannot go forward. Each side goes about establishing fortifications and defenses without daring to be the first to attack. If I want to launch a sudden attack but lack any tactical advantage, what should I do?"

The T'ai Kung said: "Make an outward display of confusion while actually being well ordered. Show an appearance of hunger while actually being well fed. Keep your sharp weapons within and show only dull and poor weapons outside. Have some troops come together, others split up; some assemble, others scatter.[22] Make secret plans, keep your intentions secret. Raise the height of fortifications, and conceal your elite troops. If the officers are silent, not making any sounds, the enemy will not know our preparations. Then if you want to take his western flank, attack the eastern one."

King Wu said: "If the enemy knows my true situation and has penetrated my plans, what should I do?"

The T'ai Kung said: "The technique for military conquest is to carefully investigate the enemy's intentions and quickly take advantage of them, launching a sudden attack where unexpected."[23]

II

MARTIAL SECRET TEACHING

13. Opening Instructions

King Wen, in the capital of Feng, summoned the T'ai Kung. "Alas! The Shang king is extremely perverse, judging the innocent guilty and having them executed. If you assist me in my concern for these people, how might we proceed?"

The T'ai Kung replied: "You should cultivate your Virtue, submit to the guidance of Worthy men, extend beneficence to the people, and observe the Tao of Heaven. If there are no ill omens in the Tao of Heaven, you cannot initiate the movement [to revolt]. If there are no misfortunes in the Tao of Man, your planning cannot precede them. You must first see Heavenly signs and moreover witness human misfortune, and only then can you make plans. You must look at the Shang king's yang aspects [his government], and moreover his yin side [personal deportment], and only then will you know his mind. You must look at his external activities, and moreover his internal ones, and only then will you know his thoughts. You must observe those distant from him and also observe those close to him, and only then will you know his emotions.

"If you implement the Tao, the Tao can be attained. If you enter by the gate, the gate can be entered. If you set up the proper forms of etiquette [*li*], the *li* can be perfected. If you fight with the strong, the strong can be conquered. If you can attain complete victory without fighting, without the great army suffering any losses, you will have penetrated even the realm of ghosts and spirits. How marvelous! How subtle!

"If you suffer the same illness as other people and you all aid each other; if you have the same emotions and complete each other; the same hatreds and assist each other; and the same likes and seek them together—then without any armored soldiers you will win; without any battering rams you will have attacked; and without moats and ditches you will have defended.

"The greatest wisdom is not wise; the greatest plans not planned; the greatest courage not courageous; the greatest gain not profitable. If you profit All under Heaven, All under Heaven will be open to you. If you harm All under Heaven, All under Heaven will be closed. All under Heaven is not the property of one man but of All under Heaven. If you take All under Heaven as if pursuing some wild animal, then All under Heaven will want to carve [the realm] up like a piece of meat. If you all ride in the same boat to cross over the water, after completing the crossing you will all have profited. However, if you fail to make the crossing, then you will all suffer the harm.[24] [If you act as if you're all on the same vessel], the empire will be open to your aim, and none will be closed to you.

"He who does not take from the people takes the people. He who does not take [from][25] the people, the people will profit. He who does not take [from] the states, the states will profit. He who does not take from All under Heaven, All under Heaven will profit. Thus the Tao lies in what cannot be seen; affairs lie in what cannot be heard; and victory lies in what cannot be known. How marvelous! How subtle!

"When an eagle is about the attack, it will fly low and draw in its wings.[26] When a fierce wild cat is about to strike, it will lay back its ears and crouch down low. When the Sage is about to move, he will certainly display a stupid countenance.

"Now there is the case of Shang, where the people muddle and confuse each other. Mixed up and extravagant, their love of pleasure and sex is endless. This is a sign of a doomed state. I have observed their fields—weeds and grass overwhelm the crops. I have observed their people—the perverse and crooked overcome the straight and upright. I have observed their officials—they are violent, perverse, inhumane, and evil. They overthrow the laws and make chaos of the punishments. Neither the upper nor lower ranks have awakened to this state of affairs. It is time for their state to perish.

"When the sun appears the myriad things are all illuminated. When great righteousness appears the myriad things all profit. When the great army appears the myriad things all submit. Great is the Virtue of the Sage! Listening by himself, seeing by himself, this is his pleasure!"

14. Civil Instructions

King Wen asked the T'ai Kung: "What does the Sage preserve?"

The T'ai Kung said: "What worries does he have? What constraints? The myriad things all naturally realize their positions. What constraints, what worries? The myriad things all flourish. No one realizes the transforming influence of government; moreover, no one realizes the effects of the passing of time.[27] The Sage preserves [the Tao of actionless action], and the myriad things are transformed. What is exhausted? When things reach the end they return again to the beginning. Relaxed and complacent he turns about, seeking it. Seeking it he gains it and cannot but store it. Having already stored it he cannot but implement it. Having already implemented it he does not turn about and make it clear [that he did so]. Now because Heaven and Earth do not illuminate themselves, they are forever able to give birth [to the myriad things].[28] The Sage does not cast light upon himself so he is able to attain a glorious name.

"The Sages of antiquity assembled people to comprise families, assembled families to compose states, and assembled states to constitute the realm of All under Heaven. They divided the realm and enfeoffed Worthy men to administer the states. They officially designated [this order] the 'Great Outline.'

"They promulgated the government's instructions and accorded with the people's customs. They transformed the multitude of crooked into the straight, changing their form and appearance. Although the customs of the various states were not the same, they all took pleasure in their respective places. The people loved their rulers, so they termed [this transformation] the 'Great Settlement.'

"Ah, the Sage concentrates on tranquilizing them, the Worthy focuses on rectifying them. The stupid man cannot be upright, therefore he contends with other men. When the ruler labors, punishments become numerous. When punishments are numerous, the people are troubled. When the people are troubled, they leave and wander off. No one, of whatever position, can be settled in his life, and generations on end have no rest. This they termed the 'Great Loss.'

"The people of the world are like flowing water. If you obstruct it, it will stop. If you open a way, it will flow. If you keep it quiet, it will be clear. How spiritual! When the Sage sees the beginning, he knows the end."

King Wen said: "How does one tranquilize them?"

The T'ai Kung: "Heaven has its constant forms, the people have their normal lives. If you share life with All under Heaven, then All under Heaven will be tranquil. The pinnacle accords with them, the next-highest transforms them. When the people are transformed and follow their government, then Heaven takes no action but affairs are complete. The people do not give anything [to the ruler] [so] are enriched of themselves.[29] This is the Virtue of the Sage."

King Wen: "What my lord has said accords with what I embrace. From dawn to night I will think about it, never forgetting it, employing it as our constant principle."

15. Civil Offensive

King Wen asked the T'ai Kung: "What are the methods for civil[30] offensives?"

The T'ai Kung replied: "There are twelve measures for civil offensives.

"First, accord with what he likes in order to accommodate his wishes. He will eventually grow arrogant and invariably mount some perverse affair. If you can appear to follow along, you will certainly be able to eliminate him.

"Second, become familiar with those he loves in order to fragment his awesomeness. When men have two different inclinations, their loyalty invariably declines. When his court no longer has any loyal ministers, the state altars will inevitably be endangered.

"Third, covertly bribe his assistants, fostering a deep relationship with them. While they will bodily stand in his court, their emotions will be directed outside it. The state will certainly suffer harm.

"Fourth, assist him in his licentiousness and indulgence in music in order to dissipate his will. Make him generous gifts of pearls and jade, and ply him with beautiful women. Speak deferentially, listen respectfully, follow his commands, and accord with him in everything. He will never imagine you might be in conflict with him. Our treacherous measures will then be settled.

"Fifth, treat his loyal officials very generously, but reduce the gifts you provide [to the ruler]. Delay his emissaries; do not listen to their missions. When he eventually dispatches other men, treat them with sincerity, embrace and trust them. The ruler will then again feel you are in harmony with him. If you manage to treat [his formerly loyal officials] very generously, his state can then be plotted against.[31]

"Sixth, make secret alliances with his favored ministers, but visibly keep his less-favored outside officials at a distance. His talented people will then be under external influence, while enemy states encroach upon his territory. Few states in such a situation have survived.

"Seventh, if you want to bind his heart to you, you must offer generous presents. To gather in his assistants, loyal associates, and loved ones, you must secretly show them the gains they can realize by colluding with you. Have them slight their work, and then their preparations will be futile.

"Eighth, gift him with great treasures, and make plans with him. When the plans are successful and profit him, he will have faith in you because of the profits. This is what is termed 'being closely embraced.' The result of being closely embraced is that he will inevitably be used by us. When someone rules a state but is externally [controlled], his territory will inevitably be defeated.

"Ninth, honor him with praise. Do nothing that will cause him personal discomfort. Display the proper respect accruing to a great power, and your obedience will certainly be trusted. Magnify his honor; be the first to gloriously praise him, humbly embellishing him as a Sage. Then his state will suffer great loss!

"Tenth, be submissive so that he will trust you, and thereby learn about his true situation. Accept his ideas and respond to his affairs as if you were twins. Once you have learned everything, subtly gather in [his power]. Thus when the ultimate day arrives, it will seem as if Heaven itself destroyed him.

"Eleventh, block up his access by means of the Tao. Among subordinates there is no one who does not value rank and wealth nor hate danger and misfortune. Secretly express great respect toward them, and gradually bestow valuable gifts in order to gather in the more outstanding talents. Accumulate your own resources until they become very substantial, but manifest an external appearance of shortage. Covertly bring in wise knights, and entrust them with planning great strategy. Attract courageous knights, and augment their spirit. Even when they are more than sufficiently rich and honored, constantly add to their riches. When your faction has been fully established [you will have attained the objective] referred to as 'blocking his access.' If someone has a state but his access is blocked, how can he be considered as having the state?

"Twelfth, support his dissolute officials in order to confuse him. Introduce beautiful women and licentious sounds in order to befuddle him. Send him outstanding dogs and horses in order to tire him. From time to time allow him great power in order to entice him [to greater arrogance]. Then investigate Heaven's signs, and plot with the world against him.

"When these twelve measures are fully employed, they will become a military weapon. Thus when, as it is said, one 'looks at Heaven above and investigates Earth below' and the proper signs are already visible, attack him."

16. Instructions on According with the People

King Wen asked the T'ai Kung: "What should one do so that he can govern All under Heaven?"

The T'ai Kung said: "When your greatness overspreads All under Heaven, only then will you be able to encompass it. When your trustworthiness has overspread All under Heaven, only then will you be able to make covenants with it. When your benevolence has overspread All under Heaven, only then will you be able to embrace it. When your grace has overspread All under Heaven, only then can you preserve it. When your authority covers the world, only then will you be able not to lose it. If you govern without doubt, then the revolutions of Heaven will not be able to shift [your rule] nor the changes of the seasons be able to affect it. Only when these six are complete will you be able to establish a government for All under Heaven.

"Accordingly, one who profits All under Heaven will find All under Heaven open to him. One who harms All under Heaven will find All under Heaven closed to him. If one gives life to All under Heaven, All under Heaven will regard him as Virtuous. If one kills All under Heaven, All under Heaven will regard him as a brigand. If one penetrates to All under Heaven, All under Heaven will be accessible to him; if one impoverishes All under Heaven, All under Heaven will regard him as their enemy. One who gives peace to All under Heaven, All under Heaven will rely on; one who endangers All under Heaven, All under Heaven will view as a disaster. All under Heaven is not the realm of one man. Only one who possesses the Tao can dwell [in the position of authority]."

17. Three Doubts

King Wu inquired of the T'ai Kung: "I want to attain our aim [of overthrowing the Shang], but I have three doubts. I am afraid that our strength will be inadequate to attack the strong, to estrange his close supporters within the court, and disperse his people. What should I do?"

The T'ai Kung replied: "Accord with the situation, be very cautious in making plans, and employ your material resources. Now in order to attack the strong, you must nurture them to make them even stronger, and increase them to make them even more extensive. What is too strong will certainly break; what is too extended must have deficiencies.[32] Attack the strong through his strength. Cause the estrangement of his favored officials by using his favorites, and disperse his people by means of the people.[33]

"Now in the Tao of planning, thoroughness and secrecy are treasured. You should become involved with him in numerous affairs and ply him with temptations of profit. Conflict will then surely arise.

"If you want to cause his close supporters to become estranged from him, you must do it by using what they love—making gifts to those he favors, giving them what they want. Tempt them with what they find profitable, thereby making them disaffected, and cause them to be unable to attain their ambitions. Those who covet profits will be extremely happy at the prospects, and their remaining doubts will be ended.

"Now without doubt the Tao for attacking is to first obfuscate the king's clarity and then attack his strength, destroying his greatness and eliminating the misfortune of the people. Debauch him with beautiful women, entice him with profit. Nurture him with flavors, and provide him with the company of female musicians. Then after you have caused his subordinates to become estranged from him, you must cause the people to grow distant from him while never letting him know your plans. Appear to support him and draw him into your trap. Do not let him become aware of what is happening, for only then can your plan be successful.

"When bestowing your beneficence on the people, you cannot begrudge the expense. The people are like cows and horses. Frequently make gifts of food and clothing and follow up by loving them.[34]

"The mind is the means to open up knowledge; knowledge the means to open up the source of wealth; and wealth the means to open up the people. Gaining the allegiance of the people is the way to attract Worthy men. When one is enlightened by Sagely advisers, he can become king of all the world."

龍韜

III

DRAGON SECRET TEACHING

18. The King's Wings

King Wu asked the T'ai Kung: "When the king commands the army he must have 'legs and arms' [top assistants] and 'feathers and wings' [aides] to bring about his awesomeness and spiritualness. How should this be done?"

The T'ai Kung said: "Whenever one mobilizes the army it takes the commanding general as its fate. Its fate lies in a penetrating understanding of all aspects, not clinging to one technique. In accord with their abilities assign duties—each one taking charge of what they are good at, constantly changing and transforming with the times, to create the essential principles and order. Thus the general has seventy-two 'legs and arms' and 'feathers and wings' in order to respond to the Tao of Heaven. Prepare their number according to method, being careful that they know its orders and principles. When you have all the different abilities and various skills, then the myriad affairs will be complete."

King Wu asked: "May I ask about the various categories?"

The T'ai Kung said: "*Fu-hsin* [Chief of Planning],[35] one: in charge of advising about secret plans for responding to sudden events; investigating Heaven so as to eliminate sudden change; exercising general supervision over all planning; and protecting and preserving the lives of the people.

"Planning officers, five: responsible for planning security and danger; anticipating the unforeseen; discussing performance and ability; making clear rewards and punishments; appointing officers; deciding the doubtful; and determining what is advisable and what is not.

"Astrologers, three: undertaking responsibility for the stars and calendar; observing the wind and *ch'i*; predicting auspicious days and times; investigating signs and phenomena; verifying disasters and abnormalities; and knowing Heaven's mind with regard to the moment for completion or abandonment.[36]

"Topographers, three: in charge of the army's disposition and strategic configuration of power when moving and stopped [and of] information on strategic advantages and disadvantages; precipitous and easy passages, both near and far; and water and dry land, mountains and defiles, so as not to lose the advantages of terrain.

"Strategists, nine: responsible for discussing divergent views; analyzing the probable success or failure of various operations; selecting the weapons and training men in their use; and identifying those who violate the ordinances.

"Supply officers, four: responsible for calculating the requirements for food and water; preparing the food stocks and supplies and transporting the provisions along the route; and supplying the five grains so as to ensure that the army will not suffer any hardship or shortage.

"Officers for Flourishing Awesomeness, four: responsible for picking men of talent and strength; for discussing weapons and armor; for setting up attacks that race like the wind and strike like thunder so that [the enemy] does not know where they come from.

"Secret Signals officers,[37] three: responsible for the pennants and drums, for clearly [signaling] to the eyes and ears; for creating deceptive signs and seals [and] issuing false designations and orders; and for stealthily and hastily moving back and forth, going in and out like spirits.

"Legs and Arms, four: responsible for undertaking heavy duties and handling difficult tasks; for the repair and maintenance of ditches and moats; and for keeping the walls and ramparts in repair in order to defend against and repel [the enemy].

"Liaison officers, two: responsible for gathering what has been lost and supplementing what is in error; receiving honored guests; holding discussions and talks; mitigating disasters; and resolving difficulties.

"Officers of Authority, three: responsible for implementing the unorthodox and deceptive; for establishing the different and the unusual, things that people do not recognize; and for putting into effect incxhaustible transformations.[38]

"Ears and Eyes, seven: responsible for going about everywhere, listening to what people are saying; seeing the changes; and observing the officers in all four directions and the army's true situation.

"Claws and Teeth, five: responsible for raising awesomeness and martial [spirit]; for stimulating and encouraging the Three Armies, causing them to risk hardship and attack the enemy's elite troops without ever having any doubts or second thoughts.

"Feathers and Wings, four: responsible for flourishing the name and fame [of the army]; for shaking distant lands [with its image]; and for moving all within the four borders in order to weaken the enemy's spirit.

"Roving officers, eight: responsible for spying on [the enemy's] licentiousness and observing their changes; manipulating their emotions; and observing the enemy's thoughts in order to act as spies.

"Officers of Techniques, two: responsible for spreading slander and falsehoods and for calling on ghosts and spirits in order to confuse the minds of the populace.

"Officers of Prescriptions, three: in charge of the hundred medicines; managing blade wounds; and curing the various maladies.

"Accountants, two: responsible for accounting for the provisions and foodstuffs within the Three Armies' encampments and ramparts; for the fiscal materials employed; and for receipts and disbursements."

19. A Discussion of Generals

King Wu asked the T'ai Kung: "What should a general be?"

The T'ai Kung replied: "Generals have five critical talents and ten excesses."

King Wu said: "Dare I ask you to enumerate them?"

The T'ai Kung elaborated: "What we refer to as the five talents are courage, wisdom, benevolence, trustworthiness, and loyalty. If he is courageous he cannot be overwhelmed. If he is wise he cannot be forced into turmoil. If he is benevolent he will love his men. If he is trustworthy he will not be deceitful. If he is loyal he will not be of two minds.

"What are referred to as the ten errors are as follows: being courageous and treating death lightly; being hasty and impatient; being greedy and loving profit; being benevolent but unable to inflict suffering; being wise but afraid; being trustworthy and liking to trust others; being scrupulous and incorruptible but not loving men; being wise but indecisive; being resolute and self-reliant; and being fearful while liking to entrust responsibility to other men.

"One who is courageous and treats death lightly can be destroyed by violence. One who is hasty and impatient can be destroyed by persistence. One who is greedy and loves profit can be bribed. One who is benevolent but unable to inflict suffering can be worn down. One who is wise but fearful can be distressed.

"One who is trustworthy and likes to trust others can be deceived. One who is scrupulous and incorruptible but does not love men can be insulted. One who is wise but indecisive can be suddenly attacked. One who is resolute and self-reliant can be confounded by events. One who is fearful and likes to entrust responsibility to others can be tricked.

"Thus 'warfare is the greatest affair of state, the Tao of survival or extinction.'[39] The fate of the state lies in the hands of the general. 'The general is the support of the state,'[40] a man that the former kings all valued. Thus in commissioning a general, you cannot but carefully evaluate and investigate his character.

"Thus it is said that two armies will not be victorious, nor will both be defeated. When the army ventures out beyond the borders, before they have been out ten days—even if a state has not perished—one army will certainly have been destroyed and the general killed."

King Wu: "Marvelous!"

20. Selecting Generals

King Wu asked the T'ai Kung: "If a king wants to raise an army, how should he go about selecting and training heroic officers and determining their moral qualifications?"

The T'ai Kung said: "There are fifteen cases where a knight's external appearance and internal character do not cohere. These are:

"He appears to be a Worthy but [actually] is immoral.

"He seems warm and conscientious but is a thief.

"His countenance is reverent and respectful, but his heart is insolent.

"Externally he is incorruptible and circumspect, but he lacks respect.

"He appears perceptive and sharp but lacks such talent.

"He appears profound but lacks all sincerity.

"He appears adept at planning but is indecisive.

"He appears to be decisive and daring but is incapable.

"He appears guileless but is not trustworthy.

"He appears confused and disoriented but on the contrary is loyal and substantial.

"He appears to engage in specious discourse but is a man of merit and achievement.

"He appears courageous but is afraid.

"He seems severe and remote but on the contrary easily befriends men.

"He appears forbidding but on the contrary is quiet and sincere.

"He appears weak and insubstantial, yet when dispatched outside the state there is nothing he does not accomplish, no mission that he does not execute successfully.

"Those who the world disdains the Sage values. Ordinary men do not know these things; only great wisdom can discern the edge of these matters. This is because the knight's external appearance and internal character do not visibly cohere."

King Wu asked: "How does one know this?"

The T'ai Kung replied: "There are eight forms of evidence by which you may know it. First, question them and observe the details of their reply. Second, verbally confound and perplex them and observe how they change. Third, discuss things which you have secretly learned to observe their sincerity. Fourth, clearly and explicitly question them to observe their virtue. Fifth, appoint them to positions of financial responsibility to observe their honesty. Sixth, test them with beautiful women to observe their uprightness. Seventh, confront them with difficulties to observe their courage. Eighth, get them drunk to observe their deportment. When all eight have been fully explored, then the Worthy and unworthy can be distinguished."

21. Appointing the General

King Wu asked the T'ai Kung: "What is the Tao for appointing the commanding general?"

The T'ai Kung said: "When the state encounters danger, the ruler should vacate the Main Hall, summon the general, and charge him as follows: 'The security or endangerment of the Altars of State all lie with the army's commanding general. At present such-and-such a state does not act properly submissive. I would like you to lead the army forth to respond to it.'

"After the general has received his mandate, command the Grand Scribe to bore the sacred tortoise shell to divine an auspicious day. Thereafter, to prepare for the chosen day, observe a vegetarian regime for three days, and then go to the ancestral temple to hand over the *fu* and *yüeh* axes.[41]

"After the ruler has entered the gate to the temple, he stands facing west. The general enters the temple gate and stands facing north. The ruler personally takes the *yüeh* ax and, holding it by the head, passes the handle to the general, saying: 'From this to Heaven above will be controlled by the General of the Army.' Then taking the *fu* axe by the handle, he should give the blade to the general, saying: 'From this to the depths below will be controlled by the General of the Army. When you see vacuity in the enemy you should advance; when you see substance you should halt.[42] Do not assume that the Three Armies are large and treat the enemy lightly. Do not commit yourself to die just because you have received a heavy responsibility. Do not, because you are honored, regard other men as lowly. Do not rely upon yourself alone and contravene the masses. Do not take verbal facility to be a sign of certainty. When the officers have not yet been seated, do not sit. When the officers have not yet eaten, do not eat. You should share heat and cold with them. If you behave in this way the officers and masses will certainly exhaust their strength in fighting to the death.'[43]

"After the general has received his mandate, he bows and responds to the ruler: 'I have heard that a country cannot follow the commands of another state's government, while an army [in the field] cannot follow central government control. Someone of two minds cannot properly serve his ruler; someone in doubt cannot respond to the enemy. I have already received my mandate and taken sole control of the awesome power of the *fu* and *yüeh* axes. I do not dare return alive. I would like to request that you condescend to grant complete and sole command to me. If you do not permit it, I dare not accept the post of general.' The king then grants it, and the general formally takes his leave and departs.[44]

"Military matters are not determined by the ruler's commands; they all proceed from the commanding general. When [the commanding general] approaches an enemy and decides to engage in battle, he is not of two minds. In this way there is no Heaven above, no Earth below, no enemy in front, and no ruler to the rear. For this reason the wise make plans for him, the courageous fight for him. Their spirit soars to the blue clouds; they are swift like galloping steeds. Even before the blades clash, the enemy surrenders submissively.

"War is won outside the borders of the state, but the general's merit is established within it. Officials are promoted and receive the highest rewards; the hundred surnames rejoice; and the general is blameless. For this reason the winds and rains will be seasonable; the five grains will grow abundantly; and the altars of state will be secure and peaceful."

King Wu said: "Excellent."

22. The General's Awesomeness

King Wu asked: "How does the general create awesomeness? How can he be enlightened? How can he make his prohibitions effective and get his orders implemented?"

The T'ai Kung said: "The general creates awesomeness by executing the great, and becomes enlightened by rewarding the small. Prohibitions are made effective and laws implemented by careful scrutiny in the use of punishments. Therefore if by executing one man the entire army will quake, kill him. If by rewarding one man the masses will be pleased, reward him. In executing, value the great; in rewarding, value the small. When you kill the powerful and the honored, this is punishment that reaches the pinnacle. When rewards extend down to the cowherds, grooms, and stablemen, these are rewards penetrating downward to the lowest. When punishments reach the pinnacle and rewards penetrate to the lowest, then your awesomeness has been effected."

23. Encouraging the Army

King Wu asked the T'ai Kung: "When we attack I want the masses of the Three Armies to contend with each other to scale the wall first, and compete with each other to be in the forefront when we fight in the field. When they hear the sound of the gongs [to retreat] they will be angry, and when they hear the sound of the drums [to advance] they will be happy. How can we accomplish this?"

The T'ai Kung said: "A general has three techniques for attaining victory."

King Wu asked: "May I ask what they are?"

The T'ai Kung: "If in winter the general does not wear a fur robe, in summer does not carry a fan, and in the rain does not set up a canopy, he is called a 'general of proper form.' Unless the general himself submits to these observances, he will not have the means to know the cold and warmth of the officers and soldiers.

"If, when they advance into ravines and obstacles or encounter muddy terrain, the general always takes the first steps, he is termed a 'general of strength.' If the general does not personally exert his strength, he has no means to know the labors and hardships of the officers and soldiers.

"If only after the men are settled in their encampment does the general retire; only after all the cooks have finished their cooking does he go in to eat; and if the army does not light fires to keep warm he also does not have one, he is termed a 'general who stifles desire.' Unless the general himself practices stifling his desires, he has no way to know the hunger and satiety of the officers and troops.

"The general shares heat and cold, labor and suffering, hunger and satiety with the officers and men. Therefore when the masses of the Three Armies hear the sound of the drum they are happy, and when they hear the sound of the gong they are angry. When attacking a high wall or crossing a deep lake, under a hail of arrows and stones, the officers will compete to be first to scale the wall. When the naked blades clash, the officers will compete to be the first to go forward. It is not because they like death and take pleasure in being wounded, but because the general knows their feelings of heat and cold, hunger and satiety, and clearly displays his knowledge of their labor and suffering."

24. Secret Tallies[45]

King Wu asked the T'ai Kung: "If we lead the army deep into the territory of the feudal lords where the Three Armies suddenly suffer some delay or require urgent action—perhaps a situation to our advantage, or one to our disadvantage—and I[46] want to communicate between those nearby and those more distant, respond to the outside from the inside, in order to supply the use of the Three Armies—how should we do it?"

The T'ai Kung said: "The ruler and his generals have a system of secret tallies, altogether consisting of eight grades.

"There is a tally signifying a great victory over the enemy, one foot long.

"There is a tally for destroying the enemy's army and killing their general, nine inches long.

"There is a tally for forcing the surrender of the enemy's walls and capturing the town, eight inches long.

"There is a tally for driving the enemy back and reporting deep penetration, seven inches long.

"There is a tally to alert the masses to prepare for stalwart defensive measures, six inches long.

"There is a tally requesting supplies and additional soldiers, five inches long.

"There is a tally signifying the army's defeat and the general's death, four inches long.

"There is a tally signifying the loss of all advantages and the army's surrender, three inches long.

"Detain all those who bring in and present tallies, and if the information from the tally should leak out, execute all those who heard and told about it. These eight tallies, which only the ruler and general should secretly know, provide a technique for covert communication that will not allow outsiders to know the true situation. Accordingly, even though the enemy has the wisdom of a Sage, no one will comprehend their significance."

King Wu said: "Excellent."

25. Secret Letters

King Wu asked the T'ai Kung: "The army has been led deep into the territory of the feudal lords and the commanding general[47] wants to bring the troops together, implement inexhaustible changes, and plan for unfathomable advantages. These matters are quite numerous; the simple tally is not adequate to clearly express them. As they are separated by some distance, verbal communications cannot get through. What should we do?"

The T'ai Kung said: "Whenever you have secret affairs and major considerations, letters should be employed rather than tallies. The ruler sends a letter to the general; the general uses a letter to query the ruler. The letters are [composed] in one unit, then divided. They are sent out in three parts, with only one person knowing the contents. 'Divided' means it is separated into three parts. 'Sent out in three parts, with only one person knowing' means there are three messengers, each carrying one part; and when the three are compared together, only then does one know the contents. This is referred to as a 'secret letter.' Even if the enemy has the wisdom of a Sage, they will not be able to recognize the contents."

"Excellent," said King Wu.

26. The Army's Strategic Power

King Wu asked the T'ai Kung: "What is the Tao for aggressive warfare?"

The T'ai Kung replied: "Strategic power is exercised in accord with the enemy's movements. Changes stem from the confrontation between the two armies. Unorthodox [ch'i] and orthodox [cheng] tactics are produced from the inexhaustible resources [of the mind]. Thus the greatest affairs are not discussed, and the employment of troops is not spoken about. Moreover, words which discuss ultimate affairs are not worth listening to.[48] The employment of troops is not so definitive as to be visible. They go suddenly, they come suddenly. Only someone who can exercise sole control, without being governed by other men, is a military weapon.

"If [your plans][49] are heard about, the enemy will make counterplans. If you are perceived, they will plot against you. If you are known, they will put you in difficulty. If you are fathomed, they will endanger you.

"Thus one who excels in warfare does not await the deployment of forces. One who excels at eliminating the misfortunes of the people manages them before they appear. Conquering the enemy means being victorious over the formless.[50] The superior fighter does not engage in battle. Thus one who fights and attains victory in front of naked blades is not a good general. One who makes preparations after [the battle] has been lost is not a Superior Sage! One whose skill is the same as the masses is not a State Artisan.

"In military affairs nothing is more important than certain victory. In employing the army nothing is more important than obscurity and silence. In movement nothing is more important than the unexpected. In planning nothing is more important than not being knowable.

"To be the first to gain victory, initially display some weakness to the enemy and only afterward do battle. Then your effort will be half, but the achievement will be doubled.

"The Sage takes his signs from the movements of Heaven and Earth; who knows his principles? He accords with the Tao of yin and yang and follows their seasonal activity. He follows the cycles of fullness and emptiness of Heaven and Earth, taking them as his constant. All things have life and death in accord with the form of Heaven and Earth. Thus it is said that if one fights before seeing the situation, even if he is more numerous, he will certainly be defeated.

"One who excels at warfare will await events in the situation without making any movement. When he sees he can be victorious, he will arise; if he sees he cannot be victorious, he will desist. Thus it is said he does not have any fear, he does not vacillate. Of the many harms that can beset an army, vacillation is the greatest. Of disasters that can befall an army, none surpasses doubt.

"One who excels in warfare will not lose an advantage when he perceives it or be doubtful when he meets the moment. One who loses an advantage or lags behind the time for action will, on the contrary, suffer from disaster. Thus the wise follow the time and do not lose an advantage; the skillful are decisive and have no doubts. For this reason when there is a sudden clap of thunder, there is not time to cover the ears; when there is a flash of lightning, there is not time to close the eyes. Advance as if suddenly startled; employ your troops as if deranged.[51] Those who oppose you will be destroyed; those who come near will perish. Who can defend against such an attack?

"Now when matters are not discussed and the general preserves their secrecy, he is spirit-like. When things are not manifest but he discerns them, he is enlightened. Thus if one knows the Tao of spirit and enlightenment, no enemies will act against him in the field, nor will any state stand against him."

"Excellent," said King Wu.

27. The Unorthodox Army

King Wu asked the T'ai Kung, "In general, what are the great essentials in the art of employing the army?"

The T'ai Kung replied: "The ancients who excelled at warfare were not able to wage war above Heaven, nor could they wage war below Earth.[52] Their success and defeat in all cases proceeded from the spiritual employment of strategic power [*shih*]. Those who attained it flourished; those who lost it perished.

"Now when our two armies, opposing each other, have deployed their armored soldiers and established their battle arrays, releasing some of your troops to create chaos in the ranks is the means by which to fabricate deceptive changes.

"Deep grass and dense growth are the means by which to effect a concealed escape.

"Valleys with streams and treacherous ravines are the means by which to stop chariots and defend against cavalry.

"Narrow passes and mountain forests are the means by which a few can attack a large force.

"Marshy depressions and secluded dark areas are the means by which to conceal your appearance.

"[Deploying] on clear, open ground without any concealment is the means by which to fight with strength and courage.[53]

"Being as swift as a flying arrow, attacking as suddenly as the release of a crossbow are the means by which to destroy brilliant plans.

"Setting up ingenious ambushes and preparing unorthodox troops, stretching out distant formations to deceive and entice the enemy are the means by which to destroy the enemy's army and capture its general.

"Dividing your troops into four and splitting them into five are the means by which by attack their circular formations and destroy their square ones.

"Taking advantage of their fright and fear is the means by which one can attack ten.

"Taking advantage of their exhaustion and encamping at dusk are the means by which ten can attack one hundred.

"Unorthodox technical skills are the means by which to cross deep waters and ford rivers.

"Strong crossbows and long weapons are the means by which to fight across water.

"Distant observation posts and far-off scouts, explosive haste and feigned retreats are the means by which to force the surrender of walled fortifications and compel the submission of towns.

"Drumming an advance and setting up a great tumult are the means by which to implement unorthodox plans.

"High winds and heavy rain are the means by which to strike the front and seize the rear.

"Disguising some men as enemy emissaries is the means by which to sever their supply lines.

"Forging [enemy] commands and orders and wearing the same clothes as the enemy are the means by which to be prepared for their retreat.

"Warfare which is invariably in accord with righteousness is the means by which to incite the masses and be victorious over the enemy.

"Honored ranks and generous rewards are the means by which to encourage obeying orders.

"Severe punishments and heavy fines are the means by which to force the weary and indolent to advance.

"Happiness and anger, bestowing and taking away, civil and martial measures, at times slowly, at others rapidly—all these are the means by which to order and harmonize the Three Armies, to govern and unify subordinates.

"Occupying high ground is the means by which to be alert and assume a defensive posture.

"Holding defiles and narrows is the means by which to be solidly entrenched.

"Mountain forests and dense growth are the means by which to come and go silently.

"Deep moats, high ramparts, and large reserves of supplies are the means by which to sustain your position for a long time.

"Thus it is said, 'One who does not know how to plan for aggressive warfare cannot be spoken with about the enemy. One who cannot divide and move [his troops about] cannot be spoken with about unorthodox strategies.[54] One who does not have a penetrating understanding of both order and chaos cannot be spoken with about changes.'

"Accordingly it is said:

"'If the general is not benevolent, then the Three Armies will not be close to him.

"'If the general is not courageous, then the Three Armies will not be fierce.

"'If the general is not wise, then the Three Armies will be greatly perplexed.

"'If the general is not perspicacious, then the Three Armies will be confounded.

"'If the general is not quick-witted and acute, then the Three Armies will lose the moment.[55]

"'If the general is not constantly alert, the Three Armies will waste their preparations.

"'If the general is not strong and forceful, then the Three Armies will fail in their duty.'

"Thus the general is their Master of Fate. The Three Armies are ordered with him, and they are disordered with him. If one obtains a Worthy to serve as general, the army will be strong and the state will prosper. If one does not obtain a Worthy as general, the army will be weak and the state will perish."

"Excellent," said King Wu.

28. The Five Notes

King Wu asked the T'ai Kung: "From the sound of the pitch pipes, can we know the fluctuations of the Three Armies, foretell victory and defeat?"

The T'ai Kung said: "Your question is profound indeed! Now there are twelve pipes, with five major notes: *kung, shang, chiao, cheng,* and *yü.*[56] These are the true, orthodox sounds, unchanged for over ten thousand generations.

"The spirits of the five phases are constants of the Tao.[57] Metal, wood, water, fire, and earth—each according to their conquest relationship—[can be employed to] attack the enemy. In antiquity, during the period of the Three Sage Emperors, they used the nature of vacuity and non-action to govern the hard and strong. They didn't have characters for writing; everything proceeded from the five phases. The Tao of the five phases is the naturalness of Heaven and Earth. The division into the six *chia*[58] is [a realization] of marvelous and subtle spirit.

"Their method was, when the day had been clear and calm—without any clouds, wind, or rain—to send light cavalry out in the middle of the night to approach the enemy's fortifications. Stopping about nine hundred paces away, they would all lift their pipes to their ears and then yell out to startle the enemy. There would be a very small, subtle sound that would respond in the pitch pipes.

"If the *chiao* note responded among the pipes, it indicated a white tiger.

"If the *cheng* note responded in the pipes, it indicated the Mysterious Military.

"If the *shang* note responded in the pipes, it indicated the Vermillion Bird.

"If you *yü* note responded in the pipes, it indicated the Hooked Formation.

"If none of the five notes responded in the pipes, it was *kung*, signifying a Green Dragon.

"These signs of the five phases are evidence to assist in the conquest, the subtle moments of success and defeat."

"Excellent," said King Wu.

The T'ai Kung continued: "These subtle, mysterious notes all have external indications."

"How can we know them?" King Wu asked.

The T'ai Kung replied: "When the enemy has been startled into movement, listen for them. If you hear the sound of the *pao* drum, then it is *chiao*. If you see the flash of lights from a fire, then it is *cheng*. If you hear the sounds of bronze and iron, of spears and halberds, then it is *shang*. If you hear the sound of people sighing, it is *yü*. If all is silent, without any sound, then it is *kung*. These five are the signs of sound and appearance."

29. The Army's Indications

King Wu asked the T'ai Kung: "Before engaging in battle I want to first know the enemy's strengths and weaknesses, to foresee indications of victory or defeat. How can this be done?"

The T'ai Kung replied: "Indications of victory or defeat will be first manifest in their spirit. The enlightened general will investigate them, for they will be evidenced in the men.

"Clearly observe the enemy's coming and going, advancing and withdrawing. Investigate his movements and periods at rest, whether they speak about portents, what the officers and troops report. If the Three Armies are exhilarated [and] the officers and troops fear the laws; respect the general's commands; rejoice with each other in destroying the enemy; boast to each other about their courage and ferocity; and praise each other for their awesomeness and martial demeanor—these are indications of a strong enemy.

"If the Three Armies have been startled a number of times, the officers and troops no longer maintaining good order; they terrify each other [with stories about] the enemy's strength; they speak to each other about the disadvantages; they anxiously look about at each other, listening carefully; they talk incessantly of ill omens, myriad mouths confusing each other; they fear neither laws nor orders and do not regard their general seriously—these are indications of weakness.

"When the Three Armies are well ordered; the deployment's strategic configuration of power solid—with deep moats and high ramparts—and moreover they enjoy the advantages of high winds and heavy rain; the army is untroubled; the signal flags and pennants point to the front; the sound of the gongs and bells rises up and is clear; and the sound of the small and large drums clearly rises—these are indications of having obtained spiritual, enlightened assistance, foretelling a great victory.

"When their formations are not solid; their flags and pennants confused and entangled with each other; they go contrary to the advantages of high wind and heavy rain; their officers and troops are terrified; and their *ch'i* broken while they are not unified; their war horses have been frightened and run off, their military chariots have broken axles; the sound of their gongs and bells sinks down and is murky; the sound of their drums is wet and damp—these are indications foretelling a great defeat.

"In general, when you attack city walls or surround towns, if the color of their *ch'i* is liked dead ashes, the city can be slaughtered.[59] If the city's *ch'i* drifts out to the north, the city can be conquered. If the city's *ch'i* goes out and drifts to the west, the city can be forced to surrender. If the city's *ch'i* goes out and drifts to the south, it cannot be taken. If the city's *ch'i* goes out and drifts to the east, the city cannot be attacked. If the city's *ch'i* goes out but then drifts back in, the city's ruler has already fled. If the city's *ch'i* goes out and overspreads our army, the soldiers will surely fall ill. If the city's *ch'i* goes out and just rises up without any direction,[60] the army will have to be employed for a long time. If, when you have attacked a walled city or surrounded a town for more than ten days without thunder or rain, you must hastily abandon it, for the city must have a source of great assistance.

"Those are the means by which to know that you can attack and then go on to mount the attack, or that you should not attack and therefore stop."

"Excellent," said King Wu.

30. Agricultural Implements

King Wu asked the T'ai Kung: "If All under Heaven are at peace and settled, while the state is not engaged in any conflicts, can we dispense with maintaining the implements of war? Can we forego preparing equipment for defense?"

The T'ai Kung said: "The implements for offense and defense are fully found in ordinary human activity. Digging sticks serve as *chevaux-de-frise* and caltrops. Oxen and horse-pulled wagons can be used in the encampment and as covering shields. The different hoes can be used as spears and spear-tipped halberds. Raincoats of straw and large umbrellas serve as armor and protective shields. Large hoes, spades, axes, saws, mortars, and pestles are tools for attacking walls. Oxen and horses are the means to transport provisions. Chickens and dogs serve as lookouts. The cloth that women weave serves as flags and pennants.

"The method that the men use for leveling the fields is the same for attacking walls. The skill needed in spring to cut down grass and thickets is the same as needed for fighting against chariots and cavalry. The weeding methods used in summer are the same as used in battle against foot soldiers. The grain harvested and the firewood cut in the fall will be provisions for the military. In the winter well-filled granaries and storehouses will ensure a solid defense.

"The units of five found in the fields and villages will provide the tallies and good faith that bind the men together. The villages have officials and the offices have chiefs who can lead the army. The villages have walls surrounding them, which are not crossed; they provide the basis for the division into platoons. The transportation of grain and the cutting of hay provide for the state storehouses and armories. The skills used in repairing the inner and outer walls in the spring and fall, in maintaining the moats and channels are used to build ramparts and fortifications.

"Thus the tools for employing the military are completely found in ordinary human activity. One who is good at governing a state will take them from ordinary human affairs. Then they must be made to accord with the good management of the six animals,[61] to the opening up of wild lands, and the settling of the people where they dwell. The husband has a number of acres that he farms, the wife a measured amount of material to weave—this is the Way to enrich the state and strengthen the army."

"Excellent," said King Wu.

虎韜

IV
TIGER SECRET TEACHING

31. The Army's Equipment

King Wu asked the T'ai Kung: "When the king mobilizes the Three Armies, are there any rules for determining the army's equipment, such as the implements for attack and defense, including type and quantity?"

The T'ai Kung said: "A great question, my king! The implements for attack and defense each have their own categories. This results in the great awesomeness of the army."[62]

King Wu said: "I would like to hear about them."

The T'ai Kung replied: "As for the basic numbers when employing the army, if commanding ten thousand armed soldiers the rules for [the various types of equipment and their] employment are as follows.

"Thirty-six Martial Protective Large *Fu-hsü* Chariots. Skilled officers, strong crossbowmen, spear bearers, and halberdiers—total of twenty-four for each flank [and the rear].[63] The chariots have eight-foot wheels. On it are set up pennants and drums which, according to the Art of War, are referred to as 'Shaking Fear.' They are used to penetrate solid formations, to defeat strong enemies.

"Seventy-two Martial-Flanking Large Covered Spear and Halberd *Fu-hsü* Chariots.[64] Skilled officers, strong crossbowmen, spear bearers, and halberdiers comprise the flanks. They have five-foot wheels and winch-powered linked crossbows which fire multiple arrows for self-protection.[65] They are used to penetrate solid formations and defeat strong enemies.

"One hundred and forty Flank-supporting Small Covered *Fu-hsü* Chariots equipped with winch-powered linked crossbows to fire multiple arrows for self-protection. They have deer wheels and are used to penetrate solid formations and defeat strong enemies.

"Thirty-six Great Yellow Triple-linked Crossbow Large *Fu-hsü* Chariots. Skilled officers, strong crossbowmen, spear bearers, and halberdiers comprise the flanks, with 'flying duck' and 'lightning's shadow' arrows for self-protection. 'Flying duck' arrows have red shafts and white feathers, with bronze arrowheads. 'Lightning's shadow' arrows have green shafts and red feathers, with iron heads.[66] In the daytime they display pennants of red silk six feet long by six inches wide, which shimmer in the light. At night they hang pennants of white silk, also six feet long by six inches wide, which appear like meteors. They are used to penetrate solid formations, to defeat infantry and cavalry.

"Thirty-six Great *Fu-hsü* Attack Chariots.[67] Carrying Praying Mantis Martial warriors, they can attack both horizontal and vertical formations and can defeat the enemy.

"Baggage Chariots [for repelling] mounted invaders, also called 'Lightning Chariots.' The Art of War refers to their use in 'lightning attacks.'[68] They are used to penetrate solid formations, to defeat both infantry and cavalry.

"One hundred and sixty Spear and Halberd *Fu-hsü* Light Chariots [for repelling] night invaders from the fore. Each carries three Praying Mantis Martial knights. The Art of War refers to them as mounting 'thunder attacks.' They are used to penetrate solid formations, to defeat both infantry and cavalry.

"Iron truncheons with large square heads weighing twelve catties, and shafts more than five feet long, twelve hundred of them. Also termed 'Heaven's Truncheon.'

"The Great Handle *Fu* Ax with an eight-inch blade, weighing eight catties, and a shaft more than five feet long, twelve hundred of them. Also termed 'Heaven's *Yüeh* Ax.'

"Also the Iron Square-headed Pounder, weighing eight catties, with a shaft of more than five feet, twelve hundred. Also termed 'Heaven's Pounder.' They are used to defeat infantry and hordes of mounted invaders.

"The Flying Hook, eight inches long. The curve of the hook is five inches long, the shaft is more than six feet long. Twelve hundred of them. They are thrown into masses of soldiers.

"To defend the Three Armies deploy *Fu-hsü* [chariots] equipped with wooden Praying Mantises and sword blades, each twenty feet across, altogether one hundred and twenty of them. They are also termed *chevaux-de-frise*.[69] On open, level ground the infantry can use them to defeat chariots and cavalry.

"Wooden caltrops which stick out of the ground about two feet five inches, one hundred twenty. They are employed to defeat infantry and cavalry, to urgently press the attack against invaders, and to intercept their flight.[70]

"Short-axle Quick-turning Spear and Halberd *Fu-hsü* Chariots, one hundred twenty. They were employed by the Yellow Emperor to vanquish Ch'ih-yu. They are used to defeat both infantry and cavalry, to urgently press the attack against the invaders, and to intercept their flight.

"For narrow roads and small bypaths, set out iron caltrops eight inches wide, having hooks four inches high and shafts of more than six feet, twelve hundred. They are for defeating retreating[71] cavalry.

"If, in the darkness of night the enemy should suddenly press an attack and the naked blades clash, stretch out a ground net and spread out two arrowheaded caltrops connected together with 'weaving women'–type caltrops on both sides. The points of the blades should be about two feet apart. Twelve thousand sets.

"For fighting in wild expanses and in the middle of tall grass, there is the square-shank, arrow-shaped spear, twelve hundred of them. The method for deploying these spears is to have them stick out of the ground one foot five inches. They are used to defeat infantry and cavalry, to urgently press the attack against invaders, and to intercept their flight.

"On narrow roads, small bypaths, and constricted terrain, set out iron chains, one hundred twenty of them, to defeat infantry and cavalry, urgently press the attack against the invaders, and intercept their flight.

"For the protection and defense of the gates to fortifications, there are small [mobile] shields with spear and halberd [tips affixed], twelve of them, and winch-driven, multiple arrow crossbows for self-protection.[72]

"For the protection of the Three Armies, there are Heaven's Net and Tiger's Drop, linked together with chains, one hundred twenty of them. One array is fifteen feet wide and eight feet tall. For the *Fu-hsü* [chariot] with Tiger's Drop and sword blades affixed, the array is fifteen feet wide and eight feet tall. Five hundred ten of them.

"For crossing over moats and ditches, there is the Flying Bridge. One section is fifteen feet wide and more than twenty feet long. Eight of them.[73] On top there are swivel winches to extend them by linked chains.[74]

"For crossing over large bodies of water, there is the Flying River, eight of them. They are fifteen feet wide and more than twenty feet long and are extended by linked chains.

"There is also the Heavenly Float with Iron Praying Mantis, rectangular inside, circular outside, four feet or more in diameter, equipped with plantern winches. Thirty-two of them. When the Heavenly Floats are used to deploy the Flying River to cross a large lake, they are referred to as 'Heaven's Huang' and also termed 'Heaven's Boat.'

"When in mountain forests or occupying the wilds, connect the Tiger's Drops to make a fenced encampment. [Employ] iron chains, length of more than twenty feet, twelve hundred sets. [Also employ] large ropes with rings,[75] girth of four inches, length of more than forty feet, six hundred; midsized ropes with rings, girth of two inches, length of forty feet or more, two hundred sets; and small braided cords with rings, length of twenty feet or more, twelve thousand.

"Wooden canopies for covering the heavy chariots, called 'Heaven's Rain,' which fit together along serrated seams, each four feet wide and more than four feet long, one for each chariot. They are erected by using small iron posts.

"For cutting trees there is the Heavenly Ax, which weighs eight catties. Its handle is more than three feet long. Three hundred of them. Also the mattock with a blade six inches wide and a shaft more than five feet long, three hundred.

"Copper rams for pounding, more than five feet long, three hundred.

"Eagle claws with square hafts, iron handles, and shafts more than seven feet long, three hundred.

"Square-shafted iron pitchforks with handles more than seven feet long, three hundred.

"Square-shafted double-pronged iron pitchforks with shafts more than seven feet long, three hundred.

"Large sickles for cutting grass and light trees with shafts more than seven feet long, three hundred.

"Great oar-shaped blades, weight of eight catties, with shafts more than six feet long, three hundred.

"Iron stakes with rings affixed at top, more than three feet long, three hundred.

"Large hammers for pounding posts, weight of five catties, handles more than two feet long, one hundred twenty.

"Armored soldiers, ten thousand. Strong crossbowmen, six thousand. Halberdiers with shields, two thousand. Spearmen with shields, two thousand. Skilled men to repair offensive weapons and sharpen them, three hundred.

"These then are the general numbers required for each category when raising an army."

King Wu said: "I accept your instructions."

32. Three Deployments

King Wu asked the T'ai Kung: "In employing the army there are the Heavenly Deployment, the Earthly Deployment, and the Human Deployment. What are these?"

The T'ai Kung replied: "When you accord with the sun and moon, the stars, the planets, and the handle of the Big Dipper—one on the left, one on the right, one in front, and one to the rear—this is referred to as the Heavenly Deployment.[76]

"When the hills and mounds, rivers and streams are similarly to your advantage to the front, rear, left, and right, this is referred to as the Earthly Deployment.[77]

"When you employ chariots and horses, when you use both the civil and martial, this is referred to as the Human Deployment."[78]

"Excellent," said King Wu.

33. Urgent Battles

King Wu asked the T'ai Kung: "If the enemy surrounds us, severing both our advance and retreat, breaking off our supply lines, what should we do?"

The T'ai Kung said: "These are the most distressed troops in the world! If you employ them explosively, you will be victorious; if you are slow to employ them, you will be defeated. In this situation if you deploy your troops into martial assault formations on the four sides, use your military chariots and valiant cavalry to startle and confuse their army, and urgently attack them, you can thrust across them."

King Wu asked: "After we have broken out of the encirclement, if we want to take advantage of it to gain victory, what should we do?"

The T'ai Kung said: "The Army of the Left should urgently strike out to the left, and the Army of the Right should urgently strike out to the right. But do not get entangled in protracted fighting with the enemy over any one road. The Central Army should alternately move to the front and then the rear. Even though the enemy is more numerous, their general can be driven off."

34. Certain Escape

King Wu asked the T'ai Kung: "Suppose we have led our troops deep into the territory of the feudal lords where the enemy unites from all quarters and surrounds us, cutting off our road back home and severing our supply lines. The enemy is numerous and extremely well provisioned, while the ravines and gorges are also solidly held. We must get out—how can we?"

The T'ai Kung said: "In the matter of effecting a certain escape, your equipment is your treasure while courageous fighting is foremost. If you investigate and learn where the enemy's terrain is empty and vacuous, the places where there are no men, you can effect a certain escape.

"Order your generals and officers to carry the Mysterious Dark Pennants and take up the implements of war. Require the soldiers to put wooden gags into their mouths. Then move out at night. Men[79] of courage, strength, and swiftness, who will risk danger, should occupy the front to level fortifications and open a passage for the army. Skilled soldiers and strong crossbowmen should compose an ambushing force which will remain in the rear. Your weak soldiers, chariots, and cavalry should occupy the middle. When the deployment is complete slowly advance, being very cautious not to startle or frighten the enemy. Have the Martial Attack *Fu-hsü* Chariots defend the front and rear and the Martial Flanking Great Covered Chariots protect the left and right flanks.

"If the enemy should be startled, have your courageous, strong risk-takers fervently attack and advance. The weaker troops, chariots, and cavalry should bring up the rear. Your skilled soldiers and strong crossbowmen should conceal themselves in ambush. If you determine that the enemy is in pursuit, the men lying in ambush should swiftly attack their rear. Make your fires and drums numerous, and [attack] as if coming out of the very ground or dropping from Heaven above. If the Three Armies fight courageously no one will be able to withstand us!"

King Wu said: "In front of us lies a large body of water, or broad moat, or deep water hole which we want to cross. However, we do not have equipment such as boats and oars. The enemy has fortifications and ramparts which limit our army's advance and block off our retreat. Patrols are constantly watchful; passes are fully defended. Their chariots and cavalry press us in front; their courageous fighters attack us to the rear. What should we do?"

The T'ai Kung said: "Large bodies of water, broad moats, and deep water holes are usually not defended by the enemy. If they are able to defend them, their troops will certainly be few. In such situations you should use the Flying River with winches and also Heaven's Huang to cross the army over. Our courageous, strong, skilled soldiers should move where we indicate, rushing into the enemy, breaking up his formations, all fighting to the death.

"First of all, burn the supply wagons and provisions, and clearly inform the men that those who fight courageously will live, while cowards will die.[80] After they have broken out [and crossed the bridges], order the rear elements to set a great conflagration visible from far off.[81] [The troops sallying forth] must take advantage of the cover afforded by grass, trees, hillocks, and ravines. The enemy's chariots and cavalry will certainly not dare pursue them too far. Using the flames as a marker, the first to go out should be ordered to proceed as far as the flames and then stop, reforming a four-sided attack formation. In this fashion the Three Armies will be fervent and sharp and fight courageously, and no one will be able to withstand us."

King Wu said: "Excellent!"

35. Planning for the Army

King Wu asked the T'ai Kung: "Suppose we have led the army deep into the territory of the feudal lords where we encounter deep streams[82] or water in large valleys, ravines, and defiles. Our Three Armies have not yet fully forded them when Heaven lets loose a torrent, resulting in a sudden flood surge. The rear can not maintain contact with the advance portion. We don't have equipment such as pontoon bridges, nor materials such as heavy grass to stem the waters. I want to finish crossing, to keep the Three Armies from becoming bogged down. What should I do?"

The T'ai Kung said: "If the leader of the army and commander of the masses does not first establish his plans, the proper equipment will not be prepared. If his instructions are not precise and trusted, the officers and men will not be trained. Under such conditions they cannot comprise a king's army.

"In general, when the army is involved in a major campaign, everyone [should be] trained to use the equipment. For attacking a city wall or surrounding a town there are [armored] assault chariots, overlook carts, and battering rams, while for seeing inside the walls there are 'cloud ladders' and 'flying towers.' If the advance of the Three Armies is stopped, then there are the Martial Assault Great *Fu-hsü* Chariots. For defending both front and rear, for severing roads and blocking streets, there are the skilled soldiers and strong crossbowmen who protect the two flanks. If you are encamping or building fortifications, there are the Heaven's Net, the Martial Drop, the *chevaux-de-frise,* and the caltrops.

"In the daytime climb the cloud ladder and look off into the distance. Set up five-colored pennants and flags. At night set out ten thousand fire-cloud torches, beat the thunder drums, strike the war drums and bells, and blow the sharp-sounding whistles.

"For crossing over moats and ditches there are Flying Bridges with plantern-mounted winches and cogs. For crossing large bodies of water there are [boats called] Heaven's Huang and Flying River. For going against the waves and up current there are the Floating Ocean [rafts] and the [rope-pulled] River Severance. When the equipment to be used by the Three Armies is fully prepared, what worries will the commander-in-chief have?"

36. Approaching the Border

King Wu asked the T'ai Kung: "Both the enemy and our army have reached the border where we are in a standoff. They can approach, and we can also advance. Both deployments are solid and stable; neither side dares to move first. We want to go forth and attack them, but they can also come forward. What should we do?"

The T'ai Kung said: "Divide the army into three sections. Have our advance troops deepen the moats and increase the height of the ramparts, but none of the soldiers should go forth. Array the flags and pennants, beat the leather war drums, and complete all the defensive measures. Order our rear army to stockpile supplies and foodstuffs without causing the enemy to know our intentions. Then send forth our elite troops to secretly launch a sudden attack against their center, striking where they do not expect it, attacking where they are not prepared. Since the enemy does not know our real situation, they will stop and not advance."

King Wu asked: "Suppose the enemy knows our real situation and has fathomed our plans. If we move, they will be able to learn everything about us. Their elite troops are concealed in the deep grass. They press us on the narrow roads and are attacking where convenient for them. What should we do?"

The T'ai Kung said: "Every day have the vanguard go forth and instigate skirmishes with them in order to psychologically wear them out. Have our older and weaker soldiers drag brushwood to stir up the dust, beat the drums and shout, and move back and forth—some going to the left, some to the right, never getting closer than a hundred paces from the enemy. Their general will certainly become fatigued, and their troops will become fearful. In this situation the enemy will not dare come forward. Then our advancing troops will [unexpectedly] not stop, some [continuing forward] to attack their interior, others the exterior. With our Three Armies all fervently engaging in the battle, the enemy will certainly be defeated."

37. Movement and Rest

King Wu asked the T'ai Kung: "Suppose we have led our troops deep into the territory of the feudal lords and are confronting the enemy. The two deployments, looking across at each other, are equal in numbers and strength, and neither dares to move first. I want to cause the enemy's general to become terrified; their officers and men to become dispirited; their battle array to become unstable; their reserve army to want to run off; and those deployed forward to constantly look about at each other. I want to beat the drums, set up a clamor, and take advantage of it so that the enemy will then run off. How can we do it?"

The T'ai Kung said: "In this case send our troops out about ten *li* from the enemy and have them conceal themselves on both flanks. Send your chariots and cavalry out about one hundred *li* [and have them return unobserved] to assume positions cutting across both their front and rear.[83] Multiply the number of flags and pennants, and increase the number of gongs and drums. When the battle is joined, beat the drums, set up a clamor, and have your men all rise up together. The enemy's general will surely be afraid, and his army will be terrified. Large and small numbers will not come to each other's rescue; upper and lower ranks will not wait for each other; and the enemy will definitely be defeated."

King Wu asked: "Suppose because of the enemy's strategic configuration of power [*shih*] we cannot conceal troops on the flanks, and moreover our chariots and cavalry have no way to cross behind them and assume positions to both the front and rear. The enemy anticipates my thoughts and makes preemptive preparations. Our officers and soldiers are dejected, our generals are afraid. If we engage in battle we will not be victorious. What then?"

The T'ai Kung said: "Truly a serious question. In this case five days before engaging in battle, dispatch distant patrols to observe their activities and analyze their forward movement in order to prepare an ambush and await them. We must meet the enemy on deadly ground. Spread our flags and pennants out over a great distance, disperse our arrays and formations. We must race forward to meet the enemy. After the battle has been joined, suddenly retreat, beating the gongs incessantly.[84] Withdraw about three *li* [beyond the ambush], then turn about and attack. Your concealed troops should simultaneously arise. Some should penetrate the flanks, others attack their vanguard and rear guard positions. If the Three Armies fervently engage in battle, the enemy will certainly run off."

King Wu said: "Excellent."

38. Gongs and Drums[85]

King Wu asked the T'ai Kung: "Suppose we have led the army deep into the territory of the feudal lords where we are confronting the enemy. The weather has been either extremely hot or very cold, and it has been raining incessantly day and night for ten days. The ditches and ramparts are all col-

lapsing; defiles and barricades are unguarded; our patrols have become negligent; and the officers and men are not alert. Suppose the enemy comes at
night. Our Three Armies are unprepared, while the upper and lower ranks
are confused and disordered. What should we do?"

The T'ai Kung said: "In general, for the Three Armies, alertness makes for
solidity, laziness results in defeat. Order our guards on the ramparts to un-
ceasingly challenge everyone. Have all those bearing the signal flags, both inside and outside the encampment, watch each other, responding to each other's orders with countersigns, but do now allow them to make any noise. All
efforts should be externally oriented.

"Three thousand men should comprise a detachment.[86] Instruct and constrain them with an oath, requiring each of them to exercise vigilance at his
post. If the enemy approaches, when they see our state of readiness and alertness, they will certainly turn around. [As a result] their strength will become
exhausted and their spirits dejected. [At that moment] send forth our elite
troops to follow and attack them."

King Wu asked: "The enemy, knowing we are following him, conceals
elite troops in ambush while pretending to continue to retreat. When we
reach the ambush their troops turn back, some attacking our front, others
our rear, while some press our fortifications. Our Three Armies are terrified,
and in confusion fall out of formation and leave their assigned positions.
What should we do?"

The T'ai Kung said: "Divide into three forces, then follow and pursue
them, but do not cross beyond their ambush. When all three forces have arrived, some should attack the front and rear, others should penetrate the two
flanks. Make your commands clear, choose your orders carefully. Fervently
attack, advancing forward, and the enemy will certainly be defeated."

39. Severed Routes

King Wu asked the T'ai Kung: "Suppose we have led the army deep into the
territory of the feudal lords where, confronting them, we have each assumed
defensive positions. The enemy has severed our supply routes and occupied
positions cutting across both our front and rear. If I want to engage them in
battle, we cannot win; but if I want to maintain our position, we cannot hold
out for long. What should we do?"

The T'ai Kung said: "In general, when you venture deep beyond the enemy's borders you must investigate the configuration and strategic advantages of the terrain, and concentrate on seeking out and improving the advantages. Rely on mountains, forests, ravines, rivers, streams, woods, and
trees to create a secure defense. Carefully guard passes and bridges, and

moreover be certain you know the advantages of terrain conveyed by the various cities, towns, hills, and funeral mounds. In this way the army will be solidly entrenched. The enemy will not be able to sever our supply routes, nor be able to occupy positions cutting across our front and rear."

King Wu asked: "Suppose after our Three Armies have passed through a large forest or across a broad marsh and are on flat, accessible terrain, due to some erroneous or lost signal from our scouts, the enemy suddenly falls upon us. If we engage them in battle, we cannot win; if we assume a defensive position, it will not be secure. The enemy has outflanked us on both sides and occupied positions cutting across our front and rear. The Three Armies are terrified. What should be done?"

The T'ai Kung said: "Now the rule for commanding an army is always to first dispatch scouts far forward so that when you are two hundred *li* from the enemy, you will already know their location. If the strategic configuration of the terrain is not advantageous, then use the Martial Attack chariots to form a mobile rampart and advance. Also establish two rear guard armies to the rear—the further one hundred *li* away, the nearer fifty *li* away. Thus when there is a sudden alarm or an urgent situation, both front and rear will know about it, and the Three Armies will always be able to complete [their deployment into] a solid formation, never suffering any destruction or harm."

"Excellent," said King Wu.

40. Occupying Enemy Territory

King Wu asked the T'ai Kung: "Suppose, being victorious in battle, we have deeply penetrated the enemy's territory and occupy his land. However, large walled cities remain that cannot be subjugated, while their second army holds the defiles and ravines, standing off against us. We want to attack the cities and besiege the towns, but I am afraid that their second army will suddenly appear and strike us. If their forces inside and outside unite in this fashion, they will oppose us from both within and without. Our Three Armies will be in chaos; the upper and lower ranks will be terrified. What should be done?"

The T'ai Kung said: "In general, when attacking cities and besieging towns, the chariots and cavalry must be kept at a distance. The encamped and defensive units must be on constant alert in order to obstruct the enemy both within and without. When the inhabitants have their food cut off—those outside being unable to transport anything in to them—those within the city walls will be afraid, and their general will certainly surrender."

King Wu said: "Suppose that when the supplies inside the city are cut off—external forces being unable to transport anything in—they clandestinely make a covenant and take an oath, concoct secret plans, and then sally forth at night, throwing all their forces into a death struggle. Some of their chariots, cavalry, and elite troops assault us from within; others attack from without. The officers and troops are confused, the Three Armies defeated and in chaos. What should be done?"

The T'ai Kung said: "In this case you should divide your forces into three armies. Be careful to evaluate the terrain's configuration and then [strategically] emplace them. You must know in detail the location of the enemy's second army as well as his large cities and secondary fortifications. Leave them a passage in order to entice them to flee. Pay attention to all the preparations, not neglecting anything. The enemy will be afraid, and if they do not enter the mountains or the forests, they will return to the large towns or run off to join the second army. When their chariots and cavalry are far off, attack the front; do not allow them to escape. Since those [remaining] in the city will think that the first to go out have a direct escape route, their well-trained troops and skilled officers will certainly issue forth, with the old and weak alone remaining. When our chariots and cavalry have deeply penetrated their territory, racing far off, none of the enemy's army will dare approach. Be careful not to engage them in battle; just sever their supply routes, surround and guard them, and you will certainly outlast them.

"Do not set fire to what the people have accumulated; do not destroy their palaces or houses, nor cut down the trees at gravesites or altars. Do not kill those who surrender nor slay your captives. Instead show them benevolence and righteousness, extend your generous Virtue to them. Cause their people to say 'the guilt lies with one man.'[87] In this way the entire realm will then submit."

"Excellent," said King Wu.

41. Incendiary Warfare[88]

King Wu asked the T'ai Kung: "Suppose we have led our troops deep into the territory of the feudal lords where we encounter deep grass and heavy growth which surround our army on all sides. The Three Armies have traveled several hundred *li;* men and horses are exhausted and have halted to rest. Taking advantage of the extremely dry weather and a strong wind, the enemy ignites fires upwind from us. Their chariots, cavalry, and elite forces are firmly concealed in ambush to our rear. The Three Armies become terrified, scatter in confusion, and run off. What can be done?"

The T'ai Kung said: "Under such circumstances use the cloud ladders and flying towers to look far out to the left and right, to carefully investigate front and rear. When you see the fires arise, then set fires in front of our own forces, spreading them out over the area. Also set fires to the rear. If the enemy comes, withdraw the army and take up entrenched positions on the blackened earth to await their assault. In the same way, if you see flames arise to the rear, you must move far away. If we occupy the blackened ground with our strong crossbowmen and skilled soldiers protecting the left and right flanks, we can also set fires to the front and rear. In this way the enemy will not be able to harm us."

King Wu asked: "Suppose the enemy has set fires to the left and right and also to the front and rear. Smoke covers our army, while his main force appears from over the blackened ground. What should we do?"

The T'ai Kung said: "In this case [assuming you have prepared a burnt section of ground], disperse the Martial Attack chariots to form a fighting barrier on all four sides, and have strong crossbowmen cover the flanks. This method will not bring victory, but will also not end in defeat."

42. Empty Fortifications

King Wu asked the T'ai Kung: "How can I know whether the enemy's fortifications are empty[89] or full, whether they are coming or going?"

The T'ai Kung said: "A general must know the Tao of Heaven above, the advantages[90] of Earth below, and human affairs in the middle. You should mount high and look out far in order to see the enemy's changes and movements. Observe his fortifications, and then you will know whether they are empty or full. Observe his officers and troops, and then you will know whether they are coming or going."

King Wu asked: "How will I know it?"

The T'ai Kung said: "Listen to see if his drums are silent, if his bells make no sound. Look to see whether there are many birds flying above the fortifications, if they were not startled [into flight]. If there are no vapors overhead, you will certainly know the enemy has tricked you with dummies.

"If enemy forces precipitously go off—but not very far—and then return before assuming proper formation, they are using their officers and men too quickly. When they act too quickly, the forward and rear are unable to maintain good order. When they cannot maintain good order, the entire battle disposition will be in chaos. In such circumstances quickly dispatch troops to attack them. If you use a small number to strike a large force, they will certainly be defeated."

豹韜

V

LEOPARD SECRET TEACHING

43. Forest Warfare

King Wu asked the T'ai Kung: "Suppose we have led our troops deep into the territory of the feudal lords where we encounter a large forest which we share with the enemy in a standoff. If we assume a defensive posture, I want it to be solid, or if we fight, to be victorious. How should we proceed?"

The T'ai Kung said: "Have our Three Armies divide into the assault formation. Improve the positions the troops will occupy, and station the archers and crossbowmen outside, with those carrying spear-tipped halberds and shields inside. Cut down and clear away the grass and trees, and extensively broaden the passages in order to facilitate our deployment onto the battle site. Set our pennants and flags out on high, and carefully encourage the Three Armies without letting the enemy know our true situation. This is referred to as 'Forest Warfare'.

"The method of Forest Warfare is to form the spear bearers and halberdiers into squads of five. If the woods are not dense, cavalry can be used in support. Battle chariots will occupy the front. When opportune, they will fight; when not opportune, they will desist. Where there are numerous ravines and defiles in the forest, you must deploy [your forces] in the Assault Formation in order to be prepared both front and rear. If the Three Armies urgently attack, even though the enemy is numerous, they can be driven off. The men should fight and rest in turn, each with their section. This is the main outline of Forest Warfare."

44. Explosive Warfare

King Wu asked the T'ai Kung: "Suppose the enemy's [advance forces] have penetrated deep into our territory and are ranging widely, occupying our land, and driving off our cattle and horses. Then their Three Armies arrive en masse and press us outside our city walls. Our officers and troops are sorely afraid; our people are in bonds, having been captured by the enemy. If we assume a defensive posture, I want it to be solid, or if we fight, to be victorious. What should we do?"

The T'ai Kung said: "[An enemy] in situations such as this is referred to as an 'Explosive Force.' Their oxen and horses will certainly not have been fed; their officers and troops will have broken their supply routes, having explosively attacked and advanced. Order our distant towns and other armies to select their elite soldiers and urgently strike their rear. Carefully consult the calendar, for we must unite on a moonless night. The Three Armies should fight intensely, for then even though the enemy is numerous, their general can be captured."

King Wu said: "Suppose the enemy divides his forces into three or four detachments—some fighting with us and occupying our territory, others stopping to round up our oxen and horses. Their main army has not yet completely arrived, but they have had their swift invaders press us below the city walls. Therefore our Three Armies are sorely afraid. What should we do?"

The T'ai Kung said: "Carefully observe the enemy. Before they have all arrived, make preparations and await them. Go out about four *li* from the walls and establish fortifications, setting out in good order our gongs and drums, flags and pennants. Our other troops will comprise an ambushing force. Order large numbers of strong crossbowmen to the top of the fortifications. Every hundred paces set up an 'explosive gate,' outside of which we should place the *chevaux-de-frise*. Our chariots and cavalry should be held outside, while our courageous, strong, fierce fighters should be secreted in this outer area. If the enemy should reach us, have our light armored foot soldiers engage them in battle, then feign a retreat. Have the forces on top of the city wall set out the flags and pennants and strike the war drums, completing all preparations to defend the city. The enemy will assume we are going to defend the wall and will certainly press an attack below it. Then release the forces lying in ambush—some to assault their interior, others to strike the exterior. Then the Three Armies should urgently press the attack—some striking the front lines, others the rear. Even their courageous soldiers will not be able to fight, while the swiftest will not have time to flee. This is termed 'Explosive Warfare.' Although the enemy is numerically superior, they will certainly run off."

"Excellent," said King Wu.

45. Strong Enemy

King Wu asked the T'ai Kung: "Suppose we have led the army deep into the territory of the feudal lords until we are opposed by the enemy's assault forces. The enemy is numerous, while we are few. The enemy is strong, while we are weak. The enemy approaches at night—some attacking the left, others the right. The Three Armies are quaking. We want to be victorious if we choose to fight and solid if we choose to maintain a defensive posture. How should we act?"

The T'ai Kung said: "In this case we refer to them as 'Shaking Invaders.' It is more advantageous to go out and fight; you cannot be defensive. Select skilled soldiers and strong crossbowmen, together with chariots and cavalry, to comprise the right and left flanks. Then urgently strike his forward forces, quickly attacking the rear as well. Some should strike the exterior, others the interior. Their troops will certainly be confused, their generals afraid."

King Wu asked: "Suppose the enemy has blocked off our forward units some distance away and is pressing a fervent attack on our rear. He has broken up our elite troops and cut off our skilled soldiers. Our interior and exterior forces cannot communicate with each other. The Three Armies are in chaos, all running off in defeat. The officers and troops have no will to fight, the generals and commanders no desire to defend themselves. What should we do?"

The T'ai Kung said: "Illustrious is your question, my king! You should make your commands clear and be careful about your orders. You should have your courageous, crack troops who are willing to confront danger sally forth—each man carrying a torch, two men to a drum. You must know the enemy's location then strike both the interior and exterior. When our secret signals have all been communicated, order them to extinguish the torches and stop beating all the drums. The interior and exterior should respond to each other, each according to the appropriate time. When our Three Armies urgently attack, the enemy will certainly be defeated and vanquished."

"Excellent," said King Wu.

46. Martial Enemy

King Wu asked the T'ai Kung: "Suppose we have led the army deep into the territory of the feudal lords where we suddenly encounter a martial, numerically superior enemy. If his martial chariots and valiant cavalry attack our left and right flanks, and our Three Armies become so shaken that their flight is unstoppable, what should I do?"

The T'ai Kung said: "In this situation you have what is termed a defeated army. Those who are skillful in employing their forces will manage a victory. Those who are not will perish."

King Wu asked: "What does one do?"

The T'ai Kung replied: "Have our most skilled soldiers and strong crossbowmen, together with our martial chariots and valiant cavalry, conceal themselves on both sides of the retreat route, about three *li* ahead and behind our main force. When the enemy pursues us, launch a simultaneous chariot and cavalry assault from both sides. In such circumstances the enemy will be thrown into confusion, and our fleeing soldiers will stop by themselves."

King Wu continued: "Suppose the enemy's chariots and cavalry are squarely opposite ours, but the enemy is numerous while we are few, the enemy strong while we are weak. Their approach is disciplined and spirited, and our formations are unable to withstand them. What should we do?"

The T'ai Kung replied: "Select our skilled soldiers and strong crossbowmen, and have them lie in ambush on both sides, while the chariots and cavalry deploy into a solid formation and assume position. When the enemy passes our concealed forces, the crossbowmen should fire en masse into their flanks. The chariots, cavalry, and skilled soldiers should then urgently attack their army—some striking the front, others striking the rear. Even if the enemy is numerous they will certainly flee."

"Excellent," said King Wu.

47. Crow and Cloud Formation in the Mountains

King Wu asked the T'ai Kung: "Suppose we have led the army deep into the territory of the feudal lords where we encounter high mountains with large, flat rock outcroppings on top of which are numerous peaks, all devoid of grass and trees. We are surrounded on all four sides by the enemy. Our Three Armies are afraid, the officers and troops confused. I want to be solid if we choose to defend our position and victorious if we fight. What should we do?"

The T'ai Kung said: "Whenever the Three Armies occupy the heights of a mountain, they are trapped on high by the enemy. When they hold the land below the mountain, they are imprisoned by the forces above them. If you have already occupied the top of the mountain, you must prepare the Crow and Cloud Formation.[91] The Crow and Cloud Formation should be prepared on both the yin and yang sides of the mountain. Some will encamp on the yin side, others will encamp on the yang side. Those that occupy the yang side must prepare against [attacks from the] yin side. Those occupying the yin side must prepare against [attacks from the] yang side. Those occupying the left side of the mountain must prepare against the right side. Those on the right, against the left. Wherever the enemy can ascend [the mountain], your troops should establish external lines. If there are roads passing through the valley, sever them with your war chariots. Set your flags and pennants up high. Be cautious in commanding the Three Armies; do not allow the enemy to know your true situation. This is referred to as a 'mountain wall.'

"After your lines have been set, your officers and troops deployed, rules and orders already issued, and tactics—both orthodox and unorthodox—already planned, deploy your assault formation at the outer perimeter of the mountain, and have them improve the positions they occupy. Thereafter, divide your chariots and cavalry into the Crow and Cloud Formation. When your Three Armies urgently attack the enemy, even though the latter are numerous, their general can be captured."

48. Crow and Cloud Formation in the Marshes

King Wu asked the T'ai Kung: "Suppose we have led the army deep into the territory of the feudal lords where we are confronting the enemy across a river. The enemy is well equipped and numerous; we are impoverished and few. If we cross the water to attack, we will not be able to advance; while if we want to outlast them, our supplies are too few. We are encamped on salty ground. There are no towns in any direction and moreover no grass or trees. There is nothing the Three Armies can plunder, while the oxen and horses have neither fodder nor a place to graze. What should we do?"

The T'ai Kung said: "The Three Armies are unprepared; the oxen and horses have nothing to eat; the officers and troops have no supplies. In this situation seek some opportunity to trick the enemy and quickly get away, setting up ambushes to your rear."

King Wu said: "The enemy cannot be deceived. My officers and troops are confused. The enemy has occupied positions cutting across both our front and rear. Our Three Armies are defeated and in flight. What then?"

The T'ai Kung said: "When you are searching for an escape route, gold and jade are essential. You must obtain intelligence from the enemy's emissaries. In this case cleverness and secrecy are your treasures."

King Wu said: "Suppose the enemy knows I have laid ambushes, so their main army is unwilling to cross the river. The general of their second army then breaks off some units and dispatches them to ford the river. My Three Armies are sorely afraid. What should I do?"

The T'ai Kung said: "In this situation divide your troops into assault formations, and have them improve their positions. Wait until all the enemy's troops have emerged, then spring your concealed troops, rapidly striking their rear. Have your strong crossbowmen on both sides shoot into their left and right flanks. Divide your chariots and cavalry into the Crow and Cloud Formation, arraying them against their front and rear. Then your Three Armies should vehemently press the attack. When the enemy sees us engaged in battle, their main force will certainly ford the river and advance. Then spring the ambushing forces, urgently striking their rear. The chariots and cavalry should assault the left and right. Even though the enemy is numerous, they can be driven off.

"In general, the most important thing in employing your troops is that when the enemy approaches to engage in battle, you must deploy your assault formations and have them improve their positions. Thereafter, divide your chariots and cavalry into the Crow and Cloud Formation. This is the unorthodox in employing your troops. What is referred to as the Crow and Cloud Formation is like the crows dispersing and the clouds forming together. Their changes and transformations are endless."[92]

"Excellent," said King Wu.

49. The Few and the Many

King Wu asked the T'ai Kung: "If I want to attack a large number with only a few, attack the strong with the weak, what should I do?"

The T'ai Kung said: "If you want to attack a large number with only a few, you must do it at sunset, setting an ambush in tall grass, pressing them on a narrow road. To attack the strong with the weak, you must obtain the support of a great state and the assistance of neighboring states."

King Wu asked: "We do not have any terrain with tall grass, and moreover there are no narrow roads. The enemy has already arrived; we cannot wait until sunset. I do not have the support of any great state nor furthermore the assistance of neighboring states. What then?"

The T'ai Kung said: "You should set out specious arrays and false enticements to dazzle and confuse their general, to redirect his path so that he will be forced to pass tall grass. Make his route long so you can arrange your engagement for sunset. When his advance units have not yet finished crossing the water, his rear units have not yet reached the encampment, spring our concealed troops, vehemently striking his right and left flanks, while your chariots and cavalry stir chaos among his forward and rear units. Even if the enemy is numerous, they will certainly flee.

"To serve the ruler of a great state, to gain the submission of the officers of neighboring states, make their gifts generous and speak extremely deferentially. In this fashion you will obtain the support of a great state and the assistance of neighboring states."

"Excellent," said King Wu.

50. Divided Valleys

King Wu asked the T'ai Kung: "Suppose we have led the army deep into the territory of the feudal lords where we encounter the enemy in the midst of a steep valley. I have mountains on our left, water on the right. The enemy has mountains on the right, water on the left.[93] They divide the valley with us in a standoff. If we choose to defend our position, I want to be solid, and victorious if we want to fight. How should we proceed?"

The T'ai Kung said: "If you occupy the left side of a mountain, you must urgently prepare [against an attack from the] right side. If you occupy the right side of a mountain, then you should urgently prepare [against an attack from the] left. If the valley has a large river but you do not have boats and oars, you should use the Heaven's Huang[94] to cross the Three Armies over. Those that have crossed should widen the road considerably in order to improve your fighting position. Use the Martial Assault chariots at the front and rear; deploy your strong crossbowmen into ranks; and solidify all your lines and formations. Employ the Martial Assault chariots to block off all the intersecting roads and entrances to the valley. Set your flags out on high ground. This posture is referred to as an 'Army Citadel.'

"In general, the method for valley warfare is for the Martial Assault chariots to be in the forefront and the Large Covered chariots to act as a protective force. Your skilled soldiers and strong crossbowmen should cover the left and right flanks. Three thousand men will comprise one detachment, which must be deployed in the assault formation. Improve the positions the soldiers occupy. Then the Army of the Left should advance to the left, the Army of the Right to the right, and the Army of the Center to the front—all attacking and advancing together. Those that have already fought should return to their detachment's original positions, the units fighting and resting in succession until you have won."

"Excellent," said King Wu.

VI

CANINE SECRET TEACHING

51. Dispersing and Assembling

King Wu asked the T'ai Kung: "If the king, leading the army, has dispersed the Three Armies to several locations and wants to have them reassemble at a specific time for battle, how should he constrain them with oaths, rewards, and punishments so that he can achieve it?"

The T'ai Kung said: "In general, the Way to employ the military, the masses of the Three Armies, must be to have the changes of dividing and reuniting.[95] The commanding general should first set the place and day for battle, then issue full directives and particulars to the generals and commanders setting the time, indicating whether to attack cities or besiege towns, and where each should assemble. [He should] clearly instruct them about the day for battle and even the quarter hour by the water clock. The commanding general should then establish his encampment, array his battle lines, put up a gnomon and the official gate, clear the road, and wait. When all the generals and commanders have arrived, compare their arrival [with the designated time]. Those who arrived before the appointed time should be rewarded. Those who arrived afterward should be executed. In this way both the near and distant will race to assemble, and the Three Armies will arrive together, uniting their strength to engage in the battle."

52. Military Vanguard

King Wu asked the T'ai Kung: "In general, when employing the army it is essential to have military chariots, courageous cavalry, a first-assault wave, a hand-picked vanguard, and then a perceived opportunity to strike the enemy. In which situations can we strike?"

The T'ai Kung said: "Anyone who wants to launch a strike should carefully scrutinize and investigate fourteen changes in the enemy. When [any of] these changes becomes visible, attack, for the enemy will certainly be defeated."

King Wu asked: "May I hear about these fourteen changes?"

The T'ai Kung said: "When the enemy has begun to assemble they can be attacked.

"When the men and horses have not yet been fed they can be attacked.

"When the seasonal or weather conditions are not advantageous to them they can be attacked.

"When they have not secured good terrain they can be attacked.

"When they are fleeing they can be attacked.

"When they are not vigilant they can be attacked.

"When they are tired and exhausted they can be attacked.

"When the general is absent from the officers and troops they can be attacked.

"When they are traversing long roads they can be attacked.

"When they are fording rivers they can be attacked.

"When the troops have not had any leisure time they can be attacked.

"When they encounter the difficulty of precipitous ravines or are on narrow roads they can be attacked.

"When their battle array is in disorder they can be attacked.

"When they are afraid they can be attacked."

53. Selecting Warriors

King Wu asked the T'ai Kung: "What is the Way to select warriors?"

The T'ai Kung replied: "Within the army there will be men with great courage and strength who are willing to die and even take pleasure in suffering wounds. They should be assembled into a company and called 'Warriors Who Risk the Naked Blade.'

"Those who have fierce *ch'i,* who are robust and courageous, strong and explosive, should be assembled into a company and called 'Warriors Who Penetrate the Lines.'

"Those who are extraordinary in appearance, who bear long swords and advance with measured tread in good order should be assembled into a company and called 'Courageous, Elite Warriors.'

"Those who can jump well, straighten iron hooks, are powerful, have great strength, and can scatter and smash the gongs and drums [and] destroy the flags and pennants should be assembled into a company and called 'Warriors of Courage and Strength.'

"Those who can scale heights and cover great distances, who are light of foot and excel at running should be assembled into a company and called 'Warriors of the Invading Army.'

"Those who, while serving the ruler, lost their authority and want to again display their merit should be assembled into a company and called 'Warriors Who Fight to the Death.'

"Those who are relatives of slain generals, the sons or brothers of generals, who want to avenge their deaths, should be assembled into a company and called 'Warriors Who Are Angry unto Death.'

"Those who are lowly, poor, and angry, who want to satisfy their desires, should be assembled into a company and called 'Warriors Committed to Death.'

"Adopted sons[96] and slaves, who want to cover up their pasts and achieve fame, should be assembled into a company and called the 'Incited Dispirited.'

"Those who have been imprisoned and then spared corporeal punishment, who want to escape from their shame, should be assembled into a company and called 'Warriors Fortunate to Be Used.'

"Those who combine skill and technique, who can bear heavy burdens for long distances, should be assembled into a company and called 'Warriors Awaiting Orders.'

"These are the army's selected warriors. You cannot neglect their examination."

54. Teaching Combat[97]

King Wu asked the T'ai Kung: "When we assemble the masses of the Three Armies and want to have the officers and men assimilate and become practiced[98] in the Way for teaching combat, how should we proceed?"

The T'ai Kung said: "For leading the Three Armies you must have the constraints of the gongs and drums by which to order and assemble the officers and masses. The generals should clearly instruct the commanders and officers, explaining the orders three times—thereby teaching them the use of weapons, mobilization, and stopping, all to be in accord with the method for changing the flags and signal pennants.

"Thus when teaching the commanders and officers, one man who has completed his study of combat instructions will extend[99] them to ten men. Ten men who have completed their study of combat instructions will extend them to one hundred men. One hundred men who have completed their study of combat instructions will extend them to one thousand men. One thousand men who have completed their study of combat instructions will extend them to ten thousand men. Ten thousand men who have completed their study of combat instructions will extend them to the masses of the Three Armies.

"When the methods of large-scale warfare are successfully taught, they will be extended to the masses of millions. In this fashion you will be able to realize a Great Army and establish your awesomeness throughout the realm."

"Excellent," said King Wu.

55. Equivalent Forces

King Wu asked the T'ai Kung: "When chariots and infantry engage in battle, one chariot is equivalent to how many infantrymen? How many infantrymen are equivalent to one chariot? When cavalry and infantry engage in battle, one cavalryman is equivalent to how many infantrymen? How many infantrymen are equivalent to one cavalryman? When chariots and cavalry engage in battle, one chariot is equivalent to how many cavalrymen? How many cavalrymen are equivalent to one chariot?"[100]

The T'ai Kung said: "Chariots are the feathers and wings of the army, the means to penetrate solid formations, to press strong enemies, and to cut off their flight. Cavalry are the army's fleet observers, the means to pursue a defeated army, to sever supply lines, to strike roving forces.

"Thus when chariots and cavalry are not engaged in battle with the enemy, one cavalryman is not able to equal one foot soldier. However, after the masses of the Three Armies have been arrayed in opposition to the enemy, when fighting on easy terrain the rule is that one chariot is equivalent to eighty infantrymen, and eighty infantrymen are equivalent to one chariot. One cavalryman is equivalent to eight infantrymen; eight infantrymen are equivalent to one cavalryman. One chariot is equivalent to ten cavalrymen; ten cavalrymen are equivalent to one chariot.

"The rule for fighting on difficult terrain is that one chariot is equivalent to forty infantrymen, and forty infantrymen are equivalent to one chariot. One cavalryman is equivalent to four infantrymen; four infantrymen are equivalent to one cavalryman. One chariot is equivalent to six cavalrymen; six cavalrymen are equivalent to one chariot.

"Now chariots and cavalry are the army's martial weapons. Ten chariots can defeat one thousand men; one hundred chariots can defeat ten thousand men. Ten cavalrymen can drive off one hundred men, and one hundred cavalrymen can run off one thousand men. These are the approximate numbers."

King Wu asked: "What are the numbers for chariot and cavalry officers and their formations?"

The T'ai Kung said: "For the chariots—a leader for five chariots, a captain for fifteen, a commander for fifty, and a general for one hundred.

"For battle on easy terrain five chariots comprise one line. The lines are forty paces apart, the chariots from left to right ten paces apart, with detachments sixty paces apart. On difficult terrain the chariots must follow the roads, with ten comprising a company and twenty a regiment.[101] Front to rear spacing should be twenty paces, left to right six paces, with detachments thirty-six paces apart. For five chariots there is one leader. If they venture off the road more than a *li* in any direction, they should return to the original road.

"As for the number of officers in the cavalry: a leader for five men; a captain for ten; a commander for one hundred; a general for two hundred.

"The rule for fighting on easy terrain: Five cavalrymen will form one line, and front to back their lines should be separated by twenty paces, left to right four paces, with fifty paces between detachments.

"On difficult terrain the rule is front to back, ten paces; left to right, two paces; between detachments, twenty-five paces. Thirty cavalrymen comprise a company; sixty form a regiment. For ten cavalrymen there is a captain. [In action] they should not range more than one hundred paces, after which they should circle back and return to their original positions."

"Excellent," said King Wu.

56. Martial Chariot Warriors

King Wu asked the T'ai Kung: "How does one select warriors for the chariots?"

The T'ai Kung said: "The rule for selecting warriors for the chariots is to pick men under forty years of age, seven feet five inches[102] or taller, whose running ability is such that they can pursue a galloping horse, race up to it, mount it, and ride it forward and back, left and right, up and down, all around. They should be able to quickly furl up the flags and pennants and have the strength to fully draw an eight-picul crossbow. They should practice shooting front and back, left and right, until thoroughly skilled. They are termed 'Martial Chariot Warriors.' You cannot but be generous to them."

57. Martial Cavalry Warriors

King Wu asked the T'ai Kung: "How do you select warriors for the cavalry?"

The T'ai Kung said: "The rule for selecting cavalry warriors is to take those under forty, who are at least seven feet five inches tall, strong and quick, who surpass the average. Men who, while racing a horse, can fully draw a bow and shoot. Men who can gallop forward and back, left and right, and all around, both advancing and withdrawing. Men who can jump over moats and ditches, ascend hills and mounds, gallop through narrow confines, cross large marshes, and race into a strong enemy, causing chaos among their masses. They are called 'Martial Cavalry Warriors.' You cannot but be generous to them."

58. Battle Chariots

King Wu asked the T'ai Kung: "What about battle chariots?"

The T'ai Kung responded: "The infantry values knowing changes and movement; the chariots value knowing the terrain's configuration; the cavalry values knowing the side roads and the unorthodox [ch'i] Way. Thus these three armies bear the same name, but their employment differs.

"In general, in chariot battles there are ten types of terrain on which death is likely and eight on which victory can be achieved."

King Wu asked: "What are the ten fatal terrains[103] like?"

The T'ai Kung replied: "If after advancing there is no way to withdraw, this is fatal terrain for chariots.

"Passing beyond narrow defiles to pursue the enemy some distance, this is terrain which will exhaust the chariots.

"When the land in front makes advancing easy, while that to the rear is treacherous, this is terrain that will cause hardship for the chariots.

"Penetrating into narrow and obstructed areas from which escape will be difficult, this is terrain on which the chariots may be cut off.

"If the land is collapsing, sinking, and marshy, with black mud sticking to everything, this is terrain which will labor the chariots.

"To the left is precipitous while to the right is easy, with high mounds and sharp hills. This is terrain contrary to [the use of] chariots.

"Luxuriant grass runs through the fields, and there are deep, watery channels throughout. This is terrain which thwarts [the use] of chariots.

"When the chariots are few in number, the land easy, and one is not confronted by enemy infantry, this is terrain on which the chariots may be defeated.

"To the rear are water-filled ravines and ditches, to the left deep water, and to the right steep hills. This is terrain on which chariots are destroyed.

"It has been raining day and night for more than ten days without stopping. The roads have collapsed so that it's not possible to advance or to escape to the rear. This is terrain which will sink the chariots.

"These ten are deadly terrain for chariots. Thus they are the means by which the stupid general will be captured and the wise general will be able to escape."

King Wu asked: "What about the eight conditions of terrain[104] that result in victory?"

The T'ai Kung replied: "When the enemy's ranks—front and rear—are not yet settled, strike into them.

"When their flags and pennants are in chaos, their men and horses frequently shifting about, then strike into them.

"When some of their officers and troops advance while others retreat; when some move to the left, others to the right, then strike into them.

"When their battle array is not yet solid, while their officers and troops are looking around at each other, then strike into them.

"When in advancing they appear full of doubt, and in withdrawing they are fearful, strike into them.

"When the enemy's Three Armies are suddenly frightened, all of them rising up in great confusion, strike into them.

"When you are fighting on easy terrain and twilight has come without being able to disengage from the battle, then strike into them.

"When, after traveling far, at dusk they are encamping and their Three Armies are terrified, strike into them.

"These eight constitute conditions[105] in which the chariots will be victorious.

"If the general is clear about these ten injurious conditions and eight victorious possibilities, then even if the enemy surrounds him on all sides—attacking with one thousand chariots and ten thousand cavalry—he will be able to gallop to the front and race to the sides and in ten thousand battles invariably be victorious."

"Excellent," said King Wu.

59. Cavalry in Battle

King Wu asked the T'ai Kung: "How should we employ the cavalry in battle?"

The T'ai Kung said: "For the cavalry there are ten [situations that can produce] victory and nine [that will result in] defeat."

King Wu asked: "What are the ten [situations that can produce] victory?"

The T'ai Kung replied: "When the enemy first arrives and their lines and deployment are not yet settled, the front and rear not yet united, then strike into their forward cavalry, attack the left and right flanks. The enemy will certainly flee.

"When the enemy's lines and deployment are well-ordered and solid, while their officers and troops want to fight, our cavalry should outflank them but not go far off. Some should race away, some race forward. Their speed should be like the wind, their explosiveness like thunder, so that the daylight becomes as murky as dusk. Change our flags and pennants several times; also change our uniforms. Then their army can be conquered.

"When the enemy's lines and deployment are not solid, while their officers and troops will not fight, press upon them both front and rear, make sudden thrusts on their left and right. Outflank and strike them, and the enemy will certainly be afraid.

"When, at sunset, the enemy wants to return to camp[106] and their Three Armies are terrified, if we can outflank them on both sides, urgently strike their rear, pressing the entrance to their fortifications, not allowing them to go in. The enemy will certainly be defeated.

"When the enemy, although lacking the advantages of ravines and defiles for securing their defenses, has penetrated deeply and ranged widely into distant territory, if we sever their supply lines they will certainly be hungry.

"When the land is level and easy and we see enemy cavalry approaching from all four sides, if we have our chariots and cavalry strike into them, they will certainly become disordered.

"When the enemy runs off in flight, their officers and troops scattered and in chaos, if some of our cavalry outflank them on both sides while others obstruct them to the front and rear, their general can be captured.

"When at dusk the enemy is turning back while his soldiers are extremely numerous, his lines and deployment will certainly become disordered. We should have our cavalry form platoons of ten and regiments of one hundred, group the chariots into squads of five and companies of ten, and set out a great many flags and pennants intermixed with strong crossbowmen. Some should strike their two flanks, others cut off the front and rear, and then the enemy's general can be taken prisoner. These are the ten [situations in which] the cavalry can be victorious."[107]

King Wu asked: "What about the nine [situations which produce] defeat?"

The T'ai Kung said: "Whenever the cavalry penetrates the ranks of the enemy but does not destroy their formation so that the enemy feigns flight, only to turn their chariots and cavalry about to strike our rear—this is a situation[108] in which the cavalry will be defeated.

"When we pursue a fleeing enemy into confined ground, ranging far into their territory without stopping, until they ambush both our flanks and sever our rear—this is a situation in which the cavalry will be encircled.

"When we go forward but there is no road back, we enter but there is no way out, this is referred to as 'penetrating a Heavenly Well,'[109] 'being buried in an Earthly Cave.' This is fatal terrain for the cavalry.

"When the way by which we enter is constricted but the way out is distant; their weak forces can attack our strong ones; and their few can attack our many—this is terrain on which the cavalry will be exterminated.

"When there are great mountain torrents, deep valleys, tall luxuriant grass, forests and trees—these are conditions which will exhaust the cavalry.

"When there is water on the left and right, while ahead are large hills, and to the rear high mountains, and the Three Armies are fighting between the bodies of water while the enemy occupies both the interior and exterior ground—this is terrain that means great difficulty for the cavalry.

"When the enemy has cut off our supply lines, and if we advance we will not have any route by which to return—this is troublesome terrain for the cavalry.

"When we are sinking into marshy ground while advancing and retreating must both be through quagmires—this is worrisome terrain for the cavalry.

"When on the left there are deep water sluices, and on the right there are gullies and hillocks but below the heights the ground appears level—good terrain for advancing, retreating, and enticing an enemy—this terrain is a pitfall for the cavalry.

"These nine comprise fatal terrain for cavalry, the means by which the enlightened general will keep [the enemy] far off and escape and the ignorant general will be entrapped and defeated."

60. The Infantry in Battle

King Wu asked the T'ai Kung: "What about when infantry engage in battle with chariots and cavalry?"

The T'ai Kung said: "When infantry engage in battle with chariots and cavalry, they must rely on hills and mounds, ravines and defiles. The long weapons and strong crossbows should occupy the fore; the short weapons and weak crossbows should occupy the rear, firing and resting in turn. Even if large numbers of the enemy's chariots and cavalry should arrive, they must maintain a solid formation and fight intensely while skilled soldiers and strong crossbowmen prepare against [attacks from] the rear."

King Wu said: "Suppose there are no hills or mounds, ravines or defiles. The enemy arrives, and it is both numerous and martial. Their chariots and cavalry outflank us on both sides, and they are making sudden thrusts against our front and rear positions. Our Three Armies are terrified and fleeing in chaotic defeat. What should we do?"

The T'ai Kung said: "Order our officers and troops to set up the *chevaux-de-frise* and wooden caltrops, arraying the oxen and horses by units of five in their midst, and have them establish a four-sided martial assault formation. When you see the enemy's chariots and cavalry are about to advance, our men should evenly spread out the caltrops and dig ditches around the rear, making them five feet deep and wide. It is called the 'Fate of Dragon Grass.'

"Our men should take hold of the *chevaux-de-frise* and advance on foot. The chariots should be arrayed as ramparts and pushed forward and back. Whenever they stop set them up as fortifications. Our skilled soldiers and strong crossbowmen should prepare against the left and right flanks. Afterward, order our Three Armies to fervently fight without respite."

"Excellent," said King Wu.

2

The Methods of the Ssu-ma

Translator's Introduction

THE *Ssu-ma Fa* is a terse, enigmatic text dating from about the fourth century B.C. when it was probably compiled from materials dating back far into antiquity.[1] Virtually every account of its inception identifies it with the state of Ch'i, which historically was the fount of the famous military studies that received their initial impetus from the T'ai Kung, who had been enfeoffed as the first king of Ch'i a few years before his death. Traditionalists thus assert that the T'ai Kung's thoughts may form part of the early material or may have otherwise provided a foundation for the work.[2] Throughout the Spring and Autumn and the Warring States periods, military studies flourished in Ch'i as represented by Sun-tzu, Sun Pin, and Wei Liao-tzu; certain families (such as Sun, T'ien, and Ch'en) were particularly noteworthy. The renowned strategist Sun Pin may have been active at the time of the *Ssu-ma Fa's* compilation and may possibly have even been a contributor; in fact, he was a distant relative of Ssu-ma Jang-chü.[3] Furthermore, the style and character of the writing reportedly identify it as a product of this era, the fourth century B.C. Apart from the two books by Sun-Tzu and Sun Pin, it has traditionally been accorded far more authenticity than any of the other military writings.

The title, *Ssu-ma Fa,* might best be translated as *The Methods of the Minister of War* because the character *fa*—whose basic meaning is law—encompasses the concepts of "methods," standards, and techniques or art, as in Sun-tzu's *Art of War.* However, no single term adequately covers the scope of the content because the *Ssu-ma Fa* discusses laws, regulations, government policies, military organization, military administration, discipline, basic values, grand strategy, and strategy.

The origin of the military title *Ssu-ma*—which literally means "the officer in charge of horses" and which, because of the horse's vital importance to the military, eventually came to designate military matters in general—remains lost in antiquity. As an official title it apparently first appeared in the earliest dynasties of the Sage Emperors, and by the Chou dynasty it had been elevated to *Ta Ssu-ma*—"Great" *Ssu-ma,* or Minister of War. Liu Yin's introduction to the *Ssu-ma Fa* provides a general appraisal of the minister's role and duties under the Chou dynasty:

> The Minister of War controlled the government of the dependent states, administered the Six Armies, and pacified the peripheral territories. Thus he ranked among the six chief ministers of state. When in court he assisted the Son of Heaven in administering the government; when he went out he was the chief general of the army of rectification, settling the rebellious.[4]

According to the traditional view espoused by scholars such as Liu Yin, the central content of the *Methods* played a historically important role; it was supposedly instrumental in providing guidance to Duke Huan of Ch'i (reigned mid-seventh century B.C.) in his successful quest to become hegemon (*pa*)—the military ruler of the realm—on the pretext of assisting the rightful king of the declining Chou state. It is therefore equally associated with Duke Huan's famous adviser, Kuan Chung, to whom a complex, composite work on government, philosophy, and military matters—the *Kuan-tzu*—is attributed.[5] Subsequently, King Ching of the same state of Ch'i (who ruled from 547 to 490 B.C.) reportedly used the teachings to help him regain land previously lost to Ch'in and subjugate several feudal lords. At that time the work was untitled, but when a court assembly was convened under King Wei[6] (reigned 378 to 342 B.C.) to gather and record all vital information on military matters, it came to be identified as *The Methods of the Minister of War.*

Another, somewhat disputed story associated with the book suggests that the famous general T'ien Jang-chü was instrumental in the great victories achieved under King Ching. Because he had held the post of *Ssu-ma* in the king's campaign, he was granted the privilege of assuming the title as a family surname. The book, when subsequently compiled under King Wei, included his ideas and thus acquired the title *Ssu-ma Jang-chü Ping-fa* (*The Military Methods of Ssu-ma Jang-chü*). His brief biography in the *Shih chi*[7] not only records these events but also illustrates the measures he felt were necessary to wrest immediate psychological control of the troops and create the awesomeness that would command obedience:

> Ssu-ma Jang-chü was a descendant of T'ien Wan.[8] During the time of Duke Ching[9] of Ch'i, Chin attacked [the major cities of] A and P'in,[10] and Yen invaded [the river district] Ho-shang.[11] Ch'i's army suffered complete defeat, and Duke Ching was sorely troubled. Yen Ying then recommended Jang-chü, saying: "Even though Jang-chü is descended from T'ien's concubine, still, as a man, in civil affairs he is able to the masses, and in martial affairs he is able to overawe the enemy. I would like my Lord to test him." Duke Ching summoned Jang-chü and spoke with him about military affairs. He was greatly pleased with him and

appointed him as General of the Army to lead the soldiers in resisting the armies of Yen and Chin.

Jang-Chü said: "I was formerly lowly and menial. If my Lord pulls me out from amidst my village and places me above the high officials, the officers and troops will not be submissive, and the hundred surnames will not believe in me. Since the man is insignificant and his authority [ch'üan] light, I would like to have one of my Lord's favored ministers, someone whom the state respects, as Supervisor of the Army.[12] Then it will be possible." Thereupon Duke Ching assented, having Chuang Ku go forth.

Jang-chü, who had already taken his leave, made an agreement with Chuang Ku, saying: "Tomorrow at midday we shall meet at the army's gate." Jang-chü raced ahead to the army, set up the gnomon,[13] and let the water [drip in the water clock], awaiting Ku. Ku, who had always been arrogant and aristocratic, assumed that since the general had already reached the army while he was [only] the Supervisor, it was not extremely urgent. His relatives from all around, who were sending him off, detained him to drink. Midday came and Ku had not arrived. Jang-chü then lay down the standard, stopped the dripping water, and went into [the encampment]. He advanced the army [and] took control of the soldiers, clearly publicizing the constraints and bonds.[14] When the constraints had been imposed it was already evening, and then Chuang Ku arrived.

Jang-chü said: "How is it that you arrive after the appointed time?" Ku acknowledged his fault, saying: "High officials and relatives saw the simple one off, thus he was detained." Jang-chü said: "On the day a general receives the mandate [of command] he forgets his home; when he enters the army and takes control of the drumsticks and urgently beats the drum he forgets himself. At present enemy states have already deeply invaded [our land]; within the state there is unrest and movement. Officers and soldiers lie brutally cut down and exposed at the borders. Our ruler does not sleep soundly nor enjoy the sweet taste of his food. The fate of the hundred surnames hangs on you, so what do you mean by being seen off?"

He summoned the provost marshal and inquired: "What is the army's law regarding those who arrive after the appointed time?" The reply: "They should be decapitated!" Chuang Ku was terrified, and he ordered a man to race back and report it to Duke Ching, asking to be saved. He had already left but not yet returned, whereupon [Jang-chü] beheaded Ku in order to publicize [the enforcement of discipline] within the Three Armies.[15] All the officers within the Three Armies shook with fear.

Somewhat later the emissary that Duke Ching had dispatched, bearing a tally to pardon Ku, raced into the army. Jang-chü said: "When the general is with the army, there are orders of the ruler which are not accepted."[16] He asked the provost marshal: "What is the law regarding racing into the army?" The provost marshal said: "He should be beheaded." The emissary was terrified. Jang-chü said: "We cannot slay the ruler's emissary." Then he beheaded the [emissary's] attendant, severed the carriage's left stanchion, and beheaded the horse on the left in order to instruct the Three Armies. He dispatched the Duke's emissary to return and report and then moved [the army] out.

The officers and soldiers next encamped, dug wells, lit the cook fires, and prepared their drink and food. He asked about those with illness, had physicians prescribe medicine, and personally looked after them. In all cases when he took the emoluments of office and his rations, he presented them to the officers and troops; he himself divided all rations equally with the officers and troops. He compared the strong and weak among them[17] and only after three days took control of the soldiers. The sick all sought to go on the march, fighting fervently to go into battle on his behalf. Chin's army heard of it, abandoned their position, and departed. Yen's army heard of it, crossed over the river, and dispersed. Thereupon he pursued and attacked them, subsequently retaking all the territory within the borders of the old fief, returning with the soldiers. Before he reached the state capital he disbanded the units, released them from military constraints,[18] swore a covenant, and thereafter entered the city. Duke Ching and the high officials greeted him in the suburbs, rewarding the troops and completing the rites, only afterward returning to rest. After that he interviewed Jang-chü and honored him as Great Master of the Horse [*Ta Ssu-ma*]. The T'ien clan daily grew more honored in Ch'i.

*   *   *

After this, subordinates of the high officials Pao, Kao, and Kuo harmed him, slandering him to Duke Ching.[19] Duke Ching forced Jang-chü to retire. Chü fell extremely ill and died. From this the followers of T'ien Ch'i and T'ien Pao bore a grudge against Kao, Kuo, and the others. Later [along] with T'ien Ch'ang they killed Duke Chien and completely exterminated the Kao and Kuo clans. Subsequently, Ch'ang's great-grandson T'ien Ho was thereby able to establish himself as King Wei of Ch'i. In employing the army to effect Ch'i's awesomeness he greatly imitated Jang-chü's methods, and the feudal lords all paid court to Ch'i.

King Wei of Ch'i had the high officials seek out and discuss the strategy of the ancient Ssu-mas, appending Jang-chü's [methods] within them. Thus [the book] is called the *Military Methods of Ssu-ma Jang-chü*.

*   *   *

The Grand Historian comments: "I have read the *Ssu-ma Ping-fa*. It is vast, expansive, deep, and far-reaching. Even the Three Dynasties, in their campaigns of rectification, still could not exhaust its meaning. Its language as well deserves some praise. [However,] how could one such as Jang-chü, commanding the army in a minor way on behalf of a small country, have the leisure to realize the *Military Methods of the Ssu-ma*? The world already has numerous copies of the *Ssu-ma Ping-fa*. For this reason I have not discussed it but have written Jang-chü's biography."

The Grand Historian's comments eventually stimulated historical doubts about Jang-chü's possible role in the book, even though the biography clearly indicates that his thoughts were merely appended among those of the early Masters of the Horse. (However, a different account found in the histories suggests that this general was evil and dissolute, hardly a figure of any merit. Any work he might have penned has subsequently been lost.[20]) Regardless of its evolution, the book apparently assumed what was essentially its final form about the middle of the fourth century B.C.—the approximate time of Mencius's youth, more than one hundred years after the death of Confucius (551–479 B.C.), and contemporary with the probable composition of Sun-tzu's *Art of War* or perhaps Sun Pin's work.

The condition and even the authenticity of the text have been matters of scholarly debate for some centuries. Unfortunately, all editions presently available—including the one translated here from the *Seven Military Classics*—appear to be merely remnants of an original, extensive work. Only 5 chapters remain out of 155 purportedly extant in the Han dynasty,[21] although they seem to have been faithfully transmitted since the T'ang dynasty. Ch'ing dynasty textual specialists particularly attacked the work as spurious, largely on the basis of the great discrepancy in the number of chapters and the book's failure to include all the fragments preserved in other writings and in various commentaries. However, recent studies have advanced arguments to sustain the claim that at the least, the modern text represents original material—even though much has been lost—and that the central kernel reports practices that date from before the Western Chou era supplemented by paragraphs dating from the Warring States period.[22] Although further discussion must be left to the notes, if the *Shih chi* account is historically valid, the disjointed, particularized character of the individual paragraphs would be appropriate to such a book. The numerous concrete statements—all focusing on aspects of military affairs—having been rescued from the mists of time by the compilers, could never be reformed and integrated to constitute the systematized work of a single author.[23]

Scope and Nature of *The Methods*

In the Later Han dynasty, Pan Ku, author of the *History of the Former Han Dynasty*, classified the *Ssu-ma Fa* under the section on *li*—"rites," or forms of propriety—when organizing his bibliographical essay. This may have been because the work was viewed as emphasizing administration, organization, and discipline rather than strategy and battlefield tactics. Within the context of Confucianism's ascending influence and the growing domination of orthodox thought in the Later Han as well as the importance being ascribed to the major works on ritual such as the *Li chi* and *Chou li* (*Rites of Chou,* with which the *Ssu-ma Fa* has some similarities), the book may naturally have been regarded as an exposition on the military forms of the ancient dynasties—including the Early Chou—and categorized accordingly.[24]

Even if the collected fragments are included, the *Ssu-ma Fa* cannot be considered a complete work because it rarely discusses tactics or any other aspect of battlefield command. Rather, it contains a variety of specific teachings—frequently couched in difficult, terse language—for initiating military activities, mastering military administration, and managing military campaigns. Limited discussions of strategy and tactics such as those typical of the *Six Secret Teachings* appear only in the last three chapters and are frequently passages common to the *Six Secret Teachings* or Sun-Tzu's *Art of War.* Equally absent are details about government and the implementation of moral measures, even though both are strongly advocated in the first two sections (leading to a theory that these two chapters preserve truly ancient, Sagely portions of the "original" text and the remaining three incorporate the cruder ideas of Ssu-ma Jang-chü himself).[25]

Warfare and Fundamental Values

As a book that focuses on military administration, the *Ssu-ma Fa* naturally postulates that warfare is vital to the state and essential to pacifying the realm. According to the conceptualization of righteousness that was becoming more prevalent in this period, warfare provides the necessary means for chastising the evil and rescuing the oppressed. Moreover, despite advocating righteousness and humane government, the *Ssu-ma Fa* expresses the startling realization that the conscious exploitation of force is the foundation of political power.[26] As depicted from within the usual historical framework characterizing the drastic decline from Virtue, the argument runs:

> In antiquity, taking benevolence as the foundation and employing righteousness to govern constituted "uprightness." However, when uprightness failed to attain the desired [moral and political] objectives, [they resorted to] authority. Authority comes from warfare, not from harmony among men. For this reason if one must kill men to give peace to the people, then killing is permissible. If one must attack a state out of love for their people, then attacking it is permissible. If one must stop war with war, although it is war it is permissible.[27](1)

It should be noted that the text warns equally strongly against becoming enthralled with war: "Thus even though a state may be vast, those who love warfare will inevitably perish. Even though calm may prevail under Heaven, those who forget warfare will certainly be endangered!"

Distinction of the Civilian and Martial Realms

Although the *Ssu-ma Fa* falls within the realist tradition, in delineating the distinction between the civilian and the martial it reflected the changing conditions of the Warring States period. Consciousness of this separation, which would become even more pronounced later in Chinese history, perhaps received impetus from the presence and growing influence of Confucian thought as popularized by the Master's true disciples and their immediate followers. In contrast to the unity of political and military functions that historically characterized the Shang and Early Chou eras, the contributors to the *Ssu-ma Fa* stressed that the military and civilian realms should be radically distinguished because of their contradictory values. The different realities are clearly perceived—perhaps emphasized—because of the growing influence of formalistic thinking about propriety and the proper forms of government that had developed extensively under the aegis of Chou civilization. As Liu Pang, founder of the Han dynasty, later discovered, he could conquer the world on horseback, but he could not maintain civilian rule without the *li* (forms of propriety) to establish his image, provide distinctions, and ensure order. The *li* created and sustained the separation necessary to elevate him above his uncouth former comrades.

Because the Chou dynasty could devote the resources necessary to nurturing intellectual pursuits during its initial period of peace and prosperity, warfare naturally became somewhat de-emphasized.[28] The products of peace were intellectual and formal; and although the basic martial values were never completely rejected, each realm was conceived as requiring a different orientation:

> In antiquity the form and spirit governing civilian affairs would not be found in the military realm; those appropriate to the military realm would not be found in the civilian sphere. If the form and spirit [appropriate to the] military realm enter the civilian sphere, the Virtue of the people will decline. When the form and spirit [appropriate to the] civilian sphere enter the military realm, then the Virtue of the people will weaken.
>
> In the civilian sphere words are cultivated and speech languid. In court one is respectful and courteous and cultivates himself to serve others. Unsummoned, he does not step forth; unquestioned, he does not speak. It is difficult to advance but easy to withdraw.
>
> In the military realm one speaks directly and stands firm. When deployed in formation one focuses on duty and acts decisively. Those wearing battle armor

do not bow; those in war chariots need not observe the forms of propriety [*li*]; those manning fortifications do not scurry. In times of danger one does not pay attention to seniority. Thus the civilian forms of behavior [*li*] and military standards [*fa*] are like left and right.[29] (2)

The atmosphere of the court is severe, remote, and yet languid; that of the military is severe, stern, and active. The civilian atmosphere clearly stifles the martial spirit, whereas in the military the critical problem is forcing men to be active and courageous and then restraining any individual, disordered expression of these attributes.[30]

The list of important virtues on which government should rely remains essentially unchanged: benevolence, righteousness, faith, trust, loyalty, Virtue, courage, and wisdom. However, compared with the formalistic nature of combat in the Early Chou era, the Warring States mileau demanded severity and total commitment. Yet the *Ssu-ma Fa* records and thereby advocates restraints, the latter affecting battle strategy and measures in terms of both conceptualization and actual tactics. The ideals of antiquity required that formations not be attacked before they had been completed or attacks pressed home with ruthless swiftness. Rather, reaction and restraint were stressed, with the approach being responsive rather than aggressive. This civility is sometimes explained in terms of strategic considerations, but such justifications appear weak. In contrast with the other *Seven Military Classics,* a different spirit obviously pervades the *Ssu-ma Fa;* it even affects the contributors, who clearly rose to positions of power and influence through military achievements.

Perhaps the best example of this advocacy of restraint can be seen in the rules for pursuing a fleeing enemy, which were attributed to antiquity for authenticity:

> In antiquity they did not pursue a fleeing enemy more than one hundred paces or follow a retreating enemy more than three days, thereby making clear their observance of the forms of proper conduct [*li*]. They did not exhaust the incapable and had sympathy for the wounded and sick, thereby making evident their benevolence. They awaited the completions of the enemy's formation and then drummed the attack, thereby making clear their good faith. They contended for righteousness, not profit, thereby manifesting their righteousness. Moreover, they were able to pardon those who submitted, thereby making evident their courage. They knew the end, they knew the beginning, thereby making clear their wisdom. These six virtues were taught together at appropriate times, being taken as the Tao of the people's guidelines. This was the rule from antiquity. (1)

In a similar passage the ideal is again expressed in terms of the *li* but with the ostensible purpose of avoiding ambushes and entrapment.[31] However, traces of the new combat reality still creep in, as witnessed in such injunctions as "when following a fleeing army do not rest; if some of the enemy stop while others run off to the side, then be suspicious."

Importance of the People

As in all of the *Seven Military Classics,* the contributors stress that "aiding" the people provides the only justification for mobilizing forces. Moreover, sharing benefits while eliminating evil and hardship should be paramount among the government's objectives. Avoiding any disruption of seasonal agricultural activity must be an integral part of governmental efforts to secure the people's willing allegiance. Furthermore, military actions that might increase the suffering of the enemy's populace should also be avoided:

> Neither contravening the seasons nor working the people to exhaustion is the means by which to love our people. Neither attacking a state in national mourning nor taking advantage of natural disasters is the means by which to love their people. Not mobilizing the army in either winter or summer is the means by which to love both our own people and the enemy's people. (1)

The proscription against mobilizing in winter is somewhat unusual because the fall was normally the time of military training, with campaigns extending into the winter—the season of withdrawal, death, and punishment.[32]

When advancing into enemy territory, actions that might inflame the people or cause them hardship and thereby antagonize them should be severely prohibited:

> When you enter the offender's territory, do not do violence to his gods; do not hunt his wild animals; do not destroy earthworks; do not set fire to buildings; do not cut down forests; do not take the six domesticated animals, grains, or implements.[33] When you see their elderly or very young, return them without harming them. Even if you encounter adults, unless they engage you in combat, do not treat them as enemies. If an enemy has been wounded, provide medical attention and return him. (1)

Because the sole justification for launching a sanctioned attack would be the eradication of governmental evil,[34] any expedition to chastise wrongdoers must maintain an image congruent with its defining values and teachings. Accordingly, the *Ssu-ma Fa* stresses both the ceremonial, accusatory nature of the preparatory formalities[35] and the vital necessity for all the soldiers' actions to be characterized by benevolence. In accord with the military writings of the age, these policies are formulated and directed toward minimizing the enemy's resistance. However, this spirit contrasts starkly with the authoritarian policies of those who advocated consciously employing warfare as the crucial means for enriching the state as well as with the brutality witnessed throughout the Warring States period when men, including those who made the fatal mistake of surrendering rather than fighting to the death, were slaughtered by the hundreds of thousands.

Warfare: General Principles and Elements

Training Is Primary

Training men for the army entails certain problems, as indicated by this perceptive passage:

> In warfare: It is not forming a battle array that is difficult; it is reaching the point that the men can be ordered into formation that is hard. It is not attaining the ability to order them into formation that is difficult; it is reaching the point of being able to employ them that is hard. It is not knowing what to do that is difficult; it is putting it into effect that is hard. Men from each [of the four quarters] have their own nature. Character differs from region to region. Through teaching they come to have regional habits, the customs of each state [thus] being different. [Only] through the Tao [Way] are their customs transformed. (4)

The two points made here are historically important. First, the ability to train men underlies their potential utilization in battle. Second, regional character differences will affect the outcome (which is why the T'ai Kung had advocated not disturbing local customs). This conscious observation of regionalism is one of the keystones of Chinese psychology, a kernel that later received extensive development.

All battlefield success results from measures previously implemented to train and prepare the troops. Once the requisite state of preparation is fully realized, factors that directly affect the battle can be considered. The general should restrict his tactics to the army's capabilities, attempt only what his men are willing to pursue,[36] and try to force the enemy to undertake tasks for which it is incapable and unwilling. The soldiers' armor must be stalwart; the weapons must be of good quality, intermixed, and integrated. The formations must be capable of effectively utilizing the weapons and equipment.

Movement should be controlled and never allowed to become chaotic. The proper balance between exertion and exhaustion must be struck; otherwise there is equal danger of laxity and unwillingness stemming from too much rest, or inability resulting from being overtired. Quiet and control in the midst of turbulence are the keys to victory.[37] Doubt must never be permitted to creep in.

The few concrete tactical suggestions that appear in the text are similar, sometimes even identical to those found in other works from the period. For example, the wise general always evaluates the enemy carefully and then attacks its weakness. He employs terrain to his advantage, such as by occupying and fortifying uphill positions, avoiding water and marshes, and being alert for ambushes when in confined areas. He should accord with Heaven, which is generally understood as consisting of the factors of climate, season, and weather but also as the auguries obtained before battle. This reflects Shang and Early Chou practices and beliefs.[38]

Spirit and Courage

The problems of motivating men, manipulating spirit, and fostering courage command extensive attention in the *Ssu-ma Fa,* and several observations are worth abstracting from the text for systematic consideration. Virtually every military thinker in Chinese antiquity devoted a few passages to the critical problem of attaining proper commitment and nurturing courage. In simple approaches either the positive effects of rewards or the negative effects of punishments were employed singly, whereas more sophisticated thinkers offered a number of positive methods to stimulate courage and to overcome fear without the greater fear of punishment and death as the sole motivator. Righteousness, beneficence, material welfare, and freedom from oppression constituted the fundamental, positive incentives—all to be thoroughly inculcated through instruction and teaching. These need not be discussed further.

The concept of *ch'i* appears prominently in the *Ssu-ma Fa,* with much of the psychology of fear and courage being conceptualized in terms of *ch'i.* For example, in protracted conflicts courage suddenly becomes crucial:

> In general, in battle one endures through strength and gains victory through spirit. One can endure with a solid defense but will achieve victory through being endangered. When the heart's foundation is solid, a new surge of *ch'i* will bring victory. (IV)

Accordingly, men who are doubtful, worried, afraid, or terrified destroy an army: "When men have minds set on victory, all they see is the enemy. When men have minds filled with fear, all they see is their fear" (4). Because the astute commander is advised to attack doubt and weakness in an enemy,[39] regaining control of the army's spirit is critical. Thus:

> Positions should be strictly defined; administrative measures should be severe; strength should be nimble; the [soldiers'] *ch'i* should be constrained; and the minds [of the officers and people] should be unified. (4)

Among the several techniques advanced for "arousing the *ch'i*," ritual oath-taking and the final admonition of the troops ranked high in importance. Properly worded, the oath would invoke the state deities, glorify the cause, set out the objectives, condemn the enemy, and generally appeal to righteousness and similar moral values:

> When the oath is clear and stimulating the men will be strong, and you will extinguish [the effects] of baleful omens and auspicious signs. ... Arouse the men's spirits with the fervor of righteousness; prosecute affairs at the right moment. (3)

The former great historical leaders apparently felt the oath would have maximum effect at particular moments, although there was considerable disagreement among them as to the appropriate timing of its administration in order to achieve the greatest psychological impact:

> Shun made the official announcement of their mission within the state [capital] because he wanted the people to first embrace his orders. The rulers of the Hsia dynasty administered their oaths amidst the army for they wanted the people to first complete their thoughts. The Shang rulers swore their oaths outside the gate to the encampment for they wanted the people to first fix their intentions and await the conflict. [King Wu] of the Chou waited until the weapons were about to clash and then swore his oath in order to stimulate the people's will [to fight]. (2)

In the field, prior to a potentially decisive battle or in dire circumstances, visibly abandoning all hope of returning home and destroying supplies were commonly espoused measures, to which (as Sun-tzu also advocates) the *Methods* adds a farewell letter:

> Writing letters of final farewell is referred to as "breaking off all thoughts of life." Selecting the elite and ranking the weapons is termed "increasing the strength of the men." Casting aside the implements of office and carrying only minimum rations is termed "opening the men's thoughts." (5)

In the *Ssu-ma Fa* rewards and punishments continue to provide the primary incentives and means for enforcement. The contributors accepted a version of the decline-from-Virtue theory that recognized the necessity for both rewards and punitive measures, which increased with the passage of time:

> In antiquity the Worthy Kings made manifest the Virtue of the people and fully [sought out] the goodness of the people. Thus they did not neglect the virtuous nor demean the people in any respect. Rewards were not granted, and punishments were never even tried.

Shun neither granted rewards nor imposed punishments, but the people could still be employed. This was the height of Virtue.

The Hsia granted rewards but did not impose punishments. This was the height of instruction.

The Shang imposed punishments but did not grant rewards. This was the height of awesomeness.

The Chou used both rewards and punishments, and Virtue declined. ...

The Hsia bestowed rewards in court in order to make eminent the good. The Shang carried out executions in the marketplace to overawe the evil. The Chou granted rewards in court and carried out executions in the marketplace to encourage gentlemen and terrify the common man. Hence the kings of all three dynasties manifested Virtue in the same way. (2)

Conceived in terms of military prowess and the need for conquest by arms:

The rulers of the Hsia rectified their Virtue and never employed the sharp blades of their weapons, so their weapons were not mixed together. The Shang relied on righteousness, so they first used the sharpness of weapons. The Chou relied on force, so they fully utilized the sharpness of their weapons. (2)

The normal admonitions about the timely imposition of punishments and granting of rewards found in the writings of the period are included. More important is the injunction to reinforce the effectiveness of the system with bold measures when combat must again be faced. An example of this advice, which is directed toward the commander, runs as follows:

If in warfare you are victorious, share the achievement and praise with the troops. If you are about to reengage in battle, then make their rewards exceptionally generous and the punishments heavier. If you failed to direct them to victory, accept the blame yourself. If you must fight again, swear an oath and assume a forward position. Do not repeat your previous tactics. Whether you win or not, do not deviate from this method, for it is termed the "True Principle." (4)

This accords with the general policy of visibly implementing rewards and punishments right after the men have prepared for battle:

After you have aroused [people's] ch'i [spirit] and moreover enacted governmental measures [such as rewards and punishments], encompass them with a benign countenance, and lead them with your speeches. Upbraid them in accord with their fears; assign affairs in accord with their desires. (3)

Although most writers in the period adhere to such doctrines, the *Methods* identifies two special situations. In the first, because of the magnitude of the victory or defeat, the sheer numbers of those involved preclude using the normal approach:

Do not reward great victories, for then neither the upper nor lower ranks will boast of their achievements. If the upper ranks cannot boast they will not seem arrogant, while if the lower ranks cannot boast no distinctions will be established among the men. When neither of them boasts this is the pinnacle of deference.

In cases of great defeat do not punish anyone, for then both the upper and lower ranks will assume the disgrace falls on them. If the upper ranks reproach themselves they will certainly regret their errors, while if the lower ranks feel the same they will certainly try to avoid repeating the offense. When all the ranks divide [the responsibility for] the detestable among themselves, this is the pinnacle of yielding. (2)

In the second unusual case, the soldiers are so terrified of the enemy that neither the incentives of large rewards nor the threat of capital punishment can affect them. A radically different approach, which focuses on gaining control of their emotions through gathering the soldiers together and executing a series of set patterns or drills before swearing an oath,[40] becomes vital:

If they are terrified, then do not threaten them with execution and severe punishments but display a magnaminous countenance. Speak to them about what they have to live for, and go about supervising them in their duties. (2)

Such physical actions as crouching and sitting in a tight formation will presumably break the individual's isolation and end his continued immersion into the fear dominating his mind, permitting the commander to turn the soldier's attention outward with an inspirational harangue focusing on the righteousness of their cause, the rewards that can be attained, and the objectives of living.[41] As the *Ssu-ma Fa* notes elsewhere, it is only through being endangered that men will truly exhaust their spirit and energies. Doubt and fear are the greatest enemies; but if plans have been well made, the righteousness of the cause thoroughly proclaimed, and the men well trained, the army should emerge triumphant.

Concept of Battle Management

A number of principles briefly raised by the text are worthy of notice, but they are self-explanatory and need not be discussed here. However, concepts related to engaging the enemy that appear throughout the last three chapters merit brief consideration. Those of particular importance are outlining the qualities required for leadership; the necessity for thoroughly analyzing the enemy, weighing the balance of forces, and employing those forces appropriately; avoiding being misled by minor advantages; concentrating force at the critical moment after moving forward in a more dispersed fashion; and ensuring harmony among the men. The advantages of terrain should be fully utilized, whereas the tactical deployment of forces depends on their relative strength and character—including training, armament, and spirit. Even though an army's numbers may be few, tactics can be fashioned to preserve those numbers and even wrest a victory. The *Ssu-ma Fa* does not discuss these principles beyond the briefest indication of method, even though they are found more extensively in the other military writings. Measure and deliberate control—perhaps evidence of the antiquity of much of the material—are stressed throughout as the basis of both survival and victory. Applying psychological principles is also important; these principles include enervating the enemy's will to fight by leaving an escape path, never forcing him into the desperate circumstances that compel fighting to the death, and sowing doubt in the enemy's mind.

1. Benevolence the Foundation

In antiquity, taking benevolence as the foundation and employing righteousness to govern constituted "uprightness." However, when uprightness failed to attain the desired [moral and political] objectives, [they resorted to] authority [*ch'üan*]. Authority comes from warfare, not from harmony among men. For this reason if one must kill men to give peace to the people, then killing is permissible. If one must attack a state out of love for their people, then attacking it is permissible. If one must stop war with war, although it is war it is permissible. Thus benevolence is loved; righteousness is willingly submitted to; wisdom is relied on; courage is embraced; and credibility is trusted. Within, [the government] gains the love of the people, the means by which it can be preserved. Outside, it acquires awesomeness, the means by which it can wage war.[1]

The Tao of Warfare: Neither contravening the seasons[2] nor working the people to exhaustion is the means by which to love our people. Neither attacking a state in national mourning nor taking advantage of natural disaster is the means by which to love their people. Not mobilizing the army in either winter or summer is the means by which to love both your own people and the enemy's people. Thus even though a state may be vast, those who love warfare will inevitably perish. Even though calm may prevail under Heaven, those who forget warfare will certainly be endangered!

When the world had attained peace the Son of Heaven had the "Ta K'ai" [Great Peace] music performed [in celebration]. Then in the spring he held the Sou hunt, and in the fall he held the Hsien hunt. In the spring the feudal lords returned their brigades in good order, while in the fall they trained their soldiers. In this way they did not forget warfare.[3]

In antiquity they did not pursue a fleeing enemy more than one hundred paces or follow a retreating enemy more than three days, thereby making clear their observance of the forms of proper conduct [*li*].[4] They did not exhaust the incapable and had sympathy for the wounded and sick, thereby making evident their benevolence. They awaited the completion of the enemy's formation and then drummed the attack, thereby making clear their good faith. They contended for righteousness, not profit, thereby manifesting their righteousness. Moreover, they were able to pardon those who submitted,[5] thereby making evident their courage. They knew the end, they knew the beginning, thereby making clear their wisdom. These six virtues were taught together at appropriate times, being taken as the Tao of the people's guidelines. This was the rule from antiquity.

* * *

The administrative measures of the Former Kings: They accorded with the Tao of Heaven; they established what was appropriate to Earth. They put the virtuous among the people into office, rectified names, and governed things.[6] They established the states, defined the hierarchy of feudal positions, and apportioned emoluments according to rank. The feudal lords were pleased and embraced them. Those beyond the seas came to submit. Punishments were eliminated and the army rested. These were the attainments of Sagely Virtue.

* * *

Next came the Worthy Kings: They ordered the rites [li], music, laws, and measures and then created the five punishments, raising armored troops to chastise the unrighteous. They made inspection tours [of the feudal lands], investigated [the customs] of the four quarters, assembled the feudal lords, and investigated differences.[7] If any [of the feudal lords] had disobeyed orders, disordered the constant,[8] turned his back on Virtue, or contravened the seasons of Heaven[9]—endangering meritorious rulers—they would publicize it among all the feudal lords, making it evident that he had committed an offense. They then announced it to August Heaven and to the sun, moon, planets, and constellations. They prayed to the Gods of Earth, the spirits of the Four Seasons, mountains, and rivers and at the Great Altar [of state]. Then they offered sacrifice to the Former Kings.[10] Only thereafter would the Prime Minister charge the army before the feudal lords, saying, "A certain state has acted contrary to the Tao. You will participate in the rectification campaign on such a year, month, and day. On that date the army will reach the [offending] state and assemble with the Son of Heaven to apply the punishment of rectification."

The Prime Minister and other high officials would issue the following orders to the army:

When you enter the offender's territory, do not do violence to his gods; do not hunt his wild animals; do not destroy earthworks;[11] do not set fire to buildings; do not cut down forests; do not take the six domesticated animals, grains, or implements. When you see their elderly or very young, return them without harming them. Even if you encounter adults, unless they engage you in combat, do not treat them as enemies. If an enemy has been wounded, provide medical attention and return him.

When they had executed the guilty, the king, together with the feudal lords, corrected and rectified [the government and customs] of the state. They raised up the Worthy, established an enlightened ruler, and corrected and restored their feudal position and obligations.

⸗   ⸗   ⸗

The Ways by which the kings and hegemons governed the feudal lords were six:
With territory they gave shape to the feudal lords.[12]
With government directives they pacified the feudal lords.
With the rites and good faith they drew the feudal lords close to them.
With men of wisdom and strength they pleased the feudal lords.
Through strategists they constrained the feudal lords. With weapons and armor they forced the submission of the feudal lords.
By sharing misfortune with them, by sharing benefits[13] with them, they united the feudal lords. They had the smaller states serve the larger ones in order to bring the feudal lords into harmony.

⸗   ⸗   ⸗

They assembled them in order to announce nine prohibitions:
Those who take advantage of weak [states] or encroach on sparsely populated ones will have their borders reduced on all sides.
Those who murder the Worthy or harm the people will be attacked [and deposed].
Those who are brutal within their state and encroach on others outside it will be purged.
Those whose fields turn wild and whose people scatter will be reduced.
Those who rely on the fastness [of natural advantages] to disobey orders will be invaded.
Those who harm or kill their relatives will be rectified.
Those who depose or slay their ruler will be exterminated.
Those who oppose orders and resist the government will be isolated.
Those who are chaotic and rebellious both within and without their borders, who act like animals, will be extinguished.[14]

2. Obligations of the Son of Heaven

The duty of the Son of Heaven must be to concentrate on modeling on Heaven and Earth and observing [the measures] of the Former Sages.[15] The duty of officers and common men must be to respectfully serve their parents and to be upright with their ruler and superiors. Even though there is an enlightened ruler, if the officers are not first instructed, they cannot be used.

When the ancients instructed the people they would invariably establish the relationships and fixed distinctions of noble and common—causing them not to encroach on each other; the virtuous and righteous not to exceed each other; the talented and technically skilled not to occlude each other; and the courageous and strong not to clash with each other. Thus their strength was united and their thoughts were in harmony.

In antiquity the form and spirit governing civilian affairs would not be found in the military realm; those appropriate to the military realm would not be found in the civilian sphere.[16] Thus virtue and righteousness did not transgress inappropriate realms.

Superiors valued officers who were not boastful for officers who do not boast are the greatest talents.[17] If they do not boast they are not self-seeking, and if they are not self-seeking they will not be contentious. When listening to affairs of state[18] superiors want to seek out their true nature, but when listening to affairs within the military they must discuss the appropriateness of matters.[19] Therefore the talented and skillful cannot conceal each other. When officers follow orders they should receive the highest rewards, when they disobey orders the most severe form of execution.[20] Then the courageous and strong will not contend with each other.

Only after effective instructions have been provided to the people can [the state] carefully select and employ them. Only after government affairs have been thoroughly ordered can the hundred offices be sufficiently provided. When instructions are thoroughly examined the people will manifest goodness. When practice becomes habit the people will embody the customs. This is the pinnacle of transformation through education.

In antiquity they did not pursue a fleeing enemy too far or follow a retreating army too closely. By not pursuing them too far, it was difficult to draw them into a trap; by not pursuing so closely as to catch up, it was hard to ambush them. They regarded the forms of propriety [*li*] as their basic strength and benevolence as [the foundation of] their victory. After they were victorious their teachings could again be employed.[21] For this reason the true gentleman values them.

╭   ╭   ╭

Shun made the official announcement of their mission within the state [capital] because he wanted the people to first embrace his orders. The rulers of the Hsia dynasty administered their oaths amidst the army for they wanted the people to first complete their thoughts. The Shang rulers swore their oaths outside the gate to the encampment for they wanted the people to first fix their intentions and await the conflict. [King Wu] of the Chou waited until the weapons were about to clash and then swore his oath in order to stimulate the people's will [to fight].

The rulers of the Hsia rectified their Virtue and never employed the sharp blades of their weapons, so their weapons were not mixed together.[22] The Shang relied on righteousness, so they first used the sharpness of weapons. The Chou relied on force, so they fully utilized the sharpness of their weapons.[23]

The Hsia bestowed rewards in court in order to make eminent the good. The Shang carried out executions in the marketplace to overawe the evil. The Chou granted rewards in court and carried out executions in the marketplace to encourage gentlemen and terrify the common man. Hence the kings of all three dynasties manifested Virtue in the same way.

╭   ╭   ╭

When the [five types of] weapons are not intermixed, it will not be advantageous. Long weapons are for protection;[24] short weapons are for defending. If the weapons are too long they will be difficult to wield against others; if they are too short they will not reach the enemy. If they are too light they will be adroitly brandished, but such facility will easily lead to chaos. If they are too heavy they will be too clumsy, and if too clumsy they will not attain their objectives.

╭   ╭   ╭

As for their war chariots, those of the rulers of the Hsia were called "hook chariots" for they put uprightness first. Those of the Shang were called "chariots of the new moon" for they put speed first. Those of the Chou were called "the source of weapons" for they put excellence first.[25]

For flags, the Hsia had a black one at the head representing control of men. The Shang's was white for the righteousness of Heaven. The Chou used yellow for the Tao of Earth.

For insignia[26] the Hsia used the sun and moon, valuing brightness. The Shang used the tiger, esteeming awesomeness. The Chou used the dragon, esteeming culture.

′   ′   ′

When the army concentrates excessively on its awesomeness the people will cower, but if it diminishes its awesomeness the people will not be victorious. When superiors cause the people to be unable to be righteous, the hundred surnames to be unable to achieve proper organization, the artisans to be unable to profit [from their work], oxen and horses to be unable to fulfill their functions while the officers insult [the people]—this is termed "excessive awesomeness," and the people will cower. When superiors do not respect Virtue but employ the deceptive and evil; when they do not honor the Tao but employ the courageous and strong; when they do not value those who obey commands but instead esteem those who contravene them; when they do not value good actions but esteem violent behavior so that [the people] insult the minor officials—this is termed "diminished awesomeness." If the conditions of diminished awesomeness prevail the people will not be victorious.

′   ′   ′

A campaign army[27] takes measure as its prime concern so that the people's strength will be adequate. Then, even when the blades clash, the infantry will not run and the chariots will not gallop. When pursuing a fleeing enemy the troops will not break formation, thereby avoiding chaos. The solidarity of a campaign army derives from military discipline that maintains order in formation, does not exhaust the strength of men or horses, and—whether moving slowly or rapidly—does not exceed the measure of the commands.

′   ′   ′

In antiquity the form and spirit governing civilian affairs would not be found in the military realm; those appropriate to the military realm would not be found in the civilian sphere.[28] If the form and spirit [appropriate to the] military realm enter the civilian sphere, the Virtue of the people will decline. When the form and spirit [appropriate to the] civilian sphere enter the military realm, then the Virtue of the people will weaken.

In the civilian sphere words are cultivated and speech languid. In court one is respectful and courteous and cultivates himself to serve others. Unsummoned, he does not step forth; unquestioned, he does not speak. It is difficult to advance but easy to withdraw.

In the military realm one speaks directly and stands firm. When deployed in formation one focuses on duty and acts decisively. Those wearing battle armor do not bow; those in war chariots need not observe the forms of propriety [*li*]; those manning fortifications do not scurry. In times of danger one does not pay attention to seniority. Thus the civilian forms of behavior [*li*] and military standards [*fa*] are like inside and outside; the civil and the martial are like left and right.

In antiquity the Worthy Kings made manifest the Virtue of the people and fully [sought out][29] the goodness of the people. Thus they did not neglect the virtuous nor demean the people in any respect. Rewards were not granted, and punishments were never even tried.

Shun neither granted rewards nor imposed punishments, but the people could still be employed. This was the height of Virtue.

The Hsia granted rewards but did not impose punishments. This was the height of instruction.

The Shang imposed punishments but did not grant rewards. This was the height of awesomeness.

The Chou used both rewards and punishments, and Virtue declined.

Rewards should not be [delayed] beyond the appropriate time for you want the people to quickly profit from doing good. When you punish someone do not change his position for you want the people to quickly see the harm of doing what is not good.

Do not reward great victories, for then neither the upper nor lower ranks will boast of their achievements. If the upper ranks cannot boast they will not seem arrogant, while if the lower ranks cannot boast no distinctions will be established among the men. When neither of them boasts this is the pinnacle of deference.

In cases of great defeat do not punish anyone, for then both the upper and lower ranks will assume the disgrace falls on them. If the upper ranks reproach themselves they will certainly regret their errors, while if the lower ranks feel the same they will certainly try to avoid repeating the offense. When all the ranks divide [the responsibility for] the detestable among themselves, this is the pinnacle of yielding.

In antiquity those on border duty were not required to serve [labor duty] for three years thereafter, and the ruler would personally observe the people's labor.[30] Upper and lower ranks recompensed each other in this fashion, which was the pinnacle of harmony.

When they had attained their aim [of pacifying the realm], they sang triumphal songs[31] to show their happiness. They stored away the implements of war, erected the Spirit Terrace,[32] and responded to the labors of the people to show that the time for rest had come.

3. Determining Rank

In general, to wage war: [First] determine rank and position; prominently record accomplishments and offenses; retain mendicant knights;[33] publicize instructions and edicts; make inquiries among the populace; seek out artisans; apply methodology to planning; fully exploit things; change [the people's] hatreds;[34] dispel doubts; nourish strength; search out and employ the skillful; and take action in accord with the people's hearts.

ɾ   ɾ   ɾ

In general, to wage war: Solidify the people; analyze the advantages [of terrain]; impose order on the turbulent; [regulate] advancing and stopping; accept upright [remonstrance]; nourish a sense of shame; constrain the laws; and investigate punishments. Minor offenders should then be executed. If minor offenders are executed, how can major [offenses] arise?

ɾ   ɾ   ɾ

Accord with Heaven; make material resources abundant; bring joy to the people; take advantage of the resources of Earth; and value military weapons. These are termed the "Five Plans." To accord with Heaven follow the seasons; to increase material resources rely on [seizing them from] the enemy. To bring joy to the people encourage and bring them into concord [with their superiors]. To take advantage of terrain defend strategic points. Valuing weapons, there are bows and arrows for withstanding attack, maces and spears for defense, and halberds and spear-tipped halberds for support.

Now each of these five weapons has its appropriate use: The long protect the short, the short rescue the long. When they are used in turn, the battle can be sustained. When they are employed all at once, [the army] will be strong. When you see [the enemy's] situation, you can be a match for it. This is termed "weighting."

ɾ   ɾ   ɾ

A defending army should stand fast, encourage the people, and bring them into accord [with their superiors]. Only after seeing the invading enemy should it move. The general's mind is focused; the minds of the people are at one with his.

Horses, oxen, chariots, weapons, relaxation, and an adequate diet are the army's strength. Instructions are simply a matter of preparation; warfare is only a question of constraints. The army's commanding general is the body, the companies are the limbs, and the squads of five are the thumb and fingers.

*   *   *

In general, warfare is a question of the strategic balance of power [*ch'üan*], and combat is a matter of courage. The deployment of formations is a matter of skill. Employ what [your men] want, and effect what they are capable of; abolish what they do not want and are incapable of. Do the opposite of this to the enemy.

*   *   *

In general, warfare is a question of having Heaven, material resources, and excellence.

When the day and time for battle have been appropriately fixed and it is not necessary to change them; when augury by the tortoise shell presages victory; and when events proceed in a subtle, mysterious fashion, this is termed "having Heaven."

When the masses have [material resources], [the state] has them. When they thereby produce what is profitable, this is termed "having resources."

When the men are practiced in the [relative] advantages of the formations, and they fully exhaust [the strength of] things in preparation [for battle], this is referred to as "attaining excellence."

When the people are encouraged to fulfill their responsibilities, they are termed "men who take pleasure [in warfare]."

*   *   *

Increasing the army and making the [formations] solid; multiplying its strength and constantly training [the troops]; relying on [exploiting the strength] of things; perceiving the [nature of] things; and responding to sudden [events] are what is meant by "effecting preparations."

Fast chariots and fleet infantrymen, bows and arrows, and a strong defense are what is meant by "increasing the army." Secrecy, silence, and great internal strength are what is meant by "making formations solid." On this basis, being able to advance and being able to withdraw are what is meant by "multiplying strength." At times of little activity the upper ranks instruct [and constantly drill the lower ranks]. This is what is meant by "training [the troops] in formations." When there are appropriate offices [for both command and administration], it is termed "relying on [exploiting the strength of] things." When in accord with this things are perceived [and managed], it is referred to as "simplifying administration."

′   ′   ′

Determine the [number of] your masses in accord with the terrain, and deploy your formations in accord with the enemy. When in attacking, waging battle, defending, advancing, retreating, and stopping, the front and rear are ordered and the chariots and infantry move in concord, this is termed a well-planned campaign. If they do not follow orders; do not trust [their officers]; are not harmonious; are lax, doubtful, weary, afraid; avoid responsibility; cower; are troubled, unrestrained, deflated, or dilatory, it is termed a "disastrous campaign." When they suffer from extreme arrogance, abject terror, moaning and grumbling, constant fear, or [frequent] regrets over actions being taken, they are termed "destroyed and broken." Being able to be large or small or firm or weak, to change formations, and to use large numbers or small groups—in all respects being a match [for the enemy]—is referred to as "[exploiting] the balance of power [ch'üan] in warfare."

′   ′   ′

In general, to wage war: Employ spies against the distant; observe the near; act in accord with the seasons; take advantage of [the enemy's] material resources; esteem good faith; abhor the doubtful. Arouse the soldiers with fervor of righteousness. Undertake affairs at the appropriate time. Employ people with kindness. When you see the enemy, remain quiet; when you see turbulence, do not be hasty to respond. When you see danger and hardship, do not forget the masses. Within the state be generous and foster good faith. Within the army be magnanimous and martial. When the blades clash, be decisive and adroit. Within the state there should be harmony; within the army there should be standards. When the blades clash, investigate [the battlefield situation]. Within the state display cooperation; within the army display uprightness; in battle display good faith.

′   ′   ′

As for military formations: When advancing, the most important thing for the ranks is to be dispersed; when engaged in battle [it is] to be dense and for the weapons to be of mixed types. Instructions to the people should be thorough; quietness is the basis of order; awesomeness becomes advantageous when it is made manifest. When people preserve each other according to righteousness, then they will be stimulated to action. When many well-conceived plans prove successful, the people submit to them. If they sincerely submit at the appropriate time, then subsequent affairs will be well ordered. When things are manifest, then the eye discerns them clearly. When plans have been decided, the mind is strong. When advancing and withdrawing are without doubt, one can give the appearance of being without plans.[35] When listening to [legal affairs] and punishing [the guilty], do not wantonly change their designations or change their flags.

Whenever affairs are well executed they will endure; when they accord with ancient ways they can be effected. When the oath is clear and stimulating the men will be strong, and you will extinguish [the effects] of baleful omens and auspicious signs.

The Tao for eliminating baleful omens [and auspicious signs] is as follows. One is called righteousness. Charge [the people] with good faith, approach them with strength,[36] establish the foundation [of kingly government], and unify the strategic power of All under Heaven. There will not be any men who are not pleased, so this is termed "doubly employing the people."

Another is called [advantages conferred by] the strategic balance of power [ch'üan]. Increase [the enemy's] excesses, seize what he loves. Then acting from without, we can cause a response from within.[37]

⸱ ⸱ ⸱

The first is termed men; the second, uprightness; the third, language; the fourth, skill; the fifth, fire; the sixth, water; the seventh, weapons. They are referred to as the Seven Administrative Affairs.

Glory, profit, shame, and death are referred to as the Four Preservations.

Being tolerant and congenial while yet accumulating awesomeness [is the way] to prevent transgressions and change intentions. In all cases this is the Tao.

Only benevolence can attract people; however, if one is benevolent but not trustworthy, then on the contrary he will vanquish himself. Treat men as men, be upright with the upright, employ appropriate language, and use fire only where is should be used.

⸱ ⸱ ⸱

As for the Tao of Warfare: After you have aroused [the people's] ch'i [spirit] and moreover enacted governmental measures [such as rewards and punishments], encompass them with a benign countenance, and lead them with your speeches. Upbraid them in accord with their fears; assign affairs in accord with their desires. When you have crossed the enemy's borders and taken control of his territory, appoint people to the tasks of government. These are termed "methods of war."

All human qualities must be sought among the masses. Test and evaluate them in terms of name and action [to see if they cohere], for they must excel at implementation. If they are to perform some action but do not, then you yourself should lead them. If they are to perform some action and do so, then ensure that they do not forget it.[38] If you test them three times successfully, then make [their talents] evident.[39] What is appropriate to human life is termed the law.

In general the Tao for imposing order on chaos consists of first, benevolence; second, credibility; third, straightforwardness; fourth, unity; fifth, righteousness; sixth, change [wrought by authority]; seventh, centralized authority.

The Tao for establishing the laws consists of first, acceptance [of constraints]; second, the laws; third, the establishment [of the talented and upright]; fourth, urgency [in administration]; fifth, distinguishing them with insignia; sixth, ordering the colors; seventh, no nonstandard uniforms among the officers.

As for the army, when the [power of the] law lies solely with oneself, it is termed "centralized." When those below the ruler all fear the law, it is termed "law." When the army does not listen to minor affairs; when in battle it does not concern itself with small advantages; and when on the day of conflict it successfully completes its plans in subtle fashion, it is termed "the Tao."

As for warfare: When upright methods do not prove effective, then centralized control of affairs [must be undertaken]. [If the people] do not submit [to Virtue], then laws must be imposed. If they do not trust each other, they must be unified. If they are dilatory, move them; if they are doubtful, change [their doubts]. If the people do not trust the ruler, then whatever is promulgated must not be revised. This has been the administrative rule from antiquity.

4. Strict Positions[40]

In general, as for the Tao of Warfare: Positions should be strictly defined; administrative measures should be severe; strength should be nimble; the [soldier's] *ch'i* should be constrained; and the minds [of the officers and people] should be unified.

ʳ   ʳ   ʳ

In general, as for the Tao of Warfare: Rank and appoint men to office who understand the Tao and display righteousness. Establish companies and squads.[41] Order the rows and files. Set the correct [spacing between] the horizontal and vertical.[42] Investigate whether names and realities [correspond].

Those soldiers who stand [in their formations] should advance and then crouch down; those who [fire from a] squatting position should advance and then kneel.[43] If they are frightened make the formations dense; if they are in danger have them assume a sitting position. If [the enemy] is seen at a distance they will not fear them; if, when they are close, they do not look at them they will not scatter.[44]

ʳ   ʳ   ʳ

When the commanding general dismounts from his chariot, the generals of the left and right also dismount, those wearing armor all sit, and the oath is sworn, after which the army is slowly advanced.[45] All officers, from the generals down to the infantry squad leaders, wear armor.[46] Calculate the deployment of the light and heavy forces. Rouse the horses to action; have the infantrymen and armored soldiers set up a clamor. If they are afraid also collapse them into a tighter unit. Those who are kneeling should squat down; those who are squatting should lie down. Have them crawl forward on their knees, then put them at ease.[47] Have them get up, shout, and advance to the drums. Then signal a halt with the bells. With gagged mouths and minimal dry rations, swear the oath. Have the troops withdraw, crawling back on their knees.[48] Seize and summarily execute any deserters to stop the others from looking about [to desert]. Shout in order to lead them.[49] If they are too terrified of the enemy, do not threaten them with execution and severe punishments but display a magnanimous countenance. Speak to them about what they have to live for;[50] supervise them in their duties.

ʳ   ʳ   ʳ

Within the Three Armies disciplinary action is not imposed on anyone for more than half a day. Confinement does not go beyond a rest period, nor is their food reduced by more than half. If you correct their doubts and delusions they can be led, can be made to submit to orders.

ʳ   ʳ   ʳ

In general, in battle one endures through strength, and gains victory through spirit. One can endure with a solid defense, but will achieve victory through being endangered. When the heart's foundation is solid, a new surge of *ch'i* will bring victory. With armor one is secure; with weapons one attains victory.

,   ,   ,

In general, the chariots realize security through close formations; the infantry becomes solid through squatting; armor becomes solid through weight;[51] victory is attained through the lightness of the weapons.

,   ,   ,

When men have minds set on victory, all they see is the enemy. When men have minds filled with fear, all they see is their fear. When these two minds intersect and determine [action], [it is essential that] the advantages [as perceived by each] are as one.[52] It is the [commander's] duty to create this unification. Only from [the perspective of] authority [*ch'üan*] can it be seen.

,   ,   ,

In general, in warfare: If you advance somewhat into the enemy's territory with a light force it is dangerous.[53] If you advance with a heavy force deep into the enemy's territory you will accomplish nothing. If you advance with a light force deep into enemy territory you will be defeated. If you advance with a heavy force somewhat into the enemy's territory you can fight successfully. Thus in warfare the light and heavy are mutually related.

,   ,   ,

When halting be careful about the weapons and armor.[54] When on the march be cautious about the rows and files. When in battle be careful about advancing and stopping.

,   ,   ,

In general, in warfare: If you are respectful [the troops] will be satisfied. If you lead in person they will follow. When orders are annoying they will be ignored. When commands are issued in proper measure they will be seriously regarded. When the drumbeat is rapid they will move quickly; when the drumbeat is more measured they will move accordingly. When their uniforms are light they will feel quick; if lustrous they will feel stalwart.

,   ,   ,

In general, when the horses and chariots are sturdy, the armor and weapons advantageous, then even a light force can penetrate deeply.[55] If you esteem equality [in rank], then no one will strive for great results. If you value taking charge, then many will die [for the cause]. If you value life, then there will be many doubts; if you honor death [itself], then they will not be victorious.

In general, men will die for love, out of anger, out of [fear of] awesomeness, for righteousness, and for profit.

In general, it is the Tao of Warfare that when they are well instructed men will regard death lightly. When they are constrained by the Tao they will die for the upright.

·   ·   ·

In general, in warfare act in accord with whether [the troops have the spirit] to be victorious or not. Accord with Heaven, accord with men.[56]

In general, in warfare: The Three Armies should not be on the alert for more than three days; a single company should not be vigilant more than half a day; while the guard duty[57] for a single soldier should not exceed one rest period.

·   ·   ·

Those that greatly excel in warfare use the foundation; next in greatness are those that employ the ends.[58] Warfare is taking control of strategy, preserving the subtle. The foundation and the ends are only a question of [exploiting] the strategic balance of power [ch'üan].

·   ·   ·

In general, regarding victory: When the Three Armies are united as one man they will conquer.

In general, as for the drums: There are drums [directing the deployment of] the flags and pennants; drums for [advancing] the chariots; drums for the horses;[59] drums for [directing] the infantry; drums for the different types of troops; drums for the head;[60] and drums for the feet.[61] All seven should be properly prepared and ordered.

·   ·   ·

In general, in warfare: When the formation is already solid, do not make it heavier. When your main forces are advancing, do not commit all of them for by doing so you will be endangered.

·   ·   ·

In general, in warfare: It is not forming a battle array that is difficult; it is reaching the point that the men can be ordered into formation that is hard. It is not attaining the ability to order them into formation that is difficult; it is reaching the point of being able to employ them that is hard. If is not know-ing what to do that is difficult; it is putting it into effect that is hard. Men from each [of the four quarters] have their own nature. Character differs from region to region. Through teaching they come to have regional habits, the customs of each state [thus] being different. [Only] through the Tao are their customs transformed.

*   *   *

In general, whether [the troops] are numerous or few, even though they have already attained victory, they should act as if they had not been victori-ous.[62] The troops should not boast about the sharpness of their weapons or speak of the stoutness of their armor or the sturdiness of their chariots or the quality of their horses; nor should the masses take themselves to be many—for they have not yet gained the Tao.[63]

*   *   *

In general, if in warfare you are victorious, share the achievement and praise with the troops. If you are about to reengage in battle, then make their rewards exceptionally generous and the punishments heavier. If you failed to direct them to victory, accept the blame yourself. If you must fight again, swear an oath and assume a forward position. Do not repeat your previous tactics. Whether you win or not, do not deviate from this method, for it is termed the "True Principle."

In general, with regard to the people: Rescue them with benevolence; en-gage in battle with righteousness; make decisions through wisdom; fight with courage; exercise sole authority through credibility; encourage them with profits; and gain victory through achievements. Thus the mind must embody benevolence and actions should incorporate righteousness. Relying on [the nature of] things is wisdom; relying on the great is courage; relying on long-standing [relations leads to] good faith. Yielding results in harmony, and the men of themselves will be deferential. If men attribute failings to themselves, they will compete to be worthy.[64] When men are pleased in their hearts, they will exhaust their strength.

*   *   *

In general, in warfare: Attack the weak and quiet, avoid the strong and quiet. Attack the tired, avoid the well trained and alert. Attack the truly afraid, avoid those that [display] only minor fears. From antiquity these have been the rules for governing [the army].

5. Employing Masses

In general, as for the Tao of Warfare: When you employ a small number they must be solid.[65] When you employ a large mass they must be well ordered. With a small force it is advantageous to harass the enemy; with a large mass it is advantageous to use orthodox [tactics].[66] When employing a large mass advance and stop; when employing a small number advance and withdraw. If your large mass encounters a small enemy force, surround them at a distance but leave one side open.[67] [Conversely,] if you divide [your forces] and attack in turn, a small force can withstand a large mass. If their masses are beset by uncertainty, you should take advantage of it. If you are contending for a strategic position, abandon your flags [as if in flight, and when the enemy attacks] turn around to mount a counterattack. If the enemy is vast, then concentrate your troops and let them surround you. If the enemy is fewer and fearful, avoid them and leave a path open.[68]

ɼ   ɼ   ɼ

In general, as for warfare: Keep the wind to your back, the mountains behind you, heights on the right, and defiles on the left. Pass through wetlands, cross over damaged roads. Complete double the normal march before encamping; select ground [for encamping] configured like a turtle's back.

In general, as for warfare: After deploying observe their actions. Watch the enemy and then initiate movement. If they are waiting [for our attack], then act accordingly. Do not drum the advance, but await the moment when their masses arise. If they attack, entrench your forces and observe them.

ɼ   ɼ   ɼ

In general, as for warfare: [Employ] large and small numbers to observe their tactical variations; advance and retreat to probe the solidity of their defenses. Endanger them to observe their fears. Be tranquil to observe if they become lax. Move to observe if they have doubts. Mount a surprise attack and observe their discipline.

Mount a sudden strike on their doubts. Attack their haste.[69] Force them to constrict their deployment. Launch a sudden strike against their order. Take advantage of [their failure] to avoid harm.[70] Obstruct their strategy. Seize their thoughts. Capitalize on their fears.

ɼ   ɼ   ɼ

In general, when pursuing a fleeing enemy do not rest. If some of the enemy stop on the road, then be wary![71]

In general, when nearing an enemy's capital, you must have a road by which to advance; when about to withdraw, you must ponder the return route.

In general, as for warfare: If you move first [it will be easy] to become exhausted. If you move after [the enemy, the men] may become afraid. If you rest, [the men may] become lax; if you do not rest, they may also become exhausted. Yet if you rest very long, on the contrary, they may also become afraid.

Writing letters of final farewell is referred to as "breaking off all thoughts of life." Selecting the elite and ranking the weapons is termed "increasing the strength of the men." Casting aside the implements of office and carrying only minimal rations is termed "opening the men's thoughts." From antiquity this has been the rule.

3

Sun-tzu's Art of War

孫子兵法

Translator's Introduction

OF THE *Seven Military Classics* only Sun-tzu's *Military Strategy,* traditionally known as the *Art of War,* has received much exposure in the West. First translated by a French missionary approximately two hundred years ago, it was reportedly studied and effectively employed by Napoleon and possibly by certain members of the Nazi High Command. For the past two thousand years it remained the most important military treatise in Asia, where even the common people knew it by name. Chinese, Japanese, and Korean military theorists and professional soldiers have all studied it, and many of the strategies have played a significant role in Japan's storied military history, commencing about the eighth century A.D.[1] Over the millennia the book's concepts have stimulated intense debates and vehement philosophical discussions, commanding the attention of significant figures in many realms. Although the book has been rendered into English numerous times, with the translations of Lionel Giles[2] and Samuel B. Griffith[3] still widely available, further translations continue to appear. Some of these are merely versions of Giles—acknowledged or otherwise—under a different cover, whereas others represent entirely new works.[4]

Sun-tzu and the Text

It has long been claimed that the *Art of War* is China's oldest and most profound military treatise, with all other works relegated to secondary status at best. Traditionalists attribute the book to the historical Sun Wu, who is recorded in the *Shih chi* and the *Spring and Autumn Annals of Wu and Yüeh* as having been active in the last years of the sixth century B.C., beginning about 512 B.C. In their view the book should therefore date from this period and should contain his theories and concepts of military strategy. However, other scholars have (1) identified numerous historical anachronisms in the extant text that encompass terms, events, technology, and philosophical concepts;[5] (2) emphasized the absence of any evidence (such as should appear in the *Tso*

149

chuan, the classic record of the period's political events) corroborating Sun Wu's strategic role in the wars between Wu and Yüeh;[6] and (3) focused on the disparity between the advanced concepts and nature of large-scale warfare discussed in the *Art of War* and the more limited, primitive battles that characterized the end of the sixth century B.C.[7]

The traditionalist interpretation derives critical support from the numerous passages from the *Art of War* that are visible in most other military writings because, it is asserted, such extensive borrowing could only have been possible from the earliest text.[8] Moreover, this widespread copying is thought to provide ample evidence that the *Art of War* was considered early on the most important military treatise and was valued far more than any other work, oral or written. The origination of certain analytical concepts, such as terrain classification, is also credited to Sun-tzu; therefore, their utilization by the compilers of the *Ssu-ma Fa* is thought to prove Sun-tzu's historical priority indisputably rather than to raise the possibility that Sun-tzu benefited from other works.

However, even if the likelihood of later accretions and revisions is disregarded, the traditionalist position still ignores the development and existence of more than two thousand years of warfare and tactics prior to 500 B.C. and attributes the virtual creation of military strategy to Sun-tzu alone.[9] The concise, often abstract nature of his passages is cited as evidence that the book was composed at an early stage in the development of Chinese writing, but an equally compelling argument can be advanced that such a philosophically sophisticated style would only be possible from a foundation of extensive battlefield experience and a solid tradition of serious military contemplation.[10] Basic concepts and common passages seem to argue in favor of a comprehensive military tradition and evolving expertise rather than creation *ex nihilo.*

Excluding the now-untenable position of those skeptics who dismissed the book as a late fabrication,[11] three major views seem to prevail regarding the composition date of the *Art of War.* The first identifies it with the historic Sun Wu, with final compilation occurring shortly after his death in the early fifth century B.C.[12] The second, which is based on internal evidence, consigns it to the middle-to-late Warring States period, or the fourth to third centuries B.C.[13] The third, also founded on internal evidence supplemented by recently discovered texts, places it somewhere in the last half of the fifth century B.C.[14] It is unlikely that a final determination can ever be realized, especially because traditionalists tend to be very emotional in their defense of Sun-tzu's authenticity. However, it seems likely that the historical figure existed and that he not only served as a strategist and possibly a general but also composed the core of the book that bears his name. Thereafter, the essential teachings were probably transmitted within the family or a close-knit school of disciples, being improved and revised with the passing decades while gradually gaining wider dissemination. The early text may even have been edited by Sun-tzu's famous descendant Sun Pin, who also extensively employed its teachings in his own *Military Methods*.[15]

The *Shih chi* incorporates the biographies of numerous distinguished military strategists and generals, including Sun-tzu.[16] However, the *Spring and Autumn Annals of Wu and Yüeh* recounts the somewhat more interesting version that follows:

> In the third year of King Ho-lü's reign Wu's generals wanted to attack Ch'u, but no action was taken. Wu Tzu-hsü[17] and Po Hsi spoke with each other: "We nurture officers and make plans on behalf of the king. These strategies will be advantageous to the state, and for this reason the king should attack Ch'u. But he has put off issuing the orders and does not have any intention to mobilize the army. What should we do?"
>
> After a while the King of Wu queried Wu Tzu-hsü and Po Hsi: "I want to send forth the army. What do you think?" Wu Tzu-hsü and Po Hsi replied: "We would like to receive the order." The King of Wu secretly thought the two of them harbored great enmity for Ch'u. He was deeply afraid that they would take the army out, only to be exterminated. He mounted his tower, faced into the southern wind, and groaned. After a while he sighed. None of his ministers understood the king's thoughts. Wu Tzu-hsü secretly realized the king would not decide, so he recommended Sun-tzu to him.
>
> Sun-tzu, whose name was Wu, was a native of Wu.[18] He excelled at military strategy but dwelled in secrecy far away from civilization, so ordinary people did not know of his ability. Wu Tzu-hsü, himself enlightened, wise, and skilled in discrimination, knew Sun-tzu could penetrate and destroy the enemy. One morning when he was discussing military affairs he recommended Sun-tzu seven times. The King of Wu said: "Since you have found an excuse to advance this *shih*, I want to have him brought in." He questioned Su-tzu about military strategy, and each time that he laid out a section of his book the king could not praise him enough.
>
> Greatly pleased he inquired: "If possible, I would like a minor test of your military strategy." Sun-tzu said: "It is possible. We can conduct a minor test with women from the inner palace." The king said: "I agree." Sun-tzu said: "I would like to have two of your Majesty's beloved concubines act as company commanders, each to direct a company." He ordered all three hundred women to wear helmets and armor, to carry swords and shields, and [to] stand. He instructed them in military methods, that in accord with the drum they should advance, withdraw, go left or right, or turn around. He had them know the prohibitions and then ordered: "At the first beating of the drum you should all assem-

ble, at the second drumming you should advance with your weapons, and at the third deploy into military formation." At this the palace women all covered their mouths and laughed.

Sun-tzu then personally took up the sticks and beat the drums, giving the orders three times and explaining them five times. They laughed as before. Sun-tzu saw that the women laughed continuously and would not stop.

Sun-tzu was enraged. His eyes suddenly opened wide, his sound was like a terrifying tiger, his hair stood on end under his cap, and his neck broke the tassels at the side. He said to the Master of Laws: "Get the executioner's axes."

Sun-tzu [then] said: "If the instructions are not clear, if the explanations and orders are not trusted, it is the general's offense. When they have already been instructed three times and the orders explained five times, if the troops still do not perform, it is the fault of the officers. According to the rescripts for military discipline, what is the procedure?" The Master of Laws said: "Decapitation!" Sun-tzu then ordered the beheading of the two company commanders, the king's favorite concubines.[19]

The King of Wu ascended his platform to observe just when they were about to behead his beloved concubines. He had an official hasten down to them with orders to say: "I already know the general is able to command forces. Without these two concubines my food will not be sweet. It would be appropriate not to behead them."

Sun-tzu said: "I have already received my commission as commanding general. According to the rules for generals, when I, as a general, am in command of the army even though you issue orders to me, I do not [have to] accept them." [He then had them beheaded.]

He again beat the drum, and they went left and right, advanced and withdrew, and turned around in accord with the prescribed standards without daring to blink an eye. The two companies were silent, not daring to look around. Thereupon Sun-tzu reported to the King of Wu: "The army is already well-ordered. I would like your Majesty to observe them. However you might want to employ them, even sending them forth into fire and water, will not present any difficulty. They can be used to settle All under Heaven."

The King of Wu was suddenly displeased. He said: "I know that you excel at employing the army. Even though I can thereby become a hegemon, there is no place to exercise them. General, please dismiss the army and return to your dwelling. I am unwilling to act further."

Sun-tzu said: "Your Majesty only likes the words, he is not able to realize their substance." Wu Tzu-hsü remonstrated: "I have heard that the army is an inauspicious affair[20] and cannot be wantonly tested. Thus if one forms an army but does not go forth to launch a punitive attack, then the military Tao will be unclear. Now if your Majesty sincerely seeks talented *shih* and wants to mobilize the army to execute the brutal state of Ch'u, become hegemon of All under Heaven, and overawe the feudal lords, if you do not employ Sun-tzu as your general, who can ford the Huai, cross the Ssu, and traverse a thousand *li* to engage in battle?" Thereupon the King of Wu was elated. He had the drum beaten to convene the army's staff, assembled the troops, and attacked Ch'u. Sun-tzu took Shu, killing the two renegade Wu generals Kai Yu and Chu Yung.[21]

The *Shih chi* biography further states that "to the West he defeated the powerful state of Ch'u and advanced into Ying. To the north he overawed Ch'i and Chin, and his name became manifest among the feudal lords. This was due to Sun-tzu's power among them." Some military historians identify him with several campaigns against Ch'u that followed, commencing in 511 B.C.—the year after his initial interview with King Ho-lü—although he is never mentioned in any recorded source as having sole command of the troops. Presumably, Sun-tzu realized the difficulty of surviving under the evolving, unstable political conditions of his time and set an example for later ages by retiring to obscurity, leaving his work behind.[22]

The *Shih chi* biography differs in another fundamental aspect from the *Spring and Autumn Annals of Wu and Yüeh* because it identifies Sun-tzu as a native of Ch'i rather than of Wu.[23] This would place his background in a state that enjoyed the heritage of the T'ai Kung's thought—one originally on the periphery of the ancient Chou political world, which was known for its diversity of views and imaginative theories. Because the *Art of War* clearly reflects many Taoist conceptions[24] and is philosophically sophisticated, Sun-tzu may well have been a man of Ch'i.

Main Concepts in the *Art of War*

Sun-tzu's *Art of War*, as transmitted through the ages, consists of thirteen chapters of varying length—each ostensibly focused on a specific topic. Although most contemporary Chinese military scholars continue to characterize the entire work as an organic whole, marked by the logical progression and development of themes from start to finish, obvious relationships between supposedly connected passages are frequently difficult to determine or are simply nonexistent. However, the major concepts generally receive frequent, logically consistent treatment throughout, which supports the attribution of the book to a single figure or a well-integrated school of thought.[25]

The military writings unearthed in the Lin-i Han dynasty tomb include a copy of the *Art of War* essentially in its traditional form, together with significant additional material such as the "King of Wu's Questions."[26] The translation that follows has been based on the heavily annotated classical version because that version reflects the understanding and views of the past one thousand years and the beliefs on which government and military officials based their actions in real history. The traditional text has been revised only when the tomb materials resolve otherwise-opaque passages, although the impact of such changes on the overall content remains minimal. Significant variations in characters and sentences are discussed in notes supplementing the translation.

Because the *Art of War* is remarkably lucid, if compressed and sometimes enigmatic, only a brief introduction of the major topics is undertaken here. General Griffith's translation, published by Oxford, remains widely available, and his detailed introduction to Sun-tzu's thought can be consulted by those who wish a more extensive, systematic English presentation.[27] The analytical literature in Chinese and Japanese is too copious to enumerate; selected works are cited in the notes because the commentators may cast light on different concepts or passages.

At the time the *Art of War* was probably composed, warfare had evolved sufficiently to endanger the very existence of virtually every state. Therefore Sun-tzu felt that mobilizing a nation for war and committing its army to battle could only be undertaken with the greatest gravity.[28] His entire approach to employing the army is thoroughly analytical, mandating careful planning and the formulation of an overall strategy before commencing the campaign. The focus of all grand strategy must be the development of a prosperous, contented populace whose willing allegiance to the ruler is unquestioned.[29] Thereafter, diplomatic initiatives can be effected, but military preparations should never be neglected. The primary objective should be to subjugate other states without actually engaging in armed combat, thereby realizing the ideal of complete victory. Whenever possible this should be achieved through diplomatic coercion, thwarting the enemy's plans and alliances, and frustrating its strategy. The government should resort to armed combat only if the enemy threatens the state with military action or refuses to acquiesce without being forced into submission through warfare. Even when exercising this option, every military campaign should focus on achieving maximum results with minimum risk and exposure, limiting as far as possible the destruction that is inflicted and suffered.

Sun-tzu emphasizes rational self-control throughout the *Art of War*, stressing the vital necessity to avoid all engagements not based on extensive, detailed analyses of the situation and combat options and of one's own capabilities.[30] Haste, fear of being labeled a coward, and personal emotions such as anger and hatred should never be permitted to adversely influence state and command decisionmaking.[31] The army should never be thrown rashly into an engagement, thrust into a war, or mobilized unnecessarily. Instead, restraint should be exercised, although measures should be implemented to ensure that the army cannot be defeated. Accordingly, certain tactical situations and configurations of terrain should be avoided and instead be turned to one's advantage when opportune. Thereafter, the focus can be directed toward realizing the predetermined campaign strategy and implementing appropriate tactics to defeat the army.

Sun-tzu's basic strategy focuses on manipulating the enemy, creating the opportunity for an easy victory. To this end he classifies the types of terrain and their exploitation; advances numerous tactics for probing, manipulating, and weakening the enemy; conceptualizes the tactical situation in terms of extensive series of mutually defining elements;[32] and advocates the employment of both orthodox (*cheng*) and unorthodox (*ch'i*) troops to wrest the victory.[33] The enemy is lured into untenable positions with prospects of gain, enervated by being wearied and exhausted before the attack, and penetrated by forces that are suddenly concentrated at vulnerable points. The army should always be active, even when assuming a defensive posture, in order to create and seize the temporary tactical advantage (*ch'üan*) that will ensure victory. Avoiding a strong force is not cowardice but indicates wisdom because it is self-defeating to fight when and where it is not advantageous.[34]

The basic principle is "go forth where they do not expect it; attack where they are not prepared." This principle can only be realized through secrecy in all activities, through complete self-control and strict discipline within the army, and by being unfathomable. Warfare is a matter of deception—of constantly creating false appearances, spreading disinformation, and employing trickery and deceit. When such deception is imaginatively created and effectively implemented, the enemy will neither know where to attack nor what formations to employ and thus will be condemned to making fatal errors.

The corollary to being unknowable is seeking out and gaining detailed knowledge of the enemy through all available means, including the rigorous employment of spies. The fundamental principle is never to rely on the goodwill of others or on fortuitous circumstances but to guarantee through knowledge, active study, and defensive preparation that the enemy cannot mount a surprise attack or gain a victory through simple coercion.

Throughout the book Sun-tzu discusses the essential problem of command: forging a clearly defined organization that is in control of thoroughly disciplined, well-ordered troops. The critical element is spirit, technically known as *ch'i*—the essential, vital energy of life.[35] This is the component associated with will and intention; when the men are well trained, properly fed, clothed, and equipped, and if their spirits are roused, they will fight vigorously. However, if physical or material conditions have blunted their spirit; if an imbalance exists in the relationship between command and troops; if for any reason the troops have lost their motivation, they will be defeated. Conversely, the commanding general must manipulate the situation so as to avoid the enemy when its spirits are strong—such as early in the day—and exploit any opportunity presented by its diminishment, attacking when its troops no longer have any inclination to fight, such as when they are about to return to camp. Prolonged warfare can only lead to enervation; therefore, careful planning is paramount to guarantee the swift execution of the campaign strategy. Certain situations, such as fatal terrain on which a desperate battle must be fought, are conducive to eliciting the army's greatest efforts. Others are debilitating, dangerous, and even fatal and must be scrupulously avoided. Rewards and punishments provide the basis for control, but every effort must be made to foster and maintain the proper attitude of desire and commitment on the part of the men. Accordingly, all detrimental stimuli, such as omens and rumors, must be prohibited.[36]

Finally, Sun-tzu sought to maneuver the army into a position where it enjoyed such a great tactical advantage that the impact of its attack, the impulse of its "strategic configuration of power" [shih,][37] would be like the sudden onrush of water cascading down from mountain peaks. Deploying the troops into a suitable configuration [hsing];[38] creating a favorable "imbalance of power" [ch'üan];[39] concentrating forces on focused targets; exploiting advantages of terrain; and stimulating the men's spirits would all be directed toward this moment, toward this decisive objective.

1. Initial Estimations[1]

Sun-tzu said:

"Warfare is the greatest affair of state, the basis of life and death, the Way [Tao] to survival or extinction. It must be thoroughly pondered and analyzed.

ʳ ʳ ʳ

"Therefore, structure it according to [the following] five factors, evaluate it comparatively through estimations, and seek out its true nature.[2] The first is termed the Tao, the second Heaven, the third Earth, the fourth generals, and the fifth the laws [for military organization and discipline].

"The Tao[3] causes the people to be fully in accord with the ruler.[4] [Thus] they will die with him; they will live with him and not fear danger.[5]

"Heaven encompasses yin and yang, cold and heat, and the constraints of the seasons.[6]

"Earth encompasses far or near, difficult or easy, expansive or confined, fatal or tenable terrain.[7]

"The general encompasses wisdom, credibility, benevolence, courage, and strictness.

"The laws [for military organization and discipline] encompass organization and regulations, the Tao of command, and the management of logistics.[8]

"There are no generals who have not heard of these five. Those who understand them will be victorious; those who do not understand them will not be victorious.

ʳ ʳ ʳ

"Thus when making a comparative evaluation through estimations, seeking out its true nature, ask:

Which ruler has the Tao?
Which general has greater ability?
Who has gained [the advantages of] Heaven and Earth?

Whose laws and orders are more thoroughly implemented?
Whose forces[9] are stronger?
Whose officers and troops are better trained?
Whose rewards and punishments are clearer?

"From these I will know victory and defeat!

꜖   ꜖   ꜖

"If a general follows my [methods for] estimation and you employ him, he will certainly be victorious and should be retained. If a general does not follow my [methods for] estimation and you employ him, he will certainly be defeated, so dismiss him.[10]

꜖   ꜖   ꜖

"After estimating the advantages in accord with what you have heard, put it into effect with strategic power [shih][11] supplemented by field tactics which respond to external factors.[12] As for strategic power, [it is] controlling the tactical imbalance of power [ch'üan] in accord with the gains to be realized.[13]

꜖   ꜖   ꜖

"Warfare is the Way [Tao] of deception.[14] Thus although [you are] capable, display incapability to them. When committed to employing your forces, feign inactivity. When [your objective] is nearby, make it appear as if distant; when far away, create the illusion of being nearby.[15]

꜖   ꜖   ꜖

"Display profits to entice them. Create disorder [in their forces] and take them.[16]
"If they are substantial,[17] prepare for them; if they are strong, avoid them.
"If they are angry, perturb them;[18] be deferential to foster their arrogance.[19]
"If they are rested, force them to exert themselves.
"If they are united, cause them to be separated.
"Attack where they are unprepared.
"Go forth where they will not expect it.
"These are the ways military strategists are victorious. They cannot be spoken of in advance.[20]

꜖   ꜖   ꜖

"Before the engagement, one who determines in the ancestral temple that he will be victorious has found that the majority of factors are in his favor. Before the engagement one who determines in the ancestral temple that he will not be victorious has found few factors are in his favor.

"If one who finds that the majority of factors favor him will be victorious while one who has found few factors favor him will be defeated, what about someone who finds no factors in his favor?[21]

"If I observe it from this perspective, victory and defeat will be apparent."

2. Waging War

Sun-tzu said:

"In general, the strategy for employing the military [is this]:[22] If there are one thousand four-horse attack chariots, one thousand leather-armored support chariots, one hundred thousand mailed troops, and provisions are transported one thousand *li,* then the domestic and external campaign expenses, the expenditures for advisers and guests, materials such as glue and lacquer, and providing chariots and armor will be one thousand pieces of gold per day. Only then can an army of one hundred thousand be mobilized.

* * *

"When employing them in battle, a victory that is long in coming will blunt their weapons and dampen their ardor.[23] If you attack cities, their strength will be exhausted.[24] If you expose the army to a prolonged campaign, the state's resources will be inadequate.

"When the weapons have grown dull and spirits depressed, when our strength has been expended and resources consumed, then the feudal lords will take advantage of our exhaustion to arise. Even though you have wise generals, they will not be able to achieve a good result.

"Thus in military campaigns I have heard of awkward speed but have never seen any skill in lengthy campaigns. No country has ever profited from protracted warfare. Those who do not thoroughly comprehend the dangers inherent in employing the army are incapable of truly knowing the potential advantages of military actions.

* * *

"One who excels in employing the military does not conscript the people twice or transport provisions a third time.[25] If you obtain your equipment from within the state and rely on seizing provisions from the enemy, then the army's foodstuffs will be sufficient.

"The state is impoverished by the army when it transports provisions far off. When provisions are transported far off, the hundred surnames[26] are impoverished.

"Those in proximity to the army will sell their goods expensively.[27] When goods are expensive, the hundred surname's wealth will be exhausted. When their wealth is exhausted, they will be extremely hard pressed [to supply] their village's military impositions.[28]

"When their strength has been expended and their wealth depleted, then the houses in the central plains will be empty.[29] The expenses of the hundred surnames will be some seven-tenths[30] of whatever they have. The ruler's irrecoverable expenditures—such as ruined chariots, exhausted horses, armor, helmets, arrows and crossbows, halberd-tipped and spear-tipped [large, movable] protective shields, strong oxen,[31] and large wagons—will consume six-tenths of his resources.

"Thus the wise general will concentrate on securing provisions from the enemy. One bushel of the enemy's foodstuffs is worth twenty of ours; one picul of fodder is worth twenty of ours.

ɼ   ɼ   ɼ

"Thus what [motivates men] to slay the enemy is anger; what [stimulates them] to seize profits[32] from the enemy is material goods. Thus in chariot encounters, when ten or more chariots are captured, reward the first to get one. Change their flags and pennants to ours; intermix and employ them with our own chariots. Treat the captured soldiers well in order to nurture them [for our use]. This is referred to as 'conquering the enemy and growing stronger.'

ɼ   ɼ   ɼ

"Thus the army values being victorious; it does not value prolonged warfare. Therefore, a general who understands warfare is Master of Fate for the people, ruler of the state's security or endangerment."

3. Planning Offensives

Sun-tzu said:

"In general, the method for employing the military is this: Preserving the [enemy's] state capital is best, destroying their state capital second-best.[33]

Preserving their army is best, destroying their army second-best.[34] Preserving their battalions is best, destroying their battalions second-best. Preserving their companies is best, destroying their companies second-best. Preserving their squads is best, destroying their squads second-best. For this reason attaining one hundred victories in one hundred battles is not the pinnacle of excellence. Subjugating the enemy's army without fighting is the true pinnacle of excellence.

⸙ ⸙ ⸙

"Thus the highest realization of warfare is to attack the enemy's plans; next is to attack their alliances; next to attack their army; and the lowest is to attack their fortified cities.

"This tactic of attacking fortified cities is adopted only when unavoidable. Preparing large movable protective shields, armored assault wagons, and other equipment and devices will require three months. Building earthworks[35] will require another three months to complete. If the general cannot overcome his impatience but instead launches an assault wherein his men swarm over the walls like ants, he will kill one-third of his officers and troops, and the city will still not be taken. This is the disaster that results from attacking [fortified cities].

"Thus one who excels at employing the military subjugates other people's armies without engaging in battle, captures other people's fortified cities without attacking them, and destroys others people's states without prolonged fighting. He must fight under Heaven with the paramount aim of 'preservation.'[36] Thus his weapons will not become dull, and the gains can be preserved. This is the strategy for planning offensives.

⸙ ⸙ ⸙

"In general, the strategy for employing the military is this: If your strength is ten times theirs, surround them; if five, then attack them; if double, then divide your forces.[37] If you are equal in strength to the enemy, you can engage him. If fewer, you can circumvent him. If outmatched, you can avoid him. Thus a small enemy that acts inflexibly[38] will become the captives of a large enemy.

⸙ ⸙ ⸙

"The general is the supporting pillar of state. If his talents are all-encompassing, the state will invariably be strong. If the supporting pillar is marked by fissures, the state will invariably grow weak.

⸲ ⸲ ⸲

"Thus there are three ways by which an army is put into difficulty by a ruler:

"He does not know that the Three Armies should not advance but instructs them to advance or does not know that the Three Armies should not withdraw and orders a retreat. This is termed 'entangling the army.'

"He does not understand the Three Armies' military affairs but [directs them] in the same way as his [civil] administration.[39] Then the officers will become confused.

"He does not understand the Three Armies' tactical balance of power [*ch'üan*] but undertakes responsibility for command. Then the officers will be doubtful.

"When the Three Armies are already confused and doubtful, the danger of the feudal lords [taking advantage of the situation] arises. This is referred to as 'a disordered army drawing another on to victory.'

⸲ ⸲ ⸲

"Thus there are five factors from which victory can be known:

"One who knows when he can fight, and when he cannot fight, will be victorious.

"One who recognizes[40] how to employ large and small numbers will be victorious.

"One whose upper and lower ranks have the same desires will be victorious.

"One who, fully prepared, awaits the unprepared will be victorious.

"One whose general is capable and not interfered with by the ruler will be victorious.

"These five are the Way [Tao] to know victory.

⸲ ⸲ ⸲

"Thus it is said that one who knows the enemy and knows himself[41] will not be endangered in a hundred engagements. One who does not know the enemy but knows himself will sometimes be victorious, sometimes meet with defeat. One who knows neither the enemy nor himself will invariably be defeated in every engagement."

4. Military Disposition[42]

Sun-tzu said:

"In antiquity those that excelled in warfare first made themselves unconquerable[43] in order to await [the moment when] the enemy could be conquered.

"Being unconquerable lies with yourself; being conquerable lies with the enemy.

"Thus one who excels in warfare[44] is able to make himself unconquerable, but cannot necessarily cause the enemy to be conquerable.

"Thus it is said a strategy for conquering the enemy can be known but yet not possible to implement.

*   *   *

"One who cannot be victorious assumes a defensive posture; one who can be victorious attacks. In these circumstances by assuming a defensive posture, strength will be more than adequate, whereas in offensive actions it would be inadequate.[45]

*   *   *

"Those who excel at defense bury themselves away below the lowest depths of Earth. Those who excel at offense[46] move from above the greatest heights of Heaven. Thus they are able to preserve themselves and attain complete victory.

"Perceiving a victory that does not surpass what the masses could know is not the pinnacle of excellence. Wrestling victories for which All under Heaven proclaim your excellence is not the pinnacle of excellence.

"Thus lifting an autumn hair cannot be considered great strength; seeing the sun and moon cannot be considered acute vision; hearing the sound of thunder cannot be considered having sensitive ears.

"Those that the ancients[47] referred to as excelling at warfare conquered those who were easy to conquer. Thus the victories of those that excelled in warfare were not marked by fame for wisdom or courageous achievement.[48] Thus their victories were free from errors. One who is free from errors directs his measures toward [certain] victory, conquering those who are already defeated.

*   *   *

"Thus one who excels at warfare first establishes himself in a position where he cannot be defeated while not losing [any opportunity] to defeat the enemy.

"For this reason, the victorious army first realizes the conditions for victory, and then seeks to engage in battle. The vanquished army fights first, and then seeks victory.

ʳ   ʳ   ʳ

"One[49] who excels at employing the military cultivates the Tao[50] and preserves the laws; therefore, he is able to be the regulator of victory and defeat.[51]

ʳ   ʳ   ʳ

"As for military methods[52]: the first is termed measurement; the second, estimation [of forces]; the third, calculation [of numbers of men]; the fourth, weighing [relative strength]; and the fifth, victory.

"Terrain gives birth to measurement;[53] measurement produces the estimation [of forces].[54] Estimation [of forces] gives rise to calculating [the numbers of men]. Calculating [the numbers of men] gives rise to weighing [strength]. Weighing [strength] gives birth to victory.

ʳ   ʳ   ʳ

"Thus the victorious army is like a ton compared with an ounce, while the defeated army is like an ounce weighed against a ton! The combat of the victorious[55] is like the sudden release of a pent-up torrent down a thousand-fathom gorge. This is the strategic disposition of force [hsing]."[56]

5. Strategic Military Power[57]

Sun-tzu said:

"In general, commanding a large number is like commanding a few. It is a question of dividing up the numbers. Fighting with a large number is like fighting with a few. It is a question of configuration and designation.[58]

ʳ   ʳ   ʳ

"What enable the masses of the Three Armies to invariably withstand the enemy without being defeated are the unorthodox [ch'i] and orthodox [cheng].[59]

"If wherever the army attacks it is like a whetstone thrown against an egg, it is due to the vacuous and substantial.[60]

✓   ✓   ✓

"In general, in battle one engages with the orthodox and gains victory through the unorthodox. Thus one who excels at sending forth the unorthodox is as inexhaustible as Heaven,[61] as unlimited as the Yangtze and Yellow rivers.[62] What reach an end and begin again are the sun and moon. What die and are reborn[63] are the four seasons.

"The notes do not exceed five, but the changes[64] of the five notes can never be fully heard. The colors do not exceed five, but the changes of the five colors can never be completely seen. The flavors do not exceed five, but the changes of the five flavors can never be completely tasted. In warfare the strategic configurations of power [shih] do not exceed the unorthodox and orthodox, but the changes of the unorthodox and orthodox can never be completely exhausted. The unorthodox and orthodox mutually produce each other, just like an endless cycle.[65] Who can exhaust them?

✓   ✓   ✓

"The strategic configuration of power [shih] [is visible in] the onrush of pent-up[66] water tumbling stones along. The [effect of] constraints[67] [is visible in] the onrush[68] of a bird of prey breaking the bones of its [target]. Thus the strategic configuration of power [shih] of those that excel in warfare is sharply focused, their constraints are precise.[69] Their strategic configuration of power [shih] is like a fully drawn crossbow, their constraints like the release of the trigger.

✓   ✓   ✓

"Intermixed and turbulent, the fighting appears chaotic, but they cannot be made disordered. In turmoil and confusion, their deployment is circular,[70] and they cannot be defeated.

✓   ✓   ✓

"[Simulated] chaos is given birth from control;[71] [the illusion of] fear is given birth from courage; [feigned] weakness is given birth from strength. Order and disorder are a question of numbers; courage and fear are a question of the strategic configuration of power [shih]; strength and weakness are a question of the deployment [of forces (hsing)].

"Thus one who excels at moving the enemy deploys in a configuration [hsing] to which the enemy must respond. He offers something which the enemy must seize. With profit he moves them, with the foundation[72] he awaits them.

ʳ   ʳ   ʳ

"Thus one who excels at warfare seeks [victory] through the strategic configuration of power [*shih*], not from reliance on men. Thus he is able to select
men and employ strategic power [*shih*].[73]

ʳ   ʳ   ʳ

"One who employs strategic power [*shih*] commands men in battle as if he
were rolling logs and stones. The nature of wood and stone is to be quiet
when stable but to move when on precipitous ground. If they are square they
stop, if round they tend to move. Thus the strategic power [*shih*] of one who
excels at employing men in warfare is comparable to rolling round boulders
down a thousand-fathom mountain. Such is the strategic configuration of
power [*shih*]."

6. Vacuity and Substance[74]

Sun-tzu said:

"In general, whoever occupies the battleground first and awaits the enemy
will be at ease; whoever occupies the battleground afterward and must race
to the conflict will be fatigued. Thus one who excels at warfare compels men
and is not compelled by other men.[75]

ʳ   ʳ   ʳ

"In order to cause the enemy to come of their own volition, extend some
[apparent] profit. In order to prevent the enemy from coming forth, show
them [the potential] harm.

ʳ   ʳ   ʳ

"Thus if the enemy is rested you can tire him; if he is well fed you can make
him hungry; if he is at rest you can move him. Go forth to positions to which
he must race.[76] Race forth where he does not expect it.[77]

ʳ   ʳ   ʳ

"To travel a thousand *li* without becoming fatigued, traverse unoccupied
terrain. To ensure taking the objective in an attack, strike positions that are
undefended. To be certain of an impregnable defense, secure positions which
the enemy will not attack.[78]
"Thus when someone excels in attacking, the enemy does not know where
to mount his defense; when someone excels at defense, the enemy does not

know where to attack. Subtle! Subtle! It approaches the formless.[79] Spiritual! Spiritual! It attains the soundless. Thus he can be the enemy's Master of Fate.

✧ ✧ ✧

"To effect an unhampered[80] advance, strike their vacuities. To effect a retreat that cannot be overtaken, employ unmatchable speed.[81] Thus if I want to engage in combat, even though the enemy has high ramparts and deep moats, he cannot avoid doing battle because I attack objectives he must rescue.

"If I do not want to engage in combat, even though I merely draw a line on the ground and defend it, he will not be able to engage me in battle because we thwart his movements.

✧ ✧ ✧

"Thus if I determine the enemy's disposition of forces [hsing] while I have no perceptible form,[82] I can concentrate [my forces] while the enemy is fragmented. If we are concentrated into a single force while he is fragmented into ten, then we attack him with ten times his strength. Thus we are many and the enemy is few. If we can attack his few with our many, those who we engage in battle will be severely constrained.

✧ ✧ ✧

"The location where we will engage the enemy must not become known to them. If it is not known, then the positions which they must prepare to defend will be numerous. If the positions the enemy prepares to defend are numerous, then the forces we will engage will be few. Thus if they prepare to defend the front, to the rear there will be few men. If they defend the rear, in the front there will be few. If they prepare to defend the left flank, then on the right there will be few men. If they prepare to defend the right flank, then on the left there will be few men. If there is no position left undefended, then there will not be any place with more than a few. The few [are the ones] who prepare against others; the many [are the ones] who make others prepare against them.[83]

✧ ✧ ✧

"Thus if one knows the field of battle and knows the day of battle, he can traverse a thousand li and assemble to engage in combat.[84] If he does not know the field of battle nor know the day for battle, then the left flank cannot aid the right nor the right flank aid the left; the front cannot aid the rear nor the rear aid the front.[85] How much more so when the distant are some tens of *li* away and the near several *li* apart? As I analyze it, even though Yüeh's army is numerous, of what great advantage is it to them for attaining victory?[86] Thus I say victory can be achieved.[87] Even though the enemy is more numerous, they can be forced not to fight.

*   *   *

"Thus critically analyze them to know the estimations for gain and loss. Stimulate them to know the patterns of their movement and stopping. Determine their disposition of force [*hsing*] to know the tenable and fatal terrain. Probe them to know where they have an excess, where an insufficiency.

"Thus the pinnacle of military deployment approaches the formless. If it is formless, then even the deepest spy cannot discern it or the wise make plans against it.

*   *   *

"In accord with the enemy's disposition [*hsing*] we impose measures on the masses that produce victory, but the masses are unable to fathom them. Men all know the disposition [*hsing*] by which we attain victory, but no one knows the configuration [*hsing*] through which we control the victory. Thus a victorious battle [strategy] is not repeated, the configurations [*hsing*] of response [to the enemy] are inexhaustible.[88]

*   *   *

"Now the army's disposition of force [*hsing*] is like water. Water's configuration [*hsing*][89] avoids heights and races downward. The army's disposition of force [*hsing*][90] avoids the substantial and strikes the vacuous. Water configures [*hsing*] its flow[91] in accord with the terrain; the army controls its victory in accord with the enemy. Thus the army does not maintain any constant[92] strategic configuration of power [*shih*]; water[93] has no constant shape [*hsing*]. One who is able to change and transform in accord with the enemy and wrest victory is termed spiritual![94] Thus [none of] the five phases constantly dominates; the four seasons do not have constant positions; the sun shines for longer and shorter periods; and the moon wanes and waxes."[95]

7. Military Combat[96]

Sun-tzu said:

"In general, the strategy for employing the army is this: [From the time] the general receives his commands from the ruler, unites the armies, and assembles the masses, to confronting the enemy and encamping, there is nothing more difficult than military combat. In military combat what is most difficult is turning the circuitous into the straight, turning adversity into advantage.

"Thus if you make the enemy's path circuitous and entice them with profit, although you set out after them you will arrive before them. This results from knowing the tactics[97] of the circuitous and the direct.

Ɡ   Ɡ   Ɡ

"Thus combat between armies is advantageous; combat between masses is dangerous.[98] If the entire army contends for advantage, you will not arrive in time. If you reduce the army's size to contend for advantage, your baggage and heavy equipment will suffer losses.

"For this reason if you abandon your armor [and heavy equipment][99] to race forward day and night without encamping, covering two days normal distance at a time, marching forward a hundred *li* to contend for gain, the Three Armies' generals will be captured. The strong will be first to arrive, while the exhausted will follow. With such tactics only one in ten will reach [the battle site]. If one contends for gain fifty *li* away, it will cause the general of the Upper Army to stumble, and by following such tactics half the men will reach [the objective]. If you contend for gain at thirty *li*, then two-thirds of the army will reach [the objective].

"Accordingly, if the army does not have baggage and heavy equipment it will be lost; if it does not have provisions it will be lost; if it does not have stores it will be lost.

Ɡ   Ɡ   Ɡ

Thus one who does not know the plans of the feudal lords cannot prepare alliances beforehand. Someone unfamiliar with the mountains and forests, gorges and defiles, the shape of marshes and wetlands cannot advance the army. One who does not employ local guides cannot gain advantages of terrain.

Ɡ   Ɡ   Ɡ

"Thus the army is established by deceit, moves for advantage, and changes through segmenting and reuniting. Thus its speed is like the wind, its slowness like the forest; its invasion and plundering like a fire;[100] unmoving, it is like the mountains. It is as difficult to know as the darkness; in movement it is like thunder.

Ɡ   Ɡ   Ɡ

"When you plunder a district, divide the wealth among your troops. When you enlarge your territory, divide the profits. Take control of the strategic balance of power [*ch'üan*] and move. The one who first understands the tactics of the circuitous and the direct will be victorious. This is the strategy for military combat.

                                    ,   ,   ,

"The *Military Administration* states: 'Because they could not hear each other they made gongs and drums; because they could not see each other they made pennants and flags.' Gongs, drums, pennants, and flags are the means to unify the men's ears and eyes. When the men have been unified the courageous will not be able to advance alone, the fearful will not be able to retreat alone. This is the method for employing large numbers.

"Thus in night battles make the fires and drums numerous, and in daylight battles make the flags and pennants numerous in order to change the men's ears and eyes.[101]

                                    ,   ,   ,

"The *ch'i* of the Three Armies can be snatched away; the commanding general's mind can be seized. For this reason in the morning their *ch'i* is ardent; during the day their *ch'i* becomes indolent; at dusk their *ch'i* is exhausted.[102] Thus one who excels at employing the army avoids their ardent *ch'i* and strikes when it is indolent or exhausted. This is the way to manipulate *ch'i*.

                                    ,   ,   ,

"In order await the disordered; in tranquility await the clamorous. This is the way to control the mind.

                                    ,   ,   ,

"With the near await the distant; with the rested await the fatigued; with the sated await the hungry. This is the way to control strength.

                                    ,   ,   ,

"Do not intercept well-ordered flags; do not attack well-regulated formations.[103] This is the way to control changes.

                                    ,   ,   ,

"Thus the strategy for employing the military: Do not approach high mountains; do not confront[104] those who have hills behind them. Do not pursue feigned retreats. Do not attack animated troops. Do not swallow an army acting as bait. Do not obstruct an army retreating homeward. If you besiege an army you must leave an outlet.[105] Do not press an exhausted invader. These are the strategies for employing the military."[106]

8. Nine Changes[107]

Sun-tzu said:

"In general, the strategy for employing the military is this. After the general has received his commands from the ruler, united the armies, and assembled the masses:[108]

"Do not encamp on entrapping terrain.[109]

"Unite with your allies on focal terrain.[110]

"Do not remain on isolated terrain.

"Make strategic plans for encircled terrain.

"On fatal terrain you must do battle.[111]

"There are roads that are not[112] followed.

"There are armies that are not attacked.

"There are fortified cities that are not assaulted.

"There is terrain for which one does not contend.[113]

"There are commands from the ruler which are not accepted.[114]

"Thus the general who has a penetrating understanding of the advantages of the nine changes knows how to employ the army. If a general does not have a penetrating understanding of the advantages of the nine changes, even though he is familiar with the topography, he will not be able to realize the advantages of terrain.

"One who commands an army but does not know the techniques for the nine changes, even though he is familiar with the five advantages,[115] will not be able to control men.

＇　＇　＇

"For this reason the wise must contemplate the intermixture of gain and loss. If they discern advantage [in difficult situations], their efforts can be trusted. If they discern harm [in prospective advantage], difficulties can be resolved.

＇　＇　＇

"Accordingly, subjugate the feudal lords with potential harm; labor the feudal lords with numerous affairs; and have the feudal lords race after profits.

✔   ✔   ✔

"Thus the strategy for employing the army: Do not rely on their not coming, but depend on us having the means to await them. Do not rely on their not attacking, but depend on us having an unassailable position.

✔   ✔   ✔

"Thus generals have five dangerous [character traits]:

"One committed to dying can be slain.

"One committed to living can be captured.

"One [easily] angered and hasty [to act] can be insulted.

"One obsessed with being scrupulous and untainted can be shamed.

"One who loves the people can be troubled.

"Now these five dangerous traits are excesses in a general, potential disaster for employing the army. The army's destruction and the general's death will invariably stem from these five, so they must be investigated."

9. Maneuvering the Army

Sun-tzu said:

"As for deploying the army and fathoming the enemy:

"To cross mountains follow the valleys, search out tenable ground,[116] and occupy the heights. If the enemy holds the heights, do not climb up to engage them in battle. This is the way to deploy an army in the mountains.

"After crossing rivers[117] you must distance yourself from them. If the enemy is forging a river to advance, do not confront them in the water. When half their forces have crossed, it will be advantageous to strike them. If you want to engage the enemy in battle, do not array your forces near the river to confront the invader but look for tenable ground and occupy the heights. Do not confront the current's flow.[118] This is the way to deploy the army where there are rivers.

"When you cross salt marshes and wetlands, concentrate on quickly getting away from them; do not remain. If you engage in battle in marshes or wetlands, you must stay in areas with marsh grass and keep groves of trees at your back. This is the way to deploy the army in marshes and wetlands.

"On level plains deploy on easy[119] terrain with the right flank positioned with high ground to the rear, fatal terrain to the fore, and tenable terrain to the rear. This is the way to deploy on the plains.

"These four [deployments], advantageous to the army, are the means by which the Yellow Emperor conquered the four emperors.[120]

$\qquad$ *   *   *

"Now the army likes heights and abhors low areas, esteems the sunny [yang] and disdains the shady [yin]. It nourishes life and occupies the substantial.[121] An army that avoids the hundred illnesses is said to be certain of victory.[122]

$\qquad$ *   *   *

"Where there are hills and embankments you must occupy the yang side, keeping them to the right rear. This is to the army's advantage and [exploits the natural] assistance of the terrain.

$\qquad$ *   *   *

"When it rains upstream, foam appears.[123] If you want to cross over, wait until it settles.

$\qquad$ *   *   *

"You must quickly get away from deadly configurations of terrain such as precipitous gorges with mountain torrents, Heaven's Well,[124] Heaven's Jail,[125] Heaven's Net,[126] Heaven's Pit,[127] and Heaven's Fissure.[128] Do not approach them. When we keep them at a distance, the enemy [is forced to] approach them. When we face them, the enemy [is compelled to] have them at their rear.

$\qquad$ *   *   *

"When on the flanks the army encounters ravines and defiles, wetlands with reeds and tall grass, mountain forests,[129] or areas with heavy, entangled undergrowth, you must thoroughly search them because they are places where an ambush or spies would be concealed.[130]

$\qquad$ *   *   *

"If [an enemy] in close proximity remains quiet, they are relying on their tactical occupation of ravines.[131] If while far off they challenge you to battle, they want you to advance [because] they occupy easy terrain to their advantage.

ˏ   ˏ   ˏ

"If large numbers of trees move, they are approaching. If there are many [visible] obstacles in the heavy grass, it is to make us suspicious.[132] If the birds take flight, there is an ambush. If the animals are afraid, [enemy] forces are mounting a sudden attack.

ˏ   ˏ   ˏ

"If dust rises high up in a sharply defined column, chariots are coming. If it is low and broad, the infantry is advancing. If it is dispersed in thin shafts, they are gathering firewood. If it is sparse, coming and going, they are encamping.

"One who speaks deferentially but increases his preparations will advance. One who speaks belligerently and advances hastily will retreat.

"One whose light chariots first fan out to the sides is deploying [for battle].[133]

"One who seeks peace without setting any prior conditions is [executing] a stratagem.

"One whose troops race off but [who] deploys his army into formation is implementing a predetermined schedule.

"One [whose troops] half advance and half retreat is enticing you.

ˏ   ˏ   ˏ

"Those who stand about leaning on their weapons are hungry. If those who draw water drink first, they are thirsty. When they see potential gain but do not know whether to advance, they are tired.

ˏ   ˏ   ˏ

"Where birds congregate it is empty. If the enemy cries out at night, they are afraid. If the army is turbulent,[134] the general lacks severity. If their flags and pennants move about, they are in chaos. If the officers are angry, they are exhausted.

ˏ   ˏ   ˏ

"If they kill their horses and eat the meat, the army lacks grain.[135] If they hang up their cooking utensils and do not return to camp, they are an exhausted invader.[136]

ˏ   ˏ   ˏ

"One whose troops repeatedly congregate in small groups here and there, whispering together, has lost the masses. One who frequently grants rewards is in deep distress. One who frequently imposes punishments is in great difficulty. One who is at first excessively brutal and then fears the masses is the pinnacle of stupidity.[137]

r   r   r

"One who has emissaries come forth with offerings wants to rest for a while.

r   r   r

"If their troops are aroused and approach our forces, only to maintain their positions without engaging in battle or breaking off the confrontation, you must carefully investigate it.

r   r   r

"The army does not esteem the number of troops being more numerous for it only means one cannot aggressively advance.[138] It is sufficient for you to muster your own strength, analyze the enemy, and take them. Only someone who lacks strategic planning and slights an enemy will inevitably be captured by others.

r   r   r

"If you impose punishments on the troops before they have become attached, they will not be submissive. If they are not submissive, they will be difficult to employ. If you do not impose punishments after the troops have become attached, they cannot be used.

r   r   r

"Thus if you command them with the civil[139] and unify them through the martial, this is what is referred to as 'being certain to take them.'[140]

r   r   r

"If orders are consistently implemented to instruct the people, then the people will submit. If orders are not consistently implemented to instruct the people, then the people will not submit. One whose orders are consistently carried out has established a mutual relationship with the people."

10. Configurations of Terrain[141]

Sun-tzu said:

"The major configurations [*hsing*] of terrain are accessible, suspended, stalemated, constricted, precipitous, and expansive.

"If we can go forth and the enemy can also advance, it is termed 'accessible.' In an accessible configuration, first occupy the heights and yang [side], and improve the routes for transporting provisions. Then when we engage in battle, it will be advantageous.

"If we can go forth but it will be difficult to return, it is termed 'suspended.'[142] In a suspended configuration, if they are unprepared go forth and conquer them. If the enemy is prepared and we sally forth without being victorious, it will be difficult to turn back and [is] not advantageous.

"If it is not advantageous for us to go forth nor advantageous for the enemy to come forward, it is termed 'stalemated.'[143] In a stalemated configuration, even though the enemy tries to entice us with profit, we do not go forth. Withdraw [our forces] and depart.[144] If we strike them when half the enemy has come forth, it will be advantageous.

"As for constricted configurations, if we occupy them first we must fully deploy throughout them in order to await the enemy.[145] If the enemy occupies them first and fully deploys in them, do not follow them in. If they do not fully deploy in them, then follow them in.

"As for precipitous configurations,[146] if we occupy them we must hold the heights and yang sides to await the enemy. If the enemy occupies them first, withdraw [our forces] and depart. Do not follow them.

"As for expansive configurations, if our strategic power [shih] is equal,[147] it will be difficult to provoke [them to] combat. Engaging in combat will not be advantageous.

"Now these six are the Tao of terrain. Any general who undertakes responsibility for command cannot but investigate them.

"Thus there are [six types of ill-fated] armies: running, lax, sinking, crumbling, chaotic, and routed. Now these six are not disasters brought about by Heaven and Earth but by the general's errors.

"Now if, when their strategic power [shih] is equal, one attacks ten, this is called 'running [off].'[148]

"If the troops are strong but the officers are weak, it is termed 'lax.'

"If the officers are strong but the troops weak, it is termed 'sinking.'

"If the higher officers are angry and insubordinate, engaging the enemy themselves out of unrestrained anger while the general does not yet know their capability, it is termed 'crumbling.'

"If the general is weak and not strict, unenlightened in his instructions and leadership; the officers and troops lack constant [duties]; and their deployment of troops into formation is askew, it is termed 'chaotic.'

"If the general, unable to fathom the enemy, engages a large number with a small number, attacks the strong with the weak while the army lacks a properly selected vanguard, it is termed 'routed.'

"Now these six are the Tao of defeat. Any general who undertakes responsibility for command cannot but investigate them.

*   *   *

"Configuration of terrain is an aid to the army. Analyzing the enemy, taking control of victory, estimating ravines and defiles, the distant and near, is the Tao of the superior general.[149] One who knows these and employs them in combat will certainly be victorious. One who does not know these nor employ them in combat will certainly be defeated.

*   *   *

"If the Tao of Warfare [indicates] certain victory, even though the ruler has instructed that combat should be avoided, if you must engage in battle it is permissible. If the Tao of Warfare indicates you will not be victorious, even though the ruler instructs you to engage in battle, not fighting is permissible.

"Thus [a general] who does not advance to seek fame, nor [fail to retreat] to avoid [being charged with the capital] offense of retreating, but seeks only to preserve the people and gain advantage for the ruler is the state's treasure.

*   *   *

"When the general regards his troops as young children, they will advance into the deepest valleys with him. When he regards the troops as his beloved children, they will be willing to die with him.[150]

"If they are well treated but cannot be employed, if they are loved but cannot be commanded, or when in chaos they cannot be governed, they may be compared to arrogant children and cannot be used.

*   *   *

"If I know our troops can attack, but do not know the enemy cannot be attacked, it is only halfway to victory. If I know the enemy can be attacked, but do not realize our troops cannot attack, it is only halfway to victory.

"Knowing that the enemy can be attacked, and knowing that our army can effect the attack, but not knowing the terrain is not suitable for combat, is only halfway to victory. Thus one who truly knows the army will never be deluded when he moves, never be impoverished when initiating an action.

"Thus it is said if you know them and know yourself, your victory will not be imperiled. If you know Heaven and know Earth, your victory can be complete."[151]

11. Nine Terrains

Sun-tzu said:

"The strategy for employing the military is [this]: There is dispersive terrain, light terrain, contentious terrain, traversable terrain, focal terrain, heavy terrain, entrapping terrain, encircled terrain, and fatal terrain.[152]

"When the feudal lords fight in their own territory, it is 'dispersive terrain.'[153]

"When they enter someone else's territory, but not deeply, it is 'light terrain.'[154]

"If when we occupy it, it will be advantageous to us while if they occupy it, it will be advantageous to them, it is 'contentious terrain.'[155]

"When we can go and they can also come, it is 'traversable terrain.'[156]

"Land of the feudal lords surrounded on three sides such that whoever arrives first will gain the masses of All under Heaven is 'focal terrain.'[157]

"When one penetrates deeply into enemy territory, bypassing numerous cities, it is 'heavy terrain.'[158]

"Where there are mountains and forests, ravines and defiles, wetlands and marshes, wherever the road is difficult to negotiate, it is 'entrapping terrain.'[159]

"Where the entrance is constricted,[160] the return is circuitous, and with a small number they can strike our masses, it is 'encircled terrain.'[161]

"Where if one fights with intensity he will survive but if he does not fight with intensity he will perish, it is 'fatal terrain.'[162]

﹐   ﹐   ﹐

"For this reason on dispersive terrain do not engage the enemy.
"On light terrain do not stop.
"On contentious terrain do not attack.[163]
"On traversable terrain do not allow your forces to become isolated.
"On focal terrain unite and form alliances [with nearby feudal lords.][164]
"On heavy terrain plunder for provisions.
"On entrapping terrain move [through quickly].[165]
"On encircled terrain use strategy.[166]
"On fatal terrain engage in battle.

﹐   ﹐   ﹐

"In antiquity those who were referred to as excelling in the employment of the army were able to keep the enemy's forward and rear forces from connecting; the many and few from relying on each other; the noble and lowly from coming to each other's rescue; the upper and lower ranks from trusting each other; the troops to be separated, unable to reassemble, or when assembled, not to be well-ordered.[167] They moved when it was advantageous, halted when it was not advantageous.

*   *   *

"If I dare ask, if the enemy is numerous, disciplined, and about to advance, how should we respond to them? I would say, first seize something that they love for then they will listen to you.

*   *   *

"It is the nature of the army to stress speed; to take advantage of the enemy's absence; to travel unanticipated roads; and to attack when they are not alert.

*   *   *

"In general, the Tao of an invader is that when one has penetrated deeply [into enemy territory], the army will be unified, and the defenders will not be able to conquer you.

*   *   *

"If one forages in the fertile countryside, then the Three Armies will have enough to eat. If you carefully nurture them and do not [over-]labor them, their *ch'i* will be united and their strength will be at maximum.

*   *   *

"When you mobilize the army and form strategic plans, you must be unfathomable.

*   *   *

"Cast them into positions from which there is nowhere to go and they will die without retreating. If there is no escape from death, the officers and soldiers will fully exhaust their strength.

*   *   *

"When the soldiers and officers have penetrated deeply into [enemy territory], they will cling together. When there is no alternative, they will fight.

"For this reason even though the soldiers are not instructed, they are prepared; without seeking it, their cooperation is obtained;[168] without covenants they are close together; without issuing orders they are reliable. Prohibit omens, eliminate doubt so that they will die without other thoughts.

ノ   ノ   ノ

"If our soldiers do not have excessive wealth, it is not because they detest material goods. If they do not live long lives,[169] it is not because they abhor longevity. On the day that the orders are issued the tears of the soldiers who are sitting will soak their sleeves, while the tears of those lying down will roll down their cheeks. However, if you throw them into a hopeless situation, they will have the courage of Chu or Kuei.

ノ   ノ   ノ

"Thus one who excels at employing the army may be compared to the *shuaijan* [snake]. The *shuaijan* is found on Mt. Ch'ang. If you strike its head the tail will respond; if you strike its tail the head will respond. If you strike the middle [of the body][170] both the head and tail will react. If I dare ask, can we make the army like the *shuaijan,* I would say we can. For example, the people of Wu and Yüeh hate each other; but if, when fording a river in the same boat they encounter severe wind, their efforts to rescue each other will be like the left and right hands.

ノ   ノ   ノ

"For this reason fettering the horses[171] and burying the chariot wheels are inadequate to rely on [to prevent the soldiers from fleeing]. Unify their courage to be as one through the Tao of administration. Realize the appropriate employment of the hard and soft[172] through the patterns of terrain.

ノ   ノ   ノ

"Thus one who excels at employing the army leads them by the hand as if they were only one man, so they cannot avoid it.

ノ   ノ   ノ

"It is essential for a general to be tranquil and obscure, upright and self-disciplined, and able to stupefy the eyes and ears of the officers and troops, keeping them ignorant.[173] He alters his management of affairs and changes his strategies to keep other people[174] from recognizing them. He shifts his position and traverses indirect routes to keep other people from being able to anticipate him.

"At the moment the general has designated with them, it will be as if they ascended a height and abandoned their ladders. The general advances with them deep into the territory of the feudal lords and then releases the trigger.[175] He commands them as if racing a herd of sheep—they are driven away, driven back, but no one knows where they are going.

"Assembling the masses of the Three Armies, casting them into danger, is the responsibility of the general.

"The nine transformations of terrain—the advantages deriving from contraction and expansion, the patterns of human emotions—must be investigated.

"In general, the Tao of the invader is [this]:[176]

"When the troops have penetrated deeply, they will be unified, but where only shallowly, they will [be inclined to] scatter.

"When [the army] has left the state, crossed the [enemy's] border, and is on campaign, it is 'isolated terrain.'

"When the four sides are open [to others], this is 'focal terrain.'

"When you have advanced deeply, it is 'heavy terrain.'

"If you have penetrated only shallowly, it is 'light terrain.'

"If you have strongholds behind you and constrictions before you, it is 'encircled terrain.'

"If there is no place to go, it is 'fatal terrain.'[177]

"For this reason on dispersive terrain I unify their will.

"On light terrain I have them group together.

"On contentious terrain I race our rear elements forward.[178]

"On traversable terrain I focus on defense.[179]

"On focal terrain I solidify our alliances.[180]

"On heavy terrain I ensure a continuous supply of provisions.[181]

"On entrapping terrain I [speedily] advance along the roads.

"On encircled terrain I obstruct any openings.[182]

"On fatal terrain I show them that we will not live.

"Thus it is the nature of the army to defend when encircled;[183] to fight fervently when unavoidable; and to follow orders when compelled [by circumstances].

⸎   ⸎   ⸎

"For this reason one who does not know the plans of the feudal lords cannot forge preparatory alliances. One who does not know the topography of mountains and forests, ravines and defiles, wetlands and marshes cannot maneuver the army. One who does not employ local guides will not secure advantages of terrain. One who does not know one of these four or five cannot [command] the army of a hegemon or a true king.[184]

⸎   ⸎   ⸎

"Now when the army of a hegemon or true king attacks a great state, their masses are unable to assemble. When it applies its awesomeness to the enemy, their alliances cannot be sustained. For this reason it does not contend with any alliances under Heaven.[185] It does not nurture the authority [ch'üan] of others under Heaven. Have faith in yourself, apply your awesomeness to the enemy. Then his cities can be taken, his state can be subjugated.

⸎   ⸎   ⸎

"Bestow rewards not required by law, impose exceptional governmental orders. Direct the masses of the Three Armies as though commanding one man. Press affairs upon them, do not explain the purpose to them. Compel them with [prospects for] profit, but do not inform them about the [potential] harm.

⸎   ⸎   ⸎

"Cast them into hopeless situations and they will be preserved; have them penetrate fatal terrain and they will live. Only after the masses have penetrated dangerous [terrain] will they be able to craft victory out of defeat.

⸎   ⸎   ⸎

"The prosecution of military affairs lies in according with and [learning] in detail the enemy's intentions.[186] If one then focuses [his strength] toward the enemy, strikes a thousand li away, and kills their general, it is termed 'being skillful and capable in completing military affairs.'

⸎   ⸎   ⸎

"For this reason on the day the government mobilizes the army, close the passes, destroy all tallies, and do not allow their emissaries to pass through. Hold intense strategic discussions[187] in the upper hall of the temple in order to bring about the execution of affairs.

⸢ ⸢ ⸢

"If the enemy opens the door, you must race in.

⸢ ⸢ ⸢

"[Attack] what they love first. Do not fix any time for battle; assess and react to the enemy in order to determine the strategy for battle.

⸢ ⸢ ⸢

"For this reason at first be like a virgin [at home]; later—when the enemy opens the door—be like a fleeing rabbit. The enemy will be unable to withstand you."

12. Incendiary Attacks

Sun-tzu said:

"There are five types of incendiary attack: The first is to incinerate men, the second to incinerate provisions, the third to incinerate supply trains, the fourth to incinerate armories, and the fifth to incinerate formations.[188]

⸢ ⸢ ⸢

"Implementing an incendiary attack depends on the proper conditions. Equipment for incendiary attack should be fully prepared before required. Launching an incendiary attack has its appropriate seasons, igniting the fire the proper days. As for the seasons, it is the time of the dry spell; as for the day, when the moon is in *chi, pi, i,* or *chen.* When it is in these four lunar lodges, these are days the wind will arise.

⸢ ⸢ ⸢

"In general, in incendiary warfare you must respond to the five changes of fire:

"If fires are started within [their camp], then you should immediately respond [with an attack] from outside.
"If fires are ignited but their army remains quiet, then wait; do not attack.

"When they flare into a conflagration, if you can follow up, then do so; if you cannot, then desist.

"If the attack can be launched from outside without relying on inside [assistance], initiate it at an appropriate time.

"If fires are ignited upwind, do not attack downwind.

ɾ   ɾ   ɾ

"Winds that arise in the daytime will persist; those that arise at night will stop.

ɾ   ɾ   ɾ

"Now the army must know the five changes of fire in order to defend against them at the astrologically appropriate times. Thus using fire to aid an attack is enlightened, using water to assist an attack is powerful. Water can be used to sever, but cannot be employed to seize.

ɾ   ɾ   ɾ

"Now if someone is victorious in battle and succeeds in attack but does not exploit the achievement, it is disastrous, and his fate should be termed 'wasteful and tarrying.' Thus it is said the wise general ponders it, the good general cultivates it.

ɾ   ɾ   ɾ

"If it is not advantageous, do not move. If objectives cannot be attained, do not employ the army. Unless endangered do not engage in warfare. The ruler cannot mobilize the army out of personal anger. The general cannot engage in battle because of personal frustration. When it is advantageous, move; when not advantageous, stop. Anger can revert to happiness, annoyance can revert to joy, but a vanquished state cannot be revived, the dead cannot be brought back to life.

"Thus the enlightened ruler is cautious about it, the good general respectful of it. This is the Tao for bringing security to the state and preserving the army intact."

13. Employing Spies

Sun-tzu said:

"When you send forth an army of a hundred thousand on a campaign, marching them out a thousand *li,* the expenditures of the common people and the contributions of the feudal house will be one thousand pieces of gold per day. Those inconvenienced and troubled both within and without the border, who are exhausted on the road or unable to pursue their agricultural work, will be seven hundred thousand families.

"Armies remain locked in a standoff for years to fight for victory on a single day, yet [generals] begrudge bestowing ranks and emoluments of one hundred pieces of gold and therefore do not know the enemy's situation. This is the ultimate inhumanity. Such a person is not a general for the people, an assistant for a ruler, or the arbiter of victory.

ʳ   ʳ   ʳ

"The means by which enlightened rulers and sagacious generals moved and conquered others, that their achievements surpassed the masses, was advance knowledge.

"Advance knowledge cannot be gained from ghosts and spirits, inferred from phenomena, or projected from the measures of Heaven, but must be gained from men for it is the knowledge of the enemy's true situation.

ʳ   ʳ   ʳ

"Thus there are five types of spies to be employed: local spy, internal spy, turned spy [double agent], dead [expendable] spy, and the living spy. When all five are employed together and no one knows their Tao, this is termed "spiritual methodology." They are a ruler's treasures.

"Local spies—employ people from the local district.

"Internal spies—employ their people who hold government positions.

"Double agents—employ the enemy's spies.

"Expendable spies—are employed to spread disinformation outside the state. Provide our [expendable] spies [with false information] and have them leak it to enemy agents.[189]

"Living spies—return with their reports.

"Thus of all the Three Armies' affairs,[190] no relationship is closer than with spies; no rewards are more generous than those given to spies; no affairs are more secret than those pertaining to spies.

ʳ   ʳ   ʳ

"Unless someone has the wisdom of a Sage, he cannot use spies; unless he is benevolent and righteous, he cannot employ spies; unless he is subtle and perspicacious, he cannot perceive the substance in intelligence reports. It is subtle, subtle! There are no areas in which one does not employ spies.

*   *   *

"If before the mission has begun it has already been exposed, the spy and those he informed should all be put to death.

*   *   *

"In general, as for the armies you want to strike, the cities you want to attack, and the men you want to assassinate, you must first know the names of the defensive commander, his assistants, staff, door guards, and attendants. You must have our spies search out and learn them all.

*   *   *

"You must search for enemy agents who have come to spy on us. Tempt them with profits, instruct and retain them. Thus double agents can be obtained and employed. Through knowledge gained from them, you can recruit both local and internal spies. Through knowledge gained from them, the expendable spy can spread his falsehoods, can be used to misinform the enemy. Through knowledge gained from them, our living spies can be employed as times require.

"The ruler must know these five aspects of espionage work. This knowledge inevitably depends on turned spies; therefore, you must be generous to double agents.

*   *   *

"In antiquity, when the Yin arose, they had I Chih in the Hsia. When the Chou arose, they had Lü Ya [the T'ai Kung] in the Yin.[191] Thus enlightened rulers and sagacious generals who are able to get intelligent spies will invariably attain great achievements. This is the essence of the military, what the Three Armies rely on to move."

4

Wu-tzu

Translator's Introduction

UNLIKE the semilegendary Sun-tzu, Wu Ch'i—who was also called Wu-tzu by later generations—was a famous historical figure. His exploits and achievements, both military and administrative, are portrayed as truly outstanding, and shortly after his death his name became inextricably linked with Sun-tzu's. According to the *Shih chi,* whenever people discussed military theory Sun and Wu were invariably mentioned together, and Ssu-ma Ch'ien's famous biographical chapter permanently canonized that bond.

Wu Ch'i was a complex man of many contradictions, and even his biography in the *Shih chi* does not depict him favorably. He was an extremely talented individual who advocated the fundamental Confucian beliefs, although his behavior visibly contradicted them. He embraced the concept of benevolence as the essential foundation for government, yet he reputedly killed his own wife. He ignored his mother's mourning rites—a heinous offense in Confucian eyes—in order to keep a vow, clearly emphasizing trustworthiness over filial emotion and its respectful expression. Although he attained great power and encouraged the development and preservation of distinctions, he personally eschewed the visible comforts available to a commanding general and shared every misery and hardship with his troops.

Born about 440 B.C. into the tumultuous era that witnessed the initial conflicts of the incessant warfare that eventually reduced the number of powerful states in China from seven to one, Wu Ch'i realized that states could survive only if they fostered both military strength and sound government. As a young man he reportedly studied with two of the founding disciples of Confucianism, perhaps for as long as three years. Subsequently, he journeyed to find a receptive ear, yet lost favor even after great accomplishments. Eventually he was murdered in Ch'u around 361 B.C., a victim of the enmity incurred because of his draconian measures to strengthen the military and the state.

According to subsequent historical writings, not only was Wu Ch'i never defeated in battle but he rarely suffered the ignominy of a stalemate, while compiling a remarkable record of decisive victories against the superior forces of entrenched states. He has been widely regarded as China's first great general—a view that obviously ignores the T'ai Kung and Ssu-ma Jang-chü—and has been credited with such notable achievements as governing and holding the West Ho region, pacifying Yüeh (the south China region), commanding the forces of Lu to gain an overwhelming victory against Ch'i, leading Wei numerous times to thrash Ch'in's growing power, and stabilizing the government of Ch'u. Thus his views and methods, to the extent that they may be preserved in *Wu-tzu,* are not merely theoretical but were founded and thoroughly tested in reality.

Wu-tzu's reputation for having made impressive administrative contributions—especially for instituting innovative measures and controls to organize the state and instill order, first as Protector of the West River commandery and later as prime minister of Ch'u—have frequently caused him to be ranked with the famous Legalist Lord Shang.[1] Numerous anecdotes describe his emphasis on certitude, one of the few virtues he both espoused and personally embodied. Stories about him abound in works originating in the centuries after his death, such as the *Chan-kuo tse* (*Intrigues of the Warring States*), the *Han Fei-tzu,* and the *Lü-shih Ch'un-ch'iu.*[2]

The *Wu-tzu* not only constitutes one of the *Seven Military Classics* but also has long been valued as one of the basic foundations of Chinese military thought. Although less strident than the *Art of War,* it seriously considers all aspects of war and battle preparation and suggests generally applicable strategies for resolving certain tactical situations. Over the centuries traditional Confucian scholars—with their classical prejudices toward style and artifice—denigrated the *Wu-tzu* because of the comparative simplicity of the language; they also condemned its realistic policies and perceived brutality.[3] However, the text remains lucid and commanding.

The core of the *Wu-tzu* was probably composed by Wu Ch'i himself, then expanded and revised by his disciples—perhaps from their own memories or from court records. Much of the original version appears to have been lost; what remains has been edited into a succinct, fairly systematic, and remarkably comprehensive work. Although earlier versions of the text apparently date back to at least the fourth century B.C., it probably assumed its present form during the Han dynasty. Fortunately, unlike some of the military classics, few textual problems exist, and only small differences are found among the various editions. Naturally, some passages are common to other, presumably later works; but the focus, concepts, and stage of development are distinctly different.[4]

Wu Ch'i's life and values were closely intertwined, and because of his apparent historical importance his biography from the *Shih chi*—which was composed around 100 B.C.—demands inclusion here:[5]

Wu Ch'i, a native of Wey, loved military operations.[6] He once studied with Tseng-tzu,[7] then went on to serve the ruler of Lu. When the state of Ch'i attacked Lu, Lu's ruler wanted to commission Wu Ch'i as a general, but since he had taken a woman of Ch'i as his wife,[8] he was suspicious. Thereupon Wu Ch'i, who wanted to become famous, killed his wife[9] to show he had no connection with Ch'i. Lu finally appointed him as a general, and in this capacity he attacked Ch'i, destroying their forces.

Someone in Lu who hated Wu Ch'i said to the ruler: "Wu Ch'i is cruel and suspicious. When he was young his family had accumulated a thousand *chin* of gold. He traveled about seeking official appointment but was never successful, eventually exhausting the family's resources. When members of his district laughed at him he killed more than thirty of his detractors and then went east, through the gate of Wey's outer wall. On parting from his mother he bit his arm [so that it bled] and swore an oath: 'Until I become a ranking minister I will not reenter Wey.' Then he went to serve Tseng-tzu. He had only been there a short while when his mother died, but he didn't return home. Tseng-tzu despised him [for failing to perform the mourning rites[10]] and severed all relationship with him.

"Wu Ch'i then went to Lu and studied military arts in order to serve you. You doubted his intentions, so he killed his wife to obtain the post of general. Now Lu is a small state, and if it should attain a reputation for being victorious in battle, the other feudal lords will plot against it. Moreover Lu and Wey are brothers, so if you employ Wu Ch'i you will be casting aside Wey."

The ruler grew suspicious of Wu Ch'i and dismissed him.

At that time Wu Ch'i happened to hear that Marquis Wen of Wei[11] was a Worthy and wanted so serve in his court. Marquis Wen questioned Li K'o[12] about him: "What sort of a man is Wu Ch'i?" Li K'o replied: "Ch'i is greedy and licentious, but in the employment of troops even the famous general Ssu-ma Jang-chü[13] could not surpass him." Upon hearing this Marquis Wen appointed him as a general. Wu Ch'i [commanded the army] in an attack on Ch'in, seizing five cities.

In his position as general, Wu Ch'i's custom was to wear the same clothes and eat the same food as the men in the lowest ranks. When sleeping he did not set out a mat, while on the march he did not ride a horse[14] or in a chariot. He personally packed up his leftover rations, and shared all labors and misery with the troops.

Once when one of his soldiers had a blister, he personally sucked out the pus for him. The soldier's mother heard about it and wept. Someone said to her:

"Your son is only an ordinary soldier, while the general himself sucked out the pus. What is there to weep about?" The mother retorted: "That isn't it. In years past Duke Wu sucked his father's blister. His father went to war without hesitating and subsequently died at the hands of the enemy. Now Duke Wu again sucks my son's blister, so I don't know where he will die. For this reason I weep."[15]

Because Marquis Wen felt that Wu Ch'i excelled in employing the army, was scrupulous and fair-handed, and able to obtain the complete allegiance of his troops, he appointed him as Protector of the West River[16] commandery to fend off the states of Ch'in and Han.

When Marquis Wen died Wu Ch'i continued to serve his son, Marquis Wu. Marquis Wu voyaged by boat down the West River. In midstream he looked back and exclaimed to Wu Ch'i: "Isn't it magnificent! The substantiality of the mountains and rivers, this is the jewel of Wei." Wu Ch'i replied: "[The real jewel] lies in Virtue, not in precipitous defiles. Formerly the Three Miao had Tung-t'ing Lake on the left and P'eng-li Lake on the right, but they didn't cultivate Virtue and righteousness and Yü obliterated them. The place where Chieh of the Hsia dynasty resided had the Yellow and Chi rivers on the left, Mt. T'ai and Mt. Hua on the right, the cliffs of I-ch'üeh in the south, and the slopes of Yang-ch'ang to the north. But in his practice of government he didn't cultivate benevolence, and T'ang displaced him. The state of [the tyrant] Chou of the Yin dynasty had Mt. Meng-men on the left, Mt. T'ai-hang on the right, Mt. Ch'ang to the north, and the great Yellow River flowing to the south, but in his practice of government he didn't cultivate Virtue, and King Wu killed him. From this perspective [the state's jewel] is Virtue, not the precipitousness of its defiles. If you do not cultivate Virtue, all the men in the boat will comprise an enemy state."[17] "Excellent!" said Marquis Wu. Thereupon he enfeoffed Wu Ch'i as Protector of the West River commandery, and his reputation grew enormously.

Wei then established the post of Minister, naming T'ien Wen to the office. Wu Ch'i was unhappy so he accosted T'ien Wen: "Could we please discuss merit and attainments?" T'ien Wen agreed. Wu Ch'i asked: "Who is better at commanding the Three Armies, causing the officers and soldiers to take pleasure in dying in battle, and ensuring that enemy states do not dare plot against us—you or me?" "I am not as capable as you," T'ien Wen replied. Wu Ch'i then asked him: "Who is better, you or I, in administering the bureaucracy, gaining the support of the people, and filling the storehouses and arsenals?" T'ien Wen again replied: "I am not as good as you." "In serving as Protector of the West River commandery so that the Ch'in troops dare not establish villages in their eastern regions, while Han and Chao act submissively as honored guests, who is better?" T'ien Wen acknowledged: "You are." Wu Ch'i then proceeded: "In all three of these you are inferior to me, yet your position has been placed above me. Why?" T'ien Wen said: "The ruler is young, the state doubtful, the major ministers not yet supportive, while the common people[18] do not trust [the government]. At this time should the role fall to you or to me?" After Ch'i was silent for a very long time he said: "It should belong to you. This is why I am placed over you." Wu Ch'i then knew he was not as good as T'ien Wen.

After T'ien Wen died Kung Shu became Minister. He had married a princess of Wei and [wanted to] damage Wu Ch'i. Kung Shu's servant said to him: "It is easy to get rid of Wu Ch'i." Kung Shu asked how, and his servant replied: "Wu Ch'i is constrained, incorruptible, and likes fame. First you should accordingly say to Marquis Wu: 'Wu Ch'i is a Worthy while your state is small. Moreover you have a border area of fertile land abutting the strong state of Ch'in. Therefore I fear Wu Ch'i will not remain loyal.' The marquis will then ask: 'What should we do,' and you should say: 'Test him by extending [an offer of marriage] with a princess. If Ch'i intends to stay he will certainly accept her; if not he will invariably decline. With this divine his intent.' Then you should summon Wu Ch'i and return with him, while also making the princess angry so that she treats you contemptuously. When Wu Ch'i sees that the princess holds you in contempt, he will certainly decline her."

Thereupon, when Wu Ch'i saw the princess treat the Minister of Wei contemptuously, he did in fact decline Marquis Wu's offer. Marquis Wu grew suspicious and did not trust him any longer. Wu Ch'i, fearing he might be charged with some offense, subsequently left and went to the state of Ch'u.

King Tao of Ch'u had previously heard that Wu Ch'i was a Worthy, so when he arrived he appointed him as Minister. Wu Ch'i made the laws clear, examined the ordinances, eliminated unimportant offices, and dispersed distant royal relatives in order to nourish and support fighting men. He emphasized strengthening the army and destroying the vociferous proponents of the horizontal and vertical alliances.[19] To the south he pacified the Pai Yüeh. In the north he seized Ch'en and Ts'ai and forced the Three Chin to withdraw. To the west he [successfully] attacked Ch'in. The other feudal lords were troubled by Ch'u's growing strength, while all the members of the royal family wanted to harm him. When King Tao died the imperial relatives and chief ministers revolted and attacked Wu Ch'i. He ran to the king's body and hid beneath it. When his assailants shot their arrows, striking him, they thereby struck King Tao as well.

When King Tao had been buried and the prince enthroned, he had the Minister of Justice execute all those who had shot at Wu Ch'i and also struck the king's corpse. Those that were judged guilty and executed, together with having their families exterminated, numbered more than seventy.[20]

The Grand Historian says: "The habit of the contemporary age, when referring to armies and regiments, is to always speak of Sun-tzu's thirteen chapters and Wu Ch'i's strategy. At this time many [people] have them. Thus I have not discussed them but instead discussed what their actions effected and established. There is a common saying: 'One able to perform an action cannot invariably speak about it; one able to speak about something is not invariably able to perform it.' Sun Pin's plotting of strategy against P'ang Chüan was enlightened, but he was still unable to extricate himself from the misfortune of suffering severe corporeal punishment.[21] Wu Ch'i [tried to] persuade Marquis Wen that the strategic advantages of power [conferred by the substantiality of the terrain's] configuration are not as good as Virtue. However, his actions in Ch'u, on account of his harsh oppressiveness and the paucity of his beneficence, caused him to lose his life. Isn't it tragic!"

Even in death Wu Ch'i managed to execute a successful strategy and gain revenge because he knew that in trying to kill him, his enemies would desecrate the king's body and eventually be executed.

Modern scholars such as Chauncey Goodrich, troubled by the inclusion of such detrimental material as Wu Ch'i killing his wife, have studied the biography in considerable detail and concluded that it is an amalgamation of the disparate, even condemnatory materials probably available to the Grand Historian.[22] Opinion is divided about Wu Ch'i's overall historical accomplishments, with much of the biographical record being viewed as romantic embellishment, anachronistic, or simply dubious. However, given the numerous references to Wu-tzu in the extant literature from the two centuries following his death, it seems likely that Wu Ch'i served in the capacities enumerated and was a highly effective strategist and commander. A brief consideration of the more significant stories and anecdotes in these other writings not only provides information about the man and his character but also indicates the important principles generally associated with his name that are illustrated prominently by his lifelong behavior.

Wu Ch'i, who is often mentioned with Lord Shang as emphasizing the role of law and revising government policies to strengthen the state, valued credibility (which can only be established through preserving one's word in complete sincerity) above everything. An anecdote preserved in the *Han Fei-tzu*, followed by Han Fei-tzu's comments, portrays this paramount commitment:

> Wu Ch'i went out and happened to encounter an old friend. He stopped him and invited him to eat dinner with him. The friend replied: "I will. In a short time I will go back and eat with you." Wu-tzu said: "I will wait for you to dine." By nightfall the friend had not come, but Wu Ch'i waited for him without eating. Early the next morning he had someone seek out his friend, and only when the friend had come back did he eat with him.
>
> [Han Fei-tzu's comment:] When small acts of faith are achieved, great faith is established. Therefore the wise ruler accumulates good faith. When rewards and punishments are not trusted, prohibitions and ordinances will not be effected. The explanation is seen in Duke Wen attacking Yüan and Chi Cheng rescuing the starving. For this reason Wu Ch'i waited for his friend to eat.[23]

Another incident from the *Han Fei-tzu* portrays Wu Ch'i as divorcing his wife for a minor transgression (rather than killing her, as reported in the *Shih*

chi biography) in order to preserve his credibility. His brother-in-law ratio-
nalizes this action in terms of a zealous commitment to the law:

> Wu Ch'i, who was a native of Tso-shih in Wey, had his wife weave a silk band.
> When he measured it and found it to be narrower than desired, he had her
> change it. "I will," she said. When it was complete he measured it again, but the
> result was still not accurate. Wu Ch'i was enraged. His wife replied: "When I be-
> gan I set the warp, and it could not be changed." Wu-tzu sent her away. She then
> asked her older brother to seek her readmission, but her brother said: "Wu Ch'i
> is a man of law. He works with the laws so that he may attain great achieve-
> ments in a large state. Therefore he must first put the laws into practice with his
> wife, and thereafter implement them [in government]. You have no hope of
> seeking to return." His wife's younger brother was well-favored by Wey's ruler,
> so she sought the ruler's intercession with Wu-tzu on her behalf. Wu-tzu did not
> listen but instead left Wey and went to Ching [Ch'u].[24]

Yet another version of the story perceives her dismissal as resulting from
working too assiduously, thereby surpassing—rather than falling short of—
what Wu Ch'i had required:

> Wu Ch'i, showing his wife a silk band, said: "Weave a silk band for me, making
> it like this." When it was finished he compared them, and the one she had made
> was especially good. Wu Ch'i said: "I had you weave a silk band, to make it like
> this one, but now this is especially good. How is that?" His wife replied: "The
> materials employed are alike, but I concentrated on making it better." Wu Ch'i
> said: "It is not what I said to do." He had her change her clothes and return [to
> her family]. Her father went to request [that he take her back], but Wu Ch'i
> said: "In the Ch'i family there are no empty words!"[25]

This explanation is in full accord with the Legalist emphasis on not exceeding one's prescribed role, which is generally proclaimed a canonical virtue by
military thinkers within the context of battlefield situations.

Another cardinal doctrine of the strategists is the inviolate nature of rewards and punishments because they embody and symbolize the credibility
of the administrative system. To motivate men successfully requires not only
both rewards and punishments but also the absolute certainty that these will
invariably be implemented in every single instance. Wu-tzu believed un-
flinchingly in the power of the "twin handles," as Lord Shang termed them,
and especially in the ability of rewards to motivate men so strongly that they
would risk their lives and chance everything. Although instruction, organization, training, and the development of a sense of shame should precede
any manipulation of the human spirit, the underlying effect of credibility in
attaining a desired objective is well illustrated by the following incident:

When Wu Ch'i was serving as Protector of the West River commandery, [the state of Ch'in] had a small fortified watchtower near the border. Wu Ch'i wanted to attack it for if he did not eliminate it, it would be extremely harmful to the farmers. However, it was not worth summoning armored troops to eliminate it. Therefore he leaned a carriage shaft against the North Gate and issued an ordinance which stated: "Anyone who can move this outside the South Gate will be rewarded with superior lands and an excellent house." For a while no one moved it, then someone did succeed in moving it. Upon his return [from the South Gate], Wu Ch'i rewarded him in accord with the ordinance. Shortly thereafter he set a picul of red beans outside the East Gate and issued an ordinance which stated: "Anyone able to move this outside the West Gate will be rewarded as in the first case." The people competed to move it. Then Wu Ch'i sent down an order: "Tomorrow when we attack the tower, whoever can ascend it first will be [enfeoffed as *ta-fu*[26]] and rewarded with superior lands and a house." The people fought to race to the tower, attacking and seizing it in a single morning.[27]

The *Shih chi* biography states that Wu Ch'i studied with Tseng-tzu; however, because this is chronologically impossible, it was probably Tseng-tzu's son Tseng Shen, with whom Wu Ch'i may have studied for as long as three years.[28] If the biography is credible and Tseng Shen condemned Wu Ch'i for blatantly violating the precepts of filial behavior—one of the cornerstones of Tseng-tzu's recension of Confucianism—Wu Ch'i may have rejected formal studies in favor of military pursuits, which were presumably his first inclination. However, throughout the *Wu-tzu* he advocates policies based on four fundamental Confucian virtues: benevolence, righteousness, the forms of propriety (*li*), and the Way (Tao) of Heaven. This accords with the new reality of the Warring States period wherein state governments had become significantly dependent on the willing consent and participation of the populace in any military enterprise.[29] The famous (probably fabricated) discussion with Marquis Wu while they were floating down the West River, which is recorded in other texts as well, clearly expresses Wu Ch'i's belief in Virtue rather than in simple strategic advantage. Another interview with the marquis at the start of his reign reflects the same concern, but it is coupled with an advocacy of practicing accessible government while retaining political power and preventing the nobles from encroaching on the people:

Marquis Wu asked Wu-tzu about the initial reign year. Wu-tzu replied: "It is said that the ruler of a state must be cautious about the beginning." "How does one go about being cautious about the beginning?" "Make it upright." "How does one make it upright?" "Make wisdom enlightened. If wisdom is not enlightened, how can you perceive the upright? Listen widely and select from what you hear so as to make wisdom enlightened. For this reason in antiquity, when the ruler

first held court, the *ta-fu* each had one speech, the officers one audience, and if
the common people requested admittance they would be heard. If the nobles
made any inquiries they would certainly be answered, and they would not re-
fuse any who came from the four quarters. This can be termed 'not plugged up
or obscured.' In apportioning salaries they made certain to extend them to everyone, while in the employment of punishments they were invariably accurate.
The ruler's mind had to be benevolent. He thought of the ruler's profit and the
elimination of the people's harm. This can be termed 'not losing the people.' The
ruler personally had to be upright, the intimate ministers carefully selected. The
ta-fu could not hold more than one office concurrently, while the handles for
controlling the people did not lie with one clan. This can be referred to as 'not
[losing] the balance of authority [*ch'üan*] and strategic power [*shih*].' This is the
meaning of the *Spring and Autumn Annals* and the basis of the initial reign
year."[30]

A dramatic passage in the *Lü-shih Ch'un-ch'iu* describes Wu Ch'i's pro-
phetic words as he departed from Wei, providing another version of the
story of slander incorporated in the *Shih chi* biography:

When Wu Ch'i governed the area outside the West River, Wang Ts'o slandered
him to Marquis Wu of Wei. Marquis Wu had an emissary summon him. When
Wu Ch'i reached the gate on the far shore, he stopped the carriage and rested.
As he looked toward the West River, several tears fell from his eyes. His servant
addressed him: "I have observed your intentions. You have cast aside the world
as if throwing away a pair of straw sandals. Yet now as you leave the West River
region you weep. Why is it?" Wu Ch'i wiped the tears away and replied: "You
do not understand. If the ruler truly knew me and had me exhaust my abilities,
Ch'in could certainly be destroyed, and with the West River region he could become a true king. But now the ruler listens to the ideas of slanderers and does
not know me. It will not be long before the West River region belongs to Ch'in.
From henceforth the state of Wei will diminish." Wu Ch'i subsequently left Wei
and entered Ch'u. Day by day Wei diminished while Ch'in grew greater every
day. This is what Wu Ch'i saw first and wept about.[31]

Wu Ch'i's radical, emotional commitment to his political beliefs and his desire to exert himself on behalf of the state clearly manifest themselves in such
passages.

Several incidents provide glimpses of Wu Ch'i's activities in Ch'u, apparently confirming that King Tao quickly entrusted him with power and influence. Seeking to strengthen the central government and thereby the state and
the army, Wu Ch'i proposed policies that invariably antagonized entrenched
interests:

Formerly, Wu Ch'i instructed King Tao of Ch'u about Ch'u's customs. "The
chief ministers are too powerful, the hereditary lords too numerous. In this sort

of situation, above they press upon the ruler while below they oppress the people. This is the Way [Tao] to impoverish the state and weaken the army. It would be better to take back all ranks and emoluments from the hereditary lords after three generations; diminish the salaries and allowances of the hundred officials; and reduce all unnecessary offices in order to support selected, well-trained officers." King Tao had implemented his suggestion for a year when he died. Wu Ch'i was then torn apart in Ch'u.[32]

Another version of the story in the *Lü-shih Ch'un-ch'iu* (which dates from the third century B.C.) provides a further explanation of Wu Chi's policy to populate the countryside and emasculate the power of the stagnant nobility:

Wu Ch'i addressed the King of Ch'u: "What Ch'u has a surplus of is land, but what is insufficient is people. Now if your lordship takes what is insufficient to increase what is in surplus, then I cannot do anything." Thereupon the king ordered the nobles to go out and fill the vast, empty lands. They all found this to be extremely bitter. When the king of Ch'u died, the nobles all came [to the capital]. The king's corpse was lying in the upper hall. The nobles, acting together, shot arrows at Wu Ch'i. Wu Ch'i yelled: "I will show you how I use weapons." He pulled out an arrow and ran. Prostrating himself over the corpse, he stuck the arrow in and yelled out: "The ministers are revolting against the king!" Then Wu Ch'i died. However, according to Ching law anyone who exposed a weapon before the king's body should be subject to the severest penalty, with the extirpation of their families to three degrees. Wu Ch'i's wisdom can certainly be said to have been acute.[33]

Chinese tradition has long held that the military arts belong to the category "contrary Virtue," a concept perhaps originally espoused by the mythical Lao-tzu and later expounded in many of the military writings, including the *Wu-tzu*.[34] Consequently, the longer one's involvement and the more extensive one's experience, the more likely it becomes that disaster will befall the individual. This is made clear in two fictional interviews found in the *Shuo yüan*:

When Wu Ch'i was serving as Protector of Yüan, during his tour of inspection of the commandery he reached Hsi where he asked Ch'ü I-chiu: "The king, not knowing that I am a petty man, has made me Protector of Yüan. Sir, how would you instruct me?" Duke Ch'ü did not reply.

After a year the king made him Director of Ordinances. During his tour of inspection of the commandery he reached Hsi. He asked Ch'ü I-chiu: "I inquired of you, but you did not instruct me. Now the king, not knowing I am a petty man, has made me Director of Ordinances. Sir, would you examine how I am acting?" Duke Ch'ü said: "What are you going to do?" Wu Ch'i said: "I am going to level the ranks of nobility in Ch'u and even their emoluments; reduce what is in excess and continue what is insufficient; and polish the armor and weapons in order to contend for All under Heaven at the appropriate time." Duke Ch'ü said: "I have heard that in the past, those that excelled at governing states did not change the old nor alter the usual. Now you are about to level the ranks of Ch'u's nobility and even their emoluments, reduce what is surplus and continue what is insufficient. This is changing the old and altering the usual. Moreover I have heard that weapons are inauspicious implements and that conflict is a contrary Virtue. Now you secretly plot the contrary Virtue and love to employ inauspicious implements. Reaching out for what men abandon is the extreme of contrariness; implementing licentious and dissolute affairs is not advantageous. Moreover when you employed the troops of Lu, you should not have gained your intentions in Ch'i, but you realized them. When you employed the troops of Wei, you should not have been able to realize your intentions against Ch'in, but you gained them. I have heard it said, 'If one is not the man for disaster, he cannot complete disaster.' I formerly found it strange that my ruler had frequently acted contrary to the Way [Tao] of Heaven but up to now not met with any misfortune. Alas, it was probably waiting for you."Wu Ch'i fearfully said: "Can it still be altered?" Duke Ch'ü said: "It cannot." Wu Ch'i said: "I plan on behalf of others." Duke Ch'ü said: "A prisoner whose punishment has been determined cannot change himself. You would best be honest and sincerely implement [the affairs of government] for the state of Ch'u has nothing more valued than raising up the worthy."[35]

From a historical perspective that had witnessed Ch'in's slow evolution to power and subsequent meteoric collapse, the milieu that saw the rise of state Confucianism and the pervasive expression of Taoism in such syncretic texts as the *Huai-nan tzu* gave voice to a condemnatory view:

On behalf of Ch'in, Lord Shang instituted the mutual guarantee laws, and the hundred surnames were resentful. On behalf of Ch'u, Wu Ch'i issued orders to reduce the nobility and their emoluments, and the meritorious ministers revolted. Lord Shang, in establishing laws, and Wu Ch'i, in employing the army, were the best in the world. But Lord Shang's laws [eventually] caused the loss of Ch'in for he was perspicacious about the traces of the brush and knife,[36] but did not know the foundation of order and disorder. Wu Ch'i, on account of the military, weakened Ch'u. He was well practiced in such military affairs as deploying formations, but did not know the balance of authority [ch'üan] involved in court warfare.[37]

From such passages it appears that Wu Ch'i actually wielded significant political power and tried to implement typically Legalist reforms. Determining whether he enjoyed such influence in Wei's central government is more problematic because although Li K'o and other ministers apparently embarked on similar programs, Wu Ch'i's administrative impact and power were probably confined to the West River region, where he may have been virtual dictator.

Fundamental Concepts and Strategies

The present text of the *Wu-tzu* consists of six chapters focusing on topics critical to military affairs: Planning for the State; Evaluating the Enemy; Controlling the Army; the Tao of the General; Responding to Change; and Stimulating the Officers. Although none of the sections concentrates solely on a single topic because strategic considerations are interspersed throughout, these traditional chapter headings essentially depict the scope of the respective subject matter.

Need for Military Forces

Wu Ch'i lived during the period in which warfare was becoming increasingly specialized, bronze weapons had attained the peak of their development, and bronze swords and numerous iron weapons had begun to appear. Chariots—which were still manned by three men (driver, bowman, and spearman) and drawn by four horses—theoretically continued to provide the fundamental offensive weapon, although they were diminishing in effectiveness and were perhaps being relegated to functioning as transport and as a command platform.[38] Use of crossbows had just become widespread, and armies were now composed of conscripted commoners and the *shih* (knights, who were now officers), who had previously shouldered the burden of fighting.

However brief the time of Wu Ch'i's devotion to formal Confucian studies, it apparently constituted a formative period during which he absorbed the fundamental beliefs he later propounded as essential to good government. However, although he was a strong proponent of benevolence and righteousness, Wu-tzu equally stressed military strength and preparation. Without an effective fighting force, the Confucian virtues would become hollow mockeries and evil would dominate the world:

> In antiquity the ruler of the Ch'eng Sang clan cultivated Virtue but neglected military affairs, thereby leading to the extinction of his state. The ruler of the Yu Hu clan relied on his masses and loved courage and thus lost his ancestral altars. The enlightened ruler, observing this, will certainly nourish culture and Virtue within the domestic sphere while, in response to external situations, putting his military preparations in order. Thus when opposing an enemy if you do not advance, you have not attained righteousness. When the dead lie stiff and you grieve for them, you have not attained benevolence. ["Planning for the State"]

Accordingly, the commanding general must be selected carefully and must be a man of complete and diverse talents who is capable of effectively directing both military and civilian administrations. Naturally, courage is basic, but other characteristics—such as wisdom and self-control—are emphatically required.

Measure in All Matters

In Wu-tzu's era the army depended heavily on the horse for its overall mobility and for powering its focal assault weapon, the chariot. Consequently, Wu Ch'i stressed that the enlightened management of horses was primary and that men were secondary. However, certain vital principles apply to both, such as ensuring proper nourishment and appropriate eating times, adequate rest periods, the erection of temporary shelters, and the implementation of extensive, ongoing training. All the equipment for the army, and especially that for the horses, must be of good quality and kept in proper repair. Only then would the army be adequately prepared for its mission and the men given the means to execute their orders without the distraction and hindrance of material failure.

People as the Basis

Because of the shift from warfare fought by the nobility to mass mobilization and reliance on a basically civilian army, the strong support and willing allegiance of the people became essential. Wu Ch'i therefore advocated enlightened Confucian policies that would provide the people with adequate material welfare, gain their emotional support, and inculcate the basic virtues. When impositions are light and the government visibly expresses its concern for the people, the populace will respond and the state can withstand external challenges. Harmony—which can then be forged—must be present in the state, the army, the formations, and among the men themselves.

Training and Unification

Harmony and organization are counterparts: Without harmony the organization will not be cohesive, but without organization harmony is ineffectual. Wu Ch'i only briefly touched on the civilian hierarchy necessary to provide this basic organization; he mainly emphasized the need for order and distinctions and urged the selection and appointment of worthy men. Self-reliance on the part of those at the pinnacle of government can only lead to disaster, whereas accepting wise counsel results in victory.

The means required to attain a disciplined, effective fighting force are quite simple: Organize properly, train extensively, and motivate thoroughly.

Thereafter it becomes a question of strategy and tactics, and most of Wu Ch'i's book is devoted to military matters such as the composition of units, methods of control, formations, and the selection of men. He also focuses on general questions of training based on the traditional composition of the Three Armies and their employment in normal formations. Repetitive training furnishes the means for coordinated, articulated movement on the battlefield. Solidarity provides the possibility of effecting strategy, whereas disorder dooms one's tactics and turns the conflict into a shambles. A small, well-disciplined force can usually defeat a numerically superior one if the latter lacks cohesion and direction. All the forces should be completely integrated and immediately responsive to the commands of one man. Then the army will not succumb to battle pressure but will emerge victorious.

Selection, Evaluation, and Motivation of Men

Men should be selected, evaluated, and assigned duties including both combat specialties and administrative positions, that are appropriate to their individual talents and expertise. Because attitude and motivation are critical, Wu-tzu suggested policies that would consciously employ his psychological insights to forge a spirited fighting force. Given a settled, well-treated populace, the essential catalyst would be shame because men striving to avoid shame would prefer death in battle to living ignominiously. On the positive side, being committed to fighting and to dying in battle would ensure the survival not only of the individual soldier but of the entire army.

In contrast to the famous Legalist thinkers of the Warring States period, Wu-tzu felt that by themselves, rewards and punishments would be unreliable and inadequate to guarantee discipline and elicit the desired forms of behavior. Excessive rewards could easily prove counterproductive, encouraging individual rather than coherent unit action, stimulating the soldiers to break ranks in their personal quests for glory and profit. The imposition of extremely strict punishments to constrain discontent would ultimately prove similarly ineffective because the offenders would simply flee rather than face the painful consequences of failure or defeat. Only when all measures were properly implemented—including honoring and sustaining the families of those who died in combat—would a disciplined, spirited, strongly motivated force result.

Waging War and Engaging in Battle

The key to victory is impartially assessing the situation, including relative strength, to discern and develop potential tactical advantages. Wu Ch'i provides extensive instructions and techniques for evaluating the enemy and its commander and correlates national character with fighting qualities. He also analyzes general classes of battlefield situations in terms of their potential, elucidating a series in which superiority dictates attacking and another in which withdrawing and defending are advisable. Finally, he considers a number of circumstances in which the enemy either enjoys a significant advantage or encounters difficulty due to terrain, weather, or other adverse conditions; and he recommends countermeasures.

Deviations from the standards of good order, training, material supply, and similar factors create the requisite opening for attack. Any sign of internal disorder or disaffection, any character flaw or excessive strength in an enemy commander promises an exploitable opportunity. Spies should ferret out vital information, and probing attacks should be undertaken to discover the enemy's tactics and degree of integrity. Probable combat behavior can be extrapolated from national character and regional differences, and tactics can be developed for predictable responses.

Some circumstances—such as confronting an exhausted enemy—are remarkably clear and require that the commander initiate aggressive movements without hesitation, whereas others indicate that engaging the enemy would be folly. The well-ordered, rested, integrated, entrenched, and properly commanded forces of an enemy state are to be avoided until feints, deception, and other techniques can be brought to bear. Certain types of terrain and disadvantageous circumstances should also be treated with caution unless they can be turned to advantage. Armies that are outnumbered or in difficulty must make every effort to utilize the natural advantages of confined terrain, inclement weather, and water.

1. Planning for the State

Wu Ch'i, wearing the distinctive garb of a Confucian, had an audience with Marquis Wen of Wei to discuss the strategic crux of warfare. Marquis Wen said: "I do not like military affairs."

Wu Ch'i replied: "From the visible I can fathom the concealed. From the past I can discern the future. How can your lordship say this topic does not accord with his thoughts? Right now, throughout the four seasons you have the skins of slaughtered animals covered with vermillion lacquer, painted with variegated colors, and embellished with glistening images of rhinoceroses and elephants. Wearing them in winter one would not be warm; wearing them in summer one would not be cool.

"You make long spear-tipped halberds of twenty-four feet and short spear-tipped halberds of twelve feet. Your leather armored chariots block the doors; their wheels are covered and the hubs protected.[1] Looking at them they are certainly not beautiful to the eye; riding in them to hunt they are certainly not mobile. I do not know how you use them!

"If you are preparing them to advance into battle or withdraw and protect [the state] without seeking men capable of employing them, the situation is comparable to a nesting hen rushing at a fox or a puppy attacking a tiger. Even though they have great fighting spirit, they will die!

"In antiquity the ruler of the Ch'eng Sang clan cultivated Virtue but neglected military affairs, thereby leading to the extinction of his state. The ruler of the Yu Hu clan relied on his masses and loved courage and thus lost his ancestral altars. The enlightened ruler, observing this, will certainly nourish culture and Virtue within the domestic sphere while, in response to external situations, putting his military preparations in order. Thus when opposing an enemy force if you do not advance, you have not attained righteousness. When the dead lie stiff and you grieve for them, you have not attained benevolence."

Thereupon Marquis Wen personally arranged a mat for Wu Ch'i, and his wife presented him with a goblet of wine. The duke then made a sacrifice in the ancestral temple, announcing his intended employment of Wu Ch'i, and posted him as general-in-chief to protect the West River commandery. While in command he fought seventy-six major battles with the other feudal lords, winning sweeping victories in sixty-four of them and faring no worse than a draw in the remainder. He expanded Wei's land in all four directions, broadening its territory some thousand *li*. All these were Wu Ch'i's accomplishments.

✔   ✔   ✔

Wu-tzu said: "In antiquity those who planned government affairs would invariably first instruct the hundred surnames and gain the affection of the common people.

"There are four disharmonies. If there is disharmony in the state, you cannot put the army into the field. If there is disharmony within the army, you cannot deploy into formations. If you lack harmony within the formations, you cannot advance into battle. If you lack cohesion during the conduct of the battle, you cannot score a decisive victory.[2]

"For this reason when a ruler who has comprehended the Way [Tao] is about to employ his people, he will first bring them into harmony, and only thereafter embark on great affairs. He will not dare rely solely on his own plans, but will certainly announce them formally in the ancestral temple, divine their prospects by the great tortoise shell, and seek their confirmation in Heaven and the seasons. Only if they are all auspicious will he proceed to mobilize the army.[3]

"Because the people know the ruler values their lives and is sorrowed by their deaths, when such circumstances arise and they must confront danger with him, the officers will consider death while advancing glorious, but life gained through retreating disgraceful."

✔   ✔   ✔

Wu-tzu said: "Now the Way [Tao] is the means by which one turns back to the foundation and returns to the beginning. Righteousness is the means by which to put affairs into action and realize accomplishments. Plans are the means by which to keep harm distant and gain profit. The essence [provides the constraints] by which to preserve duty and conserve achievements. Now if behavior does not accord with the Way [Tao], and actions do not accord with righteousness, but instead one dwells in magnificence and enjoys nobility, disaster will inevitably befall him.

"For this reason the Sage rests the people in the Way [Tao], orders them with righteousness, moves them with the forms of propriety [*li*], and consoles them with benevolence. Cultivate these four virtues and you will flourish. Neglect them and you will decline.

"Thus when Ch'eng T'ang extirpated the evil tyrant Chieh, Chieh's people rejoiced, and when King Wu of Chou attacked the vile King Chou [of the Yin dynasty], the people of Yin did not condemn him. Because their actions accorded with Heaven and Man, they were able to succeed."

ʳ   ʳ   ʳ

Wu-tzu said: "In general to govern the state and order the army, you must instruct them with the forms of propriety [*li*], stimulate them with righteousness, and cause them to have a sense of shame. For when men have a sense of shame, in the greatest degree it will be sufficient to wage war, while in the least degree it will suffice to preserve the state.[4]

"Now being victorious in battle is easy, but preserving the results of victory is difficult.[5] Thus it is said that among the states under Heaven that engage in warfare, those that garner five victories will meet with disaster; those with four victories will be exhausted; those with three victories will become hegemons; those with two victories will be kings; and those with one victory will become emperors. For this reason those who have conquered the world through numerous victories are extremely rare, while those who thereby perished are many."

ʳ   ʳ   ʳ

Wu-tzu said: "In general the reasons troops are raised are five: to contend for fame; to contend for profit; from accumulated hatreds; from internal disorder; and from famine. The names [of the armies[6]] are also five: 'righteous army,' 'strong army,' 'hard army,' 'fierce army,' and 'contrary army.' Suppressing the violently perverse and rescuing the people from chaos is termed 'righteousness.' Relying on [the strength of] the masses to attack is termed 'strong.' Mobilizing the army out of anger is termed 'hard.' Abandoning the forms of propriety [*li*] and greedily seeking profit is termed 'fierce.' While the country is in turmoil and the people are exhausted, embarking on military campaigns and mobilizing the masses is termed 'contrary.' These five each have an appropriate Way [Tao]. In the case of the righteous you must use propriety to subjugate them. Toward the strong you must be deferential to subjugate them. Against the hard you must use persuasive language to subjugate them. Against the fierce you must employ deceit to subjugate them. Against the contrary you must use the tactical balance of power [*ch'üan*] to subjugate them."

ʳ   ʳ   ʳ

Marquis Wu asked: "Could I hear about the Way [Tao] for ordering the troops, evaluating[7] men, and making the state secure?" Wu Ch'i replied:

"The enlightened kings of antiquity always exerted every effort to maintain the forms of propriety [li] between themselves and their ministers, manifest the distinctions of rank, settle and assemble the officials and people, accord with their customs to instruct them, and select and recruit the talented in order to prepare for the unexpected.

"In the past Duke Huan of Ch'i[8] enlisted the support of fifty thousand men and thereby attained hegemony over the feudal lords. Duke Wen of Chin summoned forty thousand men to serve as his lead troops and thereafter realized his intention [of becoming hegemon]. Duke Mu of Ch'in organized thirty thousand men into penetrating formations and subdued neighboring enemies.

"Thus the ruler of a strong state must evaluate his people. Among the people those who have courage and strength should be assembled into one unit. Those who take pleasure in advancing into battle and exerting their strength to manifest their loyalty and courage should be assembled into another unit. Those who can climb high and traverse far, who are nimble and fleet should be assembled into a unit. Officials of the king who have lost their positions and want to show their merit to their ruler should be assembled into a unit. Those who abandoned their cities or left their defensive positions and want to eradicate the disgrace should also be assembled into a unit. These five will constitute the army's disciplined, elite troops. With three thousand such men, from within one can strike out and break any encirclement or from without break into any city and slaughter the defenders."[9]

*   *   *

Marquis Wu inquired: "I would like to hear about the Way [Tao] for making battle formations invariably stable, defenses inevitably solid, and victory in battle certain." Wu Ch'i replied: "This can immediately be made clear, but why ask only about this? If you are able to have worthy men hold high positions and the unworthy occupy low positions, then your battle formations will already be stable. If the people are settled in their farming and homes and [are] attached to their local authorities, then your defenses will already be solid. When the hundred surnames all acclaim my lord and condemn neighboring states, then in battle you will already be victorious."

*   *   *

Once when Marquis Wu was planning government affairs, none of his numerous ministers could equal him. After dismissing the court he had a happy, self-satisfied look. Wu Ch'i entered and said: "Once in antiquity when King Chuang of Ch'u was planning state affairs, he discovered none of his ministers could equal his talents. After he had dismissed the court he wore a troubled countenance. Duke Shen inquired: 'Why does your lordship have a troubled countenance?' He replied: 'I have heard it said that there is no lack of Sages in the world and no shortage of Worthies in a state. One who can get them to be his teachers will be a king, while one who has them as his friends can become a hegemon. Now I am not talented, yet none of my ministers can even equal me in ability. Our state of Ch'u is in deep trouble.' This is what the king of Ch'u found troublesome, yet you are pleased by it. I therefore dare to be fearful!" Marquis Wu immediately looked embarrassed.[10]

2. Evaluating the Enemy

Marquis Wu addressed Wu Ch'i: "At present Ch'in coerces me on the west, Ch'u encircles me in the south, Chao collides with me in the north, Ch'i encroaches on us in the east, Yen cuts off my rear, and Han occupies land to the front. Defending against the troops of six nations in all four directions, our strategic configurations of power [*shih*] is extremely disadvantageous. I am worried. What can be done about this?"

Wu Ch'i replied: "In general first being cautious is the true treasure in the Way [Tao] for ensuring the security of the state. As you have now awakened to the trouble, disaster can be kept away. Let me discuss the character and customs of these six countries.[11]

"Although Ch'i's battle array is dense in number, it is not solid. That of Ch'in is dispersed, with the soldiers preferring to fight individually. Ch'u's formations have good order, but they cannot long maintain their positions. Yen's formations are adept at defense, but they are not mobile.[12] The battle arrays of the Three Chin are well controlled, but they prove useless.

"Now Ch'i's character is hard; their country is prosperous; the ruler and ministers are arrogant and extravagant and insulting to the common people. The government is expansive, but salaries are inequitable. Each formation is of two minds, with the front being heavy and the rear light. Thus while they are dense, they are not stable. The Way [Tao] to attack them is to divide them into three, harrying and pursuing the left and right, coercing and following them for then their formations can be destroyed.

"Ch'in's character is strong, the land treacherous, and the government severe. Their rewards and punishments are believed in; the people never yield but instead are all fiery and contentious. Thus they scatter and individually engage in combat. The Way [Tao] to attack them is to first entice them with profits for their soldiers are greedy and will abandon their generals to pursue them. Capitalizing on their misjudgment you can hunt down their scattered ranks, establish ambushes, take advantage of the moment, and then their generals can be captured.

"Ch'u's character is weak, its lands broad, its government troubling [to the people], and its people weary. Thus while they are well-ordered, they do not long maintain their positions. The Way [Tao] to attack them is to suddenly strike and cause chaos in the encampments. First snatch away their *ch'i*—lightly[13] advancing and then quickly retreating, tiring and laboring them, never actually joining battle with them. Then their army can be defeated.

"Yen's character is sincere and straightforward. Its people are careful; they love courage and righteousness and rarely practice deception in their plans. Thus they will defend their positions but are not mobile. The Way [Tao] to attack them is to strike and press them; insult them and then put distance between you; then race and get behind them so that their upper ranks will be doubtful and their lower ranks fearful. Be cautious about our chariots and cavalry, avoiding conflict on the open road, and then their general can be captured.

"The Three Chin are central countries. Their character is harmonious and their governments equitable. The populace is weary from battle but experienced in arms, and they have little regard for their generals. Salaries are meager, and as their officers have no commitment to fight to the death, they are ordered but useless. The Way [Tao] to attack them is to press [points in] their formations, and when large numbers appear oppose them. When they turn back, pursue them in order to wear them out. That then is the strategic configuration of power [*shih*] in these countries.

"Within the army you must have soldiers with the courage of tigers, the strength to easily lift tripods, and the fleetness of barbarian horses. To attack their flags and seize their generals you must have men with such abilities. If you have men such as these, select and segregate them [into special units]; favor and honor them. They are referred to as the 'army's fate.' Those who are expert in the use of the five weapons,[14] who are strong and quick and are intent on swallowing the enemy should be given rank and prominence for they can make victory decisive. If you are generous to their parents, wives, and children; encourage them with rewards; and awe them with punishments, these strong soldiers, when in formation, will solidly hold their positions for a long time. If you can discern and evaluate men such as these, you can attack a force double your strength."

Marquis Wu exclaimed: "Good!"

Wu-tzu said: "In general when evaluating the enemy there are eight conditions under which one engages in battle without performing divination.[15]

"First, in violent winds and extreme cold, they arise early and are on the march while [barely] awake, breaking ice to cross streams, unfearing of any hardship.[16]

"Second, in the burning heat of midsummer, they arise late and without delay press forward in haste, through hunger and thirst, concentrating on attaining far-off objectives.

"Third, the army has been out in the field for an extended period; their food supplies are exhausted; the hundred surnames are resentful and angry; and numerous baleful portents have arisen, with the superior officers being unable to squash their effects.

"Fourth, the army's resources have already been exhausted; firewood and hay are scarce; the weather frequently cloudy and rainy; and even if they wanted to plunder for supplies, there is nowhere to go.

"Fifth, the number mobilized is not large; the terrain and water not advantageous; the men and horses both sick and worn out; and no assistance comes from their allies.

"Sixth, the road is far and the sun setting; the officers and men have labored long and are fearful. They are tired and have not eaten; having cast aside their armor, they are resting.

"Seventh, the generals are weak; the officials irresponsible; the officers and troops are not solid; the Three Armies are frequently frightened; and the forces lack any assistance.

"Eighth, their formations are not yet settled; their encampment [is] not yet finished; or they are traversing dangerous territory and narrow defiles, half concealed and half exposed.

"In these eight conditions attack them without any doubts.

"There are six circumstances in which, without performing divination, you should avoid conflict.

"First, the land is broad and vast, the people wealthy and numerous.

"Second, the government loves the people, the ruler's beneficence extends and flows [to all of them].

"Third, rewards are trusted, punishments based on investigation, and both are invariably implemented in a timely fashion.

"Fourth, people are ranked according to their military accomplishments; they award official positions to the Worthy and employ the able.

"Fifth, their forces are massive, and their weapons and armor are all first-rate.

"Sixth, they have the assistance of all their neighbors and the support of a powerful state.

"In general in these situations you are not a match for the enemy, so without doubt avoid them. This is what is meant by 'seeing possibility and advancing, knowing difficulty and withdrawing.'"

*   *   *

Marquis Wu inquired: "From external observation of the enemy I would like to know their internal character, from studying their advance know at what point they will stop in order to determine victory and defeat.[17] May I hear about this?"

Wu Ch'i replied: "If the enemy approaches in reckless disarray, unthinking; if their flags and banners are confused and in disorder; and if the men and horses frequently look about, then one unit can attack ten of theirs, invariably causing them to be helpless.

"If the feudal lords have not yet assembled; ruler and ministers are not yet in agreement; ditches and embankments not yet complete; prohibitions and orders not yet issued; and the Three Armies clamoring—wanting to advance but being unable to, wanting to retreat but not daring to—then you can attack with half the enemy's force and never lose in a hundred encounters."

*   *   *

Marquis Wu asked: "Is there a Way [Tao] by which the enemy can invariably be attacked?"

Wu Ch'i said: "In employing the army you must ascertain the enemy's voids and strengths and then race [to take advantage of] his endangered points. When the enemy has just arrived from afar and their battle formations are not yet properly deployed, they can be attacked. If they have eaten but not yet established their encampment, they can be attacked. If they are running about wildly, they can be attacked. If they have labored hard, they can be attacked. If they have not yet taken advantage of the terrain, they can be attacked. When they have lost the critical moment and not followed up on opportunities, they can be attacked. When they have traversed a great distance and the rear guard has not yet had time to rest, they can be attacked. When fording rivers and only half of them have crossed, they can be attacked. On narrow and confined roads, they can be attacked. When their flags and banners move about chaotically, they can be attacked. When their formations frequently move about, they can be attacked. When a general is separated from his soldiers, they can be attacked. When they are afraid, they can be attacked. In general in circumstances such as these, select crack troops to rush on them, divide your remaining troops, and continue the assault— pressing the attack swiftly and decisively."

3. Controlling the Army

Marquis Wu asked: "In employing the troops what is primary?"

Wu Ch'i replied: "First make clear the four [principles] of lightness, the two of heaviness, and the one of belief."

The Duke asked: "What do you mean?"

He replied: "You should arrange the employment of terrain so that it will be easy for the horses; the horses so that they will easily pull the chariots; the chariots so that they will easily convey the men; and the men so that they will easily engage in battle. If you are clear about treacherous and easy ground, then the terrain will be light for the horses. If they have hay and grain at the proper times, the horses will easily pull the chariots. If the axles are well greased, the chariots will easily convey the men. If the weapons are sharp and armor sturdy, the men will easily engage in battle. For advancing there should be generous rewards; for retreating heavy penalties; and they should both be properly implemented so that they will be believed in. If your examination can realize this, it will be the key to victory."[18]

Marquis Wu asked: "What measures will ensure the soldiers will be victorious?"

Wu Ch'i replied: "Control[19] is foremost."

Marquis Wu again asked: "It is not large numbers?"

"If the laws and orders are not clear, rewards and punishments not trusted; when sounding the gongs will not cause them to halt or beating the drum to advance, then even if you had one million men, of what use would they be? What is meant by control is that when stationary [in camp] they observe the forms of propriety [*li*] and when in action they are awesome. When they advance they cannot be withstood; when they withdraw they cannot be pursued. Their advancing and withdrawing are measured; the left and right flanks respond to the signal flags. Even if broken off from the main order they preserve their formations; even if scattered they will reform lines. They will hold together in peace; they will hold together in danger. Their number can be assembled together, but cannot be forced apart. They can be employed, but they cannot be exhausted. No matter where you can dispatch them, no one under Heaven will be able to withstand them. They are called 'the troops of a father and son.' "[20]

Wu-tzu said: "In general the Way [Tao] to command an army on the march is to not contravene the proper measure of advancing and stopping; not miss the appropriate times for eating and drinking; and not completely exhaust the strength of the men and horses. These three are the means by which the troops can undertake the orders of their superiors. When the orders of superiors are followed, control is produced. If advancing and resting are not measured; if drinking and eating are not timely and appropriate; and if, when the horses are tired and the men weary, they are not allowed to relax in the encampment, then they will be unable to put the commander's orders into effect. When the commander's orders are thus disobeyed, when encamped they will be in turmoil, and in battle they will be defeated."

Wu-tzu said: "In general, on the battlefield—soon to become a graveyard—if the soldiers are committed to fight to the death they will live, whereas if they seek to stay alive they will die. A good general will act as if [they are] in a sinking boat or trapped in a burning building—there is not enough time for the wise to make plans or the courageous to get angry. Only engaging the enemy will do! Thus it is said that the greatest harm that can befall the army's employment [stems from] hesitation, while the disasters that strike the Three Armies are born in doubt."

Wu-tzu said: "Now men constantly perish from their inabilities and are defeated by the unfamiliar. Thus among the methods for using the military, training and causing them to be alert are first. One man who has been trained in warfare can instruct ten men. Ten men who have studied warfare can train one hundred men. And one hundred such men can train one thousand. One thousand, ten thousand; and ten thousand who have been trained in warfare can train the entire body of the Three Armies.

"With the nearby await the distant; with the well-ordered await the labored; with the surfeited await the hungry.[21]

"Have them deploy in circular formations, then change to square ones. Have them sit, then get up; move, then halt. Have them move to the left, then the right; forward and to the rear. Have them divide and combine, unite and disperse. When all these changes are familiar, provide them with weapons. These are what are termed 'the general's affairs.'"

,   ,   ,

Wu-tzu said: "The basic rule of warfare that should be taught is that men short in stature should carry spears and spear-tipped halberds, while the tall should carry bows and crossbows.[22] The strong should carry the flags and banners; the courageous should carry the bells and drums. The weak should serve in supply work, while the wise should supervise the planning.

"Districts and villages should be organized together, with squads of five and ten forming the basis for mutual protection and guarantee. To a single drum beat they should prepare their weapons; to the double beat they should drill in various deployments; to a triple beat they should hasten to eat; to a quadruple beat they should have final inspection; and to a five-beat cadence they should move out. Only after you hear the drums sound in unison should you raise the banners."

,   ,   ,

Marquis Wu asked: "Is there a Way [Tao] for advancing and halting the Three Armies?"

Wu Ch'i replied: "Do not confront 'Heaven's Furnace' or 'Dragon's Head.' Heaven's Furnace is the mouth of a deep valley. Dragon's Head is the base of a high mountain. You should keep the Green Dragon banner on the left, White Tiger on the right, Vermillion Bird in the front, Mysterious Military to the rear, with Twinkler above from where military affairs will be controlled. When about to engage in combat determine the wind's direction. If favorable, yell and follow it; if contrary, assume a solid formation and await the enemy."

,   ,   ,

Marquis Wu asked: "In general are there methods for taking care of the chariots and cavalry?"[23]

Wu Ch'i replied: "Now the horses must be properly settled, with appropriate grass and water and correct feeding so as to be neither hungry nor full. In the winter they should have warm stables, in the summer cool sheds. Their mane and hair should be kept trimmed and their hooves properly cared for. Blinders and ear protectors should be used so as to keep them from being startled and frightened. Practice their galloping and pursuit, exercise constraint over their advancing and halting. Men and horses must be attached to each other; only thereafter can they be employed.

"The equipment for the chariots and cavalry—such as saddles, bridles, bits, and reins—must all be complete and durable. Normally, the horses do not receive their injuries near the end of the battle but invariably they are injured at the start. Similarly, they are not injured so much by hunger as by being overfed. When the sun is setting and the road long, the riders should frequently dismount for it is better to have the men weary than to overlabor the horses. You should always direct movements so as to keep some strength in reserve against the enemy suddenly turning on us. Anyone who is clear about this can traverse the realm without hindrance."

4. The Tao of the General

Wu-tzu said: "Now the commanding general of the Three Armies should combine both military and civilian abilities. The employment of soldiers requires uniting both hardness and softness. In general when people discuss generalship, they usually focus on courage. However, courage is but one of a general's many characteristics for the courageous will rashly join battle with the enemy. To rashly join battle with an enemy without knowing the advantages and disadvantages is not acceptable. Now the affairs to which the general must pay careful attention are five: first, regulation; second, preparation; third, commitment; fourth, caution; and fifth, simplification. Regulation is governing the masses just as one controls a few. Preparation is going out the city gate as if seeing the enemy. Commitment means entering combat without any concern for life. Caution means that even after conquering, one maintains the same control and attitude as if just entering a battle. Simplification means the laws and orders are kept to a minimum and are not abrasive.

"To accept the mandate [of command] without ever declining, destroy the enemy, and only afterward speak about returning is the proper form of behavior [li] for a general. Thus when the army goes forth, his only thought should be of the glory that death will bring, not the shame of living."

⌐   ⌐   ⌐

Wu-tzu said: "In general warfare has four vital points: ch'i, terrain, affairs, and strength. When the masses of the Three Armies—the million soldiers of the forces—are strategically deployed in appropriate formations according to varying degrees of strength by one man, this is termed the 'vital point [chi] of ch'i.' When the road is narrow and the way perilous; when famous mountains present great obstacles; and if ten men defend a place one thousand cannot pass, this is termed a 'vital point [chi] of earth.' Being good at controlling clandestine operatives; with a few light troops harassing the enemy, causing them to scatter; and forcing rulers and ministers to feel mutual annoyance and higher and lower ranks to reproach each other, this is termed the 'vital point [*chi*] of affairs.' When the chariots have solid axles and secure pins; the boats [have] well-suited rudders and oars; the officers are thoroughly familiar with the fighting formations; and the horses practiced in pursuit and maneuvers, this is termed the 'vital point [*chi*] of strength.' One who knows these four is qualified to be a general. However, his awesomeness, Virtue [*te*], benevolence, and courage must be sufficient to lead his subordinates and settle the masses. Furthermore, he must frighten the enemy and resolve doubts. When he issues orders, no one will dare disobey them. Wherever he may be, rebels will not dare oppose him. Gaining him, the state will grow strong; losing him, the state will perish. This is what is referred to as a good general."

Wu-tzu said: "Now the different drums, gongs, and bells are the means to awe the ear; flags and banners, pennants and standards the means to awe the eye; and prohibitions, orders, punishments, and fines the means to awe the mind. When the ear has been awestruck by sound, it cannot but be clear. When the eye has been awestruck by color, it cannot but be discriminating. When the mind has been awestruck by penalties, it cannot but be strict. If these three are not established, even though you have the support of the state you will invariably be defeated by the enemy. Thus it is said that wherever the general's banners are, everyone will go, and wherever the general points, everyone will move forward—even unto death."[24]

Wu-tzu said: "In general the essentials of battle are as follows. You must first attempt to divine[25] the enemy's general and evaluate his talent. In accord with the situation exploit the strategic imbalance of power [*ch'üan*]; then you will not labor but will still achieve results. A commanding general who is stupid and trusting can be deceived and entrapped. One who is greedy and unconcerned about reputation can be given gifts and bribed. One who easily changes his mind and lacks real plans can be labored and distressed. If the upper ranks are wealthy and arrogant while the lower ranks are poor and resentful, they can be separated and divided. If their advancing and withdrawing are often marked by doubt and the troops have no one to rely on, they can be shocked into running off. If the officers despise the commanding general and are intent on returning home, by blocking off the easy

roads and leaving the treacherous ones open, they can be attacked and captured. If the terrain over which they advance is easy but the road for withdrawal difficult, they can be forced to come forward. If the way to advance is
difficult but the road for retreating easy, they can be pressed and attacked. If
they encamp on low wetlands where there is no way for the water to drain
off, if heavy rain should fall several times, they can be flooded and drowned.
If they make camp in a wild marsh or fields dense with a heavy tangle of
grass and stalks, should violent winds frequently arise you can burn the
fields and destroy them. If they remain encamped for a long time—the generals and officers growing lax and lazy, the army becoming unprepared—you
can sneak up and spring a surprise attack."

Marquis Wu asked: "When our two armies are confronting each other but
I do not know their general, if I want to fathom him what methods are
there?"

Wu Ch'i replied: "Order some courageous men from the lower ranks to
lead some light shock troops to test him. [When the enemy responds] they
should concentrate on running off instead of trying to gain some objective.
Then analyze the enemy's advance, whether their actions—such as sitting
and standing—are in unison and their organization well preserved; whether
when they pursue your retreat they feign being unable to catch you, or when
they perceive easy gain they pretend not to realize it. A commander like this
may be termed a 'wise general.' Do not engage him in battle.

"If their troops approach yelling and screaming, their flags and pennants
in confusion, while some of their units move of their own accord and others
stop, some weapons held vertically, others horizontally—if they pursue our
retreating troops as if they are afraid they will not reach us, or seeing advantage are afraid of not gaining it, this marks a stupid general. Even if his
troops are numerous they can be taken."

5. Responding to Change

Marquis Wu asked: "If the chariots are sturdy, the horses excellent, the generals courageous, and the soldiers strong, but when you suddenly encounter
the enemy they are thrown into turmoil and break formation, what can be
done?"

Wu Ch'i replied: "In general it is a rule of battle that during daylight hours
the flags, banners, pennants, and standards provide the measure, while at
night the gongs, drums, pipes, and whistles provide the constraints.[26] When

left is signaled, they should go left; when right, then right. When the drum is beaten, they should advance; when the gongs sound, they should halt. At the first blowing they should form ranks; at the second assemble together. Execute anyone who does not follow the orders. When the Three Armies submit to your awesomeness and the officers and soldiers obey commands, then in combat no enemy will be stronger than you, nor will any defenses remain impenetrable to your attack."

*   *   *

Marquis Wu asked: "If the enemy is numerous while we are few, what can I do?"

Wu Ch'i replied: "Avoid them on easy terrain, attack them in narrow quarters. Thus it is said, for one to attack ten, nothing is better than a narrow defile. For ten to attack one hundred, nothing is better than a deep ravine. For one thousand to attack ten thousand, nothing is better than a dangerous pass.[27] Now if you have a small number of troops, should they suddenly arise—striking the gongs and beating the drums—to attack the enemy on a confined road, then even though his numbers are very great, they will all be startled and move about. Thus it is said, when employing larger numbers concentrate on easy terrain; when using small numbers concentrate on naturally confined terrain."

*   *   *

Marquis Wu asked: "Their forces are extremely numerous, martial, and courageous. Behind them are ravines and dangerous passes; on their right mountains; on the left a river. They have deep moats and high ramparts and are defending their position with strong crossbowmen. Their withdrawal is like a mountain moving, their advance like a tempest. As their food stocks are also plentiful, it will be difficult to defend against them for very long. What should be done?"

Wu Ch'i replied: "A great question indeed! This is not [a problem] of the strength of chariots and cavalry[28] but [of having] the plans of a Sage. If you can prepare one thousand chariots and ten thousand cavalry and support them with foot soldiers, you can divide them into five armies, each one traversing a different route. Now if the five armies simultaneously move along five different routes, the enemy will certainly be confused and will not know where to concentrate his efforts. If the enemy fortified his defenses in order to solidify his troops, quickly dispatch spies in order to observe their plans. If they listen to our persuasions, they will abandon their positions and depart. If they do not listen to our persuasions, they will kill our emissaries and burn the treaties. Then divide your forces and engage them in five battles. However, if you win any of the battles do not pursue the retreating enemy. If you do not win then withdraw in extreme haste, thereby feigning a retreat. After reforming, swiftly attack them, with one force tying them up in the front, another cutting off their rear, while two of your armies move silently to the left and right flanks to suddenly attack them. If the five armies strike simultaneously, they will certainly gain the advantage. This is the Way [Tao] for attacking the strong."

Marquis Wu asked: "The enemy is nearby, pressing us. Even if I want to retreat, there is no road. My soldiers are terrified. What can I do?"

Wu Ch'i replied: "The technique for dealing with this is as follows. If your troops are numerous and his few, divide them and attack. If, on the contrary, his troops are numerous and yours few, then use improvised measures to harry him, never giving him any rest. Then, even though he is numerous, he can be forced to submit."

Marquis Wu asked: "If I encounter the enemy in a deep valley where gorges and defiles abound to the sides, while his troops are numerous and ours few, what should I do?"

Wu Ch'i replied: "Traverse hilly regions, forests, valleys, deep mountains, and vast wetlands quickly, departing from them posthaste. Do not be dilatory. If in high mountains or a deep valley the armies should suddenly encounter each other, you should first beat the drums and set up a clamor— taking advantage of it to advance your archers and crossbowmen, both shooting the enemy and taking prisoners. Carefully investigate their degree of control; if they are confused, then attack without doubt."

Marquis Wu asked: "On the left and right are high mountains, while the land is extremely narrow and confined. If when we meet the enemy we dare not attack them yet cannot escape, what shall we do?"

Wu Ch'i replied: "This is referred to as 'valley warfare.' Even if your troops are numerous, they are useless. Summon your talented officers to confront the enemy, the nimble-footed and the sharpest weapons to be at the forefront. Divide your chariots and array your cavalry, concealing them on all four sides several *li* apart so that they will not show their weapons. The enemy will certainly assume a solid defensive formation, not daring either to advance or retreat. Thereupon display your flags and array your banners, withdraw outside the mountains, and encamp. The enemy will invariably be frightened, and your chariots and cavalry should then harass them, not permitting them any rest. This is the Way [Tao] for valley warfare."

ʼ   ʼ   ʼ

Marquis Wu asked: "If we encounter the enemy in a vast, watery marsh where the chariot wheels sink down to the point that the shafts are under water; our chariots and cavalry are floundering; and we have not prepared any boats or oars so we cannot advance or retreat, what should we do?"

Wu Ch'i replied: "This is referred to as 'water warfare.' Do not employ chariots or cavalry, but have them remain on the side. Mount some nearby height and look all about. You must ascertain the water's condition, know its expanse, and fathom its depth. Then you can conceive an unorthodox stratagem [ch'i] for victory. If the enemy begins crossing the water, press them when half have crossed."

ʼ   ʼ   ʼ

Marquis Wu asked: "When it has been continuously raining for a long time so the horses sink into the mire and the chariots are stuck, while we are under enemy attack on all four sides and the Three Armies are terrified, what should I do?"

Wu Ch'i replied: "In general desist from employing chariots when the weather is rainy and the land wet, but mobilize them when it is hot and dry. Value high terrain, disdain low ground. When racing your strong chariots, whether advancing or halting, you must adhere to the road. If the enemy arises, be sure to follow their tracks."

ʼ   ʼ   ʼ

Marquis Wu asked: "If a savage raiding force suddenly appears—plundering our lands and fields, seizing our cattle and horses—what should I do?"

Wu Ch'i replied: "When a savage raiding force appears, you must carefully consider its strength and well maintain your defensive position. Do not respond to their attacks [by going out to engage them]. When they are about to withdraw at the end of the day, their packs will certainly be heavy and their hearts will invariably be afraid. In withdrawing they will concentrate on speed, and inevitably there will be stragglers. You should then pursue and attack them, and their troops can be overcome."

ʼ   ʼ   ʼ

Wu-tzu said: "Now as to the Way [Tao] for attacking the enemy and besieging his cities: After his cities and towns have already been shattered, enter each of the palaces, take control of their bureaucrats, and collect their implements [of administration]. However, wherever your army goes do not cut down the trees, destroy houses, take the grain, slaughter the animals, or burn their supplies. Thus you will show the populace that you do not harbor vicious intentions. Accept those who seek to surrender and settle them."

6. Stimulating the Officers

Marquis Wu asked: "Is making punishments severe and rewards clear adequate for victory?"

Wu Ch'i replied: "As to these matters of severity and clarity I do not have all the answers. Even so, they are not what can be relied on. Now if when you issue commands and promulgate orders the people take pleasure in hearing them; when you raise the army and mobilize the masses the people take pleasure in battle; and when the weapons clash and blades cross the people take pleasure in death, then these three are what a ruler of men can rely on."

Marquis Wu asked: "How does one attain this result?"

Wu Ch'i answered: "You should identify men of accomplishment and honor them with a grand feast while also stimulating those who failed to accomplish anything notable."

Thereupon Marquis Wu had sitting mats set out in the ancestral temple hall, arrayed into three rows, and held a feast for the officers and chief officials. Those distinguished by their achievements sat in the front row and were feasted with the finest foods together with three meats served on the most valuable dishes. Those who ranked next in accomplishment sat in the middle row and were feasted with fine food served on less lavish vessels. Those who had not accomplished anything noteworthy sat in the last row and were feasted with fine food served on ordinary utensils. When the feast was over and they came out, he also honored the parents and families of the meritorious outside the temple gate, again according to their accomplishments. He annually sent emissaries to call on the families of those who had died in the service of the country, bestowing aid on their parents. By so doing he showed that they would not be forgotten.

After he had performed these actions for three years, Ch'in happened to mobilize its army and approach the West River commandery. When Wei's officers heard about it, those that buckled on their armor and enthusiastically attacked them without waiting for any orders from their superiors numbered in the tens of thousands.

Marquis Wu summoned Wu Ch'i and said: "Your previous instructions have all been effected."

Wu Ch'i replied: "I have heard that men have strengths and weaknesses, that their *ch'i* flourishes and ebbs. If your lordship is willing to test fifty thousand previously undistinguished men, I would like to lead them to engage the enemy. If Ch'in is not victorious, it will be laughed at by the feudal lords and lose the balance of authority [*ch'üan*] over the world.[29]

"Now if there is a murderous villain hidden in the woods, even though one thousand men pursue him they all look around like owls and glance about like wolves. Why? They are afraid that violence will erupt and harm them personally.[30] Thus one man oblivious to life and death can frighten one thousand. Now if I can take a mass of fifty thousand and turn them into a single murderous villain, leading them to punish Ch'in, we will surely make it difficult for the enemy!"

Thereupon Marquis Wu assented to his plan, granting him another five hundred strong chariots and three thousand cavalry. They destroyed Ch'in's five-hundred-thousand-man army as a result of this policy to encourage the officers.

The day before the battle Wu Ch'i spoke to the Three Armies: "All the aides and officers must confront, follow, and capture the enemy's chariots, cavalry, and infantry. If the chariots do not make prisoners of the enemy's chariots, the cavalry does not make prisoners of the enemy's cavalry, and the infantry does not take the enemy's infantry, then even if we forge an overwhelming victory no one will be credited with any achievements." Thus on the day of the battle his orders were not onerous, but his awesomeness shook the world.

5

Wei Liao-tzu 尉繚子

Translator's Introduction

THE *Wei Liao-tzu* is purportedly named after a historical figure whose surname was Wei (although this is not the same Chinese character as the state of Wei) and personal name was Liao. The character "tzu," meaning master and indicating respect, was added by the compilers of his book. One notation suggests he had once been a student of Lord Shang, the famous Legalist theorist and fabled administrator who advocated the creation of a strong centralized government marked by strict control of the people and resources. In another tradition, Wei Liao is recorded as having been an important adviser to the first Ch'in emperor in his successful quest to wrest control over all of China, but scant historical evidence sustains either view.[1]

Whatever his personal history, Wei Liao was a brilliant strategist and a perceptive observer who realized that only by integrating the civil and the martial could a state be assured of surviving in the tumultuous Warring States environment. He never illustrated his discussions with examples from personal military experience; he is not historically noted as a commander; and the book is almost devoid of actual tactics—therefore he appears to have been strictly a theoretician. However, his extensive military knowledge is evident from the frequent inclusion of passages that are found in the present *Six Secret Teachings*, the *Art of War*, and other military books[2] and from his detailed description of army organization and discipline.[3]

One view holds that Wei Liao probably lived in the last half of the fourth century B.C., an era in which mendicant persuaders indiscriminately sought receptive ears among the feudal lords regardless of their moral qualifications or state identification. Although most of them propounded doctrines that emphatically required loyalty and good faith, they themselves apparently remained unencumbered by such virtues until being accorded respectful treatment and proper employment. Even then, as exemplified by the famous general Wu Ch'i, if times changed and favor was lost, they suffered few qualms about shifting their allegiance to another regime.

Wei was among the states confronted by the new, terrible reality of the Warring States period (as discussed in the introduction). One of the three feudal domains formed by the disintegration of Chin, Wei not only retained the strength to be numbered among the seven major powers but initially also grew in military prowess. With a western border along the future Great Wall, it encompassed the central region north of the Chou imperial domain. However, Wei's fortunes began to fade under King Hui (reigned 370–319 B.C.)[4] when it suffered two significant defeats and was forced to move its capital to Ta-liang. The major defeat was at Ma-ling at the hands of Ch'i in 341 B.C., but the next twenty years also witnessed a series of losses to Ch'in—the emerging power that eventually unified the empire in 221 B.C.— and another to the large southern state of Ch'u. After shifting the capital the king renamed the state Liang and referred to himself as the "king of Liang."

The opening chapter of the *Wei Liao-tzu* makes it appear as though the book records Wei Liao's response to King Hui's obsessive search for the military and political knowledge that would not only strengthen Wei's sagging defenses but would also furnish the means by which to defeat his enemies and avenge his losses. When Mencius—the famous Confucian standard-bearer—visited King Hui in about the same period, the king initiated their interview by saying:[5] "As for ourselves, in the east I was defeated by Ch'i, and my eldest son died there. In the west we suffered the loss of some several hundred *li* to Ch'in. In the south we have been insulted by Ch'u. I am ashamed of this."

King Hui brusquely initiated his interview with Wei Liao with the same theme: "Is it true that the Yellow Emperor, through punishments and Virtue, achieved a hundred victories [without a defeat]?" Wei Liao immediately redirected the focus with a reply that emphasized human effort:[6] "Punishment was employed to attack [the rebellious], Virtue was employed to preserve [the people]. This is not what is referred to as 'Heavenly Offices, [auspicious] hours and days, yin and yang, facing toward and turning your back to.' The Yellow Emperor's [victories] were a matter of human effort, that is all." Wei Liao departed when he failed to secure employment in Wei, apparently because the king lacked confidence in policies that in addition to military measures would require the cultivation and pursuit of virtue.

The only other textual reference to a "Wei Liao" appears in the *Shih chi* annals depicting Ch'in's ascension to power roughly eighty years later. A man identified only as "Wei Liao, a man of Ta-liang" (the capital of Wei) offers advice to the youthful king of Ch'in, the eventual unifier of the empire known as Ch'in Shih Huang-ti. In 237 B.C. the king seized the reins of power from his ministers and immediately began to expel all foreign advisers and favored retainers:

> The king had a sweeping search conducted in order to expel the foreign retainers. Li Ssu sent up a memorial [in opposition] and the king stayed the expulsion order. Li Ssu then persuaded the king of Ch'in to consider first taking Han in order to frighten the other states. Thereupon he had Li Ssu plan the fall of Han. The king of Han was worried and plotted with Han Fei-tzu how to weaken Ch'in.
>
> [At this time] Wei Liao, a native of Ta-liang, advised the king of Ch'in, saying: "With respect to [the vastness of] Ch'in's borders, the feudal lords may be compared to the rulers of provinces and districts. My only fear is that the feudal lords will form an alliance, uniting to do something unexpected. This is how Chih Po, Fu Ch'ai, and King Min perished. I request your Majesty not begrudge the expense of his wealth to bribe the great ministers and thereby cause confusion in their plans. Without expending more than thirty thousand *chin* the feudal lords can be eliminated." The king of Ch'in followed his plan, never stood on ceremony in his interviews with Wei Liao, and wore the same clothes and ate the same food.
>
> Liao said [to others]: "As for the king of Ch'in's character, he has a nose like a wasp, elongated eyes, shoulders like a vulture, and sounds like a wolf. He has little kindness and generosity for others but has the heart of a tiger or a wolf. When in straightened circumstances he easily humbles himself to others, but when he attains his ambition he will just as easily consume people. I am a common man, but when he sees me he is always very deferential. If I truly enable the king of Ch'in to gain his objective of ruling All under Heaven, then All under Heaven will become prisoners. I cannot consort with him for long." Then he departed. The king of Ch'in realized it, stopped him, and appointed him as a Commander, using his plans and strategies. Li Ssu was in charge of governmental affairs.[7]

No further mention of Wei Liao's activities or his role in Ch'in survives, although the policy he suggested was apparently implemented with considerable success.

The historical picture is complicated further by the former existence of two distinct works entitled *Wei Liao-tzu*, based on their inclusion in two different *Han shu* bibliographic categories. One, which is identified with the Wei Liao who is noted as a disciple of Lord Shang, appears in the "miscellaneous" category, whereas the other is found under "military" books. The text incorporated in the present *Seven Military Classics*, although essentially consistent, also appears to combine two distinct works. (The first twelve chapters are more philosophical and general in scope and frequently deal with grand strategy, whereas the last twelve focus on the nature and problems of organization, discipline, command, and structure.) This dichotomy has prompted various theories about the possible authors and their relationship with these texts, which are discussed in the last part of this introduction.

Scholarly interest in the *Wei Liao-tzu* has recently increased because several chapters, still fairly well preserved on bamboo slips, were discovered in 1972 in the Han dynasty tomb at Lin-i. Although there are numerous minor differences in wording—especially in the choice of particles—and the bamboo slip edition is characterized by a somewhat more philosophical orientation than the current *Wei Liao-tzu*, only a few of the differences significantly affect the traditional understanding of the historically received passages.

The style and historical content of the book suggest a composition date around the end of the fourth century B.C., and based on the bamboo slip edition,[8] the book clearly assumed its present form before the inauguration of the Han in 206 B.C.—contrary to skeptical claims that denigrate it as a much later fabrication. Therefore, it might tentatively be concluded that the *Wei Liao-tzu* may actually be based on Wei Liao's court conversations with King Hui in the fourth century B.C., perhaps with additional, detailed material about military organization appended by someone from his family or school within the century after his death.

Basic Measures and Policies

Wei Liao must have been painfully aware of the military developments and famous engagements of the fourth century B.C. as well as of the escalating magnitude and brutality of battle. When he began his audiences with King Hui, he should have been thoroughly familiar with Wei's defeats at Kui-ling and Ma-ling, and he had probably studied and reflected on the strategies employed within the context of evolving military theory. Analyzing the state's situation, he apparently concluded that only radical, thoroughly implemented policies could provide any hope for preserving the state and perhaps achieving the king's virtually unobtainable objectives. Thus his conversations—as portrayed in the *Wei Liao-tzu*—propose drastic measures requiring strict enforcement and advocate a thorough revision of the state's values, policies, and basic approach to political and military issues.

The Basis: Agriculture and the People

Because the state of Wei had suffered devastating territorial, military, and economic losses in the preceding wars, increasing the population became an immediate priority. From Wei Liao's viewpoint, a state's prosperity depended mainly on fully developing and exploiting its agricultural resources. In order to increase productivity, new lands must be cultivated and energetic farmers nurtured. Government policies that emphasize agriculture and offer incentives to attract disaffected, displaced, or vanquished migrant peoples simultaneously accomplish both objectives.[9] Greater harvests rapidly provide the populace with adequate nourishment while creating economic wealth. When they are well fed, clothed, and sheltered, the people will be healthy, strong, and content and will naturally give their allegiance to the benevolent ruler who nurtured them. They will thus become loyal citizens capable of being inculcated with values, instructed in the virtues and demands of the state.

Humanistic Values and Authoritarian Government

The government must embrace the full range of humanistic values associated with Confucianism, although the *Wei Liao-tzu* never refers to Confucius nor attributes them to his school. The ruler must be the foremost exemplar of the Tao, personally cultivating and embodying Virtue. He should severely limit his desires and follow the path of moderation and restraint.[10] His actions must always be righteous, his motives benevolent. His policies must be directed toward aiding and sustaining the people rather than toward self-aggrandizement and the glorious exercise of power. The forms of propriety, good faith, filial behavior, the family, friendship, and shame must all be fostered among the populace. When the agricultural seasons are respected and the government imposes few taxes and minimizes corvée duties, the people can be virtuous. As their faith in the government develops, they can be instructed in and rewarded for appropriate performance. When the laws, standards of propriety, and righteousness are taught, a sense of shame will develop and the government can then properly punish deviant behavior.[11] As long as the government does not exhaust the people, moral behavior and social conformance can be expected.

Although Wei Liao believed in the fundamental Confucian, humanistic virtues, he also advocated draconian measures to ensure that only those values sanctioned by the state as productive and acceptable would be honored. Therefore, he proposed strictly prohibiting heterodoxy and vigorously suppressing any tendencies inimical to agriculture and warfare, the twin foundations of the state. The government must establish the proper tone by not permitting desires nor extravagance, by eliminating decoration and frivolity. Talented administrators must be employed to supervise all the activities of both the state and the people, with the people's welfare being paramount. Commercial enterprises and the pursuit of profit, although essential to the state's economic strength and welfare,[12] must be appropriately directed and constrained to prevent them from harming the people and the entire value system. Harmony, cooperation, and unity must be fostered and ensured in all activities.

Conquest and the Path to Victory

If the government can truly establish Virtue and foster the people's welfare, the state should be able to develop the internal strength to vanquish its enemies without resorting to force of arms. Although there are many prerequisites to military success, proper preparation and thorough planning coupled with careful evaluation of the enemy and the battlefield situation are paramount. Accordingly:

> In general, [in employing] the military there are those who gain victory through the Tao; those that gain victory through awesomeness; and those that gain victory through strength. Holding careful military discussions and evaluating the enemy, causing the enemy's *ch'i* to be lost and his forces to scatter so that even if his disposition is complete he will not be able to employ it, this is victory through the Tao.
>
> Being precise about laws and regulations, making rewards and punishments clear, improving weapons and equipment, causing the people to have minds totally committed to fighting, this is victory through awesomeness.
>
> Destroying armies and slaying generals, mounting barbicans and firing crossbows, overwhelming the populace and seizing territory, returning only after being successful, this is victory through strength.
>
> (Chapter 4: Combat Awesomeness)

Wei Liao extended the mandatory observance of humanitarian measures to campaign armies, reflecting the time-honored Confucian idea that punitive military actions should be directed against evil monarchs and their cohorts and not against the populace, except as armed adults might actively attack them. Implemented as military policy, this idea includes preserving the fields and orchards; not plundering the towns nor disturbing the populace; never destroying the people's means of livelihood; and generally securing the welfare of the people.[13] In proposing such benevolent constraints, Wei Liao was probably reacting to the almost unimaginable scale of the carnage witnessed in his era—when several hundred thousand died in battles—and the brutal policies of states such as Ch'in, which awarded rank based on the number of heads taken in combat. Therefore, rather than foraging and plundering, as Sun-tzu advocated, Wei Liao felt the army should follow practices that minimize enemy opposition and encourage the enemy to surrender to the humane ruler who will return them to their lands. Although the *Wei Liao-tzu* is not alone among the *Seven Military Classics* in advocating such measures, its author differed consciously from the practices of his time, no doubt because of the policy's strategic advantages rather than from any naive commitment to virtue.

Organization and Unity

Wei Liao believed in a strict hierarchical organization solidified by a mutual guarantee system that bonds men into units of five and ten and imposed linkages at all levels.[14] The ruler exercises supreme authority, although the commanding general replaces him in the field. The civilian populace as well as the members of the army should respond as "the limbs respond to the mind." Strict enforcement of the mutual guarantee system, originated by Lord Shang, implicates all of the unit or squad members in the transgressions of any one of them. Whether in society or in battle, failure to discover and report another's crime, prevent a comrade's death, or fight with determination was punished with the same severity as if the negligent person had committed the offense himself. Contrary to Confucian belief, under this system a father could not conceal his son's crimes nor a son his father's. Systematic drilling and army training ensures that the soldiers are solidly bonded into squads, respond to commands, are fully cognizant of their responsibilities to each other and their commanders, and are capable of executing maneuvers and engaging the enemy without panicking in the chaos and stress of battle.[15]

Rewards and Punishments

Every military analyst emphasized the irreplaceable function of rewards and punishments in society and the army. Much of the *Wei Liao-tzu* is devoted to explicating the essential principles for implementing an effective system of rewards and punishments, the majority of which are common to the other military and Legalist writings of the time. The most basic principles include establishing severity in punishments and (contrary to the belief of Lord Shang) generosity in rewards, strictly imposing punishments on even the highest ranks and granting rewards to the lowest ranks, and never pardoning offenses—although certain losses and reversals in battle could be redeemed by valiant actions that result in commensurate or surpassing achievements. The standards of conduct as well as the laws and regulations must all be clear and well publicized. No deviation—such as spontaneous acts of individual courage—is to be tolerated. Rewards should be granted solely in accord with battlefield achievements, and rank should similarly be restricted to those who have proven themselves in the test of combat. Delays in punishing and rewarding should never be allowed because their impact is diminished accordingly.

Spirit and Courage

Wei Liao believed that the army's *ch'i* essentially determined a battle's outcome; thus he extensively analyzed the nature and effects of spirit and courage, virtually formulating a detailed psychology of combat. The fundamental problem is simply that people fear danger and do not want to die, even for their native state. Comprehensive measures are necessary to forge an effective army:

> People do not take pleasure in dying, nor do they hate life, [but] if the commands and orders are clear and the laws and regulations carefully detailed, you can make them advance. When, before [combat], rewards are made clear and afterward punishments are made decisive, then when [the troops] issue forth they will be able to realize an advantage, and when they move they will be successful.

(Chapter 3: Discussion of Regulations)

Wei Liao believed that by nurturing the people's allegiance to their ruler and the soldiers' love for their commander and combining the resultant positive motivation with their fear of harsh, certain punishment, a powerful, well-disciplined army could be fashioned. The key lies in ensuring that when battlefield fears of death and of the enemy inevitably arise, they are insignificant compared with the soldier's terror at the thought of the punishment they will certainly suffer for cowardice or defeat:

> Now the people do not have two things they fear equally. If they fear us then they will despise the enemy; if they fear the enemy they will despise us. The one who is despised will be defeated; the one who establishes his awesomeness will be victorious. In general, when the general is able to implement the Way [to awesomeness], his commanders will fear him. When the commanders fear their general, the people will fear their commanders. When the people fear their commanders, then the enemy will fear the people. For this reason those who would know the Tao of victory and defeat must first know about the balance of power of "fearing" and "despising."[16]

(Chapter 5: Tactical Balance of Power in Attacks)

Creating certainty and fostering commitment are paramount because when the commander exudes confidence and the orders are clear, when doubts have no chance to arise, the men will be confident and assured in their actions. Enthusiastic, unquestioned commitment will dispel doubt, carry men through battle, and terrorize the enemy—as does a warrior in the marketplace:

> If a warrior wields a sword to strike people in the marketplace, among ten thousand people there will not be anyone who does not avoid him. If I say it is not that only one man is courageous but that the ten thousand are unlike him, what is the reason? Being committed to dying and being committed to seeking life are not comparable.

(Chapter 3: Discussion of Regulations)

Wei Liao-tzu accordingly believed in Sun-tzu's tactics to "rob the enemy of his spirit," to cause fear, consternation, and confusion. A general's weaknesses can be exploited to create doubt, and deception employed to surprise and terrorize the unprepared. When neither Virtue can cause the enemy's soldiers to be ashamed and willingly submit nor awesomeness compel them to flee without being overwhelmed in battle, then such measures must be employed and the victory delivered.

Strategic and Tactical Conceptions

If we accept the *Wei Liao-tzu* as a product of the mid- to late Warring States period, the development and refinement of certain topics previously expressed in the *Ssu-ma Fa, Art of War, Wu-tzu, Mo-tzu,* and Sun Pin's *Military Methods* become apparent. Of particular importance is the new, self-reliant attitude expressed from the inception of the conversations because Wei Liao rejected not only the yin-yang practices flourishing in his time but also all reliance on Heaven and the spirits. Human effort constitutes the sole means to achievement; therefore, the ruler must ensure that the state creates regulations and implements practices appropriate to the contemporary situation and fully exploits human potential. This is attained through the development of surpassing internal strength—both economic and military—in some views synonymous with the concept of *hsing* (shape, form) and its unfolding throughout the empire as necessary as *shih* (strategic advantage conveyed by deployment of force).[17]

Wei Liao's campaign army would be characterized by a complete discipline and thorough integration that would allow great flexibility in deploying and subsequently executing complex battle plans. His tactics emphasized selected principles advanced in the other military texts, particularly speed; deception; concentration of force; assaulting weak points while avoiding strengths; acting on the most complete intelligence; seizing and maintaining the initiative; and always being active rather than passive. Sun-tzu's vision of orthodox [*cheng*] and unorthodox [*ch'i*] forces, which is generally equated with orthodox forces initiating a direct attack and unorthodox ones executing flanking or indirect attacks, evolved further into a concept of interrelationship, as one changes into the other.[18] When discipline, speed, command expertise, and the orthodox/unorthodox are integrated and fully realized, dramatic results can be attained with small forces.[19]

Wei Liao and the History of the Text

The *Wei Liao-tzu* was undoubtedly composed between the late fourth and late third centuries B.C., or roughly the middle to late Warring States period. However, contemporary scholarship continues to debate whether the early texts had any connection with either of the historical Wei Liaos, when they attained final form, and whether the present book has been accurately transmitted from the originals. Because the various positions draw radically different conclusions from the textual materials, they merit brief summation here and in the accompanying notes.

Traditional studies have all observed that the *Han shu* bibliography lists a *Wei Liao-tzu* in twenty-nine sections in the miscellaneous category[20]—with Pan Ku's annotation that it is by a Wei Liao of the Six States (Warring States) period—and another, identically titled book of thirty-one sections in the Ping *hsing-shih*[21] military subclassification. Prior to the 1972 discovery of the bamboo slip edition at Lin-i, virtually all writings from the Sung dynasty onward labeled the *Seven Military Classics* edition a forgery or bemoaned the heavy losses that had reduced the original to only twenty-four sections. Those critics who condemned the *Six Secret Teachings* as an obvious forgery because of its purported brutality and the espousal of doctrines that could not possibly have been associated with true Sages equally found fault with the *Wei Liao-tzu;* they especially objected to the passage which asserts that a truly effective commander can "kill" half of his men.[22] Among the latter group of critics, Yao Chi-heng also observed that the *Wei Liao-tzu* not coincidentally contains a passage from Mencius—which states that the "seasons of Heaven are not as good as the advantages of Earth"—and cited it as evidence that the author borrowed extensively from such writings to fabricate the book found in the miscellaneous category.[23]

Traditionalists have also tended to recognize the existence of two distinct texts, speculating on which one provides the basis for the present work. Commenting on the miscellaneous entry, Yen Shih-ku identified Wei Liao as a student of Lord Shang,[24] which caused some analysts to focus almost exclusively on this aspect and ignore many concepts historically associated with the Confucians and Taoists.[25] Others have held that the military text has been largely preserved and faithfully transmitted whereas the miscellaneous work has vanished, thus equally ignoring significant contents.[26] A third view, discussed below, proposed that there was only a single book but that it existed in different versions.

Inherently connected with the issue of textual transmission is the intricate question regarding the possible relationship of the present *Wei Liao-tzu* with the historically identified authors. One contemporary viewpoint suggests that in the absence of reliable proof to the contrary, particularly with the discovery of the bamboo slip edition, the contents should be attributed to the mendicant persuader Wei Liao because they are a record of the advice he proffered to King Hui. (The possibility of later accretions, revisions, and adjustments can easily be encompassed within this view.) This judgment is founded on the reference to Wei Liao at the beginning of the book; the continued submissive viewpoint of a subject speaking to a ruler throughout; the king's weakness and ignorance coupled with the state's debilitated condition; and the nature of the historical references.[27]

A second perspective holds that the concepts expressed within the *Wei Liao-tzu* and the scope of warfare it reflects clearly indicate that it should date from the late Warring States period and its authorship be identified with the Wei Liao who ventured to advise the king of Ch'in.[28] Moreover, this Wei Liao's surname was perhaps Liao, and he held the essentially honorary position of "*wei*," or commandant.[29] This would account for the detailed knowledge of what appears to be Ch'in's military organization preserved in the last half of the present book[30] but unfortunately not for the pretense of advising King Hui because the political realities of the two states were radically different.

Chang Lieh, who has written several articles on the dates and background of the military writings, is a proponent of the late Warring States viewpoint for several interesting reasons.[31] First, because King Hui and Lord Shang were known historical protagonists, if Wei Liao had been associated with the latter in any way or had espoused doctrines associated with him, he would hardly have dared to seek an audience with King Hui.[32] Second, the amalgamation of Confucian concepts of righteousness and benevolence with a state policy sanctioning aggressive warfare (ostensibly to chastise the evil) did not evolve until late in the Warring States period, when it was synthesized by Hsün-tzu. Earlier, during King Hui's reign—in direct opposition to Confucians such as Mencius—Lord Shang had advocated eliminating virtue and its associated concepts from society and political life and relying instead on strength, rewards, and punishments. The *Wei Liao-tzu*, on the contrary, integrates virtue and might while stressing both severe punishments and generous rewards—the latter in direct contradiction of Lord Shang. Accordingly, the historical author should intellectually and temporally postdate Lord Shang and Hsün-tzu.[33] Third, he embraces and continues other ideas of Hsün-tzu, such as relying on men rather than Heaven and enriching the people.[34] Finally, noting Wei Liao's trepidations as chronicled by the *Shih chi*, Chang suggests they stemmed from his daunting championship of virtue and righteousness within an extremely inhospitable context of brutality and militarism. Chang therefore concludes that the text was written near the end of the Warring States period and that it is properly attributed to the late historical adviser to the young king.[35]

In one of the initial articles analyzing the bamboo slips and the contemporary *Wei Liao-tzu*, Ho Fa-chou offers some general observations and conclusions.[36] First, he believes that the bamboo slip edition, the four chapters preserved in the *Ch'ün-shu chih-yao*,[37] and the text classified in the miscellaneous category were originally identical. However, he feels that the *Seven Military Classics* version originates in the one subsumed under the military category. Furthermore, an analysis of the extant writings causes him to conclude that both *Han shu* texts were originally variations of the same book, the miscellaneous version simply being characterized by more Confucian and Taoist terms and concepts. Correspondingly, the military materials in the military text were given greater prominence and the language was simplified, but the subject matter and conclusions remain congruent.[38]

Ho also raises the intriguing question as to why, if the work is posited as a forgery, it would be imputed to an unknown sophist in an obscure presentation to a ruler remembered mostly for his failures. Because the *Wei Liao-tzu* contains numerous admonitions and correctives that could only have been directed to a weak ruler—rather than to the despot of a strong state such as Ch'in—Ho concludes it must be a record of an actual audience rather than a later confabulation. Further evidence is garnered from the historical events and figures Wei Liao cites—in particular his employment of Wu Ch'i as an exemplar—and the likelihood that Wei Liao was merely continuing to espouse practices and measures in concord with Wei's strong administrative and early Legalist tradition.[39] Furthermore, Wei's debilitated condition had prompted King Hui to actively seek external advice and receive proponents of virtually every position, thus stimulating an interchange of ideas and principles among Confucians, Taoists, Legalists, and others—such as Wei Liao.[40]

Robin D. S. Yates, in a seminal article, has summarized many of these views and contributed his own interpretations.[41] He finds internal evidence for having classified the *Wei Liao-tzu* under the military subcategory "form and positional advantage" (*hsing-shih*) lacking and questions whether the extant texts are actually the ones seen by the *Han shu* bibliography's compilers.[42] He further suggests that the book's identification with Wei Liao is essentially a matter of convenient attribution to foster a sense of authority and lacks any inherent justification.[43] Based on its Confucian and Taoist materials coupled with the diatribes against the use of divination, Yates then postulates a likely composition date that is slightly post-Mencius.[44]

Finally, in the critical introduction to his 1989 annotated *Wei Liao-tzu ch'ien-shuo,*[45] Hsü Yung thoroughly reviews the above material—only to creatively revive the original theory that naively believed the historical figures, although active in two distinct periods, were actually a single individual. Unconvinced by the arguments for attributing the text to either the earlier or the later Wei Liao, Hsü emphasizes the minimal likelihood that two men with identical names could have appeared within a century of each other in the Warring States era.[46] In addition, the contents of the second part of the book clearly detail the forms of military organization and principles for army practice that probably characterized Ch'in's forces.[47] The concept of benevolence constituting the proper foundation for all warfare, which is prominent in the first part of the *Wei Liao-tzu,* is also thought to have arisen late in the Warring States period. Because Hsü Yung believes the book is basically homogeneous, he consciously draws the inevitable conclusion that it is the work of a single thinker. He is then compelled to resolve the problem apparently posed by the unbelievable longevity required for Wei Liao to have been active in two courts nearly a century apart by redefining King Hui's period of reign. In brief, Hsü calculates that King Hui did not die until 310 B.C., nine years after the traditionally ascribed date.[48] Therefore, if a very young Wei Liao—a native of Wei—had been granted an audience at a time when the king was soliciting advice from all persons and quarters, including Mencius, his subsequent interview with a very youthful king of Ch'in would have occurred when he was in his early nineties.[49] Nothing is heard of him thereafter because he probably died from old age rather than actively assuming some post.[50] Accordingly, the first twelve chapters of the present book would stem from the miscellaneous text—a product of his youth—and the remaining twelve from the writings consigned to the military classification—the work of his final years.[51] Thus in Hsü's view, all sixty sections originally existed in Pan Ku's time—with the historian perhaps separating them into two works—but they were combined, with losses and accretions over the ages, until constituting the present *Wei Liao-tzu.*[52]

1. Heavenly Offices[1]

King Hui of Liang inquired of Wei Liao-tzu: "Is it true that the Yellow Emperor, through punishments and Virtue,[2] achieved a hundred victories [without a defeat]?"

Wei Liao-tzu replied: "Punishment was employed to attack [the rebellious], Virtue was employed to preserve [the people].[3] This is not what is referred to as 'Heavenly Offices, [auspicious] hours and days, yin and yang, facing toward and turning your back to.' The Yellow Emperor's [victories] were a matter of human effort, that is all. Why was that?

"Now if there is a fortified city and one attacks it from the east and west but cannot take it, and attacks from the south and north but cannot take it, can it be that all four directions failed to accord with an [auspicious] moment that could be exploited? If you still cannot take it, it is because the walls are high, the moats deep, the weapons and implements fully prepared, the materials and grains accumulated in great quantities, and their valiant soldiers unified in their plans. If the wall is low, the moats shallow, and the defenses weak, then it can be taken. From this perspective, 'moments,' 'seasons,' and 'Heavenly Offices' are not as important as human effort.

"According to the *Heavenly Offices*,[4] 'deploying troops with water to the rear is referred to as "isolated terrain."[5] Deploying troops facing a long ridge is termed "abandoning the army."'[6] When King Wu attacked King Chou of the Shang, he deployed his troops with the Chi[7] River behind him, facing a mountain slope. With 22,500 men he attacked King Chou's hundreds of thousands and destroyed the Shang dynasty. Yet, had not King Chou deployed in accord with the Heavenly Offices?

"The Ch'u general Kung-tzu Hsin was about to engage Ch'i in battle. At that time a comet appeared, with its tail over Ch'i. [According to such beliefs] wherever the tail pointed would be victorious, and they could not be attacked. Kung-tzu Hsin said: 'What does a comet know? Those who fight according to the comet will certainly be overturned and conquered.'[8] On the morrow he engaged Ch'i and greatly defeated them. The Yellow Emperor said: 'Putting spirits and ghosts first is not as good as first investigating my own knowledge.' This means that the Heavenly Offices are nothing but human effort."[9]

2. Military Discussions

"Measure the fertility and barrenness of the earth, and then establish towns. To construct the city walls, determine the appropriate terrain.[10] In accord with the city walls, determine the appropriate [number of] men.[11] In accord with [the number of] men, determine the appropriate amount of grain. When all three have been mutually determined, then internally one can be solid in defense, and externally one can be victorious in battle.[12] Being victorious in battle externally and preparations[13] being controlled internally, victory and preparations are mutually employed,[14] like the halves of a tally exactly matching each other.

"Control of the army is as secretive as the [depths of] Earth, as dark and obscure as the [heights of] Heaven,[15] and is given birth from the nonexistent. Therefore it must be opened.[16] The great is not frivolous, the small is not vast.[17]

"One who is enlightened about prohibitions, pardons, opening,[18] and stopping up[19] will attract displaced people and bring unworked lands under cultivation.[20]

"When the land is broad and under cultivation, the state will be wealthy; when the people are numerous and well-ordered, the state will be governed.[21] When the state is wealthy and well governed, although the people do not remove the blocks [from the chariots] nor expose their armor, their awesomeness instills order on All under Heaven.[22] Thus it is said 'the army's victory stems from the court.'[23] When one is victorious without exposing his armor, it is the ruler's victory; when victory comes after deploying [the army], it is the general's victory.[24]

"The army cannot be mobilized out of personal anger.[25] If victory can be foreseen, then the troops can be raised. If victory cannot be foreseen, then [the mobilization] should be stopped. If trouble arises within a hundred *li,* do not spend more than a day mobilizing the forces. If trouble arises within a thousand *li,* do not spend more than a month mobilizing the forces. If the trouble lies within the Four Seas, do not spend more than a year mobilizing the forces.[26]

"As for the commanding general: Above he is not governed by Heaven, below he is not controlled by Earth, in the middle he is not governed by men. He should be composed so that he cannot be stimulated to anger. He should be pure so that he cannot be inveigled by wealth.[27] Now if the mind is deranged [by emotion], the eyes are blind, and the ears are deaf—to lead men with these three perversities is difficult!

"Wherever the army ventures—whether it is along byways that wind about like sheep's intestines, along roads as bumpy as a saw's teeth, curling about the mountains, or entering a valley—it will be victorious. Whether deployed in a square formation or deployed in a round formation, it will be victorious.[28]

"A heavy army is like the mountains, like the forests, like the rivers and great streams. A light force is like a roaring fire; like earthen walls it presses upon them, like clouds it covers them.[29] They cause the enemy's troops to be unable to disperse and those that are dispersed to be unable to reassemble.[30] Those on the left are unable [to rescue those on] the right, those on the right are unable [to rescue those on] the left.[31]

"The weapons are like a mass of trees, the [effects of the] crossbows like a goat's horns.[32] Every man, without exception, steps high and displays his courage. Casting off all doubts, fervently and determined, they go forth decisively!"

3. Discussion of Regulations

"As for the military, regulations must first be established. When regulations are established first, the soldiers will not be disordered. When the soldiers are not disordered, punishments will be clear. If wherever the gongs and drums direct them a hundred men all contend; to penetrate the enemy's ranks and cause chaos among his formations a thousand men all strive; and to overturn the enemy's army and kill his generals ten thousand men raise their blades in unison, no one under Heaven will be able to withstand them in battle.

"In antiquity the soldiers were organized into squads of five and ten, the chariots into companies and rows. When the drums sounded and the pennants flew,[33] it never happened that the first to scale the walls were not outstanding state soldiers of great strength! The first to die were also always outstanding state soldiers of great strength. If the enemy suffers a loss of one man and we lose a hundred, it enriches the enemy and greatly diminishes[34] us! Through the ages[35] generals have been unable to prevent this.

"When conscripts have been assigned to the army but they run off to their native places, or flee when they approach a battle, the harm caused by the deserters is great. Through the ages generals have been unable to prevent it.

"What can kill men beyond a hundred paces are bows and arrows. What can kill a man within fifty paces are spears and halberds. When the general drums [the advance] but the officers and troops yell at each other, twist their arrows to break them, smash their spears, cradle their halberds,[36] and find it advantageous to go to the rear, and when the battle commences these all occur, it will be internally self-defeating. Through the ages generals have been unable to prevent them.

"Soldiers losing their squads of five and ten; chariots losing their companies and rows; unorthodox[37] forces abandoning their generals and fleeing; the masses also running off—these are things which generals through the ages have been unable to prevent. Now if a general can prevent these four, he will be able to traverse high mountains, cross over deep rivers, and assail strong formations. Being unable to prevent these four is like losing your boat and oars and crossing the Yangtze and Yellow rivers. It cannot be done!

"People do not take pleasure in dying, nor do they hate life, [but] if the commands and orders are clear, and the laws and regulations carefully detailed, you can make them advance. When, before [combat], rewards are made clear, and afterward punishments are made decisive, then when [the troops] issue forth they will be able to realize an advantage, and when they move they will be successful.

"Order that a company [commander][38] be established for one hundred men, a Ssu-ma for one thousand men, and a general for ten thousand men. With a small number you can punish a mass, with the weak you can punish the strong. If you test my words [you will find] their techniques sufficient to ensure that within the masses of the Three Armies, if you execute a single man none will escape punishment. Fathers will not dare conceal their sons, and sons will not dare conceal their fathers, so how much the more so the citizens of the state?

"If a warrior wields a sword to strike people in the marketplace, among ten thousand people there will not be anyone who does not avoid him. If I say it is not that only one man is courageous, but that the ten thousand are unlike him, what is the reason? Being committed to dying and being committed to seeking life are not comparable. If you listen to my techniques, [you will find] they are sufficient to cause the masses of the Three Armies to become a brigand[39] committed to dying. No one will stand before them, no one will follow them. They will be able to come and go alone, being the army of a king or hegemon.

"Who led a mass of one hundred thousand and no one under Heaven opposed him? Duke Huan.[40]

"Who led a mass of seventy thousand and no one under Heaven opposed him? Wu Ch'i.

"Who led a mass of thirty thousand and no one under Heaven opposed him? Sun-tzu.

"Today among the armies led by commanders from the various feudal states, there is not one that does not reach a mass of two hundred thousand men. Yet if they are unable to succeed in establishing their merit, it is because they do not understand prohibitions, pardons, opening [the path to life], and stopping up [excessive severity]. If you make the ordinances clear so that one man will be victorious, then ten men will also thereby be victorious. If ten men can be victorious, then one hundred, one thousand, or ten thousand men can also thereby be victorious. Thus I say if you improve our weapons and equipment, nurture our martial courage, when you release [our forces] it will be like a bird attacking, like rushing down a thousand-fathom valley.[41]

"Now a state that finds itself in difficulty sends its valuable treasures out with emissaries to other states, sends its beloved sons out as hostages, and cedes land along its borders in order to obtain the assistance of All under Heaven. Although the troops [coming to assist] are said to number one hundred thousand, in actuality they do not exceed several tens of thousands. When their troops come forth there are none to whom [the ruler] has not said to his commanding general: 'Do not be beneath anyone nor be the first to fight.'[42] In reality one cannot enter battle with them.

"If we measure the population within our borders, without the [system of] five no one could order them. The ordinances regulate the mass of one hundred thousand, and the king must be able to have them wear our uniforms and eat our food. If they are not victorious in battle nor stalwart in defense, it is not the fault of our people for it was internally brought on. The various feudal states under Heaven aiding us in battle are like worn-out old horses with their manes flying trying to compete with legendary swift steeds. How can they supplement our *ch'i?*

"We should employ all the resources under Heaven for our own use, we should govern with all the regulations under Heaven as our own regulations. We should revise our commands and orders and make punishments and rewards clear. We should cause that apart from engaging in agriculture there will be no means to eat, and apart from engaging in battle there will be no means to attain rank. We should cause the people to bump into each other in competing to go out to the farms and into battle. Then under Heaven we will not have any enemies! Thus I say that when a command is promulgated, an order issued, its credibility will extend throughout the state.

"If among the populace there are those who say they can vanquish the enemy, do not allow them to speak idly but absolutely test their ability to fight.

"To look at other peoples' lands and gain them, to divide up other rulers' subjects and nourish them, one must be able to absorb their Worthies. If you are unable to bring in and employ their Worthies but want to possess All under Heaven, you must destroy armies and slay generals. In this way, even though you may be victorious in battle, the state will grow increasingly weak. Even though you gain territory, the state will be increasingly impoverished. All this proceeds from the state's regulations being exhausted."

4. Combat Awesomeness

"In general, [in employing] the military there are those who gain victory through the Tao; those that gain victory through awesomeness; and those that gain victory through strength. Holding careful military discussions and evaluating the enemy, causing the enemy's ch'i to be lost and his forces to scatter so that even if his disposition[43] is complete he will not be able to employ it, this is victory through the Tao.

"Being precise about laws and regulations, making rewards and punishments clear, improving weapons and equipment, causing the people to have minds totally committed to fighting, this is victory through awesomeness.

"Destroying armies and slaying generals, mounting barbicans and firing crossbows, overwhelming the populace and seizing territory, returning only after being successful, this is victory through strength. When kings and feudal lords know these, the three ways to victory will be complete.

"Now the means by which the general fights is the people; the means by which the people fight is their ch'i. When their ch'i is substantial they will fight; when their ch'i has been snatched away they will run off.

"Before punishment has been applied [to the enemy], before the soldiers have clashed, the means by which one seizes the enemy are five:

1. Discussing the way to victory in the court
2. Discussing [the general] receiving his mandate[44]
3. Discussing crossing the borders[45]
4. Discussing making the moats deep and the fortifications high
5. Discussing mobilizing, deploying, and applying punitive measures [to the enemy]

"In these five cases first evaluate the enemy and afterward move. In this way you can attack their voids and seize them.

"One who excels at employing the army is able to seize men and not be seized by others. This seizing is a technique of mind. Orders [unify][46] the minds of the masses. When the masses are not understood, the orders will have to be changed frequently. When they are changed frequently, then even though orders are issued the masses will not have faith in them.[47]

"Thus the rule for giving commands is that small errors should not be changed, minor doubts should not be publicized. Thus when those above do not [issue] doubtful orders, the masses will not listen to two different [versions]. When actions do not have any questionable aspects, the multitude will not have divided intentions. There has never been an instance where the people did not believe the mind of their leader and were able to attain their strength.[48] It has never been the case that one was unable to realize their strength and yet attain their deaths in battle.

"Therefore a state must have the righteousness of the forms of etiquette [li], trust, familiarity, and love, and then it can exchange hunger for surfeit. The state must first have the customs of filiality, parental love, honesty, and shame, and then it can exchange death for life. When the ancients led the people they invariably placed the rites and trust first, and afterward ranks and emoluments. They put honesty and shame first, and punishments and fines afterward; close relationships and love first, and imposed constraints on their persons afterward.[49]

"Thus those who engage in combat must take leading in person as their foundation in order to incite the masses and officers, just as the mind controls the four limbs. If their minds are not incited, then the officers will not die for honor. When the officers will not die for honor, then the masses will not do battle.

"In order to stimulate the soldiers, the people's material welfare cannot but be ample. The ranks of nobility, the degree of relationship in death and mourning, the activities by which the people live cannot but be made evident. One must govern the people in accord with their means to life, and make distinctions clear in accord with the people's activities. The fruits of the field and their salaries, the feasting of relatives [through the rites of] eating and drinking, the mutual encouragement in the village ceremonies, mutual assistance in death and the rites of mourning, sending off and greeting the troops—these are what stimulate the people.[50]

"Ensure that the members of the squads of five and ten are like relatives, the members of the companies and their officers[51] like friends. When they stop they will be like a solid, encircling wall, when they move like the wind and rain. The chariots will not wheel to the rear, the soldiers will not turn about. This is the Way to establish the foundation for combat.

"Land is the means for nourishing the populace; [fortified] cities the means for defending the land; combat the means for defending the cities.

Thus if one concentrates on plowing the people will not be hungry; if one concentrates on defense the land will not be endangered; if one concentrates on combat the cities will not be encircled. These three were the fundamental concerns of the Former Kings, and among them military affairs were the most urgent.

"Therefore the Former Kings concentrated on five military affairs: When the store of accumulated foodstuffs is not substantial, the soldiers do not set out. When rewards and salaries are not generous, the people are not stimulated. When martial warriors are not selected, the masses will not be strong. When weapons and implements are not prepared, their strength will not be great. When punishments and rewards are not appropriate, the masses will not respect them. If one emphasizes these five, then at rest [the army] will be able to defend any place it secures, and in motion it will be able to attain its objectives.[52]

"As for remaining within the state and going forth to attack, you want those remaining behind to be 'heavy.' In deploying your troops you want the formations to be solid. In launching an attack you want to make the utmost effort. And in going forth to battle you want to be of one mind.

"The state of a [true] king enriches the people; the state of a hegemon enriches the officers. A state that merely survives enriches the high officials, and a state that is about to perish enriches its own granaries and storehouses. This is termed 'the top being full while the bottom leaks.' When disaster comes there will be no means to effect a rescue.

"Thus I say that if you raise the Worthy and give responsibility to the capable, [even] without the time being propitious affairs will still be advantageous. If you make the laws clear and are cautious in issuing orders, then without performing divination with the tortoise shell or milfoil you will obtain good fortune. If you esteem achievement and nurture effort, without praying you will attain blessings. Moreover it is said, 'The seasons of Heaven are not as good as the advantages of Earth. Advantages of Earth are not as good as harmony among men.' What Sages esteem is human effort, that is all!

"Now when the army is toiling on the march, the general must establish himself [as an example]. In the heat he does not set up an umbrella; in the cold he does not wear heavier clothes. On difficult terrain he must dismount and walk. Only after the army's well is finished does he drink. Only after the army's food is cooked does he eat. Only after the army's ramparts are complete does he rest. He must personally experience the same toil and respite. In this fashion even though the army is in the field for a long time, it will be neither old nor exhausted."[53]

5. Tactical Balance of Power in Attacks

"The military is victorious through being quiet; a state is victorious through being united.[54] One whose strength is divided will be weak; one whose mind has doubts will be turned against.[55] Now when one's strength is weak, advancing and retreating will not be bold, and pursuing an enemy will not result in capturing anyone. Generals, commanders, officers, and troops should be a single body both in action and at rest. But if the commander's mind is already doubtful and the troops inclined to rebellion, then even though a plan has been decided on they will not move, or if movement has been initiated they cannot be controlled. When different mouths speak empty words, the general lacks the proper demeanor, and the troops have not had constant tests [during training], if they set out to attack they will inevitably be defeated. This is what is referred to as a 'hasty, belligerent army.' It is inadequate for engaging in warfare.

"Now the general is the mind of the army, while all those below are the limbs and joints. When the mind moves in complete sincerity, then the limbs and joints are invariably strong. When the mind moves in doubt, then the limbs and joints are invariably contrary. Now if the general does not govern his mind, the troops will not move as his limbs. Then even though the army might be victorious, it will be a lucky victory, not [the result of] the tactical imbalance of power in the attack.[56]

"Now the people do not have two things they fear equally. If they fear us then they will despise the enemy; if they fear the enemy they will despise us. The one who is despised will be defeated; the one who establishes his awesomeness will be victorious. In general, when the general is able to implement the Way [to awesomeness],[57] his commanders will fear him. When the commanders fear their general, the people will fear their commanders. When the people fear their commanders, then the enemy will fear the people. For this reason those who would know the Tao of victory and defeat must first know about the balance of power of 'fearing' and 'despising.'

"Now one who is not loved and cherished in the minds [of his men] cannot be employed by me; one who is not respected and feared in the minds [of his men] cannot be appointed by me.[58] Love follows from below, awesomeness is established from above. If they love [their general] they will not have divided minds; if they are awestruck [by their general] they will not be rebellious. Thus excelling at generalship is merely a question of love and awesomeness.

"One who engages in battle but does not invariably win cannot be said to 'do battle.' One who attacks an enemy but does not invariably seize them cannot be said to have 'attacked.'[59] If it were otherwise, their punishments and rewards were not sufficiently trusted. Credibility [must be established] before the moment of need; affairs [must be managed] before the first signs appear. Thus the masses, when once assembled, should not be fruitlessly dispersed. When the army goes forth it should not return empty-handed. They will seek the enemy as if searching for a lost son; they will attack the enemy as if rescuing a drowning man.

"One who occupies ravines lacks the mind to do battle.[60] One who lightly provokes a battle lacks fullness of *ch'i*. One who is belligerent in battle lacks soldiers capable of victory.

"Now in general, one who presumes upon righteousness to engage in warfare values initiating the conflict. One who contends out of personal animosity responds only when it is unavoidable. Even though hatreds have formed and troops have been mobilized, await them and value acting after them.[61] During the conflict you must await their advance.[62] When there is a lull you must prepare [against sudden attacks].

"There are armies that are victorious in the court; those that achieve victory in the plains and fields; and those that attain victory in the marketplace. There are those who fight and gain victory; those that submit and are lost; and those that are fortunate not to be defeated, as in cases where the enemy is unexpectedly frightened and victory is gained by a turn of events. This sort of victory 'by turn of events' is said not to be a complete victory. What is not a complete victory lacks any claim to having effected a tactical imbalance in power. Thus the enlightened ruler, on the day for the attack, will [concentrate on] having the drums and horns sound in unison and regulating their armed might. Without seeking victory he will then be victorious.

"Among armies there are those who abandon their defenses, abolish their awesomeness, and are yet victorious because they have methods. There are those who have early established the use of their weapons so that their response to the enemy is all-encompassing and their general leadership is perfected.

"Thus for five men there is a squad leader, for ten men a lieutenant, for one hundred men a company captain, for one thousand men a battalion commander, and for ten thousand men a general. [This organization] is already all-encompassing, already perfected. If a man dies in the morning, another will replace him that morning; if a man dies in the evening, another will replace him that evening. [The wise ruler] weighs the tactical balance of power with the enemy, evaluates the generals, and only thereafter mobilizes the army.

"Thus in general, when assembling an army a thousand *li* away, ten days are required and when a hundred *li,* one day, while the assembly point should be the enemy's border.[63] When the troops have assembled and the general has arrived, the army should penetrate deeply into their territory, sever their roads, and occupy their large cities and large towns. Have the troops ascend the walls and press the enemy into endangered positions. Have the several units of men and women each press the enemy in accord with the configuration of the terrain and attack any strategic barriers. If you occupy [the terrain around] a city or town and sever the various roads about it, follow up by attacking the city itself. If the enemy's generals and armies are unable to believe in each other, the officers and troops unable to be in harmony, and there are those unaffected by punishments, we will defeat them. Before the rescue party has arrived a city will have already surrendered.

"If fords and bridges have not yet been constructed,[64] strategic barriers not yet repaired, dangerous points in the city walls not yet fortified, and the iron caltrops not yet set out, then even though they have a fortified city, they do not have any defense!

"If the troops from distant forts have not yet entered [the city], the border guards and forces in other states[65] not yet returned, then even though they have men, they do not have any men! If the six domesticated animals have not yet been herded in, the five grains not yet harvested, the wealth and materials for use not yet collected, then even though they have resources they do not have any resources!

"Now when a city is empty and void and its resources are exhausted, we should take advantage of this vacuity to attack them. The Art [of War][66] says, 'They go out alone, they come in alone. Even before the enemy's men can cross blades with them, they have attained [victory].' This is what is meant."

6. Tactical Balance of Power in Defense

"In general, when the defenders go forth, if they do not [occupy] the outer walls of the cities nor the borderlands[67] and when they retreat do not [establish] watchtowers and barricades for the purpose of defensive warfare, they do not excel [at defense]. The valiant heroes and brave stalwarts, sturdy armor and sharp weapons, powerful crossbows and strong arrows should all be within the outer walls, and then all [the grain stored outside] in the earthen cellars and granaries collected, and the buildings [outside the outer walls] broken down and brought into the fortifications. This will force the attackers to expend ten or one hundred times the energy, while the defenders will not expend half of theirs.[68] The enemy aggressors will be harmed greatly, yet generals through the ages have not known this.

"Now the defenders should not neglect their strategic points. The rule for defending a city wall is that for every *chang* [ten feet], you should employ ten men to defend it—artisans and cooks not being included. Those who go out [to fight] do not defend the city; those that defend the city do not go out [to fight]. One man [on defense] can oppose ten men [besieging them]; ten men can oppose one hundred men; one hundred men can oppose one thousand men; one thousand men can oppose ten thousand men. Thus constructing [a city's] interior and exterior walls by accumulating loose soil [and tamping it down][69] does not wantonly expend the strength of the people for it is truly for defense.

"If a wall is one thousand *chang,* then ten thousand men should defend[70] it. The moats should be deep and wide, the walls solid and thick, the soldiers and people prepared,[71] firewood and foodstuffs provided, the crossbows stout and arrows strong, the spears and halberds well suited. This is the method for making defense solid.

"If the attackers are not less than a mass of at least a hundred thousand[72] while [the defenders] have an army outside that will certainly come to the rescue, it is a city that must be defended. If there is no external army to inevitably rescue them, then it is not a city that must be defended.

"Now if the walls are solid and rescue certain, then even stupid men and ignorant women will all—without exception—protect the walls,[73] exhausting their resources and blood for them. For a city to withstand a siege for one year, the [strength of][74] the defenders should exceed that of the attackers and the [strength of] the rescue force exceed that of the defenders.

"Now if the walls are solid but rescue uncertain, then the stupid men and ignorant women—all without exception—will defend the parapets, but they will weep. This is normal human emotion. Even if you thereupon open the grain reserves in order to relieve and pacify them, you cannot stop it. You must incite the valiant heroes and brave stalwarts with their sturdy armor, sharp weapons, strong crossbows, and stout arrows to exert their strength together in the front and the young, weak, crippled, and ill to exert their strength together in the rear.[75]

"If an army of a hundred thousand is encamped beneath the city walls, the rescue force must break open [the siege], and the city's defenders must go out to attack. When they sally forth they must secure the critical positions [along the way]. But the rescue forces to the rear [of the besiegers] should not sever their supply lines, and the forces within and without should respond to each other.[76]

"In this sort of rescue display a half-hearted commitment. If you display a half-hearted commitment, it will overturn[77] the enemy and we can await them. They will put their stalwarts in the rear, and place the old in the forefront. Then the enemy will not be able to advance, nor be able to stop the defenders [from breaking out]. This is what is meant by the 'tactical balance of power in defense.'"

7. Twelve Insults[78]

"Awesomeness lies in[79] not making changes. Beneficence lies in according with the seasons.[80] Perceptivity[81] lies in [promptly] responding to affairs. [Success in] warfare lies in controlling *ch'i*. [Skill in] attacks lies in fathoming externals.[82] Defense lies in manipulating external appearance. Not being excessive lies in measuring and counting. Not encountering difficulty lies in foresight and preparation. Being cautious lies in respecting the small. Wisdom lies in controlling the large. Eliminating harm lies in being decisive. Gaining the masses lies in deferring to other men.

"Regret arises from relying on what is doubtful. Evil lies in excessive executions. Prejudiced views come from frequently following one's own desires. Inauspicious events arise from detesting to hear about one's errors. Extravagance lies in exhausting the people's resources. Unenlightenment consists in accepting advice [which] separates you [from reality]. Being insubstantial stems from lightly initiating movements. Stubbornness and ignorance lie in separating yourself from the Worthy. Misfortune lies in loving profits. Harm lies in drawing common men near. Disaster lies in lacking any place to defend. Danger lies in lacking [clear] commands and orders."

8. Martial Plans

"In general, [when employing] the military do not attack cities that have not committed transgressions or slay men who have not committed offenses.[83] Whoever kills people's fathers and elder brothers; whoever profits himself with the riches and goods of other men; whoever makes slaves of the sons and daughters of other men is in all cases a brigand. For this reason the military provides the means to execute the brutal and chaotic and to stop the unrighteous.[84] Whenever the army is applied the farmers do not leave their occupations in the fields, the merchants do not depart from their shops, and the officials do not leave their offices, due to the martial plans[85] all proceeding from one man.[86] Thus even without the forces bloodying their blades, All under Heaven give their allegiance.

"A state of ten thousand chariots [concentrates on] both agriculture and warfare. A state of one thousand chariots [focuses] on rescuing [others] and on defending [itself].[87] A state of one hundred chariots [commits itself] to serving and supporting [other states].[88] Those engaged in agriculture and warfare do not seek any authority [ch'üan] outside themselves; those who rescue others and defend themselves do not seek aid outside themselves; and those who serve and support other states do not seek material resources outside themselves. Now if [one's resources] are neither sufficient to go forth to wage battle nor adequate to remain within the borders and defend the state, one must correct [the insufficiency] with markets. Markets are the means to provide for both offensive and defensive warfare. If a state of ten thousand chariots lacks states of one thousand chariots to assist it, it must have markets able to furnish one hundred chariots.

"In general, executions provide the means to illuminate the martial. If by executing one man the entire army will quake, kill him. If by rewarding[89] one man ten thousand men will rejoice, reward him. In executing, value the great; in rewarding, value the small. If someone should be killed, then even though he is honored and powerful, he must be executed, for this will be punishment that reaches the pinnacle. When rewards extend down to the cowherds and stable boys, this is rewards flowing down [to the lowest]. Now the ability to implement punishments that reach the pinnacle, and rewards that flow down [to the lowest], is the general's martial charisma. Thus rulers value their generals.[90]

"Now when the commanding general takes up the drum, brandishes the drumsticks, and approaches danger for a decisive battle so that the soldiers meet and the naked blades clash—if he drums the advance and they respond to wrest the victory, then he will be rewarded for his achievements and his fame will be established. If he drums the advance but they fail, then he himself will die and the state will perish. For this reason survival[91] and extinction, security and danger all lie at the end of the drumstick! How can one not value the general?

"Now taking up the drums and wielding the drumsticks, having the soldiers collide and the blades clash so that the ruler achieves great success through military affairs I do not find to be difficult. The ancients said, 'Attacking without chariots with protective covering,[92] defending without equipment such as the caltrops, this is what is meant by an army that does not excel at anything!' Looking without seeing and listening without hearing stem from the state not having markets.

"Now markets are offices for sundry goods.[93] [The government should] buy items which are cheap in the market and sell those that have grown expensive in order to restrain the aristocrats and people. People [only] eat one *tou*[94] of grain, and horses eat three *tou* of beans, so why is it the people have a famished look and the horses an emaciated appearance? The markets have goods to deliver, but the office lacks a controller. Now if you raise the best-trained army under Heaven but do not manage the sundry goods, this is not what is referred to as 'being able to conduct warfare.'

"[To retain men in service] straight from their mobilization to the time when their armor and helmets have become worm infested, they must be men whom we can employ. [This is like] a bird of prey pursuing a sparrow which flies into a man's arms or enters someone's dwelling. It is not that the bird is casting away its life, but that to the rear there is something to fear.

"When T'ai Kung Wang was seventy, he butchered cows at Ch'ao Ko and sold food in Meng Chin. He was more than seventy years old, but the ruler did not listen to him, and people all referred to him as a mad fellow. Then when he met King Wen he commanded a mass of thirty thousand and with one battle All under Heaven was settled. Without his understanding or martial plans, how could they have achieved this unification? Thus it is said, 'If a good horse has a whip, a distant road can be traversed; if Worthies and men of rank unite together, the Great Tao can be illuminated.'

"When King Wu attacked King Chou, the army forded [the Yellow River] at Meng Chin. On the right was the king's pennant, on the left the ax of punishment, together with three hundred warriors committed to die and thirty thousand fighting men. King Chou's formation deployed several hundred thousand men, with [the infamous ministers] Fei Liao and O Lai personally leading the halberdiers and ax bearers. Their lines stretched across a hundred *li*. King Wu did not exhaust the warriors or people, the soldiers did not bloody their blades, but they conquered the Shang dynasty and executed King Chou. There was nothing auspicious nor abnormal; it was merely a case of perfecting oneself, or not perfecting oneself, in human affairs.

"Generals of the present generation investigate 'singular days' and 'empty mornings,' divine about Hsien-ch'ih,[95] interpret full and disastrous days, accord with tortoise shell augury, look for the auspicious and baleful, and observe the changes of the planets, constellations, and winds—wanting to thereby gain victory and establish their success. I view this as very difficult!

"Now the commanding general is not governed by Heaven above, controlled by Earth below, nor governed by men in the middle. Thus weapons are evil implements. Conflict is a contrary virtue. The post of general is an office of death. Thus only when it cannot be avoided does one employ them.[96] There is no Heaven above, no Earth below, no ruler to the rear, and no enemy in the front. The [unified] army of one man is like the wolf and tiger, like the wind and rain, like thunder and lightning. Shaking and mysterious, All under Heaven are terrified by it.

"The army that would be victorious is like water. Now water is the softest and weakest of things, but whatever it collides with—such as hills and mounds—will be collapsed by it for no other reason than its nature is concentrated and its attack is totally committed.[97] Now if one has the sharpness of the famous sword Mo Yeh, the toughness of rhinoceros hide [for armor], the masses of the Three Armies, and orthodox and unorthodox methods, then under All Heaven no one can withstand him in battle.

"Thus it is said that if you raise the Worthy and employ the talented, even if the hour and day [are not auspicious], your affairs will still be advantageous. If you make the laws clear and are cautious about orders, without divining with the tortoise shell or milfoil you will obtain propitious results. If you honor achievement and nurture effort, without praying you will obtain good fortune. It is also said that 'the seasons of Heaven are not as good as the advantages of Earth; the advantages of Earth are not as good as harmony among men.' The Sages of antiquity stressed human effort, that is all.

"When Wu Ch'i engaged Ch'in in battle, wherever he encamped the army did not flatten the paths between the fields. Young saplings provided protective covering against the frost and dew. Why did he act like this? Because he did not place himself higher than other men. If you want men to die, you do not require them to perform [perfunctory acts of] respect. If you want men to exhaust their strength, you do not hold them responsible for performing the rites. Thus, in antiquity an officer wearing a helmet and armor did not bow, showing people that he is not troubled by anything.[98] To annoy people yet require them to die, to exhaust their strength, from antiquity until today has never been heard of.

"When the commanding general receives his mandate, he forgets his family. When he commands the army and they encamp in the field, he forgets those close to him. When he takes up the drumsticks and drums [the advance], he forgets himself.

"When Wu Ch'i approached the time for battle, his attendants offered their swords. Wu Ch'i said: 'The general takes sole control of the flags and drums, and that is all. Approaching hardship he decides what is doubtful, controls the troops, and directs their blades. Such is the work of the general. Bearing a single sword, that is not a general's affair.'

"When the Three Armies have assumed formation, they should advance for a day and [on the next day] make a forced march to complete a total of three days' distance.[99] Beyond three days' distance they should be like un-blocking the source of a river.[100] Observing the enemy in front, one should employ their strength. If the enemy is white, then whiten them; if they are red, then redden them.[101]

"When Wu Ch'i engaged Ch'in in battle, before the armies clashed one man—unable to overcome his courage—went forth to slay two of the enemy and return with their heads. Wu Ch'i immediately ordered his decapitation. An army commander remonstrated with him, saying: 'This is a skilled war-rior. You cannot execute him.' Wu Ch'i said: 'There is no question that he is a skilled warrior. But it is not what I ordered.' He had him executed."[102]

9. The General as a Law Official[103]

"In general, a general is an officer of the law, the ruler of the ten thousand things. It cannot be the personal domain of one man. When it is not the per-sonal domain of one man, the ten thousand things will all come [of them-selves] and be governed there, the ten thousand things will all come and be commanded there.

"The perfected man [chün-tzu] does not stop criminals more than five paces away. Even though they may shoot at him with barbed arrows, he does not pursue them. He excels at discovering the nature of a criminal's offense. Without relying on thorn branches, he can obtain a complete understanding of the offender's situation.[104]

"If you flog a person's back, brand his ribs, or compress his fingers in or-der to question him about the nature of his offense, even a state hero could not withstand this cruelty and would falsely implicate himself.[105]

"There is a saying in our age: 'One who has thousands of pieces of gold will not die; one who has hundreds of pieces of gold will not suffer corporeal punishment.' If you listen to my techniques and try them in practice, then even a person with the wisdom of Yao or Shun will not be able to affect a word [of the charge against him], nor one with ten thousand pieces of gold be able to use the smallest silver piece [to escape punishment].

"At present those in prison awaiting judgment number no less than several tens in the smallest gaols, no less than several hundred in the middle-sized jails, and no less than several thousand in the largest prisons. Ten men entan-gle one hundred men in their affairs; one hundred men drag in one thousand; and one thousand trap ten thousand. Those that have become entangled are parents and brothers; next relatives by marriage; and next those who are ac-quaintances and old friends. For this reason the farmers all leave their occu-pations in the fields, the merchants depart from their stores, and the officials leave their posts.[106] These good people have all been dragged in because of the nature of our criminal proceedings. The *Art of War* says: 'When an army of ten thousand goes forth, its daily expense is a thousand pieces of gold.'[107] Now when there are ten thousand good people thus entangled and imprisoned, yet the ruler is unable to investigate the situation—I take it to be dangerous!"

10. The Source of Offices

"Bureaucratic offices are the means to control affairs and [are] the foundation of administration. Regulations which divide the people into four groups according to their occupations are the parameters of administration.[108] Honor, rank, riches, and salaries must be appropriately determined for they are the embodiment of nobility and humbleness. Treating the good well and punishing the evil, rectifying the laws for organizing the people, and collecting taxes and impositions are implements for governing the people.[109] Making land distributions equitable and restraining taxes and other impositions on the people provide measure to what is levied and bestowed. Regulating the artisans and [ordering] the preparation of implements for use is the contribution of the master artisans.[110] Dividing the territory and occupying the strategic points is the work of eliminating oddities and stopping licentiousness. Preserving the laws, investigating affairs, and making decisions are the roles of subordinates. Illuminating the laws and examining their application are functions of the ruler. Illuminating the duties of the bureaucrats, setting responsibilities as light or heavy—these fall under the authority [*ch'üan*] of the ministers and ruler.[111]

"Making rewards and bestowals clear, being strict in executing and punishing are methods for stopping evil. Being cautious about opening and closing and preserving the single Tao are the essentials of government.[112] When [information] from below reaches to high and [the concerns of] high penetrate to below, this is the most sensitive of perceptions. By knowing the extent of the state's resources, you can plan to use the surplus.[113] Knowing the weakness of others is [the way] to embody strength; knowing the movements of others is [the way] to determine quietness.[114] Offices are divided into the civil and the martial, and only the ruler exercises power over both.

"The ceremonial vessels are all regulated for the Son of Heaven's convocation. When itinerant persuaders and spies have no means [to gain entrance], this is the technique for rectifying discussions. The feudal lords have their rites for honoring the Son of Heaven, and rulers and their people—generation after generation—continue to acknowledge the king's mandate [to rule].

If someone changes or creates new rites, alters what is normal, or contravenes the king's illustrious Virtue, then in accord with the *li* [rites] the king can attack them.[115]

"Officials with no affairs to administer, a ruler without rank or rewards [that need to be] bestowed, a populace without criminal cases or lawsuits, a state without traders or merchants[116]—how perfected the king's rule! What I have so clearly proposed should be well heeded by your Majesty."

11. Governing the Foundation

"In general, what is the Way to govern men? I say that without the five grains[117] you have nothing to fill their stomachs, without silk and hemp nothing to cover their form. Thus to fill their stomachs there are grains, and to cover their form there is thread. Husbands work at weeding and plowing, wives at weaving. If the people do not have secondary occupations, then there will be goods accumulated in the storehouses. The men should not engrave nor make decorative carving; the women should not embroider nor do decorative stitching.

"[Carved] wooden vessels emit secretions, [engraved] metal utensils smell offensive. The Sage drinks from an earthen [vessel] and eats from an earthen [vessel]. Thus when clay is formed to make utensils there is no waste under Heaven. Today [people think] the nature of metal and wood is not cold for they embroider their clothes [with them]. The original nature of horses and oxen is to eat grass and drink water, but they give them beans and grains. This is governing which has lost its foundation, and it would be appropriate to establish regulations to control it.

"If in the spring and summer the men go out to the southern fields, and in the fall and winter the women work at weaving cloth, the people will not be impoverished. Today, when their short, coarse clothing does not even cover their bodies nor the dregs of wine and husks of grain fill their stomachs, [the foundation] of government has been lost.

"In antiquity the land was not [classified] as fertile or barren, the people were not [classified] as diligent or lazy. How could the ancients have attained this, how could we have lost it now? The men do not finish plowing their fields, the women daily break their shuttles, so how could they not be hungry and cold? Probably, the administration of the ancients was fully effected, while that of today stops [before thorough implementation].

"Now what I term 'governing well' means causing the people not to have any selfish interests. If the people do not have selfish interests, then All under Heaven will be one family. In the absence of private plowing and weaving, they will suffer the cold together, they will experience hunger together. Then even if they have ten sons they will not have [the expense of] even an extra bowl of rice, while if they have one son their expenses will not be reduced by even one bowl. Thus where would there be any clamoring and drunken indulgence to ruin the good people?

"When the people stimulate each other to frivolity and extravagance, the misfortunes of the desiring mind and of the competition to seize [things] arise. Perversity begins with one fellow, and then the people seek to selfishly accumulate some extra food and have some stored wealth. If the people then commit a single offense and you arrest them and impose corporeal punishments to control them, how is one acting as the ruler of the people? Those that excel at governing take hold of the regulations, causing the people not to have any selfish interests. When those below do not dare to be selfish, there will not be any who commit evil.

"Return to the foundation, accord with principle, have all issue forth from one Tao, and then the desiring mind will be eliminated. Competition will be stopped, the jails will be empty, the fields full, and the grains plentiful. You will settle the people and embrace the distant. Then outside your borders there will not be any difficulty under Heaven, while within the state there will be neither violence nor turbulence. This is the perfection of administration.

"The azure sky—no one knows its extremity! Of the ancient emperors and Sage kings, who should be your model? Ages that have passed cannot be regained, future ages cannot be awaited. Seek them in yourself.

"There are four qualities for one referred to as the Son of Heaven: 'Spiritual enlightenment,' 'display of brilliance,'[118] 'vast discourse,'[119] and 'being without enemies.' These are the aspects of the Son of Heaven.

"Wild animals are not used for sacrificial offerings, miscellaneous studies do not make a scholar of attainment. Today people say: 'The hundred li of the sea cannot quench one man's [uncontrolled] thirst; a spring three feet deep can slake the thirst of the Three Armies.' I say: 'Desire is born from lack of measure, perversity is born from lacking prohibitions.' The highest ruler transforms in spiritlike fashion, the next relies on things, the lowest relies on not taking the people away from their seasonal work nor seizing the people's wealth. Now prohibitions must be completed through the martial, rewards must be completed through the civil."

12. Tactical Balance of Power in Warfare

"The Art of War[120] states: 'One thousand men provide the means to exercise the tactical balance of power [ch'üan], ten thousand men constitute martial prowess. If you apply the force of tactical power to the enemy first, he will not be able to commit in strength. If you apply martial prowess first, the enemy will not be able to engage you with his full awesomeness.' Thus the army values being first. If it is victorious in this, then it will conquer the enemy. If it is not victorious in this, then it will not conquer them.

"Now when we go, they come; when we come, they go. These mutually produce victory and defeat. The pattern of battle is thus.

"Now essential sincerity lies in spiritual enlightenment. The tactical balance of power [ch'üan] lies in the extremities of the Tao. If you have something, pretend not to have it; if you lack something, appear to have it.[121] Then how can the enemy trust the appearance?

"The reason the Former Kings are still heard about is that they entrusted the upright with responsibility and eliminated the deceitful. They always preserved their benevolent and congenial hearts but were decisive, without delaying, in effecting punishments. One who understands the Tao of Warfare will invariably first plan against the defeats which arise from not knowing where to stop. Why must one always advance to be successful? If you advance too lightly and seek to engage the enemy in battle, should they—on the contrary—plan to stop your going forth, the enemy will control the victory. Thus the Art of War says: 'If they seek us, pursue them; when you see them, attack. When the aggressors dare not oppose us, press the attack, and they will inevitably lose their tactical power.'[122]

"Those from whom [the initiative] has been taken have no ch'i; those who are afraid are unable to mount a defense; those who have suffered defeat have no men.[123] They are all cases of an army lacking the Tao [of the military]. When you decide to go forth and have no doubts, then follow your plan. When you rob the enemy [of his plans] and still no one confronts you, press the attack home. If you can see clearly and occupy the high ground, then overawe them [into submission]. This is the pinnacle of the Tao of the military.

"Those who are unguarded in their discussion can be clandestinely listened to. Those who come forth to insult and taunt [your forces] without proper discipline can be destroyed. Those whose attack is like water rushing forth, like lightning striking can throw their army into chaos.[124] You must settle those [of your troops who are] in crisis, eliminate their worries, and decide matters through wisdom. Be superior to the enemy through discussions in the court; be more majestic and severe than they through discussions on bestowing the mandate [of command]; and arouse their fighting spirit through discussions of crossing the enemy's borders.[125] Then the enemy state can be forced to submit without fighting."

13. Orders for Severe Punishments

"If a general commanding one thousand men or more retreats from battle, surrenders his defenses, or abandons his terrain and deserts his troops, he is termed a 'state brigand.' He should be executed, his family exterminated, his name expunged from the registers, his ancestral graves broken open, his bones exposed in the marketplace, and his male and female children pressed into government servitude. If the commander of one hundred or more men retreats from battle, surrenders his defenses, or abandons his terrain and deserts his troops, he is termed an 'army brigand.' He should be executed, his family exterminated, and his male and female children pressed into government servitude.

"If you cause the people to fear heavy punishments within the state, then outside the state they will regard the enemy lightly. Thus the Former Kings made the regulations and measures clear before making their awesomeness and punishments heavy. When punishments are heavy, then they will fear them within the state. When they fear them within the state, then they will be stalwart outside it."

14. Orders for the Squads of Five

"Within the army the regulations for organization should be as follows: Five men comprise a squad of five, with all the members being mutually responsible for each other. Ten men comprise a double squad of ten, with all the members being mutually responsible for each other. Fifty men compose a platoon, with all the members being mutually responsible for each other. One hundred men comprise a company, with all the members being mutually responsible for each other.

"If a member of the squad of five violates an order or commits an offense, should the others report it their punishment will be remitted. If they know about it but do not report it, then the entire squad will be punished. If a member of the double squad of ten violates an order or commits an offense, should the others report it their punishment will be remitted. If they know about it but do not report it, then the entire double squad will be punished. If a member of a platoon violates an order or commits an offense, should the others report it their punishment will be remitted. If they know about it but do not report it, then the entire platoon will be punished. If a member of a company violates an order or commits an offense, should the others report it their punishment will be remitted. If they know about it but do not expose him, the entire company will be punished.

"All the officers—from the level of the double squad of ten up to the generals of the right and left, superiors and inferiors—are mutually responsible for each other. If someone violates an order or commits an offense, those that report it will be spared from punishment, while those who know about it but do not report it will all share the same offense.

"Now when the [members of the] squads of five and ten are mutually bonded and the upper and lower ranks mutually linked, no perversity will remain undiscovered, no offense will remain unreported. Fathers will not be able to cover for their sons, older brothers will not be able to conceal their younger brothers. How much less so will the people of the state, living and eating together, be able to violate orders and conceal each other?"

15. Orders for Segmenting and Blocking Off Terrain

"The Central, Left, Right, Forward, and Rear armies all have their segmented terrain—each surrounded on all four sides by temporary walls—with no passage or communication among them permitted.

"The general has his segmented terrain; the regimental commander has his segmented terrain; and the company[126] commander has his segmented terrain. They should all construct ditches and sluices and make the orders blocking [communications] explicit so that it is impossible for someone who is not a member of [the company of] one hundred to pass through. If someone who is not a member [of the company] of one hundred enters, then the commander should execute him.[127] If he fails to execute him, he will share the offense with him.

"Along the roads crisscrossing the encampment, set up administrative posts[128] every 120 paces. Measure the men and the terrain. The road posts should be within sight of each other. Prohibit crossing over the roads and clear them. If a soldier does not have a tally or token issued by a general or other commanding officer, he cannot pass through. Wood gatherers, fodder seekers, and animal herders all form and move in squads of five. If they are not moving in squads of five, they cannot cross through. If an officer does not have a token, if the soldiers are not in squads of five, [the guards] at the crossing gates should execute them. If anyone oversteps the demarcation lines, execute him. Thus if within the army no one contravenes orders nor violates the prohibitions, then without there will not be any perversity that is not caught."

16. Orders for Binding the Squads of Five

"The orders which bind the squad of five state: 'Five men comprise the squad of five. They collectively receive a tally from command headquarters. If [in battle] they lose men but capture [or kill] an equivalent number of the enemy, they negate each other. If they capture members of an enemy squad without losing anyone themselves, they will be rewarded. If they lose members without capturing [or killing] equal numbers of the enemy, they will be killed and their families exterminated.

"'If they lose their squad leader but capture a squad leader, the two negate each other. If they capture a squad leader without losing their own, they will be rewarded. If they lose their squad leader without capturing an enemy squad leader, they will be killed and their families exterminated. However, if they rejoin the battle and take the head of a squad leader, then their punishment will be lifted.

"'If they lose their general but capture [or kill] one, the two negate each other. If they capture a general without losing their own, they will be rewarded. If they lose their general and do not kill an enemy general, they should be considered according to the Law for Abandoning Their Positions and Fleeing.'[129]

"The Law for Battlefield Executions states: 'The leader of a double squad of ten can execute the other nine. A company commander can execute the double squad leaders. The general of one thousand men can execute company commanders. The general of ten thousand men can execute the general of one thousand men. The generals of the Armies of the Left and Right can execute the generals of ten thousand men. The Grand General has no one he cannot execute.'"

17. Orders for Regulating the Troops

"To regulate the troops, employ the orders for regulating them to segment them into three [armies]. The Army of the Left will have green flags, and the troops will wear green feathers.[130] The Army of the Right will have white flags, and the troops will wear white feathers. The Central Army will have yellow flags, and the troops will wear yellow feathers.

"The troops will have five emblems: The front line will have green emblems, the second row red emblems, the third row yellow emblems, the fourth row white emblems, and the fifth row black emblems.

"The next [rule] for regulating the troops is that anyone who loses his emblem will be executed. The first five lines place their emblems on their heads, the next five lines place their emblems on their necks, the next five on their chests, the next five on their stomachs, and the last five on their waists.[131] In this fashion it will never happen that the troops will have someone other than their own officers nor officers other than their own troops. If someone sees a case where it is incorrect but does not inquire about it, or sees confusion but does not act to stop it, the crime will be comparable to that of the offender.

"When the drums sound for [the troops] to move and engage in battle, those lines that move forward confront the danger, while those that retreat to the rear are reviled by the people. Those who venture forward past the five lines will be rewarded; those that race past the five lines to the rear will be executed. By this means it can be known that advancing and retreating, moving to the fore and rear are achievements of the commanders.[132] Thus it is said: 'If you beat the drum and they advance like a thunderclap, they move like the wind and rain, no one will dare oppose you to the fore, no one will dare follow you to the rear.' This speaks about having regulations."

18. Orders for Restraining the Troops

"Gongs, drums, bells, and flags—these four each have their methods of employment. When the drums sound, the army should advance; when the drums are beat again, they should attack. When the gongs sound, they should stop; when the gongs are struck again, they should withdraw. Bells are used to transmit orders. When the flags point to the left, [the army should] go left; when the flags point to the right, then to the right. Unorthodox units are the opposite.[133]

"Beat the drum once and the left [foot steps forward]; beat it again and the right [foot advances].[134] If for each step there is one beat, this is the pace beat. If for ten steps there is one beat, this is the quickstep beat. If the sound is unbroken, this is the racing beat. The *shang* note is that of the general's drum. The *chiao* note is that of a regimental commander's drum. The small drum is that of a company commander. When the three drums sound together the generals, regimental commanders, and company commanders are all of one mind. The unorthodox army is the opposite of this.

"If a drummer misses a beat he is executed. Those that set up a clamor are executed. Those that do not obey the gongs, drums, bells, and flags but move by themselves are executed.

"When combat methods are taught to one hundred men, after their instruction is complete unite them [with other companies] to comprise one thousand men.[135] When the instruction of one thousand men is complete, unite them [with other regiments] to comprise ten thousand. When the instruction of [the armies of] ten thousand is complete, assemble them into the Three Armies. When the masses of the Three Armies can divide and unite, they can execute the methods of large-scale combat. When their instruction is complete, test them with maneuvers.

"In a square formation they are victorious; in a circular formation they are also victorious; in a jagged array they are also victorious; and if they encounter difficult terrain they will also emerge victorious. If the enemy is in the mountains, climb up after him. If the enemy is in the depths, plunge in after him. Seek the enemy as if searching for a lost child, follow him without any doubt. In this way you will be able to defeat the enemy and control his fate.

"Now one must make decisions early and determine plans beforehand. If plans are not first determined, if intentions are not decided early, then neither advancing nor retreating will be ordered. When doubts arise defeat is certain. Thus an orthodox army values being first; an unorthodox army values being afterward. Sometimes being first, sometimes being afterward—[this is the way] to control the enemy. Generals throughout the ages who have not known this method, after receiving their commission to go forward, were first to launch an attack—relying on courage alone. There were none who were not defeated.

"Their actions seem hesitant but are not; their movements seem to be confident but are not; their movement is at times slow, at times rapid, but is neither slow nor rapid. These three present entanglements in battle."

19. Orders for the General

"When the commanding general is about to receive his commission, the ruler must first discuss military strategy in the ancestral temple, then issue the order in the court. The ruler personally grants the *fu* and *yüeh* axes to the general,[136] saying: 'The Left, Right, and Central armies have their separate responsibilities. If anyone oversteps the bounds of their responsibility to seek the intercession of higher ranks, he shall be put to death. Within the army there cannot be two [sources of] orders. Anyone who issues a second order shall be executed. Anyone who delays the implementation of an order shall be executed. Anyone who disobeys an order shall be executed.'

"The General of the Army makes the announcement: 'To those about to go out beyond the gates of the state [capital], the time [for assembling] is set as midday. Within the encampment we shall set up a gnomon and place it at the axle gate. Those who arrive past the designated time will be subject to the provisions of the law.'[137]

"When the General of the Army has entered the encampment, he closes the gate and has the streets cleared. Anyone that dares to travel through them will be executed. Anyone that dares to talk in a loud voice will be executed. Those that do not follow orders will be executed."

20. Orders for the Vanguard

"What is referred to as 'the vanguard'[138] moves off from the main force about one hundred *li*, assembling at a designated place and an appointed time. It carries a three-day [supply of] prepared food. It moves in front of the main army. Pennants are made for uniting to engage in battle.[139] Then when a pennant for engaging in battle is raised,[140] the vanguard feasts its soldiers[141] and has them deploy into a strategic configuration of power [*shih*] for battle. They are referred to as 'racing to battle.'

"The advance army moves in front of the vanguard. When the pennant for engaging in battle is raised, it moves off from the main force double the [vanguard's] distance—about one hundred *li* ahead of the vanguard—assembling at a designated place and time. They carry a six-day [supply of] prepared food. They are ordered to prepare for the battle and deploy troops to occupy the strategic positions. If the battle turns to the [army's] advantage, they pursue the retreating enemy; if the forces are stalemated, they race into [the enemy]. If the vanguard encounters anyone who has turned back, they should execute him. What are termed the 'armies of the various generals,' consisting of four unorthodox forces,[142] will wrest victory.

"The army has its squads of ten and five and [the methods of] dividing and reuniting. Before [engaging in battle] duties are assigned, and designated units should occupy the strategic locations, passes, and bridges. When the pennant for uniting to engage in battle is raised, they should all assemble. The main army sets out with a fixed daily ration and their combat equipment all complete. The orders are issued and they move; anyone who does not follow orders is executed.

"Now determine and assign forces to the strategic points within the four borders of the state. After the advance army and vanguard have already set out, the people within the borders are not able to move about. Those who have received the king's commands, who have been given and carry the proper tallies and tokens are called 'officers acting in accord with their duties.' Officers who are not acting in accord with their duties but yet move about should be executed. When the pennant for uniting to engage in battle is raised, these officers—acting in accord with their duties—travel about and are employed to ensure that affairs are mutually regulated.[143] Accordingly, one who wants to wage warfare must first secure the interior."

21. Military Instructions I

"Orders for instructing the soldiers: Disperse them to their encampments, and have them assume formation. Those who advance or retreat contrary to orders should be punished for the crime of contravening instructions.

"The front lines are instructed [by the commander of] the front lines; the rear lines are instructed [by the commander of] the rear lines; the lines to the left are instructed [by the commander of] the lines on the left; the lines to the right are instructed [by the commander of] the lines to the right. When all five men [in a line] have been successfully instructed, their squad leader is rewarded. Failing to successfully instruct all of them will result in [being punished] as though one had committed the crime of contravening instructions.[144] If someone who has fallen ill[145] brings it to the attention of the squad by himself and the squad members jointly report it, they will be spared from punishment.

"In general, when the squad of five assumes formation for battle, if one of the men does not advance and face death at the enemy, his instructor [will be punished] as if he had committed the crime of contravening the law. The double squad of ten guarantees the ten men within it. If they lose a man and the other nine men do not fight to the death in a desperate battle with the enemy, then their instructor [will be punished] as if he had committed the crime of contravening the law. From the double squad up to the subordinate generals, if anyone does not follow the laws, their instructors [will be punished] as if they had committed the crime of contravening the law. In general, to make punishments and fines clear and incentives and rewards correct, they must fall within the laws for instructing the soldiers.

"Generals have different flags, companies have different emblems. The Army of the Left wears their emblems on the left shoulder; the Army of the Right wears their emblems on the right shoulder; the Central Army wears their emblems on the front of the chest. Record their emblems as 'a certain armored soldier' and 'a certain officer.' From front to rear, for [each platoon of] five lines the most honored emblems are placed on the head, the others accordingly lower and lower.[146]

"The squad leader instructs the other four men using a board as a drum, a piece of tile as a gong, and a branch as a flag. When he strikes the drum they should advance; when he lowers the flag they should race forward; when he strikes the gong they should withdraw. When he points [left] they should go to the left; when he points [right] they should go to the right. When the gongs and drums are struck together they should sit.

"When the squad leader has completed instructing the squad, they should be united [with another squad] under a leader for a double squad of ten. When the double squad leader has completed instructing them, they should be united under a platoon commander. When the platoon commander has completed instructing them, they should be united under a company commander. When the company commander has completed instructing them, they should be united under an army commandant.[147] When the army commandant has completed instructing them, they should be united under a subordinate general. When the subordinate general has completed instructing them, they should be united under the commanding general.

"When the commanding general has completed instructing them, he has them deploy into formation in the countryside. He sets up three large posts, one every hundred paces, and has the formation move away from them. They advance one hundred paces and practice weaponry.[148] They quickstep for a hundred paces and then race for another hundred paces. They practice battle tactics in order to attain the measure [set by the general]. Afterward, rewards and punishments should be implemented.

"From the commandant down, every officer has a flag. When the battle has been won, in each case look at the rank of the flags that have been captured in order to stimulate their hearts with clear rewards.[149]

"Victory in war lies in establishing awesomeness. Establishing awesomeness lies in uniting strength.[150] Uniting strength lies in rectifying punishments. By rectifying punishments rewards are illuminated.

"Today if the people turn their backs to the border gates and decide the issue of life and death, if they have been taught to die without hesitation there is a reason.[151] [Training and instructions] have caused the defenders to inevitably be solid; those engaged in battle to inevitably fight; perverse plans not to be put into action; perverse people not to speak; orders to be effected without any changes; the army to advance without doubt; and the light units to be like a clap of thunder—to rush at the enemy like the terrified. Raise those of merit, distinguish those of virtue, making their distinction as clear as black and white. Cause the people to follow the orders of their superiors just as the four limbs respond to the mind.

"If the forward units break up the enemy's ranks, throw his formation into chaos, and crush his hardness like water bursting through, there is a basis for it. This is termed the 'army's instructions.' They provide the means to open sealed borders, preserve the altars of state, eliminate disaster and harm, and complete Martial Virtue."

22. Military Instructions II

"I have heard that a ruler of men must attain the Tao of certain victory. Thus to be able to unite others and become expansive and great, to unify the ordinances and regulations and have his awesomeness prevail in the world, there are twelve essential matters:

"The first is called 'connected punishment' and refers to the method of joint criminal responsibility for all members of the squad of five.

"The second is 'terrain restrictions,' which refers to prohibiting and stopping passage along the roads in order to ensnare external, perverse forces.

"The third, 'preserving the chariots,'[152] refers to the chariot commanders and infantry leaders being mutually dependent, the three [officers in the chariot] and the squads of five being cohesive in order to bind them together.

"The fourth, 'opening and plugging up,'[153] refers to dividing the terrain with boundaries and having each man die performing his appointed function, securely defending his position.

"The fifth, 'demarking boundaries,' refers to the left and right restraining each other, front and rear awaiting each other, and a wall of chariots creating a solid defense in order to oppose the enemy and stop [them].[154]

"The sixth, 'commands are distinguished,' refers to the forward rows concentrating on advancing, thereby being distinguished from those in the rear who are not able to compete to be the first to ascend[155] nor overstep their positions.

"The seventh, 'five emblems,' refers to distinguishing the rows [with emblems] so that the troops will not be disordered.[156]

"The eighth, 'preserving the units,' refers to the units breaking up and following each other, each having their appointed sections.

"The ninth, 'gongs and drums,' refers to stimulating them to achievement and compelling them to virtue.

"The tenth, 'arraying the chariots,' refers to making the formation tight, with the spears deployed to the front,[157] and putting blinders on the horses' eyes.

"The eleventh, 'warriors of death,' refers to selecting the talented and wise[158] from among masses of the army to ride in the war chariots. They race forward and back, across and about, using unorthodox tactics to gain mastery over the enemy.

"The twelfth, 'strong troops,' refers to regulating the flags[159] and preserving the units. Without the flags [signaling an order], they do not move.

"When the instructions for these twelve have been successfully taught, anyone who contravenes an order should not be pardoned. If the army is weak, they will be able to strengthen it. If a ruler is unknown, they will be able to honor him. If orders become enervated, they will be able to revitalize them. If the people become migrants, they will be able to attract them. If the people are numerous, they will be able to govern them. If the territory is vast, they will be able to defend it. Without the state's chariots crossing the thresholds nor the variegated armor being taken out of the storage bags, your awesomeness will cause All under Heaven to submit.

"Soldiers have five defining commitments:[160] For their general they forget their families; when they cross the border they forget their relatives; when they confront the enemy they forget themselves; when they are committed to die they will live; urgently seeking victory is the lowest. One hundred men willing to suffer the pain of a blade can penetrate a line and cause chaos in a formation. One thousand men willing to suffer the pain of a blade can seize the enemy and kill its general. Ten thousand men willing to suffer the pain of a blade can transverse under Heaven at will."

King Wu asked T'ai Kung Wang: "In a short time[161] I want to exhaustively attain the essentials of employing men." Wang replied: "Your rewards should be like mountains, your punishments like valleys. The supreme makes no errors, the next corrects his mistakes.[162] Now anyone who, when about to be punished, requests that he not be punished should die. Anyone who, when about to be rewarded, requests that he not be rewarded should die.[163]

"Attack a country according to its changes.[164] Display riches in order to observe their poverty. Display exhaustion in order to observe their illness. If the ruler is immoral and the people disaffected, in cases such as these one has a basis for attack.

"In general, whenever about to mobilize the army, you must first investigate the strategic balance of power [ch'üan] both within and without the borders in order to calculate whether to mount a campaign. [You must know] whether the army is well prepared or suffers from inadequacies, whether there is a surplus or shortage of foodstuffs. You must determine the routes for advancing and returning. Only thereafter can you mobilize the army to attack the chaotic and be certain of being able to enter his state.

"If the territory is vast but the cities small, you must first occupy their land. If the cities are large but the land narrow, you must first attack their cities. If the country is vast and the populace few, then isolate their strategic points. If the land is confined but the people numerous, then construct high mounds in order to overlook them. Do not destroy their material profits nor seize the people's agricultural seasons. Be magnanimous toward his government [officials], stabilize [the people's] occupations, and provide relief for their impoverished for then [your Virtue] will be sufficient to overspread All under Heaven.

"Today warring states attack each other and mount large-scale assaults on the virtuous. From the squads to the platoons, from the platoons to the army, none have unified orders. They cause the people to have unsettled minds; they only incline toward arrogance and extravagance. Their plans are calamities; they are constantly involved in disputes, so the officers spend their time investigating matters. These are entanglements and moreover bring about defeat. Even after the sun has set the road remains long, and when [the soldiers] return to camp they are dispirited. The army is old, the general covetous. Since he will fight to seize material gains, he is easily defeated.

"When the general is light, the fortifications low, and the people's minds unstable, they can be attacked. If the general is weighty and the fortifications are high but the masses are afraid, they can be encircled. In general, whenever you encircle someone you must provide them with a prospect for some minor advantage, causing them to become weaker day by day.[165] Then the defenders will be forced to reduce their rations until they have nothing to eat. When their masses fight with each other at night, they are terrified. If the masses avoid their work, they have become disaffected.[166] If they just wait for others to come and rescue them and when the time for battle arrives they are tense, they have all lost their will[167] and are dispirited. Dispirit defeats an army; distorted plans defeat a state."

23. Army Orders[168] I

"Weapons are inauspicious implements. Conflict is a contrary Virtue.[169] All affairs must have their foundation. Therefore when a true king attacks the brutal and chaotic, he takes benevolence and righteousness as the foundation for it. [At the present time] the warring states then establish their awesomeness, resist their enemies, and plot against each other. Thus they cannot abandon their armies.

"The military takes the martial as its trunk, and takes the civil as its seed.[170] It makes the martial its exterior, and the civil the interior. One who can investigate and fathom the two will know victory and defeat. The civil is the means to discern benefit and harm, to discriminate security and danger. The martial is the means to contravene a strong enemy, to forcefully attack and defend.

"One who is unified will be victorious;[171] one who is beset by dissension will be defeated. When formations are tight they are solid; when the front is dispersed it can attain its [objectives].[172] One whose troops fear their general far more than the enemy will be victorious. One whose troops fear the enemy far more than their general will be defeated. Thus to know who will be victorious, who defeated, weight your general with the enemy. The enemy and your general are like a steelyard and balance. If [the general] is settled and quiet, [the troops] are well-ordered; if he is brutal and hasty, they are in chaos.[173]

"Sending troops forth and deploying the army have standard orders; the dispersal and density of the lines and squads have standard methods; and arraying the rows from front to rear has its appropriateness and suitability. Standard orders are not employed when pursuing a fleeing enemy or suddenly striking a city. If the front and rear are disordered, then [the army] loses [its integrity]. If anyone causes confusion among the lines, behead him.

"The standard deployment for formations is always facing toward the enemy. There are also internally oriented formations, externally oriented formations, standing formations, and sitting formations. Internally oriented formations provide the means to preserve the center; externally oriented formations provide the means to prepare against external threats. Standing formations are the means to move, sitting formations the means to stop. Mixed formations—with some soldiers standing, others sitting—respond to each other in accord with the need to move or stop, with the general being in the middle. The weapons of the seated soldiers are the sword and ax; the weapons of the standing soldiers are the spear-tipped halberd and crossbow; the general also occupies the middle.

"Those who excel at repulsing the enemy first join battle with orthodox troops, then [use unorthodox ones] to control them. This is the technique for certain victory.

"Array the *fu* and *yüeh* axes [for punishment], make a display of the emblems and flags [used as rewards]. Those who have merit must be rewarded; those who contravene orders must die. The preservation or destruction of the state and the life or death of the soldiers lie at the tips of the [general's] drumsticks. Even though there are those under Heaven who excel at commanding armies, no one will be able to repulse them.

"Before arrows have been shot and cross in flight, before the long blades have clashed, those who yell out first are termed 'vacuous,' those who yell out afterward are termed 'substantial,' and those who do not yell are termed 'secretive.' 'Vacuous' and 'substantial' are the embodiment of warfare."

24. Army Orders[174] II

"Units are dispatched from the main army to undertake advance preparations for defense. They should set up observation posts along the borders every three to five *li*. When they hear that the main army is making preparations to advance, mount a defense, and engage in battle, they should prohibit all movement in order to provide security to the state.

"When troops from the interior are about to set out for border duty, have the commanding officer provide them with their flags, drums, halberds, and armor. On the day for issuing forth, anyone who arrives after the commanding officer has gone out beyond the district border shall be liable for the law for late arrival for border duty.

"The term of border duty for a soldier is one year. Anyone who leaves before being replaced shall be punished analogously to the law for deserting the army. If his parents, wife, or children know about it, they will share the crime with him. If they do not know about it, pardon them.

"If a soldier arrives at the headquarters of the Grand General a day after his commanding officer, his parents, wife, and children should all share the crime with him. If a soldier abandons his post to return home for a day and his parents, wife, or children do not arrest [him], hold him, or report it, they should also share the crime with him.

"If they should lose their commanding officer in battle, or if their commanding officer should abandon his troops and flee by himself, behead them all. If a forward officer should abandon his troops and flee, any officer to the rear who is able to kill him and reassemble his troops should be rewarded. Anyone [among such troops] who has not achieved merit within the army must serve three years at the border.[175]

"If the Three Armies engage in a major battle and the Grand General dies, all of the subordinate officers commanding units of more than five hundred men who were not able to fight to the death with the enemy should be beheaded. All the troops near to the commanding general, on the left and right in [protective] formation, should be beheaded. As for the remaining officers and men in the army, those who have military merit should be reduced one grade. Those who do not have military merit should be rescripted to three years' border duty.

"If the squad of five loses a man in battle, or if a squad member dies in battle but they do not retrieve his corpse, then take away all the merit of all his squad members. If they retrieve his corpse, then their crimes should all be pardoned.

"The army's advantage and disadvantage lie with name and substance [cohering throughout] the state. Today if a person's name appears as holding a particular [military] office but in reality he is at home, then the office has not gained the substance [of his presence], and the household has not gained the [registration of] his name. When troops are assembled to compose an army, it will have an empty name without substance. Outside the state it will be inadequate to repel enemies, while within the borders it will be inadequate to defend the state. This is the way in which the army becomes insufficient, in which the general has his awesomeness taken away.

"I believe that when soldiers abandon their units and return home, the other members of their squad in the same barracks and their officers should be punished for taking their rations for their own consumption, [the deserters'] names being shown as the army's substance. Thus a person is nominally with the army, but in reality double the ration is expended.[176] The resources of the state are then empty, and the harvests of the people are naturally exhausted. How can the disaster of defeat be avoided?

"Today if they are stopped from returning home by the laws, this prevents the loss of an army and is the first military victory. When the squads of five and ten are mutually bound to the point that in battle the troops and officers will aid each other, this is the second military victory. If the general is able to establish his awesomeness, the soldiers to master and follow their instructions, while the commands and orders are clear and trusted, and attacking and defending are both properly executed, this is the third military victory.

"I have heard that in antiquity those who excelled in employing the army could [bear to] kill[177] half of their officers and soldiers. The next could kill thirty percent and the lowest ten percent. The awesomeness of one who could sacrifice half of his troops affected all within the Four Seas. The strength of one who could sacrifice thirty percent could be applied to the feudal lords. The orders of one who could sacrifice ten percent would be implemented among his officers and troops. Thus I say that a mass of a hundred ten thousands that does not follow orders is not as good as ten thousand men who fight. Ten thousand men who fight are not as good as one hundred men who are truly aroused.

"When rewards are like the sun and moon, credibility is like the four seasons, orders are like the *fu* and *yüeh* axes, and regulations are as [sharp as the famous sword] *Kan-chiang,* I have never heard of officers and troops not following orders!"

6

Three Strategies of Huang Shih-kung

黄石公三略

Translator's Introduction

Origin of the *Three Strategies*

Popular Chinese tradition has historically attributed three military writings—the *Six Secret Teachings,* the *Three Strategies of Huang Shih-kung,* and the esoteric *Yin Fu (Hidden Symbols)*—to the famous general, strategist, and political thinker Chiang Shang, best known as the T'ai Kung. As with most ancient Chinese works there are numerous problems with the text of the *Three Strategies* and the usual questions about its authenticity. However, even if the book were a "valueless forgery"—as claimed by the numerous Confucians who vehemently denounced its purported brutality—it would still demand serious study because of its antiquity, complex content, and manifest influence on subsequent military thinkers in China and eventually in Japan.[1] In its present form the language, subject matter, and presentation suggest it dates from near the end of the first century B.C.,[2] although four other views (which are summarized below) propose rather different interpretations.

The *Three Strategies* attained historical prominence through Chang Liang's critical accomplishments in establishing the power and consolidating the authority of the Han dynasty during the turmoil and violent insurrections that overthrew the repressive, short-lived Ch'in dynasty. The story of its sudden appearance typifies semilegendary Chinese historical accounts, although circumstances can be construed to suggest a possible line of transmission extending back through the obscurity of time to the T'ai Kung himself. According to this tradition, the *Three Strategies* records the aging Sage's pronouncements after being enfeoffed as king of Chi'i—a state on the periphery of Chou culture—following the conquest of the Shang dynasty. Subsequently, the individual spontaneous statements—recorded in disjointed fashion—were collected, edited, and systematized. This task was probably performed by Ch'i's official court historian, with the work thereafter being secretly preserved by successive generations because of its great military value. It is assumed that because the T'ai Kung had already composed the *Six Secret Teachings,* his comments when peace had been attained throughout the realm would mainly expand and supplement the earlier treatise. This would account for the more extemporaneous character of the material and for the absence of many focal military topics, such as battlefield command and tactics.

The book then surfaced when transmitted by a nondescript old fellow to Chang Liang a decade before he became famous and powerful. The *Shih chi* records the incident:[3]

> Once when Chang Liang was leisurely strolling across the Hsia-p'ei Bridge, he encountered an old man wearing the poor garb of a retired gentleman. When the old fellow reached the place where Chang was standing, he deliberately lost his shoe over the side of the bridge. Looking at Chang he commanded: "Young fellow, go down and fetch my shoe." Chang Liang was startled by this and wanted to beat him soundly, but because of the man's age he repressed his impulse.
>
> Chang went down below the bridge and got the shoe. Upon returning the old man ordered: "Put it on my foot." As Chang had already gone and retrieved the shoe, he formally knelt down and put it on. Once he was wearing the shoe the old man smiled and departed. Chang Liang was quite surprised and continued staring at him. After the old man had gone about a few hundred yards, he returned and said: "Son, you can be taught. Five days from now, at dawn, meet me here." Chang Liang felt this was strange, but he knelt and assented.
>
> Five days later, at dawn, Chang went to the bridge. However, the old fellow was already there, and he upbraided him: "When you make an appointment with an old man, how can you arrive after him?" He then departed, saying: "In five days we will meet even earlier." Five days later, when the cock first crowed, Chang Liang went there. However, the old fellow was first again, and once more he was angry. "How can you come after me?" As he departed he yelled: "In five more days come again, even earlier!"
>
> In another five days, before the night was half over, Chang Liang went there. In a little while the old man also arrived and was happy. "This is the way it should be," he said. Then, taking out a book, he continued: "If you read this you can become a teacher of kings. Ten years from now you will flourish. In thirteen years you will see me on the northern bank of the Chi River. The yellow rock at the foot of Ku-ch'eng Mountain will be me." Then he departed without another word, never to be seen again. In the morning Chang Liang looked at the book and discovered it to be the T'ai Kung's military strategy. He thereafter regarded it as something exceptional and constantly studied and worked over the book.

The old man may have been a proud descendant of Ch'i's official state historian, a Worthy whose family had preserved the secret teachings for generations. According to the military historian General Hsü P'ei-ken, this is suggested by his knowledge of the area, which was so detailed that he identified himself with a large yellow rock (*huang shih*)—a reference that would eventually give the book its name, *Three Strategies of the Duke of Yellow Rock*.[4] Because Ch'i was one of the last states vanquished by the infamous Ch'in, the Duke of Yellow Rock would have been amply motivated to assist in overthrowing the now-tortured dynasty. Providing this essential work of strategy to a young fugitive who was being hunted for his attempted assassination of the emperor would have been a highly appropriate gesture.

There are actually five basic views concerning the origin of the *Three Strategies,* with the first, traditional one just discussed attributing it directly to the T'ai Kung. The second, a variation on the first, ascribes it to the disciples or later military followers of the T'ai Kung. This view envisions a prototypical text that evolved around a kernel of concepts over the centuries until it eventually underwent extensive revision in the pre-Ch'in period, which accounts for the anachronistic language and concepts and for the possibility that it may also have influenced Sun-tzu and Wei Liao-tzu (rather than the reverse). The third view assumes that rather than simply handing down the writings of the T'ai Kung, Huang Shih-kung wrote the book himself shortly before the famous incident. This would equally explain the concepts and language, especially the highly visible Taoist influence. The fourth view, which is essentially identified with conservative classical scholars, derisively terms the book a blatant forgery of the Wei-Chin period or later. Some scholars, such as Cheng Yüan, characterized the *Three Strategies* as having stolen the empty words of Taoism and being a useless book,[5] whereas others excoriated its brutality or attacked the rusticity of its language.[6]

The final view—advanced by the contemporary scholar Hsü Pao-lin based on the concepts, language, and historical references incorporated in the text—concludes that the work was written around the end of the Former Han dynasty, probably by a reclusive adherent of the Huang-Lao school who had expert knowledge of military affairs.[7] In addition, this view holds that the book transmitted to Chang Liang was not the present *Three Strategies* but the *Six Secret Teachings*—the T'ai Kung's military thought—as is stated by Ssu-ma Ch'ien in the *Shih chi* biography.[8] (Huang Shih-kung's book, now known as the *Three Strategies of Huang Shih-kung*, was originally titled *The Records of Huang Shih-kung* and only acquired its present name during the Sui dynasty.[9]) This explains the reference to powerful families usurping power, the prevalence of Huang-Lao thought amid concepts from many schools, and the narrow focus on government affairs in an age of peace. Although elements of Hsü's arguments seem somewhat tenuous, in the absence of archaeological evidence to the contrary, his general conclusions should probably be accepted and the *Three Strategies* acknowledged as the last of the truly ancient works, with a likely composition date somewhere around A.D. 0.[10]

Basic Content and Focus

The tone of the *Three Strategies* is far less strident than that of the *Six Secret Teachings* and other works on which its author clearly drew, presumably because the brutal, monumental task of consolidating the empire and establishing enlightened rule had already been accomplished by the Han dynasty. Although many of the themes and ideas of the previous five *Military Classics* are represented in the *Three Strategies,* it focuses primarily on government and military administration and control. With the possible exception of a brief passage advancing a theory of strongpoints,[11] discussions of campaign strategy and battle tactics are absent. Instead the text concentrates on concepts of government; the administration of forces; the unification of the people; the characteristics of a capable general; methods of nurturing a sound material foundation; motivation of subordinates and the soldiers; implementation of rewards and punishments; ways to foster majesty—which was a critical concept—and the need to balance between the hard and the soft.

Four main threads of thought—their differences apparently reconciled and their viewpoints remarkably integrated—are clearly present in the *Three Strategies.*[12] Further study is required to determine whether the author deliberately fashioned a grand synthesis on the new intellectual ground of Huang-Lao thought, as claimed by the scholar Hsü Pao-lin, or whether contemporary researchers are simply succumbing to the temptation to creatively perceive unity after extensively pondering and analyzing the text. Generally speaking, the fundamental concepts of Confucianism—such as benevolence, righteousness, the practice of humanitarian government, the promotion of the welfare of the people, rule by Virtue, and the employment of the Worthy—underlie the entire work. Pivotal measures espoused by the Legalists—such as strengthening the state, rigorously enforcing the laws, strictly implementing rewards and punishments, and ensuring that the ruler retains power and exercises authority—supplement the original Confucian approach, bringing the entire work much closer in tenor and outlook to Hsün-tzu than Confucius and Mencius. The Taoist spirit—which emphasizes the passive, being harmonious, not contending, preserving life, the Tao and *Te* (Virtue), and especially the evilness of warfare—pervades the book but is modified to accept the reality of righteous warfare and contending for harmony.

The works of the previous military strategists—especially the *Wei Liao-tzu* and the *Six Secret Teachings* (which is sometimes quoted as the *Military Pronouncements*)—provide essential concepts for government administration, organization, and control. Many of the amalgamated Confucian and Legalist policies, such as treating the people as the basis and rigidly implementing rewards and punishments, have long traditions among the strategists. Some of these have been described as reaching their pinnacle in the *Three Strategies,* although this might merely be a question of emphasis. Clearly, the text is more complex philosphically than a simple work on military administration and therefore requires further study. Due to various limitations, such detailed analysis must be left to specialized monographs, with the introduction below supplying only a brief summary of salient points as a guide to Huang Shih-kung's world.

Hierarchy of Strategies

In its present form the work consists of three sections denominated in the traditional way as upper, middle, and lower. Unfortunately, these terms are open to two interpretations: as simple indicators of position in the work or as indicating some assigned value or priority. A passage in the book itself, which may be a commentator's interpolation rather than the author's own thoughts, clearly states that each of the sections is both necessary and appropriate to its own period of moral and political deterioration.[13] There is no identification of the hierarchy of chapters as being respectively appropriate to different styles of government and ages of virtue, as might have been expected.

Over the millennia Chinese intellectuals have conceptualized their history in terms of recurring dynastic cycles superimposed on a general pattern of moral decline. Starting with the age of true Sage Emperors, civilization became more complex, artificial, and perverse—culminating in the period when mere men usurped power and disputants had to consciously create and espouse concepts of virtue in a futile attempt to master evil. Each philosophic school interpreted this decline from its own, self-serving perspective. In extremely simplified form, the Confucians viewed the creation of culture and civilization as the great accomplishment of former Sages and culture heroes and as the means by which to ensure and preserve an ordered society wherein Virtue should prevail and morality rule. The Taoists, championed by their paragon Lao-tzu, decried the creation of concepts of virtue and the chains of civilization as serving solely to further hasten the already precipitous decline from spontaneity, simplicity, and natural harmony. The Legalists derived a very different lesson from this deterioration, envisioning it as proof of the absolute need for draconian measures: for law and authority to prevent civil disorder, foster a strong state, and guarantee the ruler's security.

Mankind's apparent passage through several dramatically different forms of government, each characterized by distinctive virtues and policies, was seen to furnish illustrative justification for these respective theories. It is tempting to view Huang Shih-kung as having directed each of the three strategies to a particular style of government and degree of aggressive administration. However, the present text makes no such assertion, and in fact the "Superior Strategy" "establishes the forms of propriety and rewards"—clearly not the method of the earliest Sages. In harmony with the Legalists, who felt that laws must be newly created for each age, Huang Shih-kung proclaims that all three theories are necessary for their respective periods of decadence. Each section provides the ruler with functionally specific techniques for attaining his administrative objectives:

> The Sage embodies Heaven, the Worthy model on Earth, and the wise find their teachers in antiquity. Thus the *Three Strategies* has been written for a period of decadence. The "Superior Strategy" establishes the forms of propriety and rewards, discriminates between evildoers and the valiant, and makes clear success and defeat. The "Middle Strategy" makes out the differences in Virtue and behavior and makes manifest changes in the balance of power [*ch'üan*]. The "Inferior Strategy" arrays the Tao and Virtue, investigates security and danger, and makes clear the calamity of harming the Worthy.
>
> Thus if the ruler thoroughly understands the "Superior Strategy" he will be able to employ the Worthy and seize his enemies. If he thoroughly understands the "Middle Strategy" he will be able to employ and control his generals and unite the people. If he thoroughly understands the "Inferior Strategy" he will be able to discern the sources of flourishing and decline and understand the regulations for governing a state. If his subordinates thoroughly understand the "Middle Strategy" they will be able to achieve merit and preserve themselves.

Despite the above passage, a close examination of the book's contents suggests this interpretation lacks a strong textual basis. Although there is some difference in emphasis among the strategies, essentially the same themes and concerns underlie all three sections. The first chapter contains most of the writing, whereas the other two introduce some new subjects and expand on others. Whether this resulted from the text having been tampered with or whether the transmission has been imperfect and large sections lost can never be known. This sort of textual imbalance is unusual, but the author may have simply expressed his ideas without concern for symmetry and length.

Concepts of Government

By accepting the historical "decline" theory, the *Three Strategies* commits itself to a program that stresses the cultivation of Virtue and the simultaneous implementation of aggressive government policies to cope with an age in decline. In concord with the *Six Secret Teachings* and the *Wu-tzu* it emphasizes nurturing the people, fostering their allegiance and willing support,[14] and integrating them under a moral leader and a vigorous government. Because the highest ideal is the Sage King, the author advocates essentially Confucian measures designed to promote the people's material welfare and engender their voluntary adherence. The ruler and also the general should act to ease distress, remove evil, and increase prosperity. Consequently, they should minimize taxes and labor duties, avoid disrupting the critical agricultural seasons, and nurture stability and tranquility. Because it is expected that the well-ordered, ideally governed state can mobilize its citizens when confronted by hostilities, military matters—apart from actual strategy and tactics—essentially become questions of civilian government and administration. Conscripts provide the basis for military strength, and defensive capabilities are stressed.

Exercise of Authority

Both the "Superior" and "Inferior Strategies" discuss the numerous problems that arise when the ruler has lost effective control of the government, the evil have gained control of offices and power, and parties and cliques dispense governmental largess. The *Three Strategies* warns against allowing these situations to develop, following the essential Legalist doctrine that the ruler himself must wield as well as theoretically hold power. The key to preventing the encroachment of the great families, the ruler's relatives, and even powerful military men is the successful employment of Sages and Worthies. (This represents a deviation from standard Legalist principles, which held that moral worth and individual talent cannot and should not be relied on. In contrast, the Mohists and Confucians stressed the role and importance of sagely paragons, a policy the author of the *Three Strategies* envisioned as "according with the subtle," "according with the Tao.") When the good are recognized and advanced and the evil removed and punished, the proper context for true, effective, benevolent government will have been established, and the people will naturally regard the court in a positive light.

Military Preparation, Management, and Execution

As mentioned above, a Taoist influence pervades the book—from the overall unification in the practice of the Way (Tao)[15] to the general recognition that warfare is inauspicious and evil and that it violates what the Taoists perceive as the natural tendency to life.[16] In contrast to the positive attitude of the *Six Secret Teachings* and other works, which still deem warfare to be of momentous importance to the nation, the negative or dark side of military affairs also commands attention in the *Three Strategies*. The army must be employed with restraint; however, when absolutely necessary to preserve the state, uphold the principles of civilization, and protect life, its use accords with the Tao. Because hesitation and doubt doom military enterprises, once the decision to employ the army has been reached, its use should be decisive: "The Sage King does not take any pleasure in using the army. He mobilizes it to execute the violently perverse and punish the rebellious. ... Weapons are inauspicious implements, and the Tao of Heaven abhors them. However, when their employment is unavoidable it accords with the Tao of Heaven." Lao-tzu's famous sentence ("the army is an inauspicious implement"[17]) has clearly been modified to accept the reality of Huang-Lao thought in the *Three Strategies*.

The foundation, the possibility of military action always remains the people. In many states the populace is impoverished and disaffected; the populace of the true ruler should be adequately nourished, clothed, rested, and strongly bound to its king and state. Immigrants and the persecuted as well as the worthy and talented should all be welcomed and granted refuge, thereby strengthening the country. Once they are brought under the sway of government policies, all the people will be forged into a cohesive, integrated whole.

Motivating the People

The *Three Strategies* discusses in some detail the age-old problem of motivation, directing attention to the entire spectrum of commoners, bureaucrats, ministers, generals, officers, and soldiers. It even identifies around twenty types of individuals by their predominant character or behavioral tendencies and suggests means to use each type to the state's advantage.[18] However, stability and prosperity are essential because without security, enjoyment becomes impossible and without prosperity, the government will lack adequate resources to offer the necessary incentives. If men are to exert themselves for the state, they must have prospects of appropriate rewards; if they are to die for it, they must be strongly stimulated with the promise of material goods as well as abstract honor.[19]

The nature and form of incentives must be suited precisely to the individual because men differ in their values and requirements. For example, although many enthusiastically pursue great profits, the pure and incorruptible are motivated only by fame, honor, and position. The proper combination of respect—both public and private—and material gain must be determined and employed. Allegiance must be gained through the benevolent, enlightened government policies discussed previously; and the submission of the men's minds (which is attained through pleasure) as opposed to just their bodies (attained through their conformance—willing or otherwise—to the forms of propriety and the laws of the land) is vital. Thereafter, virtually everyone can be attracted and utilized by playing on their characters and desires. However, only Virtue will attract the Worthy; thus the ruler and commander should continually strive to perfect themselves.

Military and Tactical Concepts

Although Huang Shih-kung focuses on problems of administrative control, several important military concepts found in the *Three Strategies* merit attention: generalship, swiftness, authority, integration and balance, and the hard and soft.

From the time of the Spring and Autumn period, the commanding general was entrusted increasingly not only with tactical command but also with complete governing authority for the military and its related, largely civilian support groups. With few exceptions the measures discussed for the civilian sphere are equally applicable in the military realm. Once the general assumes his duties his authority must be unquestioned. Because of the breadth of his powers and the range of his responsibilities, only a man of wide comprehension, decisiveness, and extensive abilities can master the problem. He should be emotionally controlled and never display doubt or indecision. Furthermore, he must be receptive to suggestions and criticism, although his authority must still be unquestioned. Swiftness, secrecy, unity, and uprightness should characterize his execise of power. His anger should be righteous and result in the punishment of offenders.

Sun-tzu initiated the idea of "swiftness rather than duration," and the *Three Strategies* continues to emphasize speed and decisiveness throughout: "Battle should be like the blowing wind. Attacks should be like a flowing river." Doubting, questioning decisions, consulting spirits or using divination, or anything else that might undermine the army's commitment and retard its actions should never be permitted.

In antiquity as today, the *image* of authority frequently constituted the real and frequently the only basis of power and means of controlling men.

Wei, which is perhaps best translated as "awesomeness," is a term commonly employed to describe the aura of the authoritative figure. According to Confucius, *wei* is the image, the impact of the man of righteousness when he dons his armor. It is the ultimate power of a general or the remoteness of a ruler wielding the might of a trembling empire.

Virtually all of the Legalists and military thinkers sought consciously to develop this awesomeness because of its critical role in governing men and causing the enemy to shiver and quake. Without it the general would be reduced to impotence because he would lose the allegiance of his men and his orders would be ignored or insulted.

The timeless foundation of administrative and actual power is the personal, unquestioned control of the twin handles of rewards and punishments. Although the theory and implications of the rigorous, severe, systematic imposition of rewards and punishments tend to be most closely identified with the Legalist school, every military thinker probably acknowledged their vital importance. When their credibility remains undoubted, the majesty, the awesomeness of the commander is established: "The army takes rewards as its form and punishment as its substance. When rewards and punishments are clear the general's majesty is effected."

The second element in the general's and ruler's awesomeness is his expert use of orders and commands. Orders must never be issued lightly, nor should they be rescinded; otherwise they lose their power and impact. His continued fearsomeness depends on the acceptance and execution of his orders; and this execution depends on the fear, respect, and willing allegiance of the men. Clearly, the most extensive efforts must be taken to preserve this interrelationship because once a crevice such as doubt appears, the collapse of authority is imminent.

An early passage in the "Superior Strategy" expands on the following quotation from a presumably ancient military text: "The soft can control the hard, the weak can control the strong." Perhaps the author intends to startle the reader because, by citing an obviously Taoist paradigm, he strikingly denies conventional military wisdom which holds that strength and hardness provide the keys to victory. Lao-tzu's recognition of the soft being able to conquer the hard—conceptualized in several of his verses[20]—leads him to believe that one should assume a passive, low posture to avoid becoming brittle, strong, and exposed. Huang Shih-kung has expanded these insights to apply them rigorously in the military sphere. However, rather than accepting the power of softness or weakness alone, he equally advocates the employment of the hard and strong—each as appropriate to the moment and conditions. Such conscious employment, in Huang Shih-kung's view, accords with the Tao (Way) of Heaven and is necessary if one is to be effective under the harsh conditions of real statecraft.

A somewhat later passage again cites the *Military Pronouncements* to substantiate Huang Shih-kung's view that appropriate implementation of all these four—softness, hardness, weakness, and strength—is required. Tending to one extreme or another will result in an unstable situation, and the state will perish. Accordingly, Virtue—which is identified as softness[21]—should be practiced, but the state should also have a strong military and prepare for righteous warfare. Some of the commentators, such as Liu Yin in the Ming dynasty, also point out the possibilities of deceit and trickery—whereby softness is feigned and hardness employed and the reverse.[22] However, there is no expansion of this theme in the *Three Strategies,* and the analysts who cite these passages as incontrovertible evidence that the work was produced by a member of the Huang-Lao school (rather than an eclectic strategist) may be overstating the case. Taoist thought has a long association with military thinking—extending back as far as Sun-tzu—and the incorporation of such observations does not automatically prove this contention.

I

SUPERIOR STRATEGY

The commander in chief's[1] method focuses on winning the minds of the valiant, rewarding and providing salaries to the meritorious, and having his will penetrate to the masses. Thus if he has the same likes as the masses, there is nothing he will not accomplish. If he has the same dislikes as the masses, there is nothing he will not overturn. Governing the state and giving security to one's family [is a question of] gaining the people. Losing the state and destroying one's family [is a question of] losing the people. All living beings[2] want to realize their ambitions.

The *Military Pronouncements*[3] states: "The soft can control the hard, the weak can control the strong."[4] The soft is Virtue. The hard is a brigand.[5] The weak is what the people will help, the strong is what resentment will attack. The soft has situations in which it is established; the hard has situations in which it is applied; the weak has situations in which it is employed; and the strong has situations in which it is augmented. Combine these four and control them appropriately.

When neither the beginning nor end has yet become visible, no one is able to know them. Heaven and Earth are spiritual and enlightened, with the myriad things they change and transform. His changes and movements should not be constant. He should change and transform in response to the enemy. He does not precede affairs;[6] when the enemy moves he immediately follows up. Thus he is able to formulate inexhaustible strategies and methods of control, sustain and complete the awesomeness of Heaven, bring tranquility and order to [the extremes of] the eight directions, and gather and settle the Nine Barbarians. Such a strategist is a teacher for an emperor or a true king.

Thus I say everyone covets strength, but rare are those capable of preserving the subtle. If someone can preserve the subtle he can protect his life. The Sage preserves it in order to respond to the slightest change in affairs. If he releases it then it will extend throughout the Four Seas. If he rolls it up it will not fill a cup. He dwells in it, but without a house. He guards it, but without city walls. He stores it away in his breast, and enemy states submit.

The *Military Pronouncements* states: "If one can be soft and hard, his state will be increasingly glorious! If one can be weak and strong, his state will be increasingly illustrious! If purely soft and purely weak, his state will inevitably decline. If purely hard and purely strong, his state will inevitably be destroyed."

Now the Way [Tao] to govern the state is to rely on Worthies and the people. If you trust the Worthy as if they were your belly and heart, and employ the people as if they were your four limbs, then all your plans will be accomplished. If your measures follow on each other as naturally as the four limbs, or the way the joints of the bones cooperate with each other, this is the Tao of Heaven, the natural. There is no gap in such skill.

The essence of the army and state lies in investigating the mind of the people and putting into effect the hundred duties of government.

Bring peace to those who are in danger. Give happiness to those who are afraid. Return those who rebel. Be indulgent to those who have grievances. Investigate [the complaints of] those who have legal suits. Raise up the lowly. Repress the strong. Destroy the enemy. Enrich the greedy. Use those that have desires. Conceal the fearful. Attract strategists. Investigate slanderers. Reproach the insulting.[7] Eliminate the rebellious. Stifle those who act willfully. Diminish the arrogant. Summon those who turn their allegiance toward you. Give life to those who submit. Release those who surrender.

If you gain a strategic position, defend it. If you get a dangerous defile, block it. If you take difficult terrain, then establish encampments [to hold it]. If you secure a city, then cut if off [to enfeoff the generals]. If you seize territory, then divide it up [as a reward for the officers]. If you obtain riches, then distribute them [among your troops].

When the enemy moves observe him; when he approaches prepare for him. If the enemy is strong, be deferential [to make him arrogant]. If the enemy is well rested, then leave him.[8] If the enemy is insulting, then wait [for his *ch'i* to decline]. If the enemy is explosive, then soothe him. If the enemy is rebellious, then treat him with righteousness. If the enemy is sincere, then lead him [to abandon his perverse ruler].

Accord [with the enemy's actions][9] to initiate measures and repress him. Rely on the strategic configuration of power [*shih*] to destroy him. Spread false words and cause him to make errors.[10] Set out your net to catch them.[11]

When you gain something, do not keep it [for yourself]. If you occupy a territory, do not set up permanent defenses. If you seize [a city], do not [keep it for yourself] for long. If you establish [a new ruler], do not take the state altars. Thus while you perform the actions yourself, those who gain by it are the officers. How does one know where the real profit lies? They become feudal lords, you become the emperor. Have the cities prepare to defend themselves, have the officers manage their appropriate positions.

Through the ages rulers managed to venerate their ancestors with the proper ceremonies, but few were able to treat the people as they should have been treated. Those who venerate their ancestors foster proper familial connections, but those who treat the people as they should be treated become rulers. To treat the people as they should be treated means concentrating on agriculture and sericulture and not disturbing the people during their vital seasonal occupations. It means keeping taxes and impositions to a minimum, not exhausting their wealth. If you impose few labor services, if you do not cause the people to be overly labored, then the state will be prosperous and the families will enjoy pleasure. Only thereafter should you select officers to control and supervise them.

Now what are termed "officers" are men of character and valor. Thus it is said, "Draw in their men of character and valor and the enemy's state will be impoverished." These valiant men are the trunk of a state. The common people are its root. If you have the trunk and secure the root, the measures of government will be implemented without resentment.

Now the essence of employing the army lies in respecting the forms of propriety [li] and making salaries generous. When the proper forms of propriety are followed, wise officers will be attracted. When salaries are generous, righteous officers will regard death lightly. Thus if when granting salaries to the Worthy you do not begrudge the expense and when rewarding the able are not dilatory, then the strength of your subordinates will be united while your enemy's state will be reduced [as the capable abandon him].

The Way to employ men is to honor them with rank and supply them generously with material goods, for then the officers will come of their own accord. Welcome them according to the forms of propriety [li], stimulate them with righteousness, and then the officers will die [for the state].

Now those who command the army must share tastes and attitudes with the officers and men and confront both safety and danger with them,[12] for then the enemy can be attacked. Thus the army will attain full victory, and the enemy will be completely destroyed. In antiquity, when outstanding generals commanded armies, there was once a case where the commander was presented with a cask of sweet wine. The general had it poured into the river and shared the drinking of the wine with the officers and men as it flowed downstream. Now a cask of wine is unable to flavor a river of water, but the officers of the Three Armies were all motivated to fight to the death because the flavor and taste reached them personally.[13]

The *Military Pronouncements* states: "When the army's wells have not yet been completed, the general does not mention thirst. When the encampment has not yet been secured, the general does not speak about fatigue. When the army's cookstoves have not yet been lit, the general does not speak about hunger. In the winter he does not wear a fur robe; in the summer he does not use a fan; and in the rain he does not set up an umbrella."[14] This is termed the proper form of behavior for a general.

He is with them in safety, he is united with them in danger. Thus his troops can be combined but cannot be forced apart. They can be employed but cannot be tired out. With his beneficence he ceaselessly gathers them together, with his plans he constantly unites them. Thus it is said that when you cultivate beneficence tirelessly, with one you can take ten thousand.

The *Military Pronouncements* states: "The basis of the general's awesomeness is his commands and orders. The basis of complete victory in battle is military administration. The reason officers treat battle lightly is the employment of commands." Thus the general never rescinds an order. Rewards and punishments must be as certain as Heaven and Earth, for then the general can employ the men. When the officers and soldiers follow orders, the army can cross the border.

Now the one who unifies the army and wields its strategic power [*shih*] is the general. The ones that bring about conquest and defeat the enemy are the masses. Thus a disordered general cannot be employed to preserve an army, while a rebellious mass cannot be used to attack an enemy. If this sort of general attacks a city it cannot be taken, while if this type of army lays siege to a town it will not fall. If both are unsuccessful then the officers' strength will be exhausted. If it is exhausted then the general will be alone and the masses will be rebellious. If they try to hold defensive positions they will not be secure, while if they engage in battle they will turn and run. They are referred to as an "old army."

When the troops are "old," then the general's awesomeness will not be effective. When the general lacks awesomeness, then the officers and troops will disdain punishment. When they disdain punishment, the army will lose its organization into squads of five. When the army loses its squads of five, the officers and soldiers will abandon their positions and run off. When they flee, the enemy will take advantage of the situation. When the enemy seizes the opportunity to profit from this situation, the army will inevitably perish.

The *Military Pronouncements* states: "The exemplary general, in his command of the army, governs men as he would want to be treated himself. Spreading his kindness and extending his beneficence, the strength of his officers is daily renewed. In battle they are like the wind arising; their attack is like the release of a pent-up river."[15] Thus our army can be seen but not withstood, can be submitted to but not be conquered. If you lead the men in person, your soldiers will become the most valiant under Heaven.

The *Military Pronouncements* states: "The army employs rewards as its external form and punishments as its internal substance." When rewards and punishments are clear, then the general's awesomeness is effected. When the proper officials are obtained, then the officers and troops are obedient. When those entrusted [with responsibility] are Worthies, enemy states will be fearful.

The *Military Pronouncements* states: "Where the Worthy go they have no enemies before them." Thus officers can be deferred to, but they cannot be arrogant.[16] The general can be pleased but cannot be troubled. Plans can be complex, but they cannot be doubted. When the officers are arrogant, their subordinates will not be submissive. When the general is troubled, his subordinates and troops will not trust each other. When plans are doubted, the enemy will be roused to confidence. If one proceeds to mount an attack under these conditions, chaos will result.

Now the general is the fate of the state. If he is able to manage the army and attain victory, the state will be secure and settled.

The *Military Pronouncements* states: "The general should be able to be pure; able to be quiet; able to be tranquil; able to be controlled; able to accept criticism; able to judge disputes; able to attract and employ men; able to select and accept advice; able to know the customs of states; able to map mountains and rivers; able to discern defiles and difficulty; and able to control military authority [*ch'üan*]."

Thus it is said that the wisdom of the benevolent and Worthy, the thoughts and plans of the Sages and illuminated, the words of the wood carriers, the discussions in court, and the affairs of ascension and decline—all of these are what the general should hear about.

If the general can think of his officers as if thirsty, his plans will be followed. But if the general stifles advice, the valiant will depart. If plans are not followed, the strategists will rebel. If good and evil are treated alike, the meritorious officers will grow weary. If the general relies solely on himself, his subordinates will shirk all responsibility. If he brags, his assistants will have few attainments. If he believes slander, he will lose the hearts of the people. If he is greedy, treachery will be unchecked. If he is preoccupied with women, then the officers and troops will become licentious. If the general has a single one of these faults, the masses will not submit. If he is marked by two of them, the army will lack order; if by three of them, his subordinates will abandon him; if by four, the disaster will extend to the entire state!

The *Military Pronouncements* states: "For the general's plans one wants secrecy. For the officers and masses one wants unity. For attacking the enemy one wants swiftness." When the general's plans are secret, treacherous impulses are thwarted. When the officers and masses are unified, then the heart of the army is united. When the attack on the enemy is swift, they will not have time to prepare. When the army has these three, their plans cannot be snatched away.

If the general's plans leak out, the army will not be able to effect the strategic disposition of power [*shih*]. If external agents spy out internal affairs, the disaster that will befall the army cannot be controlled. If wealth[17] is brought into the encampment, a myriad evildoers will assemble. If the general is marked by these three, the army will inevitably be defeated.

If the general does not carefully contemplate his course of action, his strategists will abandon him. If the general is not courageous, the officers and troops will be terrified. If the general moves the army recklessly, it will not be imposing. If he transfers his anger [to the innocent], the whole army will be afraid. As the *Military Pronouncements* states: "Contemplation and courage are what the general values; movement and anger are what the general employs." These four are the general's clear precepts.

The *Military Pronouncements* states: "If the army lacks material resources, officers will not come. If the army does not have [ample] rewards, the officers will not go into battle [with the proper commitment]."

The *Military Pronouncements* states: "Beneath fragrant bait there will certainly be dead fish. Beneath generous rewards there will certainly be courageous officers."[18] Thus the forms of propriety are what officers will turn to, while rewards are what they will die for. If you summon them with what attracts them and display what they will die for, then those you seek will come. But if you treat them respectfully and afterward express regret at doing so, then they will not remain with you. If you reward them and afterward regret it, then the officers will not respond to your commands. If you are tireless in effecting propriety and rewards, the officers will compete with each other to die.

The *Military Pronouncements* states: "A state about to mobilize its army concentrates first on making its beneficence ample. A state about to attack and seize another concentrates on first nurturing the people." Conquering the many with only a few [is a question of] beneficence. Conquering the strong with the weak [is a question of] people. Thus the good general, in nurturing his officers, treats them no differently than himself. Therefore, he is able to direct the Three Armies as if they were of one mind, and then his victory can be complete.

The *Military Pronouncements* states: "The key to using the army is to first investigate the enemy's situation. Look into his granaries and armories, estimate his food stocks, divine his strengths and weaknesses, search out his natural advantages, and seek out his vacuities and fissures." Thus if the state does not have the hardship of an army in the field yet is transporting grain, it must be suffering from emptiness. If the people have a sickly cast, they are impoverished.

If they are transporting provisions for a thousand *li,* the officers will have a hungry look. If they must gather wood and grass before they can eat, the army does not have enough food to pass one night. Accordingly, if someone transports provisions a thousand *li,* he lacks one year's food; two thousand *li,* he lacks two years' food; three thousand *li,* he lacks three years' food. This is what is referred to as an "empty state." When the state is empty, the people are impoverished. When the people are impoverished, then the government and populace are estranged. While the enemy attacks from without, the people steal from within. This is termed a situation of "inevitable collapse."

The *Military Pronouncements* states: "When a ruler's actions are cruelly violent, his subordinates will be hasty to implement harsh measures. When the taxes are onerous, impositions numerous, fines and punishments endless, while the people mutually injure and steal from each other, this is referred to as a 'lost state.' "

The *Military Pronouncements* states: "When the secretly greedy [display] an external appearance of incorruptibility; prevarication and praise can gain fame; bureaucrats steal from the state to distribute their own beneficence, causing confusion in the ranks; and people adorn themselves and [feign] the proper countenance in order to attain high office, this is referred to as 'the beginning of thievery.' "

The *Military Pronouncements* states: "If administrative officials form parties and cliques, each advancing those with whom they are familiar; the state summons and appoints the evil and corrupt, while insulting and repressing the benevolent and worthy; officials turn their backs on the state and establish their personal interests; and men of equal rank disparage each other, this is termed 'the source of chaos.' "

The *Military Pronouncements* states: "When strong clans assemble the evil, people without position are honored, and there are none who are not shaken by their majesty; when these practices proliferate and are intertwined they cultivate an image of virtue—establishing it through public beneficence—and they snatch the authority [*ch'üan*] belonging to those in official positions; when they insult the people below them, and within the state there is clamoring and backbiting, while the ministers conceal themselves and remain silent, this is 'causing chaos at the root.' "

The *Military Pronouncements* states: "Generation after generation they act treacherously, encroaching upon and stealing district offices. In advancing and retiring they seek only their own convenience, and they forge and distort documents, thereby endangering the ruler. They are referred to as 'the state's treacherous ones.'"

The *Military Pronouncements* states: "When the officials are many but the people few; there is no distinction between the honored and lowly; the strong and weak insult each other; and no one observes the prohibitions or adheres to the laws, then these effects will extend to the ruler, and the state will reap the misfortune."

The *Military Pronouncements* states: "When the ruler regards the good as good but does not advance them, while he hates the evil but does not dismiss them; when the Worthy are hidden and covered, while the unworthy hold positions, then the state will suffer harm."

The *Military Pronouncements* states: "When the branches [the ruler's relatives] and leaves [the powerful families] are strong and large, forming parties and occupying positions of authority so that the lowly and mean insult the honored, growing more powerful with the passing of time, while the ruler cannot bear to dismiss them, then the state will suffer defeat from it."

The *Military Pronouncements* states: "When deceitful ministers hold superior positions, the entire army will be clamoring and contentious. They rely on their awesomeness to grant personal favors, and act in a manner that offends the masses. Advancement and dismissal lack any basis, the evil are not dismissed, and men seek gain with any appearance possible. They monopolize appointments for themselves, and in advancements and dismissals boast of their own merits. They slander and vilify those of great Virtue, and make false accusations against the meritorious. Whether good or evil, all are treated the same by them. They gather and detain affairs of government so that commands and orders are not put into effect. They create a harsh government, changing the ways of antiquity and altering what was common practice. When the ruler employs such wanton characters, he will certainly suffer disaster and calamity."

The *Military Pronouncements* states: "When evil men of courage praise each other, they obfuscate the ruler's wisdom. When both criticism and praise arise together, they stop up the ruler's wisdom. When each person praises those he favors, the ruler loses the loyal."

Accordingly, if the ruler investigates unusual words, he will discover their beginnings. If he engages scholars and Worthies, then evil men of courage will withdraw. If the ruler appoints [virtuous] men of experience and age, the myriad affairs will be well managed. If he respectfully invites the recluses and hidden scholars to take positions, the officers will then fulfill their functions. If plans extend to the firewood carriers, achievements will be predictable. If he does not lose the minds of the people, his Virtue will flourish.

II

MIDDLE STRATEGY

Now the Three August Ones[19] never spoke, but their transformations flowed throughout the Four Seas. Thus the world had no one to whom to attribute the accomplishments.

The Emperors embodied Heaven and took Earth as their model. They spoke and issued orders, and the world attained Great Peace. Ruler and minister yielded the credit for this to each other, while all within the Four Seas were transformed without the common people being conscious of how the changes came about. Therefore, in employing subordinates they did not rely on the forms of propriety or rewards. There was the beauty of accomplishments and no harm.

Kings governed men by means of the Tao, causing their hearts to be compliant and their wills to be submissive while also establishing restrictive measures and making preparations against decline. All [the feudal lords] within the Four Seas assembled [at their courts], and the duty of kingship was not neglected. Even though they made military preparations, they never suffered the misfortune of warfare. Rulers did not doubt their subordinates, while subordinates had faith in their rulers. The state was settled, the ruler secure, and bureaucrats could resign with righteousness, so they also were able to have beauty without harm.

The hegemons governed their officers by virtue of authority—bonding them through trust, motivating them with rewards. When that trust declined the officers grew distant, and when rewards became inadequate they would not submit to orders.

The *Army's Strategic Power*[20] states: "When the army is mobilized and advances into the field, the sole exercise of power lies with the general. If in advancing or withdrawing the court interferes, it will be difficult to attain success."

The *Army's Strategic Power* states: "Employ the wise, courageous, greedy, and stupid. The wise take pleasure in establishing their achievements. The courageous love to put their will into effect. The greedy fervently pursue profits. The stupid have little regard for death. Employ them through their emotions, for this is the military's subtle exercise of authority [*ch'üan*]."

The *Army's Strategic Power* states: "Do not allow your disputatious officers to discuss the enemy's good points because they may delude the masses. Do not allow the benevolent to control the finances, for they will dispense too much and become attached to the lower ranks."

The *Army's Strategic Power* states: "Prohibit mediums and shamans from divining about the army's good or bad fortune on behalf of the officials and officers."

The *Army's Strategic Power* states: "One does not employ righteous officers with material wealth alone. Thus the righteous will not die for the malevolent. The wise will not make plans on behalf of an obtuse ruler." The ruler cannot be without Virtue, for if he lacks Virtue his ministers will rebel. He cannot be without awesomeness, for if he lacks awesomeness he will lose his authority [*ch'üan*]. A minister cannot be without virtue, for if he lacks virtue then he has nothing with which to serve his ruler. He cannot be without awesomeness, for if he lacks awesomeness the state will be weak. If he is too awesome then he himself will be overturned.

Therefore the Sage Kings—in governing the world—observed the flourishing and decline [of the seasons], measured human gains and losses, and created forms of administration. Thus the feudal lords have two armies, the regional earls have three armies, and the Son of Heaven has six.[21] When the world is turbulent, rebellion and contrariness are born. When the king's bountiful influence is exhausted, the feudal lords swear oaths [of alliance] and attack each other.

If your state's Virtue and strategic configuration of power [*shih*] are the same as those of the enemy so that neither state has the means to overcome the other, then you must win the minds of the valiant, share likes and dislikes with the common people, and only thereafter attack the enemy in accord with changes in the balance of power [*ch'üan*]. Thus without stratagems you have no means to resolve suspicions and settle doubts. Without rumor and the unorthodox you have no means to destroy evildoers and stop invaders. Without secret plans you have no means to be successful.

The Sage embodies Heaven, the Worthy model on Earth, and the wise find their teachers in antiquity. Thus the *Three Strategies* has been written for a period of decadence. The "Superior Strategy" establishes the forms of propriety and rewards, discriminates between evildoers and the valiant, and makes clear success and defeat. The "Middle Strategy" marks out the differences in Virtue and behavior and makes manifest changes in the balance of power [*ch'üan*]. The "Inferior Strategy" arrays the Tao and Virtue, investigates security and danger, and makes clear the calamity of harming the Worthy.

Thus if the ruler thoroughly understands the "Superior Strategy" he will be able to employ the Worthy and seize his enemies. If he thoroughly understands the "Middle Strategy" he will be able to employ and control his generals and unite the people. If he thoroughly understands the "Inferior Strategy" he will be able to discern the sources of flourishing and decline and understand the regulations for governing a state. If his subordinates thoroughly understand the "Middle Strategy" they will be able to achieve merit and preserve themselves.

When the soaring birds have all been slain, then good bows are stored away.[22] When enemy states have been extinguished, ministers in charge of planning are lost. Here "lost" does not mean they lose their lives but that [the ruler] has taken away their awesomeness and removed their authority [*ch'üan*]. He enfeoffs them in court, at the highest ranks of his subordinates, in order to manifest their merit. He presents them with excellent states in the central region in order to enrich their families, and bestows beautiful women and valuable treasures on them in order to please their hearts.

Now once the masses have been brought together they cannot be hastily separated. Once the awesomeness of authority [*ch'üan*] has been granted it cannot be suddenly shifted. Returning the forces and disbanding the armies [after the war] are critical stages in preservation and loss. Thus weakening [the commanding general] through appointment to new positions, taking [his authority] by granting him a state, is referred to as a "hegemon's strategy." Thus the hegemon's actions incorporate a mixed approach [of Virtue and power]. Preserving the altars of state, gathering those of character and courage—both are encouraged by the strategic power [*shih*] of the "Middle Strategy." Thus [to exercise such] power [*shih*] the ruler must be very secretive.

III
INFERIOR STRATEGY

Now one who can sustain the imperiled under Heaven can control the security of All under Heaven. One who can remove the distress of those under Heaven will be able to enjoy the pleasure [of governing] All under Heaven. One who can rescue those under Heaven suffering from misfortune will be able to gain the prosperity of All under Heaven. Therefore, when the ruler's munificence extends to the people, Worthy men will give their allegiance. When his munificence reaches the multitudinous insects, then Sages will ally with him. Whomever the Worthy give their allegiance to, his state will be strong. Whomever the Sages support, [under him] the six directions will be unified. One seeks the Worthy through Virtue, one attracts Sages with the Tao. If the Worthy depart the state will become weak; if the Sages depart the state will grow depraved. Weakness is a step on the road to danger, depravity is a sign of doom.

The government of a Worthy causes men to submit with their bodies. The government of a Sage causes men to submit with their minds. When their bodies submit the beginning can be planned; when their minds submit the end can be preserved. Their physical submission is attained through the forms of propriety; their mental submission is attained through music.[23]

What I refer to as music is not the sound of musical instruments—the stones, metal [bells], strings, and bamboo [pipes]. Rather, I refer to people taking pleasure in their families, clans, occupations, capitals and towns, orders of government, the Tao, and Virtue. One who rules the people in this fashion creates music in order to bring measure to their activities, to ensure that they do not lose their essential harmony. Thus the Virtuous ruler uses music to give pleasure to the people; the debauched ruler uses music to give pleasure to himself. One who provides pleasure to others endures and prospers; one who pleasures himself does not endure, but perishes.

One who abandons what is nearby to plan for what is distant will labor without success. One who abandons the distant to plan for the nearby will be at ease and attain lasting results. A government marked by ease has many loyal ministers. A government marked by labor has many resentful people. Thus it is said: "One who concentrates on broadening his territory will waste his energies; one who concentrates on broadening his Virtue will be strong." One who is able to hold what he possesses will be secure; one who is greedy for what others have will be destroyed. A government that verges on being destroyed will entangle later generations in the misfortune. One who enacts policies beyond proper measure will, even though successful, inevitably be defeated. Indulging oneself while instructing others is contrary [to natural order]; rectifying yourself and transforming others accords [with the Tao]. Contrariness is a summons to chaos; according with is the essence of order.

The Tao, Virtue, benevolence, righteousness, and the forms of propriety—these five—are one body. The Tao is what men tread; Virtue is what men gain; benevolence is what men approach; righteousness is what men consider appropriate; and the forms of propriety are what people embody. You cannot lack any one of them.

Thus rising in the early morning, sleeping at night are constraints of the forms of propriety. Punishing brigands and taking revenge are decisions of righteousness. The compassionate heart is an expression of benevolence. Gaining [what you want] yourself, and gaining it for other people, is the path of Virtue. Ensuring that people are equal and do not lose their place, this is the transformation of the Tao.

What proceeds from the ruler and descends to the minister is termed "commands." What is recorded on bamboo strips and silk rolls is termed "orders." What is initiated and implemented is termed "government." Now when commands are disobeyed,[24] then orders are not put into effect. When orders are not put into effect, then government is not established. When government is not established, then the Tao does not penetrate [the realm]. When the Tao does not penetrate, then depraved ministers will prevail. When depraved ministers prevail, then the ruler's majesty is injured.

To welcome Worthies a thousand li away, the road is far; to bring in the unworthy, the road is quite near. For this reason the enlightened ruler abandons the near and takes the distant. Therefore, he is able to complete his achievements. He honors [worthy] men, and his subordinates all exhaust their energies.

If you dismiss one good [man], then a myriad good [acts] will decline. If you reward one evil [man], then a myriad evils will be drawn to you. When the good are rewarded and the evil suffer punishment, the state will be secure, and the multitudes of good people will come.

When the masses are doubtful, there are no settled states. When the masses are deluded, there are no governed people. When doubts are settled and the deluded returned, then the state can be secure. When one order is contravened, then a hundred orders will be disobeyed. When one evil act is done, a hundred evils will form. Thus if you put good into effect amidst a compliant people and impose harsh measures on wicked people, orders will be implemented without any discontent.

Employing the discontented to govern the discontented is termed "contrary to Heaven."[25] Having the vengeful control the vengeful, an irreversible disaster will result. Govern the people by causing them to be peaceful. If one attains peace through purity, then the people will have their places, and the world will be tranquil.

If those who oppose the ruler are honored, while the greedy and uncivilized are enriched, then even if there is a Sage ruler he cannot realize a well-ordered government. If those who oppose the ruler are punished, while the greedy and uncivilized are arrested, then a transformation will be effected and the myriad evils eliminated.

Pure, incorruptible officers cannot be enticed with rank and salary. Self-constrained, righteous officers cannot be coerced with awesomeness or punishment. Thus when the enlightened ruler seeks the Worthy, he must observe what will attract them. To attract pure, incorruptible officers he perfects his observance of the forms of propriety. To attract self-constrained, righteous officers he perfects himself in the Tao. Only thereafter will they be attracted and the ruler's reputation preserved.

The Sage and perfected man perceive the sources of flourishing and decline, understand the beginnings of success and defeat, have attained true knowledge of the crux [chi] of governing and turbulence, and know the measure of coming and going. Such men, even in poverty, will not hold a position in a doomed state. Though lowly, they will not eat the rice of a turbulent country. They conceal their names and cling to the Way [Tao]. When the proper time comes they move, reaching the pinnacle which a subject can attain. When they encounter Virtue that accords with them, they will establish extraordinary achievements. Thus their Tao is lofty, and their names will be praised in later generations.

The Sage King does not take any pleasure in using the army. He mobilizes it to execute the violently perverse and punish the rebellious. Now using the righteous to execute the unrighteous is like releasing the Yangtze and Yellow rivers to douse a torch, or pushing a person tottering at the edge of an abyss. Their success is inevitable! Thus [when action should be taken] one who hesitates and is quiet, without advancing, seriously injures all living beings. Weapons are inauspicious instruments, and the Tao of Heaven abhors them. However, when their employment is unavoidable it accords with the Tao of Heaven. Now men in the Tao are like fish in water. If they have water they will live; if not they will die. Thus the ruler must constantly be afraid and dare not lose the Tao.

When prominent, powerful families gain control of official duties, the state's awesomeness weakens. When the power of life and death lies with the prominent, powerful families, the state's strategic power [*shih*] is exhausted. If the prominent, powerful families bow their heads in submission, then the state can long endure. When the power of life and death lies with the ruler, then the state can be secure.

When the four classes of people[26] have nothing for their use, then the state will lack all stores. When the four classes have enough for their use, then the state will be secure and happy.

When Worthy ministers are brought inside government, depraved ones will be outside. When depraved ministers are inside, Worthy ministers will perish. When within and without lose what is appropriate, disaster and disorder will last through generations.

If the major ministers doubt the ruler, a myriad evils will accumulate and gather. If the ministers usurp the respect that should be due the ruler, then the upper and lower ranks will be confused. When the ruler [effectively] occupies the position of a minister, upper and lower [ranks] lose their order.

If someone injures the Worthy, the calamity will extend three generations. If someone conceals the Worthy, he himself will suffer the harm. If someone is jealous of the Worthy, his reputation will not be complete. If someone advances the Worthy, the blessings will flow to his sons and grandsons. Thus the ruler is anxious to advance the Worthy and thereby make his good name illustrious.

If you profit one person but injure a hundred, the people will leave the city. If you profit one person and harm ten thousand, [the populace of] the state will think about dispersing. If you get rid of one and thereby profit a hundred, the people will long for your munificence. If you get rid of one and thereby profit ten thousand, your government will not be disordered.

7

Questions and Replies Between T'ang T'ai-tsung and Li Wei-kung

唐太宗

李衛公

問對

Translator's Introduction

THROUGH POLITICAL MEASURES and the brutal, unremitting implementation of aggressive military strategies, the brief Ch'in dynasty unified the empire in 221 B.C. Within two decades it had been supplanted by the glorious Han, whose reign encompassed four centuries of centralized, prosperous rule and civilization until itself perishing. Thereafter, China was again characterized by political fragmentation during the period of Disunion, which ended when the dynamic Emperor Sui Wen-ti seized power in A.D. 581. The historical legacy of his dynasty mirrors that of the Ch'in because he not only reunified the country geographically but also imposed central bureaucratic institutions that regained political control of the populace and made local bureaucracy an instrument of the state. Furthermore, he conducted extensive efforts to culturally integrate the north and the south; displace the powerful, entrenched aristocratic families; and reform the tax system. The many institutions created under his reign subsequently provided the foundation for the illustrious T'ang.[1]

Unfortunately, his heir, Sui Yang-ti (reigned A.D. 604–618), quickly displayed many of the reprehensible traits characteristic of archetypical last rulers, historically associated with the loss of Heaven's Mandate. Foremost among these traits was his extravagance, particularly in the area of public works. Millions of people were pressed into service for such projects as restoring the Great Wall, rebuilding and extending canals, and constructing the new capital. Furthermore, in the period A.D. 611 to 614, Sui Yang-ti mounted three disastrous expeditions to impose Chinese suzerainty over Korea, largely by conscripting men from the northeast region. The heritage of these onerous state policies was impoverishment, discontent, and death—inevitably stimulating more than two hundred factions to revolt.

Li Yüan, the powerful Sui official who eventually founded the T'ang dynasty (reigning under the title T'ang Kao-tsu), has traditionally been portrayed as having been forced into revolting by the combined influences of popular prophecies and the machinations of his son, Li Shih-min (T'ang

T'ai-tsung).[2] Li Yüan not only commanded the strongest provincial army but was directly related to the Sui imperial family as well as to powerful semi-barbarian aristocratic families in the northwest region. Entrusted with suppressing several of the sporadic revolts that had begun to appear in A.D. 613, his success augmented his authority and solidified his control over the strategic province of Shansi. Initiated in the fifth month of A.D. 617, the revolt quickly gathered major support from a number of other rebels and strong generals; by the eleventh month of that year, Li Yüan had captured the capital. In the fifth month of A.D. 618, the year of Sui Yang-ti's murder, he formally ascended the throne to establish the T'ang dynasty.

During the rise of both the Sui and T'ang, the nomadic powers outside the historical borders had become fragmented, with some of the Turks nominally acknowledging Chinese suzerainty and many of their tribesmen even serving in the imperial military forces. The Eastern Turks provided significant support to Li Yüan's revolt in its formative stages—not only by furnishing horses, men, and limited supplies but also by essentially foregoing any opportunistic actions to capitalize on the chaos. At the time of the establishment of the dynasty, only a limited area in the north had actually been brought under central government control; the next ten years were spent consolidating its power, extending the imperial domain in all directions—including to the agriculturally critical eastern areas—and creating a heritage of tranquility for succeeding generations.

The T'ang established itself through the talents of its skilled generals, the adoption of Sui institutions, the populist appeal of its positions, and a benevolent pacification policy—especially in the south. Three generals particularly distinguished themselves: Li Ching, the strategist to whom this seventh military classic is attributed; Li Shih-chi; and Li Shih-min, the second son of Li Yüan who became T'ang T'ai-tsung upon his usurping the throne in A.D. 627. All three were active in the founding and integration of the empire, with T'ang T'ai-tsung being depicted as heroically leading his elite troops into many pitched conflicts.

T'ang T'ai-tsung, who asks the questions and offers short observations in this military classic, apparently received a Confucian education; he therefore had thorough knowledge of the classics and histories as well as being extremely skilled in the martial arts. He reportedly commanded troops by age fifteen and after contributing to the establishment of the T'ang as both a strategist and a commander, was instrumental in subduing numerous challenges to the new state—including those mounted by segments of the Western Turks. He finally became emperor by displacing his father, although only after murdering his older brother, the designated heir. Stories of his prowess and famous horses abound in popular Chinese history.[3]

As emperor he consciously cultivated the image of a proper ruler, one responsive to the needs of the people and willing to accept criticism and advice. The country was truly unified, both politically and culturally. Measures were enacted to reduce the plight of the people and stimulate the economy. Government expenditures were reduced, and effective administration was imposed throughout the nation. With the passage of time and perhaps distance from the uncertainties of the initial period, he eventually became more independent, intolerant, and extravagant. However, the formative years of the T'ang saw the rebirth of thought and culture, the resurgence of a civilization that would dazzle Asia for three centuries.

Li Ching—who lived from A.D. 571 to 649—began his career under the Sui, serving in the northwest in a military capacity. He eventually joined the T'ang forces just after the fall of the capital, Ch'ang-an, and became one of T'ang T'ai-tsung's earliest associates and supporters. Thereafter, he commanded T'ang troops in the suppression of both internal and external challenges, the great conquest of the Western Turks (for which he became famous), and the pacification of the south. Thus if the *Questions and Replies* actually preserves his conversations with T'ang T'ai-tsung, or even a large part of them, the strategies they discuss were not only theoretical concepts but had been personally tested and employed by them in critical battles.

The book differs markedly from the earlier classics, being more of a survey of earlier works, combined with a wide-ranging discussion and appreciation of their theories and contradictions. Illustrated by historical examples from their own campaign experiences, these discussions apparently reveal the predominant strategies and tactics of their era. Although most historians consider the book to be a forgery from either the late T'ang or Northern Sung, arguments have also been advanced that—as with other compendiums summarizing the thought and actions of the period—it is at least based on an actual protowork or recorded notes.[4]

Li Ching's biography from the *Hsin T'ang-shu* not only depicts the turbulent career of a successful T'ang politician and commander but also portrays the man and his strategies in action:[5]

Li Ching, whose personal name was Yao-shih, was a native of San-yüan in the Metropolitan prefecture. Tall and elegant in appearance, he was thoroughly versed in the classics and histories. He once said to those close to him: "In this life a man wants to attain wealth and rank through accomplishments. Why must one compose passages like the Confucians?" Whenever his uncle Han Ch'in-hu discussed military affairs with him, he would sigh in amazement and say: "If one cannot discuss Sun-tzu and Wu-tzu with this man, who can one discuss them with?" When Li Ching served the Sui dynasty as Chief of the Palace Attendants, Niu Hung—Minister for the Ministry of Personnel—saw him and remarked: "This is a talent to assist a king!" The Left Vice Director [for State Affairs], Yang Su, placing his hand on his great seat, said to him: "My lord, in the end you should sit here!"

At the end of the Ta-yeh period he served as Vice Magistrate of Ma-i District. When T'ang Kao-tsu attacked the Turks, Li Ching observed that Kao-tsu was marked by extraordinary ambition. He had himself arrested [for being disloyal to Kao-tsu] in order to urgently report Kao-tsu's revolutionary intentions and sent to Chiang-tu. When he reached Ch'ang-an the road was blocked. Kao-tsu then conquered the capital [and captured Li Ching]. He was about to have him beheaded when Ching cried out: "My lord raised troops to eliminate perversity and chaos on behalf of All under Heaven. If you want to achieve the great affair [of becoming emperor], how can you slay a righteous man because of personal enmity?" The king of Ch'in [Li Shih-min] also interceded on his behalf, and he was released, being brought into the government as a member of the Three Capital Guards. He accompanied [Li Shih-min] on the campaign to pacify Wang Shih-ch'ung and for his achievements was appointed a commander.

Hsiao Hsien occupied Chiang-ling, so [Kao-tsu] issued an imperial edict to Ching to pacify the area. Accompanied by a few light cavalrymen he crossed to Chin-chou to confront several tens of thousands of Man [barbarian] Teng Shih-luo bandits encamped in the mountain valleys of the region. King Yüan of Lu-chiang had not been victorious, so Ching planned the attack for him, forcing the enemy to withdraw. They proceeded to Hsia-chou, where they were blocked by Hsien's army and could not advance. The emperor assumed he was procrastinating and issued an imperial edict to the Supervisor in Chief Hsü Shao to behead Ching. Shao entered a plea on Ching's behalf, and he was spared.

The Man peoples in K'ai-chou under Jan Chao-tse then invaded K'uei-chou. Hsiao-kung, king of Chao Commandery, engaged them in battle but without gaining any advantage. Ching led eight hundred men to destroy their encampment and strategic defiles, establishing an ambush which resulted in the beheading of Chao-tse and the capture of five thousand prisoners. The emperor exclaimed to his attendants: "Employing men of achievement is not as good as using those who have erred. This is certainly true in Li Ching's case." Thereupon he personally drafted his citation, saying: "You are blameless for what is already past. I have long forgotten previous events." Li Ching subsequently planned the strategy for ten campaigns against Hsien.

By imperial edict Ching was appointed Commander in Chief of the Campaign Army, concurrently serving as Aide to Hsiao-kung's Campaign Army, with both armies' administrative matters all being entrusted to him. In August of the fourth year of the Martial Virtue reign period [A.D. 621], he reviewed the troops in K'uei-chou. It was the time of the autumn floods, with heavy waves on the vile, overflowing waters [of the Ch'ang-chiang River].[6] Hsien believed Ching would not be able to descend, so he did not establish any defenses. Ching's generals also requested they await the calming of the river before advancing. Ching said: "For the army the most critical affair is for its speed to be spiritual. Now the men have just assembled and Hsien does not yet know it, so if we take advantage of the water to attack his fortifications, it will be like being unable to cover one's ears at a thunderclap. Even if he is able to suddenly summon his troops, he will lack the means to oppose us, and we will certainly capture him." Hsiao-kung followed his plan, and in the ninth month the navy attacked I-ling. Hsien's general Wen Shih-hung encamped at Ch'ing-chiang with several tens of thousands of troops. Hsiao-kung wanted to attack him, but Ching said: "You cannot! Shih-hung is a stalwart general, while those below him are all courageous men. Now when they have newly lost Ching-men, they will all be full of ardor to oppose us. This is an army which can rescue the defeated and cannot be opposed. It would be better to go to the southern river bank and wait for their *ch'i* [spirit] to abate, and then take them." Hsiao-kung did not listen but instead left Ching behind to guard the encampment and personally went forth to engage them in battle. After being soundly defeated, he returned. The bandits then employed boats to disperse and plunder the countryside. Ching saw their disarray and let his army loose to destroy them. They seized more than four hundred vessels, while ten thousand of the enemy drowned.

Thereupon, leading a vanguard of five thousand light cavalry, he raced to Chiang-ling. They besieged the city and encamped, [subsequently] destroying generals Yang Chün-mao and Cheng Wen-hsiu and taking four thousand armored soldiers prisoner. Hsiao-kung continued the advance, and Hsien was terrified. He summoned the troops of the Chiang-nan region, but when they did not arrive, surrendered the next day. Ching entered their capital. His orders were quiet but strict, and the army did not loot [the city].

Some [of his generals] requested that Ching confiscate the family wealth of Hsien's generals who had opposed them in order to reward the army. Ching said: "The army of a True King has sympathy for the people and seizes the guilty. They were coerced into coming, so if we confiscate their wealth because the army opposed us—what they fundamentally did not wish to do—we make no allowance for the real rebels. Now that we have just settled Ching and Ying, we should display generosity and magnanimity in order to pacify their hearts. If they surrender and we confiscate their wealth, I am afraid that from Ching south, they will strengthen their walls and increase their emplacements. Forcing them into a desperate defense is not excellence in planning." He stopped their actions and did not confiscate their wealth. Because of this the line of cities between the Chiang and Han rivers competed with each other to submit.

For his achievements he was appointed duke of Yung-k'ang District and acting prefect for Ching-chou [Prefecture]. Thereupon he crossed the mountains to
Kuei-chou and dispatched emissaries along different routes to proclaim the policy of pacification. Tribal leaders—such as Feng-ang—with their children, all
came to submit, and the entire southern region was settled. When they calcu-
lated the gains, established authority, and created offices, they had added
ninety-six commanderies in all, with more than six hundred thousand households. He was summoned by imperial edict and his efforts praised. He was
granted the titles of Pacification Commissioner for Ling-nan and acting Commander in Chief for Kuei-chou.

He felt that Ling-hai was rustic and distant and [that] for a long time [it] had
not seen [a proper display of] Virtue, so that unless he manifested awesomeness
and military majesty and displayed the rites and righteousness, he would not
have the means to transform their customs. Thus he led the army on a southern
tour. Wherever they went he inquired about the sick and suffering and saw the
elders and aged in his courtyard. He proclaimed the emperor's beneficent intentions, and near and far submitted in fear.

Fu Kung-shih occupied Tan-yang in rebellion. The emperor appointed Hsiao-
kung Commander in Chief and summoned Ching to the court where he received
the general strategy and was appointed Vice Commander under Hsiao-kung.
When they marched east on their punitive expedition, Li Shih-chi and the others—seven general officers—all received appointment as Area Commanders.
Kung-shih dispatched Feng Hui-liang with thirty thousand naval forces to invest
Tang-t'u and Ch'en Cheng-t'ung with twenty thousand infantry and cavalry to
invest the Ch'ing-lin Mountains. From Mount Liang they connected their forces
in order to sever the road to Chiang and built crescent-shaped walls stretching
out more than ten *li* from north to south in order to extend their flanks.

All the [emperor's] generals voiced their opinion: "They have strong soldiers
and unbroken palisades. Even without engaging in battle they will wear out our
army. If you directly seize Tan-yang and empty his stronghold, then Hui-liang
and the others will surrender by themselves." Ching said: "It is not so. While
those two armies are elite units, the ones under Kung-shih's personal command
are also spirited troops. Since they have already secured Shih-t'ou Mountain,
their stronghold cannot yet be breached. If we remain we will not gain our objective, but we must shun retreat. For the stomach and back to have overwhelming worries is not a completely successful plan. Moreover, Hui-liang and Cheng-
t'ung are experienced rebels of more than a hundred battles. They do not fear
combat in the wilds. Right now they are maintaining the security of their position, clinging to Kung-shih's strategy. If we do the unexpected, provoking them
and attacking their fortifications, we will certainly destroy them. Hui-liang will
be drawn out and Kung-shih captured."

Hsiao-kung listened to him. Ching, leading Huang Chün-han and the others,
advanced along water and land routes. After a bitter battle they killed and

wounded more than ten thousand men. Hui-liang and the others fled, so Ching—in command of light cavalry—went to Tan-yang. Kung-shih was afraid, but although his forces were still numerous, they were incapable of fighting, so he fled. They captured him, and the region south of the Ch'ang-chiang River was at peace.

When the Branch Department of State Affairs was established for the Southeast Circuit, Ching was made Minister for the Ministry of War. He was granted a thousand pieces of silk, a hundred female slaves, and a hundred horses. When the Branch Department of State Affairs was discontinued, he was made Acting Chief Administrator for the Yang-chou Superior Area Command. The emperor sighed and said: "Ching, could the ancient generals Han, Pai, Wei, and Huo have done any more than you in the vital affairs of Hsien and Kung-shih!"[7]

In the eighth year [625] the Turks made an incursion into T'ai-yüan. Ching, as Commander in Chief of the Campaign Army, encamped with ten thousand men from the Chiang and Huai armies in the T'ai-ku region. At this time all the other generals suffered numerous defeats, while Ching alone returned with his army intact. For a short while he was appointed Acting Commander in Chief for An-chou [Prefecture].

When T'ang T'ai-tsung ascended the throne he received appointment as Minister of the Ministry of Justice, his accomplishments were recorded, and he was enfeoffed with four hundred households, concurrently acting as Secretariat Director.

A portion of the Turks separated and revolted, so the emperor planned a strategy to advance and take them. As Minister of the Ministry of War he acted as Commander in Chief for the Campaign Army of the Ting-hsiang Circuit, leading three thousand crack cavalry through Ma-i to race to the O-yang Mountains. Hsieh-li K'o-han[8] was astonished: "If the entire T'ang Army has not been mobilized, how would Ching dare to bring his single army here?" Thereupon the soldiers were repeatedly frightened. Ching let loose his agents to sow discord among the K'o-han's trusted confidants. At night he launched a sudden attack against Ting-hsiang and destroyed it. The K'o-han managed to escape and fled to Ch'i-k'ou.

For his accomplishment Ching was advanced and enfeoffed as duke of Tai-kuo. The emperor said: "Li Ling[9] crossed the desert with five thousand infantrymen but in the end surrendered to the Hsiung-nu. His achievements were still recorded on bamboo and silk. With three thousand cavalrymen Ching trampled through blood and took their court prisoner, subsequently taking Ting-hsiang. Antiquity does not have its like. It is enough to wash away my shame at Wei River!"[10]

Hsieh-li went to secure Mount T'ieh, then dispatched an emissary to acknowledge his offense, requesting that his state could become an inner vassal. Ching, as Commander in Chief of the Ting-hsiang Circuit, was sent out to receive him. The emperor also dispatched the Chief Minister of the Court of State

Ceremonial, T'ang Chien, and General An Hsiu-jen to act as officers for the pacification. Ching [who knew Hsieh-li's submission was uncertain] spoke with his Lieutenant General Kung-chin: "The Imperial Emissary is, on the contrary, a prisoner, so Hsieh-li must feel secure. If ten thousand cavalrymen, carrying twenty days' rations, stage a sudden attack from Pai-tao, we will certainly obtain what we desire." Kung-chin said: "The emperor has already agreed to the surrender, and the administrators are with them. What about that?" Ching said: "The opportunity cannot be lost. This is the way Han Hsin destroyed Ch'i.[11] For someone like T'ang Chien, what is there to regret?"

He directed the army on an urgent advance. Whenever they encountered [enemy] patrols, they took the soldiers prisoner and had them follow. Only when they were seven *li* from his headquarters did Hsieh-li realize it. The tribesmen were terrified and scattered, and Ching's army killed more than ten thousand, making prisoners of a hundred thousand men and women. They captured Hsieh-li's son, Tieh-luo-shih, and killed [his wife] the princess of I-ch'eng. Hsieh-li fled but was captured and presented to the emperor by the Assistant Commander in Chief of the Campaign Army for the T'a-tung Circuit, Chang Pao-hsiang. Thereby the T'ang enlarged its territory from north of Mount Yi to the Great Desert.

The emperor thereupon declared a general pardon throughout the realm and bestowed five days of festivities on the people. The Censor-in Chief Hsiao Yü accused Ching of disregarding the laws while commanding the army, allowing the troops to plunder extensively, and losing a great many rarities and treasures for the state. The emperor summoned Ching and upbraided him. Ching did not offer any argument but bowed his head to the ground and acknowledged his offense. The emperor slowly said: "In the Sui when General Shih Wan-sui destroyed Ta-t'ou K'o-han, he was not rewarded, but was executed. I will not do that. I pardon your offenses, and take note of your achievements." Then he advanced him to be Left Grand Master for Splendid Happiness, presented him with a thousand pieces of silk, and increased his fief to five hundred households. When this had been done he said: "Previously, people slandered and criticized you, but now I have realized the truth." Then he bestowed an additional two thousand pieces of material and transferred him to be Vice Director on the Right for State Affairs. Whenever Ching participated in discussions he was very respectful, as if he could not speak, and was considered profound and sincere.

At the time the emperor dispatched emissaries to the sixteen circuits to travel about investigating the customs of the people and appointed Ching to be Commissioner for the Metropolitan Circuit. It happened that he suffered from a foot disease, so he beseeched the emperor to release him from this duty. The emperor dispatched the Vice Director of the Secretariat, Ts'en Wen-pen, to proclaim to him: "From antiquity those that knew how to stop after attaining riches and honor have probably been few. Although you are ill and weary, still exert yourself to go on. Now if you consider the welfare of the state, I will deeply admire it. If you want to complete your elegant objectives and become a model for the age, you must accept." Then he bestowed upon him the privilege of an Acting Lord Specially Advanced remaining in residence, and gave him a thousand pieces of silk and a superior carriage with two horses. For his salary [the emperor] continued his previous emoluments as an officer for the state and domain. Whenever his illness abated somewhat he would go to the Secretariat-Chancellery one day out of three as a Grand Councillor for the Secretariat-Chancellery and was accorded the privilege of using the staff of spiritual longevity.

A short time later the T'u-yü-hun invaded the border. The emperor addressed his attendants: "Is Ching able to again assume the post of general?" Ching went to see Fang Hsüan-ling and said: "Even though I am old, I can still undertake one more campaign." The emperor was elated and appointed him the Commander in Chief of the Campaign Army for the West Seas Circuit. Five other generals with their armies—Tao-tsung, king of Ch'eng; Hou Chün-chi; Li Ta-liang; Li Tao-yen; and Kao Tseng-sheng—were all subordinate to him. When the army arrived at the city of Fu-ssu, the T'u-yü-hun had already burned all the grass and withdrawn to secure the Ta-fei River valley. The generals all advised that since the spring grass had not yet sprouted and the horses were weak, they could not do battle. Ching decided that their strategy would be to make a deep penetration. Subsequently, they passed beyond Mount Chi-shih and engaged in more than several tens of major battles. They killed and captured great numbers, destroying their states, and most of the inhabitants surrendered. Fu-yün [Qughan of the] T'u-yü-hun, being depressed, hung himself. Ching then established [Fu-yün's son] Mu-jung Sun, [also known as] King Ta-ning, in authority and returned home.

[Early in the campaign] Kao Tseng-sheng's army, traveling by way of the salt marsh roads, arrived late. Ching upbraided him somewhat, so that after they returned Kao reviled him. Together with the Aide for Kuang-chou, T'ang Feng-i, he accused Ching of plotting to revolt. Officers investigated the charge but found it unsubstantiated. Tseng-sheng and the others were judged guilty of making false accusations. Ching then closed his doors and dwelt in seclusion, refusing the visits of guests and relatives.

The emperor changed his enfeoffment to Duke of Wei-kuo.[12] His wife died. The emperor instructed that the grave should be built in the style [indicated by] stories about Wei and Huo, making the towers like Mount T'ieh and Mount Chi-shih to manifest his accomplishments. He was advanced to Commander Unequaled in Honor.

The emperor wanted to attack Liao, so he summoned Ching to come [to the court] and said: "In the south you pacified Wu, in the north destroyed the Turks, in the west settled the T'u-yü-hun. Only Kao-li [Koguryo] has not submitted. Do you also have any inclination about this?" He replied: "In the past I relied upon the awesomeness of Heaven to achieve some small measure of merit. Now although I am weak from my illness, if your Majesty is truly unwilling to release me, my sickness will be healed." The emperor took pity on his old age and did not consent to the assignment.

In the twenty-third year [649] his illness became acute. The emperor favored him with a visit at his official residence and wept. "You have been my lifelong friend and have labored for the state. Now your illness is like this, I sorrow for you." He died at age seventy-nine. He was granted the posthumous titles Minister of Education and Auxiliary Regional Area Commander in Chief. As a loyal minister he was interred on the side of the Imperial burial grounds at Chao-ling and bestowed the posthumous title *Ching Wu*.

As may be evident from the biography, Sui and T'ang military forces consisted of crossbowmen, cavalry, and infantrymen. The chariot had long ceased to have any military significance, and bronze weapons had vanished. Great flexibility was possible due to the large number of smaller, locally based units that could be called on for a major campaign. These troops were essentially professional and were supplemented by general conscription when required. Weapons groups were specialized, the emphasis was on speed and mobility, and flanking and other indirect maneuvers received preference over brute shock action.

BOOK I

The T'ai-tsung inquired: "Kao-li [Koguryo] has encroached on Hsin-lo [Silla] several times.[1] I dispatched an emissary to command them [to desist], but they have not accepted our edict. I am about to send forth a punitive expedition. How should we proceed?"

Li Ching replied: "According to what we have been able to find out about them, Kai Su-wen[2] relies upon his own knowledge in military affairs. He says that the Central States lack the capability to mount a punitive expedition and so contravenes your mandate. I request an army of thirty thousand men to capture him."

The T'ai-tsung said: "Your troops will be few while the place is distant. What strategy will you employ to approach them?"

Li Ching said: "I will use orthodox [cheng][3] troops."

The T'ai-tsung said: When you pacified the T'u-chüeh [Turks],[4] you employed unorthodox [ch'i] troops. Now you speak about orthodox troops. How is that?"

Li Ching said: "When Chu-ko Liang[5] captured Meng Hu seven times, it was not through any other Way [Tao]. He employed orthodox troops, that's all."

ꞏ ꞏ ꞏ

The T'ai-tsung said: "When Ma Lung of the Chin dynasty[6] conducted a punitive campaign against Liang-chou, it was also in accord with the 'Diagram of Eight Formations,'[7] and he built narrow chariots.[8] When the terrain was broad he employed encampments of 'deer-horn chariots,'[9] and when the road was constricted he built wooden huts and placed them upon the chariots so they could both fight and advance. I believe it was orthodox troops which the ancients valued!"

Li Ching said: "When I conducted the punitive campaign against the T'u-chüeh, we traveled west for several thousand li. If they had not been orthodox troops, how could we have gone so far? Narrow chariots and deer-horn chariots are essential to the army. They allow controlling the expenditure of energy,[10] provide a defense to the fore,[11] and constrain the regiments and squads of five. These three are employed in turn. This is what Ma Lung learned so thoroughly from the ancients."

′   ′   ′

The T'ai-tsung said: "At the battle in which I destroyed Sung Lao-sheng, when the fronts clashed our righteous army retreated somewhat. I then personally led our elite cavalry[12] to race down from the Southern plain, cutting across in a sudden attack on them. After Lao-sheng's troops were cut off to the rear, we severely crushed them, and subsequently captured him. Were these orthodox troops? Or unorthodox troops?"

Li Ching replied: "Your majesty is a natural military genius, not one who learns by studying. I have examined the art of war as practiced from the Yellow Emperor on down. First be orthodox, and afterward unorthodox; first be benevolent and righteous, and afterward employ the balance of power [ch'üan] and craftiness. Moreover, in the battle at Huo-i the army was mobilized out of righteousness, so it was orthodox. When Chien-ch'eng[13] fell off his horse and the Army of the Right withdrew somewhat, it was unorthodox."

The T'ai-tsung said: "At that time our slight withdrawal almost defeated our great affair, so how can you refer to it as unorthodox?"

Li Ching replied: "In general, when troops advance to the front it is orthodox, when they [deliberately] retreat to the rear it is unorthodox. Moreover, if the Army of the Right had not withdrawn somewhat, how could you have gotten Lao-sheng to come forward? The *Art of War* states: "Display profits to entice them, create disorder [in their forces] and take them."[14] Lao-sheng did not know how to employ his troops. He relied on courage and made a hasty advance. He did not anticipate his rear being severed nor being captured by your Majesty. This is what is referred to as 'using the unorthodox as the orthodox.'"

The T'ai-tsung said: "As for Huo Ch'ü-ping's[15] tactics unintentionally cohering with those of Sun-tzu and Wu-tzu, was it really so? When our Army of the Right withdrew, [my father, Emperor] Kao-tsu, turned pale. But then I attacked vigorously and, on the contrary, it became advantageous for us. This unknowingly cohered with Sun-tzu and Wu-tzu. My lord certainly knows their words."

′   ′   ′

The T'ai-tsung said: "Whenever an army withdraws can it be termed unorthodox?"

Li Ching said: "It is not so. Whenever the soldiers retreat with their flags confused and disordered, the sounds of the large and small drums not responding to each other, and their orders shouted out in a clamor, this is true defeat, not unorthodox strategy. If the flags are ordered, the drums respond to each other, and the commands and orders seem unified, then even though they may be retreating and running, it is not a defeat and must be a case of unorthodox strategy. The *Art of War* says: 'Do not pursue feigned retreats.'[16] It also says: 'Although capable display incapability.'[17] These all refer to the unorthodox."

The T'ai-tsung said: "At the battle of Huo-i, when the Army of the Right withdrew somewhat, was this a question of Heaven? When Lao-sheng was captured, was this due to the efforts of man?"

Li Ching said: "If the orthodox troops had not changed to unorthodox, and the unorthodox to orthodox, how would you have gained the victory? Thus for one who excels at employing the army, unorthodox and orthodox lie with man, that is all! He changes them in spirit-like fashion, [which is] the reason they are attributed to Heaven."

The T'ai-tsung nodded his head.

The T'ai-tsung said: "Are the orthodox and unorthodox distinguished beforehand, or are they determined at the time of battle?"

Li Ching said: "According to Duke Ts'ao's *Hsin shu* [*New Book*],[18] 'If you outnumber the enemy two to one, then divide your troops into two, with one section being orthodox, and one section being unorthodox. If you outnumber the enemy five to one, then three sections should be orthodox and two sections unorthodox.'[19] This states the main point. As Sun-tzu said: 'In warfare the strategic configurations of power do not exceed the unorthodox and orthodox, but the changes of the unorthodox and orthodox cannot be completely exhausted! The unorthodox and orthodox mutually produce each other, just like an endless cycle. Who can exhaust them?'[20] This captures it. So how can a distinction be made beforehand?

"If the officers and troops are not yet trained in my methods, if the assistant generals are not yet familiar with my orders, then we must break [the training] into two sections. When teaching battle tactics, in each case the soldiers must recognize the flags and drums, dividing and combining in turn. Thus [Sun-tzu] said: 'Dividing and combining are changes.'[21]

"These are the techniques for teaching warfare. When the instructions and the evaluation [of their implementation] have been completed and the masses know my methods, only then can they be raced about like a flock of sheep, following wherever the general points.[22] Who then makes a distinction of unorthodox and orthodox? What Sun-tzu refers to as 'giving shape to others but being formless ourselves'[23] is the pinnacle in employing the unorthodox and orthodox. Therefore, such a distinction beforehand is [merely for the purpose] of instruction. Determining the changes at the moment of battle, [the changes] are inexhaustible."

The T'ai-tsung said: "Profound indeed! Duke Ts'ao must have known it. But what the *Hsin shu* teaches is only what he [conveyed] to his generals, not the fundamental method of the unorthodox and the orthodox."

↙   ↙   ↙

The T'ai-tsung said: "Duke Ts'ao states, 'Unorthodox troops attack from the flank.' My lord, what do you have to say about this?"

Li Ching replied: "I recall that, in commenting on *Sun-tzu*, Duke Ts'ao said: 'Going out first to engage in battle is orthodox; going out afterward is unorthodox.' This is different from his discussions about flank attacks. I humbly refer to the engagement of great masses as orthodox, and those which the general himself sends forth as unorthodox. Where is the restriction of first, or later, or flank attack?"

↙   ↙   ↙

The T'ai-tsung said: "If I cause the enemy to perceive my orthodox as unorthodox, and cause him to perceive my unorthodox as orthodox, is this what is meant by 'displaying a form to others?' Is employing the unorthodox as orthodox, the orthodox as unorthodox, unfathomable changes and transformation, what is meant by 'being formless?' "

Li Ching bowed twice and said: "Your Majesty is a spiritual Sage. You go back to the ancients, beyond what I can attain."

↙   ↙   ↙

The T'ai-tsung said: "If 'dividing and combining are changes,' wherein lie the unorthodox and orthodox?"

Li Ching said: "For those who excel at employing troops there are none that are not orthodox, none that are not unorthodox, so they cause the enemy never to be able to fathom them. Thus with the orthodox they are victorious, with the unorthodox they are also victorious. The officers of the Three Armies only know the victory; none know how it is attained.[24] Without being able to fully comprehend the changes, how could [the outstanding generals] attain this? As for where the dividing and combining come from, only Sun-tzu was capable [of comprehending it]. From Wu Ch'i on, no one has been able to attain it."

The T'ai-tsung said: "What was Wu Ch'i's strategy like?"

Li Ching said: "Permit me to speak about the general points. Marquis Wu of Wei asked Wu Ch'i about [the strategy to be employed] when two armies confront each other. Wu Ch'i said: 'Have some of your low-ranking, courageous soldiers go forward and attack. When the fronts first clash, have them flee. When they flee, do not punish them, but observe whether the enemy advances to take [the bait]. If they sit as one and arise as one, and do not pursue your fleeing troops, the enemy has good strategists. If all their troops pursue the fleeing forces, some advancing, some halting, in disordered fashion, the enemy is not talented. Attack them without hesitation.'[25] I think that Wu Ch'i's strategy is generally of this sort, not what Sun-tzu would refer to as 'an orthodox engagement.'

The T'ai-tsung said: "My lord, your uncle Han Ch'in-hu once said you could discuss Sun-tzu and Wu-tzu with him.[26] Was he also referring to the unorthodox and orthodox?"

Li Ching said: "How could Ch'in-hu know about the pinnacle of the unorthodox and orthodox? He only took the unorthodox as unorthodox, and the orthodox as orthodox! He never knew about the 'mutual changes of the unorthodox and orthodox into each other, the inexhaustible cycle.' "[27]

The T'ai-tsung said: "When the ancients approached enemy formations and then sent forth unorthodox troops to attack where unexpected, were they also using the method of 'mutual changes?' "

Li Ching said: "In earlier ages most battles were a question of minimal tactics conquering those without any tactics, of some minor degree of excellence conquering those without any capabilities. How can they merit being discussed as the art of war? An example is Hsieh Hsüan's destruction of Fu Chien. It was not [because of] Hsieh Hsüan's excellence but probably Fu Chien's incompetence."[28]

The T'ai-tsung ordered the attending officers to find Hsieh Hsüan's biography in the histories and report on it. After hearing the report he said: "Fu Chien's management of this affair was really not good."

Li Ching said: "I observe that Fu Chien's biography records that 'Ch'in's armies had all been broken and defeated, with only Mu-jung Ch'ui's single force still intact. Fu Chien [the Ch'in king], leading more than a thousand cavalry, raced over to join him. Ch'ui's son Pao advised Ch'ui to kill Fu Chien but without result.' From this one sees that when the Ch'in armies were in turbulence, only Mu-jung Ch'ui's force remained intact, so it is obvious that Fu Chien was probably betrayed by Ch'ui's [treachery]. Now to be betrayed by others yet still hope to conquer the enemy, is it not difficult? Thus I say that men such as Fu Chien lacked tactics."

The T'ai-tsung said: "Sun-tzu said that 'one who plans extensively will conquer one who does less planning,'[29] so thus we know some planning will conquer no planning. All affairs are thus."

ʳ ʳ ʳ

The T'ai-tsung said: "The Yellow Emperor's *Art of War*[30] has been transmitted by previous generations as *The Classic of Grasping the Unorthodox* and as *The Classic of Grasping Subtle Change*. What do you have to say about this?"

Li Ching said: "The pronunciation of the character 'unorthodox'[31] is the same as that for 'subtle change.'[32] Thus some have transmitted [the title] as the latter, but the meaning is the same. If we investigate the actual writing it says: 'Four are orthodox, four are unorthodox. The remaining forces[33] are for "grasping subtle change."' Here [the character] 'unorthodox' is 'excess.' Because of this it is pronounced '*chi.*' My foolish opinion is that there is nothing which is not subtle, so why stress 'grasping' in speaking about it? It ought to be the remainder, then it would be correct.

"Now orthodox troops receive their [mission] from the ruler, while unorthodox troops are ordered forth by the general. Sun-tzu said: 'If orders are consistently implemented so as to instruct the people, then the people will submit.'[34] These are what are received from the ruler. Moreover, he says: 'The [employment of] the troops cannot be spoken of beforehand'[35] and 'there are commands from the ruler which are not accepted.'[36] These are what the general himself issues.

"As for generals: If they employ orthodox tactics without any unorthodox ones, they are defensive generals. If they employ unorthodox tactics without any orthodox ones, they are aggressive generals. If they employ both, they are generals to preserve the state. Thus 'grasping subtle change' and 'grasping the unorthodox' are not fundamentally two methods. Students [of military strategy] thoroughly understand them both!"

          ʼ   ʼ   ʼ

The T'ai-tsung said: "[The *Classic of Grasping Subtle Change* states:] 'The number of formations is nine, with the center having the excess which the commanding general controls.[37] The "four sides" and "eight directions" are all regulated therein. Within the [main] formation, formations are contained; within the platoons,[38] platoons are contained. They [can] take the front to be the rear, the rear to be the front.[39] When advancing, they do not run quickly; when withdrawing, they do not race off. There are four heads, eight tails.[40] Wherever they are struck is made the head. If the enemy attacks the middle, the [adjoining] two heads will both come to the rescue. The numbers begin with five and end with eight.'[41] What does all this mean?"

Li Ching said: "Chu-ko Liang set stones out horizontally and vertically to make eight rows. The method for the square formation then is this plan. When I instructed the army, we invariably began with this formation. What generations have passed down as *The Classic of Grasping Subtle Change* probably includes its rough outline."

          ʼ   ʼ   ʼ

The T'ai-tsung said: "Heaven, Earth, wind, clouds, dragons, tigers, birds, and snakes—what is the meaning of these eight formations?"

Li Ching said: "There was an error made by those who transmitted them. The ancients secretly concealed these methods, so they craftily created these eight names. The eight formations were originally one, being then divided into eight. For example, 'Heaven' and 'Earth' originated in flag designations; 'wind' and 'clouds' originated in pennant names. 'Dragons,' 'tigers,' 'birds,' and 'snakes' originated in the distinctions of the platoons and squads. Later generations erroneously transmitted them. If they were cleverly creating formations in the image of animals, why would they just stop at eight?"

          ʼ   ʼ   ʼ

The T'ai-tsung said: "The numbers begin with five and end with eight, so if they were not set up as images, then they are really ancient formations. Would you please explain them for me?"

Li Ching said: "I observe that the Yellow Emperor governed the army according to the methods by which he first established the 'village and well' system.[42] Thus the 'well' was divided by four roads, and eight families occupied it. Its shape was that for the Chinese character for 'well' [see Figure 1], so nine squares were opened therein. Five were used for formations, four were empty.[43] This is what is meant by 'the numbers beginning with five.'

"The middle was left vacant to be occupied by the commanding general, while around the four sides the various companies were interconnected, so this is what is meant by 'ending with eight.'

"As for the changes and transformations to control the enemy: Intermixed and turbulent, their fighting [appeared] chaotic, but their method was not disordered. Nebulous and varying, their deployment was circular, but their strategic power [shih] was not dispersed.[44] This is what is meant by 'they disperse and become eight, reunite and again become one.'"

* * *

The T'ai-tsung said: "The Yellow Emperor's governance of the army was profound indeed! Even if later generations have men with the wisdom of Heaven and spirit-like planning ability, none will be able to exceed his scope! After this who came near to him?"

Li Ching said: "When the Chou dynasty first flourished, the T'ai Kung substantially copied his methods. He began at the Ch'i state capital by establishing the well-acreage[45] system, [constructing] three hundred chariots, and [training] three hundred Tiger Guards[46] in order to establish a military organization. [They practiced advancing] 'six paces, seven paces,' [making] 'six attacks, seven attacks,'[47] so as to teach them battle tactics. When he deployed the army at Mu-yeh, with [only] a hundred officers the T'ai Kung controlled the army[48] and established his military achievements. With forty-five thousand men he conquered King Chou's mass of seven hundred thousand.

"In the Chou dynasty the *Ssu-ma Fa* was based upon the T'ai Kung. When the T'ai Kung died the people of Ch'i obtained his bequeathed strategies. When Duke Huan became hegemon over All under Heaven, he relied on Kuan Chung[49] who again cultivated the T'ai Kung's methods. Their army was referred to as a 'restrained and governed force,' and all the feudal lords submitted."

* * *

The T'ai-tsung said: "The Confucians mostly say that Kuan Chung was merely the minister of a hegemon [rather than a true king], so they truly do not know that his military methods were founded upon a king's regulations. Chu-ko Liang had the talent of a king's supporter, and he compared himself with Kuan Chung and Yüeh I. From this we know that Kuan Chung was also

Figure 1   Chinese character for "well"

the true sustainer of a king. But when the Chou declined the king could not use him, so he borrowed the state of Ch'i and mobilized an army there."

Li Ching bowed twice and said: "Your Majesty is a spiritual Sage! Since you understand men this well, even if your old minister should die, he would not be ashamed before any of the great Worthies of antiquity.

"I would like to speak about Kuan Chung's methods for organizing the state of Ch'i. He divided Ch'i to compose three armies. Five families comprised the fundamental unit, so five men made up a squad of five. Ten fundamental family units composed a hamlet, so fifty men composed a platoon. Four hamlets constituted a village, so two hundred men composed a company. Ten villages constituted a town, so two thousand men formed a battalion. Five towns made up an army, so ten thousand men composed one army. It all proceeded from the *Ssu-ma Fa*'s meaning that one army consists of five battalions, while one battalion consists of five companies.[50] In actuality, these are all the bequeathed methods of the T'ai Kung."

The T'ai-tsung said: "People say the *Ssu-ma Fa* was composed by Jang-chü. Is this true or not?"

Li Ching said: "According to the 'Biography of Jang-chü' in the *Shih chi,* he excelled in commanding the army at the time of Duke Ching of Ch'i, defeating the forces of Yen and Chin. Duke Ching honored him with the post of Commander of the Horse [*Ssu-ma*], and from then on he was called Ssu-ma Jang-chü. His sons and grandsons were then surnamed Ssu ma. In the time of King Wei of Ch'i they sought out and talked about the methods of the ancient Commanders of the Horse [ssu-ma] and also narrated what Jang-chü had studied. This subsequently became a book in ten chapters called *Ssu-ma Jang-chü*. Moreover, what has been transmitted from the military strategists and remains today is divided into four categories: 'balance of power and plans,' 'disposition and strategic power,' 'yin and yang,' and 'techniques and crafts.' They all come out of the *Ssu-ma Fa*."[51]

The T'ai-tsung said: "During the Han, Chang Liang and Han Hsin ordered [the books on] military arts. Altogether there were one hundred and eighty-two thinkers, but after they collated and edited them to select the important ones, they settled on thirty-five. Now we have lost what they transmitted. What about this?"

Li Ching said: "What Chang Liang studied was *The Six Secret Teachings* and *The Three Strategies* of the T'ai Kung. What Han Hsin studied was the *Ssu-ma Jang-chü* and the *Sun-tzu*. But the main principles do not go beyond the Three Gates and Four Types, that is all!"

The T'ai-tsung said: "What is meant by the Three Gates?"

Li Ching said: "I find that in the eighty-one chapters of the *Plans of the T'ai Kung*, what is termed 'secret strategy' cannot be exhausted in words; the seventy-one chapters of the *Sayings of the T'ai Kung* cannot be exhausted in warfare; and the eighty-five chapters of the *Warfare of the T'ai Kung* cannot be exhausted in resources. These are the Three Gates."[52]

The T'ai-tsung said: "What is meant by the Four Types?"

Li Ching said: "These are what Jen Hung discussed during the Han. As for the classes of military strategists, 'balance of power and plans' comprises one type, 'disposition and strategic power' is one type, and 'yin and yang' and 'techniques and crafts' are two types. These are the Four Types."

The T'ai-tsung said: "The *Ssu-ma Fa* begins with the spring and winter ceremonial hunts.[53] Why?"

Li Ching said: "To accord with the seasons, secure the connections with the spirits, and stress their substance. They were the most important government affairs according to the *Chou li* [*Rites of Chou*]. King Ch'eng held the spring hunt on the southern side of Mount Ch'i. King K'ang held the assembly at Feng Palace. King Mu held the assembly at Mount T'u. These are the affairs of the Son of Heaven.

"When Chou rule declined, Duke Huan of Ch'i assembled the armies [of the feudal states] at Chao-ling, while Duke Wen of Chin made his alliance [with the feudal lords] at Ch'ien-t'u. In these cases feudal lords respectfully performed the affairs of the Son of Heaven.[54] In actuality they used the Law for Nine Attacks[55] to overawe the irreverent. They employed the pretext of the hunt to hold court assemblies, accordingly conducting tours and hunts among the feudal lords, instructing them in armor and weapons.[56] The [Ssu-ma Fa also] states that unless there is a national emergency, the army should not be wantonly mobilized, but that during the times between the agricultural seasons they should certainly not forget military preparations.[57] Thus is it not profound that it placed the hunts of spring and winter at the beginning?"

⸢ ⸢ ⸢

The T'ai-tsung said: "During the Spring and Autumn period, the 'Methods for the Double Battalion of King Chuang of Ch'u'[58] stated that 'the hundred officers should act in accord with the symbolization of things, military administration should be prepared without official instructions.'[59] Did this accord with Chou regulations?"

Li Ching said: "According to the Tso chuan, 'King Chuang's chariot battalions [kuang] consisted of thirty chariots per battalion. [Each chariot] in the battalion had a company [tsu] of infantrymen plus a platoon [liang] for the flanks.'[60] 'When the army was advancing [the ones] on the right deployed by the shafts.'[61] They took the shafts as their defining measure. Thus they stayed close to the shafts to fight.[62] These were all Chou regulations.

"[In the case of Ch'u] I refer to one hundred men as a company [tsu], while fifty men are called a platoon [liang]. Thus each chariot is accompanied by one hundred and fifty men, many more than in the Chou organization. Under the Chou each chariot was accompanied by seventy-two infantrymen and three armored officers. Twenty-five men, including an officer, formed one platoon [liang], so three Chou platoons were seventy-five men altogether. Ch'i is a country of mountains and marshes; chariots were few, men numerous. If they were to be divided into three platoons [tui],[63] then they would be [functionally] the same as the Chou."

⸢ ⸢ ⸢

The T'ai-tsung said: "During the Spring and Autumn period, when Hsün Wu attacked the Ti, he abandoned his chariots to make infantry lines.[64] Were they also orthodox troops? Or unorthodox troops?"

Li Ching said: "Hsün Wu used strategy for chariot warfare, that is all! Although he abandoned the chariots, his strategy is still found therein. One force acted as the left flank, one force acted as the right flank, and one resisted the enemy in the front. Dividing them into three units, this is one tactic for chariot warfare. Whether one thousand or ten thousand chariots, it would be the same. I observe that in Duke Ts'ao's *Hsin shu* it states: 'Attack chariots [are accompanied by] seventy-five men. To the fore, to oppose the enemy, is one unit; to the left and right corners are two more units. The defense chariots[65] have an additional unit. It consists of ten men to prepare the food, five to repair and maintain the equipment, five to care for the horses, and five to gather firewood and fetch water—altogether twenty-five men. For a pair of attack and defense chariots, altogether there are one hundred men.' If you mobilize one hundred thousand men, you would employ one thousand each of the light [attack] and heavy [defense] chariots. This is the general outline of Hsün Wu's old methods.

"Moreover, I observe that in the period from Han to Wei, army regulations had five chariots compose a platoon [*tui*], with a supervisor [to command them]. Ten chariots formed a regiment [*shih*],[66] under a chief commandant. For one thousand chariots there were two men, a general and lieutenant general. If more chariots, the organization followed this pattern. If I examine it in comparison with our present methods, then our probing force is the [old] cavalry; our frontal assault troops are the [old] infantry and cavalry, half and half; and our holding force goes forth with combined chariot tactics.

"When I went to the west to rectify and punish the T'u-chüeh, we crossed several thousand *li* of treacherous terrain. I never dared change this system, for the constraints and regulations of the ancients can truly be trusted."

The T'ai-tsung honored Ling-chou with an imperial visit. After he returned he summoned Li Ching and invited him to be seated. He said: "I ordered Tao-tsung, A-shih-na She-erh, and others to mount a campaign of rectification and punishment against Hsüeh-Yen-t'o. Several groups among the T'ieh-le peoples requested the establishment of Han bureaucratic administration, and I acceded to all their requests. The Yen-t'o fled to the west, but I was afraid they would become a source of trouble to us, so I dispatched Li Chi to attack them. At present the northern regions are all at peace, but the various groups of barbarians and Han Chinese dwell intermingled with one another. What long-term method can we employ to settle and preserve them both?"

Li Ching said: "Your Majesty has ordered the establishment of sixty-six re-lay stations from the T'u-chüeh to the Hui-ho [Uighers] to connect the for-ward observation posts. This step already implements the necessary mea-sures. However, I foolishly believe it is appropriate for the Han [defensive] forces to have one method of training and the barbarians another. Since their instruction and training are separate, do not allow them to be intermixed and treated the same. If we encounter the incursion of some other group, then at that moment you can secretly order the generals to change their insig-nia and exchange their uniforms, and employ unorthodox methods to attack them."

The T'ai-tsung said: "For what reason?"

Li Ching said: "This is the technique referred to as 'manifesting many methods to cause misperception.'[67] If you have the barbarians appear as Han Chinese, and Han Chinese masquerade as barbarians, the [enemy] will not know the distinction between barbarians and Chinese. Then no one will be able to fathom our plans for attack and defense. One who excels at em-ploying an army first strives not to be fathomable,[68] for then the enemy will be confused wherever he goes."

The T'ai-tsung said: "This truly accords with my thoughts. You may go and secretly instruct our border generals that only through this difference be-tween Han and barbarians can we manifest the methods of unorthodox and orthodox warfare."

Li Ching bowed twice and said: "Your thoughts are those of a Sage, they flow from Heaven! You hear one and you know ten. How can I fully explain it all!"

✓   ✓   ✓

The T'ai-tsung said: "Chu-ko Liang said: 'A well-organized army, [even] if commanded by an incompetent general, cannot be defeated. An army that lacks good order, [even if it] has a capable general, cannot be victorious.' I suspect that his discussion is not expressive of the highest principles."

Li Ching said: "This was something Marquis Wu [Chu-ko Liang] said to stimulate[69] the troops. I observe that Sun-tzu said: 'If the instructions and training are not enlightened, the officers and troops lack constant duties, and their deployment into formation is askew, it is termed chaotic.[70] From antiquity the number of cases in which a chaotic army brought victory [to the enemy] can never be fully recorded!'[71] As to 'the instructions and leader-ship[72] not being enlightened,' he was speaking about their instruction and in-spection lacking the ancient methods. With regard to 'the officers and troops lacking constant duties,' he was speaking about the generals and their subordinates entrusted with authority [*ch'üan*] not having held their positions very long. When he refers to 'a chaotic army inviting victory,' he was speaking about self-destruction and defeat, not about an enemy conquering them. For this reason Marquis Wu said that if the army is well organized and trained, even an ordinary general will not be defeated. If the troops themselves are in chaos, then even though the general is sagacious, they will be endangered. What doubt can there be?"

The T'ai-tsung said: "The instruction and training of the army truly cannot be slighted!"

Li Ching said: "When the training accords with method, then the officers take pleasure in being employed. When instructions do not accord with method, even though one supervises and upbraids them from morning to night, it is of no advantage. The reason I thoroughly investigated the ancient regulations and collated them with all diagrams was to realize as nearly as possible a well-regulated army."

The T'ai-tsung said: "Please select the ancient methods for formations on my behalf and diagram them all for me."

The T'ai-tsung said: "Barbarian armies only rely on their strong horses to rush forth to attack. Are they unorthodox forces? Han armies only rely on their strong crossbowmen to hamstring the enemy. Are they orthodox forces?"

Li Ching said: "According to Sun-tzu: 'Those that excel in employing the army seek [victory] through the strategic configuration of power [*shih*], not through relying upon men. Therefore they are able to select men for positions and employ strategic power.'[73] What is referred to as 'selecting men' means engaging in battle in accord with the respective strengths of the barbarians and the Han. The barbarians are strong in the use of horses. Horses are an advantage in fast-moving fighting. Han troops are strong in the use of crossbows. Crossbows are an advantage in a slow-paced battle. In this each of them naturally relies upon their strategic power [*shih*], but they are not to be distinguished as unorthodox and orthodox. Previously, I discussed how the barbarians and Han units ought to change their insignia and exchange their uniforms, a technique in which the unorthodox and orthodox mutually give rise to each other. Horses also have orthodox tactics, crossbows also unorthodox employment. What constancy is there?"

The T'ai-tsung said: "My lord, discuss the technique again in detail."

Li Ching said: "First manifest a form and cause the enemy to follow it. This is the technique."

[T'ai-tsung:[74] "I understand it now. Sun-tzu said: 'For the army, the pinnacle of military deployment approaches the formless.' And 'In accord with the enemy's disposition we impose measures upon the masses that produce victory, but the masses are unable to fathom them.'[75] This is what is meant!"

Li Ching bowed twice. "Perfect indeed! Your Majesty's sagacious thoughts have already penetrated more than half of it!"]

The T'ai-tsung said: "Recently, the remnants of the Ch'i-tan [Khitan] and Hsi peoples have all submitted. I have determined that the two [tribal] commanders in chief of the Sung Mo and Jao Le regions will be united under the An-pei Protectorate. I would like to employ Hsüeh Wan-ch'e [as governor]. What do you think?"

Li Ching said: "Wan-ch'e is not as suitable as A-shih-na She-erh, Chih-shih Ssu-li, or Ch'i-pi Ho-li. They are all barbarian subjects who thoroughly understand military affairs. I once spoke with them about the mountains, rivers, and roads of the Sung Mo and Jao Le regions, as well as the submissive and rebellious barbarians as far out as the western regions where there are tens of peoples. In every detail they can be trusted. I taught them methods of deployment, and in all cases they nodded their heads and accepted my instructions. I hope you will entrust them with the responsibility without having any doubt. [Men] like Wan-ch'e are courageous but lack planning and would find it difficult to bear the responsibility alone."

The T'ai-tsung smiled and said: "These barbarians have all been well employed by you. The ancients said: 'Using the Man and Ti to attack the Man and Ti is China's strategic power.'[76] My lord has attained it."

BOOK II

The T'ai-tsung said: "I have looked through all the military books, but none surpasses Sun-tzu. In Sun-tzu's thirteen chapters there is nothing that surpasses the 'vacuous' and 'substantial.'[77] Now when employing the army, if one recognizes the strategic power [*shih*] of the vacuous and substantial, then he will always be victorious. Our contemporary generals are only able to talk about avoiding the substantial and attacking the vacuous. When they approach the enemy, few recognize the vacuous and substantial, probably because they are unable to compel the enemy [to come] to them, but on the contrary are compelled by the enemy. How can this be? My lord, please discuss the essentials of all these in detail with our generals."

Li Ching said: "Instructing them first about the techniques for changing the unorthodox [*ch'i*] and orthodox [*cheng*] into each other and afterward telling them about the form [*hsing*] of the vacuous and substantial would be possible. Many of the generals do not know how to take the unorthodox to be the orthodox, and the orthodox to be the unorthodox, so how can they recognize when the vacuous is substantial, and the substantial vacuous?"

ґ ґ ґ

The T'ai-tsung said: "[According to Sun-tzu:] 'Make plans against them to know the likelihood for gain and loss.[78] Stimulate them to know their patterns of movement and stopping. Determine their disposition [*hsing*] to know what terrain is tenable, what deadly. Probe them to know where they have an excess, where an insufficiency.'[79] Accordingly, do the unorthodox and orthodox lie with me, while the vacuous and substantial lie with the enemy?"

Li Ching said: "The unorthodox and orthodox are the means by which to bring about the vacuous and substantial in the enemy. If the enemy is substantial, then I must use the orthodox. If the enemy is vacuous, then I must use the unorthodox. If a general does not know the unorthodox and orthodox, then even though he knows whether the enemy is vacuous or substantial, how can he bring it about?[80] I respectfully accept your mandate but will [first] instruct all the generals in the unorthodox and orthodox, and afterward they will realize the vacuous and substantial by themselves."

The T'ai-tsung said: "If we take the unorthodox as the orthodox and the enemy realizes it is the unorthodox, then I will use the orthodox to attack him. If we take the orthodox as the unorthodox and the enemy thinks it is the orthodox, then I will use the unorthodox to attack him. I will cause the enemy's strategic power [shih] to constantly be vacuous, and my strategic power to always be substantial. If you teach the generals these methods, it should be easy to make them understand."

Li Ching said: "One thousand essays, ten thousand sections do not go beyond 'compel others, do not be compelled by them.'[81] I ought to use this to teach all the generals."

The T'ai-tsung said: "I have established the Yao-ch'ih Supervisor in Chief subordinate to the An-hsi Protector-general. How shall we manage and deploy the Han [Chinese] and barbarian peoples in this area?"

Li Ching said: "When Heaven gave birth to men, originally there was no distinction of 'barbarian' and 'Han.' But their territory is distant, wild, and desert-like, and they must rely on archery and hunting to live. Thus they are constantly practicing fighting and warfare. If we are generous to them, show good faith, pacify them, and fully supply them with clothes and food, then they will all be men of the Han. As your Majesty has established this Protector-general, I request you gather in all the Han border troops and settle them in the interior. This will greatly reduce the provisions necessary to feed them, which is what military strategists refer to as the 'method for governing strength.' But you should select Han officials who are thoroughly familiar with barbarian affairs, and you should disperse defensive fortifications [throughout the region]. This will be sufficient to manage the region for a long time. If we should encounter some emergency, Han troops can then go out there."

✓ ✓ ✓

The T'ai-tsung said: "What did Sun-tzu say about governing strength?"

Li Ching said: " 'With the near await the distant; with the rested await the fatigued; with the sated await the hungry.'[82] This covers the main points. One who excels at employing the army extends these three into six: 'With enticements await their coming. In quiescence await the impetuous. With the heavy await the light. With the strictly [disciplined] await the inattentive.

With order await the turbulent. With defense await attacks.'[83] When conditions are contrary to these, your strength will be insufficient. Without techniques to govern [the expenditure of force], how can one direct the army?"

The T'ai-tsung said: "People who study Sun-tzu today only recite the empty words. Few grasp and extend his meaning. Methods for governing the expenditure of strength should be thoroughly expounded to all the generals."

*   *   *

The T'ai-tsung said: "Our old generals and aging troops are exhausted and nearly all dead. Our armies are newly deployed, so they have no experience in assuming formations against the enemy. If we want to instruct them, what should be most essential?"

Li Ching said: "I would instruct the soldiers by dividing their activities into three steps. [The men] must first be organized into squads according to the Method of Five. After this organization into squads of five is complete, provide them with [military organization] into armies and brigades.[84] This is one step.

"The method for military organization into armies and brigades is to build from one to ten, from ten to one hundred.[85] This is one step.

"Entrust them to the command of subordinate generals. The subordinate generals will unite all the platoons of a brigade. Assemble and instruct them with the diagrams for the dispositions. This is one step.

"The commanding general examines the instructions in each of these three steps and thereupon conducts maneuvers to test and evaluate their deployment into formation and their overall organization. He divides them into unorthodox [ch'i] and orthodox [cheng], binds the masses with an oath, and implements punishments. Your Majesty should observe them from on high, and all measures should be possible."

*   *   *

The T'ai-tsung said: "There are several schools of thought on the Method of Five. Whose is the most important?"

Li Ching said: "According to *Master Tso's Commentary on the Spring and Autumn Annals:* 'First the battalion [of chariots], afterward the squads of five [in the gaps].'[86] Moreover, the *Ssu-ma Fa* states: 'Five men make up the squad of five.'[87] The *Wei Liao-t'zu* has [a section entitled] 'Orders for Binding the Squads of Five.'[88] Han military organization had the one-foot [wooden strip] for records and insignia [for the squads].[89] In later ages the records and insignia were done on paper, whereupon they lost the organization.

"I have studied and contemplated their methods. From the squad of five men they changed to twenty-five. From twenty-five men they change to seventy-five, composed of seventy-two infantrymen and three armored officers. When they set aside chariots and employed cavalry, then twenty-five [infantry] men were equivalent to eight cavalrymen.[90] This then was the organization of 'five soldiers matching five.'[91] Thus among the military methods of the various strategists, only the Method of Five is important. In the minimal arrangement there are five men, in the largest twenty-five. If the latter are tripled, they become seventy-five. Multiplied by another level of five, one obtains three hundred and seventy-five. Three hundred men are orthodox forces, sixty are unorthodox [with the remaining fifteen being the armored *shih*]. In this case they can be further divided into two, forming two orthodox [companies] of one hundred and fifty men each, and two [unorthodox] platoons of thirty men, one for each flank. This is what the *Ssu-ma Fa* means by 'five men composing the unit of five, with ten squads of five being a platoon,' which is relied upon until today. This is its essence."

ᵣ ᵣ ᵣ

The T'ai-tsung said: "I have discussed military strategy with Li Chi. For the most part he agrees with what you say, but Li Chi does not thoroughly understand its origin. From what techniques did the methods by which you established the 'Six Flowers Formation' originate?"

Li Ching said: "I based them on Chu-ko Liang's Eight Formations. Large formations contain small formations; large encampments contain small encampments.[92] All the corners are interlocked, the curves and broken points correlated. The ancient system was like this, so I made the diagram in accord with it. Thus the outside is drawn to be square, but the inside environment is circular. They then become the 'Six Flowers,' as commonly termed."

The T'ai-tsung said: "What do you mean by 'the outside is square and the inside circular?'"

Li Ching said: "The square is given birth from the pace,[93] the circle is given birth from the odd. The square provides the means to keep the paces straight, the circle the means to continue their turning. For this reason the number of paces is settled by the Earth, while the demarcation of the circular responds to Heaven. When the paces are settled and the circle complete, then the army's changes will not be disordered. The Eight Formations can become the Six Flowers. This is Chu-ko Liang's old method."

The T'ai-tsung said: "By drawing the square one can evaluate the paces; by setting the circle one can evaluate the weapons. From the paces one can instruct them in 'foot' techniques; with the weapons one can instruct them in hand techniques. This is advantageous to training the hands and feet and certainly seems correct."

Li Ching said: "Wu Ch'i states: 'Although on desperate ground, they cannot be separated; even if in retreat they will not scatter.'[94] This is the method of paces. Instructing the soldiers is like placing chessmen on a board. If there were no lines to demark the paths, how could one use the chess pieces? Suntzu said: 'Terrain gives birth to measurement; measurement produces the estimation [of forces]. Estimation [of forces] gives rise to calculating [the numbers of men]. Calculating [the numbers of men] gives rise to weighing [strength]. Weighing [strength] gives birth to victory. Thus the victorious army is like a ton compared with an ounce, while the defeated army is like an ounce weighed against a ton![95] It all commences with measuring out the square and circle."

The T'ai-tsung said: "Sun-tzu's words are profound indeed! If one does not determine the terrain as near or distant, the shape of the land as wide or narrow, how can he regulate the constraints?"[96]

Li Ching said: "The ordinary general is rarely able to know what constraints are. 'The strategic configuration of power [shih] of those that excel in warfare is sharply focused, their constraints are precise. Their strategic power is like a fully drawn crossbow, their constraints like the release of the trigger.'[97] I have practiced these methods. Thus the standing infantry platoons are ten paces apart from each other, the holding platoons [of chariots] twenty paces from the main army [of infantry]. Between each platoon one combat platoon is emplaced. When advancing forward, fifty paces is one measure.[98] At the first blowing of the horn all the platoons disperse and assume their positions, not exceeding ten paces apart. At the fourth blowing they position their spears and squat down. Thereupon the drum is beaten, three strikes to three shouts,[99] and they advance thirty to fifty paces [each time] in order to control the changes of the enemy. The cavalry comes forth from the rear, also advancing fifty paces at a time. The front is orthodox, the rear unorthodox.[100] Observe the enemy's response, then beat the drum again, with the front [changing to be] unorthodox and the rear orthodox.

Again entice the enemy to come forth, discover his fissures, and attack his vacuities. The Six Flowers Formation is generally like this."

The T'ai-tsung said: "Duke Ts'ao's *Hsin shu* states: 'When you deploy your formation opposite the enemy, you must first establish the pennants, drawing the troops into formation according to the pennants. When one brigade comes under attack, any other brigade that does not advance to rescue them will be beheaded.'[101] What tactic is this?"

Li Ching said: "Approaching the enemy and then establishing the pennants is incorrect. This is a method applicable only when you are training men in the tactics of warfare. The ancients who excelled at warfare taught the orthodox, they did not teach the unorthodox. They drove the masses just as if driving a herd of sheep. The masses advanced with them, withdrew with them, but they did not know where they were going.[102] Duke Ts'ao was arrogant and loved being victorious. Contemporary generals have all followed the *Hsin shu* without anyone daring to attack its shortcomings. Moreover, if you set up pennants when about to engage the enemy, is it not too late?

"I secretly observed the music and dance you created called 'Destroying the Formations.' At the front they put out four pennants, to the rear deployed eight flags. Left and right circled about, marching and racing to the gongs and drums, each in accord with its constraints.[103] This then is the Eight Formations Diagram, the system of four heads and eight tails. The people only see the flourishing of the music and dance; how can they know that military actions are like this?"

The T'ai-tsung said: "In antiquity, when Emperor Kao of the Han settled the realm, he wrote a song that went 'Where can I get fierce warriors to guard the four quarters?' Probably, military strategy can be transmitted as ideas but cannot be handed down as words. I created the Destruction of the Formations, but only you understand its form and substance. Will later generations realize I did not carelessly concoct it?"

The T'ai-tsung asked: "Are the five flags in their different colors for the five directions for orthodox [forces]?[104] Are the pennants and banners for penetrating the enemy for unorthodox [forces]? Dispersing and reforming are changes; how does one realize the appropriate number of platoons?"

Li Ching said: "I have examined and employ the methods of old. In general, when three platoons combine, their flags lean toward each other but are not crossed.[105] When five platoons are combined, then the flags of two of them are crossed. When ten platoons are combined, then the flags of five of them are crossed. When the horn is blown, then the five crossed flags are separated, and the combined unit will again disperse to form ten [platoons]. When two crossed flags are separated, the single unit will again disperse to form five [platoons]. When the two flags leaning toward each other, but uncrossed, are separated, the single unit will again disperse to form three [platoons].

"When the soldiers are dispersed, uniting them is unorthodox; when they are united, dispersing them is unorthodox. Give the orders three times, explain them five times. Have them disperse three times, have them reform three times. Then have them reform the orthodox configuration, after which the 'four heads and eight tails' can be taught to them. This is what is appropriate to the [training] method for the platoons."

The T'ai-tsung lauded his discussion.

The T'ai-tsung said: "Duke Ts'ao had fighting cavalry, attack cavalry, and roving cavalry. What elements of our contemporary cavalry and army are comparable to these?"

Li Ching said: "According to the *Hsin shu*: 'Fighting cavalry occupy the front, attack cavalry occupy the middle, and roving cavalry occupy the rear.' If so, then each of them was established with a name and designation, so they were divided into three types. Generally speaking, eight cavalrymen were equivalent to twenty-four infantrymen accompanying chariots. Twenty-four cavalrymen were equivalent to seventy-two infantrymen accompanying chariots. This was the ancient system.

"The infantrymen accompanying the chariots were normally taught orthodox methods; cavalrymen were taught unorthodox ones. According to Duke Ts'ao, the cavalry in the front, rear, and middle are divided into three covering[106] forces, but he did not speak about the two wings, so he was only discussing one aspect of the tactics. Later generations have not understood the intent of the three covering forces, so [they assume] fighting cavalry must be placed in front of the attack cavalry; how then is the roving cavalry employed? I am quite familiar with these tactics. If you turn the formation about, then the roving cavalry occupy the fore, the fighting cavalry the rear, and the attack cavalry respond to the changes of the moment to split off. These are all Duke Ts'ao's methods."

The T'ai-tsung laughed and said: "How many people have been deluded by Ts'ao Ts'ao?"[107]

The T'ai-tsung said: "Chariots, infantrymen, and cavalry—these three have one method. Does their employment lie with man?"

Li Ching said: "According to the Yü-li formation recorded in the *Spring and Autumn Annals:* 'First the battalions [of chariots], afterward the squads of five [in the gaps].' Then in this case they had chariots and infantrymen but no cavalry. When it refers to the left and right [flanks] resisting, it is speaking about resisting and defending, that is all! They did not employ any unorthodox strategy to attain victory.

"When Hsün Wu of Chin attacked the Ti [barbarian tribes], he abandoned the chariot and had [their personnel] form rows [as infantrymen].[108] In this case numerous cavalry would have been advantageous. He only concentrated on employing unorthodox forces to gain the victory, and was simply not concerned with resisting and defending.

"I have weighed their methods: In general,[109] one cavalryman is equivalent to three infantrymen; chariots and infantrymen are similarly matched. When intermixed they are [governed] by a single method; their employment lies with men. How can the enemy know where my chariots will really go forth? Where my cavalry will really come from? Where the infantrymen will follow up [the attack]? 'Hidden in the greatest depths of Earth, moving from the greatest heights of Heaven,[110] his knowledge is spirit-like!' This saying only refers to you, your Majesty. How can I be capable of such knowledge?"

The T'ai-tsung said: "T'ai Kung's book states: 'On an area of terrain six hundred paces square or sixty paces square, set out the pennants for the twelve constellations of the zodiac.'[111] What sort of tactic is this?"

Li Ching said: "Demark a perimeter of one thousand two hundred paces, total, in a square. Each section [within it] will occupy a square of [one] hundred[112] paces on edge. Every five paces horizontally, station a man, every four paces vertically, station a man. Now two thousand five hundred men will be distributed over five occupied areas with four empty ones [remaining]. This is what is meant by a 'formation containing a formation.' When King Wu attacked King Chou, each Tiger Guard commanded three thousand men.[113] Each formation had six thousand men, altogether a mass of thirty thousand. This was the T'ai Kung's method for delineating the terrain [see Figure 2]."

The T'ai-tsung said: "How do you delineate the terrain for your Six Flower Formation?"

Li Ching said: "Large-scale maneuvers are as follows. On an area twelve hundred paces square there are six formations deployed, each occupying an area with four hundred paces [on edge]. Overall it is divided into two boxes, east and west, with an open area in the middle, one thousand two hundred paces long, for training in warfare [see Figure 3]. I once taught thirty thousand men, with each formation consisting of five thousand. One encamped; five [practiced] the square, round, curved, straight, and angular dispositions. Each formation went through all five changes, for a total of twenty-five, before we stopped."[114]

The T'ai-tsung said: "What are the Five Phase formations?"

Li Ching said: "They originally established this name from the colors of the five quarters, but in reality they are all derived from the shape of the terrain—the square, round, curved, straight, and angular. In general, if the army does not constantly practice these five during peacetime, how can they approach the enemy? 'Deception is the Way [Tao] of warfare,'[115] so they resorted to naming them the Five Phases. They described them according to the ideas of the School of Techniques and Numbers about the patterns of mutual production and conquest.[116] But in actuality the army's form is like water which controls its flow in accord with the terrain.[117] This is the main point."

The T'ai-tsung said: "Li Chi spoke about male and female, square and circular tactics for ambush. Did they exist in antiquity or not?"

Li Ching said: "The male and female methods come out of the popular tradition. In actuality they refer to yin and yang, that is all. According to Fan Li's book:[118] 'If you are last then use yin tactics, if you are first then use yang tactics.[119] When you have exhausted the enemy's yang measures, then expand your yin to the full and seize them.' This then is the subtle mysteriousness of yin and yang according to the strategists.

"Fan Li also said: 'Establish the right as the female, increase the left to be male. At dawn and dusk accord with the Tao of Heaven.' Thus left and right, dawn and dusk are different according to the time. They lie in the changes of the unorthodox and orthodox. Left and right are the yin and yang in man, dawn and dusk are the yin and yang of Heaven. The unorthodox and orthodox are the mutual changes of yin and yang in Heaven and man. If one

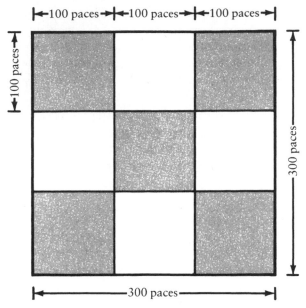

Figure 2 T'ai Kung's training array. Each sub-array (shaded areas within main array) consists of 20 men per row, 5 paces apart, and 25 men per file, 4 paces apart.

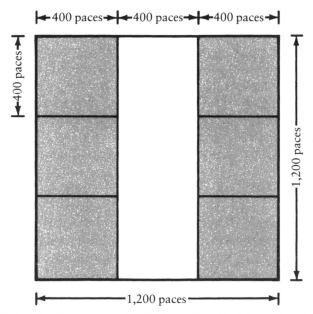

Figure 3 Li Ching's Six Flowers formation. Six formations (shaded areas) are deployed, each numbering 5,000 men. Center area is employed for drilling.

wished to grasp them and not change, then yin and yang would both deteriorate. How can one preserve only the shape of the male and female? Thus when you display an appearance to an enemy, show the unorthodox, not our orthodox. When you conquer, employ the orthodox to attack the enemy, not our unorthodox. This is what is meant by the 'orthodox and unorthodox changing into each other.'

"An 'army in ambush' does not only mean forces lying in ambush in the mountains, valleys, grass, and trees, for hiding them away is the means to [effect an] ambush. Our orthodox should be like the mountain, our unorthodox like thunder. Even though the enemy is directly opposite our front, no one can fathom where our unorthodox and orthodox forces are. At this point what shape do I have?"

⸎ ⸎ ⸎

The T'ai-tsung said: "The four animal formations also have the notes *shang, yü, wei,* and *chiao* to symbolize them. What is the reason for this?"

Li Ching said: "It is the Way [Tao] of deceit."

The T'ai-tsung said: "Can they be dispensed with?"

Li Ching said: "By preserving them one is able to dispense with them. If you dispense with them and do not employ them, deceitfulness will [grow] ever greater."

The T'ai-tsung said: "What do you mean?"

Li Ching said: "They obscured the names of the four formations [by appending] those of the four animals together with the designations of Heaven, Earth, wind, and clouds, and moreover added the notes and associated phases of *shang* and metal, *yü* and water, *wei* and fire, *chiao* and wood.[120] This was the cleverness of the ancient military strategists. If you preserve them, deceitfulness will not increase further. If you abandon them, how can the greedy and stupid be employed?"

The T'ai-tsung said: "My lord should preserve this in secrecy, not let it be leaked outside."

⸎ ⸎ ⸎

The T'ai-tsung said: "Severe punishments and imposing laws make men fear me and not fear the enemy.[121] I am very confused about this. In antiquity the Han Emperor Kuang Wu opposed Wang Mang's mass of a million with his solitary force, but he did not use punishments and laws to approach [the people]. So how did [his victory] come about?"

Li Ching said: "An army's victory or defeat is a question of the situation and a myriad factors, and cannot be decided by one element alone. In the case of Ch'en Sheng and Kuang Wu defeating the Ch'in army, could they have had more severe punishments and laws than the Ch'in? Emperor Kuang Wu's rise was probably due to his according with the people's hatred for Wang Mang. Moreover, Wang Hsün and Wang I did not understand military strategy and merely boasted of their army's masses. Thus in this way they defeated themselves.[122]

"According to Sun-tzu: 'If you impose punishments on the troops before they have become [emotionally] attached, they will not be submissive. If you do not impose punishments after the troops have become [emotionally] attached, they cannot be used.'[123] This means that normally, a general should first bind the soldiers' affection to him, and only thereafter employ severe punishments. If their affection has not yet been developed, few would be able to conquer and be successful solely by employing severe laws."

´   ´   ´

The T'ai-tsung said: "In the *Shang shu* it says: 'When awesomeness exceeds love, affairs will be successful. When love exceeds awesomeness, there will be no achievement.'[124] What does this mean?"

Li Ching said: "Love should be established first, and awesomeness afterward—it cannot be opposite this. If awesomeness is applied first and love supplements it afterward, it will be of no advantage to the prosecution of affairs. The *Shang shu* was extremely careful about the end, but this is not the way plans should be made in the beginning. Thus Sun-tzu's method cannot be eliminated for ten thousand generations."

´   ´   ´

The T'ai-tsung said: "When you pacified Hsiao Hsien, our generals wanted to appropriate the households of the traitorous officials in order to reward their own officers and troops. Only you did not concur because K'uai T'ung had not been executed by Han Kao-tsu. The regions of the Chiang and Han rivers all submitted to you.[125] From this I recall the ancients had a saying: 'The civil is able to attract and attach the masses, the martial is able to overawe the enemy.' Does this not refer to you, my lord?"

Li Ching said: "When Emperor Kuang Wu of the Han pacified the Red Eyebrows,[126] he entered the rebel encampment for a tour of inspection. The rebels said: 'King Hsiao [Emperor Kuang Wu] extends his own pure heart in sympathy unto others.' This was probably due to [the king] having previously evaluated their motives and emotions as basically not being evil. Did he not have foresight?

"When I rectified the T'u-chüeh, commanding the combined troops of both Han and barbarians, even though we went outside the pass a thousand *li,* I never killed a single Yang Kan nor beheaded a Chung Chia.[127] This, too, was [a case of] extending my innate compassionate sincerity and preserving the common good, that is all! What your Majesty has heard is excessive, putting me into an unrivaled position. If it is a question of combining both the civil and martial, how would I presume to have [such ability]?"

*   *   *

The T'ai-tsung said: "Formerly, when T'ang Chien was an emissary to the T'u-chüeh, you availed yourself [of the situation] to attack and defeat them. People say you used T'ang Chien as an 'expendable spy.'[128] Up until now I have had doubts about this. What about it?"

Li Ching bowed twice and said: "T'ang Chien and I equally served your Majesty. I anticipated that T'ang Chien's proposals would certainly not be able [to persuade them] to quietly submit. Therefore, I took the opportunity to follow up with our army and attack them. In order to eliminate a great danger I did not concern myself with a minor righteousness. Although people refer to T'ang Chien as an expendable spy, it was not my intention.

"According to Sun-tzu, employing spies is an inferior measure. I once prepared a discussion [of this subject] and at the end stated: 'Water can float a boat, but it can also overturn the boat. Some use spies to be successful; others, relying on spies, are overturned and defeated.'

"If one braids his hair and serves the ruler, maintains a proper countenance in court, is loyal and pure, trustworthy and completely sincere—even if someone excels at spying, how can he be employed [to sow discord]? T'ang Chien is a minor matter. What doubts does your Majesty have?"

The T'ai-tsung said: "Truly, 'without benevolence and righteousness one cannot employ spies.'[129] How can the ordinary man do it? If the Duke of Chou, with his great righteousness, exterminated his relatives,[130] how much the more so one emissary? Clearly, there is nothing to doubt."

*   *   *

The T'ai-tsung said: "The army values being the 'host'; it does not value being a 'guest.'[131] It values speed, not duration.[132] Why?"

Li Ching said: "The army is employed only when there is no alternative,[133] so what advantage is there in being a 'guest' or fighting long? Sun-tzu says: 'When provisions are transported far off, the common people are impoverished.'[134] This is the exhaustion of a 'guest.' He also said: 'The people should not be conscripted twice, provisions should not be transported thrice.'[135] This [comes from] the experience of not being able to long endure. When I compare and weigh the strategic power [*shih*] of host and guest, then there are tactics for changing the guest to host, changing the host to guest."

The T'ai-tsung said: "What do you mean?"

Li Ching said: "By foraging and capturing provisions from the enemy,[136] you change a guest into a host. 'If you can cause the sated to be famished and the rested to be tired,'[137] it will change a host into a guest. Thus the army is not confined to being host or guest, slow or fast, but only focuses on its movements invariably attaining the constraints[138] and thereby being appropriate."

The T'ai-tsung said: "Were there such cases among the ancients?"

Li Ching said: "In antiquity, Yüeh attacked Wu with two armies—one to the left, the other to the right. When they blew the horns and beat the drums to advance, Wu divided its troops to oppose them. Then Yüeh had its central army secretly ford the river. Without sounding their drums, they suddenly attacked and defeated Wu's army. This is a case of changing a guest into a host.

"When Shih Le did battle with Chi Chan,[139] Chan's army came from a distance. Shih Le dispatched K'ung Ch'ang to act as an advance front and counterattack Chan's forces. K'ung Ch'ang withdrew, and Chan advanced to pursue him. Shih Le then employed his concealed forces to ambush him from both sides. Chan's army was badly defeated. This is an instance of changing the tired to the rested. The ancients had many cases like this."

The T'ai-tsung said: "Were the iron caltrops and *chevaux-de-frise* created by the T'ai Kung?"

Li Ching said: "They were. But they were for resisting the enemy, that is all! The army values compelling men and does not want to resist them. In the *Six Secret Teachings* the T'ai Kung discusses equipment for defending and repelling, not what would be used in offensives."

BOOK III

The T'ai-tsung said: "The T'ai Kung has stated: 'When infantrymen engage chariots and cavalry in battle, they must take advantage of hillocks, funeral mounds, ravines, and defiles.'[140] Moreover, Sun-tzu said: 'Terrain that looks like fissures in the Heavens, hillocks, funeral mounds, and old fortifications should not be occupied by the army.'[141] What about this [contradiction]?"

Li Ching said: "The successful employment of the masses lies in their being of one mind. Unification of mind lies in prohibiting omens and dispelling doubts. Should the commanding general have anything about which he is doubtful or fearful, their emotions will waver. When their emotions waver, the enemy will take advantage of the chink to attack. Thus when securing an encampment or occupying terrain, it should be convenient to human affairs, that is all! Terrain such as precipitous gorges, deep canyons, ravines, and passes with high sides, natural prisons, and heavily overgrown areas are not suitable for human activity. Thus military strategists avoid leading troops into them to prevent the enemy from gaining an advantage over us. Hillocks, funeral mounds, and old fortifications are not isolated terrain or places of danger. If we gain them it will be advantageous, so how would it be appropriate to turn around and abandon them? What the T'ai Kung discussed is the very essence of military affairs."

The T'ai-tsung said: "I think that among implements of violence, none is more terrible than the army.[142] If mobilizing the army is advantageous to human affairs, how can one—for the sake of avoiding evil omens—be doubtful? If in the future any of the generals fails to take appropriate action because of yin and yang or other baleful indications, my lord should repeatedly upbraid and instruct them."

Li Ching bowed twice in acknowledgment, saying: "I recall the *Wei Liao-tzu* states: 'The Yellow Emperor preserved them with Virtue but attacked [the evil] with punishments. This refers to [actual] punishment and Virtue, not the selection and use of astrologically auspicious seasons and days.'[143]

Accordingly, through the 'Tao of deceit' [the masses] should be made to follow them but should not be allowed to know this.[144] In later ages ordinary generals have been mired in mystical techniques and for this reason have frequently suffered defeat. You cannot but admonish them. Your Majesty's sagely instructions should be disseminated to all the generals."

⸙   ⸙   ⸙

The T'ai-tsung said: "When the army divides and reassembles, in each case it is important that the actions be appropriate. Among the records of earlier ages, who excelled at this?"

Li Ching said: "Fu Chien commanded a mass of a million and was defeated at Fei River.[145] This is what results when an army is able to unite but cannot divide. When Wu Han conducted a campaign of rectification against Kung-sun Shu, he split his forces with Lieutenant General Liu Shang, encamping about twenty *li* apart.[146] Kung-sun Shu came forward and attacked Wu Han, whereupon Liu Shang advanced to unite with Wu Han in a counterattack, severely defeating Kung-sun Shu. This is the result that can be attained when an army divides and can reassemble. The T'ai Kung said: '[A force] which wants to divide but cannot is an entangled army; one which wants to reassemble but cannot is a solitary regiment.'[147]

The T'ai-tsung said: "Yes. When Fu Chien first obtained Wang Meng,[148] he truly knew how to employ the army and subsequently took the central plain. When Wang Meng died, Fu Chien was decisively defeated, so is this what is meant by an 'entangled army'? When Wu Han was appointed by Emperor Kuang Wu, the army was not controlled from a distance, and the Han were able to pacify the Shu area. Does this not indicate that the army did not fall into the difficulty of what is referred to as being a 'solitary regiment?' The historical records of gains and losses are sufficient to be a mirror for ten thousand generations."

⸙   ⸙   ⸙

The T'ai-tsung said: "I observe that the thousand chapters and ten thousand sentences [of the military teachings] do not go beyond 'Use many methods to cause them to make errors,'[149] this single statement."

After a long while Li Ching said: "Truly, it is as you have wisely said. In ordinary situations involving the use of the military, if the enemy does not make an error in judgment, how can our army conquer them? It may be compared with chess where the two enemies [begin] equal in strength. As soon as someone makes a mistake, truly no one can rescue him. For this reason, in both ancient and modern times, victory and defeat have proceeded from a single error, so how much more would this be the case with many mistakes?"

⸎   ⸎   ⸎

The T'ai-tsung said: "Are the two affairs of attacking and defending in reality one method? Sun-tzu said: 'When one excels at attacking, the enemy does not know where to mount his defense. When one excels at defense, the enemy does not know where to attack.'[150] He did not speak about the enemy coming forth to attack me and me also attacking the enemy. If we assume a defensive posture and the enemy also takes up a defensive position, if in attacking and defense our strengths are equal, what tactic should be employed?"

Li Ching said: "Cases such as this of mutual attack and mutual defense were, in previous ages, numerous. They all said: 'One defends when strength is insufficient, one attacks when strength is more than sufficient.'[151] Thus they referred to insufficiency as being weakness and having an excess as strength. Apparently, they did not understand the methods for attack and defense. I recall Sun-tzu said: 'One who cannot be victorious assumes a defensive posture; one who can be victorious attacks.'[152] This indicates that when the enemy cannot yet be conquered, I must temporarily defend myself. When we have waited until the point when the enemy can be conquered, then we attack him. It is not a statement about strength and weakness. Later generations did not understand his meaning, so when they should attack they defend, and when they should defend they attack. The two stages are distinct, so the method cannot be a single one."

⸎   ⸎   ⸎

The T'ai-tsung said: "I can see that the concepts of surplus and insufficiency caused later generations to be confused about strength and weakness. They probably did not know that the essence of defensive strategy is to show the enemy an inadequacy. The essence of aggressive strategy lies in showing the enemy that you have a surplus. If you show the enemy an insufficiency, then they will certainly advance and attack. In this case 'the enemy does not know where to attack.'[153] If you show the enemy a surplus, then they will certainly take up defensive positions. In this case 'the enemy does not know where to mount his defense.'[154] Attacking and defending are one method, but the enemy and I divide it into two matters. If I succeed in this matter, the enemy's affairs will be defeated. If the enemy is successful, then my aims will be defeated. Gaining and losing, success or failure—our aims and the enemy's are at odds, but attacking and defending are one! If you understand that they are one, then in a hundred battles you will be victorious a hundred times. Thus it is said: 'If you know yourself and you know the enemy, in a hundred battles you will not be endangered.'[155] This refers to the knowledge of this unity, does it not?"

Li Ching bowed twice and said: "Perfect indeed are the Sage's methods! Attacking is the pivotal point of defense, defending is the strategy for attack. They are both directed toward victory, that is all! If in attacking you do not understand defending, and in defending you do not understand attacking, but instead not only make them into two separate affairs, but also assign responsibility for them to separate offices, then even though the mouth recites the words of Sun-tzu and Wu-tzu, the mind has not thought about the mysterious subtleties of the discussion of the equality of attack and defense. How can the reality then be known?"

*   *   *

The T'ai-tsung said: "The *Ssu-ma Fa* states that 'even though a state may be vast, those who love warfare will inevitably perish' and that 'even though calm may prevail under Heaven, those who forget warfare will inevitably be endangered.'[156] Is this also one of the ways of attacking and defending?"

Li Ching said: "If one has a state and family, how could he not discuss attacking and defending? For attacking does not stop with just attacking their cities or attacking their formations. One must have techniques for attacking their minds. Defense does not end with just the completion of the walls and the realization of solid formations. One must also preserve spirit and be prepared to await the enemy. To speak of it in the largest terms, it means the Tao of rulership. To speak of it in smaller terms, it means the methods of the general. Now attacking their minds is what is referred to as 'knowing them.' Preserving one's *ch'i* [spirit] is what is meant by 'knowing yourself.'"

The T'ai-tsung said: "True! When I was about to engage in battle, I first evaluated the enemy's mind by comparing it with my mind to determine who was more thoroughly prepared. Only after that could I know his situation. To evaluate the enemy's *ch'i* I compared it with our own to determine who was more controlled. Only then could I know myself. For this reason, 'know them and know yourself' is the great essence of the military strategists. Contemporary generals, even if they do not know the enemy, ought to be able to know themselves, so how could they lose the advantage?"

Li Ching said: "What Sun-tzu meant by 'first make yourself unconquerable'[157] is 'know yourself.' 'Waiting until the enemy can be conquered'[158] is 'knowing them.' Moreover, he said that 'being unconquerable lies with yourself, while being conquerable lies with the enemy.'[159] I have not dared to neglect this admonition even for a moment."

′   ′   ′

The T'ai-tsung said: "Sun-tzu spoke about strategies by which the *ch'i* of the Three Armies may be snatched away: 'In the morning their *ch'i* is ardent; during the day their *ch'i* becomes indolent; and at dusk their *ch'i* is exhausted. One who excels at employing the army avoids their ardent *ch'i* and strikes when it is indolent or exhausted.'[160] How is this?"

Li Ching said: "Whoever has life and a natural endowment of blood, if they die without a second thought when the drums are sounded to do battle, it is the *ch'i* which causes it to be so. Thus methods for employing the army require first investigating our own officers and troops, stimulating our *ch'i* for victory, and only then attacking the enemy. Among Wu Ch'i's four vital points, the vital point of *ch'i* is foremost.[161] There is no other Tao. If one can cause his men themselves to want to fight, then no one will be able to oppose their ardor. What [Sun-tzu] meant by the *ch'i* being ardent in the morning is not limited to those hours alone. He used the beginning and end of the day as an analogy. In general, if the drum has been sounded three times but the enemy's *ch'i* has neither declined nor become depleted, then how can you cause it to invariably become indolent or exhausted? Probably, those who study the text merely recite the empty words and are misled by the enemy. If one could enlighten them with the principles for snatching away the *ch'i*, the army could be entrusted to them."

′   ′   ′

The T'ai-tsung said: "You once said that General Li Chi[162] is capable in military strategy, but can he be employed indefinitely or not? If I am no longer around to control and direct him, [I fear] he cannot be used. In the future, how should the heir apparent direct him?"

Li Ching said: "If I were to plan on behalf of your Majesty, nothing would be better than [for you] to dismiss Li Chi and have the heir apparent reemploy him. Then he would certainly feel grateful and think how to repay him. In principle, is there any harm in this?"[163]

The T'ai-tsung said: "Excellent. I have no doubts about it."

′   ′   ′

The T'ai-tsung said: "If I order Li Shih-chi and Chang-sun Wu-chi[164] to take the reigns of government together, what do you think?"

Li Ching said: "[Li] Chi is loyal and righteous. I can guarantee that he will uphold his duties. [Chang-sun] Wu-chi followed your commands and made great contributions. Because he is a relative, your Majesty has entrusted him with the office of Deputy Minister. But while in external demeanor he is deferential to other officials, within he is actually jealous of the Worthy. Thus Yü-chih Ching-te[165] pointed out his shortcomings to his face and then retired. Hou Chün-chi hated him for forgetting old [friends], and as a result he revolted and turned against you.[166] These were both brought about by Wu-chi. Since you questioned me about this, I did not dare avoid discussing it."

The T'ai-tsung said: "Do not let it leak out. I will ponder how to settle it."

ʳ ʳ ʳ

The T'ai-tsung said: "Emperor Han Kao-tsu was able to command his generals, but later on Han Hsin and P'eng Yüeh were executed, and Hsiao Ho was imprisoned.[167] What is the reason for this?"

Li Ching said: "I observe that neither Liu Pang nor Hsiang Yü were rulers capable of commanding generals.[168] At the time of Ch'in's collapse, Chang Liang originally wanted to gain revenge for his [old state of] Han, while Ch'en P'ing and Han Hsin both resented Hsiang Yü's failure to employ them.[169] Therefore they availed themselves of Han's strategic power. Hsiao Ho, Ts'ao Ts'an, Fan K'uai, and Kuan Ying were all fleeing for their lives.[170] Han Kao-tsu gained All under Heaven through relying upon them. If he had caused the descendants of the Six States to be reestablished, all the people would have embraced their old states.[171] Then even if he had the ability to command generals, who could the Han have employed? I have said that the Han gained the realm through Chang Liang borrowing [Kao-tsu's] chopsticks and Hsiao Ho's achievements in managing water transportation. From this standpoint, Han Hsin and P'eng Yüeh being executed and Fan Tseng not being used [by Hsiang Yü] are the same.[172] I therefore refer to Liu Pang and Hsiang Yü as rulers incapable of commanding generals."

ʳ ʳ ʳ

The T'ai-tsung said: "The Later Han Emperor Kuang-wu, who restored the dynasty, was thereafter able to preserve complete his meritorious generals and did not entrust them with civil affairs. Is this being good at commanding generals?"

Li Ching said: "Although Emperor Kuang-wu availed himself of the glories of the Former Han and casily attained success, still Wang Mang's strate-

gic power was not inferior to Hsiang Yü's, while [his generals] K'ou Hsün
and Teng Yü[173] never surpassed Hsiao Ho and Ts'ao Ts'an. He alone was
able to extend his pure heart, employ a genial administration, and preserve
complete his virtuous subjects, so he was far more worthy than Han Kao-
tsu. Based on this, if we discuss being able to command generals, then I
would say that Emperor Kuang-wu attained it."

ʳ   ʳ   ʳ

The T'ai-tsung said: "In ancient times when they dispatched the army and
appointed the commanding general, [the ruler] would ritually prepare by observing a vegetarian regime for three days. He would then hand a *yüeh* ax to
the general, saying: 'From this to Heaven above will be controlled by the
General of the Army.' Moreover, he would give him a *fu* ax, saying: 'From
this to Earth below will be controlled by the General of the Army.'[174] Then
he would push the hub [on the general's chariot][175] and say: 'Advancing and
withdrawing should only be timely. When you are already on the march,
those in the army will only obey the general's orders, not the ruler's commands.' I note that these rites have long been neglected. Today I would like
to establish a ceremony with my lord for commissioning and sending off the
general. What about it?"

Li Ching said: "I dare to say that the Sages created this ceremony together
with the vegetarian fast at the ancestral temple in order to borrow awesomeness and spirituality from the spirits. Granting the *yüeh* and *fu* axes together
with pushing the hub were the means by which they entrusted them with authority. Today, whenever your Majesty is about to dispatch the army, you invariably hold deliberations and discussions with your high officials, announce it at the temple, and afterward dispatch them. This, then, is inviting
the spirits to come forth. Whenever you have appointed a general, you have
always ordered him to manage affairs as circumstances may dictate. This,
then, is loaning him great authority. How does it differ from observing a vegetarian fast and pushing the hub? It completely harmonizes with the ancient
ceremony, its meaning is identical. It is not necessary to consult together to
decide [a new one]."

The ruler said "Excellent" and then ordered the nearby officials to record
these two practices as a model for later ages.

ʳ   ʳ   ʳ

The T'ai-tsung said: "Can the [divinatory] practices of yin and yang[176] be
abandoned?"

Li Ching said: "They cannot. The military is the Tao of deceit, so if we [apparently] put faith in yin and yang divinatory practices, we can manipulate the greedy and stupid. They cannot be abandoned."

The T'ai-tsung said: "You once said that selecting astrologically auspicious seasons and days are not methods of enlightened generals. Ignorant generals adhere to them, so it seems appropriate to abandon them."

Li Ching said: "King Chou perished on a day designated as *chai-tzu*; King Wu flourished on the same day. According to the astrologically auspicious seasons and days, *chia-tzu* is the first day. The Shang were in chaos, the Chou were well governed. Flourishing and perishing are different in this case. Moreover, Emperor Wu of the Sung mobilized his troops on a 'going to perish day.'[177] The army's officers all felt it to be impermissible, but the emperor said: 'I will go forth and he will perish.' Indeed, he conquered them. Speaking with reference to these cases, it is clear that the practices can be abandoned. However, when T'ien Tan was surrounded by Yen, Tan ordered a man to impersonate a spirit. He bowed and prayed to him, and the spirit said Yen could be destroyed. Tan thereupon used fire oxen to go forth and attack Yen, greatly destroying them.[178] This is the deceitful Tao of military thinkers. The selection of astrologically auspicious seasons and days is similar to this."

The T'ai-tsung said: "T'ien Tan entrusted their fate to the supernatural and destroyed Yen, while the T'ai Kung burned the milfoil and tortoise shells yet went on to exterminate King Chou. How is it that these two affairs are contradictory?"

Li Ching said: "Their subtle motives were the same. One went contrary [to the practices] and seized [the enemy], one accorded with them and implemented [his plans].[179]

"In antiquity, when the T'ai Kung was assisting King Wu, they reached Mu-yeh where they encountered thunder and rain. The flags and drums were broken or destroyed. San I-sheng wanted to divine for an auspicious response before moving. This, then, is a case where because of doubts and fear within the army, he felt they must rely on divination to inquire of the spirits. [But] the T'ai Kung believed that rotted grass and dried-up bones were not worth asking. Moreover, in the case of a subject attacking his ruler, how could there be a second chance? Now I observe that San I-sheng expressed his motives at the beginning, but the T'ai Kung attained his subsequently. Even though one was contrary to and the other in accord with [divinatory practices], their reasons were identical. When I previously stated these techniques should not be abandoned, it was largely to preserve the vital point of *ch'i* before affairs have begun to manifest themselves.[180] As for their being successful, it was a matter of human effort, that is all!"

⸴　⸴　⸴

The T'ai-tsung said: "At present there are only three real generals—Li Chi, Li Tao-tsung, and Hsüeh Wan-ch'e. Apart from Li Tao-tsung, a relative, who can undertake great responsibility?"

Li Ching said: "Your Majesty once said that when employing the army, Li Chi and Li Tao-tsung will not achieve great victories, but neither will they suffer disastrous defeats, while if Wan-ch'e does not win a great victory, he will inevitably suffer a serious defeat. In my ignorance I have thought about your Sagely words. An army which does not seek great victory but also does not suffer serious defeat is constrained and disciplined. An army which may achieve great victory or suffer horrendous defeat relies upon good fortune to be successful. Thus Sun Wu said: 'One who excels at warfare establishes himself in a position where he cannot be defeated while not losing [any opportunity] to defeat the enemy.'[181] This says that constraint and discipline lie with us."

⸴　⸴　⸴

The T'ai-tsung said: "When two formations approach each other, should we not want to fight, how can we attain it?"

Li Ching said: "In antiquity the Chin army attacked Ch'in,[182] engaged in battle with them, and then withdrew. The *Ssu-ma Fa* states: 'Do not pursue a fleeing enemy too far nor follow a retreating army too closely.'[183] I refer to those retreating as being under the control of the reins. If our army already is constrained and disciplined while the enemy's army is also in well-ordered rows and squads, how can [either side] lightly engage in combat? Thus when they [both] go forth, clash, and then withdraw without being pursued, each side is defending against loss and defeat. Sun-tzu said: 'Do not attack well-regulated formations, do not intercept well-ordered flags.'[184] When two formations embody equal strategic power [*shih*], should one lightly move he may create an opportunity for the enemy to gain the advantage and thereby suffer a great defeat. [Strategic] principles cause it to be thus. For this reason armies encounter situations in which they will not fight and those in which they must fight. Not engaging in battle lies with us; having to fight lies with the enemy."

, , ,

The T'ai-tsung said: "What do you mean 'not engaging in battle lies with us?'"

Li Ching said: "Sun Wu has stated: 'If I do not want to engage in battle, I will draw a line on the ground and defend it. They will not be able to engage us in battle because we thwart their movements.'[185] If the enemy has [capable] men, the interval between the clash and retreat cannot yet be planned. Thus I said that not engaging in battle lies with us. As for having to fight lying with the enemy, Sun Wu has stated: 'One who excels at moving the enemy deploys in a configuration to which the enemy must respond. He offers something which the enemy must seize. With profit he moves them; with his main force he awaits them.'[186] If the enemy lacks talented officers, they will certainly come forth and fight. I then take advantage of the situation to destroy them. Thus I said that having to fight lies with the enemy."

The T'ai-tsung said: "Profound indeed! The constrained and disciplined army—when it realizes appropriate strategies—flourishes, but when it lacks them perishes. My lord, please compile and record the writings of those through the ages who excelled at constraint and discipline, provide diagrams, and submit them to me. I will select the quintessential ones to be transmitted to later ages."

[Li Ching said:[187] "I previously submitted two diagrams of the Yellow Emperor's and T'ai Kung's dispositions together with the *Ssu-ma Fa* and Chu-ko Liang's strategies for the unorthodox and orthodox. They are already highly detailed. Numerous famous historical generals employed one or two of them and achieved success. But official historians have rarely understood military matters, so they were unable to properly record the substance of their achievements. Would I dare not accept your Majesty's order? I will prepare a compilation and narration for you."]

, , ,

The T'ai-tsung said: "What is of greatest importance in military strategy?"

Li Ching said: "I once divided it into three levels to allow students to gradually advance into it. The first is termed the Tao, the second Heaven and Earth, and the third Methods of Generalship. As for the Tao, it is the most essential and subtle, what the *I Ching* refers to as 'all-perceiving and all-knowing, [allowing one to be] spiritual and martial without slaying.'[188] Now what is discussed under Heaven is yin and yang; what is discussed under Earth is the narrow and easy. One who excels at employing the army is able to use the yin to snatch the yang, the narrow to attack the easy. It is what Mencius referred to as the 'seasons of Heaven and advantages of Earth.'[189]

The Methods of Generalship discusses employing men and making the weapons advantageous—what the *Three Strategies* means by saying that one who gains the right officers will prosper, and the *Kuan-tzu* by saying that the weapons must be solid and sharp."

ʳ   ʳ   ʳ

The T'ai-tsung said: "Yes. I have said that an army which can cause men to submit without fighting is the best; one that wins a hundred victories in a hundred battles is mediocre; and one that uses deep moats and high fortifications for its own defense is the lowest. If we use this as a standard for comparison, all three are fully present in Sun-tzu's writings."

Li Ching said: "We can also distinguish them if we scrutinize their writings and retrace their undertakings. For example, Chang Liang, Fan Li, and Sun Wu abandoned the world to withdraw into lofty isolation. No one knows where they went. If they had not penetrated the Tao, how could they have done it? Yüeh I,[190] Kuan Chung, and Chu-ko Liang were always victorious in battle and solid in defense. If they had not investigated and understood the seasons of Heaven and the advantages of Earth, how could they have succeeded? Next would be Wang Meng's preservation of Ch'in and Hsieh An's defense of Chin.[191] If they had not employed [outstanding] generals and selected talented man, repaired and solidified their defenses, how could they have managed? Thus the study of military strategy must be from the lowest to middle and then from the middle to highest, so that they will gradually penetrate the depths of the teaching. If not, they will only be relying on empty words. Merely remembering and reciting them is not enough to succeed."

ʳ   ʳ   ʳ

The T'ai-tsung said: "Taoists shun three generations [of a family] serving as generals.[192] [Military teachings] should not be carelessly transmitted, yet should also not be not transmitted. Please pay careful attention to this matter."

Li Ching bowed twice and went out, and turned all his military books over to Li Chi.

Appendixes, Notes, Bibliography, Glossary, and Indexes

Appendix A: The Chariot

THE ROLE and importance of chariots as well as the date of their introduction have been the subject of several articles in recent decades. Unquestionably, the chariot was introduced from the West through central Asia around the fourteenth century B.C., and then the transmission route was probably severed because subsequent major Western developments were never reflected in China. (Hayashi Minao confidently asserts that the Shang had chariots by 1300 B.C. and that they were used in hunting.[1] Edward L. Shaughnessy holds that the chariot's introduction should be dated to 1200 B.C.[2]) Support for the theory of diffusion rather than indigenous origin is seen in the absence of any precursor, such as oxen-pulled wagons or four-wheeled carts, although horses were domesticated prior to this period.[3]

Although the construction of the Chinese chariot was substantially the same as its Western prototype, the earliest chariots unearthed thus far have several distinctive characteristics: Each wheel has many more spokes—sometimes as many as forty-eight; wheel shape is conical; and the chariot box is rectangular and larger than is the case in the West and can accommodate three men standing in triangular formation.[4] (Some of these developments are also seen in an intermediate stage in the Trans-Caucasus versions discovered in this century.[5]) No major alterations occur after its introduction, although there was a historical tendency toward stronger, heavier, swifter vehicles. Significant minor innovations and refinements naturally continued over the centuries, such as in the method of mounting the chariot box on the axle and in the yoking, with a continuing differentiation into types by use. (Even the Shang apparently had specialized chariots or carriages for ordinary transport, chariots designed for combat and the hunt—perhaps in limited numbers—and something similar to wagons for conveying goods.[6])

In the Shang the chariot was a highly visible symbol of rank and power and was elaborately decorated, often being covered with imperial gifts of insignia. However, perhaps because of their greater numbers, chariots in the

Chou were more pragmatic and functional, although they still conspicuously displayed marks of royal favor.[7] Finally, in the Spring and Autumn and Warring States periods, highly specialized chariots and other wheeled vehicles were created to suit the requirements of siege warfare and other specialized assault tasks; they were equipped with large shields, towers, battering rams, movable ladders, and multiple arrow crossbows.[8]

Tradition holds that Hsi Chung—either as a minister under the Yellow Emperor or in the Hsia dynasty—created the chariot. The Shang reputedly employed either seventy or three hundred chariots to overthrow the Hsia, but this is improbable. The actual degree to which the Shang employed chariots remains somewhat controversial; some scholars find no evidence that the Shang employed chariots as a battle element,[9] whereas others—especially traditionally oriented experts such as Ku Chieh-kang—maintain qualified opposing views.[10] However, certain facts are known. For example, even in the later years of the dynasty, Shang knights were apparently fighting on foot as infantrymen rather than from chariots. Some of their enemies, however, seem to have employed them in substantial numbers compared with their overall forces.[11]

The Chou are traditionally noted for increasing the horsepower of their assault chariots, using four rather than two horses.[12] (Shang tombs also have chariots with four horses, but these may have been for funerary display rather than for actual use.) One explanation for the Chou's startling victory—apart from their superior Virtue and the support of the people—is the swiftness of their movement and their unexpected crossing of the Yellow River to the south, thereby avoiding Shang defenses to the west. (According to the *Shih chi*, the Shang ruler significantly furthered the Chou's efforts by consciously ignoring their approach until they were suddenly upon him.) In the actual battle three hundred chariots were probably employed, which matches the reported three thousand members of the Tiger Guard, assuming the ten-to-one ratio that is frequently suggested.[13] The swiftness and ferocity of the assault surprised the Shang and might be attributed to the Chou's superior and perhaps first effective use of chariot power.

Significant clashes between the Chou and their steppe neighbors in which considerable numbers of chariots were employed apparently commenced in the first centuries of Chou rule; in one such encounter 130 enemy vehicles were reportedly captured.[14] Massed chariot battles were occurring by the ninth century B.C. and continued throughout the Western Chou era and into the Spring and Autumn period. However, the effectiveness of the chariot under actual combat conditions has been questioned in recent decades by Creel[15] and others. Although the chariot promised power, speed, and mobility—at least in contrast to foot movement—it may have been more symbolic and have served largely as a command platform rather than an overwhelming assault weapon. This is not to deny that chariot combat—often involving great numbers—took place. However, as Yang Hung has discussed, the chariot demanded a large area, and the warriors positioned on either side in the back (especially the one on the right who wielded the halberd) could only engage the enemy when the chariots passed each other perfectly—neither too far apart nor too head on.[16] In addition, their stability and maneuvering ability—which were restricted by a fixed axle that rendered turning extremely difficult, especially at speed—were minimal, even on the flattest plain. (Imagine racing across a corn field without shock absorbers and attempting to fire a bow or strike a moving, equally unpredictable opponent with a shock weapon at the last instant.)

The failure of Wu and Yüeh to adopt the chariot, despite explicit efforts to inculcate them in their use around 541 B.C., further indicates a realization of terrain-imposed limitations; both states were mountainous regions crisscrossed by rivers and streams and marked by lakes, ponds, and marshes.[17] In response to these insurmountable constraints, Wu and Yüeh stressed infantry and naval forces and developed weapons for close combat—such as the sword—to such a high degree that they were famous throughout the realm; when unearthed today, they still retain their surface and edge qualities.[18]

Despite their inherent faults, chariots did permit the comparatively rapid conveyance of men, and under the direction of a skilled driver and reasonable conditions of terrain, they could undoubtedly be formidable. The romantic image of courageous knights challenging each other from their glistening, leather armored chariots rings as true for China as the West, and the chariot was particularly suited to individuals valiantly racing out and provoking the enemy into hasty action. (However, Creel has observed that the Age of Chivalry did not begin until the Spring and Autumn period.[19])

The difficulty of maintaining close formations required advancing at a measured pace (as edicted by King Wu in his prebattle instructions preserved in the *Shih chi* and *Ssu-ma Fa*) in order to coordinate not only chariots with chariots but also chariots with supporting infantry. The necessary imposition and observance of such constraints must have severely tempered an assault thrust's maximum speed and, insofar as the book reflects antique practices, no doubt underlies the *Ssu-ma Fa*'s repeated stress on adhering to proper measures. (For further discussion, see the translator's introduction and the notes to the *Ssu-ma Fa* translation.) It was possible for coordinated infantry to take advantage of the chariot's difficulties and surround, overturn, or otherwise obstruct it; according to the *Tso chuan*, they also constantly failed of their own accord—suffering broken axles, becoming mired, getting tangled in branches, and falling into unseen gullies. Perhaps because of these limitations, coupled with their cost and extensive training requirements, the only effective way for armies to expand was with infantrymen. However, the growth of infantry divisions obviously reflected changing social and political conditions as well as a number of other factors, and experts such as Yang Hung explicitly deny that the problems of chariot employment caused them to be replaced.[20]

Appendix B: The Horse and Cavalry

THE HORSE was domesticated in China in neolithic times but was not ridden. The indigenous breed, which had a distribution through the steppe region, was apparently rather small—especially compared with the mounts of the nomadic peoples who appeared on China's western borders around the fifth century B.C. (Creel dogmatically asserts that no evidence exists for mounted riders in China prior to about 300 B.C.,[1] but Shaughnessy suggests the Chinese were encountering mounted riders by the end of the Spring and Autumn period in 484 B.C.[2] Some traditional scholars, on the basis of scant archaeological evidence, have argued for a long indigenous development period and for the existence of riding and hunting as early as the Shang, but this view is largely discredited.[3] Others claim that a *Tso chuan* entry indicates that barbarians were waging mounted warfare by 664 B.C.[4] Pulleyblank[5] and Yetts[6] basically concur with Creel. However, there are historical references to the famous general Wu Ch'i [440?–361 B.C.] riding on horseback; a similar passage is found in the *Wu-tzu* [which is conveniently employed to discredit the work's authenticity]. Passages in the *Six Secret Teachings* that discuss the tactical employment of cavalry are also consigned to a late Warring States date on the basis of King Wu-ling's innovation in 307 B.C.[7])

Prior to the fifth century B.C. the nomads were still on foot and fought as infantry or employed chariots. In the fourth century the Hu peoples initiated the first mounted incursions against the northern border states of Chao and Yen. Their horses offered them the obvious advantages of speed, mobility, and freedom in targeting, immediately spreading the requirements of static defense over much larger areas. Consequently, King Wu-ling of Chao resolved to force his warriors to imitate the barbarian mode of dress (trousers and short jackets) because he believed such attire was critical in unleashing the cavalry's power. Apparently, his intent was to increase the army's aggressive potential rather than simply to cope with the Hu, who were not particularly formidable, because he subsequently attempted to flank and invade

Ch'in from the north.[8] Thereafter, the horse and cavalry grew in importance but until the Han dynasty, they remained a minor element in the army despite the tactics proposed by strategists such as Sun Pin and the T'ai Kung (of the *Six Secret Teachings* rather than the historical figure). According to their works, the cavalry provides mobility; frees the army from having its main assault weapon (hitherto the chariot) confined to level terrain; and permits the development of unorthodox maneuvers. Throughout the Warring States period, chariots remained more important than the cavalry (although in terms of power and numbers, the infantry came to play a greater role). Even the conquering Ch'in army, however, only included about ten percent cavalry. Liu Pang, founder of the Han, created an elite cavalry unit to turn the tide in his final battles with Hsiang Yü, but this still only amounted to twenty percent of his total forces.[9]

Subsequently, Han Wu-ti, the great expansionist emperor of the Former Han—determined to secure the famous, superior horses from the distant nomads—dispatched major campaign armies into central Asia to subjugate recalcitrant peoples and seize the horses by force.[10] One hundred thousand cavalry, accompanied by as many supply wagons, embarked on the campaign of 128 to 119 B.C. From this time on the chariot ceased to have any tactical fighting role (although there was an abortive attempt by Fang Kuan in the T'ang era to reconstruct and follow the antique ways). From perhaps the middle of the Former Han era, the cavalry became an independent battle element that provided focal power for orthodox tactics and flexibility for executing unorthodox tactics.[11] With the invention of stirrups and the development of an effective saddle, heavy cavalry became possible, although it was displaced again by light cavalry with the approach of the T'ang. T'ang Tai-tsung made particularly effective use of the cavalry in wresting control of the empire and was famous for his horsemanship. He was perhaps of nomadic ancestry and well understood the effectiveness of cavalry (as is seen in the military work bearing his name and the accompanying translator's introduction).

Appendix C: Armor and Shields[1]

THE PRIMITIVE ARMOR of the predynastic neolithic period and the Hsia probably consisted of animal skins, including those of the fearsome tiger, with little alteration. From the Shang through the end of the Warring States, leather—generally fashioned from cowhide, although sometimes from rhino or buffalo—comprised the basic material. When employed in conjunction with large shields, leather armor apparently provided adequate protection against the bronze weapons of the period. Based on evidence from the Chou (and assuming essential continuity between the Shang and Chou), the mighty Shang warriors wore two-piece leather armor that covered the front and back as well as bronze helmets. As the scope and intensity of conflict increased in the early Chou, construction techniques changed dramatically—shifting from two large pieces to multiple small rectangles strung into rows with leather thongs, the rows then being overlaid to create a lamellar tunic. The individual pieces were cut from leather that had been tanned, lacquered, and finally colored (frequently with red or black pigmented lacquer or perhaps decorated with fierce motifs). Due to the perishable nature of such materials, the exact course of their evolution remains indistinct, but such armor probably displaced two-piece models by the Spring and Autumn period.

Armor was apparently specialized, suited to the warrior's function and his mode of fighting. For example, that for charioteers—who remained basically stationary once ensconced in their vehicle—was generally long and cumbersome, protecting the entire body while primarily leaving the arms free. However, the infantry—which was heavily dependent on agility and foot speed for both its survival and aggressiveness—obviously fought with shorter leather tunics, fewer restrictive leg protectors, and far less overall weight. When the cavalry developed, although they could easily sustain more weight than infantrymen, their legs had to be unrestricted (but protected against outside attacks), which accounts for the adoption of barbarian-style trousers and short tunics. Furthermore, until the invention of the stirrups, excess weight would also contribute further to the rider's instability.

Thus heavy cavalry did not develop until the post-Han, only to be again displaced by swifter, lighter elements within a few centuries.

Even after the development of iron and its application for agricultural implements and weapons, iron armor—which was necessary to withstand the greater firepower of the crossbow as well as perhaps stronger iron swords—did not displace leather until well into the Han (coincident with the replacement of the bronze sword). Bronze armor may have existed in the early Chou, and the use of some combination of leather with perhaps a reinforcing bronze outer piece (particularly for the shield) is evident. However, until the advent of iron plates imitating the leather lamellar construction—thus ensuring flexibility and endurable weight—metal appears to have been extremely rare. Even in the Han and thereafter, leather never entirely disappeared, being employed in a supplementary fashion.

Shields—an essential adjunct to every warrior's defensive equipment—were generally constructed on a wooden frame over which lacquered leather or various lacquered cloth materials were stretched. All-wood shields as well as those made from reeds and rushes obviously existed in some regions and in different eras, although their history has yet to be reconstructed. But as with body armor, leather was the material of choice, sometimes with additional protective layers of bronze. With the rise of iron weapons and the crossbow, iron shields also appeared but apparently not in great numbers until late in the Warring States or the Han dynasty.

Helmets were fashioned from bronze throughout the period, although iron helmets had appeared by the beginning of the Warring States. However, as with the iron sword and armor, they did not dominate until at least the Han.

Chariots, which evolved little over the period, also used lacquered leather for reinforcement, as is noted in Wu Ch'i's initial interview with the king in the *Wu-tzu*. Protection for the horse—the prime target—was also considered important and may have originated late in the Warring States period. However, again it was not until the Han that equine armor became both massive and extensive, reflecting the newly dominant role of the cavalry and the need to protect the valuable steeds. Outside stimuli from the mounted, highly mobile steppe peoples may have also contributed to the development of armor (and perhaps some weapons), but most developments were indigenous rather than imitative.

Appendix D: The Sword

ALTHOUGH THERE ARE a few dissenting voices and much controversy about the origin, evolution, and numbers of swords, it appears that the true sword—one with the blade more than double the length of the haft—did not really develop in China until late in the Spring and Autumn period.[1] Prior to this time warriors carried daggers, spear heads, and sometimes a short sword—all of which were fashioned from bronze.[2] (However, based on recent archaeological evidence, some traditionally oriented scholars have deduced that Western Chou warriors carried bronze swords.[3] An occasional artifact from the Shang is also classified as a "sword" in the literature, but when its dimensions are considered, the blade rarely exceeds the length of the haft by much—consigning it instead to the category of short swords or long daggers.)

Swords in the Western Chou and Spring and Autumn periods were designed for piercing and thrusting, not for slashing and cutting attacks.[4] With the advent of the infantry, weapons for close combat necessarily supplemented and then began to displace the halberd and other chariot-oriented war implements. In addition to the sword, the short or hand *chi* (spear-tipped halberd capable of thrusting attacks much like a spear[5]) became very common among Warring States infantrymen—particularly in states where chariots were tactically unsuitable, such as Wu and Yüeh.[6]

Some scholars have coupled the final evolution and proliferation of the sword to the development of the cavalry in the late Warring States period and subsequently the Han dynasty.[7] Extremely long swords, especially double-edged ones, would be both dangerous and unwieldy for cavalrymen;[8] therefore, the excessively long swords that developed in the late Warring States and early Han were probably exclusively for infantrymen or were simply ceremonial.

Theories of origin range from imitation of steppe weapons to totally indigenous development without any nonmetalic precursors.[9] One theory holds that warriors in the Shang and Early Chou carried spearheads as a sort of short dagger and that from these—especially as the spearheads became longer and stronger—the short dagger with a handle and then the elongated sword, evolved.[10] As the technology of metalworking progressed, improvements in shape, durability, sharpness, and appearance rapidly followed. However, whatever their origin, swords with slashing power and considerable length in comparison with the handle really only flourished in the late Warring States, Ch'in, and Han.[11]

As the cavalry became the dominant battle element in the armed forces, the sword evolved to match its requirements. Thus from the Han onward, a single-edged sword with a ring handle—actually termed a "knife"—gradually displaced the long swords of the Warring States. Thereafter, metalworking continually improved, especially layering and surface treatment; and two distinctive trends emerged—one toward higher-quality, shorter, functional-edged weapons; the other toward purely ceremonial and elaborately decorated symbolic swords. Steel "knives" became the sword of choice for both infantrymen and cavalrymen as the T'ang—the era of the last of the *Seven Military Classics*—approached.

(Although this brief sketch is inadequate for any true understanding of the sword and its history, a more extensive consideration requires a separate book. Readers with a command of Asian languages should consult Hayashi Minao's detailed but somewhat dated work[12] and similar writings in Chinese.[13])

Appendix E: Military Organization

MILITARY ORGANIZATION in all its aspects—such as the development of administrative districts, population registration, and universal military service obligations—requires a separate study. Opinions on many aspects—including fundamentals, questions of origin, and early history—are far from unanimous. However, because knowledge of the basic organizational methods and principles is helpful to understanding much of the *Seven Military Classics,* a brief overview is undertaken here.

The critical problem in characterizing organization in the Shang dynasty is the uncertain role the chariot played because some scholars believe the chariot comprised the core element around which the company—the basic military unit—was formed. If chariots were insignificant or only played a transport role, this would obviously not be possible. Consequently, two theories must be considered: chariot-centered and clan-centered. In the former, the chariot—manned by three members of the nobility—would be accompanied by conscripted commoners, probably ten men per chariot.[1] Their function was strictly supportive; because they would be drawn from the state's farming and artisan populations as well as from each noble's personal retainers—in an age when bronze weapons were expensive and limited in numbers—they were only minimally armed.[2] Based on burial patterns, this line of thought holds that the chariots were organized into squads of five, with either three or five squads to a company. Each squad would be supported by a one-hundred-man infantry company with (in some views) a complement of twenty-five officers. A battalion composed of three or five squads with associated infantry would constitute an operational unit. (Conclusive evidence for these reconstructions is lacking.[3])

Another view—based on excavated tombs—suggests the total number per *tsu,* or company, was one hundred: three officers for the chariot and seventy-two infantry organized into three platoons, supported by a supply vehicle staffed by twenty-five. However, this conceptualization seems to derive from the later idealization found in the *Chou li* and more likely describes the state of affairs late in the Spring and Autumn.[4]

Considerable textual evidence suggests that the clan composed the basic organizational unit, with the *tsu* (a different character than that above) again numbering one hundred men.[5] The members would all be from the nobility, under the command of the clan chief—who would normally also be the king, an important vassal, or a local feudal lord. Thus organized, they probably fought as infantry units, although chariots could also have been integrated for transport and command purposes. (According to Hsü Cho-yün, clan units [*tsu*] still actively participated in the pitched battles of the Spring and Autumn.[6]) Ten such companies probably comprised a *shih,* which was basically an army of one thousand men; in fact, the term *shih* should be considered synonymous with "army" in this period.[7] The word normally translated as "army"—*chün*—does not appear until the Spring and Autumn.[8]

Early Western Chou military organization would have been essentially the same, but with the units definitely chariot-centered. As discussed in a footnote to the translation of the *Six Secret Teachings,* the three thousand famous Tiger Warriors at the epoch-making battle of Mu-yeh would appropriately work out to a ratio of ten men per chariot. Thereafter, the infantry expanded as the number associated with each chariot gradually increased, until by the early Spring and Autumn the ratio was perhaps twenty, twenty-two, or even thirty foot soldiers per vehicle.[9] In the Spring and Autumn period—the classic age of chariot warfare depicted in the *Tso chuan*—the systematic grouping of men into squads of five, with a vertical hierarchy mapped out on multiples of five, seems to have developed and become prevalent.[10] This is the period described by passages in several of the *Military Classics* and the *Chou li,* during which seventy-two infantrymen accompanied each chariot, deployed in three platoons characterized as left, center, and right. (These designations were nominal; actual positioning depended on their function. For example, on easy terrain the center platoon would follow the chariot, whereas on difficult terrain it would precede it—both as a defensive measure and to clear obstacles.[11]) Whether the officers were included among the one hundred also seems to be a matter of debate.[12]

From the *Chou li* and some of the military writings, the following chart can be constructed, with rough Western equivalents as indicated:

Unit	Strength	Possible Western Equivalents	
wu	5	squad	
liang	25	platoon	
tsu	100	company	
lü	500	battalion	(regiment)
shih	2,500	regiment	(brigade)
chün	12,500	army	(corps)

The Western equivalents are relative; their definition depends on the era and country of organization.[13] The columns represent a set of alternatives, so that if regiment is used for *lü*, then brigade (or perhaps division) should be used for *shih*. The term *lü* is an ancient one; it was originally used by the Shang to designate a military unit that reportedly expanded to ten thousand for one campaign, but it also may have referred to the standing army.[14] Subsequently, in the Spring and Autumn and Warring States periods, it was combined with the character for army—*chün*—as *chün-lü* to indicate the army or military units in general. In its original meaning, it apparently referred to "men serving under a flag."

As already noted, the term for army—*chün*—appeared only in the Spring and Autumn and then only in the central states because the peripheral states, such as Ch'u, had their own distinct forms of organization.[15] The term "Three Armies" (*san chün*) encountered throughout the military texts normally refers to the army in general, not just to three units of army strength according to the above chart.[16] Early Chou theory asserted that the king alone had the right to maintain six armies (*shih*); a great feudal lord, three armies; lesser lords, two armies; and the least of them, one army. All of the vassal armies could and would be called on to supplement the royal forces and support the dynasty in the military campaigns that were generally mounted to suppress either rebellious states or nomadic peoples. With the rise of the hegemons in the Spring and Autumn period, states such as Chin simply disregarded both the Chou house and its prerogatives, eventually fielding as many as six armies.[17]

In the earliest stage of the Shang and Chou, force size was apparently irregular; it was enumerated, constituted, and organized to meet the situation and the demand. However, with the vastly augmented scope of conflict in the Warring States and the imposition of universal service obligations, military hierarchy and discipline became essential, as is evident from the emphasis on them in the *Seven Military Classics*. Actual service demands made on the newly registered populace also increased from the Spring and Autumn into the Warring States; at first, only a single male in each family was required to serve, then all males were so required. This mirrored early Chou trends when all the people who dwelled within the state (*kuo*) trained and were obligated to fight but were universally mobilized in only the most dire circumstances.[18] With the creation and imposition of hierarchical administrative systems for the populace (both variants—the village and district—began late in the Spring and Autumn in Chin and Ch'u, perhaps originating with Kuan Chung), the male population could be quickly summoned for active duty. The village and district groups of five and twenty-five were immediately translated into squads and platoons. Local officials at all levels would immediately become officers at the respective unit level, although there were professional military personnel for the higher ranks and a standing army to form the army's core.[19] This meant that the total qualified populace could be mobilized for military campaigns, and that virtually an entire country could go to war.[20]

Notes

Abbreviations Used in the Notes

(See also the lists at the beginning of the notes to individual translations.)

AA	Acta Asiatica
AM	Asia Major
BIHP	Bulletin of the Institute of History and Philology
BMFEA	Bulletin of the Museum of Far Eastern Antiquities
BSOAS	Bulletin of the School of Oriental and African Studies
CC	Chinese Culture
CCCY	Chin-chu chin-i editions
EC	Early China
GSR	Grammata Serica Recensa (Bernhard Karlgren, BMFEA 29 [1957])
HJAS	Harvard Journal of Asiatic Studies
JAOS	Journal of the American Oriental Society
JAS	Journal of Asian Studies
JCP	Journal of Chinese Philosophy
JNCBRAS	Journal of the North Central Branch, Royal Asiatic Society
JRAS	Journal of the Royal Asiatic Society
KK	K'ao-ku hsüeh-pao
MS	Monumenta Serica
PEW	Philosophy East and West
TP	T'oung Pao
WW	Wen-wu

General Introduction and Historical Background of the Classics

1. The Confucius (551–479 B.C.) of the *Analects* demands courage and resoluteness in the practice of righteousness and requires that his disciples always do what is appropriate. He cultivated the six arts, which included chariot driving and archery, and in other texts refers to the terrible visage of the righteous man when he dons his armor. He also indicated that the *chün-tzu,* or perfected man, does not compete, which was taken by later Confucians as evidence that conflict and warfare are inappropriate for civi-

lized men. Other early Confucians, such as Mencius (371–289 B.C.) and Hsün-tzu (a Confucian of the late Warring States period who wrote extensively on military affairs), were cognizant of the inescapable necessity of wars and armies. Only after several centuries, as the Confucians became further removed from the pristine spirit of their founder and the realities of the early context, did the tendency toward pacificism, or (perhaps more correctly) the *civil,* emerge and gain ascendancy. This is a complex topic that requires an extensive separate analytic work.

2. The dates assigned to the Spring and Autumn and the Warring States periods vary somewhat depending on the writer's predilections. The *Ch'un ch'iu,* or *Spring and Autumn Annals,* which chronicles events from 722 to 481 B.C., was traditionally held to have been edited didactically by Confucius and was one of the essential *Five Classics.* (Confucius no doubt used the work for educational purposes and may have emended it to some extent, but he cannot be considered the compiler or editor in any real sense.) The *Tso chuan,* purportedly a commentary to the *Spring and Autumn Annals* but in actuality a self-existent work that portrays the period in considerable detail, covers the years 722 to 468 B.C. (or 464 B.C.; opinion seems to vary). The *Intrigues of the Warring States* contains some material from the early fifth century B.C., but it basically records the people and events of the period 403–221 B.C., when the Ch'in officially assumed the mantle of imperial rule. Thus the Spring and Autumn period should refer to 722 to 481 B.C. and the Warring States era to 403–221 B.C., traditional dates that are adopted herein. However, there is also considerable logic to dating the Spring and Autumn period from the movement of the Western Chou capital to the east in 771 B.C. and extending the Warring States period to cover the interval between the end of the *Tso chuan* material and 403 B.C. This gives dates such as those Herrlee G. Creel (*The Origins of Statecraft in China,* University of Chicago Press, Chicago, 1970, p. 47) adopts: 770–464 and 463–222 B.C.

3. Lord Shang (died 338 B.C.), although much reviled by Confucian tradition, had great impact in reforming the laws and institutions of the state of Ch'in. Among his important contributions were imposing stringent laws; advocating and implementing a severe but certain system of rewards and punishments; restricting the conferring of rank to military achievements; organizing the entire populace as well as the military into groups of five and ten, thereby creating a dual-purpose, mutual guarantee system that facilitated immediate conscription; and eliminating the boundary paths between fields, making land a salable commodity. (Some of these reforms may have had antecedents, including those involving the military. For example, see Fu Shao-chieh, *Wu-tzu chin-chu chin-i,* Shang-wu yin-shu-kuan, Taipei, 1976, p. 17.) The remnants of Lord Shang's book have been translated by J.J.L. Duyvendak as *The Book of Lord Shang* (Arthur Probsthain, London, 1928; reprint, University of Chicago Press, 1963).

4. Han Fei-tzu (died 233 B.C.), a famous Legalist and former disciple of Hsün-tzu (298–238 B.C.), left an extensive treatise, which has been translated in full by W. K. Liao (*The Complete Works of Han Fei-tzu,* 2 vols., A. Probsthain, London, 1959 [reprint of 1939 edition]), and as selections by Burton Watson (*Han Fei-tzu: Basic Writings,* Columbia University Press, New York, 1964.)

5. "Virtue," although encompassing the basic meaning of moral virtue, was the object of much complex thought in ancient China and came to have numerous nuances and technical meanings, including "power" and "potency." Some of these are discussed briefly in the footnotes to the translations. In general, "Virtue" (capitalized) is

used to translate the term *te* whenever the transcendent dimensions are critical—when the cultivation of *te* (virtue) leads to Virtue, which is synonymous with moral achievement and the inner power that accompanies it. Within the context of Taoist texts and to a certain extent military writings influenced by them, the term *te* indicates inner potency or power—generally as contrasted with and distinguished from the moral and ethical realm because the artificial constraints of rites, morals, and ethics were anathema to most Taoist-oriented thinkers (neo-Taoism and eclectic works excepted). A specialized body of literature has developed in recent years, due partly to the discovery of previously unknown manuscripts; these writings offer various conceptualizations and systematizations under the rubric of "Huang-Lao" thought, although there is by no means universal accord that these trends constitute a school or an affiliation. Specialists are no doubt aware of them, but the general reader may find Arthur Waley's classic comments on the term *te* in his introduction to *The Way and Its Power* (Grove Press, New York, 1958), or D. C. Lau's thoughts in his translation of the *Tao Te Ching* (The Chinese University Press, Hong Kong, 1982) of interest. (Also see the notes to the translator's introduction to the *Art of War* translation in the present volume, especially number 24, for further discussion and sources, and Aat Vervoorn's article "Taoism, Legalism, and the Quest for Order in Warring States China," *JCP*, Vol. 8, No. 3 [September 1981], pp. 303–324.)

Throughout we translate *te* as "virtue" when it refers to morals and ethics and as "Virtue" when it connotes the attainment of a special status—with inherent power—through the cultivation of virtue, which is not unlike the original meaning of *virtus*. The questions of its transcendent dimensions, relationship to potency, and metaphysical realization in warfare command must be left to another book and the studies of experts.

6. Every "civilized" dynasty, including the Shang, appears to have exploited "barbarian"—defined by reference to the dynasty's own self-perceived level of civilization—peoples against other, similar peoples. In many cases they were even settled in the frontier regions, just within state borders, and shouldered the burden of dynastic defense. However, this first appeared as an articulated policy in the Han era and was symptomatic of the steppe-sedentary conflict. Discussions may be found in Owen Lattimore, *Inner Asian Frontiers of China* (Beacon Press, Boston, 1962); Yü Ying-shih, *Trade and Expansion in Han China* (University of California Press, Berkeley, 1967); and Sechin Jagchid and Van Jay Symons, *Peace, War, and Trade Along the Great Wall* (Indiana University Press, Bloomington, 1989).

7. This discussion of the Shang is based on standard Western texts and monographs, such as Kwang-chih Chang's *Shang Civilization* (Yale University Press, New Haven, 1980) and Cheng Te-k'un's *Shang China* (Heffer, Cambridge, 1960), supplemented by the normal range of articles from specialist journals, such as *Early China* and *Wen wu*. They are listed in the bibliography under the sections for historical materials.

8. A major point of contention is whether slaves were used solely for domestic work and perhaps occasional agricultural activities or whether the entire Shang edifice was based on the systematic use and exploitation of a slave class of agricultural workers. Depending on whether a Marxist or another synthetic framework is employed, the evidence is defined and interpreted differently. However, it appears that enslaved prisoners and their descendants were found largely in domestic work rather than agriculture.

9. In the Shang and Chou dynasties, the presence of the lineage's ancestral temple virtually constituted the defining feature of a capital city. Naturally, various deities, spirits, and animistic forces were also worshipped, depending on the period, state, and beliefs of the time. The ruler's ancestral temple always played a critical role in prewar discussions and in prebattle ceremonies, as is evident in the *Seven Military Classics*.

10. In the past decade a number of lengthy, minutely detailed articles based on historical records, recently recovered bronze inscriptions, calendrical reconstructions, and celestial phenomena have discussed the probable date for Chou's conquest of the Shang. The traditionally held date of 1122 B.C. proposed by the Han dynasty scholar Liu Hsin has been invalidated emphatically by David Pankenier's proof that the rare five-planet conjunction recorded in the *Bamboo Annals* actually occurred on May 28, 1059 B.C. (See David W. Pankenier, "Astronomical Dates in Shang and Western Zhou," *EC* 7 [1981–1982], pp. 2–5.) Various other dates previously proposed—such as 1111, 1075 (T'ang Lan), 1027, 1025, and 1023 (Bernhard Karlgren)—have also been discarded. Current arguments, based on essentially the same evidence—including the critical five-planet conjunction—variously supplemented or interpreted, produce three theories: Pankenier's January 20, 1046 B.C. (Pankenier, "Astronomical Dates," p. 2–37, in particular p. 16); David S. Nivison's January 15, 1045 B.C. (originally proposed in his article "The Dates of Western Chou," *HJAS*, Vol. 43, No. 2 [December 1983], pp. 481–580), and 1040 (according to his note revising the *JAS* article published almost simultaneously in *Early China* [*EC* 8 (1982–1983), pp. 76–78]); and Edward Shaughnessy, who supports Nivison's first date of January 15, 1045 (see "'New' Evidence on the Zhou Conquest," *EC* 6 [1980–1981], pp. 57–79, and "The 'Current' *Bamboo Annals* and the Date of the Zhou Conquest of Shang," *EC* 11–12 [1985–1987], pp. 33–60, especially p. 45). Chou Fa-kao also supports the 1045 date in a Chinese review article ("Wu Wang k'e Shang te nien-tai wen-t'i," in *Li-shih Yü-yen Yen-chiu-so chi-k'an* [*BIHP*], Vol. 56, No. 1 [1985], Taipei, pp. 5–41). Because 1045 B.C. appears well-founded, it is adopted herein. However, for further discussions, see Chang, *Shang Civilization,* pp. 15–19; Creel, *The Origins of Statecraft in China,* pp. 487–491, who suggests accepting the traditional date of 1122 B.C. even though acknowledging it may be inaccurate; Tung Tso-pin, "Hsi-Chou nien-li-p'u," *BIHP* 23 (1951), pp. 681–760; Ch'ü Wan-li, "Hsi-Chou shih-shih kai-shu," *BIHP* 42 (1971), pp. 775–802; Jung Men-yüan, "Shih-t'an Hsi-Chou chi-nien," *Chung-hua wen-shih lun-ts'ung* 1 (1980), pp. 16–20; Ho Yu-ch'i, "Chou Wu-wang fa-Chou te nien-tai wen-t'i," *Chung-shan Ta-hsüeh hsüeh-pao* 1 (1981), pp. 64–70; and Edward L. Shaughnessy, "On the Authenticity of the *Bamboo Annals,*" *HJAS*, Vol. 46, No. 1 (June 1986), pp. 149–180.

11. The casting of massive ritual cauldrons, some weighing several hundred pounds, and the production of bronze weapons required hundreds of skilled artisans engaged in coordinated activity.

12. It is well-known that in the plains area of central China—the locus of the Shang dynasty—the soft yellowish earth can easily be dug with a sharpened wooden stick or other nonmetallic object. Naturally, agricultural efficiency improves with metal plows and hoes, but they were not essential and were rarely, if ever, used in the Shang era. (See Chang, *Shang Civilization,* p. 223; Hsu and Linduff, *Western Chou Civilization,* pp. 75 and 353; and T. R. Treger, *A Geography of China,* Aldine, Chicago, 1965, pp. 50–51.) A contrary view is taken by the traditionalist Ch'en Liang-tso in a lengthy, detailed

review of the archaeological evidence. He concludes that the Shang already had bronze agricultural implements, which were used concurrently with those made of inexpensive materials such as stone and bone. Moreover, in his view, these implements were employed extensively throughout the Chou period until they were finally displaced by iron in the Warring States era. (See Ch'en Liang-tso, "Wo-kuo ku-tai te ch'ing-t'ung nung-chü," *Han-hsüeh yen-chiu*, Vol. 2, No. 1 [June 1984], pp. 135–166, and Vol. 2, No. 2 [December 1984], pp. 363–402.)

13. Rice, which requires wet cultivation, originated in the south and was little grown in Shang central areas. (For general discussions of agriculture in China, see *Science and Civilisation in China*, Vol. 6, Part 2, *Agriculture* [by Francesca Bray], Cambridge University Press, Cambridge, 1984; Kwang-chih Chang, eds., *Food in Chinese Culture*, Yale University Press, New Haven, 1977; and E. N. Anderson, *The Food of China*, Yale University Press, New Haven, 1988.)

14. The enormous numbers of animals used in the almost continuous sacrifices, which went to feed the priestly caste and the nobility, is cited as evidence that cattle and other animals must have been raised. Cf. Chang, *Shang Civilization*, pp. 142–145, 230.

15. See ibid., pp. 195–196. The king's wives are also recorded as having commanded troops and as having personal forces.

16. Cf. Cheng Te-k'un, *Shang China*, pp. 208–212; Chang, *Shang Civilization*, p. 249. The total number in the army during wartime is sometimes estimated at thirty thousand (Cheng, *Shang China*, p. 210), which would be many measures smaller than the number of troops reported as having engaged in the battle of Mu-yeh. This suggests that the more limited figures apply only to the early to middle Shang era—perhaps with significant expansion later—as well as overstatement.

17. See Fan Yuzhou, "Military Campaign Inscriptions from YH 127," *BSOAS*, Vol. 52, No. 3 (1989) pp. 533–548; and David N. Keightley, who cites the extensive nature of the king's travels in "The Late Shang State," in *The Origins of Chinese Civilization*, University of California Press, Berkeley, 1983, pp. 552–555.

18. A later term, the Three Armies (*san chün*), was used constantly to refer to a campaign army. Whether it originates with these three divisions (*san shih*) or was simply an organizational creation (such as for upper, middle, and lower) is not clear. (Cf. Chin Hsiang-heng, "Ts'ung chia-ku pu-ts'u yen-chiu Yin Shang chün-lü-chung chih wang-tsu san-hsing san-shih," *Chung-kuo wen-tzu* 52 [1974], pp. 1–26; and the material on military organization in Appendix E.)

19. A basic distinction in the Shang and Early Chou was made between the people who dwelled within the *kuo,* the "state," and those who lived outside it. At this time a state was essentially a city fortified by surrounding walls, with the privileged class residing within its protective confines. The city dwellers furnished the warriors, whereas those outside the walls were not required to serve or were merely conscripted as menial support (if they were not alien peoples under the control of the *kuo*). This distinction declined as the scope of warfare eventually expanded in the Spring and Autumn period. (See, for example, Hsü Hsi-ch'en, "Chou-tai ping-chih ch'u-lun," *Chung-kuo-shih yen-chiu* 4 [1985], pp. 4–5.)

20. On warfare objectives, see Yang Hung, *Chung-kuo ku-ping-ch'i lun-ts'ung*, Ming wen shu-chü, Taipei, 1983, p. 8. Although agriculturally based and accordingly prosperous, the Shang ruling house required vast riches to distribute to the nobility,

whether directly or indirectly (through allowing them to retain the plunders of war). Because the Shang domain was extensive and the nobility counted in the ten of thousands of families, it was rather voracious. For example, in one battle the Shang reportedly took thirty thousand prisoners (see Chang, *Shang Civilization,* p. 194).

21. Among the peoples particularly chosen for sacrifice were the Ch'iang, from whose Chiang clan many of the principal wives of the Chou royalty came. The T'ai Kung, adviser to Kings Wen and Wu of the Chou, was also of Ch'iang origin. It seems possible that the Shang's enmity toward the Ch'iang drove them to an alliance with the Chou, although this is not known. See E. G. Pulleyblank, "The Chinese and Their Neighbors in Prehistoric and Early Historic Times," in *The Origins of Chinese Civilization,* pp. 420–421; Chang, *Shang Civilization,* p. 249.

22. In the Shang and probably the Early Chou, weapons were generally stored in government armories and were distributed only when required for military campaigns. (See Yen I-p'ing, "Yin Shang ping-chih," *Chung-kuo wen-tzu,* NS 7 [1983], p. 39.) This reflected the considerable cost of weapons and diffused any threat of an armed political revolt against the ruling family. Furthermore, because of the cost factor, some researchers believe conscripted infantrymen were generally not furnished with serious weapons until the infantry grew in significance and less expensive iron weapons became available. (For example, see Chung-kuo chün-shih-shih Pien-hsieh-tsu, *Chung-kuo chün-shih-shih,* Vol. 4: *Ping-fa,* Chieh-fang-chün ch'u-pan-she, Peking, 1988, p. 2.)

23. The dagger-ax derives its name from the dagger-like blade horizontally affixed near the top of a long wooden shaft, but it is primarily a hooking weapon. Wounds are inflicted by swinging down and pulling forward, with the curved knife-like blade cutting in and hooking the enemy (rather than delivering a crushing, chopping blow directly into the soldier as an ax blade would. The ancients also had axes, but their role seems to have been limited and perhaps largely ceremonial.) See Chou Wei, *Chung-kuo ping-ch'i shih-kao,* Ming-wen shu-chü, Taipei, 1980, pp. 64–88; Hayashi Minao, *Chūgoku In-shū jidai no buki,* Kyoto Daigaku Jimbun Kagaku Kenkyūsho, Kyoto, 1972, pp. 3–96; Lao Kan, "Chan-kuo shih-tai te chan-cheng fang-fa," *BIHP* 37 (1967), pp. 53–57; and Shih Chang-ju, "Hsiao-t'un Yin-tai te ch'eng-t'ao ping-ch'i," *BIHP* 22 (1950), pp. 59–65. A number of specialized articles have discussed this indigenous weapon, including Ma Heng, "Ko chi chih yen-chiu," *Yenching hsüeh-pao,* No. 5 (1929), pp. 745–753; Kuo Pao-chün, "Ko chi yü-lun," *BIHP,* Vol. 5, No. 3 (1935), pp. 313–326; and Li Chi, "Yü-pei ch'u-t'u ch'ing-t'ung kou-ping fen-lei t'u-chieh," *BIHP* 22 (1950), pp. 1–31.

24. The spear was already extant in Shang times and no doubt dates back to the neolithic period. Shang spears boasted bronze spearheads (as well as those made of other materials, such as stone and bone), but with the development of iron technology, iron tips appeared by the Warring States period. In addition, the longer spears suited to use with the chariot (and thus also employed by infantry) in the Shang and Early Chou tended to be too unwieldy for infantrymen and consequently were shortened somewhat in the Warring States period. Conversely, the blades tended to become longer and sharper in the early Spring and Autumn period and continued to undergo similar modifications thereafter. For detailed discussions, in addition to references listed in the bibliography, see Chou Wei, *Chung-kuo ping-ch'i shih-kao,* pp. 98–102; and Hiyashi Minao, *Chūgoku In-Shū jidai no buki,* pp. 97–130.

25. The bow was already a major part of the Shang warrior's arsenal and was generally carried by the chariot commander. Composite bows appeared early, increasing in complexity, size, and strength over the centuries with improvements in bonding and crafting technology. Various materials, including bamboo, were employed and were matched for greatest composite strength under tension. In the Shang era wooden shafted arrows generally mounted bronze points, although bone, stone, and other materials were also employed. However, bronze continued to prevail even after iron had generally appeared in the Warring States (refer to note 55 below). For an overview and detailed discussions, see Hiyashi Minao, *Chūgoku In-Shū jidai no buki*, pp. 243–299 (on bows) and 321–374 (on arrows); Yoshida Mitsukuni (who also discusses crossbows), "Yumi to ōyumi," *Tōyōshi kenkyū,* Vol. 12, No. 3 (1953), pp. 82–92; and the classic report and analysis of Shih Chang-ju, "Hsiao-t'un Yin-tai te ch'eng-t'ao ping-ch'i," pp. 25–44 (on the bow) and 44–54 (on arrows).

26. See Appendix C for an annotated discussions of the development and history of armor in ancient China.

27. In recent years there have been a number of claims for widespread use of bronze swords in the Early Chou, such as Hsu and Linduff, *Western Chou Civilization,* p. 81. However, although the innovative horizon for many weapons and technological achievements continues to be pushed earlier and earlier with each new discovery, it would seem these would best be termed daggers rather than swords, both in length and function. See Appendix D for an annotated discussion of the sword's history and some of the issues surrounding it.

28. "Chien-hsüan," *Lü-shih ch'un-ch'iu,* CCCY edition, Shang-wu yin-shu-kuan, Taipei, 1985, p. 204. Although claims that the Hsia had chariots are generally discounted, such assertions continue to be made, including in the recent PRC publication *Chung-kuo chün-shih-shih,* Vol. 4 *Ping-fa,* p. 5.

29. See Appendix A for an annotated discussion of the introduction and history of the chariot in China.

30. See the discussion of military organization in Appendix E for further information and references.

31. The *Ssu-ma Fa* discusses the practice and objectives of holding such hunts, and they are mentioned in a number of the other *Seven Military Classics* as well as in the *Tso chuan* and the "Ta Ssu-ma" section of the *Chou li*. (See the translator's introduction and notes to the *Ssu-ma Fa* translation for further information.) Also see *Ping-fa,* pp. 32–33; Yen I-p'ing, "Yin Shang ping-chih," p. 40; and Hsü Hsi-ch'en, "Chou-tai ping-chih ch'u-lun," p. 10.

The difficulty in attaining the required chariot skills and their expense are cited by some historians as the critical factors that made the rise of infantry units inevitable. Conscripts, whatever their class origin, simply could not be trained in the time available. For example, see Yang K'uan, "Ch'un-ch'iu Chan-kuo-chien feng-chien te chün-shih tsu-chih ho chan-cheng te pien-hua," *Li-shih chiao-hsüeh* 4 (1954), p. 12.

32. One tradition asserts that the Chou were descendants of the Hsia, whereas modern scholars such as K. C. Chang postulate that the peoples of the "Three Dynasties" were culturally and racially alike but politically distinct. (See K. C. Chang, "Sandai Archaeology and the Formation of States in Ancient China: Processual Aspects of the Origins of Chinese Civilization," in *The Origins of Chinese Civilization* [ed. David N. Keightley], pp. 495–521; and Chang, *Shang Civilization,* pp. 348–355.)

33. The Chou's "barbarian" origin was generally recognized in antiquity, and the *Shih chi* explicitly records Tan Fu—the Chou progenitor—as deliberately abandoning nomadic ways after his people resettled with him in the south to avoid conflict with other barbarians. (See the "Chou Annals." Further discussion is found in the translator's introduction to the translation of the *Six Secret Teachings*.)

34. King Chou of the Shang was persuaded by opulent bribes not only to release the future King Wen from detainment but also to name him "Lord of the West." Under this title he was entrusted with responsibility for defending Shang's flank and thereby afforded an excellent pretext for developing and exercising his own military powers. (See the translator's introduction to the translation of the *Six Secret Teachings* for additional information.)

35. It is generally thought that speed, mobility, and surprise marked the Chou campaign, with the chariot playing a key role. However, there are dissenting views, such as Hsu and Linduff (*Western Chou Civilization*, p. 88), who consider other factors more important (such as the effective deployment of infantry, longer swords, and superior armor [see Hsu and Linduff, p. 81]). For further discussion, see the translator's introduction to the *Six Secret Teachings* and Appendix A.

36. According to the *Shih chi*, the Shang had a one-hundred-thousand-man campaign army in the south, which could have amounted to a third or more of their total available forces and perhaps included some of their best units. King Chou of the Shang compounded his difficulties by ignoring repeated warnings about the potential danger posed by the Chou and notice of their actual advance. (Numbers from this period are extremely unreliable and should only be understood as indicative of comparative size.)

37. Because the antiquity of the *Six Secret Teachings* is almost universally denied, it seems possible that this revolutionary impulse may have been directed toward the imperial Ch'in by writers very late in the Warring States period. Their hatred of the brutal Ch'in would account for the ferocity of the policies, with such fervor being envisioned in the heroes of the ancient Chou as they gambled everything to overturn the vile despot. Whether the combatants observed any civilizing rites (such as in the early Spring and Autumn period) in the centuries prior to the battle at Mu-yeh is doubtful, but the traditional view assumes that they did. (This is discussed further in the translator's introduction to the translation of the *Six Secret Teachings*.)

38. See Edward L. Shaughnessy, "'New' Evidence on the Zhou Conquest," pp. 66–67.

39. Herrlee G. Creel's classic work, *The Origins of Statecraft in China*, still contains the most extensive reconstruction and discussion of these measures as well as of the Chou military. However, also see Hsu and Linduff, *Western Chou Civilization*.

40. See Hsu and Linduff, *Western Chou Civilization*, pp. 113–119; and Tu Cheng-sheng, "Lüeh-lun Yin i-min te tsao-yü yü ti-wei," *BIHP*, Vol. 53, No. 4 (December 1982), pp. 661–709.

41. For a discussion of the meaning of "army" in this period, see Appendix E.

42. See Cho-yün Hsu's extensive analysis, *Ancient China in Transition*, Stanford University Press, Stanford, 1965.

43. See the translator's introduction and notes to the *Ssu-ma Fa* translation. The emphasis on discipline and concerted action evident throughout the *Seven Military Classics* reflects this shift from the noble days of chariot warfare. (For additional discussion of the code of chivalry and its inevitable decline, see Frank A. Kierman, Jr.,

"Phases and Modes of Combat in Early China," in *Chinese Ways in Warfare* [ed. Franz A. Kierman, Jr., and John K. Fairbank], Harvard University Press, Cambridge, 1974, pp. 27–66.)

44. This incident, as recorded in the *Tso chuan* for the first year of Duke Chao, has historical importance because it shows the "barbarian" enemy fighting solely as infantrymen rather than mounted on horses or from chariots. In addition, the Chou's realization of the limitations of chariot warfare is clearly shown by the necessity they felt to abandon their own chariots and engage the enemy in confined valley terrain. The reluctance of at least one high official to relinquish his honored position as a charioteer and descend to the state of a foot soldier (for which he was summarily executed) also illustrates the prevailing attitude even this late in the Spring and Autumn period. (See Legge's translation of the incident, *The Chinese Classics:* Volume V, *The Ch'un Ts'ew with the Tso Chuen,* Oxford University Press, Oxford, 1872 [reprinted Chinhsüeh shu-chü, Taipei, 1968], p. 579.) Wei Shu initiated the conversion and formulated a plan whose effectiveness was augmented by its deceptiveness. To confuse the enemy he deployed the combined chariot and accompanying infantry forces in an unusual, unbalanced formation, provoking the enemy's laughter and ridicule—until the Chin forces sprang into action and routed them. "Be deceptive" was a dictum clearly in the minds of commanders in this era, a century or two before Sun-tzu's *Art of War.* (For further discussion and analysis, see *Ping-fa,* p. 36, and the *Wu-pei-chih* 53, pp. 22B–24B.) As the infantry expanded, officers from the nobility were assigned to command them, and rank was granted to everyone—regardless of status—for military achievement. Consequently, the status of the foot soldier improved dramatically, and although the old attitudes (which disdained foot assignment against the prestige of being assigned to the chariot) were never completely erased, their amelioration marked a significant change (see *Ping-fa,* p. 58).

It should be noted that chariots were not employed at this time in such peripheral southeastern states as Wu and Yüeh. Initially, this might have been because of ignorance and unsuitable terrain, but even after they were taught the skills of chariot driving and the tactics of warfare deployment, these and several other states fielded only infantry units. (For further discussion, see Appendix A and also Tu Cheng-sheng, "Chou-tai feng-chien chieh-t'i-hou te chün-cheng hsin-chih-hsü," *BIHP,* Vol. 55, No. 1 [1984], pp. 74–75, 82–89; *Ping-fa,* p. 58; Yang K'uan, "Ch'un-ch'iu Chan-kuo-chien," p. 11; and Yang Hung, *Chung-kuo ku-ping-ch'i,* p. 126.)

45. Another weapon, the *chi,* probably began to appear in some numbers around this time. The *chi,* or "spear-tipped dagger-ax," differed from the dagger-ax in one formidable aspect: It had a metal point at the top of the shaft to allow thrusting and stabbing. With the addition of this spear tip, the weapon could be used for an initial stabbing thrust, but if the target were missed, it could be pulled back or swung to catch the enemy with the knife-like horizontal blade. In the early stages it was probably made from two separate bronze parts, which were secured to a pole; this has prompted some archaeologists to argue that the *chi* has a longer history than is generally acknowledged. (After the wooden shaft had completely disintegrated, the two parts, which would be found separately, would be misinterpreted as having come from two weapons—a dagger-ax and a spear—rather than being parts of an integrated, composite one.) However, it appears that the *chi* was primarily a foot soldier's weapon, perhaps developed to better equip them to attack chariots; thus it grew in popularity as infantry

forces were augmented. In Shang tombs only *ko* (halberds, dagger-axes) are found, whereas Han excavations yield only *chi,* or spear-tipped dagger-axes. In the thousand years between the demise of the Shang and the flourishing of the Han, *chi* were probably created in the early Chou or Spring and Autumn periods, gradually becoming more popular until proliferating in the Warring States era. For detailed discussions, see Kuo Pao-chün, "Ko chi yü-lun," pp. 313–326; Kuo Mo-jo, *Yin Chou ch'ing-t'ung-ch'i ming-wen yen-chiu,* Jenmin ch'u-pan-she, Shanghai, 1954, pp. 172–186; Ma Heng, "Ko chi chih yen-chiu," pp. 745–753; Chou Wei, *Chung-kuo ping-ch'i shih-kao,* pp. 88–98; and Hayashi Minao, *Chūgoku In-Shū jidai no buki,* pp. 10–13 and 78–96.

In an article examining a multiple-blade *chi* excavated from a Warring States tomb, Sun Chi concludes that this sort of weapon was probably wielded by charioteers against foot soldiers and thus represented a response to the growth of infantry forces and their mounting threat to the chariot. (The attachment of knife blades to the wheel hubs served a similar function, as his article discusses on p. 83.) This implies further questions about the evolution of the *chi*—whether it was developed for infantrymen or for chariot-mounted warriors contending with other chariots or infantrymen—to which answers are unavailable. See Sun Chi, "Yu-jen ch'e-wei yü to-ko-chi," *WW* 1980, No. 12, pp. 83–85.

46. See Appendix D for details and also note 55 below.

47. Some of these qualifications are recorded in *Hsün-tzu* and itemized in the *Six Secret Teachings;* further discussion is found in the footnotes to the translations.

48. The Seven Strong States at the start of the Warring States period, as identified by Liu Hsiang's classic list, were Ch'i, Yen, the Three Chin (Han, Chao, Wei), and the newly powerful, originally peripheral states of Ch'u and Ch'in. Wu and Yüeh, two other so-called barbarian states, also emerged as significant forces.

49. The *Ssu-ma Fa* discusses the distinctions that mark the form and spirit of the civilian and military realms and advises against their becoming confused or intermixed. Most of the *Seven Military Classics* discuss the qualifications necessary for generalship, reflecting the rising concern with professionalism and a turning away from the preoccupation with moral qualifications found in the *Tso chuan.* Ironically, in earlier times the Shang and Chou kings as well as the local vassal lords not only governed their respective realms but also commanded the army and exercised supreme military power. Over time they became divorced from the complexities of battle.

50. Strategic points, such as passes and major road intersections, were increasingly guarded and fortified. The northern states, such as Yen and Chao, sought to diminish the mobility of mounted nomadic forces by creating static defense systems ("walls") along their lengthy, exposed borders. See Yang K'uan, "Ch'un-ch'iu Chan-kuo-chien feng-chien te chün-shih tsu-chih ho chan-cheng te pien-hua," p. 12. Also note Arthur Waldron's work on "walls"; "The Problem of the Great Wall of China," *HJAS,* Vol. 43, No. 2 (1983), pp. 643–663; and *The Great Wall of China: From History to Myth,* Cambridge University Press, Cambridge, 1990.

51. See Yang Hung, *Chung-kuo ku-ping-ch'i,* pp. 140–141; and *Ping-fa,* pp. 78–89. The Mohists were famous for their doctrine of not making distinctions in one's love for his fellow man. Under the direction of Mo-tzu (fl. 479–438 B.C.)—their founder and leader—they actively practiced their doctrine of opposing warfare, rushing to aid the defense of the besieged. See Robin D. S. Yates, "Siege Engines and Late Zhou Military Technology," in *Explorations in the History of Science and Technology*

in China (ed. Li Guohao et al.), Shanghai Chinese Classics Publishing House, Shanghai, 1982, pp. 409–451, for a discussion of the technology that appeared in this period. For the medieval period, which includes the T'ang (the era of the *Questions and Replies*), see Herbert Franke, "Siege and Defense of Towns in Medieval China," in *Chinese Ways in Warfare*, pp. 151–194.

52. Although early Chinese compound bows were extremely powerful, crossbows provided dramatically more formidable firepower; their strength and effective killing range generally increased over the centuries as their mechanisms were perfected. The earliest type was probably hand-cocked, using only arm strength. More powerful versions required leg strength, and the strongest used a rope attached to the waist to pull the sling back. (See Hsü Chung-shu, "I-she yü nu," pp. 435–438.) By the end of the Warring States period, crossbows had come into extensive use, although their strategic value was probably not exploited fully until the Han dynasty. Hand-held crossbows, which fired two bolts simultaneously, and repeating models (as well as repeating double-bolt models) dating from the Warring States period have now been excavated, reflecting the crossbow's technological sophistication and importance. (See Ch'en Yüeh-chün, "Chiang-ling Ch'u-mu ch'u-t'u shuang-shih ping-she lien-fa-nu yen-chiu," *WW* 1990, No. 5, pp. 89–96.) Larger, winch-powered models mounted on chariots or carriages, also capable of shooting multiple bolts, are described in the *Six Secret Teachings* and are discussed in the translation. (Also see Robin D. S. Yates, "Siege Engines and Late Zhou Military Technology," pp. 432–443.)

Tradition holds that the Yellow Emperor invented the crossbow, and Hsü Chung-shu, analyzing linguistic evidence, strongly believes that both the bow and crossbow are indigenous developments dating from pre-Shang times. (See Hsü Chung-shu, "I-she yü nu chih su-yüan chi kuan-yü tz'u-lei ming-wu chih k'ao-shih," pp. 417–418 and 438.) However, Hsü's classic view not withstanding, based on textual references and other linguistic evidence it appears the crossbow probably originated outside the central states area of China, perhaps in Ch'u or the southwest. (See Jerry Norman and Tsu-lin Mei, "The Austroasiatics in Ancient South China: Some Lexical Evidence," *MS* 32 [1976], pp. 293–294; Yang Hung, *Ku-ping-ch'i*, pp. 143–144; and Ch'en Yüeh-chün, "Lien-fa-nu," p. 96.) Remnants of crossbows with bronze trigger mechanisms have been found in tombs from the middle Warring States period, prompting scholars such as Kao Chih-hsi to argue for a much earlier (indigenous) invention—probably in the Spring and Autumn period—using wooden components. (See Kao Chih-hsi, "Chi Ch'ang-sha, Ch'ang-te ch'u-t'u nu-chi te Chan-kuo-mu—chien-t'an yu-kuan nu-chi, kung-shih te chi-ke wen-t'i," *WW* 1964, No. 6, pp. 41–44. Also see Ch'en Yüeh-chün, "Lien-fa-nu," p. 96. Note that as of this writing, no pre–Warring States crossbows have been discovered. See Hayashi's Minao's extensive, although dated, summary, *Chūgoku In-Shū jidai no buki*, pp. 301–330.) The first recorded tactical use appears to have been at the battle of Ma-ling in 341 B.C., as depicted in the *Shih-chi* and the text of the Sun Pin's *Ping-fa*. The *Spring and Autumn Annals of Wu and Yüeh* also contain numerous references to crossbows, but truly extensive employment probably began with the Han, who exploited their superior firepower and range.

53. See Appendix B for an annotated discussion of the cavalry in Chinese history.

54. The speed and mobility of the cavalry in all but the most impenetrable forests and marshes allowed the development of unorthodox tactics (*ch'i*) versus orthodox (*cheng*) methods. Although infantry forces can also be employed in unorthodox ways,

an essential aspect of the unorthodox is its unexpectedness, its exploitation of surprise, for which the cavalry is ideally suited. Sun-tzu is generally credited with advancing the idea of the unorthodox, and it is extensively discussed and expanded in the *Questions and Replies* (based on actual employment by T'ang T'ai-tsung and General Li in decisive battles when they were struggling to establish the T'ang). The *Six Secret Teachings* also analyzes the relative methods for employing infantry, chariot, and cavalry forces.

55. Iron was used extensively for the agricultural implements—generally manufactured and distributed under government monopoly—during the Warring States period. The Japanese scholar Sekino Takeshi has advanced the idea that cheap, readily available, mass-produced iron swords provided Ch'in's conscripted infantry forces their great killing power. (Cf. Sekino Takeshi, "Chūgoku shoki bunka no ikkōsatsu—dōtestsu katoki no kaimei ni yosete," *Shigaku zasshi,* Vol. 60, No. 10 [October 1951], pp. 867–907.) However, others strongly dispute his contention for a variety of reasons. First, the sword had always been a weapon of the nobility and was generally carried by officers rather than ordinary infantrymen. (Cf. Noel Barnard, "Did the Swords Exist," *EC* [1978–1979], pp. 62–63.) They would naturally have preferred the familiar elegance of the bronze weapon over the cruder iron sword. Second, bronze swords were probably still superior to early iron versions in the hands of the skilled warrior, and complex metal-working technology (such as layering with different alloys) produced very sharp, fine weapons. Third, few iron swords have been unearthed—even from the famous tombs of Ch'in Shih-Huang-ti, where most of the warriors are armed with bronze rather than iron weapons. (Cf. Noel Barnard, "Did the Swords Exist," p. 63; David N. Keightley, "Where Have All the Swords Gone?" *EC* 2 [1976], pp. 31–34.) Thus several scholars have concluded that the Han era marks the true ascension of iron weapons, with the bronze sword becoming an anachronism thereafter. (For a dissenting view, see Li Xueqin, *Eastern Zhou and Qin Civilizations,* Yale University Press, New Haven, 1985, chapter entitled "Iron Objects," pp. 315–329, who notes that China had cast iron, wrought iron, and steel by the Warring States era, which suggests a long prehistory in the Spring and Autumn period.)

56. See Wu Ch'i's biography in the translator's introduction to the *Wu-tzu* translation.

57. The battle of Ma-ling is apparently the first recorded conflict in which crossbows were employed. (There are also different versions regarding who exercised ultimate command—P'ang Chüan, who may have been killed at the earlier battle, or the imperial prince, who sallies forth with the home defense forces. General P'ang's character flaws and rashness were frequently cited by Chinese military analysts as evidence of the need for a constellation of virtues in any supreme commander.)

58. The complex process of analyzing language, concepts, and historical events to create a systematic textual chronology has been both complicated and simplified by the writings discovered in various tombs in recent decades. The detailed textual studies of Ch'ing dynasty scholars, although valuable for understanding the texts themselves, have led to conclusions that must now be reexamined and revised. Discussions of the provenance of the individual *Seven Military Classics* are found in each translator's introduction. For a general discussion, see Robin D. S. Yates, "New Light on Ancient Chinese Military Texts," *TP* 74 (1988), pp. 211–248.

T'ai Kung's Six Secret Teachings

Abbreviations of Frequently Cited Books

LTCC WCCS   *Liu-t'ao chih-chieh*, in *Ming-pen Wu-ching Ch'i-shu chih-chieh*, Vol. 2, Shih-ti chiao-yü ch'u-pan-she, Taipei, 1972.

LT CS   K'ung Te-ch'i, *Liu-t'ao ch'ien-shuo*, Chieh-fang-chün ch'u-pan-she, Peking, 1987.

TKLT CCCY   Hsü Pei-ken, *T'ai Kung Liu-t'ao chin-chu chin-i*, Shang-wu yin-shu-kuan, Taipei, 1976.

TKLT WCHC   *T'ai Kung Liu-t'ao*, in *Ch'ung-k'an Wu-ching hui-chieh*, Chung-chou Ku-chi ch'u-pan-she, Cheng-chou, 1989.

Notes to the Translator's Introduction

1. The tradition of Ch'i military studies requires a separate work; however, a brief discussion is found in the footnotes to the introductory section of the *Ssu-ma Fa*. (Also see T'ao Hsi-sheng, *Ping-fa san-shu*, Shih-huo ch'u-pan-she, Taipei, 1979, pp. 1–5, and "Chan-lüeh yüan-li yü ko-ming fan-kung te tao-lu," in *Ping-fa san-shu*, pp. 1–9; Hsü Pei-ken, *Chung-kuo kuo-fang ssu-hsiang-shih*, Chung-yang wu-kung-ying-she, Taipei, 1983, pp. 282–284.)

2. The T'ang imperial family's military heritage was particularly strong, and the early emperors valued the martial as much as or perhaps more than the civil. Therefore, they sanctioned the creation of separate, increasingly professional military forces and the establishment of a state temple honoring the T'ai Kung as an exemplary military figure and the progenitor of military studies. Confucians, who tended to denigrate the T'ai Kung as merely a military man rather than recognizing him as a Sage like Confucius or the Duke of Chou (despite historical records attesting to his unremitting promotion of essentially Confucian virtues), continually opposed such efforts. In their view the civil—the *li*—and concepts of virtue are all that should be required to govern well and tranquilize the realm. (They repeatedly cited Confucius's statement that he never studied military affairs [*Analects* XV:1] but ignored his famous assertion [preserved in his *Shih chi* biography] that both the civil and martial are necessary.) Eventually, they succeeded in having the state cult dismantled, although the T'ai Kung unofficially continued to be a patron figure for centuries. This unrealistic outlook no doubt greatly contributed to China's military weakness throughout the centuries, despite the empire's vast resources, technological achievements, and powerful administrative organization. (For an extensive discussion, see D. L. McMullen, "The Cult of Ch'i T'ai-kung and T'ang Attitudes to the Military," *T'ang Studies* 7 [1989], pp. 59–103; and T'ao Hsi-sheng, *Ping-fa san-shu*, pp. 1–4.)

3. Hsü Pei-ken's introduction to his modern translation particularly emphasizes the "revolutionary confrontation" aspect rather than a clash between two states. See *T'ai Kung Liu-t'ao chin-chu chin-i*, Shangwu yin-shu-kuan, Taipei, 1976, pp. 14–16.

4. See Hsü Pei-ken, *Chung-kuo kuo-fang ssu-hsiang-shih*, pp. 291–293. The Chou dynasty ruled in part through its avowed policy of cultural acculturation, transforming the diverse people within its domain through gradual assimilation (while absorb-

ing and integrating new characteristics themselves). The concept of the Central States and the Hua-Hsia identity arose with them (although the surviving states in the Warring States period still retained distinctive regional personalities and characteristics). For a general discussion, see Cho-yun Hsu and Katheryn M. Linduff, *Western Chou Civilization,* Yale University Press, New Haven, 1988, Chapters 4–6.

5. Historical materials from the Chou period and thereafter, such as the *Shih chi,* were clearly influenced by the effective propaganda efforts of the Chou both prior and subsequent to the conquest. Their vile portrait of the evil Shang ruler was amplified by later writers—especially the Confucians—for didactic purposes, although not without an occasional dissenting voice (for example, Tzu Kung, *Analects* XIX:20). This is not to deny that the Shang oppressed the people or that King Chou of the Shang was not a villain. Rather, it should simply be understood that the Chou's self-portrait depicting the cause of Virtue as naturally attracting allies and politically dominating the realm was underpinned in actuality by extensive military achievements and persuasive power.

6. The Shang's triumph over King Chieh, the last evil ruler of the Hsia, was traditionally portrayed in terms similar to those describing the Chou's conquest of the Shang, but much simplified. King T'ang—the founder of the Shang dynasty—cultivated his Virtue, pursued benevolent policies, and garnered his strength on the fringe of the Hsia empire until finally engaging in a decisive battle. There was even a sagely counterpart to the T'ai Kung, the famous minister I Yin, who may have created the indirect striking tactics that proved successful for the Shang. (See Hsü Peiken et al., *Chung-kuo li-tai chan-cheng-shih,* 18 vols., Li-ming, Taipei, 1976, revised edition, Vol. 1, pp. 49–53, and also the early chapters of the *Shang shu* [*Book of Documents*]. The *Shang shu* also portrays Shang dynasty kings acting as strong supporters of virtue and as punitive agents against the unrighteous.)

7. Although the parameters of the dynastic cycle postulate an essentially continuous decline in the power of the imperial house, with allowances for temporary resurgences, recently discovered historical materials indicate that the Shang kings continued to be vigorous monarchs, mounting military expeditions and conducting tours of inspection throughout the years. Even though the last ruler—who is recorded as having been enthroned for more than sixty years—considerably debauched the image of the king, earlier kings, such as Wu Ting, were both effective and powerful.

8. The archetypal seductress played an extensive but tragic role throughout Chinese history, with several infamous examples bringing the imperial house to ruin. Even the less famous seductresses were constant sources of tension because the almighty emperors—despite having numerous consorts, concubines, and other ladies in waiting—were easily persuaded by their favorites to grant state favors and administrative or military power to their own relatives, thereby weakening the imperial house and creating sources of dissension. The displacement of an old consort by a new beauty or the replacement of an heir also caused interminable strife and intrigue.

9. *Shih chi,* "Shang Annals," translated from *Shih-chi chin-chu,* Vol. 1, Shang-wu yin-shu-kuan, Taipei, 1979, p. 94.

10. Hou (ruler) Chi (millet) was one of the legendary deified figures traditionally credited with creating China's culture and civilization. He is identified particularly with agricultural developments, such as the domestication of wild grains, and is recorded in the "Chou Annals" as having been appointed minister of agriculture by Emperor Shun.

11. "Chou Annals," *Shih-chi chin-chu,* Vol. 1, p. 101. It should be noted that the Chou were already powerful before this confrontation with the other barbarians; therefore, the traditional account is obviously highly simplified.

12. Hsü Pei-ken, *Chung-kuo kuo-fang ssu-hsiang-shih,* pp. 274–275.

13. For further discussions of Shang-Chou relations, see Hsu and Linduff, *Western Chou Civilization,* pp. 41–49; and Herrlee G. Creel, *The Origins of Statecraft in China,* University of Chicago Press, Chicago, 1970, pp. 57–69.

King Wu Ting of the Shang is recorded as having conducted military campaigns against the Chou before they descended to the Wei River valley. Chi Li apparently acted on behalf of the Shang against troublesome tribes from the northwest quarter before being perceived as too great a threat himself. The fact that the Shang could command and imprison both Chi Li and King Wen is testimony of their regional power and the Chou's continued submission, even though Shang rulers could not completely control the outer quarters. Because both Chi Li and King Wen were married to Shang princesses and members of the Shang nobility also appear to have married women from the Chou royal house, marriage relations were another aspect of their political policies.

14. His detention is variously said to have lasted anywhere from one to six or seven years. During this period he reputedly devoted himself to serious contemplation, ordering the sixty-four hexagrams of the *I ching* and appending the Judgments—activities befitting a future cultural legend. (The texts for the individual hexagram lines are attributed to the Duke of Chou, one of his sons, and Confucius is closely identified with the book as well.) His reign, which began when he was fifty, is recorded in the *Shih chi* as having lasted fifty-five years; he died nine years after being released by the Shang. However, such great longevity (which he apparently shared with the T'ai Kung and the evil King Chou) is extremely problematic, particularly in an age in which people had short life expectancies. For discussions of the Shang and Chou chronologies, see, among others, David N. Keightley, "The *Bamboo Annals* and the Shang-Chou Chronology," *HJAS,* Vol. 38, No. 2 (1978), pp. 423–438; Edward J. Shaughnessy, "On the Authenticity of the *Bamboo Annals,*" *HJAS,* Vol. 46, No. 1 (1986), pp. 149–180; Chou Fa-kao, "Chronology of the Western Chou Dynasty," *Hsiang-kang Chung-wen Ta-hsüeh Chung-kuo Wen-hua Yen-chiu-so hsüeh-pao,* Vol. 4, No. 1 (1971), pp. 173–205; Ch'ü Wan-li, "Shih-chi Yin-pen-chi chi ch'i-t'o chi-lu-chung so-tsai Yin-Shang shih-tai te shih-shih," *Taiwan Ta-hsüeh wen-shih-che hsüeh-pao,* Vol. 14, No. 11 (1965), pp. 87–118; Jung Meng-yüan, "Shih-t'an Hsi-Chou chi-nien," *Chung-hua wen-shih lun-ts'ung* 1980, No. 1, pp. 1–21; Ch'ü Wan-li, "Hsi-Chou shih-shih kai-shu," *BIHP* 42 (1971), pp. 775–802; Tung Tso-pin, "Hsi-Chou nien-li-p'u," *BIHP* 23 (1951), pp. 681–760; and Ho Yu-ch'i, "Chou Wu-wang fa-Chou te nien-tai wen-t'i," *Chung-shan ta-hsüeh hsüeh-pao* 1981, No. 1, pp. 64–70.

15. Several Chinese military historians have stressed the importance of the location because it exposed them to constant military challenges. Not only did the Chou train for and mount military campaigns against their enemies, but they were also forced to always be prepared to instantly ward off sudden incursions. Their leaders, including the king, personally supervised them in the fields and directed their responses to such military emergencies. This experience nurtured unity, a strong spirit, and an unflinching commitment to battle. It also symbolizes the farmer-soldier ideal later bureaucrats felt characterized the practices of antiquity and came to be frequently cited whenever they sought to disparage the need for professional military men and studies. (However, as discussed in the general introduction, it should be remembered that at this time the

nobility rather than the peasants were the active members of the fighting forces.) See, for example, Hsü Pei-ken, *Chung-kuo kuo-fang ssu-hsiang-shih*, p. 276.

16. Career military men turned historians, such as Hsü Pei-ken, see the long preparatory period as not just providing the time necessary to cultivate Virtue and slowly develop the economic basis for a power state with a satisfied populace but also as being the minimum interval required to create—in accord with the T'ai Kung's strategy—the revolutionary military weapons that would permit the Chou to effect radical new strategies against their vastly superior enemies. General Hsü is a particularly strong advocate of the chariot's decisive importance at Mu-yeh, the first battle in which it was employed en masse. Based on his estimates, the Chou could probably not have constructed more than a score of chariots per year—particularly armored ones—and at least three thousand horses had to be bred and trained. Charioteers also had to become practiced in the requisite individual skills and coordinated in integrated battle tactics. Furthermore, a large number of bronze weapons had to be manufactured; thus the Chou became more skilled in metalworking techniques and developed their own styles of weapons. (See Hsü Pei-ken, *Chung-kuo kuo-fang ssu-hsiang-shih*, pp. 284–286, and *T'ai Kung Liu-t'ao chin-chu chin-i*, Shang-wu yin-shu-kuan, Taipei, 1976, pp. 14–26.)

17. According to the *Lü-shih Ch'un-ch'iu*, he was a *shih* (lowest rank of noble) of the Eastern I people. Ch'iang people with the Chiang surname apparently were early allies of the Chou after an even earlier period of conflict.

Recent scholars have questioned the veracity of the T'ai Kung's eastern origin. Yang Yün-ju, for example, noting the Chiang clan's early marriage relations with the Chou, concludes that both the Chiang and the Chou were originally members of the northwest barbarian peoples and that the Chiang did not venture eastward until after the Chou conquest. (See "Chiang-hsing te min-tsu ho Chiang T'ai-kung te ku-shih," in *Ku-shih pien* [ed. Ku Chieh-kang], Vol. 2, Shang-hai ku-chi, Shanghai, 1982 [original copyright 1930], pp. 113–117.)

18. In all the stories about the T'ai Kung found in the various Warring States and later writings, he is invariably portrayed as old, retired, and poor. For example, the *Shuo yüan* frequently uses his late, meteoric rise to power after an undistinguished life to illustrate that talent and merit alone are inadequate unless one meets the proper moment. One passage states, "When Lü Wang was fifty he sold food in Chi-chin; when he was seventy he butchered cows in Chao-ko; so if when he was ninety he commanded the army for the Son of Heaven, it was because he met King Wen." (*Shuo-yüan* CCCY, p. 581, and an additional reference on p. 562.) His "lands were inadequate to repay the cost of the seeds, (the yield from) his fishing inadequate to repay the cost of the nets, but for governing All under Heaven he had more than enough wisdom." (*Shuo-yüan* CCCY, p. 569.) "He was an old fellow whose wife had put him out, who had worked as a butcher's assistant in Chao-ko and as an inn employee in Chi-chin who welcomed guests." (*Shuo-yüan* CCCY, p. 234.) In the *Han-shih wai-chuan* he is laboring as a boatman when he encounters King Wen. (This incident is translated in James R. Hightower, *Han shih wai chuan*, Harvard University Press, Cambridge, 1952, pp. 140–142.)

19. The term "hegemon" does not appear until centuries after the events recorded in this biography, thus suggesting the dialogue is a late fabrication.

20. The story about how the T'ai Kung received his name is more than a little dubious; however, completely satisfactory explanations are lacking. He was apparently known by several names, perhaps depending on the recorder's perspective and location. "T'ai Kung" should refer to his enfeoffment as king of Ch'i and thus the state's official progenitor. "Lü" in "Lü Wang" probably refers to his place of origin, whereas Wang may have been his personal name; this is also the case for "Lü Shang." "Shih," in "Shih Shang-fu," perhaps referred to his command position, "T'ai Shih," rather than to his role as preceptor (*shih*) to Kings Wen and Wu (see note 21 below). "Shang-fu," or "Father Shang," may be an honorific referent from the two kings toward their army's commander in chief or perhaps their strategist-adviser. (See Yang Yün-ju, "Chiang-hsing," pp. 109–112.)

21. The *Shih chi* biography states he was appointed as a *shih*, which generally means "commander" but can also include didactic functions, as in "preceptor" or "teacher." Clearly, the T'ai Kung's role was far more encompassing and was related more to strategy than command. Historical references apart from the *Shih chi* do not record him as being commander in chief (normally a role the Chou king should personally have filled), but he seems to have commanded a force at the battle of Mu-yeh and led the initial charge to instigate the conflict. (See the "Chou Annals" in the *Shih chi*. Also note his superior role in the command of forces securing the area after the conquest in the *I-Chou shu*.)

Traditional sources indicate that subsequently, King Wu married the T'ai Kung's daughter and that she became one of the ten great ministers of his reign. (See Wei Ju-lin, *Chung-kuo li-tai ming-chiang chi ch'i yung-ping ssu-hsiang*, Chung-yang wen-wu kung-ying-she, Taipei, 1981, p. 2.)

22. The practice of traveling about to seek receptive rulers on whom to exercise one's persuasion is identified with the Warring States period and should be considered anachronistic. However, he may have traveled about in disguise, trying to perceive a single opportunity, or he may simply have been exceptional.

23. Mencius twice mentions that the T'ai Kung dwelled on the coast of the Eastern Sea to avoid King Chou (*Mencius*, IVA:14, VIIA:22) and also refers to him and San-i Sheng as having known King Wen (*Mencius*, VIIB:38). The *Hsin shu* mentions him "coming from the sea coast to give his allegiance" (*Hsin shu*, 10:9B).

24. Because the concept of unorthodox (*ch'i*) stratagems is attributed primarily to Sun-tzu, it is interesting to note the *Shih chi's* appraisal of the T'ai Kung's achievements in this regard. (This concept is discussed in the translator's introduction and notes to the *Art of War* translation.)

25. For a brief discussion of *ch'üan*, see the notes to the *Art of War*.

26. These conquests and alliances secured their base of operations and allowed them to expand toward the Shang domain. For further discussion, see Hsu and Linduff, *Western Chou Civilization*, pp. 89–92.

27. This very famous sentence is cited repeatedly by the T'ai Kung's detractors to support their contention that Virtue alone, rather than the T'ai Kung's despicable machinations, was enough to win the empire for the Chou.

28. Whether "Tsang-ssu" refers to a green, nine-headed river animal (originally based on a rhinoceros?) and is being invoked as a spirit to lend power to the oath or scare the men or refers to an officer for the boats is the subject of speculation.

29. The question has frequently been raised as to why King Wu did not immediately lead an attack on the Shang, particularly when they could have capitalized on the element of surprise. Various explanations have been offered, among them that King Wu felt his strength and preparations were still insufficient or that perhaps he had not expected such an overwhelming response and had neither supplies nor plans to support an attack. (Although concrete plans could have been formulated in the intervening two years, little more could have been done to dramatically alter the balance of forces.) Other suggestions include General Hsü's belief that the Chou did not bring their chariots to the assembly but concealed them for explosive use in the actual engagement and that this rally represented a sort of dress rehearsal. King Chou's minions certainly reported the events in detail, including King Wu's public acknowledgement—despite startling support to the contrary—that a subject should not attack his ruler. This sustained King Chou's complacency and arrogance—the Shang Annals indicate his disdain for any Chou threat to his power and his certainty that he would continue to enjoy the sanction of Heaven—and set the stage for the next meeting, which was then similarly regarded. King Wu thus was able to advance swiftly by an indirect southern route (fording the frozen river in an area supposedly well-known to the T'ai Kung who, according to one source, had sold rice there) and approach the capital before King Chou could muster all his forces and recall his expeditionary forces in the south. (See Hsü Pei-ken, *Chung-kuo kuo-fang ssu-hsiang-shih*, pp. 285–286, and *Chung-kuo li-tai chang-cheng-shih*, Vol. 1, pp. 74–76; and the statements attributed to King Chou in the "Shang Annals.")

30. The murder of Pi-kan and other events (such as the high officials fleeing to Chou with the sacrificial musical instruments) no doubt precipitated the king's decision to attack Shang.

The T'ai Kung's rejection of bad weather and ill portents is remarkable for an age obsessed with such beliefs. In his view, even though they claimed the Mandate of Heaven, how could the signs be auspicious for a ruler about to attack his sovereign? (Note that this incident, with additional dialogue, also appears in the *Han-shih wai-chuan*. See Hightower's translation, *Han shih wai chuan*, pp. 89–90.)

Although the T'ai Kung was obviously daring and resolute, some scholars have cited such statements as evidence that this material is fabricated because such pragmatic, unmystical views were not common until the Warring States period, when the military classics began to reject the influence of portents and signs. However, although there are serious doubts about the veracity of the details, this opinion perhaps too conveniently assumes a nonexistent homogeneity of thought and recklessly denies the possibility of the exceptional.

31. The "Shang Annals" records the manner of the king's death rather differently: "On *chia-tzu* King Chou's troops were defeated. King Chou raced back in and mounted the Deer Tower. He clothed himself in his treasures and jade, went into the fire and died. King Wu of the Chou subsequently chopped off Chou's head, hanging it up with a white pennon" (*Shih-chi chin-chu*, Vol. 1, p. 96). The *I-Chou shu* account in the "Shih-fu" chapter similarly records that King Chou immolated himself, whereas in the "Chou Annals" King Wu symbolically shoots King Chou with three arrows, then decapitates him.

32. The nine great bronze cauldrons symbolized imperial authority, and possessing them was deemed a matter of great consequence in establishing dynastic power and legitimacy.

33. An analysis and discussion of the battle of Mu-yeh merits a separate chapter. Among the many unresolved questions, perhaps the most important concerns the relative strength of the respective forces. According to the *Shih chi* and some other accounts, the Shang fielded seven hundred thousand men, whereas the Chou only had three hundred chariots, three thousand Tiger Guards, and forty-five thousand armored soldiers. The number for the Shang is extremely suspect and is subject to various explanations: It may be a general expression of size; an error for what should be seventy thousand or one hundred seventy thousand; or the total troops of the entire Shang forces, including all their allies—many of whom were already committed in other areas. The numbers for the Chou seem more reasonable but in fact may only refer to their core forces without including those of their allies. (Clearly, however, the forces of the Chou were vastly outnumbered by those of the Shang.) Depending on the source consulted, the actual battle either required little expenditure of forces—with the Shang troops offering minimal resistance to their king's morally superior enemy—or the carnage flooded the fields with blood. (Both the *Shang shu* and the *Shih chi* assert that the Shang troops "inverted their weapons" and otherwise offered little resistance.) The *I-Chou shu* lists 177,779 killed and 310,230 captured as a result of the entire campaign, which are astounding figures. (For brief discussions, see Edward L. Shaughnessy, "'New' Evidence on the Zhou Conquest," pp. 57–61.)

Notwithstanding the above evidence, the actual battle appears to have quickly turned into a rout and have ended within a few hours of the initial clash. Among the factors favoring the Chou was their commitment to the cause and consequent great fighting spirit, in contrast to the apparently reluctant, despondent Shang troops. The Chou forces were thoroughly trained and prepared, whereas the Shang were said to be deficient in both respects. The Chou unleashed an initial charge of one hundred elite stalwarts, headed by the T'ai Kung, and immediately followed with a chariot attack that moved swiftly across the plains. The combined effect both startled and terrified the Shang troops, who had not previously encountered massed chariot assaults. (Skeptics, however, such as Hsu and Linduff [*Western Chou Civilization*, pp. 81–88] believe superior infantry played the critical role and that the chariots were unimportant.) King Chou reportedly turned and fled, and his command immediately disintegrated. Because the Chou had strongly publicized (through charges possibly similar to those in the *Shang shu*) that King Chou—rather than the people—was the designated enemy, any compulsion to fight on the part of the Shang was seriously undermined. The battle and choice of battlefield were forced on the Shang because the Chou had crossed to the south—avoiding the bulwark of standing Shang defenses—and swiftly advanced. Finally, the Chou had prepared in secret, established a series of power bases, and either neutralized or gained the allegiance of states and peoples along the attack route and around the Shang. Although the Shang had obviously engineered their own self-destruction by alienating the people and eliminating effective administrators, the Chou may also have used many of the measures advocated in the Cultural Warfare chapter of the *Six Secret Teachings* to further subvert them. (For general discussions of these factors, see Chang Shao-sheng and Liu Wen-ch'an, eds., *Chung-kuo ku-tai chan-cheng t'ung-lan,* 2 vols., Ch'ang-cheng ch'u-pan-she, Peking, 1985, pp. 7–10; Li Chen, *Chung-kuo li-tai chan-cheng shih-hua,* Li-ming, Taipei, 1985, pp. 13–19; Hsü Pei-ken, *Chung-kuo kuo-fang ssu-hsiang-shih,* pp. 282–290, and *Chung-kuo li-tai chan-cheng-shih,* Vol. 1, pp. 71–84.)

34. Being in accord with local customs while still influencing the people is one of the keystones of the T'ai Kung's military thought and is consonant with postconquest Chou policies. Its wisdom was proven subsequently by numerous historical incidents, including military disasters.

35. These measures are all associated historically with the state of Ch'i and with its heritage of Legalist thought.

36. King Wu died about two years after the conquest, providing an opportunity for his brothers—in alliance with the Shang prince who was retained in heavily circumscribed, essentially symbolic power—to revolt. The Duke of Chou together with the Duke of Shao and possibly the T'ai Kung required three years to subdue the dissident peoples.

37. This charge appears in the *Tso chuan*. Cf. Legge, *The Chinese Classics: The Ch'un Ts'ew with The Tso Chuen*, Vol. 5, pp. 139–140.

38. "Expansive" should probably be understood as outgoing, energetic, active.

39. "The Hereditary House of Ch'i T'ai Kung," *Shih chi*, chüan 32, translated from *Shih-chi chin-chu*, Vol. 3, pp. 1502–1506, 1535.

40. The authenticity of *Shang shu* chapters is much debated; the consensus is that some portions may be early Chou material but that the bulk represents later composition.

41. See, for example, Edward L. Shaughnessy, " 'New' Evidence on the Zhou Conquest," pp. 60–61.

42. See Sarah Allan, "The Identities of Taigong Wang in Zhou and Han Literature," *MS*. 30 (1972–1973), pp. 57–99. Allan concludes that the T'ai Kung commanded the forces in the famous battles and was also accorded a special status in ritual affairs that was essentially equal to that of the royal clan members (p. 67). Her conclusion is based in part on early *Book of Odes* verses, which she notes as the only Western Chou references to the T'ai Kung (p. 59). However, Shaughnessy's article has proven the authenticity of the "Shih-fu" chapter of the *I-Chou shu* (which is not mentioned in Allan's article), and additional contemporary evidence shows that the T'ai Kung commanded troops and was entrusted with critical security operations. (See Shaughnessy, " 'New' Evidence on the Zhou Conquest," pp. 57 and 67. Also see Ku Chieh-kang, "I-Chou-shu 'Shih-fu' p'ien chiao-chu hsieh-ting yü p'ing-lun," *Wen-shih* 2 [1963], pp. 1–42. Ku similarly concludes that the "Shih-fu" chapter is an authentic record and provides glosses on the passage referring to the T'ai Kung on pages 6–7 of his article. It should also be noted that Allan's article states that the authentic historical material always refers to the T'ai Kung as "Shih Shang-fu" ("Taigong Wang," p. 60). However, in the *I-Chou shu* he is referred to as "T'ai Kung Wang," and in the first chapter of the recently discovered bamboo strips of the *Six Secret Teachings* he is called "Lü Shang." (See Lo Fu-i, "Lin-i Han-chien kai-shu," *WW*. 1974, No. 2, p. 33.)

43. Allan, "Taigong Wang," pp. 68–72. The Chiang, as previously discussed, were allies of the Chou and furnished troops in the decisive battles. (Unfortunately, this explanation is not entirely satisfactory because it fails to account adequately for the Ta'i Kung's early, apparently menial status—one hardly befitting an important ally. Allan suggests that the motif of recognition may underlie these legends [see discussion, pp. 89–98], and it is an important theme in Chinese thought. For example, see Eric Henry, "The Motif of Recognition in Early China," *HJAS*, Vol. 47, No. 1 [1987], pp. 5–30;

and Ralph D. Sawyer, *Knowing Men*, Kaofeng, Taipei, 1979. Henry only mentions the T'ai Kung in a footnote.)

44. It need hardly be mentioned that all of the contemporary military historians in both Taiwan and the People's Republic of China whose works have been cited in the notes above not only accept the fact of the T'ai Kung's existence but also attribute the major strategic and command role to him. Accordingly, they tend to see his thoughts as being largely preserved in the *Six Secret Teachings,* even though they have either been much revised over the centuries or were actually composed at a late date. (Western scholars, such as Hsu and Linduff, generally tend to ignore him altogether, although in his *Origins of Statecraft* [pp. 343–344] Creel posits his authenticity.)

References to the T'ai Kung are found throughout pre-Han writings—such as *Mencius,* Sun-tzu's *Art of War, Hsün-tzu, Han Fei-tzu, Lü-shih ch'un-ch'iu, Huai-nan tzu, Kuo yü,* and *Shuo yüan.* Extensive dialogues attributed to the T'ai Kung and King Wu also appear in the *Shuo yüan,* and several pages of quotations are preserved in the *T'ung tien.* That his historical authenticity has been doubted seems remarkable and perhaps symbolizes much about the nature of thought in China.

45. It is a fundamental Confucian teaching that without adequate material welfare, the development of moral behavior cannot be expected (see *Mencius,* 1A7, 3A3). Although the Legalists stressed enriching the state to make it powerful and nurturing a robust population that had the energy to fight, the military thinkers generally seem to represent a synthesis of both positions. (But see K'ung Te-ch'i's views on these policies as reflective of Legalist thought, LT CS, pp. 27, 64–65.)

46. The intent of these introductory sections is simply to provide convenient summaries of the main thoughts and principles that may act as guides in reading the text. No abstracted quotations are provided because the issues should be readily apparent in the translated material. Occasional footnotes raise additional contextual issues, but in general the introduction and explication of philosophical thought and its relationship to the material found in the *Seven Military Classics* must be left for separate works.

47. The attainment of this idealized objective is synonymous with concretely embodying Virtue. Some states will revere the aspect of Virtue; others will respect the military power it entails and therefore refrain from aggressive actions. (Unmentioned and apparently inconceivable is the possibility that yet others will greedily plot the subjugation and seizure of such a rich objective with a well-ordered populace.)

48. The universal implementation of punishments is a hallmark of Legalist thought—much in contrast to the oft-cited, simplistic reduction of the Confucian position on the idea that punishments should not extend up to men of rank nor the *li* (forms of propriety) down to the common man (see Book I of the *Li chi*). However, Lord Shang's draconian spirit is markedly absent from the *Six Secret Teachings*—evidence that, as Chang Lieh suggests, the work is an amalgamation of Confucian, Taoist, Legalist, and other viewpoints. (Cf. "*Liu-t'ao* te ch'eng-shu chi ch'i nei-jung," *Li-shih yen-chiu* 3 [1981], pp. 125–126.)

49. Such preparedness especially reflects the preoccupation of sedentary, agrarian civilizations with sudden incursions by highly mobile, mounted, nomadic steppe peoples as well as the standing threat of surprise invasions by belligerent states. It also mirrors the Chou's original position in the midst of barbarian territory, perhaps contributing to the heritage of Ch'i military thought and possibly being the remote origin of this view.

50. Wu Ju-sung, in his preface to the LT CS, and K'ung Te-ch'i view the initial secret teachings of the civil and martial as measures designed to concretely realize Sun-tzu's dictum to attack and thwart the enemy's plans, to achieve victory without fighting. This objective can best be attained by strengthening the state and the military through the measures discussed in the Civil and Martial Secret Teachings and integrating them into the state's grand strategy. Accordingly, the policies and practices for which orthodox Confucians condemned the *Six Secret Teachings* are necessary steps in defeating an enemy without suffering serious losses and even in making it practical to attack a superior foe. (K'ung believes this reflects the historical background of the Chou-Shang conflict.) (See LT CS, Preface [pp. 1–3], and pp. 25–27, 82–86.)

51. The text thus reflects the rise of the professional general as a totally independent field commander, as discussed in the general introduction. In this regard the general's appointment ceremony can therefore be seen as the culmination of a concept first articulated by Sun-tzu and considered in varying degrees in the other *Seven Military Classics.*

52. K'ung Te-ch'i points out that according to the *Six Secret Teachings,* the principal quality required for a general was loyalty, which differs significantly from previous formulations that stressed courage or wisdom. He believes this reflects the late Warring States composition date of the text, an epoch in which war had become extremely complex—using many different weapons and tactics—and generals had become extraordinarily powerful. In a world of spies, intrigue, and massive forces, a disloyal general could easily seize the rulership for himself or equally doom the state to extinction (see LT CS, pp. 118–120).

53. Chapter 18, "The King's Wings," is the first exposition of a detailed military organization with specialized functions. This chapter reflects the highly advanced nature of combat in the late Warring States.

54. Attempts to objectively classify battlefield situations, analyze the enemy, and predict the outcome of engagements assuredly began with the rise of organized combat in antiquity. The first recorded systematic efforts are found in Sun-tzu's characterizations, but the other *Seven Military Classics* also contain similar situational descriptions and tactical suggestions. However, those found in the *Six Secret Teachings* are not only far more extensive and detailed but also differ fundamentally in reflecting the complexities of large-scale mobile warfare. Particularly noteworthy are the exposition and application of separate principles for the three types of forces—cavalry, infantry, and chariot—depending on terrain, battlefield conditions, and composition of the enemy. Mobility and the use of *ch'i* (unorthodox) tactics are particularly emphasized and as K'ung Te-ch'i notes, probably reflect the results of significant battles that occurred in the fourth and third centuries B.C. wherein smaller numbers and weaker forces decisively defeated superior opposition (see LT CS, pp. 172–180). Clearly, the period in which armies first deployed then engaged in either individual or massed combat had long passed.

55. Material on siege techniques and city assault is cited as evidence of the lateness of the text, as noted below, because of precursors in *Mo-tzu* and Sun Pin's *Military Methods.*

56. As reported in the preface, the *Seven Military Classics* presently enjoy great popularity throughout Asia, often in readily accessible vernacular paperback translations and editions. Certain principles have also been consciously adopted by U.S. and

European military planners, such as in the U.S. "Air-Land Battle 2000" doctrine (which emphasizes indirect assault); copies of Sun-tzu's *Art of War* were issued to U.S. marines serving in the 1991 Middle East conflict. However, deception and surprise have generally been neglected by the West in favor of frontal assault, attrition, and technological sophistication. For insightful discussions, see Ephraim Kam, *Surprise Attack*, Harvard University Press, Cambridge, 1988; and Michael Dewar, *The Art of Deception in Warfare*, David and Charles, New York, 1989.

57. Chang Lieh, "*Liu-t'ao* te ch'eng-shu chi ch'i nei-jung," p. 122.

58. The *Han shu* "Treatise on Literature" lists a work in the Confucian category entitled *Chou-shih liu-t'ao*, or *Six Cases of Chou History*. Although the meaning of the character *t'ao* in this title is also "bowcase," it is a completely different character from the *t'ao* in the *Six Secret Teachings* (see Karlgren, *GSR*, entry 1046C). Chang Lieh, among others, disagrees with Yen's identification of the two works as identical. (See "*Liu-t'ao*," p. 123; Ch'ü Wan-li, *Hsien-Ch'in wen-shih tzu-liao k'ao-pien*, Lien-ching, Taipei, 1983, p. 479.)

59. Karlgren, *GSR* 1078G, defines it as "to wrap, cover," whereas Morohashi (entry 43189) and the *Chung-wen ta-ts'u-tien* (entry 44153) add the extended meanings of covering a bow or sword, bowcase and scabbard, and storing away. What is stored away, of course, is also concealed. (This character is apparently more recent than the one noted above, leading to the conclusion that the title could not have existed in the T'ai Kung's era.)

60. Okada Osamu, *Rikutō, Sanryaku*, Meitoku shuppansha, Tokyo, 1979, p. 7.

61. See Li Chiu-jui, *Chung-kuo chün-shih ssu-hsiang-shih*, Shun-hsien ch'u-pan kung-ssu, Taipei, 1978, p. 101. Modern scholarship generally reaches the same conclusion, but on systematic evidence. For example, Robin D. S. Yates notes the likely composition date as the late fourth to early third century B.C. ("New Light on Ancient Chinese Military Texts," p. 224).

62. For numerous examples of this view, see the passages collected on pages 791–797 of the *Wei-shu t'ung-k'ao* (Chang Hsin-ch'eng, ed.), Shangwu yin-shu-kuan, Taipei, 1970 (reprint, original edition, 1939). Among them, only Ts'ui Shu points out that in antiquity, the civil and martial were balanced and were viewed as equally necessary and appropriate (p. 796). However, he still finds the concepts and language of the book inferior—unworthy of a figure such as the historical T'ai Kung, who is cast in the role of major adviser. (Also see Hsü Pei-ken, *Liu-ta'o*, pp. 17–18.)

63. This appears to be Hsü Pei-ken's position at various points in the introduction to his modern Chinese translation, *T'ai Kung Liu-t'ao chin-chu chin-i* (see pages 6–7, 18, and 31). Also see his *Chung-kuo kuo-fang ssu-hsiang-shih*, p. 283.

64. Most of the military writings cited in note 30 above adhere to this view (for example, Li Chiu-jui, *Chung-kuo chün-shih ssu-hsiang-shih*, pp. 101–102). The question of accretion and loss is too complex to be considered within the scope of a note. However, in his "Treatise on Literature" included in the dynastic history of the Former Han (written in the Later Han), Pan Ku noted three writings associated with the T'ai Kung: "Plans" in eighty-one sections; "Words," or "Sayings," in seventy-one sections; and "Military," or "Weapons," in eighty-five sections, for a very large total of two hundred thirty-seven sections. The present *Six Secret Teachings* only contains sixty sections or chapters, although many possible remnants are scattered about in other works. Even though a partial text has been recovered from a Han tomb, textual reduc-

tions and losses apparently continued after the Han dynasty as well. (Compare the *Ch'ün-shu chih-yao* and also Wang Chung-min, *Tun-huang ku-chi hsü-lu,* Shang-wu yin-shu-kuan, Peking, 1958, p. 150. Also see Gustav Haloun, "Legalist Fragments, Part 1: Kuan-tsi 55 and Related Texts," *AM* NS, Vol. 2, No. 1 [1951–1952], pp. 85–120.) Hsü Pei-ken, who studied the text extensively for at least two decades, has speculated about the possible fate of these books. First, the military writings perhaps formed the basis for the *Six Secret Teachings,* although some more general, historically oriented materials have been included. The chapters in "Plans" may have become the essence of the *Yin-fu ching,* another work associated with his name, which is traditionally thought to have been handed down eventually through Kuei Ku-tzu to Su Ch'in. Finally, the remaining work, "Words"—which may have been a record of his pronouncements while he was ruler of Ch'i—could have been preserved by Ch'i state historians and passed down within the state to ultimately comprise the basis of the *Three Strategies of Huang-shih Kung.* (This reconstruction is not generally accepted by Western scholars. For details, see Hsü Pei-ken, TKLT CCCY, pp. 27–31.)

65. See Ch'ü Wan-li, *Hsien-Ch'in wen-shih,* p. 479; Chang Lieh, *"Liu-t'ao,"* pp. 123–124. A number of reports have been published in *Wen wu,* among the earliest being Lo Fu-i, "Lin-i Han-chien kai-shu," pp. 32–33; and Hsü Ti, "Lüeh-t'an Lin-i Yin-chüeh-shan Han-mu ch'u-t'u te ku-tai ping-shu ts'an-chien," *WW* 1974, No. 2, p. 29. K'ung Te-ch'i notes that an additional copy was recovered from another tomb in 1973 (LT CS, p. 11).

66. For examples, see the preface to LT CS, pp. 2–3, and examples cited in criticisms found in the *Wei-shu t'ung-k'ao,* pp. 792–797.

67. Numerous references to iron weapons that flourished only from the middle of the Warring States period, including arrowheads and iron caltrops, and to such sophisticated weapons as the multiple arrow repeating crossbow inevitably consign the text to the late Warring States period.

68. Although several chapters are held to be expansions of Sun-tzu's ideas, the most frequently cited source work is the *Wu-tzu.* Several other books are also mentioned as the origins for passages and concepts, including the *Wei Liao-tzu,* but serious study of their interrelationship has hardly begun. (Selected attributions are cited in notes to the individual chapters. See *Wei-shu t'ung-k'ao,* pp. 792–797.) The *Three Strategies* quotes from the *Six Secret Teachings,* or perhaps both quote from an earlier prototype text of the T'ai Kung's thought, such as the "Military" writings.

Among the more important so-called "borrowed" concepts are unorthodox tactics, mobility, the concept of a general, manipulating *ch'i,* and classifying terrains with appropriate tactics. Many passages in the various *Military Classics* are very similar and several even identical; however, the majority appear to represent discussions of essential topics in a common conceptual language, no doubt based on textual materials accessible to all these thinkers. Extensive comparative study is clearly required before the question of priorities and borrowing within the military writings can be even tentatively settled.

Conceptually, the *Six Secret Teachings* clearly falls into the late Warring States philosophical milieu. (An extended analysis is beyond the scope of this book; however, for brief discussions see LT CS, pp. 6–11; and Chang Lieh, *"Liu-t'ao,"* pp. 124–126.) A *Liu-t'ao* sentence frequently cited by skeptics as proving the book's late Han or even T'ang dynasty composition is found in Chapter 13, "Opening Instructions," and in other chapters as well: "All under Heaven is not the property of one man but of All under Heaven." Because it also appears in the *Lü-shih ch'un-ch'iu,* an eclectic work that dates to the late third century B.C., critics claim the *Liu-t'ao* authors must have copied it. However, this is simply an assumption posited as fact, and there is no independent, concrete evidence for such an assertion. Instead, it seems likely that this was a saying commonly bandied about in the third century B.C. when such concepts were flourishing. Thus in our opinion, although it is correct to date the *Six Secret Teachings* to this period on both internal and contextual grounds, dogmatic assertions about the direction of borrowing are extremely suspect (cf. LT CS, pp. 9–10).

69. Ch'ü Wan-li notes that because both the *Wu-tzu* and the *Wei Liao-tzu* are held to be forgeries, the question of borrowing remains open. (*Hsien-Ch'in wen-shih tzu-liao k'ao-pien,* p. 479. However, note that the *Wei Liao-tzu* was also recovered from the Han tomb, proving it, too, existed early in the Han, which is contrary to previous opinion.)

70. Also see the notes to the translator's introduction of the *Three Strategies of Huang-shih Kung* for further discussion in conjunction with the other writings attributed to the T'ai Kung.

71. Chang Lieh is the most visible proponent of this view. See "*Liu-t'ao* te ch'eng-shu chi ch'i nei-jung," p. 124, and his brief section in Cheng Liang-shu, ed., *Hsü Wei-shu t'ung-k'ao,* Hsüeh-sheng shu-chü, Taipei, 1984, pp. 1595–1597. In contrast, Hsü Pei-ken (TKLT CCCY, pp. 29–31) believes the *Three Strategies* was in fact the work passed along to Chang Liang and that it crystalized his intentions to overthrow the Ch'in rather than just seek personal revenge.

72. For example, see Hsü Pei-ken, *Liu-t'ao,* pp. 16–19. However, K'ung Te-ch'i classifies the first three together because they focus on planning for warfare, whereas only the last three fall under the rubric of tactical discussions (see LT CS, p. 152). K'ung offers extensive analyses of each of the various teachings, although with no speculation as to the significance of the last four names. Useful but brief overviews are also provided in *Ping-fa,* pp. 104–107.

73. This is seen by some contemporary historians as expounding a concrete program for attaining Sun-tzu's nebulous objective of unifying the people with the ruler (*Ping-fa,* p. 104).

74. See note 50 above.

Notes to the Text

1. Emended from Sage Emperor Yü to Sage Emperor Shun, based on history and Liu Yin's correction (LTCC WCCS, I:3A).

2. The *chün-tzu,* translated here as "True Man of Worth," which reflects the Confucian concept of the "perfected man" as embodying the dimensions of the ideal—including the moral and political ideal. (Originally, *chün-tzu* referred to a ruler's son and eventually designated any "gentleman" of aristocratic birth; but Confucius preempted it as a vehicle for concretely expressing the critical virtues, and it underwent further sophisticated philosophical expansion thereafter. As thus understood, the passage obviously postdates the early Confucians.)

3. Fishing may be understood as an analogy for weighing, reflecting the primary use of the term "*ch'üan*"—to weigh or balance (translated as "authority" in this passage). Depending on the size of the bait, the fisherman can entice and control larger fish.

4. *Chün-tzu,* "True Men of Worth," should not form parties or cliques, according to Confucian orthodoxy. However, when the world is in turmoil, they spontaneously gather together out of sympathy for All under Heaven, and thus the enterprise of revolution may be born.

5. *Jen,* without doubt one of the two defining virtues of Confucianism, has been variously translated as "benevolence," "true humanity," and "human-ness."

6. Perhaps an echo of Sun-tzu's "Vacuity (emptiness) and Substance."

7. Although the passage appears to discuss Yao's personal practices, all of which express the spirit and ideals found in many sections of the *Tao Te Ching,* by implication, of themselves the populace equally embraced these values and customs. Thus, the passage could well be translated more generally—"they did not adorn themselves"—as some contemporary Chinese translators have done.

8. Or possibly, "tranquilized their hearts."

9. The sentence in brackets has dropped out of the Ming edition and is restored from the Sung version.

10. The *li*—"forms of etiquette," or "forms of propriety"—were one of the cornerstones of Confucian thought and the foundation for hierarchical social organization and interaction. Far more than simply ritual forms or practices of etiquette, they both defined and reflected human relationships and directed as well as constrained the expression of human emotions.

11. By effectively confining each of the three treasures to its own area, its members were less likely to be distracted and contaminated by external stimuli and thus were not tempted to abandon their own occupations. (From the Legalist perspective, they would also be easier to monitor and control.)

12. This dictum is closely associated with Legalist thinkers but is commonly found in eclectic works as well as in the military writings. Normally, the "handles of state" are rewards and punishments, the means by which to wield authority and control power.

13. The concept of material goods being critical to the establishment and maintenance of family relations represents an extension of the generally acknowledged Confucian idea that attaining morality and harmony becomes difficult without minimal material sustenance.

14. This is the military corollary to not loaning the handles of state to other men.

15. Out of the darkness and secrecy, overt (yang) actions to overthrow the government suddenly manifest themselves. However, for the enterprise to prove effective, a true leader must appear to direct it along the proper path. (The history of China constantly witnessed the unfolding of such tragic dramas, with few centuries ever enjoying the tranquility associated with its glorious history.)

16. Several commentators understand this sentence as referring to those the ruler employs, but the scope clearly includes the entire populace. (Cf. TKLT CCCY, p. 72; LT CS, p. 53; and Okada Osamu, *Rikutō, Sanryaku,* Meitoku shuppansha, Tokyo, 1979, p. 45.)

17. Bravados, or "knights-errant," gradually appeared in the Warring States period; they became a socially and politically disruptive factor but also captured the imagination of the populace and furnished the material from which numerous romantic stories came to be fashioned. (For background, see James Liu, *The Chinese Knighterrant,* University of Chicago Press, Chicago, 1967.) Their mention further attests to the Warring States composition of the text.

18. The concept of *ch'i,* integral to discussions in many spheres—including philosophy, medicine, metaphysics, and science—is fundamental to the enterprise of military action. *Ch'i*—often identified with and translated as "spirit" or "morale"—is in fact the basis of both, being the essential energy of life, the "pneuma" or "vital breath" that circulates within the body. The military thinkers understood the difficulty of forcing men to enter battle and engage in combat, of compelling them to kill other men, and identified *ch'i* as the component whose development and surge made such actions possible. Sun-tzu, whose work follows the *Six Secret Teachings* in our chosen translation sequence, was apparently the first to realize and describe the critical role of spirit and courage in combat; he described the danger in terms of the ebb and flow of *ch'i.* The other military classics all consider ways to develop, manipulate, and ensure the proper combative spirit, the *ch'i* of their men and armies. Among the philosophers, Mencius is especially known for the cultivation of overflowing *ch'i,* although his conception differed significantly from that of the military thinkers.

The definitions, dimensions, and dynamics of *ch'i* are quite complex, entailing both metaphysical and psychological aspects. Although there are subordinate discussions in the secondary literature, the only two monographs that seriously consider the history and nature of the concept are both in Japanese: Onozawa Seiichi, Fukunaga Mitsuji, and Yamanoi Yu, eds., *Ki no shisō,* Tokyo Daigaku shuppansha, Tokyo, 1978; and Kuroda Yoshiko, *Ki no kenkyū,* Tokyo Bijustsu, Tokyo, 1977.

19. The concept of name and reality matching each other is associated primarily with the great Legalist synthesis propounded by Han Fei-tzu, a late Warring States philosopher, but it apparently originated with Shen Pu-hai. (For background, see Herrlee G. Creel, *Shen Pu-hai,* University of Chicago Press, Chicago, 1974, and "The Meaning of *Hsing-ming,*" in Søren Egerod and Else Glahn International Booksellers, *Studia Serica Bernhard Karlgren Dedicata,* Copenhagen, 1959, pp. 199–211.)

20. Hsü Pei-ken (TKLT CCCY) places this chapter at the start of the Martial Secret Teaching as Chapter 12.

21. The "subtle" (as discussed in *Questions and Replies*), or the "vital point," as employed by Wu Ch'i in the *Wu-tzu,* rather than just "opportune time" or "opportunity." (See note 32, Book I, *Questions and Replies.*)

22. All tactics advocated by Sun-tzu in the *Art of War.*

23. Another famous tactical principle from Sun-tzu (*Art of War,* Chapter 6, "Vacuity and Substance.")

24. An image common to and perhaps borrowed from Chapter 11, "Nine Terrains," of the *Art of War.*

25. The translation follows Liu Yin's understanding of "from" in parallel for each political level; otherwise, the sentences would become contradictory. Thus the ruler who does not take "from" the people, the state, or All under Heaven gains the support of these respective polities and thus "takes" them. (See LTCC WCCS, I:38; and compare TKLT CCCY, p. 84, and LT CS, pp. 70 and 72.)

26. An image common to Sun-tzu, *Art of War,* Chapter 5, "Strategic Military Power."

27. Emending the text according to the Sung edition, as Liu Yin's commentary indicates it to be correct.

28. This sentence and the passage in general reflect several concepts central to the *Tao Te Ching,* especially those expressed in Chapters 2, 7, and 51.

29. As long as the state imposes few burdens, the people will prosper. However, it is also possible to understand this as "the ruler does not give anything to the people, yet they are enriched of themselves." Because the general context of these chapters discusses the ruler providing food and clothes to the people to gather them in, both readings seem possible.

30. The civil, as distinguished from the "martial," consisted of diplomatic measures as well as political programs that clearly encompassed psychological warfare, disinformation, spying, and the creation of dissension. As noted in the translator's introduction, these measures were widely condemned by orthodox scholars, including Liu Yin, because they could not imagine that such historical paragons of Virtue as Kings Wen and Wu would need them—especially when presumably they had already gained the willing allegiance of two-thirds of the realm.

31. This passage is somewhat problematic, and the modern translators—both Chinese and Japanese—tend to elide portions of it. The general intent appears to be that by delaying his emissaries, they will appear to have been remiss in their duties, particularly when their replacements quickly succeed in their missions. (The commentators generally take *yen* as meaning "be extremely respectful toward" or "treat generously," as translated, but this seems forced, and the text may be corrupt.) Subsequently, the recently estranged officials can be used to further political objectives by playing on their disaffection and satisfying their greed. (Cf. LT CS, pp. 77–78; TKLT CCCY, p. 93; and Okada Osamu, *Rikutō*, pp. 70–71.)

32. This passage reflects fundamental concepts found in the *Tao Te Ching*, especially in Chapter 36.

33. Various interpretations are offered for how these three methods are to be employed against themselves: Increasing someone's strength stimulates him to arrogance; favored officials can best be employed to cast doubt on loyal ministers; and successfully attracting the allegiance of population segments will prove infectious, drawing ever-increasing numbers of disaffected souls. However, other possibilities obviously exist. (Cf. TKLT CCCY, pp. 102–103.)

34. The analogy comparing people with cows and horses is highly unusual and appears to suggest that if the ruler provides for the people, they will docilely follow and love him—just like horses and cattle. However, the commentators understand the sentence as translated; the ruler should follow his bestowal of material goods with more abstract measures. (Cf. LT CS, p. 82; TKLT CCCY, p. 105 [note that "the people are like cows and horses" has dropped out of the text]; and Okada Osamu, *Rikutō*, p. 80.)

35. The names of some terms, such as *Fu-hsin*, or "belly-heart" (indicating a close relationship, close confidants), in some cases are best left romanized with approximate functional equivalents indicated in brackets.

36. Their positions apparently integrated the functions of both astrologers and weather forecasters, casting an eye equally toward the interpretation of natural phenomena and the indications of baleful and auspicious moments.

37. Literally, "secret-pennants-drums."

38. All these terms probably derive from, or at least are common to, Sun-tzu's *Art of War*.

39. The first words from Chapter 1, "Initial Estimations," the *Art of War* (later echoed in *Questions and Replies* and many other military writings). Sun-tzu discusses the general's qualifications in this and other chapters.

40. Another quotation from the *Art of War,* Chapter 3, "Strategies for Attack."

41. *Fu* and *yüeh* axes in bronze date from at least the Shang dynasty, and stone precursors have also been discovered. Although the *yüeh* axe is frequently described as a larger version of the *fu* (such as by Chou Wei in his *Chung-kuo ping-ch'i shih-kao,* (Ming-wen shu-chü, Taipei, 1981, p. 106), based on archaeological discoveries of numerous examples, there are additional class distinctions. The *fu* frequently resembles a wood-splitter's ax, with the shaft passing through a hole in the upper portion. The *yüeh* resembles a Western executioner's great ax, with a wide, curved blade and a head fastened by binding the tang to the shaft. It symbolized power and authority—particularly the authority to conduct punitive expeditions—and was also employed for actual executions. (For examples and discussion, consult Ch'eng Tung and Chung Shao-i, eds., *Chung-kuo ku-tai ping-ch'i t'u-chi,* Chieh-fang-chün ch'u-pan-she, Peking, 1990.)

42. "Vacuity" (deficiencies, weaknesses, voids) and "substance" (strength) are probably derived from Sun-tzu's *Art of War,* Chapter 6, "Vacuity and Substance."

43. These practices are strongly associated with the historical Wu Ch'i and are frequently found in the military writings. (For further discussion, see the translator's inroduction and notes to the *Wu-tzu.*)

44. This ceremony is reviewed by Li Ching on behalf of T'ang T'ai-tsung in Book III of *Questions and Replies.*

45. The title of this chapter, "*Yin-fu,*" is identical with a cryptic book associated with the T'ai Kung's name, although nominally attributed to the legendary Yellow Emperor. A *Yin-fu ching,* with commentaries by other military figures such as the mysterious Kuei Ku-tzu, is presently found in the Taoist canon. However, its contents are unrelated to the material discussed in "Secret Tallies," and the brief text probably bears no relation to the T'ai Kung.

46. Because this chapter goes on to explicitly discuss military communications between the ruler and his generals, the sentence is translated as "I want to communicate" rather than "my general wants to communicate." (This differs from the start of Chapter 25, for which see note 47. Also observe the active role presumably being played by the ruler, King Wu, in directing the army, in contrast to the rise of professional commanders and the growing advocacy and acceptance of the principle of noninterference in the Spring and Autumn period. The text is clearly anachronistic in this regard because Sun-tzu and other chapters such as "Appointing the General" emphasize the general's necessary independence.)

47. Here the text clearly reads "the commanding general."

48. Echoes Lao-tzu, *Tao Te Ching,* Chapter 1.

49. These sentences appear to be misplaced. Although the referents are not specified, "plans," "deployment," "situation," and similar aspects of intelligence are clearly intended and thus are variously interpolated by the commentators.

50. Defeating them before they have deployed their forces and manifested themselves. This echoes Lao-tzu's Chapter 64.

51. As Sun-tzu advises in *Art of War,* Chapter 11, "Nine Terrains."

52. The image of attacking from above the Heavens, secreting oneself below Earth, is frequently found, however, in the military writings, including the *Art of War.*

53. This appears to be an application of Sun-tzu's principle to throw the men into a desperate position in which there is no defense except fighting to the death.

54. The concept of unorthodox (*ch'i*) tactics, made prominent by Sun-tzu and still a focal topic in *Questions and Replies,* barely appears in the *Six Secret Teachings* except for this chapter and an occasional reference in chapters that clearly describe unorthodox tactics—although not explicitly so named—such as the "Crow and Cloud Formation in the Mountains." However, much of the material in the last four secret teachings clearly falls within the category of unorthodox tactics—especially Chapter 51, "Dispersing and Assembling," which essentially amplifies the principle: "One who cannot divide and move [his troops about] cannot be spoken with about unorthodox strategies." (The entire paragraph actually paraphrases Sun-tzu.) Why the authors of the *Six Secret Teachings* failed to include such discussions, particularly after Sun Pin had further developed the application of unorthodox tactics and the cavalry had provided the mobility that made the realization of these tactics possible, remains unknown. (For a discussion of the unorthodox and orthodox, see the notes to the translator's introduction for the *Art of War.*)

55. The "moment" (*chi*), the subtle shifting of events.

56. For a discussion of the five notes and their correlation with other phenomena associated with the five phases, see Joseph Needham et al., *Science and Civilisation in China,* Vol. 2, Cambridge University Press, Cambridge, 1962, pp. 216–268.

57. The Sung edition and the modern LT CS include an additional phrase not found in the Ming edition, "by which one can know the enemy."

58. "Six *chia*" is variously understood by the traditional commentators. (Unfortunately, the modern Chinese translations—such as the LT CS edition—either ignore the difficulty or, as Hsü Pei-ken in his CCCY edition, deprecate the chapter as being a late interpolation of the yin-yang school and thus apparently not worth translating and annotating (cf. LT CS, p. 111, and TKLT CCCY, p. 138). The most common explanation is that the term stands for the entire sixty-element cycle created by sequentially pairing the ten stems with the twelve branches. (For general information about the cycle, see Needham, *Science and Civilisation in China,* Vol. 3, 1970, section 20h, especially pp. 396–398. There is also an extensive, readily accessible secondary literature on the origin and concepts of five phase thought.)

Alternatively, the six double characters headed by *chia* within the cycle of sixty may be the subject of this passage (see Okada, *Rikutō,* p. 118). In this case the sentence should be understood as stating that the division into six *chia* provides the categories for the associations with the six subtle, marvelous spirits (which are themselves associated with the five phases. Cf. LTCC WCCS, I:83B).

For a discussion of the concept of tonal response that underlies this chapter, see Derk Bodde, "The Chinese Cosmic Magic Known as Watching for the Ethers," reprinted in *Essays on Chinese Civilization* (Charles Le Blanc and Dorothy Borei, eds.), Princeton University Press, Princeton, 1981, pp. 351–372.

59. *Ch'i,* previously encountered in discussions of "spirit" or "morale," was also associated with five phase theory and various prognosticatory practices and even had military applications, as seen in this chapter. (For further discussion, see Onozawa Seiichi, Fukunaga Mitsuji, and Yamanoi Yu, eds., *Ki no shisō,* pp. 146–162; and Kuroda Yoshiko, *Ki no kenkyū,* pp. 165–172.)

60. The Sung edition has "stop" rather than *chu*—"rule"—and the sentence would accordingly be translated as "without stopping" instead of "without any direction."

61. The six domesticated animals were the horse, oxen, sheep, chickens, dogs, and pigs.

62. This chapter and the previous one on agricultural implements, which are historically important and merit separate research articles or monographs, describe the variety of equipment—especially chariots—employed by late Warring States armies. Whether this chapter is an amalgamation of earlier materials and not all the equipment was current at the time of final composition or additional sections were added in the Ch'in-Han period is not immediately clear. Similarly, many of the terms remain to be properly studied and explicated because later commentaries have not been particularly helpful in this regard and the reconstructed drawings of the T'ang and beyond are frequently misleading and unreliable. Our translation therefore must be considered tentative, although many weapons and previously nebulous pieces of equipment are becoming increasingly clear as archaeological discoveries provide concrete verification of the details. (For an introductory discussion, see Robin D.S. Yates, "Siege Engines and Late Zhou Military Technology." Further light should be cast by the volume on military technology in Needham's *Science and Civilisation* series.)

63. Based on numerous sources, each chariot was supposedly accompanied by seventy-two men, with three officers manning the chariot. Thus there would be a platoon of twenty-four for each flank and a third platoon for the rear (or front, depending on the deployment and mode of action). However, Liu Yin reads the text as indicating twenty-four men in total (LTCC WCCS, II:2A), as does K'ung Te-ch'i (LT CS, p. 132), who also has them pushing the vehicle—thereby implying that it is a cart rather than a chariot. However, others concur with seventy-two men in total per chariot. (Cf. Okada, *Rikutō*, p. 129; and TKLT CCCY, p. 148, where Hsü Pei-ken suggests that four horses were hitched to it.)

64. The name suggests it had spear tips protruding from the body of the chariot.

65. Winch-powered linked crossbows capable of firing multiple arrows in a repeating mode, presumably deriving their cocking power from the chariot's axle, only developed very late in the Warring States period. Thus this passage clearly indicates both the advanced state attained by Chinese military technology and the late composition date of this chapter. (For a discussion of such weapons based on recent archaeological discoveries, see the references included in Appendix C.)

66. The intermixed use of both bronze and iron arrowheads is to be noted.

67. According to Liu Yin (LTCC WCCS, II:3A), they were specifically designed for flank attacks.

68. As noted by Liu Yin (LTCC WCCS, II:3B), the text seems to be corrupt. The use of baggage wagons for "lightning attacks" is highly incongruous, and parts of the passage have clearly been lost because there is no mention of the number of such vehicles to be employed.

69. The text appears corrupt because the devices being described have no intrinsic relationship to chariots, yet the term *Fu-hsü* appears in conjunction with them. (The translation follows Okada, *Rikutō*, p. 138.)

70. This formulaic phrase seems out of place because it is difficult to imagine the caltrops being used in anything more than a passive role, to impede attacks and constrain the direction of an enemy's flight rather than to "urgently press an attack against invaders."

71. Following the Ming edition, which has *tsou*—"to flee" or "run off"—rather than the Sung edition, which has *pu*—"infantry."

72. Although termed "small," they must have been fairly large and been mounted on wheels or carts so as to be pushed by several men. The shields would have been essentially vertical, presenting a daunting front to aggressors. (It is also possible that they were some sort of small watchtower mounted on chariots and that instead of being accompanied by spearmen and halberdiers, as in the previous passages, speartips and halberd tips were affixed to their walls to repel invaders.)

73. Following suggestions to revise the order of the text in parallel with the previous descriptions, rather than having eight winches on each section.

74. Presumably, the chains are stretched across the water from shore to shore.

75. Lengths of rope with iron rings at each end for linking together.

76. Although the translation indicates "stars and planets" in general, it is also possible that the "morning star" is intended, which would provide exactly four items with which to orient the deployment. Modern commentators, however, tend to deemphasize what they apparently perceive as the nonscientific aspect of this chapter, preferring to interpret these phenomena in terms of winds and weather—contrary to the rich tradition of military formations and heavenly phenomena (cf. TKLT CCCY, pp. 150–151; LT CS, p. 154).

77. Liu Yin, in accord with principles found in the *Art of War* and the *Six Secret Teachings*, expands this sentence as "To the right and rear mountains and mounds, to the fore and left water and marshes, to seize convenience and advantage. This is what is meant by the Earthly Deployment" (LTCC WCCS, II:8A).

78. As Liu Yin points out, the civil is employed to attach the masses, the martial to overawe the enemy (LTCC WCCS, II:8A).

79. Throughout our translation of the *Six Secret Teachings*, which the authors have purported to be an ancient text dating from Early Chou times, the term *shih*—originally a minor rank of nobility—is frequently translated as "officer." This is to correspond to the *shih*'s status in the Early Chou era, especially when compared with the commoners who made up the "troops" in support. As the infantry grew in importance, members of the nobility gradually assumed command roles rather than simply engaging in individual combat, as discussed in the general introduction; and the *shih* especially grew in professional competence, being too low on the feudal hierarchy to benefit much from the family's wealth and power or receive any substantial inheritance. With the further passage of time into the Warring States period and the displacement and disenfranchisement of a large portion of the nobility, the scope of the term broadened even further to include "warriors" in general—especially men with martial qualifications that distinguished them from the common infantryman—and also to encompass what might be termed noncommissioned officers, such as squad leaders. Thus, depending on context, the term will be translated as "officers," "warriors," or just "men" and "soldiers"—preserving wherever possible distinctions the authors may have assumed or intended in the various passages.

80. Techniques from Sun-tzu's "Nine Terrains" designed to create the ultimate commitment to "fight to the death" and thereby live.

81. Literally, set up a "cloud of fire" to act as a highly visible marker for the troops to orient themselves while escaping through whatever natural cover might be available.

82. Following the Ming edition, which has "mountain stream," *hsi.* The Sung edition has *ch'i,* "valley" or "deep gorge."

83. The intent being to make it seem they have truly gone off. However, a hundred *li* seems excessive, especially when they are to return surreptitiously and assume positions in close proximity to the enemy.

84. Emending the Ming edition from "and stop" to the Sung's "without stopping," "incessantly," in the light of the succeeding sentence, which directs a retreat of three *li* before turning about. Because beating the gongs is the signal to retreat, incessant beating would presumably lure the enemy into assuming an uncontrolled, massive flight is underway.

85. The reason for this title is obscure because there is no mention of either gongs or drums in the chapter.

86. The term translated as "detachment" (*t'un*) apparently indicates an integral unit for temporary defensive purposes rather than the usual "encampment" because the siege presumably confines the army in a single location.

87. That is, the evil ruler whose actions have brought about the punitive actions directed toward him. The phrase reflects Chou history because it is associated with Chou's attack on the tyrannical Shang king.

88. Although Sun-tzu devotes a chapter to incendiary warfare, his focus is on aggressive actions rather than the defensive employment of fire in desperate situations. Surprisingly, the use of fire and water is little discussed in the *Seven Military Classics.*

89. For ease in understanding, we have translated *hsü*—rendered as "vacuous" in the *Art of War*—as "empty." (Normally, *k'ung* is translated as "empty.")

90. "Advantages," following the Ming edition. The Sung edition has "principles" instead. The former echoes Mencius and is perhaps more common.

91. As defined by the T'ai Kung at the end of the next chapter, "the Crow and Cloud Formation is like the crows dispersing and the clouds forming together." Flexibility is stressed in its realization.

92. Echoing Sun-tzu's concepts of the unending changes and transformations of the five notes in the *Art of War,* Chapter 5, "Strategic Military Power."

93. According to Sun-tzu in the *Art of War,* Chapter 9, "Maneuvering the Army," this would be a disadvantageous position.

94. Described in Chapter 31, "The Army's Equipment."

95. "Dispersing and assembling," or "dividing and combining," reappears as a key topic in *Questions and Replies,* where it is seen as essential to the execution of unorthodox strategies. The concept's significance was perhaps first realized by Sun-tzu (see the *Art of War,* Chapter 7, "Military Combat").

96. Sons adopted through marriage assumed their wive's surnames, thereby abandoning their own families, betraying their ancestral responsibilities, and generally violating common Confucian beliefs. Normally forced to take such drastic action because of lowly status and poverty, they would be especially motivated to escape their living ignominy by distinguishing themselves in combat.

97. A central concept in several of the military writings, including the *Ssu-ma Fa,* *Wu-tzu,* and *Questions and Replies.*

98. The Sung edition has "selected warriors" for "assimilate and become practiced."

99. The concept of training men by extending the teachings is seen in several other writings as well, including the *Wu-tzu* ("Controlling the Army") and *Questions and Replies* (Book II). In the latter the focus is on instructing the officers first, as appears to be the case here (see notes 84 and 85, Book II).

100. This chapter is significant for its unique discussion of the equivalency of various types of forces, which was possible only late in the Warring States period when all three types—chariots, infantry, and cavalry—were actively employed, although the role of chariots was increasingly diminished (cf. LT CS, pp. 199–202). Li Ching cites these equivalents in his discussions with T'ang T'ai-tsung in *Questions and Replies*.

101. A number of unusual terms are used in this chapter, whose precise position in a military hierarchy remains nebulous. Approximate functional equivalents have been used wherever possible.

102. Five feet seven inches tall in modern terms.

103. "Fatal terrain" is one of Sun-tzu's categories, advanced in "Nine Changes" and "Nine Terrains." Sun-tzu, Wu Ch'i, and others all discuss types of terrain and the tactics appropriate to them and to exploiting weaknesses in the enemy's condition.

104. Although the text states "terrain"—apparently in parallel with the ten deadly terrains described just above—seven of the eight simply characterize weaknesses in the enemy that can be exploited to advantage, as discussed earlier in the book and in other military writings. Whether sections have been inadvertently juxtaposed or the original lost and supplements provided is unknown.

105. Literally, "terrain."

106. Reflecting Sun-tzu's theory of striking the enemy when his spirit—his *ch'i*—has abated (see *Art of War,* Chapter 7, "Military Combat").

107. As most of the commentators have noted, only eight situations are described; two have apparently been lost over time.

108. Literally, "terrain."

109. "Heavenly Well" or "Heaven's Well" is among the deadly configurations of terrain Sun-tzu warns against in the *Art of War,* Chapter 9, "Maneuvering the Army."

The Methods of the Ssu-ma

Abbreviations of Frequently Cited Books

SMF CCCY   Liu Chung-p'ing, *Ssu-ma Fa chin-chu chin-i,* Shang-wu yin-shu-kuan, Taipei, 1975.

SMF CS   T'ien Hsü-tung, *Ssu-ma Fa ch'ien-shuo,* Chieh-fang-chün ch'u-pan-she, Peking, 1989.

SMF WCCS   *Ssu-ma Fa chih-chieh,* in *Ming-pen Wu-ching Ch'i- shu chih-chieh,* Vol. 1, Shih-ti chiao-yü ch'u-pan-she, Taipei, 1972.

SMF WCHC   *Ssu-ma Fa,* in *Ch'ung-k'an Wu-ching hui-chieh,* Chung-chou Ku-chi ch'u-pan-she, Cheng-chou, 1989.

Notes to the Translator's Introduction

1. Determining exactly how far back the materials may date requires systematic study, including comparison with passages from the *Spring and Autumn Annals* and

the *Tso chuan*. Some writers assert that the current book includes pre–Western Chou source material, but this seems doubtful unless the passages have been reworked into the style of the late Spring and Autumn and Warring States periods. (Cf. Chung-kuo Chün-shih-shih Pien-hsieh-tsu, *Chung-kuo chün-shih-shih,* Vol. 4: *Ping-fa,* Chieh-fang-chün ch'u-pan-she, Peking, 1988, pp. 48–53.)

2. Liu Chung-p'ing cites Sun Hsing-yen in asserting that the thoughts and strategies of the Duke of Chou together with those of the T'ai Kung provide the basis for the book. SMF CCCY, p. 4 (of the introduction).

3. T'ien Shu, another of T'ien Wan's descendants, was granted the surname *Sun* by Duke Ching for his achievements. Sun Wu (the famous Sun-tzu) and thereafter Sun Pin were descendants and therefore were all members of the same clan as T'ien Jang-chü. (Cf. Li Hsüeh-le's introduction, SMF CS, p. 1, and also pp. 16–17.)

The tradition of Ch'i military studies requires a separate extensive work as well as resolution of the thorny problems of verbal transmission and family specialization. Because the Han tomb containing the military works belonged to a person surnamed *Ssu-ma*, it has been suggested that this provides evidence of the continuity of Ch'i studies right into the Han. (Parts of the *Ssu-ma Fa* were also recovered, proving it could not have been a forgery of the Sui or T'ang dynasties.) Modern Western scholars, to a large degree following Ch'ing skeptics, vehemently deny the possibility that the T'ai Kung's or the Duke of Chou's thoughts provide the foundation of any of these works, if only because of the style and characteristics of the language. However, this ignores the possibility of gradual rephrasing over centuries of oral transmission. Further epigraphic materials will perhaps provide additional answers.

4. SMF WCCS, 1A. A more detailed description of the Great Ssu-ma's duties is found in the *Chou li,* under the "Offices of Summer" (*chüan* 7 and 8). Cf. Lin Yin, *Chou li chin-chu chin-i,* Shang-wu yin-shu-kuan, Taipei, 1972, pp. 297ff.

5. The *Kuan-tzu* is being translated by W. Allyn Rickett, *Guanzi,* Vol. 1, Princeton University Press, Princeton, 1985.

6. King Wei, originally a member of the T'ien clan, is also noted in the *Shih chi* biography (translated below) as being related to Ssu-ma Jang-chü.

7. *Chüan* 62. The translation is based on the text found in the *Shiki kaichū kōshō,* one-volume reprint, I-wen yin-shu-kuan, Taipei, 1972, pp. 840–842. Several other editions have also been consulted, including Ma Ch'ih-ying, *Shih-chi chin-chu,* Vol. 4, Shang-wu yin-shu-kuan, Taipei, 1979, pp. 2200–2202; and Han Ssu-ma, *Hsin-chiao Shih-chi san-chia chu,* Vol. 4, Shih-chieh shu-chü, Taipei, pp. 2157–2160.

8. T'ien Wan, who was originally surnamed Ch'en, had served Duke Huan of Ch'i and been enfeoffed for his contributions, taking the name T'ien. T'ien Jang-chü was a third- or fourth-generation collateral descendant of commoner status.

9. Ch'i declined precipitously after Duke Huan's hegemony, due primarily to a succession of debauched and incompetent rulers, becoming easy prey for the other feudal states. Duke Ching proved no exception to the other rulers and was saved from immediate doom only through the efforts of T'ien Wen-tzu and members of the Pao and Kao clans. T'ien Wen-tzu apparently practiced benevolent policies on behalf of the government, but the duke continued his dissolute ways until shaken by the appearance of a comet in the northwest, which presaged the invasion and collapse of Ch'i. (Cf. Ch'en Wu-t'ung and Su Shuang-pi, eds., *Chung-kuo li-tai ming-chiang,* Vol. 1, Honan jen-min ch'u-pan-she, Honan, 1987, p. 3.)

10. Some *Shih chi* commentaries identify P'in as a district rather than a city. Obviously, the surrounding territory as well as the cities would have been occupied. (The *Shih-chi k'ao-cheng* suggests that these place names did not exist at such an early period, thereby throwing into question the authenticity of the entire story or at least its association with Duke Ching.)

11. Literally, the area above the Yellow River.

12. At this time the supervisor apparently served just below the commander in chief and therefore above all other generals.

13. A staff set up to observe when the shadow of the sun was shortest and thus determine midday.

14. The commander would impose his rules for discipline, the measures for camp order, and the meaning of the various directions and commands.

15. One of the fragments of the *Ssu-ma Fa* is a three-character phrase: "Behead in order to instruct" (SMF CS, p. 132).

16. This statement—which appears in several of the *Seven Military Classics*—reflects the growing independence, professionalism, and power of the commanding generals and the realization that military campaigns were becoming so complex that the ruler—who previously, in the Shang and Early Chou, usually commanded in person—should not interfere. A similar story appears in Sun-tzu's biography. The *Ssu-ma Fa* fragments include the statements: "Affairs outside the gate (of the state's outer wall) are administered by the general" (No. 40, SMF CS, p. 131).

17. He apparently tested and evaluated the men in order to remove the weak and sick from the active ranks.

18. So as not to enter the state as an armed host, thereby keeping separate the martial and civil, as discussed in the text itself. He simultaneously defused any threat his loyal army might be seen as presenting to the political ruler.

19. They were the powers behind the throne of the dissolute ruler and thus enjoyed his confidence.

20. A Ssu-ma Jang-chü is also mentioned in the *Chan-kuo ts'e* as holding power under King Min of Ch'i (reigned 300 to 284 B.C.) and refusing to countenance his overthrow. (Cf. Yang Chia-lo, ed., *Chan-kuo ts'e*, Vol. 1, Shih-chieh shu-chü, Taipei, 1967, p. 243 [*chüan* 13, Book 6 of the state of Ch'i].)

21. One hundred fifty-five represents the total number of sections collected, perhaps before collation and elimination of duplicates. Although much has undoubtedly been lost, if the sections were fairly brief, their rearrangement might reduce the number considerably without any actual sacrifice of material.

22. Cf. note 1, above; SMF CCCY, p. 4. Also note the general discussion, pp. 4–22, and the conclusion, p. 22, in SMF CS.

23. Notwithstanding, each chapter is organized around an ostensible theme.

24. The *Chou li* discusses the offices and duties of the Chou dynasty in great detail. Although it paints a very idealized, systematic portrait, it no doubt has a substantial basis—one that is being confirmed with each new archaeological and epigraphic discovery. The fragments collected by Ch'ing scholars—collated and further analyzed in the SMF CS—contain extensive material on military organization not found in the present text. With their inclusion, the ancient book would become an even better candidate for classification under the *li* (cf. SMF CS, pp. 6–12). Liu Chung-p'ing (SMF

CCCY, p. 2) asserts that the title should not contain the word "*ping*," or military, because it should be considered a book of laws or standards rather than a book of strategy, or "methods of war."

25. SMF CS, pp. 17–18.

26. This is expressed despite their emphasis on benevolence as the foundation of the state and thus as the basis of citizen support, which is therefore synonymous with power. Note also the last paragraph of Chapter 3, where the parallel imposition of strong measures—the law—occurs in the absence of proper obedience: "When upright methods do not prove effective, then centralized control of affairs [must be undertaken]. [If the people] do not submit [to Virtue], then laws must be imposed."

27. The recognition, even advocacy of employing force to stop force, war to halt war, is not unique to this text. Mencius was a strong advocate of military activism, and such eclectic texts as the *Kuan-tzu* contain similar materials. One of the *Ssu-ma Fa* fragments states: "If men, for a reason, kill men, killing them is permissible" (SMF CS, p. 136).

28. Leaders in the very early years were still confronted with rebellion, barbarian challenges, and the problems of consolidation, but under the first few rulers the state enjoyed relative stability and tranquility.

29. Part of this passage is also repeated at the start of Chapter 2.

30. The danger of martial values predominating, affecting individuals who pursue their own paths and wield power, is also raised in Chapter 2 under the subject of "excessive awesomeness."

31. "In antiquity they did not pursue a fleeing enemy too far nor follow a retreating army too closely. By not pursuing them too far it was difficult to draw them into a trap; by not pursuing so closely as to catch up it was hard to ambush them. They regarded the *li* as their basic strength" (Chapter 2).

32. The commentators suggest it can be explained by concern for the cold that would affect the men. Campaigns in antiquity, although generally of short duration, were initiated after the fall harvest and could easily extend into the winter.

33. This contradicts the policy of having the army forage for food and the *Ssu-ma Fa*'s advocacy of confiscating rations from the enemy. For example, "To increase material resources rely on [seizing them from] the enemy" and "take advantage of [the enemy's] material resources" (Chapter 3).

34. A list of concrete justifications for undertaking a campaign of rectification is found at the end of Chapter 1.

35. These formalities are described in the middle of Chapter 1.

36. This does not imply that the general commands simply at the whim of his soldiers or that he is a passive element. Rather, through preparatory activities—such as education, drills, and training—he must ensure that their spirit is disciplined, that their martial capabilities are fully honed. However, in particular circumstances they may still not be prepared, or they may be confronted by situations beyond their skill and spirit. The astute commander must accurately discern these difficulties and react accordingly, such as by whipping up the army's enthusiasm or employing delaying tactics.

37. The repeated emphasis on measure, control, and quiet is seen as indicating material describing—or at least based on—antique forms of warfare wherein the chariots

and accompanying infantry had to be closely coordinated because gaps or disorder (which would be induced by haste) would doom the army to defeat. Cf. *Ping-fa*, pp. 48–49. (Please refer to the passage notes for further historical observations.)

38. T'ien Hsü-tung stresses this point (cf. SMF CS, p. 72).

39. "If their masses are beset by uncertainty, you should take advantage of it." [5] "Mount a sudden strike on their doubts. Attack their haste. ... Capitalize on their fears." [5]

40. As discussed in the first third of Chapter 4.

41. That is, the prospect of life, of being spared when they would normally be executed for dereliction of duty or desertion.

Notes to the Text

1. This contrasts sharply with the idealized view that a Sage King need only cultivate his Virtue to achieve rulership of the world, as discussed in the translator's introduction.

2. Such as by imposing corvée labor duties or mounting military campaigns during the prime agricultural seasons. Military actions in themselves would also violate the natural cycle of growth if undertaken during spring and summer, the period when yang is ascending and peaking.

3. The "Great Peace" or "Great Joy," apparently a triumphant musical performance that included dance, was held to welcome the victorious troops who had just pacified the realm and to simultaneously redirect the people's anger—the emotional basis of warfare—into happiness and joy (SMF WCHC 3:4–5A). Thereafter, to remain vigilant against the necessity of reluctantly employing the army against external enemies, the emperor held great hunts in the spring and fall, which the feudal lords were mandated to attend. In the early Chou, these not only provided opportunities to reinforce feudal bonds and secure a considerable meat supply but were also the chance to instill organization, practice command, and exercise the feudal members in wielding arms. Because the nobility made up the military class, even with their retainers and servants there would not be more than a few thousand participants.

In the spring the participants would be led back in "good order" and then dismissed, whereas in the fall, after training, they would embark on military campaigns if necessary (cf. SMF CCCY, notes to pp. 8–9).

One of the collected fragments describes how the various feudal lords would be ordered to pay court on a seasonal basis, with the intent and objective of each season varying (cf. SMF CS, p. 107). Another seems to reflect archaic remnants, correlating seasons with directions and military activities: "In the spring do not conduct campaigns of rectification in the east; in the fall do not undertake attacks in the west. If there is a lunar eclipse withdraw the army. In this way one is cautious (or reduces) warfare" (SMF CS, p. 99).

4. The *li*, the forms of proper behavior (also frequently translated as "rites"), evolved and became detailed systematically much later than the idealized period being portrayed. However, the code of chivalry ostensibly governing combat should be well noted because it disappears with the rise of infantry armies and the maturation of large-scale warfare. (The *Chung-kuo chün-shih-shih* notes that at the battle of Han Yüan in 645 B.C., the commander felt the correct execution of the *li* took precedence

over capitalizing on a tactical opportunity to attack an enemy that had not yet formally deployed in battle lines. In 638 B.C. the same scrupulous observation of the *li* resulted not in a glorious victory suffused with an aura of righteousness but in ignominious defeat. Thereafter, the turn toward realism accelerated, until by the end of the Spring and Autumn period—when ironically the *li* were becoming more important in all aspects of life and were later given theoretical foundation by early Confucians—such self-imposed restraint became a mark of idiocy (cf. *Ping-fa*, pp. 49–50).

5. In contrast with the Warring States period, when rank and rewards were based on the number of heads taken, and prisoners were routinely killed. (Unmentioned is the historical fact that prisoners were generally enslaved in the ancient period, including the Shang, and were often sacrificed.)

6. Offices were established to control and supervise productive activities, such as farming and the skilled crafts.

7. With a view to eliminating differences and harmonizing practices among all the states.

8. This includes relations among the ranks, standards of the state, observances of the realm.

9. Initiating activities in disharmony with the natural tendencies, such as executing in spring, the season of growth; holding military drills or hunts in summer; or perhaps wearing black in summer, when red or yellow would be appropriate.

10. Throughout the *Seven Military Classics* the importance of announcing military plans in the ancestral temple, before the spirits and before the ancient kings, is constantly emphasized.

11. Such as dikes and irrigation ditches, both of which would have required extensive, onerous labor service and if damaged would have seriously impoverished the people.

12. They constrained the feudal lords with territorial boundaries (as well as by location), thereby limiting their resources and power.

13. Literally, "profits." The Legalists emphasized the motivational power of profits, whereas Confucians such as Mencius vociferously disdained them.

14. Fragment N. 24, SMF CS, pp. 122–123, also states that one mobilizes to attack the unrighteous—defining the latter as those who violate the proper order in laws, disregard the rites, and offend the hierarchy under Heaven.

15. The ruler should actively study the traces of the Former Sages with a view to employing them himself. This is the classical Confucian view subsequently denounced by the Legalists.

16. The cryptic text states that "state deportment did not enter the military; military deportment did not enter the state." In antiquity, as discussed in the general introduction, "states" consisted basically of walled cities that encompassed the ruler, his family members, other members of the feudal nobility, and the artisans. The fields were normally outside the walled city, and state affairs were administered from within the city. However, as several books and articles have pointed out, in the Shang and early Chou states, rulers—including the king and the local feudal lords—governed and participated in military and civil affairs equally. Accordingly, the reference to "within the state" should be taken as "within the court," within the administrative center. The military would be mobilized for campaigns outside the state (unless the city itself were un-

der siege). Thus the form, spirit, behavior, deportment, and so forth appropriate to one realm would not be found in the other. (This passage is repeated later in the chapter.)

17. Although the word translated as talents is *ch'i*, it is unlikely to refer to Confucius's famous dictum that "a gentleman is not a utensil (*ch'i*)."

18. Although several commentators understand this as referring to lawsuits, it hardly seems necessary to so restrict it—particularly in an age when there were very few "lawsuits" and they constituted only a minor element in state affairs. (Epigraphic materials indicate, however, that disputes were reasonably common.)

19. Rather than base decisions on adherence to some other virtue.

20. Execution could take many forms, some more painful and terrifying than others. In later ages execution came to involve the extermination of family members as well.

21. Because their objective was benevolent and their actions would be restrained to accord with the aim of simply punishing the evil, their behavior would be consistent with their teachings, and their teachings could again be taught after the victory without any inconsistency. (The major restraints are discussed in Chapter 1, in the paragraph containing note 11.)

22. Because they had no need to employ their weapons, the "five weapons" did not have to be deployed in effective fighting combinations.

23. As Liu Yin points out (SMF WCCS, 20B), this discussion focuses solely on the predominant strength of each dynasty. Obviously, the earlier dynasties were also forced to employ military strength to subjugate their enemies.

24. As Robin D.S. Yates has pointed out, the character *wei* cannot be construed to mean "attack" even though the passage seems to require it. The long weapons are described here as protecting the men wielding shorter ones and the shorter weapons as defending those wielding longer ones. However, in chariot warfare—the presumed basis of this text—charioteers attack with long weapons and rely on short weapons for defense only when engaged in close quarters.

25. The basis for these names, if in fact they are accurate, is lost in the mists of time. The commentators offer various obscure explanations, but none seems satisfactory. Our translation of the names is speculative. Specialists may consult the various commentators: SMF WCCS, 31A–32B; SMF CCCY, pp. 41–42; SMF CS, p. 51, and also the fragment on p. 102; SMF WCHC, 3:21–22.

26. The insignia were placed on flags and worn as emblems by the soldiers in addition to their other emblems of rank. Other discussions are found in the *Six Secret Teachings* and the *Wei Liao-tzu*. Fragment No. 4, SMF CS, p. 103, also discusses the choice of weapons, with their colors and significance.

27. The term means "army," or military in general, but may also mean an "army on the move," or campaign army, as throughout this passage.

28. This repeats and expands the second passage of the chapter (refer to note 16 above).

29. Acts of goodness should not go unnoticed; therefore, they sought to learn of them.

30. Kingdoms were extremely limited, so the king could personally observe those serving border duty during his tours of inspection. (Liu Yin understands the sentence as referring to the king rather than to superiors in general. Cf. SMF WCCS, 27B.)

31. Such as the "Ta K'ai" mentioned in the first chapter.

32. The Spirit Terrace was supposedly first erected by King Wen of the Chou dynasty. Beneath it he greeted the triumphant army and welcomed those returning from border and other service. Thus it was associated with welcoming men back from labors, military or otherwise. (Another tradition holds that the tower allowed the king to look out over the four quarters and observe the conditions of the people. Cf. Liu Yin's notes, SMF WCCS, 27B; and SMF CCCY, p. 56.)

In general, terraces were an anathema to the people in antiquity, enslaving their labor without providing them with any visible benefit or enjoyment. They therefore symbolized the ruler's conspicuous consumption and generally became focal objects for hatred. For example, in his famous interview with King Hui of Liang, Mencius develops his theme of sharing wealth with the people around a reference to King Wen's ponds and terraces (IA2).

33. Some commentators take these as mendicant persuaders, whose ideas and talents could also be drawn on to develop policies and strategies (cf. SMF WCCS, 28B). However, persuaders or sophists did not really appear until the rise of social mobility toward the end of the Spring and Autumn period. The Spring and Autumn conflicts disenfranchised many members of the nobility, creating a class of stateless wanderers with a wide array of talents—martial, technical, and administrative.

34. The ruler should enquire about the people's hatreds to ensure they are directed toward the enemy, not toward annoying policies in government.

35. A phrase or two appears to be missing from the text. One other possible translation is: "If advancing and withdrawing are without doubt, [it is because plans have been settled]. If [the commander] sees the enemy and lacks plans, then listen to his case and punish him" (following Liu Yin, SMF WCCS, 38A). Another possibility would be: "When advancing and withdrawing are without doubt, one can make plans when the enemy is seen." However, because creating false impressions is a cornerstone of Chinese military thought, we prefer the translation given in the text.

36. Liu Yin understands this as referring to the enemy, preventing them from advancing, which seems doubtful (SMF WCCS, 38B).

37. This appears to be a disconnected fragment discussing techniques similar to those found in the *Six Secret Teachings*.

38. It is unclear who should not forget it—the ruler, superiors, people in general, or the person who performed the action.

39. Some commentators take this as referring to policies rather than individuals.

40. The chapter takes its title from the first line; however, the main theme is controlling the spirit (*ch'i*) of the men.

41. Liu Yin understands this as "establish officers for the companies and squads" (SMF WCCS, 43A).

42. This appears to mean the number of paces between each man in both the rows and files, such as four paces horizontally and five vertically. However, it may also be understood as establishing the direction of their movement (cf. SMF WCCS, 43A; SMF CS, p. 78; SMF CCCY, p. 98).

43. The translation of this and several subsequent sentences is extremely tentative due to the apparently corrupt state of the text. In the context of what follows, some commentators suggest this line describes the performance of military courtesies, even

though the *Ssu-ma Fa* generally emphasizes the inappropriateness of such behavior in the military realm (cf. SMF WCHC, p. 148). However, in our opinion it describes the postures or methods of advancing for the two different types of fighting formations. Crouching down and advancing by crawling would minimize exposure to projectiles (cf. *Ping-fa*, p. 52). The remainder of the passage would then describe additional drills to be implemented under conditions of fear and terror.

44. When the enemy first appears, the men are distant and appear insignificant. Plans to contain and defeat them are formulated; accordingly, the soldiers are not afraid. When the enemy is engaged the men should focus on fighting, on their roles and duty, not on looking at the enemy's army (cf. SMF WCHC, p. 149).

45. The translation generally follows the suggestions of Liu Chung-p'ing, SMF CCCY, pp. 99–100. However, it could also be translated as "the squad leaders deploy the men to the left and right; all below the commander wearing armor sit; the oath is sworn; and then the army is slowly advanced." (Cf. Liu Yin's comments, SMF WCCS, 43B–44A; and SMF CS, p. 78.)

46. This may also be understood as everyone, from those holding rank down through the infantrymen, wears armor. However, a distinction was just made in the previous sentence between those wearing armor who are ordered to sit and apparently those who are not. The latter may be confined to support personnel, but presumably they would not be involved in the actual combat. The question revolves on to what period the passage refers—Early Chou, when armies were small and consisted of nobility, or later in the Spring and Autumn or Warring States periods, when infantry had become the major component and the troops all wore armor.

47. One commentary in the SMF WCHC suggests that the severity of military law requires these actions, but then the commander can relax the discipline, putting the men at ease. This would allow him to manipulate their spirit prior to battle, when they were struck with terror. By performing these exercises, these rites, the commander could wrest control of their emotions (cf. SMF WCHC, p. 149 [3:57A]).

48. Understanding *"tu'i"* as push back, withdraw, after performing the *li* (cf. SMF WCHC, p. 149 [3:57]).

49. Personal leadership was thought to be the key to commanding the troops.

50. Presumably, this would include not only family and state but also the remission of their offenses—such as attempted desertion—if they performed valiantly in battle.

51. Or "soldiers become stalwart through the weight of their armor."

52. As the commentators note, this passage appears to be missing characters. The first two lines of the paragraph, however, become an extremely well-known axiom in the martial arts.

Some of the commentators assert that this principle of the fearful mind refers to the soldiers' fear of their commander. In the *Seven Military Classics* the thought is frequently expressed that if the troops fear their commander more than they fear the enemy, they will advance into battle. Therefore, the commander's duty is to ensure that this fearful mind is exploited so that the advantage of so preying on it—fighting the enemy—will be the same as the advantage of seeing only victory.

53. Literally, "if with the light one advances light." The understanding of territory as light or heavy appears to have been common to the period, and Sun-tzu devotes considerable space to such tactical considerations. However, an alternative is to simply read the passage as a comparison of force (cf. *Ping-fa*, p. 52): "If you advance with a

light force against a light enemy, you will be endangered. If you advance with a heavy force against a heavy enemy, you will accomplish nothing. If you advance with a light force against a heavy enemy, you will be defeated. If you advance with a heavy force against a light enemy, you will be successful. Thus in warfare the light and heavy are mutually related." It is also possible to consider the passage as discussing methods for employing the forces, such as the light in a light fashion, but this seems less likely.

54. That is, maintain vigilance; do not simply cast aside weapons and armor while resting.

55. Following Liu Yin, SMF WCCS, 47B. However, the text simply says "the light will be heavy," perhaps referring to the army's power.

56. A dictum that several commentators note is rather impractical. The commander would have to manipulate the men into developing the spirit for victory and discern ways to take advantage of the conditions of season and weather.

57. In an earlier passage, the same wording indicated confinement as a measure of discipline. This raises questions about the meaning of both paragraphs.

58. The foundation would be benevolence, civil measures; the ends would be the exercise of righteousness, the martial, force.

59. Liu Yin, writing during the Ming dynasty, understands the horses as referring to cavalry. However, this is unlikely if the text was composed prior to 300 B.C. and is describing earlier conditions of warfare (cf. SMF WCCS, 49B).

60. Drums for the head apparently referred to drums that direct the attention of the troops (and therefore their movements) in one direction or another.

61. Drums for the feet would no doubt have indicated the beat or speed of advancing.

62. The various editions record a critical difference in one character, which changes the understanding of the entire passage. The translation follows the reading of *chi*, "already" victorious, rather than *juo*, "whether" victorious. The import of the second reading would carry throughout, translating as "if one may be victorious or not; if one cannot speak about the sharpness of the weapons; cannot speak about the sturdiness of the armor; cannot speak about the sturdiness of the chariots; nor speak about the quality of the horses; nor can the masses take themselves to be many, then the Tao has not yet been attained." (Cf. SMF WCHC, p. 154 [3:67]; SMF WCCS, 50B [where Liu Yin's commentary indicates the character was originally "already"]; SMF CCCY, pp. 117–118.)

63. Here the Tao refers to the ultimate objective of pacifying the realm, gaining final victory. Understanding as in note 62, the Tao would then refer to the Tao of Warfare, the realization of a victorious army.

64. Liu Yin indicates that this refers to the upper ranks, but it need not be so restricted (cf. SMF WCCS, 52A).

65. Some of the modern Chinese translators believe this sentence refers to assuming a defensive position. However, the context does not so delimit it, and in fact the text just below discusses harassing the enemy with a small force (cf. SMF CS, p. 92).

66. "Unorthodox" tactics (*ch'i*) are not specifically mentioned in the *Ssu-ma Fa*, although there are references to using craft and subterfuge in the fragments (cf. No. 31, SMF CS, p. 127) and a few brief discussions of unusual tactics applicable to special circumstances. The concept of the orthodox/unorthodox received its greatest theoretical expression in Sun-tzu's *Art of War* and was refined and expanded thereafter.

67. See fragment No. 30, which is similar (SMF CS, pp. 126–127).

68. To avoid forcing them onto desperate ground, another concept common to Sun-tzu. Note fragment No. 49, SMF CS, pp. 134–135, which advises not pursuing or pressing an enemy too severely.

69. This may also mean "attack their confusion" or "add to their confusion."

70. The Ming commentator Liu Yin believes the character "avoid" should be understood as "prepare." However, there is no need nor justification for this view. The enemy fails to recognize danger or miscalculates its own strength and thus does not avoid fatal situations (cf. SMF WCHC, p. 158).

71. Some editions have the character *pu*—"not"—instead of *yü*—"at" or "on." Consequently, their commentators read the sentence as "If the enemy stops or deviates from the road, be wary!" (Cf. SMF CCCY, pp. 132–133.)

Sun-tzu's Art of War

Abbreviations of Frequently Cited Books

SS AS	Amano Shizuo, *Sonshi, Goshi,* Meiji shoin, Tokyo, 1972.
SS AY	Asano Yuichi, *Sonshi,* Kodansha, Tokyo, 1986.
SS HT	Hosokawa Toshikazu, *Sonshi, Goshi,* Gakken kenkyūsha, Tokyo, 1982.
SS MM	Murayama Makoto, *Sonshi, Goshi,* 3d ed., Tokuma shoten, Tokyo, 1986.
SS NT	Nakatani Takao, *Sonshi,* Kyōikusha, Tokyo, 1987.
SS TY	Tadokoro Yoshiyuki, *Sonshi,* Meitoku shuppansha, Tokyo, 1970.
ST CCCY	Wei Ju-lin, *Sun-tzu chin-chu chin-i,* Shang-wu yin-shu-kuan, Taipei, 1972.
STPF CS	Wu Ju-sung, *Sun-tzu ping-fa ch'ien-shuo,* Chieh-fang-chün ch'u-pan-she, Peking, 1983.
STPF HC	Chün-k'o-yüan chan-cheng li-cheng-pu, ed., *Sun-tzu ping-fa hsin-chu,* Chung-hua shu-chü, Peking, 1981.
STPF SY	Chu Chün, *Sun-tzu ping-fa shih-i,* Hai-ch'ao ch'u-pan-she, Peking, 1990.
STPF TC	Wei Ju-lin, *Sun-tzu ping-fa ta-ch'uan,* Li-ming, Taipei, 1970.
STPF WC	Wang Chien-tung, *Sun-tzu ping-fa,* Chih-yang ch'u-pan-she, Taipei, 1989.
ST SCC	*Sun-tzu shih-chia-chu,* Shih-chieh shu-chü, Taipei, 1984.
ST WCHC	*Sun-tzu,* in Ch'ung-k'an Wu-ching hui-chieh, Chung-chou Ku-chi ch'u-pan-she, Cheng-chou, 1989.
SWTCC WCCS	*Sun Wu-tzu chih-chieh,* in *Ming-pen Wu-ching Ch'i-shu chih-chieh,* Vol. 1, Shih-ti chiao-yü ch'u-pan-she, Taipei, 1972.

Notes to the Translator's Introduction

1. For a basic history of the text, including its influence in Japan, see the introduction and appendixes to Samuel B. Griffith's translation (cited in note 3, below). Over the centuries there have been numerous Japanese translations of varying quality, in-

cluding both scholarly renditions and extremely simplified popular editions—even comic book versions—in this century. Although several have been consulted for our translation, they will be noted only where they differ significantly from the traditional Chinese texts.

2. Lionel Giles, tr., *Sun-tzu on the Art of War,* Luzac and Co., London, 1910.

3. Samuel B. Griffith, *The Art of War,* Oxford University Press, London, 1963. Griffith also supplements the translated text with selected materials from the most important commentaries.

4. For example, Thomas Cleary's *The Art of War,* Shambhala Publications, Inc., Boston, 1988. The introduction contains a discussion of the *Art of War* as a Taoist book, and the translation incorporates extensive quotations from the commentaries.

5. For example, see Ch'i Ssu-ho, in *Hsü Wei-shu t'ung-k'ao,* 3 vols., (Cheng Liang-shu, ed.), Hsüeh-sheng shu-chü, Taipei, 1984, pp. 1599, 1602–1603. Subsequent historical events and later concepts are both noted within the *Art of War.* The former include references to Su Ch'in, and the development of the five phase theory (as now explicated by the Lin-i text entitled "The Yellow Emperor Conquers the Red Emperor")—which is necessary to understand one passage—should be counted among the latter. (See Li Ling in *Hsü Wei-shu t'ung-k'ao,* pp. 1606–1607. Also see Ch'ü Wan-li, *Hsien-Ch'in wen-shih tzu-liao k'ao-pien,* Lien-ching, Taipei, 1983, pp. 433–435; and Chang Hsin-ch'eng, ed., *Wei-shu t'ung-k'ao,* 2 vols., Shang-wu yin-shu-kuan, Taipei, 1970 [reprint of 1939 edition], Vol. 2, pp. 797–801.) Other examples are cited in the notes to the translation.

6. For example, see Li Ling in *Hsü Wei-shu t'ung-k'ao,* pp. 1614–1617; Ch'i Ssu-ho in *Hsü Wei-shu t'ung-k'ao,* pp. 1598–1599; and Chang Hsin-ch'eng, *Wei-shu t'ung-k'ao,* Vol. 2, pp. 797–800. The absence of Sun Wu's name and accomplishments from the *Tso chuan,* which is well noted for portraying Wu's events in comparative detail, is considered fatal to any claim of historicity. However, a few scholars argue that many persons and events pivotal to the history of various minor states went unrecorded, so the absence of Sun-tzu's name should not be considered remarkable.

7. For example, see Li Ling (*Hsü Wei-shu t'ung-k'ao,* pp. 1608–1613) and Ch'i Ssu-ho (*Hsü Wei-shu t'ung-k'ao,* pp. 1599–1602.) Ch'i asserts that the scope of warfare described in the *Art of War,* such as mobilizing one hundred thousand men and one thousand chariots for a single battle, did not occur until the middle of the Warring States period; protracted sieges were not known in the Spring and Autumn because cities were small and had little fortification, whereas in the Warring States they had become important, strongly fortified economic and strategic centers. It was not until the Warring States period that military offices became distinct from the normal hierarchy of nobility and personal command was relinquished by the ruler. Li Ling also avers (p. 1612) that deceit and the use of *ch'i* (unorthodox) tactics never characterized Spring and Autumn conflicts. Others have also pointed out that the forms of organization and the extensive emphasis on speed and mobility characterize infantry rather than chariot warfare and therefore reflect another transition that did not occur until the Warring States period. (Also see Chang Hsin-ch'eng, *Wei-shu t'ung-k'ao,* Vol. 2, pp. 797–801; and Ch'ü Wan-li, *Hsien-Ch'in wen-shih tzu-liao k'ao-pien,* pp. 424–425.)

The contrary view is also held—namely, that this specialization, the growing use of infantry, and a new emphasis on speed all mark evolutions found in the last years of the Spring and Autumn period. (See, for example, Wu Ju-sung, STPF CS, pp. 8–12.) Tsun

Hsin interprets these factors similarly: He feels speed is indicative of the growing use of infantry; assaults on cities were neither desirable nor sustainable because even in the developing economy of the late Spring and Autumn period, cities were not yet significantly profitable targets; and the bronze weapons of the era were designed for close combat and thus were inadequate to undertake sustained assaults against cities. Furthermore, state economies of that era could not sustain protracted campaigns; therefore, Sun-tzu emphasized speed, not duration. In contrast, the increased value of cities—which grew rapidly into major economic and strategic centers in the Warring States period—is witnessed in Sun Pin's treatise, which analyzes the types of cities and provides rudimentary tactics for both defending and besieging them. (See Tsun Hsin, "*Sun-tzu ping-fa* te tso-che chi ch'i shih-tai," *WW* 1974, No. 12, pp. 20–24. The *Six Secret Teachings* and the *Wei Liao-tzu* also consider the tactics of siege warfare, as does the *Mo-tzu*.)

8. See, for example, Cheng Liang-shu's analysis of the terms, concepts, and passages borrowed from Sun-tzu in two relatively early works, Sun Pin's *Military Methods* and the *Wei Liao-tzu,* in *Hsü Wei-shu t'ung-k'ao,* pp. 1617–1625.

9. Wu Ju-sung, in the introduction to his *Ch'ien-shuo,* briefly notes some important military events that historically predate Sun-tzu (see STPF CS p. 14). In the *Art of War* Sun-tzu also quotes from preexisting military works.

10. The question of the *Art of War*'s placement within a fairly continuous evolution of written styles is also the subject of debate. For example, Li Ling (*Hsü Wei-shu t'ung-k'ao,* pp. 1613–14) and Robin D.S. Yates ("New Light on Ancient Chinese Military Texts: Notes on Their Nature and Evolution, and the Development of Military Specialization in Warring States China," *TP* 74 [1988], pp. 218–219) view the text as somewhat advanced over the basic verbatim, summary format of the *Analects,* with some conjoined passages and a logical division of topics but less so than Sun Pin and far less than Hsün-tzu and other late Warring States–period philosophers. They note its similarities with the *Mo-tzu*'s style, and Yates believes many of the connectives are later additions that were provided in an attempt to integrate the text. Yates suggests a date of approximately 453–403 B.C., with later additions, whereas Li Ling ascribes the book to a somewhat later date—roughly the middle of the Warring States period. (Yates also advances the thought that the military works were perhaps the first private books to appear in China.) However, Ch'i Ssu-ho and others—concurring with the general view that private books did not really appear until the Warring States period—observe that Sun Wu should have been approximately contemporaneous with Confucius, but the language and presentation are more sophisticated than is apparently characteristic of this early period. Ch'i believes Lord Shang and Wu Ch'i initiated the first books, followed by Sun Pin and others, and that the *Art of War* represents the confluence of Confucius's theory of kingship, Lao-tzu's concepts of nonaction and unorthodox/orthodox, and Mo-tzu's defensive strategies. He therefore concludes that it is not the work of a single person but that it evolved over a considerable period and was composed in the middle to late Warring States period (see Ch'i Ssu-ho in *Hsü Wei-shu t'ung-k'ao,* pp. 1604–1605).

11. Skeptics abound from the Sung dynasty onward. Some, based on Tu Fu, accused Ts'ao Ts'ao (the first commentator) of butchering the text; others doubted Sun-tzu's existence or felt the work must be a later forgery (see citations in note 6, above). Their skepticism was based in part on the *Han shu* bibliographical notation of a *Sun-tzu* in

eighty-two *pien* (sections, or chapters), despite the *Shih chi* reference to thirteen sections, which gave rise to the charges against Ts'ao Ts'ao. The discovery of the bamboo slip edition in the tomb at Lin-i in 1972, although it comprises only a third of the present edition, at least proves conclusively that the book existed in roughly its current form early in the Han dynasty. Ch'ü Wan-li and others therefore suggest that the thirteen-section work had to be complete before Sun-tzu's interview with the king of Wu because the king mentions this number; the additional sections—if thirteen is not an outright error—probably consisted of materials such as those found at Lin-i, including further dialogues between the king and Sun-tzu (see Ch'ü Wan-li, *Hsien-Ch'in wen-shih tzu-liao k'ao-pien,* pp. 433–434). For further fragmentary materials, including possible evidence for a sixteen-section version of the text, see "Ta-t'ung Shang-sun-chia chai Han-chien shih-wen," *WW* 1981, No. 2.) Later notations describe the Sun-tzu in three *chüan,* or rolls, indicating the difficulty of reconstructing textual lineages with such obscure materials.

Because of its realistic approach (employing spies and deception) designed to ensure the state's survival, the *Art of War* was also vehemently condemned by Confucian literati throughout late Chinese history (and by numerous Westerners early in this century who unfortunately displayed the same attitude as that of Secretary of State Stimson in his unimaginable quashing of code-breaking activities in a hostile world). Sun Wu's existence and role as well as the book itself accordingly were viewed as late fabrications, unworthy of consideration except by the morally reprehensible.

12. After studying both traditional and newly recovered materials, Cheng Liang-shu concludes that the *Shih chi* account is basically accurate and that the *Art of War* was probably composed between 496 and 453 B.C. (see *Hsü Wei-shu t'ung-k'ao,* pp. 1617–1626).

13. See, for example, Ch'i Ssu-ho, who consigns it to the late Warring States period (*Hsü Wei-shu t'ung-k'ao,* pp. 1598–1605).

14. Yates, for example, accepts the view (which is based on internal evidence in comparison with historical events) that the text was composed between 453 and 403 B.C. (see "New Light," pp. 216–219).

15. Sun Pin, a descendant of Sun-tzu, was a brilliant strategist whose achievements have been dramatically preserved in the *Shih chi* and essentially corroborated by the Lin-i texts. His work, entitled *Ping-fa,* is best translated as *Military Methods* to distinguish it from Sun-tzu's work by the same name. Although early bibliographical data indicated the existence of these two distinct works, Sun Pin's book was apparently lost by the end of the Han, and confusion arose as to which Sun actually penned the traditionally transmitted text of the *Art of War.* (A separate, otherwise unknown chapter on cavalry has been preserved in the *T'ung-tien.*) Numerous modern Chinese and Japanese translations have already appeared; primary reports of the find appeared in *Wen wu* in 1974 and are largely contained in the articles cited in note 26, below.

16. Sun Wu and Sun Pin's connected biographies in the *Shih chi, chüan* 65, are translated by Griffith in his introduction (*The Art of War,* pp. 57–62).

17. Wu Tzu-hsü, who is largely credited with playing the major role in Wu's ascendancy, became the subject of a popular cult and numerous stories because of his achievements and perverse execution. (See David Johnson, "The Wu Tzu-hsü *Pien-wen* and Its Sources," Part I, *HJAS* 40.1 [June 1980], pp. 93–156, and Part II, *HJAS* 40.2 [December 1980], pp. 465–505.) The fact that Sun-tzu is not mentioned in the

Tso chuan is sometimes justified by pointing out that Wu Tzu-hsü was such a dominant figure as well as Sun-tzu's direct superior—he simply eclipsed Sun-tzu when credit for Wu's military success was apportioned (cf. Wei Ju-lin, ST CCCY, p. 5).

18. According to most other writings, Sun Wu was actually a native of Ch'i, as is discussed below.

19. Ch'i Ssu-ho, among others, does not believe Sun-tzu would ever have been allowed to commandeer palace women to illustrate his theories of military discipline nor that the execution of the two captains would have been understood as having proved anything. He therefore views the entire episode as an exaggeration (see *Hsü Wei-shu t'ung-k'ao,* p. 1598). Wu Ju-sung believes that rather than being a lesson about discipline, the incident illustrates Sun-tzu's fundamental teaching that a general—once he is in command of the army—does not accept orders from the ruler; this is in accord with his particular understanding of Sun-tzu's major contribution as having been the isolation and characterization of the professional general (STPF CS, p. 3).

20. This and similarly worded phrases appear frequently in the *Seven Military Classics* as well as in the *Art of War.* Essentially a quotation from the *Tao Te Ching,* it is generally taken as evidence of Taoist influence on military thought. However, perhaps this single saying was simply adopted by various military strategists because of their sobering experience in actual warfare, without reference to or acceptance of any other aspects of philosophical Taoism.

21. Yang Chia-lo, ed., *Wu Yüeh ch'un-ch'iu, chüan* 4, "Ho-lü nei-chuan." The translation follows the 1967 SPKY edition reprinted as *Wu Yüeh ch'un-ch'iu,* 2 vols., Shih-chieh shu-chü, Taipei, 1980, Vol. 1, pp. 91–95. The biography continues with Sun-tzu advising the king not to press the attack against Ch'u because the people are already exhausted. Although his name is mentioned several more times in the chapter, except in a single case where he briefly offers tactical advice, it is always coupled with that of Wu Tzu-hsü. Insofar as the *Wu Yüeh ch'un-ch'iu* is attributed to the first century A.D., nearly two centuries after the *Shih chi,* it is not considered reliable evidence for Sun-tzu's activities. However, recent PRC popular military histories frequently contain biographies of Sun-tzu that are based on such remote material (including many writings from the late Warring States and Ch'in periods) reconstructed in some detail. For example, see Ch'en Wu-t'ung and Su Shuang-pi, eds., *Chung-kuo li-tai ming-chiang,* 2 vols., Honan jen-min ch'u-pan-she, Honan, 1987, Vol. 1, pp. 13–18. Virtually every modern edition and translation cites the *Shih chi* biography and assumes Sun-tzu's authenticity, although the *Chung-kuo ku-tai chang-cheng t'ung-lan* (Chang Shao-sheng and Liu Wen-ch'an, eds., Ch'ang-cheng ch'u-pan-she, Peking, 1988, Vol. 1, pp. 74–81) nevers even mentions his name in its account of the war between Wu and Yüeh.

22. Based on the *Shih chi* account, Wu Ju-sung believes—despite intrigues and treachery—the historical Sun-tzu was active in Wu for roughly thirty years, from 512 to 482 B.C. (see STPF CS, p. 4). Chan Li-po suggests a more limited period, 512 to 496 ("Lüeh-t'an Lin-i Han-mu chu-chien *Sun-tzu ping-fa,*" WW 1974, No. 12, p. 15).

23. Later reconstructions of Sun-tzu's life trace his lineage back to the T'ien clan, which had risen to power in Ch'i after the period of Duke Huan, the first hegemon. Sun Wu's grandfather, as a reward for military achievement in a campaign against Lü, was granted the surname *Sun.* Although the T'ien lineage was among the four major ones contending energetically for power in Ch'i, they were largely successful, and skeptics

thus question why Sun-tzu would have ventured into Wu and then remained unknown for some period—during which he befriended Wu Tzu-hsü. Clearly, his family background in military studies would have provided him with expertise that would have been equally useful to his lineage, which was immersed in Ch'i's turmoil.

24. The monumental issue of the relationship between Taoist and military thought in antiquity—including questions of origins, modification of concepts, and direction of influence—obviously requires a voluminous study in itself. Many secondary works in Chinese contain at least brief ruminations on the subject, but almost all of them tend to treat it simplistically and ineffectually. (Hsü Wen-chu's chapter "Sun-tzu ho Lao-tzu ssu-hsiang pi-chiao," found in his book *Sun-tzu yen-chiu* [Kuang-tung ch'u-pan-she, Taipei, 1980, pp. 192–208] is an exception.) In the West, Christopher C. Rand has initiated the analytical effort with an intriguing, if complex, article that provides a conceptual framework for dissecting the various approaches to certain felt problems. (See "Chinese Military Thought and Philosophical Taoism," *MS* 34 [1979–1980], pp. 171–218, and "Li Ch'üan and Chinese Military Thought," *HJAS*, Vol. 39, No. 1 [June 1979], pp. 107–137.) Insofar as it is impossible to compress a meaningful, comparative presentation of Taoist ideas and military thought into a few pages of closely packed notes, we have opted to introduce appropriate comments at relevant points in the translations and other introductory material. (Ch'en Ch'i-t'ien's *Sun-tzu ping-fa chiao-shih* [Chung-hua shu-chü, Taipei, 1955 (reprint of 1944 edition)] contains a succinct analysis of the major philosophical schools' attitudes toward warfare that corrects some general misimpressions found throughout Chinese history [see pp. 231–251]. Kagakuraoka Masatoshi's article "Sonsi to Roshi" [*Tōhō shukyō* 37 (April 1971), pp. 39–50] also initiates specialist studies of this nature.)

25. The *Art of War* is classified by the *Han shu* under the subcategory "*ping ch'üan mou*," roughly "military (imbalance of) power and planning." (See notes 39 and 37 for further discussion of *ch'üan* and concepts of *shih*, to which it is closely related.) *Ch'üan* is frequently identified with expediency, with military measures that stress volatile tactics, swiftness, and indirection to achieve their aims. Books in this category are aptly described as follows: "(Experts in) *ch'üan* and *mou* preserve the state with the orthodox (*cheng*, the upright) and employ the army with the unorthodox (*ch'i*). Only after first estimating (the prospects for victory) do they engage in warfare. They unite the disposition of troops (*hsing*) and strategic power (*shih*), embrace yin and yang, and utilize (those skilled in) technology and the crafts." (A similar partial statement is found in Verse 57 of the *Tao Te Ching*: "Govern the state with the orthodox, employ the army with the unorthodox.") Other works found in this section are Sun Pin's *Military Methods* and the *Wu-tzu;* books by Lord Shang and the T'ai Kung were deleted from the original *Ch'i lüeh* listing (cf. Yates, "New Light," pp. 214–224).

26. The bamboo slip edition discovered at Lin-i constitutes slightly more than one-third of the present *Art of War* arranged in thirteen sections with many chapter headings identical to those in the current text. Although some discrepancies in extant versions (such as those found in the *Ten Commentaries* edition and the *Seven Military Classics* edition) have long been noted, they are essentially the same as—although more extensive than—the Lin-i reconstructed text. Additional material uncovered in the tomb, including a brief conversation recorded between the king of Wu and Sun-tzu (which is generally felt to be a reasonably authentic record of their initial interview), sustains the opinion that the original form of the *Art of War* was in thirteen sections, as

recorded in the *Shih chi,* and suggests that Ssu-ma Ch'ien drew on materials now lost when writing the Suns's biography. (The bamboo slip edition, of course, only proves that this particular version existed prior to—or at least early in—the Han dynasty. Scholars continue to argue about the further implications, including whether the section now entitled "Interview with the King of Wu" provides evidence for Sun Wu's existence and the early origin of the text. See, for example, Li Ling, *Hsü Wei-shu t'ung-k'ao,* pp. 1606–8.) For a brief English overview, see Yates, "New Light," pp. 211–220.

Among the most important original reports are the following: Shantung Sheng Po-wu-kuan Lin-i Wen-wu-tsu, "Shantung Lin-i Hsi-Han-mu fa-hsien *Sun-tzu ping-fa* ho *Sun Pin ping-fa* teng chu-chien te chien-pao," *WW* 1974, No. 2, pp. 15–21; Hsü Ti, "Lüeh-t'an Lin-i Yin-chüeh-shan Han-mu ch'u-t'u te ku-tai ping-shu ts'an-chien," *WW* 1974, No. 2, pp. 27–31; Lo Fu-i, "Lin-i Han-chien kai-shu," *WW* 1974, No. 2, pp. 32–35; and Chan Li-po, "Lüeh-t'an Lin-i Han-mu chu-chien *Sun-tzu ping-fa,*" *WW* 1974, No. 12, pp. 13–19. (Chan Li-po points out several instances in which the bamboo slip edition's reading is completely opposite that of the present text. In some sentences this radically alters the meaning, resolving otherwise contorted and opaque constructions. These and other views, such as those of Chu Chün, are cited in the notes to the translation.) Also see Li Ling's summary reprinted in *Hsü Wei-shu t'ung-k'ao,* pp. 1605–1608. (Li concludes that the discovery is not adequate evidence to revise a much later dating that has been derived from internal evidence.)

27. D. C. Lau, in a rather critical review of Griffith's translation, has discussed several of the main ideas and problems of the text. See "Some Notes on the *Sun Tzu,*" *BSOAS* 28 (1965), pp. 317–335. (Lau's views, although preliminary, are important to understanding the text and are taken into account in the translation.)

28. Wu Ju-sung emphasizes Sun-tzu's dictum that warfare is the greatest affair of state, as distinguished from the Shang-Chou tradition, which identifies both sacrifice and warfare as equally important matters. Wu feels that Sun-tzu's view reflects the new reality emerging late in the Spring and Autumn period and the clash of economic interests between the newly landed class and the old nobility, which had monopolized military power and authority (see STPF CS, pp. 9–12).

29. The *Art of War,* although expressing the basic view found throughout the *Seven Military Classics* that the state must always be prepared for warfare and must nurture adequate material welfare, advocates keeping the people essentially ignorant and manipulating them in battle as though they were sheep. Accordingly, PRC scholars in particular have concluded that the author lived after the rise of early Legalist thought because such measures were characteristic of that approach, and they even termed him a Legalist strategist. See, for example, Tsun Hsin, "*Sun-tzu ping-fa* te tso-che chi ch'i shih-tai," pp. 22–24; Ch'i Ssu-ho in *Hsü Wei-shu t'ung-k'ao,* p. 1603; Li Ling in *Hsü Wei-shu t'ung-k'ao,* p. 1613; and Chan Li-po, "Lüeh-t'an Lin-i Han-mu chu-chien *Sun-tzu ping-fa,*" pp. 14–15. (Keeping the people simple and ignorant is also a pronounced doctrine in the *Tao Te Ching.* However, also see note 173 of the translation.)

30. Extensive, detailed calculations were performed in the ancestral temple prior to mobilizing for a campaign, and presumably similar, although more limited, calculations were performed by the commander before individual engagements in the field. These calculations apparently were based on quantified estimates that assigned numerical values to the strength of systematically examined aspects (as discussed in note 32 below and listed especially in the first chapter of the book itself) for both the enemy

and oneself. (Cf. Lau, "Some Notes on the *Sun-tzu*," pp. 331–332; and Hsü Wen-chu, *Sun-tzu yen-chiu*, pp. 168–169.)

31. Sun-tzu's discussion of the critical qualities that should mark a general is viewed as evidence that professional commanders had already appeared on the historical stage, displacing personal field command by hereditary rulers (see note 19 above; and STPF SY, p. 12). Further confirmation is provided by his insistence that the ruler should not interfere with the commander once the latter has assumed the mantle of authority and ventured forth, as is illustrated by the famous incident from his biography.

32. Sun-tzu's descriptive method for analyzing the tactical aspects of battle is founded on around forty paired, mutually defined, interrelated categories. (This may reflect Taoist thinking about names and their mutual, interrelated definitions, as is sometimes claimed, or simply be the product of his own analytical reflection.) Among these are Heaven-Earth, offense-defense, advance-retreat, and unorthodox-orthodox. (Cf. T'ang Ching-wu, *Sun-tzu ping-fa tsui-hsin-chieh,* self-published, Taipei, 1981 [rev. ed.], pp. 25–27 for an extensive list.)

33. The military concepts and applications of the unorthodox (*ch'i*) and orthodox (*cheng*) probably originated with Sun-tzu, although the *Art of War* does not discuss them extensively. (Note that the text always orders them as *ch'i/cheng*, unorthodox/orthodox, rather than as prioritized in the West—orthodox/unorthodox. The implications, if any, remain to be explored, although against a background of correctness and uprightness, the choice seems deliberate. The military was generally regarded as *ch'i*, in accord with Lao-tzu's dictum: "With the orthodox govern the state; with the unorthodox employ the army.") The later military classics—such as the *Wei Liao-tzu, Six Secret Teachings,* and especially *Questions and Replies*—devote considerable energy to discussing *ch'i* and *cheng* and their employment.

Although the subject clearly requires a separate article or book, in essence "orthodox" tactics include employing troops in the normal, conventional, "by-the-book," expected ways—such as massive frontal assaults—while stressing order and deliberate movement. "Unorthodox" tactics are realized primarily through employing forces— especially flexible ones—in imaginative, unconventional, unexpected ways. Therefore, instead of direct chariot attacks, unorthodox tactics would mount circular or flanking thrusts. Instead of frontal assaults, they would follow indirect routes to stage unexpected, behind-the-lines forays. Their definition, of course, is dependent on normal expectation within a particular battlefield context as well as on the enemy's actual anticipations; therefore, they are mutually defining, mutually transforming, and circular in essence. Thus, as discussed in the other military classics, the orthodox may be used in unorthodox ways, and an orthodox attack may be unorthodox when it is unexpected precisely because it is orthodox—whereas a flanking or indirect assault would thereby be considered normal and therefore orthodox. A frontal feint by a large force, designed to distract or lure an enemy, would be unorthodox.

The concept lends itself to extreme complexities of thought and has often been misunderstood throughout Chinese history or dismissed as simplistic, when in fact it is quite the opposite. However, in essence it remains a descriptive tool for tactical conceptualization, for characterizing and manipulating forces within and exploiting an enemy's matrix of expectations, rather than a transformational mode to be actualized in the concrete reality of men and weapons the way a military formation is deployed. (There is nothing mysterious or mystical about *ch'i* and *cheng* and their mutually productive realtionship, yet later commentators and strategists have sometimes become seriously confused. Under such circumstances, a useful tactical conceptualization becomes an unnecessary obstacle to clear, strategic thinking.)

The concept's origins remain unclear, although speculation tends to identify it with the conflation of thought that crystalized as Taoism or as originating in divinatory practices. The interrelationship of *ch'i* and *cheng* mirrors that of yin and yang, and at least one writer attributes the concept's roots to the yin-yang principles found in the *I Ching.* The orthodox is identified with the firm or hard, whereas the unorthodox correlates with the soft or yielding. (See Hsiao T'ien-shih, *Sun-tzu chan-cheng-lun,* Tzu-yu ch'u-pan-she, Taipei, 1983 [reprint; original, 1942], pp. 197–199.) The observation that reversal characterizes the natural world figures prominently in the *Tao Te Ching,* which is traditionally ascribed to Lao-tzu. *Cheng* turns into *ch'i,* things revert to their opposites (in complementary, dynamic tension) after reaching their pinnacle, as do yin and yang. (Cf. Hsü Wen-chu, *Sun-tzu yen-chiu,* Kuang-tung ch'u-pan-she, Taipei, 1980, pp. 206–208. Hsü observes that although Sun-tzu speaks about the mutually productive relationship of *ch'i* and *cheng,* he emphasizes the unorthodox. Also see Kagakuraoka, "Sonsi to Roshi," especially pp. 44–46.)

In the introduction to his translation, General Griffith states that *cheng* forces engage or engage and fix the enemy, whereas *ch'i* forces defeat him, often through flanking and rear attacks (see *The Art of War,* pp. 34–35). He also characterizes *cheng* forces as the normal or direct and *ch'i* forces as extraordinary or indirect; similarly, as fixing and flanking (or encircling) or again as "the force(s) of distraction and the force(s) of decision" (see p. 42). He goes on to stress that *ch'i* operations are always strange, unexpected, and unorthodox and also notes the reciprocal relationship between *ch'i* and *cheng.* Finally, Griffith adds that the realization of *ch'i* and *cheng* is not confined to tactical levels but may also be implemented on strategic ones (p. 43).

D. C. Lau's criticism of Griffith's translation emphasizes the abstract nature of these two terms, as opposed to invariably identifying them with forces, and suggests that they might best be translated as "straightforward" and "crafty" (see "Some Notes on the *Sun-tzu,*" pp. 330–331).

Benjamin E. Wallacker—in a brief, often-cited etymological article—concludes that *cheng* refers to military operations that pin down or "spike" an enemy, whereas *ch'i* operations are maneuvers that force the enemy off balance and thus bring about his defeat. (He further speculates that Sun-tzu's "formulations" seem likely to have been derived from experience with cavalry forces. This would require revising the date of composition to roughly the dawn of the third century B.C.) See "Two Concepts in Early Chinese Military Thought," *Language,* Vol. 42, No. 2 (1966), pp. 295–299.

Roger T. Ames conceptually translates the terms as "irregular deployments" and "regular deployments" (*The Art of Rulership,* University of Hawaii Press, Honolulu, 1983, p. 68). "Irregular" is perhaps an unfortunate choice because it is inherently burdened with adverse military connotations. Extreme order and control are necessary to employ forces in *ch'i* maneuvers. Thus Rand's choice of "extraordinary" and "normal" seems to be better phraseology (see "Chinese Military Thought," p. 118).

The Chinese secondary literature on Sun-tzu is overwhelming; however, for *ch'i/cheng* most analysts essentially repeat the definitions found in the *Art of War* and later military classics, emphasizing the realization of these abstract concepts in concrete forces. Flexibility, maneuverability, and swiftness are stressed especially when discussing *ch'i* forces, although in Sun-tzu's view they should equally characterize all military units. (For example, see the anonymous Ming dynasty work, *Ts'ao-lu ching-lüeh,* reprinted as *Chung-kuo ping-hsüeh t'ung-lun,* Li-ming, Taipei, 1986, pp. 107–110; and Hsiao T'ien-shih, *Sun-tzu chan-cheng lun,* pp. 197–199. In the Ming dynasty Chao Pen-hsüeh noted that very few generals excelled at employing the unorthodox [*Sun-tzu-shu chiao-chieh yin-lei,* Chung-hua shu-chü, Taipei, 1970 (reprint), p. 79]).

34. Note that Wu Ju-sung believes it is not generally recognized that the *Art of War,* as with some Taoist writings, discusses means and methods for wresting victory with a small force and fewer numbers (see STPF CS, p. 17).

35. The concept of *ch'i* is both integral and fundamental to many aspects of Chinese thought, ranging from metaphysics to medicine and science through religion. One popular view holds that the character originally represented the vapors rising from cooking rice and is thus symbolic of nourishment in every sense. Unfortunately, this critical concept lacks any comprehensive or systematic Western language study. However, two extensive works (cited in note 59 of the translation of the *Six Secret Teachings*) have appeared in Japanese.

36. Sun-tzu's materialistic concept of Heaven and his opposition to consulting omens are seen by Wu Ju-sung as evidence of a new attitude and approach, in contradistinction with the old concepts held by the Chou nobility and the earlier Shang (see STPF CS, p. 18). However, yin-yang and such other concepts as five phase theory, which also appear in the *Art of War,* thereafter developed into an influential school of thought—apparently affecting military theory and even command practices although they were condemned in such other *Seven Military Classics* as the *Six Secret Teachings* and the *Wei Liao-tzu.*

37. The concept of *shih* figures prominently in both ancient military and Legalist thought, perhaps originating with the former. Although many contemporary monographs on the Legalist thinkers attribute its origin to Shen Tao and then trace its appropriation and integration in Han Fei-tzu's systematized thought, studies of *shih* in the military works are just beginning to emerge. (Among the best of the former are Wang Pang-hsiung, *Han Fei-tzu te che-hsüeh,* Tung-ta t'u-shu, Taipei, 1977, pp. 165–179; Hsieh Yün-fei, *Han Fei-tzu hsih-lun,* Tung-ta t'u-shu, Taipei, 1980, pp. 95–100; and Wu Hsiu-ying, *Han Fei-tzu chiu-i,* Wen-shih-che ch'u-pan-she, Taipei, 1979, pp. 86–91. Roger Ames essentially initiated the study of *shih* as a primary, discrete concept with a lengthy chapter in *The Art of Rulership* [University of Hawaii Press, Honolulu, 1983], entitled "*SHIH* [Strategic Advantage/Political Purchase]," pp. 65–107, which is discussed below.)

Unfortunately, *shih* is another topic whose complexities require a book-length study to resolve a number of fundamental questions, including: (1) the concept's definition and character in individual works, such as the *Art of War* (where it is used in several apparently distinct ways); (2) the evolution of the concept in the military works, especially the military classics (presuming the present tentative dating scheme is valid); (3) whether it and other, related concepts are as technically distinct as is frequently assumed, or whether the earlier stages reflect a rather generalized interchangeability of terms and concepts (such as *hsing*—form—and *shih*—power); and (4) the concept's interrelationship with developments in Legalist thought, and whether the later military classics—such as the *Three Strategies*—reflect new dimensions or orientations imposed on essentially tactical military vocabulary under the influence of newly formulated Legalist views.

A complicating factor is the cryptic nature of many of the texts. Statements and even complete sections are generally brief and often enigmatic and apparently represent only notes or cursive summaries of extensive, complex, systematized thought—most of which has either been lost or was never cohesively formulated in writing. (The development of private books may have largely coincided with the rise of specialist military studies. See note 10 above and for general background—although military books are not discussed—Burton Watson's early study, *Early Chinese Literature*, Columbia University Press, New York, 1962; Tsuen-hsuin Tsien, *Written on Bamboo and Silk*, University of Chicago Press, Chicago, 1962; and Joseph Needham et al., *Science and Civilisation in China, Chemistry and Chemical Technology*, Vol. 5, Part 1: *Paper and Printing*, Cambridge University Press, Cambridge, 1985.) Moreover, the assumption that concepts are used in a consistent and precise way in these early books, although necessary for analytical studies, is not invariably valid and also needs to be sustained.

The scope of these issues precludes incorporating an intensive examination of the nature and function of *shih* in an already massive book directed to presenting translations of the *Seven Military Classics*. However, a brief characterization of the dimensions of the concept, a short review of previous studies, and an assessment of various translation possibilities remain unavoidable. Although we must defer any systematic justification of the terms chosen to translate *shih* and its related concepts, some indication of our reasoning is warranted. (Additional notes that briefly explicate the concept within concrete contexts, drawing selectively on the extensive classical commentaries, are appended to the translations.)

Giles (see note 2 above) tends to be criticized severely for his mistranslation and misunderstanding of the *Art of War*, although not always justifiably. His English equivalents for *shih* include "circumstances," "energy," "latent energy," "combined energy," "shape" (where the usage is synonymous with *hsing*—"shape," or "form"), and "strength"; he also simply elides the term by not translating it. None of these seems particularly appropriate, although "latent energy" characterizes situational potential most accurately in several contexts.

General Griffith—an experienced military officer with expert knowledge of strategy and tactics as well as their conceptions and precise vocabulary—also uses a number of distinct, context-dependent terms. (Note that he is generally criticized by D. C. Lau for a lack of consistency in his terminology, as mentioned in note 33 above, but the sense of this term definitely varies within the *Art of War*.) These terms include "circumstances," "situation" (including at least one instance in which it seems highly inappropriate), "momentum," "strength," and "tactical power" (which merits serious consideration as an equivalent for *shih*). He also offers a valuable note to the title of the fifth chapter: "*Shih*, the title of this chapter, means 'force,' 'influence,' 'authority,' 'energy.' The commentators take it to mean 'energy' or 'potential' in some contexts and 'situation' in others" (Griffith, *Art of War*, p. 90). In contrast, for his 1988 translation (see note 4), Cleary selected "force of momentum," "formation," "conditions," and "forces."

The concept appears in the *Book of Lord Shang* and the *Kuan-tzu*, both of which probably (for the most part) date to somewhat after the *Art of War*. For the former,

J.J.L. Duyvendak (*The Book of Lord Shang,* University of Chicago Press, Chicago, 1963 [reprint of 1928 edition]) translates the term as "condition," "power," and "condition of power," with the following note: "Power would really express better the sense of what is meant. Power, that is, which relies on the general condition and trend of things, as an abstract idea, and well distinguished from brute force" (p. 98; also see his general discussion, pp. 97–100). W. Allyn Rickett, in his new translation of the *Kuan-tzu* (Guanzi, Princeton University Press, Princeton, 1985, Vol. 1) uses "circumstances," "situation," "force of circumstances," and " 'authority' derived from a specific position or situation." (See pp. 45, 58–59. He also notes that *ch'üan,* which is discussed separately, refers to "whatever is expedient under varying circumstances" [p. 45] and cites a passage from the *Han chi* that defines the temporal nature of *shih* [pp. 81–82].)

Other translations (with reference to *Han Fei-tzu*) include A. C. Graham's "power-base" and sometimes just "power." He expands on it as "a situation of strength, or on occasion weakness, in relation to circumstances, for example, strategic position on the battlefield" (*Disputers of the Tao,* Open Court, LaSalle, 1989, p. 278). Others include Christopher Rand's "circumstantial power" ("Chinese Military Thought and Philosophical Taoism," p. 174); Yates's "positional advantage" ("New Light," p. 224); and Burton Watson's "advantageous circumstances" (*Hsun-tzu: Basic Writings,* Columbia University Press, New York, 1963, p. 57 and others). D. C. Lau, despite his incisive criticism, does not offer either a definition or a translation for the term in his review article.

Roger Ames's chapter devoted to *shih* traces the concept's evolution from the military thinkers (Sun-tzu and Sun Pin) through its adoption by the Legalists and into later, eclectic texts—such as the *Huai-nan tzu*—and provides extensive material and careful analysis. After noting the various meanings (and close relationship with the term for form, *hsing*), he summarizes his findings as follows: "In the *Sun Tzu,* then, the term *shih* has at least three dimensions of meaning: (1) 'circumstances' or 'conditions'; (2) 'physical disposition' in connection with the deployment of troops; and (3) occupation of a superior position and access to the potential advantages it confers" (Ames, *The Art of Rulership,* p. 68). Because of the apparently close connection between the concept and the strategic advantage derived from occupation of superior positions, Ames elects to use the interesting, if perhaps somewhat unknown, term "purchase." His analysis and arguments are well documented and readily available, so it is only necessary to note that he consciously discards "power" and "force" as being too vague; he believes that "*shih* usually refers to something quite different from the actual strength required to accomplish something" (note 11, p. 222).

From the foregoing it seems clear that the concept of *shih* is generally thought to entail the idea of advantage resulting from superior position. However, this aspect of positional advantage has perhaps been overemphasized, thus overlooking the essential role the element of mass (the army's forces) fulfills in creating impact. The paradigm example is Sun-tzu's analogy of a log or stone perched atop a hill, which, although temporarily stabilized, has great potential energy. According to the concepts of modern physics, the momentum that can be developed and thus the amount of force that can be transferred when a rolling stone collides with an object in its path depend on the original height; the final speed at the moment of impact (which will have been reduced from the theoretical maximum as it passes over objects and encounters resistance); and its weight. Clearly, a stone will transfer less energy at the moment of impact than a much larger boulder, and the total destructive potential is inherently related to the mass of the object.

Accordingly, after studying the nature of the concept in the *Seven Military Classics*, especially in the *Art of War*, two equally important factors appear to be integrated within this concept and should be expressed by any translation: first, the strategic advantage conveyed by superior position, and second, the power of the forces involved. ("Power" refers to the army's overall capability in all aspects—including endurance, spirit, discipline, equipment, command, and physical condition—rather than strength of numbers alone.) Obviously, as the commentator Chiang Pai-li has noted, strategic advantage has a pronounced temporal character; therefore, it should not be confined to exploiting the advantages of terrain, as it is usually characterized.

Strategic advantage *in essence* is a comparative term, not an absolute one, although a vast force will naturally possess great power. (In an extreme case the advantages of terrain perhaps become negligible. A minimal force, such as a platoon or company, represents one extreme, a vast army the other.) Accordingly, we have chosen to translate the term *shih* as "strategic configuration of power" and will use this meaning throughout except where a different sense, such as shape or circumstances, seems to have been intended. Although "strategic power" is basically an acceptable abridgement and perhaps is adequate in itself, "configuration" will generally be added as a reminder that the power results from configuring the military's armed might in accord with and to the exploitation of the terrain in order to gain a strategic advantage. However, when the term is conjoined with others—such as "military" or "army"—or the text would read awkwardly, "strategic power" will be used by itself, with "configuration" understood. Finally, in the context of confined battlefield situations, where "strategic" is inappropriate in scope, *shih* is translated as "tactical configuration of power" or "tactical power."

Insofar as two military forces may be described comparatively, there are some difficulties, and the question might be posed: Does *shih* exist in the absence of an enemy? Is it inappropriate to refer to the *shih* of an army if the two forces are equally matched and poised across a valley, with both—in their static positions—enjoying equal positional advantage relative to a potential battlefield between them and each other? Because Sun-tzu refers to *shih chün*, "strategic power that is equal," the term would seem to refer to a general evaluation versus terrain—and thus configuration of power—rather than specifically confined to being defined relative to an enemy's position and deployment. ("*Ch'üan*," which is discussed below, refers to this relative imbalance of forces.) To facilitate such inquiry, which we intend to address in a separate article, "*shih*" will generally be added parenthetically whenever the term is translated.

(It should also be noted that *shih* and *hsing*—central concepts in the *Art of War*—are also found in an important verse of the *Tao Te Ching*, which can be translated as follows: "The Tao gives them birth, *Te* [Virtue] nurtures them, things give them form [*hsing*], *shih* [power] completes them" [Verse 51].)

38. *Hsing* primarily means shape or form and thus should generally refer to the disposition of the troops or the configuration of forces. However, it also appears in other uses, such as situation or context, and may be nearly synonymous with *shih* at times. We will normally translate the term as "disposition of forces" when it appears alone to avoid confusion with "configuration of power." When in compound use, such as *hsing*

shih—translated by Yates as "form and positional advantage"—the meaning of the two terms probably melds more than previously acknowledged (except perhaps in the *Han shu* classification). In such cases we will normally translate as "configuration of forces and strategic power," with appropriate annotations at each appearance.

39. *Ch'üan* is another difficult term to isolate and define precisely, and the classical commentators assign a wide range of meanings to it. Virtually everyone agrees that in ancient times it referred to the "weight of a steelyard" and thus meant "to weigh" (cf. Kalgren, *GSR*, entry 158/0). With reference to its use in the Mohist classics, Graham, for example, defines it as the " 'weighing' (of benefit and harm)," and " 'positional advantage' used for leverage" (*Disputers of the Tao*, pp. 145, 157, 209, and 164). Duyvendak notes it implies the "deciding influence and authority" (*The Book of Lord Shang*, note 1, p. 260). Other translators assign a wide range of equivalents, such as "power," "authority," "circumstances," and "expediency." (See, for example, Rickett, *Guanzi*, p. 45, where he notes its closeness to *shih*, suggests that translation of "political power," and comments that it can also refer to whatever might be expedient.) The classical Chinese commentators tend to stress the sense of weighing, of balancing forces, as well as its meaning of "authority." However, *ch'üan* is also set off against *cheng*—that is, the "expedient" (associated with the exercise of power, particularly military power) compared with the "upright" or "correct," the measures of proper government and the civil. (See, for example, T'ao Hsi-sheng, *Ping-fa san-shu*, pp. 5–6.) In some usages, the simple equivalent of "authority" is clearly adequate; however, in others the term appears to refer to the strategic imbalance of power or the strategic advantage obtained from such an imbalance and will therefore be translated as "strategic (im)balance of power." Within limited battlefield contexts, in parallel with the translation for *shih*, *ch'üan* is rendered as "tactical balance of power."

Notes to the Text

Insofar as the *Art of War* has been the most studied of the *Seven Military Classics*, numerous editions and commentaries are readily available, with additional modern works appearing annually. Therefore, in contrast to the notes for the other translations, in general only a single reference or two—if any—is provided for the commentators' views. Scholars with expertise in the relevant languages can easily refer to the passages in such standard works as the *Shih-chia chu, Shih-i-chia chu,* or those listed in the abbreviations at the beginning of the notes to the *Art of War.*

The discovery of the Han dynasty bamboo slips (hereafter abbreviated BS) has occasioned close scrutiny of the traditionally transmitted texts, including the Sung/Ming *Seven Military Classics* edition. However, although many contemporary scholars uncritically accept the BS as preserving *the* original text of the *Art of War,* many questions remain. A more balanced view is provided by Chu Chün and is cited in the notes as appropriate. Variations in meaning caused by character differences are also noted, but not simple differences caused by the presence or absence of connectives or particles or minor inversions in textual order. Furthermore, given the fragmentary nature of the text, phrases and sentences missing in the BS are not cited unless they radically affect the meaning.

1. "Estimations" in the sense of objectively estimating the relative strength and weakness of oneself and the enemy for a series of factors. Although twelve such factors are discussed in this chapter, as noted in the translator's introduction there are several

tens of paired factors that could be employed equally well in making such determinations.

The character translated as "estimations"—*chi*—also has the meaning "plans," leading some to translate the title as "Initial Plans," or "First Plans."

2. It is frequently assumed that the factors to be compared are the seven enumerated several paragraphs below because the five that immediately follow are already subsumed under "structure it according to [the following] five factors" (cf. ST SCC, p. 2; and STPF CS, p. 30). However, it seems clear that the "five factors" define the domain for comparative calculations.

Historically, some commentators did not accept the addition of "affairs" following the world "five," the correctness of which has been sustained by the BS, which also lack "factors." (Cf. Ch'en Ch'i-t'ien, *Sun-tzu ping-fa chiao-shih*, Chung-hua shu-chü, Taipei, 1955, p. 65. Chu Chün [STPF SY, pp. 2–3] believes "factors" should not be excised, despite its absence in the BS.)

3. Not the metaphysical Tao of the Taoists but the Tao of government, understood as legal and administrative measures and policies. Liu Yin (SWTCC WCCS, I:2A) understands it in terms of the usual array of Confucian virtues. However, Kuan Feng has observed that the concept is never made explicit in the *Art of War*. See Kuan Feng, "Sun-tzu chün-shih che-hsüeh ssu-hsiang yen-chiu," *Che-hsüeh yen-chiu* 1957, No. 2, p. 72.

4. The character translated as "ruler"—*shang*—may also be understood as "superiors," and the commentators espouse both possibilities. Although Liu Yin is somewhat ambivalent (SWTCC WCCS, I:2A), the translation follows STPF CS, p. 30; and SS AS, p. 26.

5. "Thus" is added from the bamboo slips, although it is implied in any case. The BS conclude the sentence with the phrase "the people will not deceive/contravene him" rather than the traditional "not fear danger." However, Chu Chün believes the traditional reading is preferable (STPF SY, p. 3). Note that the term "deceive" also occurs in the famous sentence somewhat later: "Warfare is the Tao of deception."

Commentators who stress the Legalism in Sun-tzu's thought understand the sentence as "they will die for him, they will live for him." They especially cite Sun-tzu's directive to the commanding general to manipulate his troops in combat like sheep, keeping them ignorant (cf. STPF CS, pp. 30–34). Although Sun-tzu does not advocate positive measures directed to fostering the people's welfare—such as are found in the other *Military Classics*—he does discuss gaining the allegiance of the masses before they can be employed, not impoverishing them, and the importance of benevolence in a commander. Most scholars thus have understood the ideal as being exemplified historically by King Wu of the Chou, who had garnered the willing support of the people. (For further discussion, see Wu Shu-p'ing, "Ts'ung Lin-i Han-mu chu-chien *Wu-wen* k'an Sun Wu te Fa-chia ssu-hsiang," *WW* 1975, No. 4, pp. 6–13.)

6. The BS add: "according with and going contrary to, [the basis of] victory in warfare." Neither STPF CS nor STPF SY includes it. (STPF HC, p. 150.)

7. Terrain classification is one of the keystones of Sun-tzu's strategic analysis, as will become clear from the extensive materials in Chapters eight, ten, and eleven (where these terms are further defined).

The BS add "high or low" at the start of the classifications (STPF SY, p. 3).

8. These terms are variously understood by the commentators. "The Tao of command" may refer to the exercise of command or to the establishment of military hierarchy, the chain of command. "Management of logistics" probably encompasses everything from the types and nature of the army's equipment to the provision and management of that equipment in campaigns. (For summaries, see SS AS, p. 27; STPF SY, pp. 9–10; and ST SCC, p. 8.)

Wu Ju-sung also equates the "laws" with the last four items in the series of questions for comparative evaluation: the implementation of laws and orders, strong forces, well-trained officers and troops, and clear rewards and punishments (See STPF CS, pp. 37–38).

9. "Forces" could also be translated as "weapons and masses" rather than understood as "army masses" or "infantry and masses." However, "masses" emphasizes the contrast with the next criterion for evaluation, the trained "officers and troops" (cf. STPF SY, p. 11; STPF CS, p. 30).

10. Ch'en Hao early interpreted this passage as referring to Sun Wu himself staying or leaving, rather than retaining or dismissing a general. In addition, he identifies the "general" as the king of Wu, because he frequently commanded the army himself, and interprets Sun-tzu's statement as a barb to gain employment (SWT SCC, pp. 11–12. Cf. SS AS, p. 34. However, "retaining him" as a translation seems more reasonable than the sense of "remaining with him").

Liu Yin (SWTCC WCCS, I:6B) makes an odd distinction between the first "general" in the sentence, which he believes refers to the Grand General in his consultations with the ruler, and the second general, which he sees as referring to any subordinate general appointed to implement the chosen strategy (also see STPF SY, p. 12).

11. Liu Yin believes this should refer to the subordinate generals entrusted with field command, "listening to the estimations" and resulting plans (SWTCC WCCS, I:6), but others believe it refers to the king of Wu—the "you" in the translation (cf. SS AS, p. 35, ST SCC, p. 12). *Shih* is discussed in the introductory notes.

12. This is also understood as "outside the normal realm of tactics," using the unorthodox (cf. ST SCC, p. 12; SS AS, p. 36).

13. The imbalance of power should be created with the objective of facilitating and attaining the "gains to be realized." Merely creating an imbalance of power would be pointless, and such an imbalance is already inherently dependent on the advantages one possesses (cf. STPF SY, pp. 13–14, for a similar view and an example). *Ch'üan* is discussed in the introductory notes.

14. The term "deception" here inadequately conveys both the positive and negative aspects of the matter. We prefer to translate as "deception and artifice" because much craft is involved in not only concealing appearance, which is the simplest form of deception, but also in creating false impressions.

The fourteen sentences that follow should be understood as tactical principles flowing from this realization. They are also believed to reflect or to be a distillation of tactical experience gained through combat situations in the Spring and Autumn period (STPF CS, pp. 39–40).

15. Translators often take this as "when you are nearby make it appear as if you are distant," but this would clearly be contrary to reality. It would be impossible for the enemy not to know—through reconnaissance and observation—an army's actual position, although attempts were initiated routinely to diminish the accuracy of such per-

ceptions (such as by dragging brush and increasing or reducing the number of cook fires at night). More likely, the position to which the army is about to move, an objective that is about to be attacked, is intended as translated (following Liu Yin, SWTCC WCCS, I:9A. Compare ST SCC, p. 14). Chu Chün notes this might also be understood temporally, as immediate future and some distant time (STPF SY, p. 14).

16. Two readings of these laconic sentences are possible. The critical question is whether the first term in each of them and the several that follow below should be read in the light of the Tao of Warfare and thus as explications of craft and deception and ways to manipulate the enemy, as Sun-tzu discusses extensively, or simply as a series of individual items. In the latter case, it is possible that they were simply conjoined here—rather than being the product of Sun Wu's systematic analysis—from preexisting rubrics about military action. It is tempting to read them all in parallel, with the first term always describing an aspect of the enemy and the second an action to be applied, but in our opinion the imposition of such parallelism—which is frequently invalid even for two phrases within a single short sentence—is too artificial.

Accordingly, for the first sentence, one reading would be that "If the enemy [desires] profit, entice them"—understanding "with the prospect of profit," which is somewhat redundant. The translation emphasizes the active approach because we should assume that armies will generally move for tactical advantage. At the same time we must remember that a frequently discussed (and readily exploitable) flaw in some commanding generals is greed.

For the second sentence, two additional renderings are variously suggested: "If they are disordered, seize them," and "Show [apparent] disorder [in your own forces] and seize them." The commentators cite a number of historical examples in support of the latter, but the former has adherents as well, and decisive evidence for a definitive reading is lacking. (Measures such as enticing them with profits, sowing rumors, and fostering their licentiousness would all cause the sort of disorder that could easily be capitalized on.) The translation follows Liu Yin. (SWTCC WCCS, I:9B. Cf. ST SCC, p. 15. Also note the extensive analysis, with examples of these and the following sentences, in Tzu Yü-ch'iu, ed., *Mou-lüeh k'u,* Lan-t'ien ch'u-pan-she, Peking, 1990, pp. 70–76.)

The term "take them" is said to indicate an easy victory rather than a difficult conflict (cf. ST SCC, p. 15).

17. The "substantial" and the "vacuous" (or empty) form a correlative pair that is closely identified with Sun-tzu's thought, although the terms may have predated him. One of his fundamental principles is exploiting voids, weaknesses, fissures, and vacuities. The opposite, the "substantial" (*shih*)—corresponding roughly to strong, well-organized, disciplined, expertly commanded, entrenched forces—is generally to be avoided rather than attacked with ineffectual and wasteful frontal assaults. (Wang Chien-tung, STPF WC, p. 31, notes the phrase can also be understood as "be substantial and prepare for them," although this appears less appropriate.) The theme of Chapter 6 is "Vacuity and Substance."

18. The military thinkers generally advocate fostering and exploiting anger because it blinds the general to the realities of the battlefield and takes away the troops' judgment. Consequently, suggestions that *jao* means "avoid them" are probably not accurate, even though Sun-tzu does recommend avoiding an army when it is at the peak of its fervor. (An alternative translation would be "anger and perturb them.")

19. Again, two readings are possible, the alternative being "if they are humble/lowly, make them arrogant" (cf. Tau, ed., *Mou-lüeh k'u,* pp. 71–73; STPF SY, p. 15). The translation follows Liu Yin, SWTCC WCCS, I:10B–11A. Logically, if they are "humble" they already lack combative spirit, and it would be foolish to raise their anger to no purpose. (On the other hand, they may also simply be restrained and composed.)

20. The text appears to suggest the general cannot transmit or divulge his determinations with regard to these factors before the battle. However, it may also entail the idea that they cannot be rigidly or arbitrarily determined before the situation develops. Commentators embrace both views (cf. ST SCC, pp. 20–21; STPF CS, p. 31).

21. The procedure for strategic analysis in the ancestral temple apparently assigned relative values to the various factors, including those discussed in this chapter. D. C. Lau (see "Some Notes on the *Sun-tzu,*" pp. 331–332) suggests that counting sticks were used for each factor and then the totals taken. Some form of relative weighing was probably used because certain factors would be more significant than others, and a simple total is probably misleading. (The translation follows Liu Yin. Also compare STPF CS, p. 31; Ch'en's *Chiao-shih,* pp. 72–73; Kuan Feng's comments on the various factors in "Sun-tzu chün-shih che-hsüeh ssu-hsiang yen-chiu," pp. 71–75; and Yü Tse-min, "Shih-hsi Chung-kuo ku-tai te chan-lüeh kai-nien," in *Ping-chia shih-yüan* [ed. Chün-shih li-shih yen-chiu-hui], Chün-shih k'o-hsüeh ch'u-pan-she, Peking, 1990, Vol. 2, pp. 221–226.) Giles errs in understanding "no points" as simply failing to perform any strategic calculations.

22. D. C. Lau ("Some Notes on the *Sun-tzu,*" pp. 321–325) has pointed out that initial phrases in Sun-tzu passages are often captions or summaries. The five-character phrase introducing this section appears to be one of these; however, others are less clear. Traditionally, such introductory captions have simply been made the subject of a sentence, understanding a term such as "requires" to bridge the subject and its expansion (cf. ST CCCY, p. 86; STPF WC, p. 52; and STPF CS, p. 42). Our translations generally adopt Lau's insight wherever captions apparently precede material of any length.

23. Griffith (*The Art of War,* p. 73) and some modern Chinese editions (such as STPF WC, p. 53) insert a character meaning "to value" or "esteem" in this sentence, citing (in Griffith's case) the *Seven Military Classics* edition, However, neither the latter nor the ST SCC edition contains it; Liu Yin merely uses it in his commentary explaining the passage (cf. SWTCC WCCS, I:15A; and ST SCC, p. 23).

24. This and similar sentences, as discussed in the translator's introduction, are cited as evidence for the undeveloped state of offensive and siege warfare and the relative economic unimportance of cities.

25. This sentence has various interpretations. Generally, it is agreed that the campaign should be won with only a single mobilization and conscription, which would be reasonably possible given the nature and still-limited scope of warfare in Sun-tzu's era (cf. STPF SY, pp. 27–28). Not transporting provisions a third time is understood in two distinct ways: The army is provisioned only once—when about to depart—and thereafter it must plunder and forage, securing provisions on the march and in the field. Moreover, when the troops return they are not reprovisioned (cf. SWTCC WCCS, I:16B). A second, more common, and more logical interpretation holds that they are provisioned at the commencement of the campaign and supplied again on returning

after recrossing the state's borders but must fend for themselves when in the field (cf. ST SCC, pp. 26–27; and SS AS, p. 54).

26. As noted in the general introduction, in the Early Chou period the "hundred surnames" were essentially the members of the aristocracy, the free men. As time passed and their status declined, they lost their privileged status and became the common people. The usage of the term in Sun-tzu reflects a period when the earlier meaning was becoming eclipsed but the term was probably not yet simply equivalent to "common people." From the context it is apparent that the hundred surnames farm the land, have the material wealth to pay taxes, and have the leisure to fulfill military obligations. Because the *Art of War* specifically uses this term, it is distinguished from terms that mean "the people" or the "common people" in the translation.

27. The bamboo slips have "market" for "army," with the phrase reading "the market nearby" ("the army" then being understood).

28. Military expeditions thus impose heavy direct and indirect burdens on the populace. Under the military taxation system (imposed in varying degrees and different forms) in Sun-tzu's era, hamlets and villages—depending on their classification, acreage tilled, and population—had to provide men to serve in the military effort and furnish weapons, equipment, and draft animals. If they could not obtain the weapons and supplies from their own inventory or stock, they had to be purchased. Moreover, the cost of such items for the village's own use concurrently escalated, depleting everyone's financial resources. Thus wartime inflation would strike them especially hard. (For further commentary, see Liu Yin, SWTCC WCCS I:17B; Ch'en, *Chiao-shih*, pp. 78–79; and STPF WC, p. 64.)

29. The BS are somewhat different, reading "They will exhaust their strength on the central plains, while in the interior their houses will be empty" (cf. STPF SY, p. 30). The term for "empty" is actually the much stronger term "vacuous," or "void."

30. The BS have "six-tenths" rather than "seven-tenths."

31. The term translated as "large oxen" is literally "village oxen." The meaning seems to have originated with the reported practice of having each village of sixteen "well-fields" (with eight families to each of the latter) raise one ox, which presumably remained the ruler's property. It would be employed for military purposes when required. This might explain how such oxen were viewed as expenditures from the ruler's treasury rather than as a tax contribution from the people (cf. SWTCC WCCS, I:17B; and SS AS, p. 55).

32. "Profits," understood as profits for the state. However, the term also means "advantage," as in military advantage, and the sentence could equally well be understood as "What [stimulates them] to seize advantage from the enemy is material goods." Wang Hsi views this sentence as referring simply to the establishment of rewards as incentives because "If you cause the masses to covet profits and take them for themselves, then perhaps they will violate the constraints and [military] discipline" (ST SCC, p. 31).

33. The translation follows Liu Yin's commentary on the *Seven Military Classics* and expresses the traditional viewpoint—namely, that preserving the enemy's state is the primary objective; destroying it is only second best. This accords with Sun-tzu's overall emphasis on speedily wresting victory and subjugating one's enemies without engaging in battle if at all possible. (Modern Chinese commentators cite the example

of Germany nourishing its rancor and hatred subsequent to World War I until militarily reasserting itself in World War II. See, for example, STPF WC, pp. 76–83.)

However, D. C. Lau ("Some Notes on the *Sun-tzu,*" pp. 333–335) argues that the sentence should be translated as "It is best to preserve one's own state intact; to crush the enemy's state is only a second best." Although he advances a cogent argument, the traditional understanding appears more appropriate. Whether from a Confucian, Taoist, or Legalist perspective, the idea of gaining victory while inflicting the least amount of damage on the enemy is generally fundamental. Except perhaps when blindly exacting revenge, all commanders seek to minimize their own losses while maximizing the gains that can be realized. Occupying a thoroughly devastated state was never espoused by any ancient Chinese military thinker, although scorched earth policies were prominently exploited by "barbarian" tribes later in Chinese history, and mass slaughter accompanied by wartime rampages that resulted in the wholesale destruction of cities did characterize the late Warring States period.

34. Unit force levels are discussed in Appendix E.

35. These earthworks are variously identified as mounds for overlooking and assaulting the city and as protective walls that allow the besiegers shielded movement outside the city's walls, beneath potentially withering fire (cf. STPF SY, p. 44).

36. This continues the thought of the first passage because a ruler whose objectives include "preserving" others is more likely to be welcomed by the populace. (It also accords with the Confucian ideal of King Wu, previously noted.)

37. Following Liu Yin, SWTCC WCCS, I:24B–25A; and SS AS, p. 74. D. C. Lau ("Some Notes on the *Sun-tzu,*" p. 320) believes this sentence refers to dividing the enemy, which is equally possible. However, with double strength, as Liu Yin (following Ts'ao Ts'ao) notes, one can mount a frontal assault with one part to fix them and then employ a flanking (i.e., unorthodox) attack to overwhelm them. This understanding also seems more congruent with the next sentence, which still allows for engaging the enemy if you are merely equal in strength. Forcing the enemy to divide his troops is a hallmark of Sun-tzu's thought. By dividing one's forces to launch a secondary front, the enemy would be forced to respond or face the loss of his other position. Thus he would also have to divide his forces, thereby accomplishing Sun-tzu's objective. (See Tu You's commentary and also the divergent views in ST SCC, p. 44, and Chu's analysis, STPF SY, pp. 47–49.)

38. Such as by assuming a desperate position to fight to the death or mounting a defense when flight would be appropriate.

39. As discussed in the translator's introduction, Sun-tzu is writing after the early rise of the professional commander and the increasing estrangement of many rulers from field command. The distinction between the forms of administration, discipline, and temperament appropriate to the civil and the martial is more pronounced in the other *Military Classics,* such as the *Ssu-ma Fa.* (For discussion, see the introductory section to the translation.) However, even here Sun-tzu is already warning of the dangers posed by inappropriately intermixing them.

Some editions have *ssu*—"direct" or "manage"—rather than *t'ung*—"the same as"—which resolves a somewhat awkward passage. However, both the Sung and Ming editions have *t'ung,* which can be understood as translated. (The next sentence also contains "same as [the civil]," which has been left untranslated because it can also be understood as the ruler uniting the authority for the joint command in his own hands. Cf. STPF SY, pp. 51–52; and STPF CS, p. 47. Also note the explanations in SS AS, pp.79–80.)

40. The BS have *chih,* "to know" or "to understand," rather than "recognizes."

41. The BS read "Thus, in warfare, one who knows them (the enemy) and knows himself ..."

42. The BS contain two versions of this chapter, the second basically somewhat shorter than the first.

43. "Unconquerable" rather than "invincible" because the latter tends to connote a permanence inappropriate to fluctuating battlefield conditions. The invincible are never conquerable, whereas an army—due to its disposition, exploitation of terrain, and other factors—may be temporarily unconquerable.

44. The BS lack "in warfare."

45. Contrary to our usual practice, in this rare case the translation is based on the Han bamboo text rather than the traditional *Seven Military Classics.* The latter has perturbed commentators because of its apparent inconsistency with Sun-tzu's thought and the logical development of the paragraph. The traditional text simply reads: "If one defends then he is [or will be] insufficient; if he attacks then he will [have] a surplus." This is understood by commentators such as Liu Yin to mean that one defends *because* his strength is inadequate and attacks because his force is more than abundant (cf. SWTCC WCCS, I:30). However, this contorts the grammar because it requires that the term be reversed: "If insufficient one defends" (cf. ST SCC, p. 56; STPF CS, p. 59. Also note Chu Chün's balanced appraisal, STPF SY, pp. 58–59).

46. The phrase "One who excels at offense" does not appear in the BS. The sentences would then be elided to read: "One who excels at defense buries himself away below the lowest depths of Earth and moves from above the greatest heights of Heaven." There are also unimportant, minor variations in the BS versions (cf. STPF CS, pp. 60–61; STPF SY, p. 60).

47. The BS lack "the ancients."

48. From the two BS versions, the original sentence apparently read: "Thus the battles of those who excelled did not have unorthodox victories, nor fame for wisdom, nor courageous achievements of courage" (cf. STPF CS, pp. 58–59; STPF SY, p. 60).

49. The BS have "Thus one who excels cultivates the Tao."

50. "Tao" is variously explained by the commentators as referring to such Confucian virtues as benevolence and righteousness—implemented to attract the people—or the military principles essential to being unconquerable. Cf. SWTCC WCCS, I:32B; ST SCC, pp. 61–62.

51. The BS have *cheng*—"upright," "to rectify," "to regulate"—instead of *cheng*—"government." However, as Chu Chün notes, the former could have been a loan for the latter because the two were somewhat interchangeable at that time. He therefore rejects the emendation suggested by the bamboo slips. The translation reflects the traditional text, but with the character for government understood as "regulator," rather than following commentaries that read it as "government" and produce a translation that reads "Therefore he is able to conquer defeated governments" (cf. STPF CS, p. 59; STPF SY, pp. 60–61; and ST SCC, pp. 61–62).

52. The caption for this sentence, literally "military *fa,*" is considered to be a book title by Tadokoro Yoshiyuki (SSTY, p. 118) and Ch'en Ch'i-t'ien (*Chiao-shih,* p. 105),

translatable as the "Art of Methods." This is the same title as the *Art of War* (which is best translated as "Military Methods," but we have adopted the traditional rendering). *Fa* encompasses the meanings of "laws" and "methods," with the latter more appropriate here. Rather than the title of a preexistent book or section of a work (which is also referred to in several other military classics), it should be understood as the fundamental methods for warfare, the measures that then follow (cf. STPF SY, p. 61; SS AS, p. 104). In the BS only the term *fa* appears, but Chu Chün retains "military methods" (STPF SY, p. 61).

53. "Measurement" is generally understood by the commentators as referring not only to the extent and dimensions of the terrain but also its classification according to the categories advanced in the various chapters that follow.

54. "Estimation" is variously described as referring to types of forces suitable for segments of the terrain, such as crossbowmen for the hills, or the quantities of materials required to sustain the battle. All these terms are not otherwise discussed in the *Art of War*, and their referents thus remain a matter of speculation.

55. The BS add "weighing" and "the people" to the traditional text, producing "weighing the victory of a combative people." Although this is accepted by Wu Jung-sung (STPF CS, p. 58), Chu Chün appears correct in opting for the traditional text (and thereby avoiding an awkward grammatical construction). Cf. STPF SY, p. 61.

56. As D. C. Lau has pointed out ("Some Notes on the *Sun-tzu*," pp. 332–333), the use of *hsing* (shape, configuration) here is nearly identical to *shih* (strategic power).

57. The BS merely have *Shih*, "Strategic Power," for the title.

58. The terms translated as "configuration" and "designation" are *hsing*—"form" or "shape"—and *ming*—"name." Within the context of Sun-tzu's thought, the first seems to indicate the form or configuration of forces, as in formations and standard deployments. The second appears to refer to naming the units, designating them in some fashion—such as by flags with specific symbols. However, the earliest commentary, which is by the great general Ts'ao Ts'ao, equated *hsing*/form with flags and *ming*/name with gongs and drums. Liu Yin and others extrapolate on this thought, but some scholars—such as Tu Mu—identify *hsing* with deployments and *ming* with flags (see SWTCC WCCS, I:35; ST SCC, pp. 66–67; STPF CS, pp. 67–68; and Wang Chien-tung's overview, STPF, WC, pp. 144–146). Robin D.S. Yates ("New Light," pp. 220–222), based on his extensive research on the *Mo-tzu*, believes both terms refer to flags and that the historically and philosophically significant term *hsing-ming* originates with the military thinkers. (For an early discussion of *hsing-ming*—often translated as "performance and title"—as well as the issue of which character is appropriate for the term *hsing*, see Herrlee G. Creel, "The Meaning of *Hsing-ming*," reprinted in *What is Taoism*, University of Chicago Press, Chicago, 1970, pp. 79–91.)

59. For "invariably" the BS have "entirely/altogether." (Cf. STPF CS, p. 65; and STPF SY, p. 74. Chu Chün [STPF SY] does not accept the revision.)

Unorthodox (*ch'i*) and orthodox (*cheng*) are discussed in the notes to the translator's introduction. An intriguing view is also advanced by Kuan Feng, equating the orthodox with movements designed to realize advantage and the unorthodox with actions that turn disadvantageous situations into advantageous ones. See "Sun-tzu chün-shih che-hsüeh," pp. 81–82.

60. See note 17 for an explanation of the vacuous and substantial.

61. The BS have "Heaven and Earth" rather than just "Heaven."

62. The BS have "rivers and seas" or "Yellow River and the seas" rather than the "Yangtze and Yellow rivers."

63. The Sung and Ming editions have *keng* rather than *fu*. Although Sun-tzu does not continue the explicit comparison, all the commentators make it clear that the unorthodox and orthodox are mutually related just like these further examples of cyclic phenomena (SWTCC WCCS, I:36B; ST SCC, p. 69).

64. Although the character *pien*, "change," has generally been translated as "transformation," we have opted to preserve the (possibly artificial) distinction between *pien* ("change") and *hua* ("transformation") throughout our translation of the *Seven Military Classics*. As a tentative basis for employing "change" rather than "transformation," it might be observed that musical notes are not transformed in substance when producing new sounds, only changed in effect. Similarly, the composition of a military force is untransformed when its employment is changed from orthodox to unorthodox. However, this is a topic that requires further study, and an illuminating paper by Nathan Sivin should appear coincident with the publication of this book.

65. The BS version is slightly different; it lacks the character *shun* but adds another *huan*, so it would read: "The unorthodox and orthodox in circle [fashion] mutually produce each other, just like an endless circle" (cf. STPF CS, p. 65; and STPF SY, p. 75).

66. The BS lack "pent-up" (or "accumulated") water. Most translators use the term "torrent" to describe the flow, but the essential idea in the Sung/Ming edition is that water has been restrained and has accumulated and then—when suddenly released— flows violently, turbulently, carrying even stones along. (This is not to deny that some very swift currents can tumble stones, but the pent-up water image is more appropriate to the idea of potential power unleashed and is used in many other military writings— perhaps quoted from Sun-tzu—in this fashion.)

67. The term translated as "constraints" is *chieh*, commonly used to indicate constraints or measures imposed on troops. The term lacks a satisfactory English rendering because it encompasses the concepts of "control," "timing," and "measure." The commentators generally agree it refers to the modulation of both time and space. Sun-tzu apparently intends "constraints" to encompass the deliberate structuring of actions to ensure that the timing is precise and that the impulse of strategic power is imparted at the proper moment to the objective at a critical position. When the target is moving, such as a bird or an enemy, controlling action to attain this objective becomes more difficult. The final stage should be kept short so as to minimize the enemy's ability to avoid the onslaught or effect countermeasures, as Sun-tzu states below. Liu Yin notes it also refers to the control or measurement of strength so that the objective will be reached and not missed. (SWTCC WCCS, I:37B. Also see ST SCC, pp. 71–72; ST CCCY, p. 124; and SS AS, pp. 119–120.)

68. The same term as for the "onrush" of the water, although "to attack" is clearly assumed.

69. Literally, "short." Whether in a temporal or spatial dimension, briefness is synonymous with precision and effectiveness.

70. The meaning of the circular formation has stimulated voluminous commentaries. Essentially, the army seems to be involuntarily compressed into a circular formation and is therefore vulnerable. However, such a formation presents no exposed points or positions yet offers the possibility of numerous fixed deployments and the employment of both orthodox and unorthodox tactics through unfolding. Conse-

quently, in some views it is chosen deliberately rather than forced on the army to allow flexibility while creating the similitude of difficulty and apparent defeat (cf. SWTCC WCCS, I:38A; ST SCC, pp. 72–75).

71. The translation follows Liu Yin's commentary, understanding the sentence as expressing some bases for practicing the art of deception (SWTCC WCCS, I:38A). However, there are other possible frames of reference for "Chaos is given birth from control," among them that one's own troops may become chaotic despite being well controlled. This might result from overcontrol, lack of flexibility, too fragile an organization, a shift in battlefield conditions, or laxity in maintaining discipline and organization (cf. ST SCC, pp. 74–76; STPF SY, p. 84; SS AS, pp. 122–123).

72. "Foundation," following the Sung/Ming text. However, many other texts—including the BS and the SCC—have "troops," which most modern commentators feel is correct. "Foundation" presumably refers to the general's well-disciplined, well-organized army, so indirectly it means "forces." (Cf. SWTCC WCCS, I:39A; ST SCC, p. 78; STPF SY, p. 75. Wu Jung-sung retains *pen,* "foundation," and translates it as "heavy forces." STPF CS, p. 67.)

73. Liu Yin comments: "Thus one who excels at warfare seeks (victory) through the certain victory of the army's strategic power, not through reliance on untalented men. Thus he is able to select the talented among men and entrust them with strategic power" (SWTCC WCCS, I:39B). Although many others follow Liu Yin's thoughts, a second line of commentary observes that by relying on strategic power, men can be employed according to their talents in the quest for victory. Within the context of surpassing power, even the timid will become assertive and perform their roles—something rewards, punishments, and the laws may not be able to accomplish. Furthermore, men will not be forced to attempt actions they are unable to perform (cf. ST SCC, pp. 79–80; SS AS, p. 127; STPF SY, pp. 86–87).

74. The chapter is so named because key paragraphs advance the concept of striking and exploiting any voids or weaknesses in the enemy's deployment. The substantial should always be avoided rather than confronted. (In the BS, the title characters are reversed: "Substance and Vacuity.")

75. Controlling others, rather than being controlled by others, is one of Sun-tzu's fundamental principles, and many of his tactical measures are devoted to appropriately manipulating the enemy.

76. The *Seven Military Classics* edition reads "Go forth to places he will not race to," whereas the ST SCC edition emends the "not" to "must" (cf. SWTCC WCCS, II:2B–3A; ST SCC, p. 87). D. C. Lau also supplies a perceptive note on the error of this emendation ("Some Notes on the *Sun-tzu,*" p. 321), but the recovered bamboo text indicates the original reading is "must," and collateral evidence appears in the "T'ai-p'ing yü-lan" (hereafter TPYL) quotation. (However, Chu Chün prefers the traditional text. See STPF SY, pp. 90–91, 96.) This coheres well with the preceding sentence, and the traditional text has been altered accordingly. Also note that some commentators and translators would understand the traditional sentence as "Go by way of places he will not race to."

77. Because this sentence does not appear in the bamboo text, some modern commentators view it as a later, inappropriate accretion (see STPF CS, p. 78). However, these coupled sentences are frequently quoted in other military works and have an inherent parallelism that tends to suggest their correctness (cf. SS AS, p. 134).

78. STPF CS, based on the BS, emends "will not attack" to "must attack" (STPF CS, p. 73). There is also collateral evidence for this reading in the TPYL. However, "will not attack" accords with the chapter's trend of thought, particularly in light of such sentences below as "When someone excels at defense the enemy does not know where to attack" and "If I do not want to engage in combat, even though I merely draw a line on the ground and defend it, they will not be able to engage me in battle because we thwart his movements." If the defense is impregnable, the enemy will be deterred from foolishly attacking and uselessly expending his forces. (Cf. STPF SY, p. 91; SS AS, pp. 137–138; and ST SCC, pp. 88–89.) Wu Ju-sung notes that tacticians of Sun-tzu's generation valued defense over offense, although his text accepts the BS version "must attack" (see STPF CS, pp.77–78).

79. Formless, "not *hsing,*" having no form or discernible configuration.

80. The BS have "an advance which is unresponded to" rather than "unhampered" (or "not repulsed").

81. There are two differences in the BS: "stopped" for "pursued" and "distance" for "speed." Thus it would read "To effect a retreat that cannot be stopped, employ unreachable distance." These are variously accepted or rejected by modern commentators. (Cf. STPF CS, p. 73; STPF HC, pp. 91–92; and the traditional commentaries, ST SCC, pp. 90–91.)

82. This sentence has occasioned rather divergent views. Although the translation reflects the chapter's progression, another possibility is understanding the "*hsing chih*" at the beginning of the sentence in a causative sense, as causing them to betray their form (STPF SY, p. 99). A radically different view—expressed by Liu Yin, among others—suggests that through the employment of unorthodox and orthodox tactics, one creates and displays a deceptive form or disposition to the enemy while actually being formless (SWTCC WCCS, II:5B). Others simply interpret it as displaying a form to the enemy (see STPF CS, p. 75; ST SCC, p. 93; and SS AS, p. 144).

In the BS the sentence begins with "Thus those who excel at command ... "

83. Note that D. C. Lau also understands the sentence in this way, as do several commentators. Cf. "Some Notes on the *Sun-tzu,*" pp. 329–330.

84. The BS invert the sequence of "field of battle" and "day of battle" and also lack the character for "Assemble."

85. The sequence of left/right and front/rear is reversed in the BS.

86. Presumably a comment directed to the king of Wu by Sun-tzu. However, Chang Yü comments that "I" is an error for Wu, the State's name (which seems unlikely). SWTCC WCCS, II:8A; ST SCC, p. 97.

87. The BS have "solely" or "monopolized" for "achieved." Accordingly, "Thus I say victory can be monopolized."

88. Predictability means having form; therefore, repeating previously successful tactical methods would completely contradict Sun-tzu's principle of being formless. Through flexibility and variation the configuration of response attains to the inexhaustible.

89. The BS have "move/moving" rather than "configuration." Because "configuration" is used consistently throughout the chapter, it seems preferable.

90. The BS have "victory" rather than "configuration."

91. Again the BS have "move" rather than "flow." (Chu Chün, among others, prefers the traditional text. See STPF SY, p. 93.)

92. The BS have "complete," so the phrase would be translated as "completed (fixed) configuration of power."

93. The BS lack "water," so the last part of the sentence would also describe the army.

94. The BS only have "transform" rather than "change and transform" and also lack "wrest victory."

95. The BS have two characters at the end, *shen yao*—perhaps an additional comment by an unknown hand with the meaning "Spiritual Essentials."

96. The title does not refer to actual combat but to achieving the conditions that make contention possible. The main themes are therefore the considerations of rapid versus measured advance; exploitation and avoidance of terrain and obstacles; and the critical element of *ch'i*, the army's spirit.

97. "Tactics" or "plans," but also the same character as "estimations" and therefore suggestive of comparatively valuing the effects of various routes.

98. The translation follows the *Military Classics* edition (SWTCC WCCS, II:14B). However, other editions (such as the ST SCC, p. 106; STPF CS, p. 81; STPF SY, p. 109) and the BS all have the character for "army" (*chün*) rather than "masses" (*chung*), so both parts read in parallel: "Thus combat between armies can be advantageous; combat between armies can be dangerous." Both readings are congruent with the chapter's content because fighting with an undisciplined mass is dangerous, whereas it is the nature of warfare to entail both gain and loss.

99. Following STPF WC, p. 215, and SS AS, p. 169. They literally "roll up their armor" and presumably leave it behind with the baggage train so as to allow greater foot speed. (Heavy equipment is implied from the sentences below, which all couple the baggage and heavy equipment.)

100. In the *Art of War* and the *Ssu-ma Fa*, the concept of plundering and then dividing the spoils among the troops remains evident. In contrast, the later *Military Classics* strongly advocate a policy of neither harming the general populace nor seizing their possessions.

101. Night battles did not commence until late in the Spring and Autumn period and were not common because the confusion wrought by the darkness made the results uncertain. The exact reason for multiplying the numbers of flags and fires is a subject of debate among the commentators: It was done either to ensure that their effect as tools for communication and signaling literally overwhelmed the soldiers or (and possibly as well as) to confuse the enemy by confronting it with a myriad stimuli (cf. SWTCC WCCS, II:19B–20; ST SCC, pp. 117–118).

In the BS, this passage immediately follows the quotation from the *Military Administration* (STPF CS, p. 81).

102. Following D. C. Lau's gloss on *kuei* ("Some Notes on the *Sun-tzu*," p. 320).

103. Or "majestic formations."

104. The BS have *ni*—"go against," "go contrary to"—rather than *ying*—"to meet," "to confront." This reading is also preferred by Chu Chün (STPF SY, p. 112).

105. The BS have "leave an outlet"; the Ming text has "must/outlet," the "leave" being understood. (Cf. STPF SY, p. 112, for Chu's rejection of the Ming edition.)

106. Liu Yin notes that this last paragraph is apparently repeated from the next chapter. However, only the Ming edition has the passage in the next chapter as well, where it is apparently an accidental accretion.

The BS have "masses/large numbers" for "military."

107. Chapter titles in the extant editions of the ancient classics have frequently been appended by later hands—whether compilers, subsequent authors adding material, or commentators. Many were simply drawn from the first few words of the chapter, others from a salient sentence within it; therefore, they may be largely unrelated to the chapter's overall subject matter. "Nine Changes" forces the commentators to somehow justify "changes" because the chapter's admonitions against certain courses of action on particular terrains do not constitute changes. For example, Chang Yü asserts that the chapter refers to employing the expedient—the "unusual" rather than the "normal"—in these situations, but his view lacks justification. Although the concept of flexible response is critical to Sun-tzu's tactics, it hardly seems to be the topic of this chapter. Others—including Liu Yin—suggest the chapter is badly mangled, and because the BS preserve only about forty words, they offer little help. In addition, the BS fragments lack a title. Finally, "nine" may simply be used here as a cognomem for "many" or "numerous," such as "Nine Heavens" (STPF SY, pp. 128–129). A minority view holds that "nine" might also be an error for "five" because five terrains are discussed (see SWTCC WCCS, II:24–25; ST SCC, p. 131; SS AS, pp. 194–195; and STPF CS, pp. 89–91).

108. This repeats the formula used previously to introduce the topic. Five classifications of terrain follow, all of which also appear in subsequent chapters in similar descriptive lists—frequently with definitions. Although some notes are provided below, also refer to Chapters 10 and 11 for further explication. (For additional discussion of the terms together with comments on previous translations and a full translation of the relevant lost material on terrain classification from the *Art of War* that is preserved in other texts, see Ralph D. Sawyer, "The Missing Chapter of Sun-tzu," *IKF* 6 [1987], pp. 77–98.)

109. "Entrapping terrain" is traditionally understood as low-lying ground, perhaps surrounded by hills or mountains and characterized by bodies of water such as marshes or swamps. It is thought to be land that can be inundated, possibly by heavy rains or by breaking restraining banks (as was done in China in World War II) and consequently involves heavy slogging for the chariots and men. However, there is considerable disagreement as to its defining characteristics (See STPF SY, pp. 125–126; ST CCCY, p. 165; ST SCC, p. 131). The *Six Secret Teachings*, among other works, discusses the dangers posed by similar terrain in Chapter 58. The BS have *fan*—"overflow" or "inundate"—rather than *p'i*, which means "subvert(ed)" or "defeated." Chu Chün prefers the original because the scope is wider and is capable of encompassing any terrain through which passage is difficult (STPF SY, pp. 125–126). There is another, nearly identical character *i*, which means "bridge" or "embankment"; its existence raises further, although unexplored, possibilities.

110. "Focal" terrain (following Griffith's apt term) is defined in Chapter 11 as "land of the feudal lords surrounded on three sides such that whoever arrives first will gain the masses of All under Heaven." The characters literally mean "terrain where highways intersect"; therefore, narrowly defined it would be land that is accessible from several directions over prepared roads.

111. Several sentences follow in the Ming edition of the *Seven Military Classics* that have been duplicated erroneously from other sections. Neither the Sung dynasty edi-

tion of the *Seven Military Classics* nor other editions—such as the SCC—contains them, and they are therefore omitted here.

112. Emending "can" to "not," following the Sung edition. Cf. ST SCC, pp. 132–133.

113. With this sentence there are already nine principles.

114. Wu Ju-sung notes that in the so-called "lost" fragments from the bamboo slips, the following sentences appear: "There are orders from the ruler which are not implemented. If the ruler orders anything contrary to these four, then do not implement it." "Four" refers to the last four in the series (see STPF CS, pp. 89–91). The "Nine Changes" would therefore be encompassed by the series listed prior to the strong statement about not accepting certain orders from the ruler, which is consonant with the view of commentators such as Wang Hsi, rather than being an arbitrary number (cf. STPF CS, pp. 89–91; ST SCC, p. 131; STPF WC, p. 254).

115. "Five advantages" is found in almost all editions, including the Sung and Ming, and is generally understood as referring to the advantages of the first terrains characterized at the start of this chapter. However, there may be errors in the characters because the "five" are not advantageous but rather are disadvantageous terrains, and much circumlocution is required to convert them to "advantage." One suggestion is that this should read "advantages of terrain"—the advantages and terrains, however, remaining unspecified. (See ST CCCY, p. 164; and SS AS, pp. 201–203. Compare ST SCC, pp. 136–137.)

116. Literally, "espy life"—generally understood as "look for tenable ground," terrain that can be fought on or defended. Some commentators identify it with the yang side, the side looking toward the sun (facing south or east). (Cf. SWTCC WCCS, II:35A; ST SCC, pp. 144–145; STPF WC, pp. 273–274.)

117. Sun-tzu rarely discusses the military problems posed by water—streams, rivers, lakes—no doubt reflecting an early heritage of plains warfare. As the scope of conflict expanded, the problems entailed in fording rivers, crossing wetlands, and negotiating lakes grew enormously, stimulating the development of naval forces in the southeast. Accordingly, the later military classics address these concerns somewhat extensively. (The character translated as "rivers"—*shui* rather than *ch'uan*—originally a graph of running water, can refer to rivers or to bodies of water in general. Because Sun-tzu speaks about the current's direction, rivers appear to be intended here.)

118. This is understood as meaning that armies should not assume positions downstream from an enemy because of such potential dangers as being inundated by suddenly released flood waters or felled by drinking water drawn from a poisoned river (see SWTCC WCCS, II:36A; ST SCC, p. 147).

119. Presumably, terrain easy for chariots to negotiate and for supply wagons to cross.

120. Fragments recovered from the Han tomb (as well as materials in the *Shih chi*) briefly summarize the Yellow Emperor's conquest over the other four (evil) emperors, striking each in turn in his associated quarter (that is, the Black Emperor in the north, the White Emperor in the west, and so on). This conflict, which is denied vigorously by the Confucians, was popularly understood as marking the (mythological) inception of military conflict and strategy in China. See "Lin-i Yin-ch'üeh-shan Han-mu ch'u-t'u *Sun-tzu ping-fa* ts'an-chien shih-wen," *WW* 1974, No. 12, p. 12.

121. Life-supporting terrain is obviously ground that has sunlight, grass for the animals, brush and trees for firewood, and especially potable water. Liu Yin and others equate the "substantial" with high ground (SWTCC WCCS, II:38A. Cf. ST SCC, p. 150, and STPF SY, pp. 142–143).

122. The BS lack "is said to be certain of victory," so the sentence is read as being linked with the start of the next passage (cf. STPF SY, p. 137).

123. Chu Chün points out that observing the presence of bubbles or foam on the river, which indicates rain upstream, exemplifies Sun-tzu's approach to analyzing and fathoming the enemy and battlefield situations. From the bubbles one can deduce that it has rained and can anticipate a surge in the river's flow and level. Such a surge could prove disastrous for an army encamped too close to the shore or caught suddenly in midstream (STPF SY, p. 137).

124. Although the commentators differ somewhat on the details of this and the following dangerous, natural configurations of terrain—several of which are concrete cases of Sun-tzu's more general classifications—their defining characteristics are clear (cf. SWTCC WCCS, II:38B–39A; ST SCC, pp. 151–153).

Heaven's Well is so named because it is a significant depression, such as a valley, surrounded on four sides by hills or mountains. It is dangerous because the runoff of rainwater from unexpected storms can inundate the lowlands.

125. Heaven's Jail is a valley with steep hills or mountains on three sides. Forces that carelessly enter it can be easily bottled up, unable to ascend the sides to escape.

126. Heaven's Net refers to any area of extensive, dense growth—including heavy forests or dense vegetation (including jungle-like growth of underbrush and vines) that will obstruct the passage of vehicles or entangle the men.

127. Heaven's Pit refers to an area characterized by soft, probably muddy terrain, perhaps marked by wetlands, that will mire both men and vehicles.

128. Heaven's Fissure refers to terrain that suggests a fissure in the earth. Therefore, it encompasses long, narrow passages constrained by hills or forests from which an enemy might advantageously dominate the passage.

129. The BS have "small forests," or woods.

130. The BS have "which could conceal hidden (forces)" right after "entangled undergrowth" and "places of evildoers" at the end of the sentence. (Neither the STPF CS nor the STPF SY takes note of these.)

131. The occupation of ravines was of particular interest to the classical strategists (as evidenced by material in both the *Six Secret Teachings* and *Wei Liao-tzu*); this is generally seen as indicating weakness and the need to avail oneself of advantages of terrain.

132. Easily visible obstacles have been made deliberately detectable in order to create the suspicion of ambush or the emplacement of entangling devices and thereby beguile the ordinary commander to divert his forces to the enemy's advantage.

133. Presumably, to define the field of battle and pre-position for the infantry advance.

134. They lack military discipline, grumble and move about, are noisy, and obey orders reluctantly.

135. The translation follows the *Seven Military Classics* edition. Other editions (cf. ST SCC, pp. 161–162) are somewhat different, combining this and the following sen-

tence to read: "If they feed grain to the horses and eat meat while the army does not hang up its cooking utensils nor return to camp, they are an exhausted invader."

136. These are all signs that they are preparing to launch a desperate attack; otherwise, they would need the horses and draft animals as well as their cooking utensils. (In Chapter 11 Sun-tzu advises breaking the cooking utensils and similar measures to dramatically impress on the soldiers the hopelessness of their situation and increase their determination for a last-ditch engagement.)

137. The commander, through his ill-conceived measures, has lost control over them and fears they will revolt.

138. This sentence probably refers to one's own troops. That is, it is not important that you be more numerous than the enemy because if you are not, you merely have to conceive good tactical measures. The BS lack "esteem," which accordingly is understood. "Aggressively" or "in martial fashion" (*wu*) is thought here to refer to actions taken without basis, manifesting bravado without forethought (cf. ST SCC, pp. 164–165; STPF SY, p. 147).

139. Another dimension to the civil-martial relationship.

140. Generally translated as "certain victory" or "certain conquest," the characters do not contain "victory/conquer." Rather, this is the term encountered previously for easily seizing the enemy (see note 16 above).

141. Configurations (*hsing*) of terrain, with their tactical implications. Unfortunately, the configurations are named rather than defined; parts of the text have apparently been lost, and none are preserved in the BS. Each configuration correlates the topography with the basic maneuvers possible in the situation on the assumption that two armies are confronting each other.

142. "Suspended," or "hung up." Although the text seems simple enough, there is a hidden question of perspective that the commentators have not noticed. If the situational analysis refers to the army's present position, when it goes forth it will not be able to return. Accordingly, the terrain it initially occupied would best be termed "irrecoverable." From the perspective of the position to which it advances, it becomes "hung up." Presumably, the "suspended configuration" encompasses both the initial and final positions across the terrain. (Cf. ST SCC, pp. 169–170; STPF SY, p. 154; SS AS, p. 246; and STPF CS, p. 105.)

143. "Stalemated" describes the tactical situation, although the exact character is *chih*—"branch," or "to support." Both sides are supported, so they are in a stalemate. The commentators suggest a lengthy standoff (cf. ST SCC, p. 170).

144. This might also be understood as to "draw off (our forces) to make them (i.e., the enemy) depart." That is, by withdrawing one *compels* the enemy to depart from his entrenched, advantageous position. Withdrawing one's forces and departing is the means through which the enemy's departure is accomplished in either case, but the conclusion—of stimulating them to movement—is implicit in the text translation and is necessary for the next sentence—striking when the enemy is half out.

145. "Constricted" configurations are generally described as extensive mountain valleys. Others also identify them with river or lake crossings. (Cf. SWTCC WCCS, II:48B; STPF SY, p. 154; STPF CS, p. 106; and ST SCC, p. 171.) Furthermore, the commentators generally understand the sentence as referring to occupying the mouth; however, there is no textual reason to so restrict it because the sentence simply advises to "fully" occupy it. (By leaving the entrance unobstructed, enemy forces can be lured

into the killing zone created by deploying forces on both sides throughout the valley, as in several famous historical battles.)

146. "Precipitous," invoking the image of steep mountain gorges or ravines ("ravines" being the translation in other contexts). It is difficult terrain to traverse; therefore, occupying the heights is paramount. (Cf. SWTCC WCCS, II:48B, STPF SY, p. 154; ST SCC, pp. 171–172.)

147. Following Liu Yin, taking "strategic power being equal" as an additional condition. (See SWTCC WCCS, II: 49a. Cf. STPF CS, p. 106.)

148. The odds are so insurmountable that any sort of direct attack can only result in failure and the retreat of the forces so foolishly flung at the enemy (SWTCC WCCS, II:49B).

149. Following SWTCC WCCS and ST SCC. The *T'ung-tien* has "estimating the fullest extent of the difficult and easy, advantageous and harmful, distant and near" (cf. ST SCC, p. 176; and Lau, "Some Notes on the *Sun-tzu*," p. 328). "Ravines" is the same character translated previously as "precipitous" for the configurations of terrain.

150. Here—unlike the earlier passage, which is open to some interpretation—the text clearly means "with" rather than "for" him (refer to note 5 above).

151. Following the Sung, Ming, and SCC editions. However, some others have "inexhaustible" rather than "complete" (cf. STPF SY, p. 153; SS AS, pp. 261–262).

152. The nine terrains analyzed in this chapter appear in two sequences, with some variation. In addition, some of the terms appeared previously in Chapters 8 and 10; others are new but apparently overlap with earlier configurations. This suggests that essential materials have been lost, the text has been corrupted, or the concepts were in a state of flux and not yet rigidly defined.

153. Following Giles and Griffith, who use the appropriate term "dispersive." The commentators generally understand "dispersive" as referring to the tendency of the men, while fighting within their native state, to be thinking of their homes and families and to be inclined to return there. Consequently, they are neither unified nor aroused to a fighting spirit. (Cf. SWTCC WCCS, II:56A; ST SCC, p. 182; and STPF SY, p. 168.) Note that later in the chapter the commander must unify their will on dispersive terrain (before invading enemy territory), and Sun-tzu also advises against engaging the enemy on dispersive terrain. This was perhaps a strategy designed to vitiate an invader's strength before engaging him in battle.

154. Apparently, the soliders still do not regard the enterprise too seriously and continue to think about home and family. Because it remains relatively easy to withdraw but dangerous to forge ahead, it is termed "light" terrain. (Cf. SWTCC WCCS, II:56Aa; STPF SY, p. 168; and ST SCC, p. 183. Griffith uses "frontier," Giles "facile.")

155. This is ground for which one contends, therefore "contentious" terrain. (Giles also translates as "contentious," Griffith as "key ground," and it is unquestionably a strategic point.) The configurations of terrain previously warned against in the last chapter are probably prime objectives under this category because of their great tactical potential if they can be seized and exploited. (Cf. ST SCC, pp. 183–184; STPF SY, p. 169.)

156. In Chapter 10 this is termed "accessible" terrain. Army movement is unhampered.

157. Following Griffith's apt term, "focal." Presumably, this is territory in which major highways intersect and is accessible to major powers on various sides. Its occu-

pation is the key to controlling vast territory. (See note 110 above, where the term first appears. Also compare ST SCC, p. 185; and STPF SY, p. 170.)

158. Griffith translates as "serious." This term contrasts with "light terrain," the severity of their situation now being clearly apparent to the soldiers. Their minds are unified, their courage united. (Cf. SWTCC WCCS, II:57A; and ST SCC, pp. 185–186.) Chu Chün sees the critical element as the cessation of food supplies, with the soldiers suddenly having to forage and plunder to sustain themselves, as stated slightly later in the chapter. This weighs heavily on them (STPF SY, pp. 170–171).

159. This seems to also encompass Heaven's Pit and Heaven's Net. The term is first discussed in Chapter 8.

160. "Constricted" is the same term as that used for one of the configurations in Chapter 10. (It can also mean a "gorge.")

161. The term for "encircled" can also be translated as "besieged" in other contexts and clearly carries such implications (see ST SCC, p. 186). The emphasis here is on the necessity to pass through a narrow opening or along a narrow passage, which constrains the flow of men and materials and thereby makes them vulnerable to being surrounded and attacked by even a small force.

162. Sun-tzu consistently advocates exploiting "ground of death" because when troops are deployed on it, the situation forces them to fight valiantly. The commentators think it would be terrain with solid obstacles to the front—such as mountains—and water to the rear, preventing a withdrawal. (Cf. ST SCC, pp. 187–188; and STPF SY, pp. 171–172.)

163. If you cannot occupy it first, do not attack an entrenched enemy. (SWTCC WCCS, II:58A; and ST SCC, p. 189.)

164. In Chapter 8 it states, "Unite with your allies on focal terrain."

165. In Chapter 8 it states, "Do not encamp on entrapping terrain."

166. Chapter 8: "Make strategic plans for encircled terrain."

167. Some commentators take this as referring to "uniting with the enemy in battle." However, the general import of the paragraph does not restrict the techniques strictly to combat measures.

168. There is disagreement over what is actually obtained without being sought (cf. ST SCC, p. 187).

169. The BS have "deaths" instead of "lives," but the difference is ignored by the STPF CS and STPF SY.

170. This phrase, which is implicit in any case, appears in the BS.

171. Following Chao Pen-hsüeh, *Sun-tzu-shu chiao-chieh yin-lei*, II:36B. Liu Yin (SWTCC WCCS, II:64B–65A) cites one commentator who emends the character translated as "fetter" to "release," understanding the sentence to refer to "releasing the horses."

172. Some commentators incorrectly equate "hard and soft" with "strong and weak." The two pairs are clearly distinguished in the *Military Classics*.

173. Literally, "keeping them stupid." Chu Chün believes this merely refers to preserving all plans in total secrecy rather than being a policy to keep the soldiers stupid (STPF SY, p. 176).

174. Especially the enemy.

175. Analogous with releasing the trigger of a cocked crossbow. In some editions, such as the ST SCC (p. 203), the following sentence appears: "They burn their boats and smash their cooking pots."

176. This paragraph again discusses the nine types of terrain, but from the perspective of acting as an invader. Some commentators believe it is redundant or erroneous, but others—such as the modern military historian General Wei Ju-lin—stress the difference between principles for general combat and those for invading another's territory (see ST CCCY, p. 222–224).

177. The BS are somewhat different: "If you have strongholds behind you and the enemy before you, it is 'fatal terrain.' If there is no place to go, it is 'exhausted terrain.'"

178. Some commentators take this as referring to the enemy's rear, but the context of the preceding statements indicates it should refer to actions taken with regard to one's own army. (Cf. STPF CS, p. 115; and STPF WC, p. 370.) The BS have "I will cause them not to remain."

179. The actions to be taken for four of the terrains are somewhat reversed in the BS. In this case the BS have the conclusion to the next sentence: "I solidify our alliances."

180. The BS have "I focus on what we rely on."

181. The BS have "I race our rear elements forward."

182. Liu Yin explains this as meaning that the general closes off any openings deliberately offered by the enemy to lure his forces out of their encirclement (SWTCC WCCS, II:69A). Leaving such an opening was a common way to keep the defenders from mounting a last-ditch, pitched defense. (Both the *Six Secret Teachings* and the *Wei Liao-tzu* discuss this technique.)

183. The BS preface the sentence with a fragment that apparently means "It is the nature of the feudal lords. ..."

184. Reading *pa wang* as two distinct terms rather than "hegemonic king" (cf. STPF CS, p. 115).

185. This is sometimes understood as not contending with others to form alliances, which would miss the main point of the passage.

186. This sentence is somewhat problematic. Most of the commentators interpret it in the light of Sun-tzu's policy of being deceptive, and in fact the character for "details" might also be an error for a similar character meaning "to deceive." Thus they understand it as "accord with and pretend to follow the enemy's intentions." (Cf. SWTCC WCCS, II:73A; ST SCC, p. 212.) The translation essentially follows STPF SY, p. 184. Wu Ju-sung (STPF CS, p. 115) understands it as simply finding out the details of the enemy's intentions.

187. Literally, "grind (it out)" in the temple, which presumably means somberly work out the plans and estimations. The SCC text has "incite" rather than "grind." (SWTCC WCCS, II: 73B–74A; ST SCC, p. 214. Compare STPF SY, p. 183.)

188. The fifth objective is variously interpreted as shooting flaming arrows into an encampment, burning their weapons, or attacking their formations, as translated (cf. ST SCC, p. 218).

189. When the deceit is discovered, they are murdered or executed.

190. The BS have "relationship" rather than "affairs."

191. The BS add "Shuai Shih-pi in the Hsing. When Yen arose, they had Su Ch'in in Ch'i." Because Su Ch'in was active in the second half of the fourth century B.C.—al-

most two centuries after Sun Wu presumably advanced his tactics—this is obviously a later accretion.

Wu-tzu

Abbreviations of Frequently Cited Books

HFTCC   *Han Fei-tzu chi-chieh*, Shih-chieh shu-chü, Taipei, 1969.

LSCC   *Lü-shih ch'un-ch'iu* (SPKY ed.), 4 volumes, Shih-chieh shu-chü, Taipei, 1958.

TPYL   *T'ai-p'ing yü-lan* (SPTK ed.), 7 volumes, Shang-wu yin-shu-kuan, Taipei, 1975 reprint.

WT CCCY   Fu Shao-chieh, *Wu-tzu chin-chu chin-i*, Shang-wu yin-shu-kuan, Taipei, 1976.

WT CS   Li Shou-chih and Wang Shih-chin, *Wu-tzu ch'ien-shuo*, Chieh-fang-chün ch'u-pan-she, Peking, 1986.

Notes to the Translator's Introduction

1. Lord Shang reportedly studied in Wei and served as a household tutor around four decades after Wu Ch'i left. Accordingly, he may have been influenced by Wu Ch'i's thought and political heritage. See WT CCCY, p. 1; Kuo Mo-jo, *Kuo Mo-jo ch'üan-chi*, Jen-min ch'u-pan-she, Peking, 1982, Vol. 1, pp. 506, 526 (the "Shu Wu Ch'i" chapter in the original 1943 work, *Ch'ing-t'ung shih-tai*).

2. Although the Harvard-Yenching Index Series contains references to Wu Ch'i in several works, the most important are found in the *Han Fei-tzu, Lü-shih ch'un-ch'iu, Chan-kuo ts'e, Huai-nan tzu,* and *Shuo yüan.* However, little material from the actual text is preserved in these or other books, and only a handful of passages are found in the *T'ai-p'ing yü-lan* (hereafter TPYL).

3. For example, see T'ao Chi-heng's comment as recorded in the *Wei-shu t'ung-k'ao,* entry for the *Wu-tzu,* p. 802. Typical condemnatory remarks deprecating Wu Ch'i's lack of virtue and reliance on harsh realism are found in the *Huai-nan tzu,* 9:21A and 13:7A, and in his *Shih chi* biography (translated below). However, as Kuo Mo-jo has pointed out, most of these were probably fabricated by his detractors because he was committed to the values of Confucianism as well as to creating a well-ordered state. See "Shu Wu Ch'i," pp. 527–528.

4. The most systematic analysis of the *Wu-tzu*'s composition date and authorship is found in Li and Wang's WT CS, pp. 3–12. In brief, they attribute the book to Wu-tzu himself, with allowances for serious losses, revisions, and accretions across the years and the recognition that his disciples obviously penned the portions describing his activities. Justification for this view is claimed from both historical references and the book's content and (somewhat rearranged) can be summarized as follows:

First, the works of Sun-tzu and Wu-tzu were known to be in wide circulation in the late Warring States period, based on Han Fei-tzu's comment that "Within the borders everyone speaks about warfare, and everywhere households secretly store away the books of Sun and Wu." Furthermore, his book was obviously studied and discussed throughout the ages, including by Han dynasty writers and famous Three Kingdoms' generals. (Ssu-ma Ch'ien makes a comment similar to that of Han Fei-tzu [which is found at the end of Wu Ch'i's translated biography in the translator's introduction], thereby attesting to the *Wu-tzu*'s circulation in the Former Han dynasty.) The fact that it was the focus of such attention provides evidence for the book's continuous transmission through the centuries, starting with the original work composed by Wu Ch'i and his disciples. (Constant interest should have ensured that the book was preserved in exemplary condition, but the bibliographic descriptions in successive dynasties indicate that either a major portion was lost or it was continually edited and revised, perhaps deliberately producing a very compact edition.)

Second, concepts and actual passages from the *Wu-tzu* are found in several Warring States military writings, including Sun Pin's *Military Methods*, the *Wei Liao-tzu*, and the *Six Secret Teachings*. This suggests it preexisted them, especially because Sun Pin's work had been lost for two thousand years and passages thus could not have been lifted from it to forge the *Wu-tzu* just prior to the T'ang dynasty. (Obviously, this does not preclude a Former Han dynasty forgery date, for which see Kuo Mo-jo's theory below.)

Third, the philosophical content reflects the integration of the Confucian and Legalist perspectives—the Confucian humanistic values and the Legalist emphasis on the unremitting, equitable implementation of rewards and punishments that developed in the Warring States period and found expression especially in the military writings.

Fourth, as noted in the translator's introduction, Wu Ch'i was both a civilian and military administrator, a historical figure who excelled brilliantly in both realms. This dual capability quickly vanished in the Warring States period with the necessarily increased specialization of military and civilian offices and officials. Thus his life and the book's approach reflect the earlier period.

Finally, Ch'ing scholastic criticisms of the text based on claims of historical anachronism, such as the playing of pipes in camp or the inclusion of terms whose origins presumably postdate Wu Ch'i's era, can be dismissed because evidence to the contrary is available. Moreover, recent archaeological discoveries have confirmed the early existence of items such as astrological banners, which the Ch'ing pedants could not have known about.

Li and Wang thus present a cogent argument, although they fail to resolve one particularly troubling criticism: The *Wu-tzu* prominently discusses employing the cavalry and refers to a cavalry force of three thousand. This indicates that one of the authors lived not only after the cavalry's appearance but also after it had become at least a supplementary force. The first mention of cavalry has previously been attributed to Sun Pin's book, and supposedly the cavalry did not become an active military element until near the end of the Warring States period. Therefore, if the authenticity of the *Wu-tzu* is accepted and its main authorship is attributed to Wu Ch'i—albeit revised by his disciples—use of the cavalry must have started in China much earlier than is now generally believed. If the cavalry dates to after 300 B.C., then at least parts of the *Wu-tzu* are later accretions or the entire text is a late Warring States or Han dynasty creation. Li and Wang do not address this problem satisfactorily. (See Appendix B for a discussion of the history of the cavalry in China. Some of the horse's equipment listed in the *Wu-tzu*, including the saddle, did not develop until the Later Han.)

The Han tomb, which contains so many other military works, does not include any portions of the *Wu-tzu*. This in itself is not fatal to claims of early origin because there are many possible explanations and other writings are also absent. However, on the basis of its absence from the tomb, the presence of references to the cavalry, and other anachronisms in terms—such as mentioned above—Kuo Mo-jo concludes that the original *Wu-tzu* has been lost and that the extant work is a later, probably Former Han forgery. (See Chung-kuo chün-shih-shih Pien-hsieh-tsu, *Chung-kuo chün-shih shih,* Vol. 4: *Ping-fa,* Chieh-fang-chün ch'u-pan-she, Peking, 1988, pp. 149ff.)

In view of the cavalry's significant appearance in the *Wu-tzu,* our own provisional conclusion is that contents of the work are substantially from Wu Ch'i himself but that in the course of transmission and revision, later Warring States strategists (and probably Han students)—perhaps in an effort to "update" the work—added passages on the cavalry and otherwise emended some of the terminology. Furthermore, it appears that a portion of the book has been lost or deliberately excised, but whether this loss is an extensive as claimed is somewhat doubtful, given that Wu Ch'i was clearly a man of action perhaps with little time for writing voluminously. (Cf. Wang Hsien-ch'en and Hsü Pao-lin, *Chung-kuo ku-tai ping-shu tsa-t'an,* Chieh-fang-chün ch'u-pan-she, Peking, 1983.)

5. Readers interested in another translation of this biography are encouraged to consult Chauncey S. Goodrich's article in *Monumenta Serica* (35 [1981–1983], pp. 197–233) entitled "Ssu-ma Ch'ien's Biography of Wu Ch'i," hereafter referred to as "Biography." Goodrich analyzes the text and provides extensive footnotes on critical references, figures, and historical questions. Kuo Mo-jo ("Shu Wu Ch'i," pp. 506–533) has also extensively analyzed the various stories and legends surrounding Wu Ch'i and has critically dismissed many of them, including the reported killing of his wife. Although many of the accounts are obviously suspect, perhaps some truth underlies them.

The translation is based on Takigawa Kametarō's widely acclaimed *Shiki kaichu kaōshō,* I-wen yin-shu-kuan, Taipei, 1972 (1-vol. reprint; original edition, 10 vols., Tokyo, 1932–1934), pp. 845–847.

6. Or "loved weapons."

7. Because Confucius died about 479 B.C. and Tseng-tzu (505–436 B.C.) was one of his original disciples, it is generally assumed that Wu Ch'i studied with Tseng-tzu's son, Tseng Shen, about seventy years thereafter. For further discussion, see Goodrich, "Biography," note 6, p. 218; *Lü-shih ch'un-ch'iu* (hereafter LSCC), 2:16b; and WT CCCY, pp. 10–11, where Fu Shao-chieh suggests that Wu Ch'i, Marquis Wen, and Li K'o all studied with Tzu Hsia—one of the original disciples known coincidentally for great longevity. (Kuo Mo-jo similarly concludes that it was Tseng-tzu's son and that Wu Ch'i may have studied with Tzu Hsia. See "Shu Wu Ch'i," pp. 506–509.)

8. A Ch'i high official had arranged for Wu Ch'i to marry his daughter after meeting him in Lu and being strongly impressed. Cf. *Chung-kuo li-tai ming-chiang,* p. 28.

9. Although this incident is also cited in Chapter 34 of the *Han Fei-tzu* (*Han Fei-tzu chi-chieh* [hereafter HFTCC], Shih-chich shu-chü, Taipei, 1969, p. 232) as an illustration of action "against emotions," its veracity has long been questioned, as is discussed below. Cf. also Goodrich, "Biography," pp. 203–204, for his view that the story was fabricated by Wu Ch'i's detractors. (Goodrich concurs with Kuo Mo-jo. See "Shu Wu Ch'i," pp. 511–515.)

10. Tseng-tzu was identified particularly with the development of theories about filial obligations and their emotional expression in the *li*, the forms of propriety. Authorship of the *Classic of Filial Piety* was frequently attributed to him as well, a view that is no longer accepted. For further discussion, refer to Goodrich, "Biography," note 9, p. 219; and some of Tseng-tzu's pronouncements in the *Analects:* I:9, XIX:17, and XIX:18.

11. Marquis Wen typified the strong rulers who forged powerful states through the implementation of enlightened policies and the active solicitation of knowledgeable advisers. He governed at Wei's inception when the great state of Chin fragmented into Han, Wei, and Chao—also termed the Three Chin. Cf. also Goodrich's note 12, "Biography," pp. 219–220.

12. Li K'o and Hsi-men Pao were two famous Worthies who assisted Marquis Wen in reforming the state and formulating new policies. Their actual scholarly affiliations and political orientations—nominally Confucian but visibly activist—are the subjects of considerable speculation.

13. The famous general Ssu-ma Jang-chü is discussed in the translator's introduction to the *Ssu-ma Fa*.

14. This reference to Wu Ch'i riding a horse is cited as perhaps indicating an earlier mastery and use of horses than the dramatic introduction by the state of Chao later in the fourth century. Cf. Goodrich, "Biography," note 16, p. 220.

15. This story also appears in the *Han Fei-tzu*, HFTCC, p. 206; and *Shuo yüan*, 6:19b.

16. The West River is actually a portion of the Yellow River that happens to run north and south. Cf. Goodrich, "Biography," note 19, p. 221.

17. This incident is also recorded in the *Shuo yüan*, 5:3b–4a; and *Chan-kuo ts'e*, 22:2b.

18. Literally, the "hundred surnames"—members of the original nobility, as opposed to the serfs and mean people.

19. As scholars have long noted, this statement is problematic. If it really refers to the proponents of the "horizontal and vertical alliances," it is anachronistic because they did not appear for another fifty years (cf. Goodrich, "Biography," note 36, p. 224). This passage is frequently cited as evidence of the *Wu-tzu*'s late composition.

20. Capital political offenses inevitably entangled entire families, with the most serious resulting in the extermination of all family members through the third degree of relationship. These policies reflected Chinese conceptions of the extended family and mutual responsibility.

21. Sun Pin—a descendant of Sun-tzu—was a famous strategist, military adviser, and the author of the recently discovered work, *Military Methods*. He suffered severe, mutilating punishment as the victim of an intrigue spawned by jealousy.

22. Cf. Goodrich, "Biography," pp. 203, 214–217; Kuo Mo-jo, "Shu Wu Ch'i," pp. 511–515.

23. HFTCC, p. 214.

24. Ibid., p. 246.

25. Ibid., p. 246.

26. This phrase is not found in all the editions. The *ta-fu* would be a member of the nobility who was holding a high government rank.

27. HFTCC, p. 171. There is a similar story about moving a post in LSCC, 25:15.

28. As discussed in note 7.

29. The mass mobilization of farmers to serve as combat infantrymen rather than simply as support troops meant their volitional consent had to be sought as well as coerced. They could easily flee to other states, most of which were beginning to welcome people to bring new lands under cultivation and increase the state's agricultural wealth.

30. *Shuo yüan,* 3:1.

31. LSCC, 11:15b–16a; repeated, with slight character variations, in LSCC, 20:30b–31a.

32. HFTCC, p. 67.

33. LSCC, 21:14b–15.

34. The clearest expression in the *Tao Te Ching* is found in Chapter 31: "Now weapons are inauspicious implements. There are things that abhor them." The first part is subsequently repeated. Please refer to the discussion in the introductory material for Sun-tzu's *Art of War* and also note the last passage of *Questions and Replies.*

35. *Shuo yüan,* 15:2.

36. The brush was already being used to write characters on bamboo and other wooden slips, whereas the knife was used to excise errors (by scraping them off).

37. *Huai-nan tzu chu,* Shih-chieh shu-chü, Taipei, 1969, p. 366.

38. For a general discussion of the limitations of chariots, please see the general introduction.

Notes to the Text

1. The chariots are so numerous that they even block the palace doors. An alternative reading would be that their doors as well as the hubs, are protected. The wheels were probably covered to prevent enemy soldiers from inserting a pole between the spokes or otherwise seizing them, whereas the hubs had to be protected from being forced off. Impressions of wooden chariots with such protective coverings have been discovered in recent tomb excavations. These measures indicate how vulnerable chariots were to infantrymen except on the most level ground, where their speed would exceed that of swift runners.

2. Another version of this passage, but with only three disharmonies, is found in TPYL, 272:2B.

3. The psychological and ritual importance of seeking the sanction of departed ancestors by formally announcing the planned commencement of military activities to them in the temple is reiterated in other military texts. Resorting to divination, however, is clearly opposed by some texts, and this passage seems to express the beliefs of a previous age, possibly suggesting an earlier date for the composition.

4. Confucius observed the importance and the role of shame in human behavior (*Analects,* II:3, XIII:20, IV:22, and V: 25), and the Confucian school turned the development of a sense of shame into the foundation of the philosophy and psychology of the *li*—the forms of propriety—in such works as *Li chi.* The military strategists also

seized on its catalytic power, playing on a man's fear of disgracing himself before his comrades. Wu-tzu clearly felt rewards and punishments alone would be inadequate to ensure the requisite battlefield performance. (For a discussion of the role of shame in the Greek phalanx, compare Chapter 10 in Victor Hanson, *The Western Way of War,* Alfred A. Knopf, New York, 1989.)

5. An alternative but nontraditional reading of the first sentence would be "Being victorious in battle is easy, but being victorious through defensive [nonaggressive] measures is difficult." Although the passage continues by focusing on the number of battles, thereby supporting the traditional interpretation, gaining the world through a single victory would be the conquest of Virtue over the unopposed. It could only be accomplished through preserving one's stance rather than by waging external, violent warfare.

6. Or possibly "warfare." However, from the view of the virtuous, fighting against a "contrary army" is still a righteous cause.

7. Not just a simple enumeration of men or a discrete population count but rather the classification and numbering of men according to their abilities, such as great strength or speed. Their selection and employment is discussed below and in the next chapter.

8. The famous Duke Huan was the first of the hegemons—strongmen who ruled under the guise of supporting the Chou.

9. The *Six Secret Strategies,* Chapter 53, "Hand-Picked Warriors," proposes similar measures to attain dramatic results.

10. This well-known passage is also found in the *Han Fei-tzu,* HFTCC, p. 360.

11. Hsun-tzu similarly characterized these states and summarized their military tactics in the "Discussion of the Military," Chapter 15. Cf. Wang Hsien-ch'ien, *Hsün-tzu chi-chieh,* Shih-chieh shu-chü, Taipei, pp. 180–181.

12. Some commentators understand this to mean "they will not run off."

13. Some commentators suggest this means "light troops" rather than as translated. However, it seems clear that the manner of provocation is being described because the enemy is being slighted, treated "disdainfully." "Lightly advancing" is also parallel to "quickly retreating."

14. The identification of the "five weapons" varies. Fu (WT CCCY, note 46, p. 75) suggests they may have been the bow and arrow, halberd, spear, fighting staff, and the spear-tipped halberd. (The identification of the "fighting staff" is a matter of some disagreement. According to the *Chou li,* it was a composite weapon made from bamboo and was octagonal in shape. However, this probably represents a later [Han dynasty] idealization because examples found in tombs are round and formed from a single wood.) For a detailed discussion, consult Hayashi Minao's extensive work, *Chūgoku In-Shū jidai no buki,* Kyoto Daigaku Jimbun Kagaku Kenkyūsho, Kyoto, 1972, pp. 237–241. Other lists include both offensive and defensive implements; the *Huai-nan tzu* mentions the knife (or dagger), sword, spear, spear-tipped halberd, and arrows. In the earliest periods the halberd and ax figured most prominently.

15. This and the following paragraph suggest an age when divination still had believers, but the rationality of military strategy should dominate battlefield decisions.

16. This sentence is somewhat problematic. It may also mean "They have arisen early and are still on the march late." Similarly, they may be deliberately breaking the ice to ford rivers or perhaps to use boats on a lake, as translated, or they may unwit-

tingly be breaking through the ice as they attempt to cross. The former seems more likely, given the apparently severe conditions of wind and cold.

17. Similar material is also found in the *Six Secret Teachings*.

18. Also found in the TPYL, 313:6.

19. Literally, "governing" or "administering"—here translated as "control" because for Wu-tzu it subsumes all aspects of organization, discipline, and training.

20. The troops and their commander (and ruler) are characterized by a relationship similar to the idealized one between father and son: it is characterized by benevolence, righteousness, beneficence, good faith, and love from the parent with the reciprocal virtues of trust, love, respect, and obedience from the son.

21. This passage, which closely echoes one in Sun-tzu's Chapter 6, "Vacuity and Substance," is evidently misplaced here.

22. Cf. TPYL, 297:4A.

23. Passages such as these are cited as evidence that the *Wu-tzu* must be a spurious work because cavalry—to the best of available evidence—had not yet been introduced in Wu Ch'i's era. However, cavalry tactics are not discussed, only the use of horses for riding. As already noted, Wu Ch'i's biography preserves his reputation for walking rather than riding when the men are weary, providing further evidence that riding existed at the start of the fourth century.

24. Cf. TPYL, 270:8.

25. The character used is "to divine," but the subsequent discussion focuses solely on the rational evaluation of character and ability.

26. The use of pipes and whistles at night is cited by T'ao Nai as evidence that the text must have been composed in the Six Dynasties period because military music did not include this use until after the Wei-Chin period (Ch'ü Wan-li, *Hsien-Ch'in wen-shih tzu-liao k'ao-pien,* Lien-ching, Taipei, 1983, p. 480). This of course presumes their function was identical, rather than simply sounding as signals, and that someone revising an earlier text did not simply fill out a phrase to reflect contemporary practice. (However, note that Li and Wang deny the validity of this claim, asserting that evidence exists that these instruments were used in such fashion much earlier. See note 4 above to the introductory section and the citations contained therein.)

27. The tactical exploitation of confined spaces to restrict the movement of both chariots and men is advanced in many military writings. This might suggest a common body of tactical knowledge, extensive cross-borrowing, or simply common sense developed through bitter experience.

28. This is obviously an explicit reference to employing cavalry as a battlefield force rather than just using horses to perhaps carry the officers. Similar references follow in this chapter.

29. This passage is commonly understood as referring to Wu Ch'i, the speaker, suggesting that if it (the state of Wei) fails it will be laughed at; therefore, he has forged a force that has the total commitment of the enraged bandit in the marketplace. However, this runs contrary to the logic of persuasion because if Wei fails with only a limited force, although its audacity might be laughable, defeat would be expected. However, if—contrary to all expectation—the mighty Ch'in should be vanquished, they would certainly be laughed at, and Wei's army would be correspondingly glorified for its great accomplishment.

30. Also cited in TPYL, 33:7.

Wei Liao-tzu

Abbreviations of Frequently Cited Books

BS	Bamboo Slips: The text as given by the bamboo slips, which may be cited from the YCS CP or other texts and commentaries.
RT	Reconstructed Text: the text reconstructed by Hsü Yung in WLT CS, based on the traditionally transmitted texts, revised and supplemented by the materials preserved in the *Ch'ün-shu chih-yao* and the bamboo slips (YCS CP). The RT generally follows the work of Chung Chao-hua, as recorded in the latter's extensive footnotes in the WLT CC.
WLT CC	Chung Chao-hua, *Wei Liao-tzu chiao-chu,* Chung-chou shu-hua-she, Honan, 1982.
WLT CS	Hsü Yung, *Wei Liao-tzu ch'ien-shuo,* Chieh-fang-chün ch'u-pan-she, Peking, 1989.
WLT CY	Hua Lu-tsung, *Wei Liao-tzu chu-i,* Chung-hua shu-chü, Peking, 1979.
WLT CCCY	Liu Chung-p'ing, *Wei Liao-tzu chin-chu chin-i,* Shang-wu yin-shu-kuan, Taipei, 1975.
WLT WCHC	*Wei Liao-tzu,* in *Ch'ung-k'an Wu-ching hui-chieh,* Chung-chou Ku-chi ch'u-pan-she, Cheng-chou, 1989.
WLTCC WCCS	*Wei Liao-tzu chih-chieh,* in *Ming-pen Wu-ching Ch'i-shu chih-chieh,* Shih-ti chiao-yü ch'u-pan-she, Taipei, 1972, 2 vols.
YCS CP	Yin-ch'üeh-shan Han-mu Chu-chien Cheng-li Hsiao-tsu, "Yin-ch'üeh-shan chien-pen *Wei Liao-tzu* shih-wen (fu chiao-chu)," *WW* 2 (1977), pp. 21–27.

Notes to the Translator's Introduction

1. These and other issues regarding the historical Wei Liao and the evolution of the text are discussed at the end of this translator's introduction.

2. The interrelationship of these texts, especially the *Wei Liao-tzu* and *Six Secret Teachings,* remains to be clarified. Their sequence of completion and whether they incorporate passages from other, now-lost works cannot be resolved until the discovery of new textual materials. The *Wei Liao-tzu* clearly postdates Sun-tzu's *Art of War,* the *Mo-tzu,* Sun Pin's *Military Methods,* and the *Wu-tzu;* it adopts and advances many of Wu Ch'i's concepts and principles. (In his notes to the individual chapters, Hsü Yung discusses Wei Liao-tzu's thought in relation to Sun-tzu and Wu Ch'i but oddly neglects the numerous materials borrowed from the *Six Secret Teachings.* Some points regarding the latter and many other common concepts are found in our notes to the translation, but space precludes more than cursory references.)

3. PRC orthodox military historians now regard the *Wei Liao-tzu* as the earliest work to systematically discuss military training. See, for example, Tung Chien, "Ch'ien-t'an *Wei Liao-tzu* te 'ping-chiao' ssu-hsiang," in Chün-shih li-shih yen-chiu-hui, ed., *Ping-chia shih-yüan,* Vol. 2, Chün-shih k'o-hsüeh ch'u-pan-she, Peking, 1990, pp. 283–291.

4. The dates for King Hui's reign are discussed in the section on textual history.

5. The first book of the *Mencius* begins with several interviews between Mencius and King Hui (and King Hui's son, King Hsiang, after he ascends the throne) and therefore has traditionally been entitled "King Hui of Liang." Mencius strongly condemns King Hui in VIIB1.

6. A main theme of the *Wei Liao-tzu* is relying on human effort rather than looking to the Heavens or spirits, as is discussed in textual notes 1–9 below.

7. "Annals of Ch'in Shih Huang," *Shih chi, chüan* 6. The translation is based on Takikawa Kametarō, *Shiki kaichū kōshō*, I-wen yin-shu-kuan, Taipei, 1972 (one-volume reprint of original 1934 edition), pp. 107–108.

8. The style of the characters and the presence of characters that should be avoided if the scribe were copying the text after the Han's ascension indicate that the slips, and thus the *Wei Liao-tzu,* are pre-Han.

9. The *Wei Liao-tzu* thus reflects the massive population displacements resulting from the large-scale warfare seen in the middle and especially the late Warring States period.

10. The *Wei Liao-tzu* also incorporates Taoist concepts, although Legalism—somewhat modified by Confucian concerns with benevolence and virtue—predominates. Key passages are noted in the translation as they arise.

11. In contrast to the *Wei Liao-tzu,* from the Legalist view concepts of virtue, righteousness, and shame are detrimental.

12. Wei Liao recognized the importance of cities as economic centers and the vital need for trade and other commercial activities to create the wealth required to finance military forces and campaigns. Thus his policies differed radically from Lord Shang's condemnation of commercial enterprise (see Chung-kuo Chün-shih-shih Pien-hsieh-tsu, *Chung-kuo chün-shih-shih,* Vol. 5: *Ping-chia,* Chieh-fang-chün ch'u-pan-she, Peking, 1990, p. 140). At the same time, these activities must be directed to the state's benefit and not be permitted to injure the people and their primary occupations. His tactics include principles for attacking and defending cities and further advancing concepts found in Mo-tzu's and Sun Pin's writings while clearly reversing Sun-tzu's advice to avoid becoming entangled in sieges and city assaults (as discussed in the translator's introduction to the *Ssu-ma Fa*). Wei Liao also identified economic conflict as the root cause of war (see WLT CS, pp. 40–41).

13. The first chapter of the *Ssu-ma Fa* advocates identical concepts and measures.

14. Bonding into squads of five remained the foundation of military organization throughout Chinese history. Contemporary Western military theory, based on behavioral analysis of performance in World War II, recognizes small groups of six or seven men as constituting the basic identifiable and motivational unit—essentially validating the ancient insight.

15. Also see Tung Chen's discussion, "Ch'ien-t'an *Wei Liao-tzu* te 'ping-chiao' ssu-hsiang," pp. 283–291.

16. These issues are considered extensively in the *Ssu-ma Fa* as well. Military historians will recognize contemporary Western theory in these powerful manipulations.

17. See Wu Ju-sung's foreword to Hsü Yung's *Wei Liao-tzu ch'ien-shuo,* pp. 5–12. For the concepts of *hsing* (form, shape) and *shih* (strategic configuration of force [or power], advantage conveyed by the strategic deployment of force), which largely originate with Sun-tzu, refer to the translator's introduction to the *Art of War.*

18. The text rarely mentions unorthodox tactics by name, but Hsü Yung's detailed analysis identifies them in Wei Liao-tzu's concrete tactics and measures. (See WLT CS, pp. 34–35, and his notes to the individual chapters. Also see the translator's introduction and notes to Sun-tzu's *Art of War* for an elucidation of *ch'i* and *cheng*.) The absence of any mention of the cavalry in the *Wei Liao-tzu*, evidence for a fourth-century composition date, confines the possibilities for implementing unorthodox tactics to chariots and infantry. However, note that Sun Pin already employs cavalry, which raises further questions about the chronological relationship of the texts—although cavalry may have been considered in the now-lost portions of the extant *Wei Liao-tzu*.

19. As Hsü Yung points out, Wei Liao valued a spirited, highly trained, and disciplined force over large numbers. See WLT CS, p. 38.

20. The "miscellaneous" category contains books whose contents were not attributable to a single school, such as the Confucians or Taoists. Thus "miscellaneous" refers to the amalgamated contents of an individual work, not to a collection of various books.

The *Han shu* bibliography (Chapter 30), based essentially on Liu Hsiang's and Liu Hsin's earlier *Chi lüeh*, contains a "military" section subdivided into four classifications: "*Ping mou-ch'üan*," or "Military Plans and Balance of Power"; "*Ping hsing-shih,* " or "Military Shape (or Disposition) and Advantage Conveyed by Strategic Deployment of Force"; "*Yin-yang*"; and "*Ping Chi-ch'iao*," or "Military Techniques and Crafts." (For further discussion, see Robin D.S. Yates, "New Light on Ancient Chinese Military Texts: Notes on Their Nature and Evolution, and the Development of Military Specialization in Warring States China," *TP* 74 [1988], pp. 211–247.)

21. See note 17 above for *hsing* and *shih*.

22. For example, see Yao Chi-heng's comments collected in the *Wei-shu t'ung-k'ao* (ed. Chang Hsin-ch'eng), Shangwu yin-shu-kuan, Taipei, 1970 (reprint) (original ed., 1939), p. 803. Yao also opportunely condemns the view that some historical commanders deliberately sought out transgressions immediately prior to battle so as to dramatically execute up to one hundred soldiers and vividly affect the troops.

Note that Hsü Yung vigorously disputes the traditional understanding of this phrase, believing it refers to a commander fighting with forces reduced by the indicated amount—such as half or 30 percent—in comparison with the enemy. (See WLT CS, pp. 167–175. Also see notes 174–177, which accompany the translation for this passage.) Hua Lu-tsung, among contemporary scholars, embraces the view that this "killing" refers to the degree to which the commander is willing to inflict capital punishment to enforce discipline and compel his troops to fight fervently (*Wei Liao-tzu chu-i*, Chung-hua shu-chü, Peking, 1979, p. 6).

23. *Wei-shu t'ung-k'ao*, p. 803. This is hardly a crippling criticism because Mencius is not necessarily the originator of the saying, whereas Wei Liao may have been reacting to and appropriating a statement that accorded with his own thoughts. See, for example, the contemporary view advanced in *Ping-chia*, p. 144.

24. Yen Shih-ku cites a statement from Liu Hsiang's (no longer extant) *Pie lüeh*. However, if Wei Liao had his interview in King Hui's last year (320 B.C.), unless he were already over forty it is unlikely that he could have studied with Lord Shang, who died in 338 B.C. Furthermore, Lord Shang was active in the foreign state of Ch'in, whereas Wei Liao was presumably from Wei.

25. The recent *Chung-kuo chün-shih-shih* (Chieh-fang-chün ch'u-pan-she, Peking, 1988), for example, focuses mainly on the continuation of Lord Shang's ideas in its brief analysis. See Vol. 4: *Ping-fa,* pp. 102–103.

26. Hu Ying-lin is prominently identified with this view. Chung Chao-hua, in an article emphasizing the distinctiveness of the descriptions for each category, concludes that all the extant texts are variants of the same original and that the miscellaneous text has been lost. (See Chung Chao-hua, "Kuan-yü *Wei Liao Tzu* mou-hsieh wen-t'i te shang-ch'üeh," *WW* 1978, No. 5, pp. 60–63, or the slightly abridged reprint in the *Hsü Wei-shu t'ung-k'ao* [ed. Cheng Liang-shu], Hsüeh-sheng shu-chü, Taipei, 1984, pp. 1639–45.)

27. For example, see Hua Lu-tsung's introduction to his modern edition, WLT CY, pp. 1–4. (An abridged abstract is also found in the *Hsü Wei-shu t'ung-k'ao,* pp. 1631–1632.) Also see Chung Chao-hua, WLT CC, pp. 3–5; and Hsü Yung's summary of this position, WLT CS, pp. 16–17. All historical references are confined to individuals who lived before King Hui's time; the absence of famous generals thereafter is presumed to indirectly establish the latest date of composition. Another issue is the question of "*shih chiang,*" or hereditary generals. Their mention is considered evidence of early composition; however, Yates has pointed out that this view appears mistaken (see "New Light," pp. 226–227. Also see Hsü Yung, WLT CS, pp. 24–25).

28. These issues are discussed below. For a comprehensive overview, see Hsü Yung, WLT CS, p. 17. Among the main contentions is that Wei Liao's reference to armies of two hundred thousand would only be accurate late in the Warring States period. However, as Hsü points out, armies varied in size, and the sentence might refer to a state's entire standing army rather than a campaign force (see WLT CS, p. 25).

29. This view apparently originated with Ch'ien Mu. See Ch'ü Wan-li, *Hsien-Ch'in wen-shih tzu-liao k'ao-pien,* Lien-ching, Taipei, 1983, p. 489; and Hsü Yung, WLT CS, p. 23.

30. Obviously, if it were not for the distinct character of the two halves of the present book, the issue of authorship could be simply resolved by attributing it to the original Wei Liao, allowing for accretions and revisions and perhaps assuming the second historical figure is simply an erroneous reference.

31. Chang Lieh's article ("Kuan-yü *Wei Liao-tzu* te chu-lu ho ch'eng-shu," *Wen shih,* Vol. 8, No. 3 [1980], pp. 27–37) is cited from the abridged reprint in the *Hsü Wei-shu t'ung-k'ao,* pp. 1646–1652.

32. *Hsü Wei-shu t'ung-k'ao,* p. 1647. In support of the text being properly attributed to the earlier Wei Liao, Hua Lu-tsung makes a similar argument: Ch'in's historical enmity with Wei would have (theoretically) prevented Wei Liao from illustrating his thoughts with references to Wu Ch'i when speaking to the king of Ch'in (WLT CY, p. 3; also see *Ping-chia,* pp. 139–140).

33. *Hsü Wei-shu t'ung-k'ao,* pp. 1648–50. Note that other scholars dismiss Hsün-tzu's view as incomplete, as idealistically favoring benevolence while neglecting the realities of military power and operations (see Wu Jung-sung's foreword to the WLT CS, p. 8).

Whether the military texts first synthesized benevolence and military might—perhaps on a Confucian basis in response to the growing scope of warfare and social upheaval rather than simply incorporating a preexistent position—seems to be an interesting, open question. Hsün-tzu could equally well have borrowed from the *Wei Liao-*

tzu if it had been composed late in the fourth century B.C. (Note Change Lieh's comments on the sudden increased scope of brutality under the Ch'in, perhaps stimulating a realization that benevolence and a humane approach to warfare were essential. See *Hsü Wei-shu t'ung-k'ao,* pp. 1649–1650.)

34. Ibid., pp. 1650–1651.

35. Ibid., p. 1652.

36. "*Wei Liao-tzu* ch'u-t'an," *WW* 1977, No. 2, pp. 28–34. An abridged reprint, in traditional characters, is also found in *Hsü Wei-shu t'ung-k'ao,* pp. 1632–1639. (All citations refer to the original article.) A simplified character transcription of the bamboo fragments also appeared in the same issue of *WW*: "Yin-ch'üeh-shan chien-pen *Wei Liao-tzu* shih-wen," pp. 21–27.

37. The *Ch'ün-shu chih-yao,* compiled in the T'ang dynasty, abstracted the essential chapters from the classics, histories, and philosophers—thereby preserving many valuable materials that would otherwise be lost.

38. For detailed analysis, see "*Wei Liao-tzu* ch'u-t'an," pp. 28–31.

39. Ibid., pp. 32–33. (Also see *Ping-chia,* pp. 139–140.) Apart from Wu Ch'i, who instituted strong administrative policies in the regions under his authority (see the translator's introduction to the translation of the *Wu-tzu*), Li Li and Hsi-men Pao were particularly prominent. Ho believes that Wei Liao is more appropriately identified with them than with Lord Shang, who had also been influenced by this earlier heritage.

40. "*Wei Liao-tzu* ch'u-t'an," pp. 33–34. This intellectual activity, made famous by Mencius, was probably well-known in the late Warring States period and thus was the probable basis for attributing the forgery to Wei Liao-tzu at the court of Liang. (Also see Chang Lieh, *Hsü Wei-shu t'ung-k'ao,* pp. 1651–1652.)

41. See note 20, above.

42. "New Light," p. 230. However, in a foreword to the WLT CS that focuses on the appropriateness of including the text in this category, Wu Ju-sung arrives at the opposite conclusion. He stresses the prewar development of surpassing strength (which he equates with *hsing*) and its rapid realization in execution (which he identifies as *shih*). See WLT CS, pp. 5–12.

43. "New Light," p. 230.

44. Ibid., p. 232.

45. Hsü Yung, WLT CS, pp. 13–31.

46. Ibid., p. 16.

47. Ibid., p. 17.

48. Ibid., p. 18. Based on the *Shih chi,* as corrected by the *Bamboo Annals,* King Hui's demise has generally been dated to 319 B.C. (See D. C. Lau, *Mencius,* 2 vols., The Chinese University Press, Hong Kong, 1984, II:309–312.)

49. Various dates are given for the respective interviews. For example, Hua Lu-tsung ascribes Wei Liao's audience to somewhat after 334 B.C.—when King Hui urgently sought external advice—and the subsequent appearance in Ch'in to 237 B.C. (WLT CY, p. 4). D. C. Lau believes Mencius probably visited Wei shortly before King Hui's death, or about 320 B.C. (*Mencius,* p. 310). Hsü's date would be about 312 or 311 B.C. Chung Chao-hua, in the introduction to his WLT CC (p. 3), espouses the standard view—calculating the time from the first year after King Hui's death (318 B.C., when other scholars think he may have had interviews with King Hsiang) to the certain

date of his arrival at the Ch'in court, 236 B.C., as eighty-two years. Chang Lieh dates the arrival to 237 B.C. (*Hsü Wei-shu t'ung-k'ao*, p. 1652).

50. WLT CS, pp. 18–20.

51. Ibid., p. 23.

52. Ibid., pp. 27–28. Hsü Yung also discusses extensively the questions of accretion and loss raised by many historians over the years and the variations in the number of sections found in the different texts. For details of this specialized question, see ibid., pp. 26–30.

Notes to the Text

1. The title of this chapter, "Heavenly Offices," appears several times within it—apparently with two different referents. Although some commentators (WLT CCCY, p. 2) take it simply as a book title, most consider that in some instances, it refers instead to a body of astrological judgments and proscriptions based on assigning auspicious and inauspicious interpretations to celestial phenomena. The translation follows the consensus in demarking such occurrences. (Cf. WLT CY, pp. 2–3; WLT CC, p. 2. Note that in WLT CS, it is never considered a book title. See WLT CS, pp. 46–47.)

2. "Punishments and Virtue" is also subject to different interpretations. Although Hsü Yung (WLT CS, p. 46) takes it as a book title, as thus conjoined the terms are generally thought to refer to a system of beliefs about auspicious and inauspicious times. *Hsing*—"punishment"—is associated with yin, the dark (*hsüan*), and the (Earthly) branches in the double character cycle of days; whereas *Te*—"Virtue"—is associated with yang, the bright, and the (Heavenly) stems in the cyclic sequence. Each would have portents associated with it and in the military realm, appropriate times for the initiation of activities; the initial direction and orientation for the campaign could also be specified. "Punishment" is also associated with death, "Virtue" with life.

3. The author of the *Wei Liao-tzu* thus defines punishment and Virtue in terms of government action, thereby focusing exclusively on human effort—human affairs—rather than on structuring actions in accord with metaphysically auspicious phenomena. (All references to "Wei Liao-tzu" hereafter should be understood as generic, indicating the author or authors of the *Wei Liao-tzu* text rather than a historic person.)

4. Many of the commentators take this occurrence of Heavenly Offices as a book title. The Sung edition includes additional characters meaning "According to the deployments in the *Heavenly Offices*. ..."

5. Literally, "severed terrain," here translated as "isolated terrain" consistent with our translation of the term in the *Art of War*, where it appears in Chapter 8, "Nine Terrains." By deploying in this orientation, forces are arrayed inauspiciously with their backs turned to the water. This differs conceptually from a purely strategic evaluation that presumably would fault any deployment that lacked the possibility of ordered withdrawal.

6. This is an example of inauspiciously facing toward, being turned toward.

7. Probably an error for the Ch'ing River because the former does not flow through the Mu-yeh battlefield region, whereas the latter does (see WLT CC, note 11, p. 3).

8. There appears to be some logical inconsistency in this sentence, and the commentators offer several different understandings. Clearly, Kung is expressing the thought that the comet is irrelevant and that despite its baleful omen, they will be victorious.

However, another interpretation is "If we were to employ the comet to fight, we would have to turn the tail over before we could be victorious" (WLT CS, p. 47).

9. The Sung edition has "seasons of Heaven" instead of "Heavenly Offices." The thought expressed in this chapter reflects the theme of the entire work and is also picked up by Li Ching in Book III of *Questions and Replies*.

10. These sentences echo a passage in Chapter 4 of the *Art of War*. This chapter is particularly complex, not because of the ideas expressed or any shortage of textual materials but because of the extensive reconstructions possible with the recovered tomb materials (YCS CP) supplemented by the *Ch'ün-shu chih-yao*. In this instance, the RT reads: "Measure the fertility and barrenness of the earth, and then establish towns and construct city walls. In accord with the city walls, determine the appropriate terrain" (WLT CS, p. 53).

11. The RT: "In accord with the terrain, determine the appropriate number of men" (WLT CS, p. 53).

12. The RT: "These three having been mutually determined, when one withdraws he can thereby be solid in defense, and [when he advances can thereby] be victorious in battle" (WLT CS, p. 53).

13. The bamboo slips read "*fu*" (blessings, good fortune, prosperity) rather than "*pei*" (preparations). In full, the RT: "Being victorious in battle externally, prosperity being produced internally, victory and prosperity respond to each other ..." (see WLT CC, notes, p. 6; WLT CS, p. 53).

14. The Sung edition has "respond," as translated in note 13.

15. An image from Chapter 4 of the *Art of War*.

16. Hsü Pei-ken believes "open" is an error for "closed" because military affairs should be secretive and obscure (cf. WLT CCCY, p. 15).

17. RT: "Closing it, it is small but not. ... Thus, for one who is king, the people turn to him as flowing water, look up to him as the sun and moon, return to him like their father and mother. Thus it is said ..." (serial periods indicate a damaged or lost portion in the text).

18. Understood as opening the path to life, nourishing the people (cf. WLTCC WCCS, I:5).

19. Liu Yin understands "stopping up" as referring to stopping the excessively harsh correction of minor transgressions (ibid.). Others see the efforts directed toward stopping extravagance and profligate customs (cf. WLT CY, p. 5; WLT CS, p. 56). The RT adds: "His taking of All under Heaven will be like a transformation. One whose state is impoverished he will be able to make rich" (cf. WLT CS, p. 53).

20. The RT adds: "Those who do not respond to the [constraints of] the four seasons, he will be able to bring it about that they respond to them" (WLT CS, p. 53).

21. Both phrases in the RT use a double negative for emphasis: "cannot but be wealthy," "cannot but be governed" (ibid.).

22. The RT: "As for a state that is well governed and moreover wealthy, even though they do not remove the blocks from the chariots, nor is the armor taken out from the bags, their awesomeness causes All under Heaven to submit" (ibid.).

23. In accord with Sun-tzu's approach to warfare. However, the RT adds a series of phrases indicating that victory comes in the fields, marketplaces, and so forth (ibid.).

24. As the sentence stands, the implication is that once the army is in the field, any victory is attributable to the general. However, the RT adds phrases that change the

meaning somewhat: "If one engages in battle and then is victorious, it is the high officers' victory. If one is victorious a second time, it is equivalent to a defeat. 'If an army of a hundred thousand goes forth, the daily expenses will be a thousand pieces of gold.' 'Therefore, attaining a hundred victories in a hundred battles is not the pinnacle of excellence. Subjugating the enemy's army without fighting is the true pinnacle of excellence'" (ibid.). These phrases reflect Sun-tzu's admonition against protracted fighting and Wu-tzu's emphasis on winning decisively and avoiding numerous battles.

25. This echoes Sun-tzu's admonition in the *Art of War,* Chapter 12.

26. Unfortunately, this relatively simple sentence is subject to several interpretations by the commentators. Literally, "do not mobilize one day's army" can be understood as translated; as meaning do not mobilize for only a day (because this would be negligent and haphazard and would doom the forces to defeat); and as meaning do not mobilize in just a day because again this would be too hasty. (The translation follows Liu Yin's emphasis on acting quickly and decisively so as not to lose an opportunity. See WLTCC WCCS, I:6, and compare WLT CS, p. 56; WLT CY, p. 6; and WLT CCCY, pp. 18–19.) The RT adds a long, supplementary passage.

27. The RT adds a lengthy, broken passage on the general and the senses.

28. The RT adds, "Deployed in an elongated formation it will be victorious" (WLT CS, p. 54).

29. Another, broken passage follows in the RT that appears to have inappropriate sentences as well.

30. A paraphrase from the *Art of War,* Chapter 11. The RT adds, "Those whose heads are bowed cannot raise them; those whose heads are raised cannot bow them" (WLT CS, p. 54).

31. Another paraphrase from the *Art of War,* Chapter 6. (Note that this describes the plight of a general who lacks intelligence and knowledge of the battlefield.) The RT adds, "Wise officers cannot offer plans, courageous officers cannot (take action?)" (ibid.).

32. Liu Yin understands the image as "like a whirlwind" (WLTCC WCCS, I:8A).

33. Drums were used to sound the advance, pennants to direct the troops.

34. The Sung edition has "harms" instead of "diminishes."

35. Following Liu Yin (WLTCC WCCS, I:9) and WLT CCCY (p. 29), *shih chiang* is understood as "generals through the ages." However, other interpretations are "hereditary generals"—those whose families have served as generals for generations (with the implication that they are unqualified)—and "contemporary generals" of their age. The latter seems least likely. (Cf. WLT CS, p. 62; WLT CY, p. 10; WLT CC, p. 13.)

36. Some editions have *t'o,* "to drag", rather than *pao,* "to embrace."

37. The concept of *ch'i* ("unorthodox") forces is discussed in the translator's introduction and notes to the *Art of War.*

38. Following the consensus of the commentators that "commander" should be understood in parallel with the succeeding phrases referring to the *ssu-ma* and the general.

39. See note 5 to *Three Strategies of Huang Shih-kung.*

40. Duke Huan, who ruled Ch'i from 685 to 634 B. C., was the first of the five hegemons, or strongmen who exercised de facto power over the entire realm in the name of supporting the now-weakened hereditary house of Chou.

41. Analogies from Sun-tzu's "Strategic Military Power" (*Art of War*, Chapter 5).

42. The Sung edition has "Heaven" for "man," changing the sentence to "Do not be the first under Heaven to engage in battle."

43. Reading "disposition," "shape," "form" in accord with the Sung edition, rather than the Ming edition's "punishment."

44. The modern commentators generally understand this sentence as translated. However, it may also refer to receiving the Mandate of Heaven to go forth and punish the evil. (Cf. WLT CCCY, p. 51; WLT CS, p. 72; WLT CY, p. 16; WLT CC, p. 19.)

45. For other possible interpretations, such as "speed," see WLT CS, p. 72; WLT CC, p. 19; and WLT CY, p. 16.

46. "Unify" is implied and is also found in several of the variant editions.

47. The RT adds considerable material from the *Ch'ün-shu chih-yao,* with the important sentences then reading as follows: "Military affairs rely on the strength of the masses. If you are not extremely careful about actions taken, you will have to change them several times. When you change them several times, then even though affairs are initiated, the masses will be perturbed" (WLT CS, p. 71). The fostering of certainty in the general's orders and avoiding doubt in both their minds and in the mind of the commander are important themes in most of the *Seven Military Classics.*

48. The translation follows the Ming text (note WLT CCCY, pp. 53–54; and WLT CY, p. 17). However, the RT provided by the WLT CS is somewhat more consistent: "In antiquity, among those who led the people it never happened that they were unable to gain their minds and yet able to gain their strength" (WLT CS, p. 71).

49. The RT variant merits note: "Only after the people will die for their ruler just as for their families should you constrain them with regulations. Thus in antiquity those who engaged in warfare would invariably take *ch'i* as their foundation in order to stimulate the will, and stimulate the will in order to employ the four limbs, and the four limbs in order to employ the five weapons. Thus when the will is not stimulated, the soldiers will not die for honor. When the soldiers will not die for honor, even though they constitute a multitude, they will not be martial" (WLT CS, p. 71).

50. As Liu Yin discusses, the ruler should accord with the people's desires and social affairs to further structure and direct their activities (WLTCC WCCS, I:20).

51. Following the Ming text and the understanding of WLT CCCY, p. 59, and WLT CY, p. 16, which assume the terms are correct as they stand—meaning a "company" and a "*po,*" the officer for the company. However, note that WLT CS emends the text to the terms for the paths crisscrossing (and defining) the ancient agricultural fields and therefore, by implication, referring to the organizational cohesiveness of the agricultural community (cf. WLT CS, pp. 71–72. However, this seems contextually inappropriate). The WLT CC (p. 22) understands *po* as a larger unit, perhaps something like a double company or regiment, but the appearance of the term in Chapter 15 of the *Wei Liao-tzu* clearly shows it to be one hundred men, a company.

52. The RT prefaces the passage with "the Former Kings" (WLT CS, p. 71). In this case the remaining sentences would continue the description of the ancient practices by discussing their results rather than stating a general conclusion, as translated; the latter would be appropriate for a contemporary listener such as King Hui.

53. An "old" army is a prominent concept in the "Superior Strategy" of *Huang Shih-kung.* The proper behavior for a general exercising personal leadership is discussed in many military writings, including Chapter 23 of the *Six Secret Teachings*

("Encouraging the Army") and the "Superior Strategy" of *Huang Shih-kung*. They both contain descriptions similar to the ones found in this chapter.

54. The BS read "The military is solid through being quiet and victorious through being united." (WLT CS, p. 80; WLT CY, p. 22; WLT CC, p. 27.)

55. This clearly continues the observations and principles of the last chapter.

56. In Sun-tzu's conception, one of the commander's aims is to create a tactical balance of power (*ch'üan*) that dramatically favors him, resulting in an easy, overwhelming victory. Failing to effect this imbalance, the victory can only be viewed as fortuitous. (Cf. Sun-tzu's *Art of War*, Chapter 1, "Initial Estimations." Also refer to the notes to the translator's introduction and translation for a brief discussion of *ch'üan*, which is translated as "tactical balance of power" or sometimes "imbalance" of power to emphasize the desired orientation.)

57. The BS have "die for the Tao/Way" rather than "able to implement the Tao/Way" (WLT CC, p. 28). Note the discussion of the general's awesomeness and the problem of doubt in the "Superior Strategy" of *Huang Shih-kung*, where the analogy of the mind and limbs is also used.

58. There are several interpretations of this seemingly simple sentence. Rulers frequently, and generals sometimes, are spoken of as "loving their people" or "loving their men." However, the phrase "loving and cherishing the minds of their men" is unusual and in the context of the passage that follows, seems to require understanding in a causative sense: "causing the minds of their men to love and cherish them," just as "causing their minds to fear and respect them." (Liu Yin's comment accords with the simple "loving the minds of the men"; our translation agrees with WLT CY, p. 23; and WLT CCCY, p. 78.) Another possibility is "Those who are not able with love and solicitude to cause their officers and troops to cherish them and submit cannot be employed by me; those who are unable with awesomeness and severity to cause the officers and troops to respect and fear them cannot direct the army for me" (see WLT CS, p. 82).

59. Possibly reflecting Sun-tzu's concepts in *Art of War*, Chapters 3 and 4, insofar as the wise general will not undertake an assault unless he can be victorious.

60. The term translated as "occupies ravines" is also the title of Chapter 50 in the *Six Secret Teachings*, "Divided Valleys." Throughout the *Six Secret Teachings* the authors advocate seizing and occupying such strategic points when outnumbered or otherwise at a disadvantage. The BS read somewhat differently: "Those imprisoned in a ravine have no mind to fight." (WLT CC, p. 28. See Chung's note 19 for a discussion of relevant ideas from Sun-tzu. However, he does not consider whether this situation is desperate enough to force the men's spirits to ultimate commitment.)

61. Following the Ming edition and Liu Yin, WLTCC WCCS, I:27B. Armies marching forth under the banner of righteousness, such as the effort led by King Wu of the Chou dynasty against the Shang, presumably have fervent public support and should therefore initiate action. Those contending over lesser, "nationalistic" state issues should respond rather than initiate action, probably to generate public support. The BS are completely contradictory: "One who awaits the enemy values being first" (WLT CC, p. 29, followed by WLT CS, p. 80).

62. BS have "During the conflict you must be timely" (WLT CC, p. 29).

63. This directive emphasizes speed in reaching the marshaling point for the offensive, apparently to take advantage of the enemy's unpreparedness; this is similar to the concept found in *Art of War*, Chapter 2, "Military Discussions." However, note that

Sun-tzu clearly advised against this sort of exhaustive employment of military forces because it would make them susceptible to being defeated by any well-rested forces that might await them (see *Art of War,* Chapter 7, "Military Combat"). Although minor advances in transport technology may have occurred between the writing of the *Art of War* and the first chapters of the *Wei Liao-tzu,* even if more than two or three centuries had passed, without the advent of the cavalry, chariots and infantry would still only be able to cover roughly thirty *li* a day on an extended march.

64. Following WLT CCCY, p. 88; WLTCC WCCS, I:30A (Liu Yin's commentary); and WLT CS, p. 84. Two editions understand "*fa,*" translated as "to construct," as "broken" or "destroyed," which seems unlikely (WLT CY, p. 22; WLT CC, p. 30). Constructing fording points (or possibly "ferries") and bridges would facilitate the general movement of defense forces; however, destroying them could thwart an enemy's advance, particularly in a concrete situation in which the invader's objective might be clear.

65. Literally, "guests," which should probably be understood as forces invading another state's territory—thus generally called a "guest" in military terms—or perhaps stationed inside foreign territory, just beyond the border, to prevent incursions.

66. Although these sentences certainly reflect Sun-tzu's thinking, they are not found in the *Art of War.*

67. Following WLT CCCY, p. 92. The commentators generally understand the term *yü* as "borders" or "border defense works."

68. The context clearly describes policies designed to deny all material aid and shelter to the invaders, forcing them to transport provisions extreme distances and thus expend great energy to maintain their siege. (Compare the ideas in the "Superior Strategy" of *Huang Shih-kung.*) Therefore, although a certain amount of preparatory destruction and loss is entailed, in general the defenders expend only a fraction of the enemy's energy to collect their foodstuffs, bring in their knocked-down shelters (rather than destroyed, as the commentators would have it), and prepare for the siege. The translation follows Liu Yin's commentary, WLTCC WCCS, I:31A, with which both the CCCY and CY editions agree. However, Hsü Yung's CS edition, apparently misunderstanding it completely, views it as a discussion of *ch'i* (understood as spirit rather than effort or energy). Thus he translates it into modern Chinese as "In this fashion it causes the aggressor's spirit (*ch'i*) to grow and expand and the defenders' spirits to drop" (WLT CS, p. 89). Apparently in the belief that the passage continues the initial condemnation of inept actions, based on the YCS BS, he then translates the next sentence as "Once they encounter the enemy's advance and attack, the defending army will then sustain great losses" (WLT CS, p. 89).

69. From the earliest period down into the Warring States era, walls were generally made from tamped earth, sometimes packed within a permanent retaining form built of stones that then made up the exterior faces. Consequently, great effort was required to move the dirt necessary for a wall of any functional dimensions, and such walls—if never put to defensive use—would appear to be a wanton waste of energy.

70. Emending "wall" to "defend," according to the Sung edition.

71. The YCS CP have "the soldiers, people, and masses selected" (WLT CS, p. 88; WLT CC, p. 32).

72. Here the YCS CP text resolves a murky passage quite well, adding to the number of besieging forces the critical words "to balance," "to be suitable." Thus the sen-

tence would read "The attackers must not be less than a mass of more than one hundred thousand to be suitable [to the task]" (cf. WLT CS, pp. 88–89).

73. Liu Chung-p'ing interprets this as shielding and protecting the somewhat fragile earthen walls against damage from the natural elements, such as wind and rain (WLT CCCY, p. 97).

74. Strength broadly construed rather than simple numerical superiority, as some commentators suggest.

75. The YCS CP have a connective "then" between the two halves of the sentence. Accordingly, the weak would be incited by the strong taking their stance at the forefront and would willingly assume positions at the rear (cf. WLT CS, p. 88).

76. The BS version differs significantly: "If a mass of fifty thousand ... [the city] truly must be rescued. Contain their rear, go forth through their strategic points. Lightly strike their rear, do not allow provisions to pass through." Hsü Yung assumes the fifty thousand refers to the rescuing forces. (Cf. WLT CS, p. 88. His text, p. 86, differs slightly from the annotations in the CC edition, p. 33, including "truly not be rescued" instead of "truly must be rescued.") The tactical concerns raised here reflect those found in Chapter 40 of the *Six Secret Teachings,* "Occupying Enemy Territory," although in the latter the perspective is that of the besieging forces.

77. *Tao,* literally "turn over," generally taken as "to confuse," as in confuse the enemy (cf. WLT CY, p. 26; WLTCC WCCS, I:33B). However, the ruse of a half-hearted effort can also be understood as "turning their army around" because they reverse their deployment, putting their stalwarts to the rear.

78. The primary meaning of the second word in the title is "mound," and its secondary meaning is "insult." The basic idea appears to be that if one is conscientious about following the twelve recommended practices, the state will become strong and therefore will be able to display an attitude of superiority toward others and to "insult" its enemies. Similarly, if a state falls into the twelve ill habits, other states will soon be able to insult it as it grows weaker and becomes easy prey for its enemies. The chapter thus continues the thoughts found in Chapter 5, "Tactical Balance of Power in Attacks."

79. The twenty-four practices are couched in a formulaic phrase, "X lies in Y," the term "lies in" being *tsai yü.* The latter can also be translated as "be at," "depends upon," "consists in," and "be present in." Our translation adopts slight variations in accord with the implications of the terms. In all cases the fundamental idea is that the root of a certain condition lies in a certain practice.

80. The government should avoid interfering with the people's seasonal occupations and should also actively foster and observe ritual practices that accord with the activities of the seasons.

81. The commentators generally take *chi* as "planning," "making strategy." However, the term's fundamental meaning is "the subtle," the "moment," and therefore sensitivity to the small, or perceptivity. (In *Wu-tzu* it means "vital point." See Chapter 4, "The Tao of the General." Also see note 32 of *Questions and Replies.*)

82. By penetrating the external form and then formulating plans to take advantage of the situation.

83. The first passage can be understood as a normative description of how a righteous army should behave, or how the ideal armies of antiquity—in particular, those of the Chou dynasty—actually managed their campaigns and constrained their behavior.

84. These are among the justifications stated in Book I, "Benevolence the Foundation," of the *Ssu-ma Fa* for undertaking a punitive expedition. (Also see note 55 of *Questions and Replies*.)

85. The title of the chapter is apparently derived from this phrase, which appears here and elsewhere in the text. However, the title can also be understood as "Martial Discussions" or "Military Discussions," as Liu Yin suggests in his commentary (cf. WLTCC WCCS, I:35B).

86. Hua Lu-tsung notes that another interpretation is that all these plans are directed toward a single objective—the evil ruler. Although this would accord with the Chou's pronounced theory of extirpating only the evil, it seems unlikely here (cf. WLT CY, p. 32).

87. Some commentators understand the phrase as "rescuing oneself," but this seems unlikely. (Compare the modern Chinese translations in WLT CY, p. 34; and WLT CS, p. 98.)

88. Following WLT CCCY, p. 112. However, Liu Yin notes that a small state "takes pleasure in nourishing the people" (I:37A), and WLT CY (p. 34) understands the state as nurturing itself rather than serving others. However, in the reality of the Spring and Autumn and Warring States periods, a small state would have to subjugate itself to a significant power in order to exist, and therefore "serve and support" seems more likely.

89. Emending the text according to an identical sentence in essentially the same paragraph in the *Six Secret Teachings* (Chapter 22, "The General's Awesomeness"). Both the Sung and Ming texts have "execute" instead of "reward," and the paragraph proceeds to draw conclusions about both punishments and rewards in parallel, justifying the emendation.

90. The last sentence is restored from the Sung edition.

91. Emending "flourishing" in the Ming edition to "exist" from the Sung version.

92. Some commentators have identified this as a form of boat or other vessel as well as various types of assault vehicles for attacking cities. Cf. WLT CC, p. 39, for a summary.

93. This might equally refer to a "sundry goods official" and could also be understood as "markets manage the sundry goods." Cf. WLT CCCY, p. 118; WLT CY, p. 33; and WLT CC, p. 39.

94. A *tou*—at least in the Han dynasty—is generally taken as having been equivalent to 1.996 modern liters, or slightly more than two quarts. This would presumably have been the minimum dry rations (before cooking) for a month. The amount for a horse, however, would be completely inadequate unless computed on a per-day basis and supplemented with hay. (Note that in Chapter 11 Wei Liao-tzu condemns feeding grain to horses as an extravagant practice.)

95. A star's name (WLT CY, p. 34).

96. For a discussion of these sentences and their origination in the Taoist classic, the *Tao Te Ching*, see the translator's introduction and notes to the *Three Secret Strategies*. A similar passage appears in the third section, "Inferior Strategy."

97. Clearly sentences and an analogy from Lao-tzu's *Tao Te Ching*, Chapter 78. Sun-tzu also uses the power and imagery of water to illustrate his principles in *Art of War*, Chapters 5 and 6.

98. The radical difference between the perfunctory obligations of the civil realm and the brusque, unfettered martial realm, including this concrete example, are discussed in the second chapter of the *Ssu-ma Fa,* "Obligations of the Son of Heaven."

99. The commentators offer various explanations for this sentence, although generally taking it to mean that on the second day the army will complete an additional three days' distance. However, this runs contrary to every principle advanced by virtually every military strategist, including Sun-tzu. (See especially *Art of War,* Chapter 7, "Military Combat," where Sun-tzu specifically condemns rushing forward a hundred *li* to engage in combat; the *Ssu-ma Fa,* Book II, "Obligations of the Son of Heaven"; and Wu Ch'i, *Wu-tzu,* Chapter 2, "Evaluating the Enemy.") Covering double the normal distance in a single day would have already exhausted the troops and animals; a triple days' march would be virtually impossible and would ensure that the army would be easy prey for any forces that follow Sun-tzu's principles and await them well rested. (Probably only a regular day's march, or roughly thirty *li,* could be accomplished on the first day due to the normal disorganization at the outset, whereas a double pace would be possible on the second day because presumably the men would still be fresh. The author is obviously stressing the realization of speed to surprise the enemy relatively unprepared, as Sun-tzu also strongly advocates in *Art of War,* Chapter 9.)

100. The pent-up river analogy also appears in the "Superior Strategy" section of the *Three Secret Teachings.*

101. The text couches it in terms of applying a mineral of the same color to them. This is generally understood either as responding in kind to their strength, such as employing chariots to confront chariots (presumably to cause their rapid disintegration by confronting and smashing their strength), or as using banners of identical colors to cause confusion. (For the former, see WLT CCCY, p. 133; for the latter, WLT CY, p. 37; and WLT CS, p. 101.)

102. In accord with Wu Ch'i's dictum, "Execute anyone who does not follow orders" (Chapter 5, "Responding to Change," *Wu-tzu*). Only through such draconian measures could the army be unified and realize its potential effectiveness.

103. The title of the chapter, *Chiang Li,* by itself would normally be understood as "Principles of Generalship" or the "General's Principles." However, the chapter opens with a discussion of the general's role as an impartial administrator of the law and proceeds with a strong condemnation of the criminal practices of his day, including the system of extended guilt or culpability. (In the latter the criminal's relatives and associates are implicated in various ways and are also severely punished or executed.) The first sentence identifies the general with this role of *administrator* (of the law) (cf. WLT WCHC, 5:57).

104. The commentators and modern Chinese translators have produced much-simplified and also very contorted versions of the first two sentences of this paragraph. The first problem arises with determining the appropriate meaning for *ch'iu,* translated as "stop" but found primarily with the meaning "help," "aid," or "assist" as well as "to stop" and "to correctively manage." (It may also be an error for a somewhat similar character, "to seek," or for another, "to pursue.") Most of the modern editions simply state the apparent implications of the sentences: namely, that in his administration of law cases, the perfected man does not seek for evidence or crimes beyond the case that is immediately present. Thus, even if the criminal has shot at him in the past, this

does not implicate him in the present. However, such explanations are not very satisfactory. (Cf. WLTCC WCCS, 1:4; WLT CS, p. 106; WLT CY, pp. 39–40; WLT CC, p. 44.)

105. The BS edition concludes rather differently and much less effectively for the point of Wei Liao-tzu's argument: "A state hero would overcome [the false accusation], while the 'mean man' would [falsely accuse himself]" (WLT CC, p. 45; and WLT CS, pp. 104–105). This fragment obviously assumes a great capacity for enduring pain on the part of the state hero.

106. This describes a situation exactly contrary to the ideal just portrayed in Chapter 8.

107. Although somewhat similar expressions occur in isolation in Chapters 2 and 13 of Sun-tzu's *Art of War,* the entire sentence does not.

108. The four groups were the officials (aristocrats), farmers, artisans, and merchants.

109. The BS text has "calculate the migrant peoples" (cf. WLT CC, p. 48; and WLT CS, pp. 109–110). This would reflect Wei Liao-tzu's advocacy of state policies to attract immigrants and displaced persons, as discussed in earlier chapters.

110. "Master artisans," following WLT CC, p. 48.

111. The BS have "root" rather than "authority," which changes the last part of the sentence to read "is the root/basis of ruler and ministers" (cf. WLT CC, p. 48; WLT CS, p. 110). There is disagreement as to whether the term *ch'en chu* refers to "the ministers and the ruler" or just the ruler (cf. WLT CCCY, p. 149; WLT CY, p. 43).

112. "Opening and closing" (or "stopping up") was encountered in Chapter 3, "Discussion of Regulations." The "single Tao" may refer either to the combination of agriculture and warfare or to those policies designed to unify the people and integrate the government and the people (also see note 18).

113. Understood by Hsü Yung as "this is the basis for ensuring that resources will have a surplus" (WLT CS, p. 110).

114. Because the government's domestic policies are being discussed, some commentators take this sentence as referring to the status of activities within the state (WLT CY, p. 43). However, it is generally understood as referring to evaluating the enemy, knowing the enemy's weakness and movement (WLTCC WCCS, I:52B; WLT CCCY, p. 150; WLT CS, pp. 110–111).

115. The *li* (rites) defining the relationship between ruler and subject, king and feudal lord. (The *Chou li* [under the Office of the Ssu-ma] and the *Ssu-ma Fa* contain similar justifications in terms of aberrant behavior, in accord with the *li* understood as furnishing the parameters of government, for mounting a punitive expedition. Two are mentioned in Chapter 8, above [see note 84].)

116. The state is apparently so ideal that people concentrate on basic occupations and are neither contentious nor motivated by rewards. However, this depiction markedly contradicts Wei Liao-tzu's advocacy of markets and commercial activity as the essential foundation of the state's prosperity and the bulwark of military financing.

117. The five grains are variously identified, even in antiquity. Millet was the basis of northern diets, and one early list includes two types of millet. Other grains were rice, wheat, barley, and legumes. (See Francesca Bray, *Agriculture, Science and Civilisation in China,* Vol. 6, Part II, Cambridge University Press, Cambridge, 1984, pp. 432ff.)

118. The ruler's Virtue and enlightened rule shine throughout the world.

119. Presumably on the proper structure for human relations. Liu Yin refers to "The Great Plan" in the *Shu Ching* in illustration, in which case the ruler's discourse would be all-encompassing (WLTCC WCCS, I:56A).

120. These sentences do not appear in the present text of Sun-tzu's *Art of War*.

121. Reflecting Sun-tzu's principles, particularly as expressed in the *Art of War*, Chapter 1.

122. This quotation, which is not found in the present text of the *Art of War*, has as many interpretations as there are commentators and modern translators. Our translation largely follows Liu Yin (WLTCC WCCS, I:61A), but for other variations compare WLT CS, p. 120; WLT CY, p. 50; and WLT CCCY, pp. 176–177.

123. The last phrase can also be understood in the past tense, as "those who suffered a defeat [in reality] had no men."

124. The analogies of rushing water and lightning are commonly found in the military writings, normally to advocate and describe the swiftness and effect of an overwhelming, onrushing attack. Although most of the strategists also raised the specter of the chaos and disorder inherent in such precipitousness (and advised capitalizing on it whenever possible), in general they still emphasized employing it.

125. As described in Chapter 4, "Combat Awesomeness." (The commentators and translators erroneously tend to ignore "discussions," interpreting the character as "plans" or simply deleting it altogether. This misses Wei Liao-tzu's emphasis on planning and detailed discussions, as Sun-tzu advocated, to realize victory without engaging in combat.)

126. The term translated as "company commander" is *po,* which was encountered previously in Chapter 4, "Combat Awesomeness" (see note 51). In the passage that follows, the number of men under his command is explicitly recorded as one hundred men, making the unit a company.

127. Throughout this chapter we translate *chu,* which means "punish" or "execute/kill," as "execute" in accord with the general—although not unanimous—view of the commentators. Military law was strict, and the tradition from Shang Yang on down embodied the belief that only thoroughness in implementing the severest punishments would cause the people and soldiers to follow the laws and orders.

128. The commentators differ on whether these are guard posts—possibly kiosks or watchtowers—or simply some sort of marker, such as posts or pennants. (Cf. WLT CCCY, p. 195; WLT CY, p. 57; WLT CC, p. 58; WLT CS, p. 130.)

129. Possibly other provisions of the law that would cover the offenses committed by the officers, as described in "Orders for Severe Punishment," Chapter 13.

130. Presumably, the feathers are affixed to their caps or helmets to provide a marker that jutts into the air and is more easily visible than any marking on their uniforms.

131. Many commentators assume this means that the soldiers in the first line of five wore their emblems on their heads, those in the next line wore them on their necks, and so forth. However, this would be redundant because the members of the lines would already be clearly distinguished by the color of their emblems. It is more likely that it applies to the subgroup of five squads within the company of one hundred, as our translation expresses. (Compare WLTCC WCCS, II:3B; WLT CCCY, p. 203; and WLT CY, p. 61.)

132. Literally, "commanders of the troops," as the context makes clear (cf. WLTCC WCCS, II:4a; WLT CY, p. 61; and WLT CCCY, p. 207). However, some scholars understand this as "commanders and troops" (cf. WLT CS, p. 136).

133. A similar passage appears in the *Wu-tzu,* Chapter 5, "Responding to Change."

134. The translation follows the suggestion of Robin D.S. Yates. The commentators and modern translators take it (both here and in other texts) as "Beat the drum once and the army goes left; beat it again and it goes to the right" (cf. WLT CY, p. 63; and WLT CS, p. 139). Liu Chung-p'ing offers a unique explanation: Within the pair of drumsticks, the left one is much heavier and thus makes a larger, deeper sound, whereas the right one is lighter and is more suitable for a lighter, rapid sound. However, he fails to offer a satisfactory translation of this sentence, although his theory could describe a distinction between the heavier, slow beat and a rapid, racing beat (see WLT CCCY, pp. 211–213).

135. Except for a few characters in preface, this passage is identical to one found in Chapter 54 "Teaching Combat," in the *Six Secret Teachings* and is almost identical to a (presumably earlier) one found in Chapter 3, "Controlling the Army," of the *Wu-tzu.* Wu Ch'i apparently sought to establish the systematized training of the troops through ever-widening concentric circles. One man—presumably an officer—taught ten men. These ten men were then responsible for transferring the instructions to one hundred and the one hundred in turn to one thousand. Consequently, this is similar to the practice of having instructions radiate down from the higher-ranking officers to the lower ones and then to the troops, as in *Questions and Replies.* The passage in the *Six Secret Teachings* begins with the statement "When teaching the commanders and officers," clearly indicating that it, too, is founded on a downward radiation concept. However, the passage in the *Wei Liao-tzu* lacks these prefatory characters and has the character *ho,* "to unite" or "join with," rather than *ch'eng,* "to complete" (with the implication of "to extend"). Although *ho* can be glossed as *ch'eng,* in the *Wei Liao-tzu* it appears that the authors understand these perhaps common sentences differently. Consequently, when the training at each smaller unit level is complete, it is united with other such units to make up the next-larger tactical unit and then undergo joint training. Thus the translation differs somewhat from the previous passages. (Cf. WLT CY, pp. 63–64; WLT CS, p. 139; and WLT CCCY, pp. 214–215.)

136. Compare with the ceremony described in Chapter 21 of the *Six Secret Teachings,* "Appointing the General," and see textual note 41 for an explanation of the axes.

137. See the similar description in Chapter 51, "Dispersing and Assembling," of the *Six Secret Teachings.*

138. The term translated as "vanguard," *chung chün,* has traditionally been understood as designating a rear guard force, an army that "follows in the rear" (WLTCC WCCS, II:8B; WLT CCCY, pp. 226–232). This explanation was based on *chung* meaning the "heel of the foot" and "to follow in the footsteps of." However, modern commentators understand it as referring to a "vanguard" because this chapter speaks of it as following behind the advance army (cf. WLT CC, p. 65; WLT CY, pp. 67–68; WLT CS, pp. 146–147).

139. Understanding *piao* as a type of command pennant (cf. WLT CC, p. 65). The chapter refers to these pennants several times, and various explanations are offered by the commentators. One is that flags or pennants were emplaced at the assembly point or on the designated battlefields and that the various forces then marched to them.

Others suggest they were a sort of marker post that functioned similarly (cf. WLTCC WCCS, II: 8B–9A). Still another view is that *piao* refers to a prearranged schedule and that actions should be taken in accord with it (cf. WLT CY, p. 68). Finally, some feel that they conveyed a prearranged signal or command and were possibly a pennant or flag of some type (cf. WLT CS, p. 136). In the latter case, *ho piao* might refer to uniting the halves of the command, thereby authenticating it.

140. Raised, or possibly presented to the commander.

141. The soldiers are not just fed but are ceremoniously feasted to raise their morale for battle.

142. This sentence is thought by some commentators to be a misplaced fragment because it bears little relation to the context. The explanations for the four unorthodox forces include the main army, advance army, vanguard, and the division of troops. (The latter is clearly forced, as is the whole explanation. Any force can be used in unorthodox tactics; they are not inherently unorthodox despite a force perhaps having special training.) Others suggest they are four main types of battle array (WLT CC, pp. 65–66) or corner positions on the formation (WLT CS, pp. 9–10.)

143. The commentators differ on the meaning of *hsiang tsan*; some take it as "to participate in planning military affairs," others as "to investigate and check each other," and still others as translated. (Cf. WLT CCCY, p. 232; WLT CS, pp. 146–147; WLT CC, p. 66.)

144. Although the text is ambiguous, clearly both the squad leader—who is responsible for the behavior and attainments of his men—and the instructor will be liable to punishment.

145. The term translated as "falls ill" is variously understood—from leaving formation and thus not participating in the drills to falling down, lying on the ground. In the latter case the soldier would obviously not need to report his illness himself. (Cf. WLT CY, p. 70; WLT CC, p. 68; and WLT CS, p. 151.) Liu Yin suggests that the term is not clear but may mean "commit an offense" (WLTCC WCCS, II:11B; also see WLT CCCY, p. 236).

146. As discussed in Chapter 17, "Orders for Regulating the Troops."

147. A mid-echelon officer apparently in charge of eight hundred men (WLT CS, p. 151).

148. Following the commentators who gloss *chüeh* as to engage in archery or weapons practice rather than as a term designating foot-speed measure (WLT CC, p. 69; WLT CY, p. 70).

149. No doubt the rewards—which would be based strictly on objectively quantifiable battlefield achievements such as the number of heads, prisoners, and flags captured—also included the awarding of flags of rank. Thus everyone would be able to observe the basis for such awards and also the promotions themselves.

150. The commentators generally understand *lu li* as "uniting strength," probably based on a *Kuo yü* gloss. However, in this case the meaning of the original character— "kill," "slay in war," "massacre"—would perhaps be more appropriate. The sentence would then read "Establishing awesomeness lies in [attaining] killing power."

151. Following WLT CY, p. 70; WLT CC, p. 69.

152. Certain variant texts have "army" for "chariots." However, the passage is more comprehensible if it refers to the three chariot officers and the squads of five, reflecting the stage of growing chariot and infantry cooperation (WLT CC, p. 71).

153. These terms have been encountered previously with a different meaning. See note 19, the text of chapter 3, and note 112.

154. Or possibly to stop in the sense of encamping. (Cf. WLTCC WCCS, II:16A; WLT CC, p. 71; and WLT CS, p. 154.)

155. As in ascend a wall, mount a parapet.

156. Emending "first" to "causes," as Liu Yin's commentary suggests (WLTCC WCCS, II:16B).

157. Apparently the aim is to make the formation as dense as possible, with the spears almost touching (cf. WLTCC WCCS, II:17A). Some have understood this as referring to their deployment when encamped, but it need not be so restricted (cf. WLT CY, p. 75).

158. The Sung edition has "strong" rather than wise. However, because the chariot also served as a command platform, "strong" is not invariably correct.

159. Emending "their" to "flags," following the Sung edition.

160. This passage is similar to those found in several texts describing the commitments required of generals being commissioned.

161. Following the Sung edition rather than the Ming, although both can mean "within a short period." (Liu Yin explains the Ming text as "a few spies," which seems rather inappropriate to the context [WLTCC WCCS, II:19A].)

162. This presumably refers to the ruler in his implementation of the system of rewards and punishments.

163. Based on the context, these two sentences could also be understood as referring to those who presumed to interfere with the implementation of the law. Thus, "If someone should be punished, execute anyone who requests that he be spared. If someone should be rewarded, execute anyone who requests that he not be rewarded."

164. Their internal changes, deviations from the ideal and the proper. The sentences that follow suggest using probing stimuli to elicit changes, similar to the techniques used by the T'ai Kung in evaluating men discussed in Chapters 6 and 20.

165. A principle espoused in Chapter 40 of the *Six Secret Teachings,* "Occupying Enemy Territory." The prospect of achieving an opening or some other advantage will presumably lead them to commit their forces to the enterprise, thereby wearing them down without throwing them into such a completely hopeless situation that they will fight a desperate, pitched battle. (Much of the earlier material in the chapter on attacking cities while sparing the people also reflects Chapter 40.)

166. They are thinking of leaving, escaping.

167. Literally, "their minds have been lost," to which Liu Yin adds the interesting comment that when they have "lost their minds, how can they possibly make plans?" This explains the problem of "distorted plans," noted in the chapter's last sentence.

168. Either this chapter has been deliberately condensed during the course of transmission, or significant portions have simply been lost. The *Ch'ün-shu chih-yao* and the bamboo slips supplement the received Ming (Sung) text in numerous places but do not represent sufficiently radical changes to necessitate revising the latter in view of our objective of translating the integral Sung/Ming text. However, for the convenience of readers interested in this material, rather than appending a confusing array of sentences section by section, we provide a tentative complete translation after the notes for this chapter. (The translation follows the reconstructed text found in the WLT CS, pp. 159–160.)

169. A saying from the *Tao Te Ching* previously encountered in this and other military classics.

170. Some commentators suggest that "trunk" should be understood as "pillars" and "seed" as "foundation" (cf. WLT CY, p. 79).

171. The translation follows Liu Yin's division of the text. However, some commentators understand this sentence as referring to integrating and unifying the martial and civil, continuing the thread of the previous sentence. (See WLT CY, p. 79; and also the RT translation below.)

172. Following the Ming text, which asserts the principle that an advance front should be dispersed in order to be effective. (Cf. WLTCC WCCS, II:22B and the slightly different view in WLT CY, p. 79.) Other commentators understand *ta*, which can mean "to penetrate" in the passive sense—as "be penetrated"—so that being dispersed would be harmful. (This is apparently based on the absence of "advance front" in the RT, for which see the translation below.) Also recall this statement from Book III of the *Ssu-ma Fa*: "When advancing, the most important thing for the ranks is to be dispersed; when engaged in battle, to be dense."

173. Following Liu Yin's suggestion that the sentence refers to the general and the troops, respectively (WLTCC WCCS, II:23A).

Translation of the reconstructed text: "Weapons are inauspicious implements; combat is a contrary Virtue; conflict is the last of affairs. The true king attacks the brutal and chaotic to settle benevolence and righteousness. They are the means by which the warring states establish their awesomeness and encroach on their enemies, what weak states are unable to abandon.

"The military takes the martial as its ridge beam and takes the civil as its pillars. It takes the martial as the exterior, and takes the civil as the interior. It makes the martial the external, and makes the civil the internal. One who can investigate and fathom these three will then know the means to victory and defeat. The martial is the means to insult an enemy, to determine life and death. The civil is the means to discern benefit and harm, examine security and danger. The martial is the means to contravene an enemy, the civil is the means to defend. The military's employment of the civil and martial is like an echo responding to a sound, like a shadow following a body.

"An army is victorious through being unified and defeated through being beset by dissension. Through tightness formations are inevitably solid; when dispersed they are porous. A general who has awesomeness will survive; one who loses his awesomeness will die. One who has awesomeness will be victorious; one without awesomeness will be defeated. When the troops have a general, then they will fight; when they are without a general, then they will flee. When they have a general, they will die; when without a general, they will be disgraced. What is meant by awesomeness is rewards and punishments. One whose troops fear their general more than the enemy will be victorious in battle. One whose troops fear the enemy more than their general will flee from battle. Thus to know who will be victorious, who defeated, before engaging in battle, definitely weigh your general with the enemy. The enemy and your general are like a steelyard and balance.

"The army is ordered through being settled and quiet, and becomes chaotic through brutality and haste. Sending troops forth and deploying the army definitely have constant orders; the dispersal and density of the lines and squads definitely have constant methods; and arraying the rows from front to rear has its appropriateness and suitability. Constant orders are not for pursuing a fleeing enemy or suddenly striking a city. If the front and rear are disordered, then [the army] loses [its integrity]. If the front loses [their order], the rear beheads them.

"As for the army's constant formations, there are those which face toward the enemy; those which are internally oriented; standing formations; and sitting formations. Formations which face toward the enemy provide the means to prepare against external threats. Internally oriented ones are the means to preserve the center. Standing formations are the means to move, sitting formations the means to stop. Mixed formations—with some soldiers standing, others sitting—respond to each other in accord with the need to advance or stop, the general being in the middle. The weapons of the seated soldiers are the sword and ax; the weapons of the standing soldiers are the spear-tipped halberd and crossbow; the general also occupies the middle.

"Those who excel at repulsing the enemy first join battle with orthodox troops, then [use unorthodox ones] to control them. This is the technique for certain victory.

"Generals and their troops do not have the closeness of fathers and sons, nor the intimacy of blood relationship nor the personal connections of the six degrees of family relationship. Yet, although before them there is a thousand-fathom-deep valley or the abyss of a precipitous mountain gorge, when they see the enemy they race at them as if returning home, and when they see the enemy entering water or fire they follow them in, it is because before them they see the clarity of rewards and preservation, while behind them they see the punishment of certain death. If in front of them the general is not able to make clear his [rewards and behind them he is not able to make his punishments severe], then it defeats the army, causes the death of the general and the capture of the troops. The general who is able to control his officers and troops, [both] within the encampment and when practicing formations, makes his corporeal punishments and fines severe, and makes his various rewards clear. Then, when they issue forth they will realize complete achievement.

"Array the *fu* and *yüeh* axes [for punishment], make a display of the emblems and flags [used as rewards]. Those who have merit must be rewarded; those who contravene orders must die. When the point is reached that the two enemies are confronting each other, the deployed formations are pressing close upon each other, and the general takes up the drumsticks and drums the advance, then surviving and perishing, life and death, lie in the tips of the drumsticks. Even though there are those under Heaven who excel at commanding armies, [no one] will be able to repulse them after the great drumming. When the troops have gone forth, the armies have been deployed, and the arrayed formations see the enemy—looking across at each other's emblems and flags, before the arrows have been shot and cross in flight, before the long blades have clashed—those who yell out first are termed 'vacuous,' those who yell out afterward are termed 'substantial,' and those who do not yell are termed 'secretive.' 'Vacuous,' 'substantial,' and 'secretive' are the embodiment of warfare."

174. As with "Army Orders I," a tentative translation of the RT found in the WLT CS (pp. 160–161) follows the chapter notes below.

175. The punishment for men involved in such flight is thus an extended three-year tour of duty on the border, in contrast to the earlier-mentioned single year's obligation.

176. The double expenditure is generally understood as referring either to the rations for an empty position plus those consumed by a man at home or, more likely, to

two rations covering only a single man at the front. (Cf. WLT CS, p. 165; WLT CY, p. 83; WLT CCCY, p. 291.)

177. Although the text seems straightforward, this sentence has caused considerable discussion over the centuries. As mentioned in note 22 to the translator's introduction, it has frequently been taken as referring to administering capital punishment to the troops, apparently to put them in greater awe of their own commander than of the enemy. More likely, it should be understood as translated: "The general is able to bear having half of his men killed to achieve victory." (See Hsü Yung's lengthy discussion in the WLT CS, pp. 166–175.)

Translation of the reconstructed text: "Districts which are a hundred *li* from the army should all make preparations for defense and for repelling [the enemy] just as a city which lies on the borders. When there is an order to mobilize the army, the commanding officers should receive their drums and flags, halberds and armor. On the day for issuing forth, anyone who goes out across the district borders after his commanding officer shall be liable for the law for late arrival for border duty.

"After serving on border duty for a year, anyone who subsequently deserts and does not follow the commanding officer's orders shall be punished analogously to the law for deserting the army. If his parents, wife, or children know about it, they will share the crime with him. If they do not know about it, pardon them.

"If a soldier arrives at the headquarters of the Grand General a day after his commanding officer, his parents, wife, and children should all share the crime with him. If a soldier abandons his post to return home for a day and his parents, wife, or children do not arrest him, hold him, or report it, they will also share the crime with him.

"If they should lose their commanding officer in battle, or if their commanding officer should be killed in battle and the troops flee by themselves and return [to the rear], they deserve to all be beheaded. If a commanding officer should command his troops in a retreat, anyone who beheads him and seizes his troops should be rewarded. Anyone [among them] in the army who has not achieved merit must serve three years at the border.

"If the army engages in a major battle and the Grand General dies, all the subordinate officers commanding units of more than five hundred men who were not able to fight to the death with the enemy deserve to be beheaded. All the troops near the commanding general, on the left and right in [protective] formation, deserve to be beheaded. As for the remaining officers and men, those who have achieved military merit should be reduced one grade of merit. Those who have not achieved military merit should be rescripted to three years' border duty.

"If the squad of five loses a man in battle, or if a squad member dies in battle but they do not retrieve his corpse, then take away all the merit of all his squad members. [Those without military merit] should be rescripted to three years' border duty. If they retrieve his corpse, then their crimes should be pardoned.

"If the troops escape and return home ... it is a great harm to the army and a great waste to the state. If the generals are unable to stop it, this is the way to become internally weak of oneself.

"The army's advantage and disadvantage lie with name and substance in the state. Today if a person's name appears on the military [rolls] but in reality he is at home, then the [army] has not gained the substance [of his presence], and the household has not gained the [registration of] his name. When troops are assembled to compose an army, it will have an empty name and no substance. Outside the state it will be inadequate to repel enemies, while within the borders it will be inadequate to defend the state. This is the way in which the army becomes insufficient, in which the general has his awesomeness taken away.

"I believe that when soldiers abandon their units and return home, the other members of their squad in the same barracks and their officers take their rations for their own consumption while the person is eating at home. Thus a person is nominally with the army, but in reality double the ration is expended. The resources of the state are then empty and completely exhausted, and the harvest is outside. [Alternative reading: (The troops) are outside for years.] How can the number fleeing to the interior [be reduced]?

"If they can be stopped from returning home, it prevents the loss of an army and is the first military victory. If the squads of five and ten are caused to be mutually bonded to the point that in battle the troops and officers will aid each other, this is the second military victory. If the general is able to establish his awesomeness, the soldiers to master and follow their instructions, while the commands and orders are clear and trusted, and attacking and defending are both properly executed, this is the third military victory.

"In antiquity those who excelled in employing the army could [bear to] kill half of their officers and soldiers. The next could kill 30 percent and the lowest 10 percent. The awesomeness of one who could sacrifice half of his troops is established within the Seas. The strength of one who could sacrifice 30 percent could be applied to the feudal lords. The orders of one who could sacrifice 10 percent would be implemented among his officers and troops. I have heard that a mass of a hundred ten-thousands that does not fight is not as good as the corpses of ten thousand men. Ten thousand men who do not die are not as good as the ghosts of one hundred men.

"When rewards are as clear as the sun and moon and as credible as the four seasons; when orders are as strict as the *fu* and *yüeh* axes and as sharp as [the famous sword] *Kan-chian,* it has never been heard of that there were officers and troops who would not die in the lists!"

Three Strategies of Huang Shih-kung

Abbreviations of Frequently Cited Books

HSK CCCY   Wei Ju-lin, *Huang Shih-kung San-lüeh chin-chu chin-i,* Shang-wu yin-shu-kuan, Taipei, 1975.

HSK CS   Hsü Pao-lin, *Huang Shih-kung ch'ien-shuo,* Chieh-fang-chün ch'u-pan-she, Peking, 1986.

HSK WCHC   *Huang Shih-kung San-lüeh,* in *Ch'ung-k'an Wu-ching hui-chieh,* Chung-chou Ku-chi ch'u-pan-she, Cheng-chou, 1989.

HSKCC WCCS   *San-lüeh chih-chieh* in *Ming-pen Wu-ching Ch'i-shu chih-chieh,* Vol. 2, Shih-ti chiao-yü ch'u-pan-she, Taipei, 1972.

SL MK   Manabe Kureo, *Sanryaku,* Kyōikusha, Tokyo, 1987.

SL OK   Okada Osamu, *Rikuto, Sanryaku,* Meitoku Shuppansha, Tokyo, 1979.

Notes to the Translator's Introduction

1. For an extensive discussion, refer to Hsü Pao-lin, HSK CS, pp. 26–33, and especially pp. 29–30 for the history of the text in Japan.

2. For a general discussion, see ibid., pp. 1–18.

3. From *Shih chi* 55, "The Hereditary House of Marquis Liu." The translation is based on Takigawa Kametaro, *Shiki kaichū kōshō,* 1-volume reprint, I-wen yin-shu-kuan, Taipei, 1972 (Tokyo, 1932–1934), original edition, pp. 784–785.

4. Cf. Hsü Pei-ken, *T'ai-kung Liu-t'ao chin-chu chin-i,* Shang-wu yin-shu-kuan, Taipei, 1976, pp. 29–31.

5. Quoted in Ch'ü Wan-li, *Hsien-Ch'in wen-shih tzu-liao k'ao-pien* (hereafter *Hsien-Ch'in,* Lien-ching, Taipei, 1983, p. 481.

6. A Sung scholar, Chang Shang-ying—who is closely identified with the *Su shu* (for which he wrote an introduction and a commentary), claimed that the famous work given to Chang Liang was neither the *Three Strategies* nor the *Six Secret Teachings* but instead was the *Su shu.* He further asserted that Chang Liang had ordered the book entombed with him to prevent the unworthy from obtaining it and that it had resurfaced only when discovered by grave robbers in the Chin dynasty. Although it is generally accepted that Chang forged the *Su shu* himself, the concept of burying works to prevent their transmission is worth noting. For a brief discussion of the *Su shu,* see Ch'ü Wan-li, *Hsien-Ch'in,* p. 481; and Chang Hsin-ch'eng, ed., *Wei-shu t'ung-k'ao* (hereafter *Wei-shu*), Vol. 2, Taiwan Shangwu yin-shu-kuan, Taipei, 1970 (reprint) (original edition, 1939), pp. 808–809.

7. Cf. Hsü Pao-lin, HSK CS, pp. 6–18.

8. Slightly later in his biography the Grand Historian writes, "Chang Liang exercised his persuasion on the Duke of P'ei (Liu Pang) with the military strategies of the T'ai Kung" (Takigawa, *Shiki,* p. 785). Chang Lieh advances the same conclusion. See Cheng Liang-shu, ed., *Hsü Wei-shu t'ung-k'ao* (hereafter *Hsü Wei-shu*), Vol. 3, Hsüeh-sheng shu-chü, Taipei, 1984, pp. 1594–1597.

9. Cf. Hsü Pao-lin, HSK CS, pp. 6–9.

10. The former Han officially ended with Wang Mang usurping the throne and declaring himself the first emperor of the Hsin dynasty in A.D. 9. He was a member of the imperially related Wang family who exploited the family's power and influence, became regent for two youthful emperors, and finally reigned under his own authority. Accordingly, Hsü Pao-lin believes the *Three Strategies* describes the conditions leading to this usurpation, itemizing the dangers of powerful imperial relatives monopolizing power and of skilled politicians controlling affairs. However, rulers at every level of the old feudal hierarchy were equally confronted with such problems throughout ancient Chinese history, and many other strategists and intellectuals—including Han Fei-tzu—decried the situation. Hsü's argument that the passage about reducing the power of commanding generals after a campaign refers to the period following the establishment of the Han also lacks the singularity of uniqueness. Clearly, the Ch'in had also been confronted with demobilizing a tremendous force—a mass no longer bound to the land (cf. Owen Lattimore, *Inner Asian Frontiers of China,* Beacon Press, Boston, 1960, pp. 441–443)—as had other states after massive efforts and significant strategic victories during the Warring States period.

11. Hsü Pao-lin perceives a new realization of the value of strategic strongpoints in the *Three Strategies,* one that results from experiences gained in the increasingly vast

scope of conflict leading to the establishment of the Han dynasty. This may, however, be a case of projecting historical events into strategic thought. The *Six Secret Teachings* had already advanced tactical methods for systematically exploiting configurations of terrain (as Hsü acknowledges), and the passage on which his view is based consists of only three four-character phrases. Cf. Hsü, HSK CS, pp. 22, 74–75.

12. See Wei Ju-lin's running comments throughout the HSK CCCY; and Hsü Pao-lin, HSK CS, especially pp. 10–13, as well as his running commentary and analysis. Hsü has perhaps artificially isolated Legalist elements that are an integral part of prior strategic thought. Wei's commentary tends to emphasize the book's continuity with previous military writings, especially the *Six Secret Teachings*.

13. Hsü, HSK CS, pp. 87–88, does not accept the possibility that it might be an interpolation.

14. Hsü believes the *Three Strategies* expresses a new, significantly advanced attitude toward the people because they are seen as being as essential as the general to attaining victory. Moreover, the general should have his intentions penetrate to the masses rather than simply commanding them while keeping them ignorant, as Sun-tzu advocated (see Sun-tzu, the *Art of War*, Chapter 11). Effective government presumably responds to the people's problems and needs, so a new relationship is thereby created (see Hsü, HSK CS, pp. 20–21, 57–58). However, Wei Ju-lin takes the opposite view (HSK CCCY, p. 39).

15. HSK CS, pp. 52, 108–111.

16. This spirit clearly pervades the entire *Tao Te Ching*. Readers unfamiliar with this Taoist classic can consult the readily available translations by D. C. Lau (see note 17), Wing-tsit Chan, or Arthur Waley.

17. This famous phrase is from Verse 31 and may also be translated "Weapons are inauspicious implements." It is followed by a second phrase, "There are things that abhor them" rather than "The Tao of Heaven abhors them." In his translation (*Tao Te Ching*, Chinese University Press, Hong Kong, 1982, p. 49) D. C. Lau notes that this verse lacks Wang Pi's commentary, leading to the suspicion that it may be a commentator's interpolation. At the same time the concept appears elsewhere, as in Kou Chien's biography in the *Shih chi*, 41 (Takigawa, *Shiki*, p. 654), and Chapter 12 of the *Six Secret Teachings* (cf. HSK CCCY, p. 123).

18. See Hsü, HSK CS, pp. 64, 96–97. It seems doubtful that the *Three Strategies* represents the most advanced conceptualization of character usage up until that time, as Hsü asserts.

19. Note how the concept of shame—which is vital to Confucian thought, the *Wu-tzu*, and other military writings—has been superseded.

20. The pivotal expression is found in the *Tao Te Ching*, Verse 78, "Under Heaven nothing is softer or weaker than water, but for attacking the firm and strong nothing is able to surpass it." Also note Verse 76.

21. The *Three Strategies* does not really expand on the referents of the hard and soft, the weak and strong, but merely mentions them in two passages. Once the duality is established, prolific speculation is possible.

22. Liu Yin, HSKCC WCCS, "Superior Strategy," 3B–4A.

Notes to the Text

1. Although this sentence is usually taken as referring to the "commander in chief" rather than the ruler, the subsequent content of the passage suggests it might be translated as "The ruler's method for command focuses on winning the minds of the valiant."

2. "All living beings" is actually expressed as "the category of [beings] containing *ch'i*." The conceptualization of men in terms of *ch'i* underlies the military psychology of courage, discipline, and *ch'i* manipulation, as can be seen in the other military classics as well.

3. "Pronouncements" appears to be the best English rendering for the term *ch'en* (Matthews #181, where the pronunciation is given as "*ch'an*"; Morohashi, #36144; and *Ta Chung-wen ts'u-tien*, #36986), which basically means prophecy or verification. However, these "pronouncements" generally seem to be based on military experience and common sense rather than on prognostications about the future. They predict the results that will be obtained from following particular courses of action in certain situations and also provide abstracted wisdom. The original source for these quotations, if one existed, has been lost. As discussed in the translator's introduction, Hsü Pao-lin cites the use of this term as evidence that the text was composed in the Han period, based on his assertion that the character *ch'en* does not appear before the Ch'in dynasty (HSK CS, p. 15). Also note HSK CCCY, p. 40.

4. This sentence is cited as evidence of the Taoist influence in the text. The *Three Strategies* obviously differs from a purely passive posture in advocating the appropriate use of both the hard and soft, even though in a relativistic sense, the soft can overcome the hard. Accordingly, Hsü Pao-lin asserts that the work is a product of Huang-Lao Taoism and therefore could not have been written until Huang-Lao thought developed and flourished in the Former Han era (HSK CS, pp. 10–13).

5. "Brigand" appears to be the best translation for the term *tsei*, which originally carried the strong meaning of harming or killing people and committing crimes against the established order (such as an officer killing his superior or ruler). It also had a class or social status basis because presumably the mean or common people could only commit *tao*, which primarily meant robbery but also included the murder of officials. Cf. Tu Cheng-sheng, "Ch'uan-t'ung fa-tien shih-yüan—ch'ien lun Li Li Fa-ching te wen-t'i," in Hsü Cho-yün, *Chung-kuo li-shih lun-wen-chi,* Shang-wu yin-shu-kuan, Taipei, 1986, pp. 433–438. *Tsei* may also be translated as "bandit" and "murderer."

6. Wei Ju-lin believes there must be an error in the text because basic military thought dictates seizing the active role rather than responding. See HSK CCCY, p. 42. (However, permitting affairs to begin to unfold may also allow taking control and therefore still being the manipulator.)

7. This four-character phrase is somewhat problematic. According to the Ming commentator Liu Yin (I ISKCC WCCS, I:8), the enemies who harm and insult the ruler are to be overturned. (However, the character may be a loan for "investigated" rather than overturned.) Those whose offenses are not serious are to be tolerated to see whether they reform. Hsü Pao-lin glosses it as "to warn" (HSK CS, pp. 35 and 42). Alternatively, this may be a fragment that means "restore the decimated."

8. Some commentators, including Hsü Pao-lin (HSK CS, p. 35), interpret this causatively—make the enemy depart so as to tire him. Others read it more simply, as to depart yourself. The latter seems preferable, even though it is a general principle of the military works that one should exhaust an enemy by moving him about. Note Sun-tzu, the *Art of War,* Chapters 5 and 6.

9. Liu Yin elaborates this as "Accord with the desires of the people to initiate appropriate measures" rather than simply responding in an active fashion to his plans and movements. See HSKCC WCCS, I:9B.

10. Another interpretation would be "Spread accusations and point out his errors," which would be a basic propaganda measure in psychological warfare.

11. Liu Yin believes this sentence should be understood as "Set out a net of principles to catch the Worthy" (HSKCC WCCS, I:9B). Hsü's modern translation has "Establish ambushes on all four sides to encircle and destroy them" (HSK CS, p. 43).

12. Wu Ch'i both advocated and embodied this principle.

13. This incident (circa 375 B.C.) involved Kou Chien, king of Yüeh, prior to the war that annihilated the state of Wu. Consequently, it is argued that the *Three Strategies* must have been written after 375 B.C. (assuming the incident is not a later interpolation).

14. This is virtually a quotation from Wu Ch'i's biography in the *Shih chi,* which has been translated in the translator's introduction to the *Wu-tzu.* A similar passage is also found at the end of Chapter 4 in the *Wei Liao-tzu.*

15. This echoes, if not copies, Sun-tzu's analysis in the *Art of War,* Chapter 5, "Strategic Configuration of Power."

16. There are two interpretations of this passage. One is expressed by the translation; the other would run "Thus officers can be treated with deference, but they cannot be treated arrogantly."

17. Wealth may refer here to the general's possessions, goods brought in by merchants, excessive materials for the army, or perhaps the gifts and bribes of other states. In all cases temptation arises, and evil follows.

18. This is essentially a summation of the allegory used by the T'ai Kung in his initial interview with King Wen of the Chou dynasty, as preserved in the first chapter of the *Six Secret Teachings.*

19. The Three August Ones are variously identified; however, they represent the ultimate embodiment of government through radiant Virtue and profound nonaction. The five legendary emperors, again variously identified, followed them and were much more active—creating culture and the essential artifacts of civilization. In the Taoist view, as civilization declined from Virtue into artifice, rulers became more active—increasingly interfering in people's lives and creating laws, taxes, and bureaucratic burdens. The Confucians held a similar "decline from Virtue" view, attributing the world's problems to a lack of such Sages and the failure of moral values to be practiced—not because of the activity of the great rulers but in spite of it.

20. The *Army's Strategic Power* is presumably another lost text. Whether this was an actual book or merely a convenient title created by the authors to attribute sayings—actual or conveniently concocted—that justified their thoughts is unknown.

21. This hierarchy of armies allocated on the basis of feudal rank perhaps represented the conditions at the start of the Chou dynasty, but by the middle of the Spring and Autumn period, the stronger states had five or more such armies—assuming an army to be 12,500 men.

22. This sentence is cited as evidence that the work was composed after the Han dynasty had restored peace and tranquility. Hsü Pao-lin further asserts that it comes from a dialogue recorded in a *Shih chi* biography, proving a post–*Shih chi* date of composition (HSK CS, p. 15).

23. The character for "pleasure" and "music" is the same but with different pronunciations. Because the Confucians believed that the forms of propriety and music were essential elements of the foundation of personal development and education, the character is translated as music. However, "pleasure" would work equally well, reading: "Their physical submission is attained through the forms of propriety; their mental submission is attained through pleasure. What I refer to as pleasure is not the sound of musical instruments." The senses are never mutually exclusive. Mencius has a famous discussion with King Hui of Liang on music, pleasure, and the responsibilities of rulership (Book I), which this passage clearly draws on. In addition, numerous passages in the *Hsün-tzu* and the *Li chi* couple the forms of propriety—the *li*—with music. Although proper, volitional practice of the *li* results in self-cultivation and emotional alchemy, music is recognized as being truly influential in harmonizing and developing the emotions. Hsü Pao-lin's comments agree with the present translation (ibid., p. 100). Most commentators simply avoid the question by merely repeating the character for music/pleasure in their notes without further elaboration.

24. Literally, "lost." Some commentators, such as Hsü Pao-lin, take this as referring to the ruler's errors in framing commands. Others understand it as failures in execution at the highest level, which then work down to affect even the lowest officials. See ibid., pp. 105 and 123.

25. The "discontented" might also refer to the source of discontent, the laws that are causing the problem (cf. Hsü, ibid., p. 105, who understands it in this way).

26. The four classes of people are the *shih* (officers, old nobility, members of the bureaucracy, literati), farmers, artisans, and merchants.

Questions and Replies Between T'ang Tai-tsung and Li Wei-kung

Abbreviations of Frequently Cited Books

LWK CC	Wu Ju-sung and Wang Hsien-ch'en, *Li Wei-kung wen-tui chiao-chu,* Chung-hua shu-chü, Peking, 1983.
LWK CCCY	Tseng Chen, *T'ang T'ai-tsung Li Wei-kung wen-tui chin-chu chin-i,* Shang-wu yin-shu-kuan, Taipei, 1975.
LWK WCCS	*T'ang T'ai-tsung Li Wei-kung wen-tui chih-chieh* in *Ming-pen Wu-ching Ch'i-shu chih-chieh,* Shih-ti chiao-yü ch'u-pan-she, Taipei, 1972, 2 vols.

TLWT WCHC　　*T'ang Li wen-tui,* in *Ch'ung-k'an Wu-ching hui-chieh,* Chung-chou Ku-chi ch'u-pan-she, Cheng-chou, 1989.

Notes to the Translator's Introduction

1. In addition to the Sui and T'ang dynastic histories, the general introduction is based primarily on the following works: Denis Twitchett and John K. Fairbank, general eds., *The Cambridge History of China,* Vol. 3: *Sui and T'ang China, 589–906, Part I,* Cambridge University Press, London, 1979; Arthur F. Wright, *The Sui Dynasty,* Alfred A. Knopf, New York, 1978; Arthur F. Wright and Denis Twitchett, eds., *Perspectives on the T'ang,* Yale University Press, New Haven, 1973; René Grousset, *The Empire of the Steppes: A History of Central Asia,* Rutgers University Press, New Brunswick, 1970; Fu Yüeh-ch'eng, *Chung-kuo t'ung-shih,* 2 vols., Ta-Chung-kuo t'u-shu kung-ssu, Taipei, 1985 (reprint) (original ed., 1960); Hsü Cho-yün, ed., *Chung-kuo li-shih lun-wen-chi,* Shang-wu yin-shu-kuan, Taipei, 1986; and Hsü Pei-ken et al., *Chung-kuo li-tai chan-cheng-shih,* Li-ming, Taipei, 1976 (rev. ed.), Vol. 7 and Vol. 8.

2. The historical portrait of T'ang T'ai-tsung's role and activities in the founding and consolidation of the T'ang dynasty has been the subject of considerable reevaluation and revision in recent times. It is generally thought that the emperor heavily influenced the official records from which posterity would fashion the dynastic history. Thus his father's role—which is much diminished in the traditional accounts—should probably be augmented and his determination, intelligence, and overall abilities accorded significantly greater recognition. (See Twitchett and Fairbank, *Sui and T'ang China,* pp. 38–47 on T'ang sources and pp. 155ff.)

3. T'ang T'ai-tsung's six horses are especially famous; they have been memorialized by stone reliefs and even became the subject of early Western articles (see the notes to Appendix B). His actions in deposing and imprisoning his father and murdering his elder brother were of course contrary to all the ethical dictates of Confucianism.

4. Unlike the earlier military classics, the textual history of *Questions and Replies* has not benefited from any startling discoveries or recently recovered renditions. Consequently, although analytical studies have become more incisive, the fundamental question of authorship and the period of composition remain essentially unresolved.

In the Ming and Ch'ing dynasties, orthodox scholars reviled the text as a forgery characterized by uncouth language, limited concepts, and erroneous interpretations of historical events. (For examples, see Chang Hsin-ch'eng, ed., *Wei-shu t'ung-k'ao,* Vol. 2, Shang-wu yin-shu-kuan, Taipei, 1970 [reprint of 1939 ed.], pp. 810–812; and LWK CC, pp. 84–96.) In the last century a few voices have begun to cautiously criticize these strident expressions of personal opinion, but no one has yet ventured to attribute the book to Li Ching or to assert that it constitutes an actual record of the conversations.

Briefly summarized, there are two main views: One holds that the book is a forgery of the Northern Sung period, the other that it was compiled by unknown scholars late in the T'ang or early Sung. These views are based mainly on the absence of any reference to a book by this title in the bibliographical sections in either the *History of the T'ang* or the *History of the Sung* (which does, however, suddenly contain the names of seven works associated with Li Ching) and on claims of Northern Sung military scholars to have seen a draft of the work by Yüan I, who purportedly forged it. The concurrence of several contemporaries regarding these claims prompted later generations of orthodox thinkers, who were already predisposed to view the text as an inferior work, to readily accept the forgery story as fact. Finally, the *T'ung-tien*, which was compiled by Tu Yu at the end of the eighth century A.D., contains numerous excerpts from a work entitled *Li Ching ping-fa* and quotes Li Ching extensively but without ever mentioning the *Questions and Replies*.

Evidence discrediting the Yüan I forgery theory is based on Emperor Shen-tsung's edict mandating the study and exegesis of "Li Ching's ping-fa" because the text (or texts) had become unreadable in the Northern Sung. Thereafter, the emperor also ordered the compilation and editing of the ancient military works, resulting in the present *Seven Military Classics*. The latter's initial circulation is believed to have predated the forgery story by about ten years; therefore, the *Questions and Replies* must have been in existence prior to its supposed creation by Yüan I. Furthermore, analysts question how the best military scholars—in a period when they were fervently investigating military theory for the urgent purpose of defending the state—could all have been deceived. Accordingly, they conclude that the forgery story must be false.

Wu and Wang (LWK CC) have suggested that historical references to the emperor ordering the exegesis of "Li Ching's ping-fa" should be understood as referring to his military writings in general rather than to a particular text entitled *Li Ching's Art of War*, which is similar to Sun-tzu's *Art of War*. After condensation and editing, the resulting integrated work was retitled *Questions and Replies*, thereby eclipsing the texts from which it was derived. (Unfortunately, although they discredit the forgery theory, Wu and Wang do not offer any alternatives. See LWK CC, pp. 1–5.)

Adherents of the Yüan I theory generally assumed he based his draft on material from the *T'ung-tien*. However, Wang Tsung-hsi's analysis in the Ch'ing era proved this view to be erroneous. (Wang compiled a text entitled *Wei-kung ping-fa chi-pen* from the extant materials attributed to Li Ching that were preserved from early sources. Although based mainly on the *T'ung-tien*, the text was supplemented by quotations from Tu Yu's commentary on Sun-tzu *Art of War* and later encyclopedic works. Comparing the contents of his work with the *Questions and Replies* requires a separate study. For further discussion and analysis, see Teng I-tsung, *Li Ching ping-fa chi-pen chu-i*, Chieh-fang-chün ch'u-pan-she, Peking, 1990; Chung-kuo Chün-shih-shih Pien-hsieh-tsu, *Chung-kuo chün-shih-shih*, Vol. 5: *Ping-chia*, Chieh-fang-chün ch'u-pan-she, Peking, 1990, pp. 433–436; and Wang Hsien-ch'en and Hsü Pao-lin, *Chung-kuo ku-tai ping-shu tsa-t'an*, Chieh-fang-chün ch'u-pan-she, Peking, 1983, pp. 84–86.) Others who accepted the forgery theory believed that rather than amplifying original materials, Yüan I developed his own military concepts, enhancing them with the borrowed veracity of a famous strategist.

Generally speaking, military historians perceive advances over previous texts in theory and conceptualization in the *Questions and Replies* and believe the book must come from the hands of an experienced strategist, even if it does not record the actual discussions between Li Ching and T'ang T'ai-tsung. (This does not preclude court notes or other material having been available.) Consequently, it might have been compiled or forged at the end of the T'ang or early in the Sung and presumably was modeled on the *Chen-kuan cheng-yao*—a summary of government discussions, achievements, and policies during T'ang T'ai-tsung's administration (cf. Twitchett and Fairbank, *Sui and T'ang China*, pp. 240–241). However, based on certain textual material, the authors of the *Chung-kuo chün-shih-shih*, Vol. 4: *Ping-fa*, pp. 208–210, conclude that such concepts as "infantry dominating cavalry"—which are expressive of Sung thought—inevitably consign it to the Northern Sung.

Detailed, specialized studies of the text's provenance are clearly required. However, we can tentatively conclude that final compilation probably occurred in the Northern Sung—perhaps under Emperor Shen-tsung's mandate—from earlier materials. Whether the original materials were extensively supplemented or were simply rephrased in contemporary language and judiciously expanded upon remains unknown. (For further analysis and attribution of materials, see Chung-kuo Chün-shih-shih Pien-hsieh-tsu, *Chung-kuo chün-shih-shih*, Vol. 4: *Ping-fa*, pp. 158–162, 204–210; *Chung-kuo chün-shih-shih*, Vol. 5: *Ping-chia*, pp. 428–436; and Hsü Pao-lin, *Chung-kuo ping-shu t'ung-chien*, Chieh-fang-chün ch'u-pan-she, Peking, 1990, pp. 130–135.)

5. The translation of Li Ching's biography follows the version found in "Lieh-chuan" 18, 93:1A–6A, in the *T'ang shu* (*Erh-shih-wu shih*, Vol. 26: *T'ang shu*, Vol. 2, I-wen yin-shu-kuan, Taipei, undated, pp. 1308–1310), supplemented with reference to his biography in the *Chiu T'ang shu* ("Lieh-chuan" 17, 67:1A–8A, *Erh-shih-wu shih*, Vol. 23: *Chiu T'ang shu*, Vol. 2, pp. 1199–1202). The biography and useful notes are also found in Tseng Chen's modern translation of the entire military classic, LWK CCCY, pp. 1–30, and very extensive materials in the 1980 monograph on Li Ching by Lei Chia-chi (*Li Ching*, Lien-ming wen-hua, Taipei, 1980). Translations of the complex T'ang dynasty titles follow Charles O. Hucker's *A Dictionary of Official Titles in Imperial China* (Stanford University Press, Stanford, 1985).

6. The Chiang River refers to the Ch'ang-chiang, best known in the West as the Yangtze.

7. Han Hsin, Pai Ch'i, Wei Ch'ing, and Huo Ch'ü-ping. Pai Ch'i was a famous Ch'in general whose exploits are recorded in Warring States writings. Wei Ch'ing was an outstanding Han major general noted for his success against barbarian forces in remote regions. (His biography appears in *chüan* 111 of the *Shih chi* and has been translated by Burton Watson ["The Biographies of General Wei Ch'ing and the Swift Cavalry General Ho Ch'ü-ping," in *Records of the Grand Historian of China*, Vol. 2, Columbia University Press, New York, 1961, pp. 193–216].) For Han Hsin, see note 11 below; for Huo Ch'ü-ping, see note 15 to the translation.

8. The "K'o-han" (as phoneticized in Chinese) is better known as the "Great Khan," or Qaghan.

9. Li Ling was a famous but ill-fated Han general who went deep into Hsiung-nu territory with a small force, fought heroically, and was finally captured (or surrendered) after protracted fighting against insurmountable odds for days in succession. A brief biography appears within the portrait of Li Kuang in the *Shih chi* (cf. Watson, *Records of the Grand Historian of China*, Vol. 2, pp. 153–154), and a fuller record of his life is found in the *Han shu*, *chüan* 54. (For a translation, see Burton Watson, *Courtier and Commoner in Ancient China*, Columbia University Press, New York, 1974, pp. 24–33.) Ssu-ma Ch'ien's vocal but ill-advised defense of Li Ling resulted in his own condemnation and punishment.

10. An interesting comment from the T'ai-tsung because the historical records do not portray the Wei River confrontation as the ignominious defeat (or coercion) it ap-

pears to have been. In A.D. 626, shortly after the T'ai-tsung usurped the throne, the Eastern Turks advanced far down the banks of the Wei River, close to the capital. The T'ai-tsung failed to defeat them militarily and was probably forced to propitiate them through extensive bribes, perhaps even on the advice of Li Ching (see Twitchett and Fairbank, *Sui and T'ang China*, pp. 220–221).

11. Han Hsin, a great general and strategist, was instrumental in the founding of the Han dynasty. The incident regarding T'ang Chien is similar in that the king of Han (the future Han Kao-tsu) had already dispatched an emissary to persuade Ch'i to submit to his authority, although without rescinding Han Hsin's mandate to attack Ch'i. Han Hsin therefore proceeded with the campaign and—availing himself of Ch'i's newly relaxed defenses—effected a considerable, victorious advance. Naturally, the envoy was killed when Han Hsin's attacks materialized contrary to the promised truce. (Han Hsin's biography, which preserves the outlines of his strategies and contains several interesting applications of principles from Sun-tzu's *Art of War*, appears in the *Shih chi* [*chüan* 92] and has been translated in full by Burton Watson ["The Biography of the Marquis of Huai-yin (Han Hsin)," in *Records of the Grand Historian of China*, Vol. 1, pp. 208–232].)

12. Li Ching's enfeoffment as duke of Wei (Wei Kung) is thus reflected by his formal name in the book's title: Li, Duke of Wei.

Notes to the Text

1. During the Three Kingdoms period (57 B.C. to A.D. 668) in Korea, Koguryo (phoneticized as Kao-li in Chinese) occupied roughly the north, Paekche (Pai-chi) the southwest, and Silla (Hsin-lo) the southeast. From the Han on, Chinese dynasties had attempted—with varying degrees of success—to exercise suzerainty over the Korean peninsula. At the outset of the T'ang, they were opposed by Koguryo in the north but received grudging recognition and requests for support from Silla, which was being militarily pressured by the alliance of Koguryo and Paekche. Silla eventually came to dominate when T'ang forces defeated Koguryo in A.D. 668; thereafter, it began to resist Chinese attempts to directly rule the area. (See LWK CCCY, pp. 31–36; and Twitchett and Fairbank, *Sui and T'ang China*, pp. 231–235 for background.)

2. Yon Kae-so-mun—a charismatic leader who deposed the king—wielded despotic military power, fervently opposed the T'ang, and forged the alliance that challenged Silla.

3. The concepts of *ch'i* and *cheng*, "unorthodox" and "orthodox," dominate Li Wei-kung's strategic thought. (For definitions and discussion of these terms, which perhaps originated with Sun-tzu, refer to the translator's introduction and footnotes to the *Art of War* translation.) They are discussed concretely with reference to earlier historical conflicts and to the battles culminating in the T'ang's overthrow of the Sui. (For a strategic overview of the T'ang conquest, see "T'ang t'ung-i Chung-kuo te chancheng," in *Chung-kuo chün-shih-shih*, Vol. 2, Part 2: *Ping-lüeh*, Chieh-fang-chün ch'u-pan-she, Peking, 1988, pp. 43–75.)

4. The pacification campaign against the Turks is summarized in Li Wei-kung's translated biography in the translator's introduction.

5. The famous, often romanticized strategist in the Three Kingdoms period.

6. A famous general who was active in the mid- to late fourth century A.D. in the Western Chin period (see LWK CCCY, pp. 41–43).

7. A famous diagram created by Chu-ko Liang for deploying combined troops—including infantry, chariots, and cavalry. However, it also had precursors that were attributed to various figures.

8. Commentators disagree on whether the chariots were simply narrow chariots that were specially constructed or modified for use on constricted terrain or were a different type of vehicle, such as a cart (cf. LWK CCCY, pp. 44–45; and LWK CC, p. 3).

9. "Deer-horn chariots" apparently were named for the blades affixed to the front, which protruded out to prevent an enemy from approaching. The commentators differ as to whether these were permanently affixed or were mounted when the chariots were deployed in a circular formation to protect the encampment. In such a configuration, they would presumably have been "head to tail," perhaps mounting the blades just to the outside. However, because the commentators generally emphasize that this deployment equally constrained the men within the camp, the use of permanently mounted blades turning within cannot be completely ruled out. Yet another view holds that the name is derived from the overall formation, with the horns being spikes partially buried in the ground just next to the chariots. Because the number of spikes was apparently small, they probably did not constitute a palisade. (See LWK CC, p. 3; LWK CCCY, p. 45; and TLWT WCHC, IV:2–4.)

10. One of Sun-tzu's main themes, techniques for which include manipulating the enemy as well as directly controlling one's own activities and degree of movement. (Cf. LWK CC, p. 3; and TLWT WCHC, IV:2–4.)

11. "Defense to the fore" rather than "moving against opposition," as sometimes suggested. The "deer-horn" chariots would be particularly effective in this regard. (Cf. LWK CCCY, p. 47; and TLWT WHCH, IV:2–4A.)

12. The term translated as "elite" cavalry originally meant "iron" cavalry, designating armored fighters (cf. LWK CC, p. 5).

13. Li Chien-ch'eng was the T'ai-tsung's ill-fated elder brother, who was eventually murdered as a preliminary to the T'ai-tsung displacing his father from the throne.

14. Sun-tzu, the *Art of War*, Chapter 1, "Initial Estimations." Also see note 16 to the text.

15. One of Han Wu-ti's famous generals, noted for his achievements despite his pronounced disdain for the ancient military writings. His *Shih-chi* biography (*chüan* 111) is translated by Burton Watson as "The Biographies of General Wei Ch'ing and the Swift Cavalry General Ho Ch'ü-ping," in *Records of the Grand Historian of China*, Vol. 2, pp. 193–216.

16. Sun-tzu, the *Art of War*, Chapter 7, "Military Combat." This is a common theme in the military writings.

17. Ibid., Chapter 1, "Initial Estimations."

18. Duke Ts'ao, popularly known as Ts'ao Ts'ao, was a famous general and eventually a warlord who was active in the disintegration of the Han dynasty and the subsequent rise of the Three Kingdoms. He wrote the first known commentary on Sun-tzu's *Art of War*, and what remains of his thoughts are found therein, the *Hsin shu* being lost.

19. His statements are apparently based in part on Sun-tzu's analysis of tactics appropriate to relative advantages of strength in the *Art of War,* Chapter 3, "Strategies for Attack."

20. Ibid., Chapter 5, "Strategic Military Power."

21. Ibid., Chapter 7, "Military Combat." (In the Ming edition, "combining" has inadvertently dropped out but is retained in the Sung version.)

22. An image from *Art of War,* Chapter 11, "Nine Terrains."

23. Ibid., Chapter 6, "Vacuity and Substance." However, note that the translation differs from our translation of Sun-tzu: "Thus if I discern the enemy's disposition of forces (*hsing*) while I have no perceptible form, I can concentrate while the enemy is fragmented." Li Ching clearly takes the sentence to refer to creating false impressions and feigning deployments. Although this is one of Sun-tzu's basic techniques, in the *Art of War* this sentence refers to the contrast between fathoming the enemy and being unfathomable oneself, as the chapter emphasizes (also see note 82 to the *Art of War* translation).

24. This echoes Sun-tzu's basic thought, especially as seen in ibid., Chapter 6, "Vacuity and Substance," and is one reason People's Republic of China scholars term him a Legalist thinker.

25. From Chapter 4 of the *Wu-tzu,* "The Tao of the General," a chapter more oriented to fathoming enemy generals than to focusing on tactics. Li Ching's memory of the text is unusually deficient; he has abridged and somewhat altered it.

26. His purported comment is recorded in Li Ching's biography.

27. From Sun-tzu, the *Art of War,* Chapter 5, "Strategic Military Power."

28. Fu Chien was emperor of a consciously sinicized Tibetan "barbarian" state, who was active in the early part of the so-called "Five Barbarian and Sixteen Kingdoms period." (The "Five Barbarians" refers to the five "barbarian" powers that established their authority over parts of China between 317 and 589, whereas the "Sixteen Kingdoms" refers to the successive states contending for power from 304 to 439.) At the battle of Fei River described in the text, Emperor Fu Chien—despite leading a million-man force—was defeated and his empire lost. A description of Fu Chien's achievements and defeat is found in the *History of the Chin.* For further discussion, see LWK CCCY, pp. 80–85. (Also note Yeh Shih's scathing comments on Li Ching's evaluation of Fu Chien's capabilities, LWK CC, p. 87.)

29. Sun-tzu, the *Art of War,* Chapter 1, "Initial Estimations." This is the conclusion to the chapter and is translated differently from our *Art of War* version because the understanding appears different and the text is abridged. In the original, Sun-tzu is apparently discussing the use of tallies to calculate the probability of winning, whereas the T'ai-tsung's rough recpitulation seems to stress the planning aspect rather than the calculations. (See note 21 to "Initial Estimations"; and LWK CC, p. 12, which reflects one traditional understanding, as does the T'ai-tsung.)

30. A terse, enigmatic text of approximately 360 characters associated with the legendary Yellow Emperor and also attributed to Feng Hou, his minister. A book with this title is preserved in several collections, generally with commentary by the Han scholar Kung-sun Hung. Although ascribed to the Yellow Emperor, it clearly postdates Sun-tzu, even employing some phrases from the *Art of War* and perhaps originates late in the Warring States period. Ma Lung, who is highly regarded by Li Ching and the T'ai-tsung and who appears on the first page of this chapter, is also noted as having written

a commentary for it. (Note that there are some minor differences between the extant text and the portions quoted in *Questions and Replies*. Editions are found in the *Pai-pu ts'ung-shu chi-ch'eng* from I-wen in Taipei and in a recent paperback from Shanghai ku-chi.)

31. The Chinese character for unorthodox—normally pronounced *ch'i*—has a less common second pronunciation—*chi*—when it refers to a "remainder" or "excess." This second meaning and associated pronunciation are the basis for Li Ching's explanation.

32. *Chi* (Karlgren, *GSR* 547C) is perhaps best understood as "motive force," "spring of change," "subtle change," "moment," or "impulse"—perhaps derived from the meaning of *chi* (*GSR,* 547A, the same character without the wood radical, glossed as "small, first signs") in *Chuang-tzu.* Although it is generally understood by the commentators as referring to "opportunity," this seems to be a derived meaning. Sun-tzu consistently speaks about change, both the changes that a commander should effect and those found in the evolving battlefield situation. The commander needs to grasp such changes as they develop, thereby converting them into "opportunities" that can be exploited. (Cf. LWK CC, pp. 12–13; LWK CCCY, pp. 87–91; LWK WCCS, I:16B–17B; and TLWT WCHC, 4:15–16.)

33. "Remaining forces," *yü chi,* the second character being the character for "unorthodox" in the alternate pronunciation.

34. Sun-tzu, the *Art of War,* Chapter 9, "Maneuvering the Army."

35. Essentially identical to a statement in *Art of War,* Chapter 1, "Initial Estimations."

36. Ibid., Chapter 8, "Nine Changes" (cf. note 114 to the *Art of War* translation). This dictum is not confined to Sun-tzu.

37. Literally, "grasps."

38. "*Tui,*" translated as "platoon," a term the *Classic of Grasping Subtle Change* and Li Ching both use to designate a body of men. Although in most contexts it indicates a specific, small number, in some instances it stands as a more general reference to a "force" or "group." From the Warring States period on, it consisted of fifty (frequently specialized) infantrymen, which was also its strength as a fundamental organizational unit in the T'ang military system.

39. The overall orientation, which is both flexible and indeterminate, can be defined at will. Accordingly, "the front can be taken as the rear, the rear taken as the front." One commentator suggests that facing south would be the "normal" orientation, with the north then being the rear (TLWT WCHC, 4:17B).

40. Liu Yin states that any of the four unorthodox or four orthodox formations can be the head. Similarly, any of the nine formations (deployed throughout the matrix)—including the general's in the center—can be the focus of an enemy attack, and the remaining eight will respond, thereby constituting the tails (LWK WCCS, I:19). This differs from the orientation of the entire formation, which is normally determined by the direction of its forward movement, and pertains instead to conditions of engagement.

An alternative explanation identifies the "four heads" as being the outer positions on the horizontal and vertical axes (or roads) that are formed by the four lines (cf. TLWT WCHC, 4:17).

41. "Five" refers to the main horizontal and vertical directions or axes in the "well" configuration (front, rear, left, and right) supplemented by the "center." The forces de-

ployed in the outer boxes formed by the parallel lines defining the axes can be dispersed to fully occupy all eight outer positions. Thus formations occupying "five" positions can effectively cover all "eight" outer positions (Cf. LWK CC, pp. 8–12, 15; LWK CCCY, p. 92; TLWT WCHC, 4:17B–18A.) Note that the overall formation as well as contiguous positions react like the *shuaijan* in Sun-tzu, the *Art of War,* Chapter 11, "Nine Terrains,"

42. A legendary administrative system to organize the people and promote agriculture—one of several variants found in or attributed to antiquity. The Chinese character for "well" (*ching*) resembles a tic-tac-toe board, with a slight outward curve in the downward left leg. (For further discussion, for example, see Li Chia-shu, "Ts'ung *Shih-ching* k'an Hsi-Chou mo-nien i-ch'i Ch-un-ch'iu chung-yeh ch'i-chien-fen feng-chih, tsung-fa-chih, ching-t'ien-chih tung-yao," *Chung-kuo wen-hua yen-chiu-so hsüeh-pao* 19 [1988], pp. 191–216.)

43. Entire volumes have been written about this and similar formations, with extensive disagreement about their use (cf. *Chung-kuo chün-shih-shih,* Vol. 4: *Ping-fa,* pp. 67–78, for some examples). However, in this case it appears the four corners were left open, with the army's forces filling the middle positions horizontally and vertically as well as the middle. However, the middle is not counted as being "filled" (as discussed in the text immediately following) because these are "excess" or "unorthodox" forces under the personal direction of the commanding general himself (cf. Liu Yin's comments, LWK WCCS, I:21).

44. This echoes a similar statement in Sun-tzu, the *Art of War,* Chapter 5, "Strategic Military Power."

45. As distinguished from the "well-field" system described by Mencius (III:A3) and the "village-well" system attributed to the Yellow Emperor just above. (Cf. Tu Cheng-sheng, "Chou-tai feng-chien chieh-t'i-hou te chün-cheng hsin-chih-hsü," *BIHP,* Vol. 55, No. 1 [1984], pp. 96–109.)

46. Most historical sources state the number as three thousand rather than three hundred, as do some editions. (For a discussion of the T'ai Kung and the efforts of the Chou to construct the weapons of war, including the three hundred chariots, refer to the translator's introduction. Also note Yeh Shih's vehement criticism of Li Ching's ascription of monumental achievements to the T'ai Kung, LWK CC, p. 87.)

47. Quoted from the "Chou Annals" in the *Shih chi* and also found in the *Shu ching.* The concept of measured constraint, associated with the Chou scope of battle, is prominently preserved in the *Ssu-ma Fa.*

48. Translating from the Ming edition. Others have "incited the army." Historically, the Annals record the T'ai Kung as leading this elite band of one hundred in the initial, sudden assault against the Shang army.

49. The *Kuan-tzu,* recently translated by W. Allyn Rickett (*Guanzi,* Princeton University Press, Princeton, 1985) is an eclectic work associated with his name.

50. No longer extant in the present *Ssu-ma Fa,* only in fragments dispersed in other works. However, multiples of five were basic throughout the Chou. (For a brief discussion, see Appendix E; and, for example, Tu Cheng-sheng, "Chou-tai feng-chien chieh-t'i-hou te chün-cheng hsin-chih-hsü," pp. 73–113, and especially 79–81; and LWK CCCY, pp. 102–103. There is an entire category of books on military organization, many noted in the recent work by Hsü Pao-lin, *Chung-kuo ping-shu t'ung-chien,* Chieh-fang-chün ch'u-pan-she, Peking, 1990, pp. 217–280. Foremost among them is

the modern *Li-tai ping-chih ch'ien-shuo* (ed. Wang Shao-wei and Liu Chao-hsiang), an extensive analysis and revision of the *Li-tai ping-chih*, Chieh-fang-chün ch'u-pan-she, Peking, 1986.)

51. For a discussion of these categories, see note 20 to the translator's introduction to the *Wei Liao-tzu*. Li Ching is basically following Ssu-ma Ch'ien's history of the *Ssu-ma Fa* as found in Ssu-ma Jang-chü's *Shih chi* biography. (The biography appears in full in the translator's introduction to the *Ssu-ma Fa* translation.)

52. These three works are now lost. For a discussion of the extant text and its relationship to them, see the translator's introduction to the translation.

53. Surprisingly, this appears to be erroneous. The extant *Ssu-ma Fa* discusses the "spring and fall hunts" near the beginning, not the "spring and winter" hunts. Although winter was considered the season of death, the *Ssu-ma Fa* decries winter mobilization because of the extreme hardship the soldiers would suffer from the cold. Of course, the text reflects an early age of limited battles. (The *Chou li, chüan* 7, "Summer Offices, Ssu-ma," discusses hunts for all four seasons. However, in analyzing these regulations, Lao Kan also notes that according to the *Kuo-yü,* military activities should be conducted in winter. See "Chou-tai ping-chih ch'u-lun," *Chung-kuo-shih yen-chiu* 1985, No. 4, p. 10.)

54. The term used, "respectfully performed the affairs of," usually refers to a subject respectfully accepting and executing his ruler's commands. However, in reality, the feudal lords had simply usurped power and sought to legitimize their actions through such claims.

55. The *Chou li* (*chüan* 7, "Summer Offices, Ssu-ma") lists the nine reasons the ruler would rectify a subject state, such as harming the people or killing their own lord. This list is identical to the "nine prohibitions" the king should publicize before the assembled feudal lords, found at the end of the first chapter of the *Ssu-ma Fa*.

56. "Armor and weapons," the arts of warfare. At the same time, they would order and rectify the affairs of the submissive states, curtailing any impulse toward defiance or independence.

57. The practice of training in the intervals between the seasons is not found in the present *Ssu-ma Fa*. However, the concept of spring and fall hunting exercises providing such training, and thus the means by which "not to forget warfare," is prominent in the first chapter. Constant preparation and training are of course underlying themes in most military writings.

58. One of the five hegemons. The term translated here as "battalion" is *kuang*. Generally, *lü*—normally a unit of five hundred men—is translated as "battalion" throughout this book. However, "battalion" is the lowest-strength Western military unit that is functionally equivalent to *kuang*.

The paragraphs that follow are somewhat confusing because of the introduction of different organizational terms and the relative lack of English equivalent units. They are further complicated by Li Ching's sweeping overview of military history and his tendency to redefine terms. There is great disagreement among commentators on the original *Tso chuan* text as well, and therefore in some parts the translation is somewhat tentative. For convenience in following the details of the argument, the Chinese unit term is indicated after the English translation.

59. Quoted from Shih Hui's appraisal of Ch'u (Chin's enemy) and Sun-shu Ao's selection of classic regulations to organize Ch'u's government and army. (*Tso chuan,*

twelfth year of Duke Hsüan. For a complete translation, see the sixth month: James Legge, *The Ch'un Ts'ew with the Tso Chuen,* Oxford University Press, 1872 [reprint Chin-hsüeh shu-chü, Taipei, 1968], p. 312, tr. p. 317; Burton Watson, *The Tso chuan,* Columbia University Press, New York, 1989, p. 87.) Although the meaning of the second half of the sentence is clear (the military should always be prepared without having specific instructions or orders), the first part—"on the symbolization of things"— has elicited divergent comments. Essentially, each officer should act in accord with his designated responsibility, as symbolized and thus defined and directed by his pennant. (Apparently, the pennants had animals and objects depicted on them, with associated duties and responsibilities within the hierarchy of military command. Of course, insignia could also function in this manner, and there is no evidence to preclude this meaning as well—particularly because the narrative also discusses them.) Thus, whether in action or not, the officers knew their duties and would act accordingly. However, the commentators advance other views as well, including one that interprets the phrase as referring to commands conveyed by flags with appropriate objects on them. (Thus Watson translates as "the various officers move in accord with the objects displayed on the flags," essentially the same translation as that of Legge. [See Watson, *The Tso chuan,* p. 87, including his note 10.] This follows Chang Ping-lin's understanding of the sentence as referring to the wielding of central command, which Wu and Wang also accept [LWK CC, p. 21].) Cf. Yang Po-chün, *Ch'un-ch'iu Tso-chuan chu,* Chung-hua shu-chü, Peking, 1990 (rev. ed.), Vol. 2, p. 724.

60. The commentators offer several interpretations for these sentences in an attempt to make sense of the numbers implied. The translation reflects Li Ching's apparent understanding, which may not be the original meaning. Thus the term for company, *tsu,* is taken as referring to the number of men accompanying each chariot rather than to a full battalion of chariots, and the problematic phrase *"tsu pian chih liang"* is understood as emplacing an additional company to the flanks. (This might have originally meant a company of twenty-five, so two companies for the two flanks would yield fifty for a total of one hundred fifty men per chariot, as Li Ching asserts. However, his definition of *liang* requires that it be fifty men, so one *liang* is obviously split between the two flanks of each chariot.)

Other views, derived solely from the *Tso chuan,* range from one hundred men per chariot to one hundred fifty men per *kuang* or battalion, which is variously accounted as thirty or fifteen chariots. Attempts are made to force these numbers to conform to figures derived from the *Ssu-ma Fa* (portions no longer extant), but Yang Po-chün believes they should all be thrown out because the discussion simply refers to chariots and the definition of a chariot battalion and has nothing to do with infantrymen. (See *Ch'un-ch'iu Tso-chuan chu,* pp. 731–732; Li Tzung-t'ung, *Tso-chuan chu-shu chi pu-cheng,* Shih-chieh shu-chü, Taipei, 1971, Vol. 1, 23:13B–14A; and *Chung-kuo chün-shih-shih,* Vol. 4: *Ping-fa,* pp. 13–15.)

The original statement in the *Tso chuan* is perhaps translated as follows: "The ruler's personal guard is divided into two battalions. For each battalion there is a company [*tsu*] and a platoon [*liang*] to the flanks of the company." It is otherwise recorded in the *Tso chuan* that a battalion consisted of thirty chariots, although both Watson and Legge translate as if the entire guard corps was only thirty chariots, or one *kuang* (Legge: "Its ruler's own chariots are divided into two bodies of fifteen each. To each of them are attached 100 men, and an additional complement of 25 men" [Legge, *The*

Ch'un Ts'ew with the Tso Chuen, p. 318]). Arguments advanced that the speaker was defining the nature of the *tsu* in the second part of the sentence seem inappropriate to an extemporaneous battlefield analysis of an enemy's military preparedness and organization.

The original sentence continues by describing how the right wing stands on alert from early morning and the left wing thereafter, thereby illustrating that their forces are constantly prepared. Li Ching has apparently extrapolated this laconic statement to describe Ch'u forces in general, although the commentators all agree that it refers to the king's personal guards or chariots.

61. Another quotation from slightly earlier in the narrative, the twelfth year of Duke Hsüan. Again, the original and its meaning in Li Ching's analysis are open to at least two possible interpretations. First, as translated in the text, it indicates that the contingent of infantrymen assigned to the right are deployed close to the shafts, whereas (in the original) those assigned to the left are dispatched to "search for fodder." (This "searching for fodder" seems highly unlikely because it commits half the ruler's personal troops to a menial, although important, activity. [It has been suggested that this might be a phrase from some other dialect, with a rather different—but unknown—meaning.] They might have been sent forth to scour the environment for enemy troops in concealment and to otherwise provide security functions.) Second, *yu yüan* might refer to the Army of the Right taking its direction from the commanding general's chariot, as symbolized by the "shaft." (Cf. Yang Po-chün, *Ch'un-ch'iu Tso-chuan chu,* p. 723; Legge, *The Ch'un Ts'ew with the Tso Chuen,* p. 317; Watson, *The Tso chuan,* p. 87; LWK CC, p. 22; and LWK CCCY, pp. 113–114.) A third possibility is that the infantrymen deployed to the right of each chariot simply follow the direction of the general's shaft during an advance, without any redeployment to protect both flanks. (Left flank coverage for each chariot would presumably be provided by the chariot company positioned to the left in all cases but one.) Li Ching exploits both senses in his statements that immediately follow.

62. Li Ching thus apparently concludes that the regulations stipulate that the formation's orientation is determined by the direction of the chariots' advance, which (perhaps because of the vulnerability of the chariots, as discussed in the general introduction and Appendix A) required the soldiers attached to the chariot battalion to remain close to the flanks during combat. Examples of reorienting the general's chariot shafts and thus the army's direction occur in the *Tso chuan's* narrative of this battle and its preliminary actions.

63. *Tui,* platoons with a strength of fifty men (see note 38 above). A *tui* was equal to two *liang.*

64. Recorded in the *Tso chuan,* the first year of Duke Chao. As discussed in the general introduction, this pivotal battle is generally regarded as marking the inception of a shift from chariot warfare to infantry warfare. (Unfortunately, the battle is not included in Burton Watson's translation of the *Tso chuan* but can be found in Legge [*The Ch'un Ts'ew with the Tso Chuen,* text p. 572, translation p. 579]. For further analysis, see LWK CCCY, pp. 113–115; LWK CC, p. 22; Tu Cheng-sheng, "Chou-tai," p. 88; and especially *Chung-kuo chün-shih-shih,* Vol. 4: *Ping-fa,* pp. 24–26.)

65. These are generally regarded by the commentators as supply vehicles. (Also see *Chung-kuo chün-shih-shih,* Vol. 4: *Ping-fa,* p. 14.)

66. *Shih* is the ancient term for army, later more equivalent to "regiment." Here company or battalion would more appropriately suggest its strength.

67. Wu Tzu-hsü's statement recorded in the *Tso chuan,* thirtieth year of Duke Chao, is cited as the source for this quotation (LWK CC, p. 25; Legge, *The Ch'un Ts'ew with the Tso Chuen,* p. 733, translation p. 735). However, it obviously summarizes Sun-tzu's approach to warfare and the thought of most traditional strategists thereafter.

68. Such as by employing deception, being formless, and preserving secrecy. (Note that the idea of Han Chinese pretending to be barbarians contravenes the most fundamental beliefs of many orthodox officials and therefore fell beyond the realm of possibility. See, for example, Yeh Shih's vehement denouncement of this tactic, LWK CC, p. 88.)

69. Following LWK CCCY, p. 124.

70. Chapter 10, "Configurations of Terrain." In the *Art of War* the sentence begins "If the general is weak and not strict, unenlightened in his instructions and leadership. ..." Li Ching dropped the first phrase and changed "leadership" to "training."

71. Ibid., Chapter 3, "Planning Offensives." The *Three Strategies* ("Superior Strategy") also incorporates this belief.

72. Here the text matches the original, having the character for "leadership" rather than "training."

73. From Sun-tzu, the *Art of War,* Chapter 5, "Strategic Military Power." The original has "excels at warfare" rather than "excels in employing the army."

74. The section in brackets, to the end of Li Ching's comment, does not appear in the Ming edition but is preserved in the Sung version.

75. Two statements from Sun-tzu, the *Art of War,* Chapter 6, "Vacuity and Substance."

76. The tradition of employing barbarians against barbarians, especially partially sinicized or submissive ones against more brutal hordes, was consciously attempted throughout Chinese history. Even the Shang had used the "barbarian" Chou as a military buffer against more aggressive peoples to the west. (For a discussion of the "barbarian against barbarian" policy, see Yü Ying-shih, *Trade and Expansion in Han China,* University of California Press, Berkeley, 1967, pp. 14ff.)

77. A concept advanced in Sun-tzu, the *Art of War,* Chapter 6, "Vacuity and Substance."

78. The calculation of gain and loss is derived from Sun-tzu's first chapter, "Initial Estimations."

79. Ibid., Chapter 6, "Vacuity and Substance."

80. "How can he bring it about?" This is understood as referring to manipulating the enemy, bringing them into a position from which victory can be effected (cf. Liu Yin's comments, LWK WCCS, II:2B).

81. Sun-tzu, the *Art of War,* Chapter 6, "Vacuity and Substance." Sun-tzu states, "Thus one who excels at warfare compels men and is not compelled by other men." (For further discussion of the phrase "compels men and is not compelled by men," see Tzu Yü-ch'iu, ed., *Mou-lüeh k'u,* Lan-t'ien ch'u-pan-she, Peking, 1990, p. 171.)

82. Sun-tzu, the *Art of War,* Chapter 7, "Military Combat."

83. Although the six do not comprise an actual quotation from Sun-tzu, most express his thoughts and principles—especially employing enticements to draw the en-

emy forth (cf. LWK CCCY, pp. 140–141). "Heavy" and "light" can refer to "substance" as contrasted with the "light" or insubstantial or to the types of troops.

84. The term *"chün-chiao"* is variously understood as a rank of officer or the units of organization (as taken in the translation). Cf. LWK CC, p. 33; LWK CCCY, pp. 143–144; TLWT WCHC, *chüan* 4, II:6–7.

85. Units are integrated hierarchically by tens (rather than fives). Thus ten squads of five compose a platoon and ten platoons a battalion or regiment. The basic idea is to effect training from the fundamental unit up the scale of organization. (This is different, however, from the idea of one man teaching five and five men then teaching five more, thereby spreading the skills through horizontal training—as found in Wu Ch'i's "Controlling the Army" [*Wu-tzu,* Chapter 3].) Thus higher-level instruction is directed to the officers, possibly such as the *chün-chiao* (if the term is understood as an officer) and subordinate generals.

86. From the fifth year of Duke Huan (Cf. Legge, *The Ch'un Ts'ew with the Tso Chuen,* pp. 44, 46). The chariots provided the front, the infantrymen filled in the gaps.

87. See note 50 above.

88. Chapter 16 in the extant *Wei Liao-tzu.*

89. In antiquity, until the development of paper in the late Han, and its growing use thereafter, wooden slips were employed for all recording purposes—including recording commands and the achievements and offenses of the squad of five, which is probably the intended reference here. A squad's insignia symbolized its inescapable participation in a mutually bonded unit, with severe consequences for failing to preserve unit integrity. (Cf. LWK CC, p. 34; LWK CCCY, pp. 145–146; LWK WCCS, II:7.)

90. In terms of functional organization, twenty-five infantrymen composed a *liang* (platoon), and eight cavalrymen similarly constituted a platoon. Thus the organization for cavalry—although identical in principle—was significantly different and lacked the squad level.

91. Following Liu Yin. Many commentators take this as a quotation from the *Ssu-ma Fa,* Chapter 3, "Determining Rank." There the text goes on to discuss the five types of weapons and their appropriate, integrated use. However, this would seem to misread the *Questions and Replies* (even though the *Ssu-ma Fa* emphasizes the use of "five" throughout) because there is no justification for introducing any discussion of weapons.

92. As with the formations from the *Classic of Grasping Subtle Change,* the main deployment consists of formations suborganized into smaller copies. Thus each brigade, for example, is able to execute changes that mirror the overall deployment in responding to attacks in the area of responsibility.

93. The Ming edition of the *Seven Military Classics,* which is the basis for our translation, has the character *pu*—"pace" or "step"—and is followed by some later editions. The Sung edition has the character *cheng*—"orthodox" or "upright"—and is followed by such modern editions as LWK CC. If the text is emended to *cheng,* it would then read "The square is given birth from the orthodox; the circle is given birth from the unorthodox [*ch'i*]." Cf. LWK CC, p. 34; LWK CCCY, pp. 148–149; LWK WCCS, II:10B–11A; TLWT WCHC, *chüan* 4, II:9A.

94. *Wu-tzu,* Chapter 3, "Controlling the Army." The original is somewhat different: "Even if broken off from the main order they preserve their formations, even if scattered they will reform lines."

95. Sun-tzu, the *Art of War,* Chapter 4, "Military Disposition."

96. For *chieh, "constraints,"* see the notes to *Art of War,* Chapter 5, "Strategic Military Power." *Chieh* is used in two rather distinct senses in the ensuing discussion: first, in the sense found in Sun-tzu, which has the essential meaning of an "impulse" or "decisiveness" (Giles)—that which occurs in a brief, finite moment—and second, in the normal sense of "measure," of imposing fixed measure on actions—whether spatial or temporal.

97. A quotation from *Art of War,* Chapter 5, "Strategic Miitary Power."

98. *Chieh.*

99. The commentators generally take this to mean one beating of the drum for each shout; however, it has also been suggested that it means a thrust at the enemy for each shout.

100. Although this seems to refer to spatial dimensions, as front and rear, it could also refer to temporal order, as first and later.

101. A rather curious statement because such automatic responses could easily be exploited by enemy strategists.

102. This sentence paraphrases one from Sun-tzu, the *Art of War,* Chapter 11, "Nine Terrains": "He commands them as if racing a herd of sheep—they are driven away, driven back, but no one knows where they are going."

103. The concept of "constraints" reappears here, more properly rendered as "measure" or perhaps "rhythm" in accord with its use in music and dance.

104. In accord with "five phase" concepts, each of the directions was correlated with one of the five phases, and a whole array of aspects was further grouped around each phase. (Cf. Joseph Needham, *Science and Civilization in China,* Vol. II, *History of Scientific Thought,* Cambridge University Press, Cambridge, 1962, pp. 232–265.) Liu Yin notes them as follows: east—green; south—red; west—white; north—black; center—yellow (LWK WCCS, II:15B).

105. Cf. TLWT WCHC, p. 190.

106. *"San fu,"* translated as "three covering forces," refers to the division into three operational units that apparently have responsibility for "covering" or "protecting" each other (understanding *fu* in the sense of "overspread," "cover." Cf. Karlgren, *GSR,* entry 1034m). Whether they represent units available for executing flexible—including unorthodox—tactics or three ambushing forces is the subject of disagreement (cf. LWK CC, p. 39).

107. Through their own misunderstanding of the *Hsin shu,* not because of Duke Ts'ao's ignorance of military tactics.

108. See note 64 to the text of *Questions and Replies.*

109. Following the Sung edition of the *Seven Military Classics,* which has *fan* rather than *jen*—the latter clearly a copyist's error.

110. A partial quotation from Sun-tzu, the *Art of War,* Chapter 4, "Military Disposition." The original reads: "One who excels at defense buries himself away below the lowest depths of Earth. One who excels at offense moves from above the greatest heights of Heaven." "Lowest depths" is literally "nine layers of Earth," "greatest heights" is "nine layers of Heaven."

111. Although the *Six Secret Teachings* discusses the selection and training of men, this passage does not appear in the extant writings.

112. Emending the text to read "hundred" instead of "twenty." (See Appendix E for a diagram.)

113. "Three thousand" is definitely an error. "One hundred" would yield the historically appropriate force strength. (However, the discussion is even more complex. Cf. Liu Yin's notes, LWK WCCS, II:20–21A.) The "Tiger Guards" are discussed in the translator's introduction to the *Six Secret Teachings;* their role was apparently that of an elite force rather than officers in a command structure.

114. There are five changes rather than four because the fifth change is to reassume the initial formation.

115. A famous dictum from Sun-tzu, the *Art of War,* Chapter 1, "Initial Estimations." "Deceit" alone is inadequate; the phrase should perhaps be translated "The essence of warfare is deception and artifice."

116. The five phases were systematically correlated into a number of relationships, principal among them the production and conquest cycles. For example, wood gives birth to fire, whereas fire conquers (i.e., smelts) metal. (For further discussion, see Needham, *History of Scientific Thought,* pp. 253–265.) Once the formations are assigned phase names, they naturally fall into these patterns of relationships, suggesting various dynamics.

117. An analogy from Sun-tzu, the *Art of War,* Chapter 6, "Vacuity and Substance": "Water configures its flow in accord with the terrain, the army controls [its measures] for victory in accord with the enemy."

118. Fan Li was a thinker and political adviser in the Spring and Autumn period who evolved military theories based on the unending cycle of yin and yang. His writings—if any—have been lost, although fragments have been preserved in other works from the period.

119. "Last" and "first" could also be understood spatially, as "in front" and "behind," or "to the rear."

120. As discussed in note 104 above, the five phases had many aspects correlated with them, including musical notes.

121. This echoes the *Ssu-ma Fa* and early Legalist thinkers.

122. Emperor Kuang Wu succeeded in conquering all the dissident forces as well as Wang Mang to restore the Han dynasty, thereafter known as the Eastern or Later Han.

123. Sun-tzu, the *Art of War,* Chapter 9, "Maneuvering the Army."

124. "The Punitive Expedition of Yin," in the "Book of the Hsia," the *Shang Shu (Book of Documents).* Cf. James Legge, tr., *The Shoo King,* in the *Chinese Classics,* Oxford University Press, undated Hong Kong reprint, p. 163.

125. This incident is recorded in his biography.

126. The "Red Eyebrows," who derived their name from their custom of painting their eyebrows red to conspicuously distinguish themselves in battle, were among the groups that arose in opposition to the usurper Wang Mang (who held power from A.D. 8–23).

127. Yang Kan and Chung Chia were two minor figures in the Spring and Autumn period, preserved in the historical records for their offenses against military regulations. The former was spared although his driver was executed, but the latter was beheaded (LWK CC, p. 47).

128. Sun-tzu advanced the concept of the "expendable spy" in the *Art of War,* Chapter 13, "Employing Spies." There he defines them as agents "employed to spread

disinformation outside the state." Literally, the term is "dead spy" because they are likely to be killed once the true situation is known. (Li Ching's biography presumably records his decision and actions in the case of T'ang Chien.)

129. A quote from ibid.

130. The Duke of Chou, who is discussed in the general introduction, was compelled by his great righteousness to command armies against his own brothers when they revolted against the enthronement of King Wu's son. (There were other contributing factors as well, including the revolutionaries' apparent belief that the Duke of Chou was using the pretext of acting as regent for the underage king to seize power for himself.)

131. A "host" generally fights on his own terrain, usually on his own terms, whereas an invader is generally termed a "guest." However, these terms are simplistic and often nominal, as Li Ching's discussion shows.

132. This is one of Sun-tzu's main themes, found especially in the *Art of War,* Chapter 2, "Waging War."

133. A concept central to all the strategists in the *Seven Military Classics* as well as the *Tao Te Ching.*

134. *Art of War,* Chapter 2, "Waging War."

135. Ibid. "One who excels in employing the army does not conscript the people twice nor transport provisions a third time."

136. These policies were hallmarks of Sun-tzu's approach and were markedly different from those of later theorists (although no doubt common practice).

137. A quote from Sun-tzu, the *Art of War,* Chapter 6, "Vacuity and Substance." The order of the phrases has been reversed from the original: "If the enemy is rested you can tire him; if he is sated you can make him hungry."

138. Again the concept of "constraint" or "measure" appears.

139. An incident from the Sixteen Kingdoms period.

140. A quotation from Chapter 60 of the *Six Secret Teachings,* "The Infantry in Battle." The original differs slightly, reading "mounds" rather than "funeral mounds."

141. This sentence does not appear in the extant *Art of War.* However, Sun-tzu does discuss several classifications of terrain and their inherent dangers in various chapters. Tseng Chen has pointed out the wisdom of such seemingly obscure policies: Deserted places of former habitation as well as funeral grounds were more likely to harbor disease vectors and environmental poisons (LWK CCCY, pp. 190–191).

142. Many commentators understand *ping* as referring to "weapons" rather than "army," but because all weapons are inherently "implements of violence" and the passage continues with a discussion about mobilizing the army, "army" seems more appropriate here.

143. The reference to *t'ien-kuan* is somewhat problematic, with some commentators understanding it as the title of a lost traditional text (*Heavenly Offices*) and others thinking it refers to the astrological interpretation of heavenly phenomena. (See the notes to Chapter 1 of the *Wei Liao-tzu,* "Heavenly Offices," and also LWK CCCY, p. 193; and LWK CC, p. 52.) Accordingly, the phrase *t'ien kuan shih jih* is translated throughout as "astrologically auspicious seasons and days," thereby emphasizing the intentional structuring of actions to accord with auspicious times and avoid baleful moments.

144. This continues the discussion found in Book II of using animal names and such other designations as the five notes to obscure the actuality of military formations.

145. Previously discussed in Book I; see note 28.

146. Kung-sun Shu, a commandery governor under Wang Mang's reign, had proclaimed himself emperor in the chaotic period prior to the establishment of the Later Han. When Emperor Kuang-wu deputed Wu Han to dislodge Kung-sun Shu from his power base and vanquish him, he admonished him to avoid an immediate, direct confrontation (see LWK CCCY, p. 194).

147. Not found in the extant *Six Secret Teachings*. The term "entangling the army" also appears in Chapter 3 of the *Art of War,* "Strategies for Attack."

148. Wang Meng was a reclusive expert on military affairs who was accidentally discovered and eventually employed by Fu Chien. Just prior to his own death he advised Fu Chien against undertaking the doomed campaign against Chin, but his warning was obstinately disregarded. Fu Chien was subsequently defeated at Fei River.

149. Essentially a summation of Sun-tzu's approach to warfare.

150. From Sun-tzu, the *Art of War,* Chapter 6, "Vacuity and Substance."

151. This is a quotation from the traditionally transmitted text of the *Art of War,* Chapter 4, "Military Disposition."

152. Ibid.

153. Ibid., Chapter 6, "Vacuity and Substance." The T'ai-tsung has expanded Sun-tzu's basic principles regarding relative force and manipulating the enemy to create new tactical principles.

154. Ibid.

155. Ibid., Chapter 3, "Planning Offensives."

156. *Ssu-ma Fa,* Book I, "Benevolence the Foundation."

157. Sun-tzu, the *Art of War,* Chapter 4, "Military Disposition."

158. Ibid.

159. Ibid.

160. Ibid., Chapter 7, "Military Combat."

161. *Wu-tzu,* Chapter 4, "The Tao of the General." (See note 32 to the text of *Questions and Replies* for a discussion of the concept of "vital points.")

162. Li Chi, who had a distinguished military career, began as the leader of a small band of rebels and eventually threw his allegiance to the T'ang (whereupon he changed his original surname, Hsü, to Li. He was compelled to drop his middle character, "shih," because it was identical to that in Li Shih-min's name and thus was proscribed by imperial taboo. Accordingly, he became known as Li Chi instead of Li Shih-chi.) A highly successful military strategist and general, he commanded troops during the consolidation of the empire, undertook desert campaigns, and later supported the invasion of Koguryo—which he frequently directed in person. He also held a number of high civil positions when not deputed on military duties.

163. Although there may not be "any harm" in it, later commentators—such as Liu Yin—find it rather unbelievable, for a variety of reasons (see LWK WCCS, III:11–12).

164. Chang-sun Wu-chi was T'ang T'ai-tsung's brother-in-law, adviser, and confidant from childhood. Distinguished for his military achievements, he also furthered the T'ai-tsung's usurpation of the throne and was appointed to the highest civil offices.

Although instrumental in establishing Kao-tsung (Li Chih's) claim to the throne and entrusted with exercising the greatest power, he was eventually banished for "plotting against" the emperor through the machinations of Empress Wu.

165. An outspoken, apparently irascible but highly capable and successful general and administrator in the early T'ang.

166. Another high-ranking, meritorious official and general who eventually—apparently out of dissatisfaction—became caught up in the internecine intrigues between Ch'eng-ch'ien and Li Tai to succeed the T'ai-tsung and was executed. He was particularly noted for his tenacity and success in the desert campaign against Karakhoja and the T'u-yü-hun (in conjunction with Li Ching).

167. As a strategist and commander, Han Hsin had been among those instrumental in Liu Pang's rise to power; but that same talent and success endangered him, and he eventually became entangled in rebellion. (See his biography in Burton Watson's translation of the *Shih chi,* "The Biography of the Marquis of Huai-yin," *Records of the Grand Historian of China,* Vol. 1, pp. 208–232.)

As a commoner, P'eng Yüeh gathered a band of men who sought to capitalize on Ch'in's disintegration. Eventually, he supported Liu Pang, and after several years of varying degrees of success, participated in the decisive battle against Hsiang Yü. Finally, he suffered the inescapable fate of the successful—he was accused of plotting to revolt and was executed. (See his biography in Watson, *Records of the Grand Historian of China,* "The Biographies of Wei Pao and P'eng Yüeh," Vol. 1, pp. 191–195.)

Hsiao Ho began as a minor, but apparently conscientious and successful official under the Ch'in. His position allowed him to assist Liu Pang, and he later governed the Han dynasty's primary area of recruitment and supply, sustaining Liu Pang through his darkest days (thus the reference later in the text to his skill in utilizing the water transport system). Among his other achievements was seizing the charts and maps of the empire when Liu Pang first entered the Ch'in palaces, guaranteeing vital strategic information when others were greedily fighting over riches and jewels. Ironically, in his efforts to avoid even the appearance of becoming a threat to the emperor, he was eventually imprisoned. (See his biography, "The Hereditary House of Prime Minister Hsiao," in Watson, *Records of the Grand Historian of China,* Vol. 1, pp. 125–133.)

168. Liu Pang—eventually Han Kao-tsu—and Hsiang Yü contended for the empire following the destruction of the Ch'in dynasty in perhaps the most famous conflict in Chinese history between two men of dissimilar backgrounds, talents, and personalities. (For background, see Denis Twitchett and John K. Fairbank, eds., *The Cambridge History of China,* Vol. I: *The Ch'in and Han Empires,* Cambridge University Press, London, 1986, pp. 110–119; and Watson, *Records of the Grand Historian of China,* Vol. 1, "The Basic Annals of Hsiang Yü," pp. 37–74, and "The Basic Annals of Emperor Kao-tsu," pp.77–119.)

169. Ch'en P'ing, a strategist who switched his allegiance to Liu Pang after Hsiang Yü failed to employ him, had significant tactical impact.

170. Ts'ao Ts'an served as a minor police official in Kao-tsu's native area and staunchly supported him from the early days. He participated in numerous battles and major campaigns and later held high civil positions. (His biography is found in

Watson, *The Records of the Grand Historian of China,* Vol. 1, "The Hereditary House of Prime Minister Ts'ao," pp. 421–426.)

Fan K'uai and Kuan Ying both rose from menial backgrounds to become closely associated with Liu Pang very early in the revolt and dramatically assisted his campaign to gain control of All under Heaven. (Their biographies appear together in the *Shih chi, chüan* 95.)

171. The Six States Ch'in had systematically extinguished, as discussed in the general introduction. Members of their vanquished royalty still harbored hopes of restoring their houses to their former glory, and the inhabitants had closer emotional ties and regional identification with their local states than with an abstract empire. The restoration of these former states and the question of reestablishing feudal kingdoms as regional bastions for imperial support were heatedly debated topics and adumbrated events in the history of the Former Han. (There were similar echoes in the T'ang.)

In the "chopsticks incident" that follows in the text, Chang Liang reportedly borrowed Liu Pang's chopsticks when the latter was at dinner. It might be imagined that he thereby illustrated the dangers of reestablishing the Six States because without them, the future emperor suddenly lacked the means to eat and should have realized dramatically the inherent dangers in restoring diffuse power bases. However, the historical record offers no explanation; perhaps, as Watson suggests, he somehow used them to punctuate his points. (Possibly there were enough chopsticks to "score" the estimation of the various factors raised in his discussion, as in Sun-tzu's first chapter, "Initial Estimations.") For the incident, see Watson's translation of Chang Liang's biography, *Records of the Grand Historian,* Vol. 1, "The Heriditary House of the Marquis of Liu," pp. 143–144.

172. Fan Tseng skillfully plotted military strategy for Hsiang Yü, providing him several times with opportunities to slay Liu Pang. However, he eventually lost favor as the result of deliberate disinformation and became disaffected. (For the latter, see ibid., Vol. 1, "Prime Minister Ch'en," pp. 157–158. He is also mentioned numerous times in the Annals cited in note 168, above.)

173. Two other famous generals and confidants from Liu Pang's early days.

174. The extant *Six Secret Teachings* includes four chapters that focus on the qualifications, selection, and commissioning of generals. The quotation, which is slightly different, comes from Chapter 21, "Appointing the General." (For the types of axes used, see the notes to the original translation.)

175. The ceremony sketchily preserved in the *Six Secret Teachings* does not contain any reference to pushing the hub of the general's chariot (understanding "*ku*" as "hub" rather than "wheel" or "axle," based on Hayashi Minao, "Chūgoku sen-Shin jidai no basha," *Tōhō Gakuhō* 29 [1959], pp. 216–222).

176. The practices or techniques of yin and yang encompassed classifying natural phenomena, including astronomical events and stellar objects, within a matrix of auspicious and inauspicious indications. (Some of this material survives in the traditional almanacs published annually in several Asian countries.) In addition, various divinatory practices were integral to these beliefs, including the interpretation of cracks induced on tortoise shells and animal bones and the use of milfoil stalks to cast the *I Ching* hexagrams.

177. Within the cyclic classification of days, one day was considered particularly baleful for initiating military engagements; it was a "going to perish" day. In the inci-

dent raised, when advised that he was about to act on such an inauspicious day, the future emperor retorted, "We will 'go' forth, and they will 'perish'; how is this not advantageous?" (The quotation marks are added to emphasize the word play by which he contemptuously dismissed such beliefs.)

178. This battle marked a dramatic reversal of fortune for Ch'i because through it, Ch'i extricated itself from near-extinction and went on to defeat Yen's forces and restore its own ruling house. T'ien Tan, who had been besieged at Chi-mo—one of the two strongholds to which Ch'i had been reduced by the onslaught of forces from five other states—managed to have Yüeh I, commander of the joint expedition, removed through a subterfuge. He then used "fire oxen"—in what was to become a famous historical stratagem—to break out of confinement. Up until that moment, Yen believed Ch'i was withering away in a hopeless situation and thus never expected a bold counterattack. T'ien Tan had the thousand oxen within the fortress decorated with multicolored images of dragons and then affixed knife and sword blades to the horns. Thereafter, they tied oil-soaked kindling to the tails, breached holes in the walls, and in the middle of the night—while setting up a great clamor—drove the oxen toward the enemy's encampment, simultaneously igniting the kindling to force the animals to race wildly about in terror. Naturally, the Yen forces were startled, terrified, overwhelmed, and then easily massacred by the five thousand experienced troops—the final remnants of Ch'i's forces—that pressed the attack. (These tactics and their implications are discussed in our upcoming work on famous battles within the historical context of military development in ancient China.)

179. It seems clear that T'ien Tan accorded with popular beliefs (even though he deliberately manipulated them to his own ends), whereas the T'ai Kung dramatically ignored them and thus went contrary to them. However, Liu Yin understands it in contrary fashion, for unknown reasons (LWK WCCS, II:21B).

180. Again, San I-sheng's actions—which expressed his desire to discover their prospects before initiating action—should thus be in accord with the common practice of divining before an undertaking, and the T'ai Kung's bold course should be contrary to the use of divination to assess prospects and make decisions. However, Ts'eng Chen understands it in opposite fashion (cf. LWK CCCY, p. 229).

181. Sun-tzu, the *Art of War,* Chapter 4, "Military Disposition."

182. The WCCS edition has Chin attacking Ch'in, as translated, and Liu Yin's notes on the engagement. However, other editions vary, and the editors of LWK CC would emend the text to have Ch'in attack Chin. (Cf. LWK WCCS, III:23; LWK CC, p. 64.)

183. *Ssu-ma Fa,* "Obligations of the Son of Heaven."

184. Sun-tzu, the *Art of War,* Chapter 7, "Military Combat." The order is reversed from the original.

185. Ibid., Chapter 6, "Vacuity and Substance."

186. Ibid., Chapter 5, "Strategic Military Power." The original has *shih* rather than *pen,* "main force."

187. The section demarked by brackets does not appear in the Ming edition of the *Seven Military Classics* and is restored from the Sung edition.

188. A sentence found in the *Hsi tz'u,* one of the famous commentaries deriving from the Confucian school that is appended to the *I Ching.*

189. *Mencius*, IIB:1. The terms appear at the very beginning of the chapter, introducing a rather interesting passage that emphasizes the importance of man over Heaven and Earth. The initial sentence reads, "The seasons of Heaven are not as [important] as the advantages of Earth [terrain]; advantages of Earth are not as [important] as harmony among men."

190. Yüeh I, a man of Yen, was commander of the joint forces of the five states that attacked and largely vanquished Ch'i. He was eventually displaced though T'ien Tan's clever use of spies, and his victories were reversed (see note 178, above).

191. One of the joint commanders of the Chin forces at the Fei River battle in which they defeated Fu Chien and his Ch'in armies.

192. This saying appears in Pai Ch'i's biography in the *Shih chi* and probably does not stem from the Taoists (cf. LWK CCCY, p. 243).

Notes to the Appendixes

Appendix A: The Chariot

1. See Hayashi Minao, "Chūgoku sen-Shin jidai no basha," *Tōhō Gakuhō* 29 (1959), p. 225.

2. Cf. Edward L. Shaughnessy, "Historical Perspectives on the Introduction of the Chariot into China," *HJAS*, Vol. 48, No. 1 (1988), p. 190.

3. Cf. ibid., pp. 192 and 208.

4. Cf. Cheng Te-k'un, *Chou China*, W. Heffer & Sons, Ltd., Cambridge, 1963, pp. 265–272.

5. Cf. Stuart Piggott, "Chariots in the Caucasus and in China," *Antiquity* 48 (1974), pp. 16–24.

6. Cf. Shih Chang-ju, "Yin-hsü tsui-chin chih chung-yao fa-hsien," *Chung-kuo k'ao-ku hsüeh-pao*, No. 2 (1947), p. 20.

7. See, among others, Shaughnessy, "Historical Perspectives," p. 198.

8. Cf. Ku Chieh-kang and Yang Hsiang-k'uei, "Chung-kuo ku-tai ch'e-chan k'ao-lüeh," *Tung-fang tsa-chih*, Vol. 34, No. 1 (1937), pp. 52–53; and also the descriptions in the *Six Secret Teachings*.

9. Cf. Shaughnessy, "Historical Perspectives," pp. 199, and 213–221; Herrlee G. Creel, *The Origins of Statecraft in China*, University of Chicago Press, Chicago, 1970; p. 271; and Hayashi, "Basha," p. 278.

10. Cf. Ku and Yang, "Ch'e-chan," pp. 39–54.

11. Cf. Shaughnessy, "Historical Perspectives," p. 217; for Creel's doubts about barbarians employing chariots, see *Statecraft*, p. 266.

12. Cf. Cheng, *Chou*, p. 266; Kawamata Masanori, "Higashi Ajia no kodai sensha to Nishi-Ajia," *Koshi Shunjū* 4 (1987), pp. 38–58; for a dissenting opinion, see Shih Chang-ju, "Yin-shü," p. 22.

13. Cf. Ku and Yang, "Ch'e-chan," p. 49.

14. Cf. ibid., p. 44; and Shaughnessy, "Historical Perspectives," pp. 224–225.

15. Cf. Creel, *Statecraft*, pp. 262–269.

16. Cf. Yang Hung, "Ch'e-chan yü chan-ch'e," *WW* 1977, No. 5, pp. 82–90 (also incorporated into his book, *Chung-kuo ku-ping-ch'i lun-ts'ung*, Wen-wu ch'u-pan-she, Peking, 1980).

17. Cf. Shaughnessy, "Historical Perspectives," pp. 222–223.

18. Cf. Yang Hung, *Ku-ping-ch'i,* p. 126; Li Xueqin, *Eastern Zhou and Qin Civilizations,* Yale University Press, New Haven, 1985, pp. 198 and 272.

19. See Creel, *Statecraft,* pp. 256–262.

20. Cf. Yang Hung, *Ku-ping-ch'i,* p. 100.

Appendix B: The Horse and Cavalry

1. Creel, *Statecraft,* note 61, pp. 262–263.

2. Shaughnessy, "Historical Perspectives," p. 227.

3. See Shih, "Yin-shü," pp. 21–22.

4. Cf. Chan Li and Chou Shih-ch'ü, "Shih-t'an Yang-chia-wan Han-wu ch'i-ping-yung," *WW* 1977, No. 10, p. 22.

5. E. G. Pulleyblank, "Tribe and State: Prehistoric and Historic Times," in *The Origins of Chinese Civilization* (ed. David N. Keightley), University of California Press, Berkeley, 1983, p. 450.

6. W. Perceval Yetts, "The Horse: A Factor in Early Chinese History," *Eurasia Septentionalis Antiqua* 9 (1934), p. 236.

7. These passages are discussed in the footnotes to the translations. For a summary of the current view, including comments on Sun Pin's brief statements, see Chauncey S. Goodrich's article, "Riding Astride and the Saddle in Ancient China," *HJAS,* Vol. 44, No. 2 (1984), pp. 280–281.

8. Pulleyblank, "Tribe and State," p. 450.

9. Cf. Yang Hung, *Ku-ping-ch'i,* pp. 28–29.

10. Cf. Yetts, "The Horse," pp. 231–236; Herrlee G. Creel, "The Role of the Horse in Chinese History," in Creel, *What is Taoism and Other Studies in Chinese Cultural History,* University of Chicago Press, Chicago, 1970, pp. 160–186; and Friedrich Hirth, "The Story of Chang K'ien, China's Pioneer in Western Asia," *JAOS* 37 (1917), pp. 89–116.

11. Cf. Chan and Chou, "Han-mu," pp. 26–27.

Appendix C: Armor and Shields

1. A summary based primarily on Yang Hung, *Ku-ping-ch'i,* pp. 4–96; Chou Wei, *Chung-kuo ping-ch'i shih-kao,* Ming-wen shu-chü, Taipei, 1980, pp. 169ff.; and Albert E. Dien, "A Study of Early Chinese Armor," *Artibus Asiae* 43 (1981–1982), pp. 5–66.

Appendix D: The Sword

1. See, among many others, Yang Hung, *Ku-ping-ch'i,* p. 93; Noel Barnard, "Did the Swords Exist," *EC,* No. 4 (1978–1979), p. 62; Kuo Yü-kou, "Yin Chou te ch'ing-t'ung wu-ch'i," *KK,* No. 2 (1961), pp. 114–115; and Max Loehr, "The Earliest Chinese Swords and the Akinakes," *Oriental Art* 1 (1948), pp. 132–136.

2. Cf. Barnard, "Did the Swords Exist," p. 62.

3. T'ung En-cheng, "Wo-kuo Hsi-nan ti-ch'ü ch'ing-t'ung-chien te yen-chiu," *KK* 1977, No. 2, pp. 35–55. Also see Cho-yun Hsu and Katheryn M. Linduff, *Western Chou Civilization,* Yale University Press, New Haven, 1988, pp. 77–81.

4. Yang Hung, *Ku-ping-ch'i,* pp. 125–126.

5. Cf. Chou Wei, *Chung-kuo ping-ch'i shih-kao,* pp. 88–98.

6. Cf. Yang Hung, *Ku-ping-ch'i,* p. 126.

7. Cf. Kwang-chih Chang, "The Chinese Bronze Age: A Modern Synthesis," in Wen Fong, ed., *The Great Bronze Age of China,* Knopf, New York, 1980, p. 45; Chang, *Chung-kuo ch'ing-t'ung shih-tai,* Chung-wen Ta-hsüeh ch'u-pan-she, Hong Kong, 1982, p. 13.

8. Cf. Emma C. Bunker, "The Steppe Connection," *EC* 9–10 (1983–1985), pp. 72–73.

9. Cf. Loehr, "The Earliest Chinese Swords," pp. 132–142.

10. Cf. Chou Wei, *Chung-kuo ping-ch'i shih-kao,* pp. 112–116.

11. Cf. Yang Hung, *Ku-ping-ch'i,* p. 129.

12. Hayashi Minao, *Chūgoku In-Shū jidai no buki,* Kyoto Daigaku Jimbun Kagaku Kenkyūsho, Kyoto, 1972, pp. 199–236.

13. Chou Wei, *Chung-kuo ping-ch'i shih-kao,* pp. 109–157. The number of articles that have appeared in PRC archaeological publications since 1970 is too great to list in detail. However, a number of important ones are listed in the bibliography.

Appendix E: Military Organization

1. Tu Cheng-sheng, "Chou-tai feng-chien chieh-t'i-hou te chün-cheng hsin-chih-hsü—pien-hu ch'i-min te yen-chiu chih-erh," *BIHP,* Vol. 55, No. 1 (1984), p. 75.

2. Yang K'uan, "Ch'un-ch'iu Chan-kuo-chien feng-chien te chün-shih tsu-chih ho chan-cheng te pien-hua," *Li-shih chiao-hsüeh,* No. 4 (1954), pp. 7–8.

3. For discussion, see K. C. Chang, *Shang Civilization,* Yale University Press, New Haven, 1980, pp. 195–196; Hsu and Linduff, *Western Chou Civilization,* p. 85.

4. Cf. Yen I-p'ing, "Yin-Shang ping-chih," *Chung-kuo wen-tzu,* NS 7 (1983), pp. 24–28; and *Chung-kuo chün-shih-shih,* Vol. 4: *Ping-fa,* Chieh-fang-chün ch'u-pan-she, Peking, 1988, pp. 7–13.

5. Cf. Yen I-p'ing, "Yin-Shang ping-chih," p. 38.

6. Hsu and Linduff, *Western Chou Civilization,* p. 164.

7. Lao Kan, "Chan-kuo shih-tai te chan-cheng fang-fa," *BIHP* 37 (1967), p. 48.

8. Chin Hsiang-heng, "Ts'ung chia-ku pu-ts'u yen-chiu Yin Shang chün-lü-chung chih wang-tsu san-hsing san-shih," *Chung-kuo wen-tzu* 52 (1974), pp. 7B–14A; *Ping-fa,* p. 14. Chin believes *chün* represents an expansion of *shih* and that the Chou only used the term *shih.*

9. Tu Cheng-sheng, "Hsin-chih-hsü," p. 78.

10. Cf. ibid., pp. 75 and 78.

11. Cf. *Ping-fa,* pp. 15–25, for a discussion of basic deployment principles. Additional comments are found in the footnotes to the translations.

12. Cf. Yen I-p'ing, "Yin-Shang ping-chih," p. 24. A decade-based system is found in the *Wei Liao-tzu,* as discussed in the footnotes to the translation.

13. For Western terms, see John I. Alger, *Definitions and Doctrine of the Military Art,* Avery Publishing Group, Wayne, N.J., 1985.

14. Cf. Chang, *Shang Civilization,* p. 195.

15. Cf. Lao Kan, "Chan-kuo shih-tai," p. 47.

16. Cf. Tu Cheng-sheng, "Hsin-chih-hsü," p. 92. The term designates the armies of the left, center, and right; but when more than three armies are fielded, then it refers to

the left and right flanks and the center force, depending on how they are integrated and commanded.

17. Yang K'uan, "Ch'un-ch'iu pien-hua," p. 11; Chin Hsiang-heng, "San-hsing san-shih," p. 9A.

18. Cf. Hsü Hsi-ch'en, "Chou-tai ping-chih ch'u-lun," *Chung-kuo-shih yen-chiu,* No. 4 (1985), pp. 4–6; Chang, *Shang Civilization,* pp. 161–165.

19. Cf. Hsü, "Chou-tai ping-chih," pp. 6–8; and Yang K'uan, "Ch'un-ch'iu pien-hua," pp. 8–10.

20. Cf. Tu Cheng-sheng, "Hsin-chih-hsü," p. 74.

Selected Bibliography

BECAUSE FULL BIBLIOGRAPHIC information for all works cited in the introductions and annotations is provided in the footnotes, only selected items from among them—together with additional, essential books and articles—are included herein. For the convenience of readers interested in pursuing focal topics, the entries are divided into several categories. With the great proliferation of academic books and articles in both Asia and the West, works of a tangential nature and a myriad others that provide general contextual material cannot be included. Unfortunately, for every item listed several more are necessarily excluded, even though the bibliography must therefore be slightly less comprehensive. In addition, variant editions of other ancient texts and the extensive Japanese secondary literature on numerous historical topics—both well-known to scholars—are only minimally represented. Preference has been given to items that are reasonably available to interested readers and to Chinese scholarship on fundamental historical issues as well as to reports on selected archaeological finds and their interpretation. Writings on intellectual history by such famous scholars as Fu Ssu-nien, except where directly relevant or cited in the notes, also have not been included.

Basic Texts

武經七書:
   王雲五主編, 宋刊本武經七書, 商務印書館, 台北, 3 vol., 1971 (1935).
   [宋刊武經七書], 中國兵書集成, 解放軍出版社, 遼沈書社, 北京, vol. 1, 2, 1987.
   嚴一萍選輯, 百部叢書集成 (宋本子部), 藝文印書館, 台北, 1965.
武經七書直解 (劉寅):
   景印明本武經七書直解, 史地教育出版社, 台北, 2 vol., 1972.
   武經七書直解, 中國兵書集成, 解放軍出版社, 遼沈書社, 北京, vol. 10, 11, 1990.

Abbreviations

AA	*Acta Asiatica*
AM	*Asia Major*
BIHP	*Bulletin of the Institute of History and Philology*
BMFEA	*Bulletin of the Museum of Far Eastern Antiquities*
BSOAS	*Bulletin of the School of Oriental and African Studies*
CC	*Chinese Culture*
EC	*Early China*
GSR	*Grammata Serica Recensa* (Bernhard Karlgrean, *BMFEA* 29 [1957])
HJAS	*Harvard Journal of Asiatic Studies*
JAOS	*Journal of the American Oriental Society*
JAS	*Journal of Asian Studies*
JCP	*Journal of Chinese Philosophy*
JNCBRAS	*Journal of the North Central Branch, Royal Asiatic Society*
JRAS	*Journal of the Royal Asiatic Society*
KK	*K'ao-ku hsüeh-pao*
MS	*Monumenta Serica*
PEW	*Philosophy East and West*
TP	*T'oung Pao*
WW	*Wen-wu*

General Historical Works, Important Translations, and Specialized Monographs on the Period of the *Seven Military Classics*

Ames, Roger T., *The Art of Rulership*, University of Hawaii Press, Honolulu, 1983.

Baker, Hugh D.R., *Chinese Family and Kinship*, Columbia University Press, New York, 1979.

Balaz, Etienne, *Chinese Civilization and Bureaucracy*, Yale University Press, New Haven, 1964.

Beasley, W. G., and E. G. Pulleyblank, eds., *Historians of China and Japan*, Oxford University Press, London, 1961.

Bielenstein, Hans, *The Bureaucracy of Han Times*, Cambridge University Press, Cambridge, 1980.

————, *The Restoration of the Han Dynasty*, Elanders Boktryckeri Aktiebolag, Goteborg, 1953.

Bishop, John L., ed., *Studies in Governmental Institutions in Chinese History*, Harvard University Press, Cambridge, Mass., 1968.

Bodde, Derk, *China's First Unifier: A Study of the Ch'in Dynasty as Seen in the Life of Li Ssu*, Hong Kong University Press, Hong Kong, 1967 (1938).

————, *Essays on Chinese Civilization*, (Charles Le Blanc and Dorothy Borei, eds.), Princeton University Press, Princeton, 1981.

Chang, K. C., *Art, Myth, and Ritual: The Path to Political Authority in Ancient China*, Harvard University Press, Cambridge, Mass., 1983.

_____, ed., *Studies of Shang Archaeology,* Yale University Press, New Haven, 1986.

Chang, Kwang-chih, ed., *Food in Chinese Culture,* Yale University Press, New Haven, 1977.

_____, *Shang Civilization,* Yale University Press, New Haven, 1980.

_____, *The Archaeology of Ancient China,* Yale University Press, New Haven, 1977 (3d edition).

Cheng Te-k'un, *Archaeology in China,* 3 vols., W. Heffer & Sons, Ltd., Cambridge: *Chou China,* 1963; *Prehistoric China,* 1966; *Shang China,* 1960.

_____, *New Light on Prehistoric China,* W. Heffer & Sons, Ltd., Cambridge, 1966.

_____, *Studies in Chinese Archaeology,* Chinese University Press, 1982.

Ch'ü T'ung-tsu, *Han Social Structure,* University of Washington Press, Seattle, 1967.

_____, *Law and Society in Traditional China,* Mouton and Company, The Hague, 1965 (rev. ed.) (1961).

Cotterall, Arthur, *The First Emperor of China,* Penguin, London, 1981.

Creel, Herrlee G., *The Origins of Statecraft in China:* Vol. 1, *The Western Chou Empire,* University of Chicago Press, Chicago, 1970.

_____, *Shen Pu-hai: A Chinese Political Philosopher of the Fourth Century B.C.,* University of Chicago Press, Chicago, 1974.

Crump, J. I., Jr., *Chan-kuo Ts'e,* Oxford University Press, Oxford, 1970.

Dawson, Raymond, ed., *The Legacy of China,* Oxford University Press, Oxford, 1964.

de Crespigny, Rafe, *Official Titles of the Former Han Dynasty,* Australian National University Press, Canberra, 1967.

Dubs, Homer H., *The History of the Former Han Dynasty,* 3 vols., Waverly Press, Baltimore, 1938–1955.

Duyvendak, J.J.L., *The Book of Lord Shang,* Arthur Probsthain, London, 1928.

Eberhard, Wolfram, *Conquerors and Rulers: Social Forces in Medieval China,* E. J. Brill, Leiden, 1970.

Fairbank, John K., ed., *Chinese Thought and Institutions,* University of Chicago Press, Chicago, 1957.

_____, ed., *The Chinese World Order: Traditional China's Foreign Relations,* Harvard University Press, Cambridge, Mass., 1968.

Falkenhausen, Lothar Von, *Shang Civilization, Early China,* Supplement 1, Berkeley, 1986.

Feng Han-yi, *The Chinese Kinship System,* Harvard University Press, Cambridge, Mass., 1967 (reprint of 1948 edition; originally published in *HJAS* 2 [1937], pp. 141–275).

Fong, Wen, ed., *The Great Bronze Age of China: An Exhibition from the People's Republic of China,* Knopf, New York, 1980.

Fung Yu-lan, *A History of Chinese Philosophy,* Translated by Derk Bodde, 2 vols., Princeton University Press, Princeton, 1952 (1931) and 1953 (1934).

Gardner, Charles S., *Chinese Traditional Historiography,* Harvard University Press, Cambridge, Mass., 1938.

Graham, A. C., *Later Mohist Logic, Ethics, and Science,* Chinese University Press, Hong Kong, 1978.

Grousset, René, *The Empire of the Steppes: A History of Central Asia,* Translated by Naomi Walford, Rutgers University Press, New Brunswick, N.J., 1970 (1939).

Herrmann, Albert, *An Historical Atlas of China,* Aldine Publishing Co., Chicago, 1966 (rev. ed.) (1935, edited by Norton Ginsburg).

Ho, Ping-ti, *The Cradle of the East,* Chinese University Press, Hong Kong, 1975.

Hook, Brian, ed., *The Cambridge Encyclopedia of China,* Cambridge University Press, Cambridge, 1982.

Hsu, Cho-yun, *Ancient China in Transition: An Analysis of Social Mobility,* Stanford University Press, Stanford, 1965.

_____, *Han Agriculture,* University of Washington Press, Seattle, 1980.

Hsu, Cho-yun, and Katheryn M. Linduff, *Western Chou Civilization,* Yale University Press, New Haven, 1988.

Hsü Shihlien, *The Political Philosophy of Confucianism,* Curzon Press, London, 1932.

Hucker, Charles O., *A Dictionary of Official Titles in Imperial China,* Stanford University Press, Stanford, 1985.

Hulsewe, A.F.P., *Remnants of Han Law,* Vol. 1, E. J. Brill, Leiden, 1955.

Jagchid, Sechin, and Van Jay Symons, *Peace, War, and Trade Along the Great Wall: Nomadic-Chinese Interaction Through Two Millennia,* Indiana University Press, Bloomington, 1989.

Kao, George, *The Translation of Things Past,* Chinese University of Hong Kong, Hong Kong, 1982.

Keightley, David N., *Sources of Shang History: The Oracle-bone Inscriptions of Bronze Age China,* University of California Press, Berkeley, 1978.

_____, ed., *The Origins of Chinese Civilization,* University of California Press, Berkeley, 1983.

Lattimore, Owen, *Inner Asian Frontiers of China,* Beacon Press, Boston, 1960 (1940).

Lau, D. C., *The Analects,* Penguin Books, London, 1979.

_____, *Mencius,* 2 vols., Chinese University Press, Hong Kong, 1984.

_____, *Tao Te Ching,* Chinese University Press, Hong Kong, 1982.

Le Blanc, Charles, *Huai Nan Tzu,* Hong Kong University Press, Hong Kong, 1985.

Legg, Stuart, *The Barbarians of Asia,* Dorset Press, New York, 1990 (1970).

Leslie, Donald D., Colin Mackerras, and Gungwu Wang, *Essays on the Sources for Chinese History,* Australian National University Press, Canberra, 1973.

Li Chi, *Anyang,* University of Washington Press, Seattle, 1977.

_____, *The Beginnings of Chinese Civilization,* University of Washington Press, Seattle, 1968 (1957).

Li Guohao, Zhang Mengwen, and Cao Tianqin, eds., *Explorations in the History of Science and Technology in China,* Shanghai Chinese Classics Publishing House, Shanghai, 1982.

Li Xueqin, *Eastern Zhou and Qin Civilizations,* Translated by K. C. Chang, Yale University Press, New Haven, 1985.

Liao, W. K., *The Complete Works of Han Fei-tzu,* 2 vols., Arthur Probsthain, London, Vol. 1 1959 (1939), Vol. 2 1959.

Liu, James, *The Chinese Knight-errant,* University of Chicago Press, Chicago, 1967.

Lowe, Michael, *Crisis and Conflict in Han China*, George Allen and Unwin, London, 1974.

_____, *Records of Han Administration*, 2 vols., Cambridge University Press, Cambridge, 1967.

Nakayama, Shigeru, and Nathan Sivin, eds., *Chinese Science: Explorations of an Ancient Tradition*, MIT Press, Cambridge, Mass., 1973.

Needham, Joseph, *Clerks and Craftsmen in China and the West*, Cambridge University Press, Cambridge, 1970.

_____, *The Development of Iron and Steel Technology in China*, Newcomen Society, London, 1958.

_____, *The Grand Titration*, George Allen and Unwin Ltd., London, 1969.

_____, et al., *Science and Civilisation in China*, Cambridge University Press, Cambridge, 1962 (fourteen physical volumes to date, including Vol. 5, Part 7: *Military Technology*).

Nivison, David S. and Arthur F. Wright, eds., *Confucianism in Action*, Stanford University Press, Stanford, 1959.

Pirazzoli-t'Serstevens, Michéle, *The Han Dynasty (Le Chine des Han)*, Translated by Janet Seligman, Rizzoli International Publications, Inc., New York, 1982.

Pye, Lucian W., *Asian Power and Politics: The Cultural Dimensions of Authority*, Harvard University Press, Cambridge, Mass., 1985.

Reischauer, Edwin O., *Ennin's Travels in T'ang China*, Ronald Press, New York, 1955.

Reischauer, Edwin O., and John K. Fairbank, *East Asia: The Great Tradition*, Vol. 1, Houghton Mifflin Company, Boston, 1958.

Rickett, W. Allyn, *Guanzi*, Vol. 1, Princeton University Press, Princeton, 1985.

Roy, David T., and Tsien Tsuen-hsuin, eds., *Ancient China: Studies in Early Civilization*, Chinese University Press, Hong Kong, 1978.

Sailey, Jay, *The Master Who Embraces Simplicity*, Chinese Materials Center, Inc., San Francisco, 1978.

Schram, Stuart R., ed., *Foundations and Limits of State Power in China*, Chinese University Press, Hong Kong, 1987.

_____, ed., *The Scope of State Power in China*, Chinese University Press, Hong Kong, 1985.

Science Press, *Atlas of Primitive Man in China*, Science Press, Peking, 1980.

Swann, Nancy Lee, *Food and Money in Ancient China*, Princeton University Press, Princeton, 1950.

Tregear, T. R., *A Geography of China*, Aldine, Chicago, 1965.

Tsien Tsuen-hsuin, *Written on Bamboo and Silk: The Beginnings of Chinese Books and Inscriptions*, University of Chicago Press, Chicago, 1962.

Tung Tso-pin, *Chronological Tables of Chinese History*, Hong Kong University Press, Hong Kong, 1960.

Twitchett, Denis, and John K. Fairbank, eds., *The Cambridge History of China*, Cambridge University Press, London. Vol. 1: *The Ch'in and Han Empires, 221* B.C.–A.D. *220*, 1986; Vol. 3, Part 1: *Sui and T'ang China, 589–906*, 1979.

Waley, Arthur, *The Analects of Confucius*, George Allen and Unwin Ltd., London, 1938.

————, *The Way and Its Power,* Grove Press, New York, 1958.

Wang Gungwu, *The Structure of Power in North China During the Five Dynasties,* Stanford University Press, Stanford, 1967 (1963).

Wang Zhongshu, *Han Civilization,* Translated by K. C. Chang, Yale University Press, New Haven, 1982.

Watson, Burton, *Basic Writings of Mo Tzu, Hsün Tzu, and Han Fei Tzu,* Columbia University Press, New York, 1967.

————, *The Complete Works of Chuang-tzu,* Columbia University Press, New York, 1968.

————, *Courtier and Commoner in Ancient China,* Columbia University Press, New York, 1974.

————, *Early Chinese Literature,* Columbia University Press, New York, 1962.

————, *Records of the Grand Historian of China,* 2 vols., Columbia University Press, New York, 1961.

————, *Ssu-ma Ch'ien: Grand Historian of China,* Columbia University Press, New York, 1958.

————, *The Tso chuan,* Columbia University Press, New York, 1989.

Watson, William, *Cultural Frontiers in Ancient East Asia,* Edinburgh University Press, Edinburgh, 1971.

Wheatley, Paul, *The Pivot of the Four Quarters,* Edinburgh University Press, Edinburgh, 1971.

Wing-tsit, Chan, *The Way of Lao-tzu,* Bobbs-Merrill, New York, 1963.

Wright, Arthur F., ed., *The Confucian Persuasion,* Stanford University Press, Stanford, 1960.

Wright, Arthur F., *The Sui Dynasty,* Alfred A. Knopf, New York, 1978.

Wright, Arthur F., and Denis Twitchett, eds., *Perspectives of the T'ang,* Yale University Press, New Haven, 1973.

Yang Lien-sheng, *Excursions in Sinology,* Harvard University Press, Cambridge, Mass., 1969.

————, *Studies in Chinese Institutional History,* Harvard University Press, Cambridge, Mass., 1969.

Yü Ying-shih, *Trade and Expansion in Han China: A Study in the Structure of Sino-barbarian Economic Relations,* University of California Press, Berkeley, 1967.

Western Language Articles on Ancient and Medieval History

*(Articles of particular relevance, excluding those found in
collected works listed under books or those that pertain generally
to intellectual or scientific history)*

Allan, Sarah, "Drought, Human Sacrifice and the Mandate of Heaven in a Lost Text from the *Shang Shu*," BSOAS 47 (1984), pp. 523–539.

An Zhimin, "The Neolithic Archaeology of China: A Brief Survey of the Last Thirty Years," Translated by K. C. Chang, EC 5 (1979–1980), pp. 35–45.

Barnard, Noel, "Chou China: A Review of the Third Volume of Cheng Te-k'un's *Archaeology in China*," *MS* 24 (1965), pp. 307–459.

———, "Chou Hung-hsiang, *Shang-Yin ti-wang pen-chi*" (review of), *MS* 19 (1960), pp. 486–515.

———, "A Preliminary Study of the Ch'u Silk Manuscript," *MS* 17 (1958), pp. 1–11.

Blakely, Barry, "In Search of Danyang. I: Historical Geography and Archaeological Sites," *EC* 13 (1988), pp. 116–152.

Broman, Sven, "Studies on the Chou Li," *BMFEA* 33 (1961), pp. 1–88.

Bunker, Emma C., "The Steppe Connection," *EC* 9–10 (1983–1985), pp. 70–76.

Chang Ch'i-yün, "The Period of the Ch'un-ch'iu: A General Survey," *CC* 27:2 (1986), pp. 1–29.

Chen Ch'i-yün, "Han Dynasty China: Economy, Society, and State Power," *TP* 70 (1984), pp. 127–148.

Cheng Chung-ying, "Legalism Versus Confucianism: A Philosophical Appraisal," *JCP* 8 (1981), pp. 271–302.

Cheng Te-k'ung, "The Origin and Development of Shang Culture," *AM* NS 6:1 (1957), pp. 80–98.

Cheung, Frederick Hok-Ming, "Conquerors and Consolidators in Anglo-Norman England and T'ang China: A Comparative Study," *Asian Culture* 13:1 (1985), pp. 63–85.

Chou Fa-kao, "Chronology of the Western Chou Dynasty," *Hsiang-kang Chung-wen Ta-hsüeh Chung-kuo Wen-hua Yen-chiu-so hsüeh-pao* 4:1 (1971), pp. 173–205.

Chun, Allen J., "Conceptions of Kinship and Kingship in Classical Chou China," *TP* 76 (1990), pp. 16–48.

Cikoski, John S., "Toward Canons of Philological Method for Analyzing Classical Chinese Texts," *EC* 3 (1977), pp. 18–30.

De Crespigny, Rafe, "Politics and Philosophy Under the Government of Emperor Huan 159–168," *TP* 66:1–3 (1980), pp. 41–83.

Egan, Ronald C., "Narratives in *Tso Chuan*," *HJAS* 37:2 (1977), pp. 323–352.

Fields, Lanny B., "The Legalists and the Fall of Ch'in: Humanism and Tyranny," *Journal of Asian History* 17 (1983), pp. 1–39.

Fu Pei-jung, "On Religious Ideas of the Pre-Chou China," *CC* 26:3 (September 1985), pp. 23–39.

Graham, A. C., "A Neglected Pre-Han Philosophical Text: *Ho-Kuan-Tzu*," *BSOAS* 52:3 (1989), pp. 497–532.

Haloun, Gustav, "Legalist Fragments," *AM* 2:1 (1951–1952), pp. 85–120.

Harper, Donald, and Jeffrey Riegel, "Mawangdui Tomb Three: Documents" (Abstract), *EC* 2 (1976), pp. 68–72.

Henricks, Robert G., "Examining the Ma-wang-tui Silk Texts of the Lao-tzu," *TP* 65:4–5 (1979), pp. 166–199.

———, "On the Chapter Divisions in the *Lao-tzu*," *BSOAS* 45:3 (1982), pp. 501–524.

———, "The Philosophy of *Lao-tzu* Based on the Ma-wang-tui Texts: Some Preliminary Observations," *SSCR Bulletin* 9 (Fall 1981), pp. 59–78.

Henry, Eric, "The Motif of Recognition in Early China," *HJAS* 47:1 (1987), pp. 5–30.

Hsü Cho-yün, "Some Working Notes on the Western Chou Government," *BIHP* 36 (1966), pp. 513–524.

Hu Pingsheng, "Some Notes on the Organization of the Han Dynasty Bamboo 'Annals' Found at Fuyang," *EC* 14 (1989), pp. 1–24.

Huber, Louisa G., "The Bo Capital and Questions Concerning Xia and Early Shang," *EC* 13 (1988), pp. 46–77.

———, "A Commentary on the Recent Finds of Neolithic Painted Pottery from Ta-ti-wan, Kansu," *EC* 9–10 (1983–1985), pp. 1–19.

Hulsewe, A.F.P., "The Ch'in Documents Discovered in Hupei in 1975," *TP* 64:4–5 (1978), pp. 175–217.

———, "Watching the Vapours: An Ancient Chinese Technique of Prognostication," *Nachrichten* 125 (1979), pp. 40–49.

———, "The Wide Scope of *Tao*, 'Theft,' in Ch'in-Han Law," *EC* 13 (1988), pp. 166–200.

Jacobson, Esther, "Beyond the Frontier: A Reconsideration of Cultural Interchange Between China and the Early Nomads," *EC* 13 (1988), pp. 201–240.

Jan Yün-hua, "Tao, Principle, and Law: The Three Key Concepts in the Yellow Emperor Taoism," *JCP* 7 (1980), pp. 205–228.

———, "*Tao Yüan* or *Tao: The Origin*," *JCP* 7 (1980), pp. 195–204.

Kamiya Masakazu, "The Staffing Structure of Commandery Offices and County Offices and the Relationship Between Commanderies and Counties in the Han Dynasty," *AA* 58 (1990), pp. 59–88.

Karlgren, Bernhard, "The Book of Documents," *BMFEA* 22 (1950), pp. 1–81.

———, "The Early History of the Chou Li and Tso Chuan Texts," *BMFEA* 3 (1931), pp. 1–59.

———, "Glosses on the Book of Documents, I," *BMFEA* 20 (1948), pp. 39–315.

———, "Glosses on the Book of Documents, II," *BMFEA* 21 (1949), pp. 63–206.

———, "Legends and Cults in Ancient China," *BMFEA* 18 (1946), pp. 199–356.

———, "Some Sacrifices in Chou China," *BMFEA* 40 (1968), pp. 1–31.

Keightley, David N., "The *Bamboo Annals* and the Shang-Chou Chronology," *HJAS* 38:2 (1978), pp. 423–438.

———, "Reports from the Shang: A Corroboration and Some Speculation," *EC* 9–10 (1983–1984), pp. 20–54.

———, "The Shang State as Seen in the Oracle-bone Inscriptions," *EC* 5 (1979–1980), pp. 25–34.

Lau, D. C., "The Treatment of Opposites in *Lao Tzu*," *BSOAS* 21 (1958), pp. 344–360.

Li Zehou, "Confucian Cosmology in the Han Dynasty," *Social Sciences in China* 7 (1986), pp. 81–116.

Loewe, Michael, "Han Administrative Documents: Recent Finds from the Northwest," *TP* 72 (1986), pp. 291–314.

———, "The Han View of Comets," *BMFEA* 52 (1980), pp. 2–31.

MacCormack, Geoffrey, "The *Lü Hsing*: Problems of Legal Interpretation," *MS* 37 (1986–1987), pp. 35–47.

McLeod, Katrina C.D., and Robin D.S. Yates, "Forms of Ch'in Law: An Annotated Translation of the *Feng-chen shih*," *HJAS* 41:1 (1981), pp. 111–163.

Negata Hidemasa, "A Diplomatic Study of the Chü-yen Han Wooden Strips," *AA* 58 (1990), pp. 38–57.

Nivison, David S., "1040 as the Date of the Chou Conquest," *EC* 8 (1982–1983), pp. 76–78.

Pang Pu, "Origins of the Yin-Yang and Five Elements Concepts," *Social Sciences in China* 6:1 (1985), pp. 91–131.

Pankenier, David W., "Astronomical Dates in Shang and Western Zhou," *EC* 7 (1981–1982), pp. 2–37.

———, "*Mozi* and the Dates of Xia, Shang, and Zhou: A Research Note," *EC* 9–10 (1983–1985), pp. 175–183.

Rawson, Jessica, "Late Western Zhou: A Break in the Shang Bronze Tradition," *EC* 11–12 (1985–1987), pp. 285–295.

Riegel, Jeffrey, "A Summary of Some Recent *Wenwu* and *Kaogu* Articles on Mawangdui Tombs Two and Three," *EC* 1 (1975), pp. 10–14.

Rosement, Henry, Jr., "State and Society in the *Hsün Tzu:* A Philosophical Commentary," *MS* 29 (1970–1971), pp. 38–78.

Rubin, V. A., "Tzu-Ch'an and the City-state of Ancient China," *TP* 52 (1965), pp. 8–34.

Shaughnessy, Edward L., "The 'Current' *Bamboo Annals* and the Date of the Zhou Conquest of Shang," *EC* 11–12 (1985–1987), pp. 33–60.

———, "The Date of the 'Duo You *Ding*' and Its Significance," *EC* 9–10 (1983–1985), pp. 55–69.

———, "Historical Geography and the Extent of the Earliest Chinese Kingdoms," *AM* Third Series 2:2 (1989), pp. 1–22.

———, "'New' Evidence on the Zhou Conquest," *EC* 6 (1980–1981), pp. 57–79.

———, "On the Authenticity of the *Bamboo Annals*," *HJAS* 46:1 (June 1986), pp. 149–180.

———, "Recent Approaches to Oracle-Bone Periodization: A Review," *EC* 8 (1982–1983), pp. 1–13.

Silbergeld, Jerome, "Mawangdui, Excavated Materials, and Transmitted Texts: A Cautionary Note," *EC* 8 (1982–1983), pp. 79–92.

Thorp, Robert L., "The Growth of Early Shang Civilization," *HJAS* 45 (1985), pp. 5–75.

Turner, Karen, "The Theory of Law in the *Ching-fa*," *EC* 14 (1989), pp. 55–76.

Wallacker, Benjamin E., "Chang Fei's Preface to the Chin Code of Law," *TP* 72 (1986), pp. 229–268.

Wang Gung-wu, "The Chiu Wu-tai shih and History-writing During the Five Dynasties," *AM* NS 6:1 (1957), pp. 1–22.

Wang Ningsheng, "Yangshao Burial Customs and Social Organization: A Comment on the Theory of Yangshao Matrilineal Society and Its Methodology," Translation by David N. Keightley, *EC* 11–12 (1985–1987), pp. 6–32.

Watson, Walter, "Principles for Dealing with Disorder," *JCP* 8 (1981), pp. 349–370.

Wu Hung, "From Temple to Tomb: Ancient Chinese Art and Religion in Transition," *EC* 13 (1988), pp. 78–115.

Yamada Katsuyoshi, "Offices and Officials of Works, Markets and Lands in the Ch'in Dynasty," *AA* 58 (1990), pp. 1–23.

Yates, Robin D.S., "Social Status in the Ch'in: Evidence from the Yün-meng Legal Documents. Part One: Commoners," *HJAS* 47:1 (1987), pp. 197–237.

Yu Weichao, "The Origins of the Cultures of the Eastern Zhou," Translated by Terry Kleeman, *EC* 9–10 (1983–1985), pp. 307–314.

Zhang Jinfan, "Administration and Administrative Law in Ancient China," *Social Sciences in China* 7:3 (1986), pp. 169–196.

Western Language Articles on Weapons, Technology, and the Evolution of Mobility

Chariot and Horses

Bishop, C. W., "The Horses of T'ang T'ai-Tsung: Of the Antecedents of the Chinese Horse," *Museum Journal* (University of Pennsylvania) 9 (1911), pp. 244–273.

Ferguson, John C., "The Six Horses of T'ang T'ai-Tsung," *JNCBRAS,* 67 (1936), pp. 1–6.

Fernald, Helen E., "The Horses of T'ang T'ai-Tsung and the Steele of Yu," *American Oriental Society Journal* 55 (1935), pp. 420–428.

Goodrich, Chauncey S., "Riding Astride and the Saddle in Ancient China," *HJAS* 44:2 (1984), pp. 279–306.

Piggott, Stuart, "Chariots in the Caucasus and in China," *Antiquity* 48 (1974), pp. 16–24.

Shaughnessy, Edward L., "Historical Perspectives on the Introduction of the Chariot into China," *HJAS* 48:1 (1988), pp. 189–237.

Yetts, W. Perceval, "The Horse: A Factor in Early Chinese History," *Eurasia Septentionalis Antiqua* 9 (1934), pp. 231–255.

Weapons, Armor, and Related Technology

An Zhimin, "Some Problems Concerning China's Early Copper and Bronze Artifacts," Translated by Julia K. Murray, *EC* 8 (1982–1983), pp. 53–75.

Barnard, Noel, "Did the Swords Exist" (Rejoinder), *EC* 4 (1978–1979), pp. 60–65.

Beveridge, H., "Oriental Crossbows," *Asian Review* Series 3, *The Imperial and Asiatic Quarterly Review* 32 (1911), pp. 344–348.

Dien, Albert E., "A Study of Early Chinese Armor," *Artibus Asiae* 43 (1981–1982), pp. 5–66.

_____, "Warring States Armor and Pit Three at Qin Shihuangdi's Tomb" (Research Note), *EC* 5 (1979–1980), pp. 46–47.

Gardner, Charles W., "Weapon of Power," *Military History* 12 (1989), pp. 16–74.

Gordon, D. H., "Swords, Rapiers, and Horse-riders," *Antiquity* 27 (1953), pp. 67–78.

Huslewe, A.F.P., "Again the Crossbow Trigger Mechanism," *TP* 64:4–5 (1978), p. 254.

Karlgren, Bernhard, "Some Weapons and Tools of the Yin Dynasty," *BMFEA* 17 (1945), pp. 101–144.

Keightley, David N., "Where Have All the Swords Gone? Reflections on the Unification of China," *EC* 2 (1976), pp. 31–34.

LaPlante, John D., "Ancient Chinese Ritual Vessels: Some Observations on Technology and Style," *EC* 13 (1988), pp. 247–273.

Loehr, Max, "The Earliest Chinese Swords and the Akinakes," *Oriental Art* 1 (1948), pp. 132–142.

McEwen, E., R. Miller, and C. Bergman, "Early Bow Design and Construction," *Scientific American* 6 (1991), pp. 76–82.

Rogers, Spencer L., "The Aboriginal Bow and Arrow of North America and Eastern Asia," *American Anthropologist* NS 42 (1940), pp. 255–269.

Sun Shuyun and Han Rubin, "A Preliminary Study of Early Chinese Copper and Bronze Artifacts," Translated by Julia K. Murray, *EC* 9–10 (1983–1985), pp. 261–289.

Trousdale, William, "Where All the Swords Have Gone," *EC* 3 (1977), pp. 65–66.

Wilbur, C. Martin, "The History of the Crossbow, Illustrated from Specimens in the United States National Museum," *Smithsonian Institution Annual Report* (1936), pp. 427–438.

Western Language Monographs and Articles on Chinese Military History, Texts, and Topics

Allan, Sarah, "The Identities of Taigong Wang in Zhou and Han Literature," *MS* 30 (1972–1973), pp. 57–99.

Balmforth, Edmund E., *A Chinese Military Strategist of the Warring States: Sun Pin,* unpublished Ph.D. dissertation, Department of History, Rutgers University, 1979.

Chang Ch'un-shu, "Military Aspects of Han Wu-ti's Northern and Northwestern Campaigns," *HJAS* 26 (1966), pp. 148–173.

Duyvendak, J.J.L., "An Illustrated Battle-account in the *History of the Former Han Dynasty, TP* 34 (1939), pp. 244–264.

Fan Yuzhou, "Military Campaign Inscriptions from YH 127," *BSOAS* 52:3 (1989), pp. 533–548.

Goodrich, Chauncey S., "Ssu-ma Ch'ien's Biography of Wu Ch'i," *MS* 35 (1981–1983), pp. 197–233.

Johnson, David, "The Wu Tzu-hsü *Pien-wen* and Its Sources," Part I, *HJAS* 40:1 (June 1980), pp. 93–156; Part II, *HJAS* 40:2 (December 1980), pp. 465–505.

Kierman, Frank A., Jr., and John K. Fairbank, eds., *Chinese Ways in Warfare,* Harvard University Press, Cambridge, Mass., 1974.

Lau, D. C., "Some Notes on the *Sun-tzu,*" *BSOAS* 28 (1965), pp. 317–335.

Marsh, Susan H., "Frank A. Kierman, Jr., and John K. Fairbank (eds.), *Chinese Ways in Warfare*" (review of), *JCP* 3 (1975), pp. 97–104.

Rand, Christopher C., "Chinese Military Thought and Philosophical Taoism," *MS* 34 (1979–1980), pp. 171–218.

———, "Li Ch'üan and Chinese Military Thought," *HJAS* 39:1 (June 1979), pp. 107–137.

———, *The Role of Military Thought in Early Chinese Intellectual History,* unpublished Ph.D. dissertation, Department of History and East Asian Languages, Harvard University, 1977.

Vervoorn, Aat, "Taoism, Legalism, and the Quest for Order in Warring States China," *JCP* 8:3 (September 1981), pp. 303–324.

Wallacker, Benjamin E., "Two Concepts in Early Chinese Military Thought," *Language* 42:2 (1966), pp. 295–299.

Yates, Robin D.S., *The City Under Siege: Technology and Organization as Seen in the Reconstructed Text of the Military Chapters of Mo-tzu,* unpublished Ph.D. dissertation, Harvard University, 1980.

––––––, "The Mohists on Warfare: Technology, Techniques, and Justification," *Journal of the American Academy of Religion* Thematic Studies Supplement 47:3 (1980), pp. 549–603.

––––––, "New Light on Ancient Chinese Military Texts: Notes on Their Nature and Evolution, and the Development of Military Specialization in Warring States China," *TP* 74 (1988), pp. 211–248.

––––––, "Siege Engines and Late Zhou Military Technology," in *Explorations in the History of Science and Technology in China* (Li Guohao et al., eds.), Shanghai Chinese Classics Publishing House, Shanghai, 1982, pp. 409–451.

General Works on History and Fundamental Writings in Chinese and Japanese

Amano Shizuo, *Sonshi, Goshi,* Meiji shoin, Tokyo, 1972.

Chang Ch'i-yün, *Chung-hua wu-ch'ien-nien shih,* 9 vol., Chung-kuo wen-hua ta-hsüeh ch'u-pan-she, Taipei, 1981 (1961).

Chang I-jen, "Ts'ung *Kuo-yü* yü *Tso-chuan* pen-chih-shang te ch'a-i shih-lun hou-jen tui *Kuo-yü* te p'i-p'ing," *Han-hsüeh yen-chiu:* Part I, 1:2 (December 1983), pp. 419–453; Part II, 2:1 (June 1984), pp. 1–22.

Chang Kuang-yüan, "Ts'ung shih-yen-chung t'an-so wan-Shang chia-ku ts'ai-liao cheng-chih yü pu-k'e te fang-fa," *Han-hsüeh yen-chiu:* Part I, 2:1 (June 1984), pp. 57–107; Part II, 2:2 (December 1984), pp. 447–509.

Chang Ya-ch'u and Liu Yü, "Ts'ung Shang-Chou pa-kua shu-tzu fu-hao t'an shih-fa te chi-ke wen-t'i," *KK* 1981:2, pp. 155–163.

Chang Yin-lin, *Chung-kuo shih-kang,* Cheng-chung shu-chü, Taipei, 1982 (1951).

Chao Po-hsiung, *Chou-tai kuo-chia hsing-t'ai yen-chiu,* Hunan chiao-yü ch'u-pan-she, Ch'angsha, 1990.

Ch'en Chi-yu, *Han Fei-tzu chi-shih,* 2 vols., Edited by Yang Chia-lo, Shih-chieh shu-chü, Taipei, 1972.

––––––, *Lü-shih ch'un-ch'iu chiao-shih,* 2 vols., Hsüeh-lin ch'u-pan-she, Shanghai, 1984.

Ch'en Li-kuei, *Chan-kuo shih-ch'i te Huang-Lao ssu-hsiang,* Lien-ching ch'u-pan-she, Taipei, 1991.

––––––, "*Kuan-tzu* chung te Huang-Lao ssu-hsiang," *Shih-fan Ta-hsüeh Kuo-wen hsüeh-pao* 19:6 (1990), pp. 33–64.

Ch'en Liang-tso, "Wo-kuo ku-tai te ch'ing-t'ung nung-chü," *Han-hsüeh yen-chiu* 2:1 (June 1984), pp. 135–166; and 2:2 (December 1984), pp. 363–402.

Ch'en P'an, "Ch'un-ch'iu Chan-kuo shih-kao shang-ch'üeh," *Han-hsüeh yen-chiu* 2:2 (December 1984), pp. 343–361.

_____, "Ch'un-ch'iu lieh-kuo te chiao-t'ung," *BIHP* 37 (1967), pp. 881–932.

_____, "*Chung-kuo shang-ku-shih* tu-chi," *Han-hsüeh yen-chiu* 1:2 (December 1983), pp. 455–473.

Cheng Liang-shu, "Lun Shang-chün-shu 'Keng-fa' pien yü Chan-kuo-ts'e 'Chao-ts'e' te kuan-hsi," *Ku-kung hsüeh-shu chi-k'an* 1986:3–4, pp. 101–110.

Ch'eng Wu, "Han-ch'u Huang-Lao ssu-hsiang ho Fa-chia lu-hsien," *WW* 1974:10, pp. 43–47.

Chin Wei-no, "T'an Ch'ang-sha Ma-wang-tui san-hao Han-mu po-hua," *WW* 1974:11, pp. 40–44.

Ch'iu Chen-sheng, *San-kuo yen-i tsung-heng-t'an,* Hsiao-yüan ch'u-pan, Taipei, 1991.

Chou Shih-jung, "Yu-kuan Ma-wang-tui ku-ti-t'u te i-hsieh tzu-liao ho chi-fang Han-yin," *WW* 1976:1, pp. 28–32.

Chu T'ing-hsien, *Shang-shu yen-chiu,* Shang-wu yin-shu-kuan, Taipei, 1987.

Chu Yu-tseng, *I-Chou-shu chi-hsün chiao-shih,* Edited by Yang Chia-lo, Shih-chieh shu-chü, Taipei, 1980.

Ch'ü Wan-li, "Hsi-Chou shih-shih kai-shu," *BIHP* 42 (1971), pp. 775–802.

_____, "Shih-chi Yin-pen-chi chi ch'i-t'o chi-lu-chung so-tsai Yin-Shang shih-tai te shih-shih," *Taiwan Ta-hsüeh wen-shih-che hsüeh-pao* 14:11 (1965), pp. 87–118.

Chung-kuo K'o-hsüeh-yüan K'ao-ku Yen-chiu-so and Hunan-sheng Po-wu-kuan Hsieh-tso Hsiao-tsu, "Ma-wang-tui erh, san-hao Han-mu fa-chüeh te chu-yao shou-huo," *KK* 1975:1, pp. 47–57, 61.

Fu Yüeh-ch'eng, *Chung-kuo t'ung-shih,* 2 vols., Ta-Chung-kuo t'u-shu kung-ssu, Tai-pei, 1985 (reprint), (original ed. 1960).

Han Lien-ch'i, "Lun Ch'un-ch'iu shih-tai fa-lü chih-tu te yen-pien," *Chung-kuo-shih yen-chiu* 1983:4, pp. 1–12.

Han Yang-min, *Ch'in-Han wen-hua shih,* Lo-t'o ch'u-pan-she, Taipei, 1987.

Ho Kuan-piao, "San-kuo chih Sui-T'ang chan-hou yün-ch'i chih chu-tso k'ao-lüeh," *Han-hsüeh yen-chiu* 7:2 (December 1989), pp. 123–136.

Ho Yu-ch'i, "Chou Wu-wang fa-Chou te nien-tai wen-t'i," *Chung-shan Ta-hsüeh hsüeh-pao* 1 (1981), pp. 64–70.

Hosokawa Toshikazu, *Sonshi, Goshi,* Gakken kenkyūsha, Tokyo, 1982.

Hou Chia-chü, "Chou-li-chung te cheng-chih ssu-hsiang chi chih-tu," *Yu-shih hsüeh-chih* 18:2 (1984), pp. 1–26.

_____, "Yu-kuan Chou-li te li-tai yen-chiu," *Shu-mu chi-k'an* 18:2 (1984), pp. 22–27.

Hsiao Han, "Ch'ang-she Ma-wang-tui Han-mu po-shu kai-shu," *WW* 1974:9, pp. 40–44.

Hsiung T'ieh-chi, *Ch'in Han hsin-Tao-chia lüeh-lun kao,* Jen-min ch'u-pan-she, Shanghai, 1984.

Hsü Cho-yün, *Chung-kuo li-shih lun-wen-chi,* Shang-wu yin-shu-kuan, Taipei, 1986.

Hu-nan-sheng Po-wu-kuan Chung-kuo K'o-hsüeh-yüan K'ao-ku Yen-chiu-so, "Ch'ang-sha Ma-wang-tui erh, san-hao Han-mu fa-chüeh chien-pao," *WW* 1974:7, pp. 39–48.

Jung Meng-yüan, "Shih-t'an Hsi-Chou chi-nien," *Chung-hua wen-shih lun-ts'ung* 1980:1, pp. 1–21.

Kao Yu, *Huai-nan tzu chu,* Edited by Yang Chia-lo, Shih-chieh shu-chü, Taipei, 1969.

Kuo Ch'ing-fan, *Chiao-cheng Chuang-tzu chi-shih,* 2 vols., Edited by Yang Chia-lo, shih-chieh shu-chü, Taipei, 1971.

Kuo Pao-chün, *Chung-kuo ch'ing-t'ung-ch'i shih-tai,* Lo-t'o ch'u-pan-she, Taipei, 1987.

Kuroda Yoshiko, *Ki no kenkyū,* Tokyo Bijustsu, Tokyo, 1977.

Li Chia-shu, "Ts'ung *Shih-ching* chung k'an tsao-Chou she-hui te mien-mao—ping lun Hsi-Chou she-hui hsing-chih wen-t'i," *Hsiang-kang Chung-wen Ta-hsüeh Chung-kuo Wen-hua Yen-chiu-so hsüeh-pao* 17 (1986), pp. 163–200.

Li Shu-t'ung, *Chung-kuo-shih hsin-lun,* Hsüeh-sheng shu-chü, Taipei, 1985.

Lu Tien, *Ho Kuan-tzu chieh,* Edited by Yang Chia-lo, Shih-chieh shu-chü, Taipei, 1967.

Lu Wen-ch'ao, *Ch'ün-shu shih-pu,* Edited by Yang Chia-lo, Shih-chieh shu-chü, Taipei, 1963.

Matsui Takeo, *Goshi,* Meitoku shuppansha, Tokyo, 1971.

Ma-wang-tui Han-mu Po-shu Cheng-li Hsiao-tsu, "Ch'ang-sha Ma-wang-tui san-hao Han-mu ch'u-t'u ti-t'u te cheng-li," *WW* 1975:2, pp. 35–48.

Onozawa Seiichi, Fukunaga Mitsuji, and Yamanoi Yu, eds., *Ki no shisō,* Tokyo Daigaku shuppansha, Tokyo, 1978.

Ozaki Hotsuki, *Goshi,* Kyoikusha, Tokyo, 1987.

P'an Ying, *Chung-kuo shang-ku-shih hsin-t'an,* Ming-wen shu-chü, Taipei, 1985.

Shih Chang-ju, "Yin-hsü tsui-chin chih chung-yao fa-hsien (fu lun Hsiao-t'un ti-ts'eng)," *Chung-kuo k'ao-ku hsüeh-pao* 2 (1947), pp. 1–81.

Ssu-ma Kuang, *Hsin-chiao Tsu-chih t'ung-chien,* 16 vols., Edited by Yang Chia-lo, Shih-chieh shu-chü, Taipei, 1972.

T'ang Lan, "*Huang-ti ssu-ching* ch'u-t'an," *WW* 1974:10, pp. 48–52.

T'ao Hsi-sheng, *Chung-kuo cheng-chih ssu-hsiang shih,* 4 vols., Shih-huo ch'u-pan-she, Taipei, 1972 (1954).

Ting Shan, "Yu San-tai tu-i lun ch-i min-tsu wen-hua," *BIHP* 5:3 (1935), pp. 87–129 (plus four plates).

Tu Cheng-sheng, "Lüeh-lun Yin i-min te tsao-yü yü ti-wei," *BIHP* 54:3 (December 1982), pp. 661–709.

———, " 'Pien-hu ch'i-min' te ch'u-hsien chi ch'i li-shih i-i," *BIHP* 54:3 (1983), pp. 77–111.

———, "Ts'ung chüeh-chih lun Shang Yang pien-fa so-hsing-ch'eng te she-hui," *BIHP* 56:3 (1985), pp. 485–544.

Tung Tso-pin, "Hsi-Chou nien-li-p'u," *BIHP* 23 (1951), pp. 681–760.

T'ung Chu-ch'en, "Ts'ung Erh-li-t'o lei-hsing wen-hua shih-t'an Chung-kuo te kuo-chia ch'i-yüan wen-t'i," *WW* 1975:6, pp. 29–33.

Wang Hsiao-po, *Hsien-Ch'in Fa-chia ssu-hsiang shih-lun,* Lien-ching ch'u-pan, Taipei, 1991.

Wang Hsien-ch'ien, *Hsün-tzu chi-chieh,* Edited by Yang Chia-lo, Shih-chieh shu-chü, Taipei, 1974.

Wang Shih-chang and Wang Ta-hua, *Chung-kuo cheng-chih ssu-hsiang shih,* San-min shu-chü, Taipei, 1970.

Wei Chin, "Ts'ung Yin-ch'üeh-shan chu-chien k'an Ch'in Shih-huang fen-shu," *WW* 1974:7, pp. 1–4.

Wei Wei and Hsiao Te-yen, *Chu-tzu chih-yao,* Edited by Yang Chia-lo, Shih-chieh shu-chü, Taipei, 1967.

Wu-tzu chih-chieh, in *Ming-pen Wu-ching Ch'i-shu chih-chieh,* Vol. 1, Shih-ti chiao-yü ch'u-pan-she, Taipei, 1972.

Yang Chia-lo, ed., *Chan-kuo ts'e,* 3 vols., Shih-chieh shu-chü, Taipei, 1967.

_____, ed., *Chu-shu chi-nien pa-chung,* Shih-chieh shu-chü, Taipei, 1977.

_____, ed., *Li-tai jen-wu nien-li t'ung-pu,* Shih-chieh shu-chü Taipei, 1974.

_____, ed., *Lun-yü chu-shu chi pu-cheng,* Shih-chieh shu-chü, Taipei, 1963.

_____, ed., *Shang-shu chu-shu chi pu-cheng,* Shih-chieh shu-chü, Taipei, 1973.

_____, ed., *Shih-t'ung t'ung-shih,* 2 vols., Shih-chieh shu-chü, Taipei, 1981.

_____, ed., *Tso-chuan chu-shu chi pu-cheng,* 3 vols., Shih-chieh shu-chü, Taipei, 1971.

_____, ed., *Wu Yüeh ch'un-ch'iu,* 2 vols., Shih-chieh shu-chü, Taipei, 1967.

Yang Po-chün, *Ch'un-ch'iu Tso-chuan chu,* 3 vols., Chung-hua shu-chü, Peking, 1990 (rev. ed.).

_____, "Sun Pin ho *Sun Pin ping-fa* tsa-k'ao," *WW* 1975:3, pp. 9–13.

Yen Keng-wang, *Chung-kuo ti-fang hsing-cheng chih-tu shih,* Chung-yang Yen-chiu-yüan, Taipei, 1974.

Works on Military History and Topics in Chinese and Japanese

Anonymous, *Chung-kuo ping-hsüeh t'ung-lun* (original title: *Ts'ao-lu ching-lüeh*), Li-ming, Taipei, 1986.

Chan Li-po, "Ma-wang-tui Han-mu ch'u-t'u te shou-pei-t'u t'an-t'ao," *WW* 1976:1, pp. 24–27.

Chang Chen-che, *Sun Pin ping-fa chiao-li,* Ming-wen shu-chü, Taipei, 1985.

Chang Ch'i-yün, *Chung-kuo chün-shih shih-lüeh,* Chung-hua wen-hua ch'u-pan-she, Taipei, 1956.

Chang Shao-sheng and Liu Wen-ch'an, eds., *Chung-kuo ku-tai chan-cheng t'ung-lan,* 2 vols., Ch'ang-cheng ch'u-pan-she, Peking, 1985.

Chao Pen-hsüeh, *Sun-tzu-shu chiao-chieh yin-lei,* Chung-hua shu-chü, Taipei, 1970 (reprint).

Ch'en Ch'i-t'ien, *Sun-tzu ping-fa chiao-shih,* Chung-hua shu-chü, Taipei, 1955 (reprint of 1944 edition).

Ch'en Ts'e, *Chu-ko Liang ping-fa,* Wu-ling ch'u-pan-she, Taipei, 1980.

Ch'en Wu-t'ung and Su Shuang-pi, eds., *Chung-kuo li-tai ming-chiang,* 2 vols., Honan jen-min ch'u-pan-she, 1987.

Chiang I-ch'ing, *Chung-kuo ping-fa chih ch'i-yüan,* Lien-ya ch'u-pan-she, Taipei, 1982.

Chin Hsiang-heng, "Ts'ung chia-ku pu-ts'u yen-chiu Yin-Shang chün-lü-chung chih wang-tsu san-hsing san-shih," *Chung-kuo wen-tzu* 52 (1974), pp. 1–26 (plus illustrations).

Chou Fa-kao, "Wu Wang k'e Shang te nien-tai wen-t'i," *BIHP* 56:1 (1985), pp. 5–41.

Chu Shao-hou, *Chün-kung chüeh-chih yen-chiu,* Jenmin ch'u-pan-she, Shanghai, 1990.

Ch'üeh Hsün-wu, ed., *Chung-kuo ku-tai chün-shih-chia chuan-chi hsü-chu,* Yüeh-lu shu-she, Ch'ang-sha, 1985.

Chün-shih Li-shih Yen-chiu-hui, *Ping-chia shih-yüan,* Chün-shih k'o-hsüeh ch'u-pan-she, Peking, 1990.

Chung-kuo Chün-shih-shih Pien-hsieh-tsu, *Chung-kuo chün-shih-shih,* Vol. 5: *Ping-chia,* Chieh-fang-chün ch'u-pan-she, Peking, 1990.

_____, *Chung-kuo chün-shih-shih,* Vol. 4: *Ping-fa,* Chieh-fang-chün ch'u-pan-she, Peking, 1988.

_____, *Chung-kuo chün-shih-shih,* Vol. 6: *Ping-lei,* Chieh-fang-chün ch'u-pan-she, Peking, 1991.

_____, *Chung-kuo chün-shih-shih,* Vol. 2: *Ping-lüeh* (part II), Chieh-fang-chün ch'u-pan-she, Peking, 1988.

Hsiao T'ien-shih, *Sun-tzu chan-cheng-lun,* Tzu-yu ch'u-pan-she, Taipei, 1983 (reprint of 1942 edition).

Hsieh Yün-fei, *Han Fei-tzu hsin-lun,* Tung-ta t'u-shu, Taipei, 1980.

Hsü Hsi-ch'en, "Chou-tai ping-chih ch'u-lun," *Chung-kuo-shih yen-chiu* 1985:4, pp. 3–12.

Hšu Pei-ken, *Chung-kuo kuo-fang ssu-hsiang-shih,* Chung-yang wu-kung-ying-she, Taipei, 1983.

Hsü Pei-ken and Wei Ju-lin, *Sun Pin ping-fa chu-shih,* Li-ming wen-hua, Taipei, 1976.

Hsü Pei-ken et al., *Chung-kuo li-tai chan-cheng-shih* (compiled by the San-chün Ta-hsüeh), 18 vols., Li-ming, Taipei, 1980 (reprint of 1976 revised edition; original edition, 1965).

Hsü Wen-chu, *Sun-tzu yen-chiu,* Kuang-tung ch'u-pan-she, Taipei, 1980.

Hu Wen-ping, *Ch'ing-pao hsüeh,* self-published, Taipei, 1989.

Huang Ying-shan, *Chung-kuo ping-chia chih kuan-li ssu-hsiang,* Chung-kuo ching-chi, Taipei, 1986.

Huo Yin-chang, *Sun Pin ping-fa ch'ien-shuo,* Chieh-fang-chün ch'u-pan-she, Peking, 1986.

Kagakuraoka Masatoshi, "Sonsi to Roshi," *Tōhō shūkyō* 37 (April 1971), pp. 39–40.

Kao Ts'ung-tao, ed., *Chung-kuo wu-hsüeh ts-u-tien,* Ch'ang-ch'un-shu shu-fang, Taipei, 1986.

Ku Chieh-kang, "I-Chou-shu 'Shih-fu' p'ien chiao-chu hsieh-ting yü p'ing-lun," *Wen-shih* 2 (1963), pp. 1–42.

Kuan Feng, "Sun-tzu chün-shih che-hsüeh ssu-hsiang yen-chiu," *Che-hsüeh yen-chiu* 1957:2, pp. 70–90.

Lao Kan, "Chan-kuo shih-tai te chan-cheng fang-fa," *BIHP* 37 (1967), pp. 47–63.

Li Chen, *Chiang-hsiao ts'ai-te, ling-tao yü mou-lüeh,* Li-ming wen-hua, Taipei, 1986.

_____, *Chung-kuo li-tai chan-cheng shih-hua,* Li-ming wen-hua, Taipei, 1985.

_____, ed., *Chung-kuo chün-shih chiao-yü shih,* Chung-yang wen-wu kung-ying-she, Taipei, 1983.

Li Chiu-jui, *Chung-kuo chün-shih ssu-hsiang-shih,* Shun-hsien ch'u-pan kung-ssu, Taipei, 1978.

Lin-t'ung-hsien Wen-hua-kuan, "Shanhsi Lin-t'ung fa-hsien Wu-wang cheng Shang kuei," *WW* 1977:8, pp. 1–7.

Lu Chien-jung, *Ts'ao Ts'ao*, Lien-ming wen-hua, Taipei, 1980.

Ma-wang-tui Han-mu Po-shu Cheng-li Hsiao-tsu, "Ma-wang-tui san-hao Han-mu ch'u-t'u chu-chün-t'u cheng-li chien-pao," *WW* 1976:1, pp. 18–23.

Okada Isao, "Sokoku to Goki henpō," *Rekishigaku kenkyū* 490, pp. 15–30.

T'ang Ching-wu, *Chung-kuo ping-hsüeh chen-fa shih*, 2 vols., self-published, Taipei, 1985.

_____, *I-ching ping-chen ta-fa*, self-published, Taipei, 1981.

_____, *Sun-tzu ping-fa tsui-hsin-chieh*, self-published, Taipei, 1981.

T'ao Hsi-sheng, *Ping-fa san-shu*, Shih-huo ch'u-pan-she, Taipei, 1979.

T'ao Yin, *Chu-ko Liang ping-fa*, Kuo-chia ch'u-pan-she, Taipei, 1991.

Teng I-tsung, *Li Ching ping-fa chi-pen chu-i*, Chieh-fang-chün ch'u-pan-she, Peking, 1990.

Tseng Kuo-yüan, *Hsien-Ch'in chan-cheng she-hsüeh*, Shang-wu yin-shu-kuan, Taipei, 1972.

Tu Cheng-sheng, "Chou-tai feng-chien chieh-t'i-hou te chün-cheng hsin-chih-hsü," *BIHP* 55:1 (1984), pp. 73–113.

Tung Tso-pin, "Wu-wang fa-Chou nien-yüeh-jih chin-k'ao," *Taiwan Ta-hsüeh wen-shih-che hsüeh-pao* 1951:12, pp. 177–212.

Tzu Yü-ch'iu, ed., *Mou-lüeh k'u*, Lan-t'ien ch'u-pan-she, Peking, 1990.

Wang Fu-i and Chu Ch'ing-tse, ed., *Ku-tai chiang-shuai chih-chün ch'ü-wen-lu*, Chün-shih k'o-hsüeh ch'u-pan-she, Peking, 1987.

Wang Pang-hsiung, *Han Fei-tzu te che-hsüeh*, Tung-ta t'u-shu, Taipei, 1977.

Wang Shao-wei and Liu Chao-hsiang, *Li-tai ping-chih ch'ien-shuo*, Chieh-fang-chün ch'u-pan-she, Peking, 1986.

Wei Ju-lin, *Chung-kuo li-tai ming-chiang chi ch'i yung-ping ssu-hsiang*, Chung-yang wen-wu kung-ying-she, Taipei, 1981.

Wu Hsia et al, *Chung-kuo ku-tai chün-shih san-pai t'i*, Shanghai ku-chi ch'u-pan-she, Shanghai, 1989.

Wu Hsiu-ying, *Han Fei-tzu chiu-i*, Wen-shih-che ch'u-pan-she, Taipei, 1979.

Wu Ju-ts'ung, ed., *Chung-hua chün-shih jen-wu ta-ts'u-tien*, Hsin-hua ch'u-pan-she, Shanghai, 1989.

Wu Kuo-ch'ing, *Chung-kuo chan-cheng-shih*, Chin-ch'eng ch'u-pan-she, Peking, 1990.

Yang K'uan, "Ch'un-ch'iu Chan-kuo-chien feng-chien te chün-shih tsu-chih ho chan-cheng te pien-hua," *Li-shih chiao-hsüeh* 4 (1954), pp. 7–13.

Yeh Ta-hsiung, "Hsi-Chou ping-chih te t'an-t'ao," *Taiwan Ta-hsüeh Li-shih-hsüeh-hsi hsüeh-pao* 1979:6, pp. 1–16.

Yen I-p'ing, "Yin Shang ping-chih," *Chung-kuo wen-tzu* NS 7 (1983), pp. 1–82.

Yü Sheng-wu, "Li-k'uei ming-wen k'ao-shih," *WW* 1977:8, pp. 10–12.

Yüan Chung-i, "Ch'in Shih-huang-ling tung-ts'e ti-erh, san-hao yung-k'eng chün-chen nei-jung shih-t'an," in *Chung-kuo k'ao-ku she-hui ti-i-tz'u nien-hui lun-wen-chi*, Wen-wu ch'u-pan-she, Peking, 1979, pp. 315–322.

Yuasa Kunihiro, "*Utsuryoshi* no fukoku kyohei shisō," *Tōhōgaku* 69 (1985), pp. 30–43.

Works on Chariots, Cavalry, Weapons, and Technology in Chinese and Japanese

Chan Li and Chou Shih-ch'ü, "Shih-t'an Yang-chia-wan Han-mu ch'i-ping-yung," WW 1977:10, pp. 22–32.

Ch'en Han-chang, "Li-tai ch'e-chan k'ao," *Wu-yin ts'ung-p'ien* (1939), pp. 1–17.

Ch'en Jui-li, "Chan-kuo shih-tai te i-pa pao-chin-chien," *BIHP* 37:1 (1967), pp. 221–235 (plus twelve plates).

Ch'en Meng-chia, "Hsi-Chou t'ung-ch'i tuan-tai, V," *KK* 1956:3, pp. 105–130.

Ch'en Yao-chün, "Chiang-ling Ch'u-mu ch'u-t'u shuang-shih ping-she lien-fa-nu yen-chiu," WW 1990:5, pp. 89–96.

Ch'eng Tung and Chung Shao-i, eds., *Chung-kuo ku-tai ping-ch'i t'u-chi,* Chieh-fang-chün ch'u-pan-she, Peking, 1990.

Ch'in Ming, "Ch'in-yung-k'eng ping-ma-yung chün-chen nei-jung chi ping-ch'i shih-t'an," WW 1975:11, pp. 19–23.

Chou Wei, *Chung-kuo ping-ch'i shih-kao,* Ming-wen shu-chü, Taipei, 1980.

Emura Haruki, "Shunju Sengoku jidai no doka, geki no hennen to meibun," *Tōhō Gakuhō* 52 (1982), pp. 63–122.

Hao Pen-hsing, "Hsin-cheng 'Cheng-Han ku-ch'eng' fa-hsien i-p'i Chan-kuo t'ung-ping-ch'i," WW 1972:10, pp. 32–37.

Hayashi Minao, *Chūgoku In-Shū jidai no buki,* Kyoto Daigaku Jimbun Kagaku Kenkyūsho, Kyoto, 1972.

_____, "Chūgoku sen-Shin jidai no basha," *Tōhō Gakuhō* 29 (1959), pp. 155–284.

Hsü Chung-shu, "I-she yü nu chih su-yüan chi kuan-yü tz'u-lei ming-wu chih k'ao-shih," *BIHP* 4 (1934), pp. 417–439.

Kao Chih-hsi, "Chi Ch'ang-sha, Ch'ang-te ch'u-t'u nu-chi te Chan-kuo-mu—chien-t'an yu-kuan nu-chi, kung-shih te chi-ke wen-t'i," WW 1964:6, pp. 33–45.

Kao Ch'ü-hsün, "Tao-fu-tsang-chung te t'ung-tao," *BIHP* 37:1 pp. 355–381 (plus seven plates).

Kawamata Masanori, "Higashi Ajia no kodai sensha to Nishi-Ajia," *Koshi Shunjū* 4 (1987), pp. 38–58.

Ku Chieh-kang and Yang Hsiang-k'uei, "Chung-kuo ku-tai ch'e-chan k'ao-lüeh," *Tung-fang tsa-chih* 34:1 (1937), pp. 39–54.

Kuo Mo-jo, *Yin Chou ch'ing-t'ung-ch'i ming-wen yen-chiu,* Jenmin ch'u-pan-she, Shanghai, 1954.

Kuo Pao-chün, "Ko chi yü-lun," *BIHP* 5:3 (1935), pp. 313–326.

_____, "Yin-Chou te ch'ing-t'ung wu-ch'i," *KK* 2 (1961), pp. 111–118.

Li Chi, "Yü-pei ch'u-t'u ch'ing-t'ung kou-ping fen-lei t'u-chieh," *BIHP* 22 (1950), pp. 1–31.

Li Po-ch'ien, "Chung-yüan ti-ch'ü Tung-Chou t'ung-chien yüan-yüan shih-t'an," WW 1982:1, pp. 44–48.

Lin Shou-chin, "Lun Chou-tai t'ung-chien te yüan-yüan," WW 1963:11, pp. 50–55.

_____, "Tung-Chou-shih t'ung-chien ch'u-lun," *KK* 2 (1962), pp. 75–84 (plus two plates).

Lin Yün, "Chung-kuo Tung-pei-hsi t'ung-chien ch'u-lun," *KK* 2 (1980), pp. 139–161.

Liu Chan-ch'eng, "Ch'in-yung-k'eng ch'u-t'u te t'ung-p'i," WW 1983:3, pp. 12–14.

Liu Hsü, *Chung-kuo ku-tai huo-p'ao-shih,* Jen-min ch'u-pan-she, Shanghai, 1989.

Liu Teng-jung, Fang Li-chung, and P'i Tsao-shen, *Ping-ch'i ts'u-tien,* Nung-ch'un tu-wu ch'u-pan-she, Peking, 1988.

Ma Heng, "Ko chi chih yen-chiu," *Yen-ching hsüeh-pao* 5 (1929), pp. 745–753.

P'an Chi-hsing, *T'ien-kung k'ai-wu tao-tu,* Pa-shu shu-she, Szechwan, 1988.

Sekino Takeshi, "Chūgoku shoki bunka no ikkōsatsu—dōtestsu katoki no kaimei ni yosete," *Shigaku zasshi* 60:10 (October 1951), pp. 867–907.

Shih Chang-ju, "Hsiao-t'un Yin-tai te ch'eng-t'ao ping-ch'i (fu Yin-tai te ts'e)," *BIHP* 22 (1950), pp. 19–79.

Sun Chi, "Yu-jen ch'e-wei yü to-ko-chi," *WW* 1980:12, pp. 83–85.

T'ang Lan, "Hsi-Chou shih-tai tsui-tsao te i-chien t'ung-ch'i li-kuei ming-wen chieh-shih," *WW* 1977:8, pp. 8–9.

T'ang Yü-ming, "Kao-ch'eng T'ai-hsi Shang-tai t'ieh-jen t'ung-yüeh wen-t'i te t'an-t'ao," *WW* 1975:3, pp. 57–59.

T'ung En-cheng, "Wo-kuo Hsi-nan ti-ch'ü ch'ing-t'ung-chien te yen-chiu," *KK* 1977:2, pp. 35–55.

Wen Jen-chün, *K'ao-kung chi tao-tu,* Pa-shu shu-she, Szechwan, 1988.

Yang Hung, "Ch'e-chan yü chan-ch'e," *WW* 1977: 5, pp. 82–90.

———, *Chung-kuo ku-ping-ch'i lun-ts'ung,* Wen-wu ch'u-pan-she, Peking, 1980 (also edited and reprinted in Taipei, Ming-wen shu-chü, 1983).

Yoshida Mitsukuni, "Yumi to ōyumi," *Tōyōshi kenkyū* 12:3 (1953), pp. 82–92.

Works on Textual Dates and Recovered Texts in Chinese and Japanese

Chan Li-po, "Lüeh-t'an Lin-i Han-mu chu-chien *Sun-tzu ping-fa,*" *WW* 1974:12, pp. 13–19.

———, "*Sun Pin ping-fa* ts'an-chien chieh-shao," *WW* 1974:3, pp. 40–47.

Chang Hsin-ch'eng, ed., *Wei-shu t'ung-k'ao,* Shang-wu yin-shu-kuan, Taipei, 1970 (reprint) (original edition 1939).

Chang Lieh, "Kuan-yü *Wei Liao-tzu* te chu-lu ho ch'eng-shu," *Wen-shih* 8:3 (1980), pp. 27–37.

———, "*Liu-t'ao* te ch'eng-shu chi ch'i nei-jung," *Li-shih yen-chiu* 1981: 3, pp. 122–126.

Chao T'ieh-han, "Kuei Ku-tzu k'ao-pien," Part I: *Talu tsachih* 14:5 (1957), pp. 137–141; Part II: *Talu tsachih* 14:6 (1957), pp. 186–191.

Cheng Liang-shu, *Hsü Wei-shu t'ung-k'ao,* 3 vols., Hsüeh-sheng shu-chü, Taipei, 1984.

Ch'iu Hsi-kuei, "Ma-wang-tui *Lao-tzu* chia-i-pen-chüan ch'ien-hou i-shu yü 'Tao-Fa-chia,'" *Chung-kuo che-hsüeh* 2 (1980), pp. 69–84.

Chu Kuo-chao, "Shang-sun-chia chai mu-chien ch'u-t'an," *WW* 1981:2, pp. 27–34.

Ch'ü Wan-li, *Hsien-Ch'in wen-shih tzu-liao k'ao-pien,* Lien-ching, Taipei, 1983.

Chung Chao-hua, "Kuan-yü *Wei Liao-tzu* mou-hsieh wen-t'i te shang-ch'üeh," *WW* 1978:5, pp. 60–63.

Erh-ling-pa-i Pu-tui Fang-hua-lien Li-lun Hsiao-tsu, "Sun Pin p'u-su te chün-shih pien-cheng-fa," *WW* 1975:4, pp. 1–5.

Ho Fa-chou, "*Wei Liao-tzu* ch'u-t'an," *WW* 1977:2, pp. 28–34.

Hsü Pao-lin, *Chung-kuo ping-shu t'ung-chien,* Chieh-fang-chün ch'u-pan-she, Peking, 1990.

Hsü Ti, "Lüeh-t'an Lin-i Yin-ch'üeh-shan Han-mu ch'u-t'u te ku-tai ping-shu ts'an-chien," *WW* 1974:2, pp. 27–31.

Kao Heng and Chih Hsi-ch'ao, "Shih-t'an Ma-wang-tui Han-mu-chung te po-shu *Lao-tzu,*" *WW* 1974: 10, pp. 1–7.

Kuo-chia Wen-wu-chü Ku-wen-hsien Yen-chiu-shih, Ta-t'ung Shang-Sun-chia chai Han-chien Cheng-li Hsiao-tsu, "Ta-t'ung Shang-Sun-chia chai Han-chien shih-wen," *WW* 1981:2, pp. 22–26.

Kuo Mo-jo, "Shu Wu Ch'i," *Kuo Mo-jo ch'üan-chi,* Jen-min ch'u-pan-she, Peking, 1982, Vol. 1, pp. 506–533. (Originally published in *Ch'ing-t'ung shih-tai,* 1945, pp. 202–230.)

Li Ling, "Kuan-yü Yin-ch'üeh-shan chien-pen *Sun-tzu* yen-chiu te shang-ch'üeh," *Wen-shih* 7 (December 1979), pp. 23–34.

Liang Chia-ping, "Kuei Ku-tzu k'ao," *Ta-lu tsa-chih* 10:4 (1953), pp. 112–115.

Ling Hsiang, "Shih-lun Ma-wang-tui Han-mu po-shu *I Yin, Chiu chu,*" *WW* 1974:11, pp. 21–27, 44.

Lo Fu-i, "Lin-i Han-chien kai-shu," *WW* 1974:2, pp. 32–35.

Ma-wang-tui Han-mu Po-shu Cheng-li Hsiao-tsu, "Ch'ang-sha Ma-wang-tui Han-mu ch'u-t'u *Lao-tzu* i-pen chüan-ch'ien ku-i-shu shih-wen," *WW* 1974:10, pp. 30–42.

———, "Ma-wang-tui Han-mu ch'u-t'u *Lao-tzu* shih-wen," *WW* 1974:11, pp. 8–20.

Shantung Sheng Po-wu-kuan Lin-i Wen-wu-tsu, "Shantung Lin-i Hsi-Han-mu fa-hsien *Sun-tzu ping-fa* ho *Sun Pin ping-fa* teng chu-chien te chien-pao," *WW* 1974:2, pp. 15–21.

Tsun Hsin, "*Sun-tzu ping-fa* te tso-che chi ch'i shih-tai," *WW* 1974:12, pp. 2–24.

Wang Chung-min, *Tun-huang ku-chi hsü-lu,* Shang-wu yin-shu-kuan, Peking, 1958.

Wang Hsien-ch'en and Hsü Pao-lin, *Chung-kuo ku-tai ping-shu tsa-t'an,* Chieh-fang-chün ch'u-pan-she, Peking, 1983.

Wang Ming, "Shih-lun *Yin-fu ching* chi ch'i wei-wu-chu-i ssu-hsiang," *Che-hsüeh yen-chiu* 5:1 (1962), pp. 59–68.

Wei Ju-lin, "Ta-lu Han-mu ch'u-t'u *Sun-tzu ping-fa* ts'an-chien shih-wen chih yen-chiu," *Hua-hsüeh yüeh-k'an* 49:1 (1976), pp. 38–46.

Wu Shu-p'ing, "Ts'ung Lin-i Han-mu chu-chien *Wu-wen* k'an Sun Wu te Fa-chia ssu-hsiang," *WW* 1975:4, pp. 6–13.

Yin-ch'üeh-shan Han-mu Chu-chien Cheng-li Hsiao-tsu, "Lin-i Yin-ch'üeh-shan Han-mu ch'u-t'u *Sun Pin ping-fa* shih-wen," *WW* 1975:1, pp. 1–11, 43.

———, "Lin-i Yin-ch'üeh-shan Han-mu ch'u-t'u *Wang-ping* p'ien shih-wen," *WW* 1976:12, pp. 36–43.

———, "Yin-ch'üeh-shan chien-pen *Wei Liao-tzu* shih-wen (fu chiao-chu)," *WW* 1977:2, pp. 21–27.

———, "Yin-ch'üeh-shan chu-shu *Shou-fa, Shou-ling* teng shih-san-p'ien," *WW* 1985:4, pp. 27–43.

Glossary of Selected Terms with Chinese Characters

A-shih-na She-erh 阿史那社爾
abandon the army 廢軍
action 動
administration 制, 治, 政
  civil 文制, 文治
  military 軍制, 軍政, 軍治
advance 進
advance force 前鋒
advantage 利
afraid 恐
agents (spies) 間
  double 反間
  expendable 死間
  internal 內間
  living 生間
  local 鄉間
agriculture 農, 耕
All under Heaven 天下
alliances 交
altars (of state) (國) 社
ambush 伏
ancestral temple 廟
archers 弓者
armor 甲
army 軍, 師
  contrary 逆軍
  fierce 暴軍
  hard 剛軍

  of the Center 中軍
  of the Left 左軍
  of the Right 右軍
  righteous 義軍
  Six (Armies) 六師
  strong 強軍
  Three (Armies) 三軍
Army's Strategic Power 軍勢
artifice 譎
artisans 工, 工匠
ascension and decline 盛衰, 興衰
assemble 合
  and divide 分合
attack 攻
  incendiary 火攻
  orthodox 正攻
  sudden 突攻, 襲
  unorthodox 奇攻
augury 卜
auspicious 吉
authority (*ch'üan*) 權
awesomeness 威
ax
  fu 斧
  yüeh 鉞

balance of power and plans 權謀

bamboo slips 竹簡
barbarian 狄, 蠻, 番, 夷, 胡
  dress 胡服
barricade 塞
battalion 旅, 廣
battle 戰
battle array 戰陣, 陣
bells 鈴
beneficence 惠
benevolence 仁
besiege 圍
bestowals 賚
boats and oars 舟檝, 楫
border 境, 垠
bows and arrows 弓矢
brigade 師
brigand 賊
brutal 暴

calculate 算, 數
caltrops 蒺藜
capture 擒
cavalry 騎, 騎兵
  armored 甲騎
  attack 陷騎
  elite 鐵騎, 選騎, 銳騎
  fighting 戰騎
  heavy 重騎
  light 輕騎
  roving 游騎
  swift (fast) 疾騎
certitude 信
Chang Liang 張良
Chang-sun Wu-chi 長孫無忌
change 變
  and transformation 變化
Chao (state of) 趙
Chao Ling 召陵
chaos 亂
character 性
  evaluating 知人, 考人
  flaws 隙, 過

chariot 車
  assault 衝車
  attack 攻車
  battle 戰車
  deer-horn 鹿角車
  defensive 守車
  fu-hsü 扶胥車
  great covered 大櫓
  heavy 重車
  light 輕車
  martial flanking 武翼
  narrow 偏箱車
Ch'en P'ing 陳平
Ch'en Sheng 陳勝
cheng 徵
Ch'eng T'ang 成湯
chevaux-de-frise 行馬
Chi River 濟水
Chi Tan 姬澹
ch'i (pneuma, breath) 氣
Ch'i (state of) 齊
  Duke Huan of Ch'i 齊桓公
Ch'i-pi Ho Li 契苾何力
Ch'i-tan (Khitan) 契丹
Ch'i Tu 岐都
Ch'i Wei Wang 齊威王
Ch'i Yang 岐陽
chiao 角
chieh (constraint, measure) 節
chien-tu 簡牘
Chih-shih Ssu-li 執失思力
Chin (state of) 晉
Chin Wen-kung 晉文公
Ch'in (state of) 秦
Ch'in Shih Huang-ti 秦始皇帝
Chou 周
  Duke of 周公
  dynasty 周朝
  Eastern 東周
  Western 西周
Chou li (Rites of Chou) 周禮
Ch'u (state of) 楚

Chu-ko Liang 諸葛亮
ch'üan 權
  authority 權
  tactical balance of power 權
Chuang Chia 莊賈
Ch'un ch'iu 春秋
Chung Kuo (Central States) 中國
circuitous 迂
circular formation 圓 (陣)
city 城
civil 文
  and martial 文武
civil (cultural) offensive 文伐
civil virtue 文德
civilian affairs 文事
clamorous 譁
clarity (clearness) 明
clique 派, 朋
cloud ladder 雲梯
combat 戰
combat platoon 戰隊
comet 彗星
command 命, 號
commandant 尉
common people 平民, 老百姓
company 卒, 閭
compel others 致人
concentration of force 集力
configuration and designation 形名
configuration of power 勢
confront 當, 向
Confucius 孔子
confuse 惑
confusion 亂, 惑, 擾亂
conquer 勝, 克, 剋
constant 常
constraints 節
contrary virtue 逆德
counterattack 反攻, 逆擊
courage 勇

court 朝
crack troops 銳兵
credibility 信
criminal 罪者
crossbow 弩
  winch-powered linked 絞車連弩

danger 危
death 死
deceive 詭, 詐
decline 衰
defeat 敗
defense 守
defiles 阻
deflated in spirit 失氣
deploy 陣
deployment 陣
depths of Earth 九地之下
desert 逃
designation 名
desire 欲
destroy 破
dilatory 慢, 失時
disadvantage 害, 不利
disaster 災, 殃
discipline 兵制, 兵治
disharmony 不和
disordered 擾, 不治
dispirited 失氣, 挫氣, 傷氣
disposition and strategic power 形勢
disposition of force 形
disposition of power 勢
ditches 溝, 洫, 瀆
divine (divination) 卜筮
doubt 疑, 狐疑
Dragon's Head 龍頭
drums 鼓

Earth 地
Earthly Deployment 地陣
elite force 銳士

embankment 隄防
emblem 章
emolument 祿
emotionally attached 親附
emotions 情
employing men 用人
employing the military 用兵
empty 空
encampment 營
encircle(d) 圍
enemy 敵
entice 利之, 動之以利, 誘
error 過, 失
estimate 計
estimation 計
evaluate 考, 策, 察, 測
  enemy 察敵情, 料敵
  men 考人, 察才
evil 凶, 惡
evil implement 凶器
excess 奇
excess (flaw) 過
execute 誅
exterior 表
external 外

failure 失, 敗
Fan K'uai 樊噲
Fan Li 范蠡
Fan Tseng 范增
fatal 死
fathom (the enemy) 相, 測, 占
  (敵)
fear 畏
Fei River 淝水
feigned retreats 佯北
Feng Kung 酆宮
feudal lords 諸侯
few 少
fields 野, 田
fines 罰
fire 火

five 五
  affairs 五事
  colors 五色, 五彩
  flavors 五味
  grains 五穀
  notes 五音
  phases 五行
  weapons 五兵
flag 旗
flanks 偏, 旁
flee (run off) 走
flourish and decline 勝衰
flying 飛
  bridge 飛橋
  hook 飛鉤
  river 飛江
  tower 飛樓
foodstuffs 食
foot soldiers 步兵
force
  heavy 重兵
  light 輕兵
ford (rivers) 渡 (水), 濟 (水)
forest 林
formation 陣
  assault 衝陣
Former Kings 先王
formless 無形
forms of etiquette (*li*) 禮
fortification 城, 壘, 保, 堡
foundation 本
four 四
  Heads and Eight Tails
  四頭八尾
  limbs 四肢
  quarters 四方
  Seasons 四季
four-sided martial assault
  formation 四武衝陣
fragrant bait 香餌
frightened 驚懼
front 前

frontal assault force 戰鋒隊
Fu Chien 符堅
full 實
funeral mounds 墳墓

gate 門
general 將帥
  commanding 主將
  enlightened 明將
  Grand 大將
  ignorant 闇將
  subordinate 副將, 裨將
ghost 鬼
glory 榮
gnomon 表
gong 金
gorge 谿
grain 粟
granary 倉
guarantee units 保
guest 客

halberd 戈
Han (people) 漢
Han Ch'in-hu 韓擒虎
Han dynasty 漢朝
Han Hsin 韓信
Han Kao-tsu 漢高祖
handles of state 國柄
hard 剛
  and strong 強
harm 害
harmony 和
hasty 疾, 急
Heaven 天
Heavenly
  Deployment 天陣
  float 天浮
  Offices 天官
Heaven's
  Fissure 天隙
  Furnace 天竈
  Huang 天潢

  Jail 天牢
  Net 天羅
  Pit 天陷
  Well 天井
heavy force 重兵
hegemon 霸
heights 高
heights of Heaven 九天之上
helmet 盔, 冑
hero 雄, 傑
high official 大夫
hillock 丘
holding force 駐隊
honor 貴
horse 馬
host 主
Hsia dynasty 夏朝
Hsiang Yü 項羽
Hsiao Ho 蕭何
Hsiao Hsien 蕭銑
Hsieh An 謝安
Hsieh Hsüan 謝玄
Hsin Lo 新羅
Hsin shu (*New Book*) 新書
hsing (form) 形
Hsüeh Wan-ch'e 薛萬徹
Hsüeh-yen-t'o 薛延陀
Hsün Wu 荀吳
Huang Shih-kung 黃石公
Hui-ho (Uighurs) 回紇
Human Deployment 人陣
human effort (affairs) 人事
human emotions 人情
hundred 百
  illnesses 百病
  surnames 百姓
Huo Ch'ü-ping 霍去病

I Yin 伊尹
implements 器
impositions 斂
incendiary attack 火攻

nurturing the people 養人, 養民

oath 誓

observation post 斥侯, 長關

observe (the enemy) 觀, 伺 (敵)

occupy 佔, 居, 處

offense 攻

officers 士, 吏

officials 吏, 官

old army 老兵

omen 兆

opportunity 機

oppose 當, 拒

order 令

ordinance 律

orthodox (*cheng*) 正

pardon 赦, 舍

party 黨

pennant 旌

people 人, 民

perverse 邪

pipes and whistles 笳笛

plains 原

plan 計, 策

platoon 隊, 倆 (兩) 屬

pleasure 樂

power 勢

pray 祈禱

Praying Mantis Martial Knights
  螳螂武士

precipitous 險

preservation 全

press (the enemy) 逼, 壓, 薄, 迫

pretend 偽

probe (the enemy) 刺 (敵), 角之

probing force 跳盪 (隊)

profit 利

prohibitions 禁

prolonged 久

protracted fighting 戰久

provisions 糧

punish 罰

punishment 罰

punitive expedition 討

pursue 追

Questions and Replies 問對

raiding force 寇

rain 雨

ramparts 壘

rank 爵

ravine 險

rear 後

rectify 正

Red Eyebrows 赤眉

regiment 旅, 師

regimental commander 帥

regulations 律, 制

repel 禦

repress 挫

resentment 怨

responsibility 任

rested 佚

retreat 退, 北

rewards 賞
  and punishments 賞罰

righteous 義

rites (see *li*) 禮

river 川, 水

rows and files 行列

ruler 主
  enlightened 明主
  obtuse (ignorant) 無知之主

rules 法

rumor 讒譖

Sage 聖人

salary 祿

San I-sheng 散宜生

sated 飽

scouts (遠) 斥

seasonal occupations 時事,
  季事

secret plans 陰計

secret tallies 陰符

security 安

segmenting and reuniting 分合
seize 奪
sericulture 蠶, 織桑
sever 絕, 斷
shaman 巫
shame 恥
Shang 商
  dynasty 商朝
  king of 商王
Shang shu 尚書
shape (*hsing*) 形
shield 盾
shih (strategic power) 勢
Shih chi 史記
Shih Le 石勒
short weapons 短兵
shuaijan (snake) 率然
Shun (Emperor) 舜
siege 圍
six (domestic) animals 六畜
Six Flowers Formation 六花陣
Six Secret Teachings 六韜
soft 軟
soldiers 卒, 兵, 士
solid 固
Son of Heaven 天子
spear 矛
spies (see agents) 間
spirit (morale) 氣
spirits 神
Spring and Autumn 春秋
squad 伍
square formation 方陣
Ssu-ma 司馬
Ssu-ma Fa 司馬法
stalwart 堅
standoff 相拒
stimulate (the enemy) 作 (敵)
storehouse 庫
stratagem 謀, 計策
strategic
  advantage 利, 地利

configuration of power (*shih*)
勢
  point 要, 要塞, 要點, 塞, 險
strategy 計, 法, 兵法
strength 力
strike 擊
strong 強
substantial 實
subterfuge 陰謀
subtle 微, 機
subtle change 機
Sun Pin 孫臏
Sun-tzu 孫子
Sun Wu 孫武
Sung Lao-sheng 宋老生
Sung Wu-ti 宋武帝
supply wagon 輜
sword 劍, 長劍

ta-fu 大夫
T'ai Kung 太公
take (the enemy) 取 (敵)
tally 符
T'ang Chien 唐儉
T'ang Kao-tsu 唐高祖
T'ang T'ai-tsung 唐太宗
Tao (Way) 道
  of men 人道
  of the military 兵道, 軍道
  of Warfare 戰道, 兵道
taxes 賦
technique 術
techniques and crafts 技巧
terrain
  accessible 通地
  advantage of 地利
  broken-off 絕地
  classification of 分地
  configurations of 地形
  confined 狹地
  constricted 隘地
  contentious 爭地
  deadly (fatal) 死地

dispersive 散地
easy 易地
encircled 圍地
entrapping 圮地
expansive 遠地
fatal (deadly) 死地
focal 衢地
heavy 重地
isolated 絕地
light 輕地
precipitous 險地
sinking 圮下
stalemated 支地
suspended 挂地
traversable 交地
treacherous 險地
terrified 恐懼
Three Armies 三軍
Three Chin 三晉
Three Strategies 三略
Ti 狄
T'ieh-le 鐵勒
T'ien Tan 田單
tiger drop 虎落
Tiger Guards 虎賁
tired 勞, 困
tomb 墓
tortoise shell 龜殼
town 邑
training 練, 習
tranquil 靜
transformation 化
troubled 憂
true humanity 仁
True Man of Worth (*chün-tzu*) 君子
trust 信
trustworthy 有信, 可信
Ts'ao Ts'ao 曹操
Tso chuan 左傳
T'u-chüeh (Turks) 突厥
T'u Shan 塗山

unconquerable 不可勝
unity 一, 專一
unorthodox (*ch'i*) 奇
uprightness 正

vacillate 猶豫
vacuity 虛
vacuous 虛
valley 谷
vanguard 踵軍
victory 勝
by turn of events 曲勝
village 村
villain 賊
virtue 德
vital point 機
vulnerable point 空點, 弱點, 虛點 (地)

wage war 作戰
wall 牆, 城
Wang Hsün 王尋
Wang I 王邑
Wang Mang 王莽
Wang Meng 王猛
war 戰
ward off 拒
warfare 兵, 戰
explosive 突戰
forest 林戰
mountain 山戰
Warring States 戰國
warrior 士, 武
armored 甲士
water 水
weak 弱
weapons 兵器
Wei (state of) 魏
Wei Liao-tzu 尉繚子
Wei Yang 渭陽
well 井
wetlands 沮, 澤, 沛
withdraw 却

Worthy 賢人
Wu Ch'i 吳起
Wu Han 吳漢
Wu Kuang 吳廣
Wu-tzu 吳子

yang 陽
Yang Kan 楊干
Yangtze River 揚子江
Yao (Emperor) 堯

Yellow Emperor 黃帝
Yellow River 黃河, 河
Yen (state of) 燕
yin 陰
yin and yang 陰陽
Yin-fu ching 陰符經
yü 羽
Yü-chih Ching-te 尉遲敬德
Yü-li 魚麗
Yüeh (state of) 越

Indexes

EXTREMELY COMMON TERMS, such as "army" or "soldier," are noted only where of significance or where discussed in the introductory material. References to the reputed authors of the various military classics, such as Wu Ch'i in the *Wu-tzu,* and the other figures participating in the dialogues are not provided when they appear as speakers in their own works, but only where they occur in either introductory material or other texts. Historical individuals cited in the texts, unless extremely prominent, are also omitted.

In order to facilitate the study of these military writings for the widest possible audience, two indexes have been provided. The first enumerates the basic strategic and tactical principles found embedded in the texts; lists essential tactics used to realize these basic principles; and concludes with a summation of commonly encountered battlefield situations and suggested responses. In compiling this index the emphasis has been upon selecting significant, illuminating passages rather than upon comprehensiveness.

For a more complete listing of relevant topics, the second index—presented in the traditional format—should be consulted.

INDEX OF STRATEGIC AND
TACTICAL PRINCIPLES

Statements of General Principles

Essential Principles

Selected Concrete Measures Used to Implement General Principles

GENERAL INDEX